Social Media in Employee Selection and Recruitment

Richard N. Landers • Gordon B. Schmidt
Editors

Social Media in Employee Selection and Recruitment

Theory, Practice, and Current Challenges

Springer

Editors
Richard N. Landers
Department of Psychology
Old Dominion University
Norfolk, VA, USA

Gordon B. Schmidt
Division of Organizational Leadership and Supervision
Indiana University-Purdue University Fort Wayne
Fort Wayne, IN, USA

ISBN 978-3-319-29987-7   ISBN 978-3-319-29989-1 (eBook)
DOI 10.1007/978-3-319-29989-1

Library of Congress Control Number: 2016938158

Printed on acid-free paper

This Springer imprint is published by Springer Nature
The registered company is Springer International Publishing AG Switzerland

I dedicate this book to Owen, who will probably find it delicious.

—Richard Landers

This book is dedicated to my wife and our family of Wiegands, Smiths, and Schmidts; especially my mother, Priscilla; sister, Brenda; and the memory of my father, Eugene.

—Gordon Schmidt

Contents

Editors and Contributors

About the Editors

Richard N. Landers, Ph.D. is an Associate Professor of Industrial/Organizational Psychology at Old Dominion University, where he has worked since earning his Ph.D. at the University of Minnesota. His research program focuses upon improving the use of Internet technologies in talent management, especially the measurement of knowledge, skills and abilities, the selection of employees using innovative technologies, and learning conducted via the Internet. Recent topics have included big data, unproctored Internet-based testing, mobile devices including smartphones and tablets, immersive 3D virtual environments and virtual reality, game-based learning, game-based assessment, gamification, and social media and online communities. His research and writing has been featured in *Forbes*, *Business Insider*, *Science News Daily*, *Popular Science*, *Maclean's*, and *Chronicle of Higher Education*, among others. He currently serves as Associate Editor of *Computers in Human Behavior, Simulation & Gaming,* and the *International Journal of Gaming and Computer-Mediated Simulations* as well as the editorial board of *Technology, Knowledge and Learning*. He was Old Dominion University's 2014 and 2015 nominee for the State Council for Higher Education in Virginia Rising Star Outstanding Faculty Award. He is also an author of a statistics textbook, *A Step-by-Step Introduction to Statistics for Business*. Finally, he maintains a science-popularization blog spreading news about technology, business, and psychology at http://neoacademic.com.

Richard N. Landers, Ph.D., Department of Psychology, Old Dominion University, Norfolk, VA, USA

Gordon B. Schmidt, Ph.D. is an Assistant Professor of Organizational Leadership & Supervision at Indiana University-Purdue University Fort Wayne. He received his Ph.D. in Organizational Psychology from Michigan State University in 2012. His primary research interests relate to how social media can significantly impact the worker-organization relationship. Recent work has looked at legal aspects of employment terminations due to worker social media behavior. He has examined the use of compensated crowdsourcing sites, such as Amazon Mechanical Turk, by organizations. He has also examined how social media can play a part in virtual leadership and virtual team behavior. He has an upcoming book chapter on how social media can be a medium for organizational politics. He is well connected with the field of I/O Psychology through social media, being a top 10 contributor on the I/O Psychologist social media site My.SIOP, a moderator of the I/O Psychology subreddit, and running a Twitter account devoted to disseminating knowledge on psychology, management, higher education, and technology (http://www.twitter.com/iopsychology).

Gordon B. Schmidt, Ph.D., Division of Organizational Leadership and Supervision, Indiana University-Purdue University Fort Wayne, Fort Wayne, IN, USA

Contributors

Yalcin Acikgoz, M.A. has received his M.A. in Industrial/Organizational Psychology and Human Resource Management in Appalachian State University. Currently pursuing his Ph.D. in Middle East Technical University, Mr. Acikgoz's research focuses on using social media for employee recruitment and applicant withdrawal from the job application process. Mr. Acikgoz also works as a workforce analyst in a public sector organization in Turkey.

Yalcin Acikgoz, M.A., Department of Psychology, Middle East Technical University, Cankaya, Ankara, Turkey

Michael B. Armstrong, M.S. is a doctoral student studying industrial-organizational psychology at Old Dominion University. He received his Bachelor of Arts degree in psychology from Western Kentucky University in 2013 and his Master of Science degree in industrial-organizational psychology from Old Dominion University in 2015. Michael's research focuses on the use of the Internet and technology to enhance organizational training, assessment, employee selection, and workplace motivation. He has co-authored and published several journal articles and book chapters on the use of gamification and games to improve outcomes in the workplace.

Michael B. Armstrong, M.S., Department of Psychology, Old Dominion University, Norfolk, VA, USA

Julia L. Berger, Ph.D. is an industrial-organizational psychologist currently working in one of the largest nonprofit healthcare organizations in the Midwest. Her primary research interests involve personnel selection, psychometrics, and attitudes, such as employee engagement and satisfaction. She has presented her research at international and regional conferences.

Julia L. Berger, Ph.D., Human Resources—Organizational Development, ProMedica, Toledo, OH, USA

Shawn M. Bergman, Ph.D. is the founding Director of the Office of Research Consultation, Director of the HR and Analytics Research Lab, and Associate Director for the Center for Analytics Research and Education at Appalachian State University and the President of B&F Consulting. His research focuses on using social media and analytics to meet organizational objectives, legal issues surrounding the use of social media for employment decisions, and applying analytics to human resources. He has served on multiple panels at national conferences discussing the use of social media in organizational settings.

Shawn M. Bergman, Ph.D., Department of Psychology, Appalachian State University, Boone, NC, USA

Mark N. Bing, Ph.D. is an Associate Professor of Management at the University of Mississippi. From 2001 to 2005, he served as the US Navy's SUBSCREEN Principal Investigator. His research interests include personnel selection, personality measurement, test faking, CWBs, and research methods. He has served on various journal editorial boards, such as the *Journal of Applied Psychology* and *Organizational Research Methods*. His work has been published in journals such as the *Journal of Applied Psychology*, *Organizational Behavior and Human Decision Processes*, *Journal of Management*, and *Organizational Research Methods*. He is a fellow of SIOP and the APA.

Mark N. Bing, Ph.D., Department of Management, School of Business Administration, University of Mississippi, University, MS, USA

Stephanie L. Black, M.B.A. has experience working with corporations in various executive positions and as an owner of various businesses. Her academic background started at Southern Methodist University with a B.A. in Foreign Languages and Ibero-American studies. She then received an M.I.M./M.B.A. from the American Graduate School of International Business. Presently, she is finishing her Ph.D. in Management at the University of Texas at San Antonio, and she holds a dual appointment in the Department of Management at the University at Albany in entrepreneurship and in the Department of Life Sciences for the commercialization of technology. In this role, she enjoys working with students preparing them to be better global minded business leaders and researching in the use of technology in the workforce, minority entrepreneurship, sustainability, and small business development. She is also active within the business community, where she strives to help small businesses to become more innovative, entrepreneurial, and profitable.

Stephanie L. Black Department of Management, School of Business, University at Albany, Albany, NY, USA

Anita Blanchard, Ph.D. is an Associate Professor of Psychology and Organization Science at the University of North Carolina at Charlotte. Dr. Blanchard studies how information and communication technology affects communities and organizations as well as the people within them, including the health and functioning of the people, their organizations, and their communities. She is particularly interested in the feelings of community that develop in online groups. Her new research interest includes feelings of groupness online, particularly the social and technological components that affect communication partners' feelings of entitativity in traditional computer communication and new social media.

Anita Blanchard, Ph.D., Department of Psychology, University of North Carolina at Charlotte, Charlotte, NC, USA

Caleb T. Carr, Ph.D. (Ph.D., Michigan State University) conducts research addressing how new media alter communicative processes, including how social media are used for organizational uncertainty reduction, in group collaborations, and to create and maintain identity online. He is currently an Assistant Professor of Communication at Illinois State University.

Caleb T. Carr, Ph.D., School of Communication, Illinois State University, Normal, IL, USA

Andrew B. Collmus is a Ph.D. student in the Industrial-Organizational Psychology program at Old Dominion University. He holds a Bachelor of Science degree in psychology with an I/O concentration that he earned at Colorado State University. Andrew's research focuses on assessment and technology. He is a student member of SIOP, APA, SHRM, and APS.

Andrew B. Collmus Department of Psychology, Old Dominion University, Norfolk, VA, USA

H. Kristl Davison, Ph.D. is an Instructor of Management at the University of Memphis. Her research interests include employment discrimination, gender and diversity issues, organizational justice and ethics, counterproductive workplace behavior, applicant faking, and personnel selection. She has published her research in journals such as *Journal of Applied Psychology, Organizational Behavior and Human Decision Processes, Personnel Psychology, Journal of Vocational Behavior, Organizational Research Methods*, and *Journal of Business and Psychology*. She has served on the Editorial Board of *Organizational Research Methods* and chaired the Awards Committee for the Society for Industrial and Organizational Psychology (SIOP).

H. Kristl Davison, Ph.D., Department of Management, Fogelman College of Business & Economics, University of Memphis, Memphis, TN, USA

Nikki M. Dudley, Ph.D. (Ph.D., George Mason University) is a Director and Partner at Shaker. She has worked with numerous Fortune 100 clients, managing large-scale projects to create cutting edge mobile and web-based assessment solutions used in the USA and internationally. Current research interests include innovative measurement methodologies for knowledge, skills, and personality, job simulations, and applicant reactions, and she has multiple publications on these topics. She has also received the Edwin A. Fleishman Award for her research on knowledge and skill measurement and the G. Klopfer Award for distinguished contribution to the literature in personality.

Nikki M. Dudley, Ph.D., SHAKER, Beachwood, OH, USA

Jared Z. Ferrell, M.A. is the Research and Development Team Lead at Shaker and is currently a Ph.D. candidate in Industrial-Organizational Psychology program at the University of Akron. He earned his M.A. in Industrial-Organizational Psychology from the University of Akron in 2011. Jared has been involved in the development and validation of numerous pre-hire assessments across a wide variety of industries and roles. He has also presented at numerous professional conferences and published in peer-reviewed journals, as well as books on personnel selection. His research interests include applicant reactions to assessments, social networking websites, and legal issues pertaining to personnel selection.

Jared Z. Ferrell, M.A., SHAKER, Beachwood, OH, USA

Noelle B. Frantz, M.A. studied Industrial-Organizational Psychology at the University of Akron where she earned a master's degree and is currently completing her dissertation, the last requirement for earning a Ph.D. In her time at Shaker, Noelle has served both researcher and consultant roles. With a background in engineering coursework and research, Noelle brings a different perspective to the development of science-based solutions designed to meet clients' selection and assessment needs. Her research interests include assessment through science and innovation, targeted selection, performance management, and the use of technology to enhance business management.

Noelle B. Frantz, M.A., SHAKER, Beachwood, OH, USA

Sarah Guilfoyle, M.A. is a graduate of the Industrial-Organizational Psychology and Human Resource Management (IOHRM) master's program at Appalachian State University. While working toward her degree, Sarah was an active member of the Society for Human Resource Management (SHRM) and worked to build the Center for Analytics Research and Education (CARE) at Appalachian State University. She also presented on big data and social media at a local Industrial-Organizational Psychology conference. Sarah is currently pursuing an M.B.A. at Appalachian State University.

Sarah Guilfoyle, M.A., Department of Psychology, Appalachian State University, Boone, NC, USA

Shahar Gur is a Ph.D. student in Organizational Science at the University of North Carolina at Charlotte. She holds a bachelor's degree in psychology from UNC Chapel Hill. Her research focuses on prosocial behaviors and group interactions.

Shahar Gur Organizational Science, University of North Carolina at Charlotte, Charlotte, NC, USA

Christopher Hartwell, Ph.D. is an Assistant Professor in the management department of the Jon M. Huntsman School of Business at Utah State University. He received his Ph.D. in Organizational Behavior and Human Resource Management from Purdue University. His research interests include employee selection, performance management, social media in the workplace, and leadership. Chris also has more than 8 years of professional work experience in the field of human resources, including recruiting, selection, performance management, compensation and benefits administration, and employee training and development. He is a certified HR professional through both the Society for Human Resource Management and the HR Certification Institute.

Christopher Hartwell, Ph.D., Management Department, Jon M. Huntsman School of Business, Utah State University, Logan, UT, USA

Donald H. Kluemper, Ph.D. is an Assistant Professor of Management and Director of the Institute for Leadership Excellence and Development (iLEAD) at the University of Illinois at Chicago. Don's research centers around the topics of individual differences, workplace mistreatment, and leadership. His work has been published in outlets such as the *Journal of Applied Psychology*, *Journal of Management*, *Personnel Psychology*, *Organizational Behavior and Human Decision Processes*, *Journal of Organizational Behavior*, and *Leadership Quarterly*. In addition, some of Don's research on social networking websites has been featured in media outlets such as the *Wall Street Journal*, *Time Magazine*, and National Public Radio.

Donald H. Kluemper, Ph.D., Department of Managerial Studies, University of Illinois–Chicago, Chicago, IL, USA

Julia Levashina, Ph.D. is an Associate Professor at Kent State University. She is teaching and conducting research across a range of areas in human resource management. She has conducted empirical research on faking and faking detection in structured employment interviews, the use of the response elaboration technique and bogus items to detect and decrease faking in biodata measures, and the use of blatant extreme responding and unlikely virtue scales in personality tests. She has published her research in management and psychology journals including the *Journal of Applied Psychology*, *Personnel Psychology*, and *International Journal of Selection and Assessment*.

Julia Levashina, Ph.D., College of Business Administration, Kent State University, Kent, OH, USA

Kimberly E. O'Brien, Ph.D. is an assistant professor of psychology at Central Michigan University. Her research on social media has mainly focused on the negative outcomes of social networking misuse. Her research program, more broadly, includes organizational citizenship behavior, counterproductive behavior, and job stress. She considers herself a champion for using appropriate statistical analyses and has given workshops on moderated mediation, item response theory, and relative weight analysis. She received her Ph.D. in industrial/organizational psychology from the University of South Florida in 2008.

Kimberly E. O'Brien, Ph.D., Department of Psychology, Central Michigan University, Mount Pleasant, MI, USA

Kimberly W. O'Connor is a licensed Indiana attorney and a professor in the Department of Organizational Leadership and Supervision at Indiana University-Purdue University Fort Wayne. Her research areas include employment law, Internet law, and corporate social responsibility.

Kimberly W. O'Connor, Division of Organizational Leadership and Supervision, Indiana University-Purdue University Fort Wayne, Fort Wayne, IN, USA

Elizabeth S. Pears, M.A. is an Industrial-Organizational Psychology Ph.D. candidate at the University of Akron. She received her bachelor's degree in psychology from Washington and Lee University and her master's degree in Industrial-Organizational Psychology from the University of Akron. Elizabeth has been with Shaker since August 2014. Her research interests include performance management, coaching, selection, and assessments.

Elizabeth S. Pears, M.A., SHAKER, Beachwood, OH, USA

Jonathan Powers, M.A. is a second-year graduate student in the Industrial/Organizational Psychology and Human Resource Management program at Appalachian State University. Jonathan is an active member of the Society for Human Resource Management, is a project leader in the HR and Analytics Research Lab, and has worked with the Center for Analytics Research and Education at Appalachian State University. He has authored publications proposing the utility of text analytics in educational interventions targeting underprivileged high-school students and is currently working on the research examining the incremental validity of using text analytics from data gathered from social media to predict job performance.

Jonathan Powers, M.A., Department of Psychology, Appalachian State University, Boone, NC, USA

Philip L. Roth, Ph.D. is a professor of management at Clemson University. Phil's research interests involve employee selection, including the use of social media in employee selection. His methodological interests center on meta-analysis. His work appears in the *Journal of Applied Psychology*, *Personnel Psychology*, *Journal of Management*, etc. He is a fellow of SIOP and the APS. He has served as chair of the Research Methods Division of the Academy of Management and currently serves as member at large for the Human Resources Division of the Academy. His Ph.D. is from the University of Houston.

Philip L. Roth, Ph.D., Department of Management, College of Business, Clemson University, Clemson, SC, USA

Nicolas Roulin, Ph.D. is an Assistant Professor of Human Resources Management in the Asper School of Business, University of Manitoba. His research interests are organized around the interactions, strategies, and behaviors of job market actors, especially during the selection process. For instance, he investigates the use and detection of impression management and faking tactics during the employment interviews, applicants' strategies when entering competitive job markets, and the use of social networking websites as selection instruments. His research has been published in journals including the *Journal of Applied Psychology*, *Personnel Psychology*, or *International Journal of Selection and Assessment*.

Nicolas Roulin, Ph.D., Asper School of Business, University of Manitoba, Winnipeg, MB, Canada

Enrica N. Ruggs, Ph.D. is an Assistant Professor of Psychology and Organizational Science at the University of North Carolina at Charlotte. She received her Ph.D. in Industrial-Organizational (I-O) Psychology from Rice University. Dr. Ruggs examines diversity, inclusion, and discrimination in organizations. Her research focuses on understanding the manifestations, consequences, and reduction of workplace discrimination. Dr. Ruggs is particularly interested in factors that influence discriminatory behavior and the magnitude of influence of interpersonal discrimination on organizations.

Enrica N. Ruggs, Ph.D., Department of Psychology, University of North Carolina at Charlotte, Charlotte, NC, USA

Brandon Shields received his B.A. in Economics and is working toward his M.B.A. at Kent State University, where he is spending his second year in France at the ESC Rennes School of Business on exchange. As a result of his concentration in human resources, his research interests include international selection, social media as a tool for hiring, and applicant deception.

Brandon Shields College of Business Administration, Kent State University, Kent, OH, USA

J. William Stoughton, Ph.D. is a Principal Client Advisor at SHL Talent Measurement of CEB. His primary responsibility is advising CEB's new and prospective customers on talent measurement best practice during the sales process, providing: needs diagnosis, proposal recommendations, and presentations on assessment technical elements. He continues to maintain an active research program on the intersection of social networking and personnel selection. Will's research has been featured in popular media outlets such as *Fortune*, Ars Technica, *Slate*, *Time*, NBC Radio News, *Scientific American*, and National Public Radio. Will earned his Ph.D. in Industrial-Organizational Psychology from North Carolina State University.

J. William Stoughton, Ph.D., CEB, SHL Talent Measurement, Minneapolis, MN, USA

E. Daly Vaughn, Ph.D. is a Senior Associate at Shaker. He holds a Ph.D. from Auburn University and has developed and implemented innovative, custom, web- and mobile-based measures including measures of cognitive ability, situational judgment, biodata, qualitative responses, personality, and work simulations for a variety of Fortune 500 clients across a broad range of industries. His research interests include studying where innovative technology intersects with traditional human resource functions, including gamification, implicit attitude measurement, legal challenges introduced by new technology, and the use of social media within a recruitment and selection context.

E. Daly Vaughn, Ph.D., SHAKER, Beachwood, OH, USA

Sarah Singletary Walker, Ph.D. obtained a doctorate degree in Industrial-Organizational Psychology from Rice University. She is an Associate Professor at the University of Houston-Downtown. Dr. Walker's training in industrial organizational psychology provides her specific expertise in diversity, recruitment, selection, training, testing, and measurement. Her research interests include diversity, discrimination remediation, leadership, employee selection, and other areas related to human resource management. Her research has been published in the *Journal of Applied Psychology*. She is a reviewer for journals and also consults on applied projects related to recruitment, selection, and performance appraisal for both public and private companies.

Sarah Singletary Walker, Ph.D., Department of Management and Marketing, University of Houston-Downtown, Houston, TX, USA

Montressa L. Washington, Ph.D. has over 20 years of management consulting experience with Fortune 100 companies. She is a management consulting veteran with expertise in human capital management, change integration, technology assimilation, and business transformation. Montressa's research interests include strategic human resources, technology, innovation, and organizational behavior. Montressa has taught at schools of business for Villanova University, Morgan State University, and Johns Hopkins Carey Business School. Montressa's academic history—Ph.D., Case Western Reserve University—Weatherhead School of Management, MBA International Business and Marketing—Johns Hopkins University and BA English—University of Maryland College Park.

Montressa L. Washington, Ph.D., Weatherhead School of Management, Case Western Reserve University, Cleveland, OH, USA

Nathan Weidner, Ph.D. currently works as an assistant professor at Missouri S&T. He received his Ph.D. in Industrial-Organizational Psychology from Wayne State University in 2012. His research broadly focuses on the impacts of technology on organizational functioning with an emphasis on the impacts of social media in particular. He also studies how implicit theories of leadership and motivation can influence attributions made about leader behaviors and the workplace in general. He is a passionate teacher that loves to incorporate new technology into his classes and is experienced in teaching a variety of courses at both the undergraduate and master's levels.

Nathan Weidner, Ph.D., Department of Psychological Science, Missouri S&T, Rolla, MO, USA

Kevin T. Wynne, M.S. is a doctoral candidate in the industrial/organizational psychology Ph.D. program at Wayne State University. Kevin graduated cum laude with a B.A. in Psychology from the Ohio State University. He also holds an M.S. in Management from Mays Business School at Texas A&M University. Kevin has both internal and external consulting experience but is currently conducting basic and applied research on the Human Insight and Trust team at the US Air Force Research Laboratory. His research interests fall into three primary domains: (a) trust in autonomy, (b) work-life integration, and (c) social media and the workplace.

Kevin T. Wynne, M.S., Department of Psychology, Wayne State University, Detroit, MI, USA

Michael J. Zickar, Ph.D. is Professor of Psychology and Department Chair at Bowling Green State University. He has published widely in the areas of psychometrics, personnel selection, and the history of applied psychology. He is on the editorial boards of *Journal of Applied Psychology*, *Organizational Research Methods*, *Journal of Management*, and *Journal of Business and Psychology*. He is a Fellow of the Society for Industrial-Organizational Psychology.

Michael J. Zickar, Ph.D., Department of Psychology, Bowling Green State University, Bowling Green, ON, USA

Part I
Introduction

Chapter 1
Social Media in Employee Selection and Recruitment: An Overview

Richard N. Landers and Gordon B. Schmidt

Abstract Although social media are increasingly used in the employee selection and recruitment process, six significant challenges remain. First, reliability and validity is unknown. Second, even if reliable and valid, social media data may not be practical. Third, even if practical, the use of such information may not be legal. Fourth, even if legal, their use may not be ethical. Fifth, even if ethical, it is unclear how to optimally include them in existing systems. Sixth, even if optimal strategies are developed, they may be rendered obsolete at a pace too quick for academic researchers to match, at least as academic research in this domain is currently published and disseminated. This does not frame such research as useless but rather highlights the need for a faster and more comprehensive approach to studying it.

Keywords Social media • Social network sites • Personnel selection • Selection • Recruitment • Reliability • Validity • Practical • Ethical • Legal

1.1 Introduction

Social media, defined as the Internet-based platforms based upon Web 2.0 that allow users to generate and exchange their own content (Kaplan & Haenlein, 2010), are playing an increasingly important role in human resource (HR) management in general and employee hiring in particular. As noted by Segal (2014), "Social media is no longer cutting-edge; it is mainstream. For HR to overlook it today would be like ignoring e-mail 20 years ago." Yearly surveys by CareerBuilder have found continuous growth in the number of employers reporting finding social media content that has led

---

R.N. Landers, Ph.D. (✉)
Department of Psychology, Old Dominion University,
250 Mills Godwin Building, Norfolk, VA 23529, USA
e-mail: rnlanders@odu.edu

G.B. Schmidt, Ph.D.
Division of Organizational Leadership and Supervision, Indiana University-Purdue University Fort Wayne, Neff 288D 2101 East Coliseum Blvd., Fort Wayne, IN 46805, USA
e-mail: schmidtg@ipfw.edu

R.N. Landers, G.B. Schmidt (eds.), *Social Media in Employee Selection and Recruitment*, DOI 10.1007/978-3-319-29989-1_1

to the rejection of a job applicant, up to 51 % as of the 2014 survey (Grasz, 2014). Many employers now consult social media when making hiring decisions, often without the awareness of applicants. There is no longer any doubt as to this reality.

As is often the case following the introduction of new HR technologies, practice has far outpaced research on using social media in selection. Although people making hiring decisions are consulting social media, researchers have a poor understanding of how such consultations take place or what might affect the accuracy and efficiency of their judgments. There is ample evidence to suggest that although off-the-cuff evaluations of people contain much information relevant to their character, there is also a high degree of error, especially when only a single person makes such judgments (Connelly & Ones, 2010). As a result, most current advice in the practice of social media-assisted hiring is informal, unsystematic, and anecdotal.

Thus, the overall purpose of this book is to begin building a cohesive research literature surrounding social media in selection. We do so here by organizing and presenting relevant research perspectives around key themes in this emerging domain. In developing this book, we sought authors across both academia and industry to provide their perspectives on fourteen major themes. We did this both to minimize overlap between chapters and to ensure broad value for all readers. We also asked authors to write to particular audiences. Specifically, the book presents a set of chapters targeted primarily at researchers, a set of chapters targeted primarily at practitioners, then a set of chapters targeted at both while highlighting the challenges and limitations of social media when used as part of employee selection and recruitment.

In this introductory chapter, we provide a brief description of the research challenges facing selection researchers as a result of the introduction of social media into the selection process. We break these challenges down into six key dimensions, describing the major issues that define each. Next, we offer brief synopses of each chapter within the text, all focused upon answering these six questions, followed by some early conclusions.

1.2 Major Concerns in Social Media in Selection

To frame the content of this book, it is important to first distinguish selection from other aspects of the hiring process. Specifically, selection refers to the system that employers use to determine the qualifications of job applicants and the decision-making process used to act upon that information (Farr & Tippins, 2010). Although social media is increasingly permeating all aspects of human resource management, this book focuses upon selection. Specifically, we seek to explore how social media are and can be used to make decisions about the qualifications of job applicants and how social media can be used to increase the number of job applicants to be evaluated by such systems.

Social media is itself a complex term, so we must first carefully define it. Much of the early examination of social media was in fact on a specific type of social media called social network sites. Social network sites have three major characteristics: (1) they allow users to create a public or partially public personal profile within an online system, (2) they can specify a list of connections with other people using the site (e.g., Facebook's "friends"), and (3) users can view and explore content from both their own connections and the connections of others (Boyd & Ellison, 2008). Current major social network sites as of this writing include Facebook, Twitter, and LinkedIn. Social media, in contrast, include a broader set of social technologies which may not meet all the definitional elements of social network sites. For example, blogs enable users to share content with either a target group or the Internet in general. Thus, blogs are a type of social media but not a type of social network site. In this book, we are concerned with social media of all types, thus including any Internet technology that enables the sharing of content created by users with other users.

As noted earlier, the practice of incorporating information acquired via social media into the selection process is now quite common, and to a degree, this is due to the ease and attractiveness of social media as sources of information. Social media are themselves an outcome of Web 2.0, a design standard in which web applications are driven largely by content provided by users (O'Reilly, 2007). Connectivity and information-sharing are the implicit goals of social media. In the selection context, people provide a great deal of information about themselves via their online behaviors within such software, and these online behaviors can be observed, captured, and acted upon by employers. What remains unclear for both researchers and practitioners is what that information truly represents and how to best take advantage of it.

We have identified six key dimensions to this overall problem which we present here and represent the core research questions addressed by this book. First and most fundamental, there is a question of the reliability and validity of information available via social media. Job applicants may not represent themselves honestly, even going so far as to create false identities to represent themselves. Job applicant profiles may be contaminated with the behaviors of others; for example, other people may post information that appears within the social media content of a job applicant, contaminating it. Alternatively, false identities and the postings of friends may still contain job-relevant information, useful in creating predictive models of job performance.

Second, even if the information is valid from the perspective of its psychometric properties, such scores may not be practically useful. There have been several attempts to develop predictive models of later behavior based upon social media profile information, including algorithmic approaches (Youyou, Kosinski, & Stillwell, 2015). Attempts relying upon human judgment have been less successful (Van Iddekinge, Lanivich, Roth, & Junco, in press). This lack of interpretability may be because information about job applicants obtained via social media is by definition a behavioral outcome. Social media platforms bring with them online cultural norms and standards that influence user behavior. When social media postings are observed by those making hiring decisions, they are observing a person–situation interaction. This is important because observers must consider the influence of the situation when making judgments about personality (Tett & Burnett, 2003).

If employers are attempting to make judgments about people using information obtained from social media platforms they do not understand, this may harm their ability to identify relevant information (for more about such judgments, see Funder, 1995). Even more problematic, newly invented social media technologies may change the nature of the situation on a day-to-day basis.

Third, even if that information is practically useful, it may not be legal to consult it. Although information posted on the Internet is generally considered "public," many legal systems bar the consultation of particular types of information by those making hiring decisions. This produces several situations of unclear legality. For example, an employee may submit an application to an organization and choose not to share any social media profile information directly with the organization. A bored hiring manager decided to search for the candidate online, discovering several social media profiles containing information about the applicant's sex, religion, race, skin color, and national origin. Although this information is publically available, it may now unduly influence the hiring manager's decision, either intentionally or unintentionally. This influence could lead to violation of existing national legal protections, such as Title VII protections in the United States. Varying access to social media by socioeconomic status and population differences in social media platform membership may also influence the legality of such consultations.

Fourth, even if information can be viewed in such a way that it is legal to do so, it may not be ethical. In the case described above, the applicant chose not to provide social media profile information on any materials submitted to the employer, yet the employer located that information and browsed it anyway. A similar case in a more traditional context might be the following. A person applies to a job while currently employed, listing that place of employment on the vita. A hiring manager for the prospective employer travels to that place and waits for the applicant to leave work, following them home and taking pictures of everything they do along the way. Although all information collected by this hiring manager is public, such an act would be a significant invasion of privacy with repercussions for applicant reactions. Yet a similar judgment is not made when a parallel act is conducted on the Internet despite potentially similar effects on reactions.

Fifth, even if information can be acquired legally and ethically, it is unclear how it should be included procedurally in selection decisions. Currently, social media is included in selection systems generally at the discretion of the person making the decision. Few selection systems so far formalize the perusal and collection of social media data, although there are notable exceptions (O'Brien, 2014). If such decisions become part of the selection process, it is unclear where in that process they would be best incorporated. Importantly, the question of training has also been left mostly unaddressed empirically, despite evidence that trained raters tend to produce higher quality judgments than untrained raters in such situations (Connelly & Ones, 2010).

Sixth, even if we can identify an ideal way to include current social media profile information into selection systems, changes in technology may render those implementations obsolete or alter their relevance in a relatively short time. For example, game-thinking has emerged as a popular strategy for human resource managers to influence employee attitudes and behaviors (Armstrong, Landers, & Collmus, in press), and game-thinking plays a major role in social media. If social media platforms continue to evolve toward including game-thinking as a major motivational component—or if other, new technological inventions even more fundamentally change the experience of social media—it is unclear how useful these systems or any guidelines and recommendations developed from them will be even 5 years from now.

Although these six concerns are significant, addressing them creates the possibility for a significant and transformative new source of data about job applicants, capable of providing information about applicants that employers have never had before. In the quest for increasingly accurate and useful selection systems, this is still a worthwhile goal, despite a long road ahead. The chapters included in this book approach each of these six questions from a variety of perspectives and theoretical frameworks, and we believe they overall present a compelling case for this potential.

1.3 An Overview of this Volume

This volume looks to offer valuable information for both researchers and practitioners in pursuit of answers to the questions enumerated above. To accomplish this goal, the volume is divided into five sections: Introduction to the Book (this chapter), Current Applications of Social Media in Selection (researcher-focused), Practical Guidelines for Social Media in Selection (practitioner-focused), Challenges and Limitations (both audiences), and Future Directions (both audiences). This division is not intended to suggest that value will not be found for both audiences across the entire text. Instead, we designed the sections to ensure that the major perspectives of likely greatest interest to readers would be explored in adequate depth. As a result, we hope this volume will broadly provide value across chapters for all readers interested in the use of social media in the hiring process.

1.4 Chapter Structure and Synopses

1.4.1 Part 1: Introduction to the Book

This section is made up of only this chapter, the purpose of which is to orient the reader with the general structure of the book. It also briefly introduces the use of social media in selection and recruitment to the reader.

1.4.2 Part 2: Current Applications of Social Media in Selection

The second section of this volume is made up of five chapters and is focused upon developing a researcher perspective on social media use in selection and recruitment. The chapters in this section are intended to synthesize and review current research in the area while offering development and application of theoretical models to social media use in selection and recruitment processes. The purpose here is to help build a strong theoretical basis for how we understand social media use in selection and recruitment, with these models having the potential to drive future empirical examination.

In Chap. 2, "Social Media as a Personnel Selection and Hiring Resource: Reservations and Recommendations," Davison, Bing, Kluemper, and Roth offer a review of existing research on social media use in selection and recruitment. They examine the legality, standardization, reliability, and validity of job candidate data obtained via social media based on currently available research and theory. They offer their reservations regarding the practice of using social media in selection and recruitment, also giving practical advice on use to organizations.

In Chap. 3, "Theoretical Propositions about Cybervetting: A Common Antecedents Model," Berger and Zickar discuss the practice of cybervetting, where human resource professionals utilize the Internet as a means of performing supplemental background checks in prescreening and selection by googling job applicants and reviewing their profiles on social network sites. They advance a common antecedents model, where an applicant's general mental ability and personality impact both workplace behaviors and online behaviors. Their model offers a way for cybervetting to be standardized and systematized in both research and practice.

In Chap. 4, "An Uncertainty Reduction Approach to Applicant Information-Seeking in Social Media: Effects on Attributions and Hiring," Carr looks at organizations examining social media in selection through the lens of uncertainty reduction theory. He discusses the affordances of extracting data from social media and how social media could be used to supplement information predicting an applicant's performance on job-related tasks and fit with the social structure of an organization.

In Chap. 5, "Social Media Use: Antecedents and Outcomes of Sharing," Weidner, O'Brien, and Wynne examine the how and why of individuals and organizations using social media. They find the outcomes of use by individuals and organizations to be contradictory in nature with significant positive and negative outcomes.

In Chap. 6, "Game-Thinking within Social Media to Recruit and Select Job Candidates," Collmus, Armstrong, and Landers apply the developing area of game-thinking to how social media is used in selection and recruitment. They discuss current organizations utilizing social media games and apply relevant game-thinking theory to the application of game-thinking in social media recruitment and selection.

1.4.3 Part 3: Practical Guidelines for Social Media in Selection

The third part of this volume consists of four chapters that focus on giving practical advice to human resource professionals and organizations that are using or thinking of using social media in selection and recruitment processes. These chapters include examination of factors to consider when using social media data, how the social media used will differ based on country, and how organizations can keep up with rapidly changing social media sites and how users engage with them.

In Chap. 7, "Social Media, Big Data, and Employment Decisions: Mo' Data, Mo' Problems?," Guilfoyle, Bergman, Hartwell, and Powers focus on social media use in employment decisions as an application of big data examined through analytics. The authors discuss the potential use of social media big data for revolutionizing HR as well as a number of possible unforeseen negative consequences that can arise based on how they are used.

In Chap. 8, "Comparing the Social Media in the United State and BRIC Nations, and the Challenges Faced in International Selection," Shields and Levashina discuss the different usage of social media sites in BRIC Nations (Brazil, Russia, India, and China) and how it can impact international selection. The authors apply information systems research to propose a social media features framework that can be used to better understand and gain more knowledge on social media sites.

In Chap. 9, "Social Media and Employee Recruitment: Chasing the Run Away Bandwagon," Acikgoz and Bergman examine how social media is being used in the recruitment process. The authors discuss how recruiters use social media sites, their perceptions of best practices, and how candidates perceive the value of social media sites in the job search process.

In Chap. 10, "How to Stay Current in Social Media to Be Competitive In Recruitment and Selection," Black, Washington, and Schmidt discuss the real-world problem faced by HR professionals and organizations that the social media sites used by applicants can change significantly over time. The authors offer processes by which organization can keep current on social media site usage by applicant pools, audit their use of social media sites for recruitment and selection over time, and consider the credibility of social media sites and content.

1.4.4 Part 4: Challenges and Limitations

Part 4 of this volume consists of five chapters that focus on cautionary notes and particular considerations organizations need to consider when using social media is selection and recruitment. These chapters cover a wide range of topics that need to be highlighted and considered when using social media in employment selection and recruitment. Social media is often viewed as a powerful "big data" tool for hiring, so this section is intended to provide a dose of realism when considering the utility of social media content. Thus, the issues contained here are relevant to and targeted at both researchers and practitioners.

In Chap. 11, "Impression Management and Social Media Profiles," Roulin and Levashina examine how applicants may engage in impression management through social media to impact the selection process. The authors draw together research on traditional selection process impression management with research showing that social media users engage in impression management to create a positive online identity. They propose a framework for job applicants' impression management through social media.

In Chap. 12, "Applicant Reactions to Social Media in Selection: Early Returns and Future Directions," Stoughton discusses and offers a model related to how applicants react to the use of social media data in the selection process. Stoughton then discusses how the model and current research can be applied by practitioners in their own social media-based selection processes.

In Chap. 13, "Legal Concerns When Considering Social Media Data in Selection," Schmidt and O'Connor discuss existing laws that have been applied to social media and selection-related cases as well as existing laws that could be applied. The authors consider the existing US body of law as well as highlight three examples of laws from other countries that could impact organization selection processes that use social media.

In Chap. 14, "Online Exclusion: Biases That May Arise When Using Social Media in Talent Acquisition," Ruggs, Walker, Blanchard, and Gur discuss the significant concern that biases can arise when social media data is examined in the selection process. The authors draw on Stigma Theory, Attraction-Selection-Attrition, and Social Information Processing Theory to explain why minority job applicants may experience heightened negative bias during selection processes that use social media.

In Chap. 15, "Is John Smith Really John Smith? Misrepresentations and Misattributions of Candidates Using Social Media and Social Networking Sites," Frantz, Pears, Vaughn, Ferrell, and Dudley discuss how psychological factors can impact how users present themselves on social media sites as well as how those users are in turn perceived by others. The possible biases of those who are responsible for selecting candidates are discussed as to how they may impact the candidate as well as how social media data is interpreted.

1.4.5 Part 5: Future Directions

This final section includes one chapter by Landers and Schmidt with the explicit goal of drawing together topics and controversies across chapters, looking to the future to determine what topics are of highest priority. To facilitate this, a survey was conducted of this book's authors on a number of topics related to if and how social media be used in selection and recruitment as well as future areas of needed understanding. The survey results are discussed, highlighting a range of different opinions and perspectives on social media use in selection and recruitment. The future of social media use in selection and recruitment is also discussed, as well as needed areas of future theoretical and empirical research.

1.5 Conclusion

We conclude from this chapter list that this book is the single most comprehensive resource currently available for both researchers and practitioners trying to understand how social media are currently and could potentially be used in employee selection and recruitment. Importantly, we must simultaneously develop theory as well as straightforward practical recommendations, and these chapters are intended to do just that. Many organizations are already using social media, and even more organizations are adding social media to their decision-making process every year. In the face of this reality, we are obligated to provide trustworthy scientific guidance to them regarding how to do so most effectively.

References

Armstrong, M. B., Landers, R. N., & Collmus, A. B. (in press). Gamifying recruitment, selection, training, and performance management: Game-thinking in human resource management. In D. Davis & H. Gangadharbatla (Eds.), *Handbook of Research on Trends in Gamification.* Hershey, PA: Information Science Reference.

Boyd, D. M., & Ellison, N. B. (2008). Social network sites: Definition, history, and scholarship. *Journal of Computer-Mediated Communication, 13*, 210–230.

Connelly, B. S., & Ones, D. S. (2010). An other perspective on personality: Meta-analytic integration of observers' accuracy and predictive validity. *Psychological Bulletin, 136*, 1092–1122.

Farr, J. L. H., & Tippins, N. T. (2010). An introduction and overview. In *Handbook of Employee Selection* (pp. 1–6). New York: Routledge.

Funder, D. C. (1995). On the accuracy of personality judgment: A realistic approach. *Psychological Review, 102*, 652–670.

Grasz, J. (2014). Number of employers passing on applicants due to social media posts continues to rise, according to new CareerBuilder survey. Retrieved from http://www.careerbuilder.com/share/aboutus/pressreleasesdetail.aspx?sd=6%2F26%2F2014&id=pr829&ed=12%2F31%2F2014.

Kaplan, A. M., & Haenlein, M. (2010). Users of the world, unite! The challenges and opportunities of Social Media. *Business Horizons, 53*, 59–68.

O'Brien, J. (2014). Big data is changing the game for recruiters. *Mashable*. Retrieved from http://mashable.com/2014/06/11/big-data-recruiting/.

O'Reilly, T. (2007). What is Web 2.0: Design patterns and business models for the next generation of software. *Communications & Strategies, 1*, 17–37.

Segal, J. A. (2014). Social media use in hiring: Assessing the risks. *HR Magazine, 59*(9). Retrieved from https://www.shrm.org/publications/hrmagazine/editorialcontent/2014/0914/pages/0914-social-media-hiring.aspx.

Tett, R. P., & Burnett, D. D. (2003). A personality trait-based interactionist model of job performance. *Journal of Applied Psychology, 88*, 500–517.

Van Iddekinge, C. H., Lanivich, S. E., Roth, P. L., & Junco, E. (*in press*). Social media for selection? Validity and adverse impact potential of a Facebook-based assessment. *Journal of Management*.

Youyou, W., Kosinski, M., & Stillwell, D. (2015). Computer-based personality judgments are more accurate than those made by humans. *Proceedings of the National Academies of Science, 112*, 1036–1040.

Part II
Current Applications

Chapter 2
Social Media as a Personnel Selection and Hiring Resource: Reservations and Recommendations

H. Kristl Davison, Mark N. Bing, Donald H. Kluemper, and Philip L. Roth

Abstract Employers are often using Internet searches, social networking websites, and social media to examine detailed public information about job candidates, and sometimes private information about these job candidates as well. Such social media prescreening and human resource (HR) selection practices may have the potential to offer value-added information above and beyond that which is assessed using more traditional HR selection methods. However, details concerning the legality and the appropriateness or inappropriateness of these social media screening methods are only now emerging. Here we examine the legality, standardization, reliability, and job-relevance (i.e., validity) of job candidate data obtained via social media, along with reservations regarding this practice. We also provide recommendations for HR practitioners in using social media for selection purposes, should they choose to do so and hopefully with an awareness of the caveats that we provide. Suggestions for future research on social media HR selection practices are also discussed.

H.K. Davison, Ph.D.
Department of Management, Fogelman College of Business & Economics,
University of Memphis, Memphis, TN 38152, USA
e-mail: kristl.davison@memphis.edu

M.N. Bing, Ph.D. (✉)
Department of Management, School of Business Administration, University of Mississippi,
233 Holman Hall, P.O. Box 1848, University, MS 38677, USA
e-mail: mbing@bus.olemiss.edu

D.H. Kluemper, Ph.D.
Department of Managerial Studies, University of Illinois Chicago,
601 S. Morgan St. 2204 UH, Chicago, IL 60607-9308, USA
e-mail: kluemper@uic.edu

P.L. Roth, Ph.D.
Department of Management, College of Business, Clemson University,
Clemson, SC 29634-1305, USA
e-mail: rothp@clemson.edu

R.N. Landers, G.B. Schmidt (eds.), *Social Media in Employee Selection and Recruitment*, DOI 10.1007/978-3-319-29989-1_2

Keywords Social networking websites • Social media • Personnel selection • Reliability • Validity • Employment discrimination • Fair Credit Reporting Act • Labor relations • Best practices

2.1 Introduction

In May of 2015, an anonymous software engineer had to choose between two jobs with San Francisco tech companies, Zenefits and Uber. Unsure of which to select, he posted his dilemma on Quora, an online venue where people ask questions and others answer. One of the people who saw his posting was Parker Conrad, the CEO of Zenefits. Conrad told the engineer that he should go work for Uber, because Conrad was revoking the job offer. Notably, Conrad suggested that the engineer was not a good fit for Zenefits, as he values people who are action-oriented and decisive, rather than hesitant, and if someone was debating about whether they want to work at Zenefits, that would be a "bad sign" (Petrone, 2015).

The above scenario really happened and is a prime example of the "Wild West" world of personnel selection that is occurring in the realm of social media. There are clearly different ways in which one can interpret this particular event. Some may not fault the CEO of Zenefits for withdrawing a job offer based on a candidate's indecision with respect to joining the company—after all, a company may want someone who will be engaged and committed from the outset of an employment contract and has enthusiastically decided to choose that company as its future employer. Of course, such an unquestioning desire to work at a company *may* signal, or be a manifest indicator of, such potential commitment and enthusiasm. The candidate's indecision and/or questioning between two potential employers *may* indicate a lack of such enthusiasm. Alternatively, the job candidate's actions could be indicative of desirable employee traits, such as taking one's time to question various options and also listening to others' opinions regarding those options, and Conrad's actions could have been overly hasty in rejecting the candidate for his web-based inquiry.

However, the question that is of importance and relevance to personnel selection is whether social media assessments of various sorts are related to job performance and what other implications might such practices have for organizations. In the current example, the withdrawing of the job offer and thus the rejection of the job applicant based on his social media posting could very well have been based on job-irrelevant information, and thus ill-advised from a personnel selection standpoint. In all likelihood, the CEO of Zenefits was attempting to draw conclusions of person-organization fit, or rather misfit, from the social media posting, but such inferences from social media may very well be inaccurate and thus lead to poor HR hiring practices.

In the current chapter, we will examine the issues of whether social media is a valuable and legal source of information about job candidates. First, we will provide an overview of what social media is and how it is currently being used as a selection device. We will also provide a brief comparison of how it differs from and is similar to more traditional selection devices. Next, we discuss the laws relevant to using social media for selection. In this section, we make an important distinction between whether (or under what circumstances) it is legal to even use social media for selection, vs. whether considering the content of social media can be legally defended. We then discuss the potential usefulness of social media from the perspective of traditional psychometric properties, including standardization, reliability, and validity, also with particular attention paid to the legal issues. Finally, we provide guidance as to why, and why not, to use social media for selection and detail best practices for those managers and human resource (HR) professionals who wish to use social media in selection.

2.2 Overview of Social Media as a Selection Device

The evaluation or assessment of social media or social networking websites (SNWs) is a relatively recent development in the arena of personnel selection, but over last 10 years or so, it has become somewhat mainstream. For example, a society for human resource management (SHRM, 2013) study found that 20 % of the participating organizations surveyed used SNWs for screening, with another 12 % planning to use SNWs. This is not a trivial amount of use for a single, intended predictor of job performance as cognitive ability tests are used by approximately 16–20 % of employers, and approximately 42 % use aptitude tests (Rogelberg, 2006; Society for Industrial & Organizational Psychology, 2001). However, about 68 % of the SHRM (2013) study respondents indicated that they have never used SNWs for screening job candidates and do not plan to, a percentage which has stayed roughly consistent since 2008. This is interesting, suggesting that the use of SNWs for personnel selection has leveled out somewhat, and that perhaps SNW screening has not become the panacea that it was once touted to be. However, here it should be noted that the SHRM (2013) survey may represent a more HR-sophisticated audience than other organizational audiences or populations who might also make organizational hiring decisions. For example, according to Stoughton, Thompson, and Meade (2015), the use of Google or other social media screens by organizations in general often ranges from 27 % to roughly 65 %.

In particular, the SHRM survey indicated that employers seem to have more concerns about legality and job-relevance of evaluating the information on SNWs than they did in 2008. For example, in 2008, 54 % of the respondents who did not use SNWs for screening indicated that they had "concern[s] about legal risks/discovering information about protected characteristics"; by 2013, 74 % of the respondents shared that concern. Concerns about the job relevance of the information obtained from SNWs also increased from 36 % in 2008 to 63 % in 2013 and concerns about whether the SNWs provide information about candidate fit for the organization also increased from 26 to 61 % over that same time period.

In considering these findings, it appears that perhaps HR community members, or those HR professionals with enhanced training and education, have begun to decide that social media might not be as useful for making inferences regarding the future performance of job candidates as once believed, and that its use for such a purpose carries greater legal risks than originally assumed. The SHRM (2013) study findings with respect to the most common websites used may support this supposition. For example, LinkedIn remains the most commonly used SNW for screening (92 %, up from 85 % in 2011), and use of professional or association SNWs has also increased (from 9 % in 2011 to 14 % in 2013). In contrast, use of Facebook and MySpace for screening has declined over that period (from 78 % to 58 % and from 13 % to 4 %, respectively). However, we should note that the reduced use of MySpace, for example, could be due to the more general decline in use of that site, and the decline in the use of Facebook might be due in part to increased use of privacy settings by users, reducing its usefulness for employers. However, Twitter use for screening purposes rose from 11 % to 31 % from 2011 to 2013, which could be due to its greater openness than Facebook or MySpace, as well as greater familiarity with Twitter by organizations. Thus, although use of more job-relevant SNWs appears to be on the rise, we cannot necessarily conclude that employers are using the more personal SNWs (e.g., Twitter) less for screening purposes. At the very least, recent evidence suggests that the 20 % base-rate of SNW use for selection purposes (SHRM, 2013) is comparable with the base-rate of situational judgement test use (23 %), personality testing (22 %), and interviews with behaviorally anchored rating scales (26 %; Meinert, 2015).

Though again, surveys of possibly less sophisticated HR populations appear to show rather high use rates, and perhaps as high as 65 % (Stoughton et al., 2015). Indeed, we suspect that managers who have the power to hire and assess applicants and yet are less familiar with employment laws and standard HR practices will be highly likely to take the route of the CEO of Zenefits because (a) it is so easy to, for example, Google a job applicant at this point and thus (b) is very tempting to do so. In fact, we would go so far as to assert that it may very well be fun and entertaining for the assessor to conduct such web-based searches on potential future work colleagues, and thus the 65 % found by Stoughton et al. (2015) may very well be closer to the norm of the use of social media for selection purposes.

We consider the greater use of job-oriented websites when it is used for assessment to be a positive development, given the concerns that we detail in the following sections. Specifically, in the remainder of this chapter, we address the various legal issues of using SNWs for selection, as well as the psychometric and ultimately the very practical issues of whether any reliable and job-relevant information can be gleaned from SNWs. We also provide a series of recommendations and best practices for using social media in selection and conclude with suggestions for future research in this area.

2.3 Legal Issues of Using Social Media for Selection

In examining whether social media should be used from a legal perspective, it is important to make a distinction between whether evaluating social media for screening is legal or not, or under what conditions it may be considered, vs. whether use of the *content* in social media can be legally defensible. We should note here that we are primarily focusing on US Federal law, although some important issues that cross national borders may be raised. We should also note that our discussion here is also largely with reference to the dominant platforms such as LinkedIn, Facebook, and Twitter, although the concerns enumerated here will also be applicable to various other platforms (e.g., MySpace).

2.3.1 Laws Relevant to the Legality of Using Social Media in Selection

Our first question is whether examination of social media for use in selection is legal. In this respect, the major issue revolves around violations of job applicants' privacy. Certainly, there are many things that individuals post on SNWs, whether illegal, embarrassing, or simply personal in nature, which they would like to keep private, and SNWs have also responded by updating the privacy settings (Mgrditchian, 2015). Many of these things that individuals wish to keep private are things that employers would like to learn about prospective employees, whether to determine if the candidate lacks job-relevant skills, would be a performance problem, could represent a liability, or simply fits with the organization.

Given that job candidates can make their SNW profiles private or inaccessible, some employers turned to requiring job candidates to disclose their usernames and passwords as part of the screening process. For example, several years ago the Maryland Department of Corrections requested that applicants login to their SNW accounts so an interviewer could scroll through, ostensibly looking for indications of gang connections (Sullivan, 2012). Although such a practice likely violates the SNW terms, some employers persisted in this practice. As a result, at least 18 states have passed legislation that prohibits employers from asking for access to current or prospective employees' personal social media accounts, and another 28 states are considering such laws or have them underway (Wright, 2014). For example, a recent law review made an analogy between requiring job candidates to disclose their private SNW account login information to requiring the disclosure of "...whether they are in a relationship, contents of their recent correspondence matters between family and friends, whether they have children, what their political thoughts are, their social agendas, and a list of books and movies they have read and watched" (Lusk, 2014).

However, there is currently no national legislation that broadly protects the privacy of SNW users from employers, although it has been proposed and struck down at least twice (Wright, 2014). There are other federal laws that apply in specific cases, however. For example, the Fourth Amendment of the US Constitution provides privacy protections to public employees. This is not an unlimited right to privacy, however, as the government employer could have cause to view an employee's SNW, as in cases of harassment, defamation, trade secrets, etc. (Naito, 2012), and it is possible that screening of applicants' SNWs might also be justified.

With respect to private employers, there is legal debate as to whether privacy torts provide protection for users of SNWs. In particular, the tort of "intrusion upon seclusion" may provide protection for users' expectation of privacy in social media (Lusk, 2014). Although some courts have recognized this expectation of privacy, others have not. The central debate seems to be on the concept of "seclusion," which depends on whether a user has "a reasonable expectation of privacy in information that has been shared with some, yet kept private from the public" (Lusk, 2014). Thus, under tort law, there may be some privacy protection, but it is by no means guaranteed.

Other laws that are not explicitly about privacy nonetheless are also relevant here. The Stored Communications Act (SCA; a part of the Electronic Communications Privacy Act of 1986) was created to provide privacy protections comparable to those of the Fourth Amendment in online communications (Feuer, 2011), and thus is potentially applicable to both public and private employees. Specifically, the SCA prohibits "intentional and unauthorized access to online stored communications" (Lusk, 2014). In particular, the SCA was intended to stop theft of data by hackers, but could also apply to searches of SNWs for information that the user intended to be private (Juffras, 2010).

Compliance with the Fair Credit Reporting Act (FCRA) is also increasingly a concern for employers in using SNWs for screening purposes. The FCRA "promotes the accuracy, fairness, and privacy of information in the files of consumer reporting agencies" (Federal Trade Commission, 2015), where a "consumer reporting agency" is "any person which, for monetary fees … engages … in the practice of assembling or evaluating consumer credit information or other information on consumers for the purpose of furnishing consumer reports to third parties…" (Federal Trade Commission, 2012). The FCRA is relevant to HR practice insofar as individuals must give consent for reports to be given to employers, and individuals must be informed if information in their credit file or another type of consumer report has been used to deny them employment, insurance, or generate another adverse action. Individuals also have the right to know what information about them is in the files of a consumer reporting agency and to dispute incomplete or inaccurate information. Consumer reporting agencies also must correct or delete information determined to be inaccurate, incomplete, or unverifiable and may not report outdated negative information (Federal Trade Commission, 2015).

Thus, the FCRA comes into play when an employer contracts out the screening of SNWs to a third party (e.g., companies such as Social Intelligence) that would be considered a consumer reporting agency. In this case, the FCRA requires that job candidates provide their consent before a background check can be conducted by any consumer reporting agency (Ebnet, 2012), and if a candidate receives an adverse employment decision on the basis of such a check, notice must be provided to that candidate (Lusk, 2014). As third-party screening may be becoming more common given concerns about discrimination and standardization issues (as discussed in the following sections), many employers may nonetheless be violating the FCRA by failing to realize that the FCRA does apply to such employment-related checks as well.

Finally, employers need to be particularly cautious when considering international hires. Other nations have even more restrictive privacy regulations, including the European Union's Data Privacy Directive (Davison, Maraist, Hamilton, & Bing, 2012). With respect to screening of applications using social media, the Data Privacy Directive requires, among other things, that European applicants give explicit permission for searching SNWs (see Dowling, 2009; Massey, 2009). Insofar as organizations become increasingly global in orientation, we should expect the Data Privacy Directive to become more of an issue when conducting assessments of SNWs for screening purposes. Of particular issue would be the fact that avoiding the use of such social media information for the screening of European applicants, done in order to prevent violating the European Union's Data Privacy Directive, while assessing such information for applicants who are US citizens, could potentially be a violation of Title VII of the Civil Rights Act of 1964 based on national origin (i.e., disparate treatment in the hiring process).

2.3.2 Laws Relevant to the Legality of Using the Content of Social Media in Selection

Thus, even if it is determined to be legal to evaluate social media content for selection purposes, the question remains as to whether the content obtained on SNWs is legal to consider in selection. In particular, concerns in this area revolve around violations of the major US civil rights laws that affect private employers, namely Title VII of the Civil Rights Act (CRA) of 1964, the Age Discrimination in Employment Act (ADEA) of 1967, and the Americans with Disabilities Act (ADA) of 1990, amended in 2008. These three laws protect individuals from discrimination on the basis of their class of race, color, religion, sex, national origin (Title VII), age 40 and over (ADEA), and disability (ADA). When considering social media, it is quite clear that a variety of protected class information is readily available on SNWs. For example, pictures of a job candidate posted on LinkedIn or Facebook can reveal not only sex and race, but also color and even age. A candidate's affiliations or postings can provide details as a candidate's membership in any of these protected classes, including national origin (e.g., membership in cultural societies or clubs), religion (e.g., church membership), age (e.g., high school reunions, dates of college graduation), and possibly disability (e.g., postings about "awareness days"; see Disabled World, 2015). Even a platform such as Twitter, which relies on short texts for communication, rather than on rich detail (e.g., as with Facebook), can communicate a great deal of protected class information, via not only the content of the tweets but also potentially the use of certain phraseology that is indicative of age, race, national origin, etc.

In addition, a more recent law, the Genetic Information Nondiscrimination Act (GINA) of 2008, prohibits discrimination on the basis of genetic information, including "information about an individual's genetic tests and the genetic tests of an individual's family members, as well as information about the manifestation of a disease or disorder in an individual's family members (i.e., family medical history)" (EEOC, 2015). Insofar as individuals post information about their health or the health of their family members online (e.g., "please pray for my mother who is having surgery for breast cancer"), the content of these posts could fall under the protection of GINA. A hiring manager who views such posts and decides not to interview or hire a candidate with a genetic condition or whose family members have medical condition could thus be liable under GINA.

Employees of the US Federal Government have additional protections under the Civil Service Reform Act of 1978, including protection from discrimination on the basis of marital status, political affiliation, sexual orientation, and conduct not adversely affecting job performance (US Securities & Exchange Commission, 2015). Marital status and political affiliation, like age, are often readily available from the candidate's profile. Sexual orientation can be determined from one's memberships or postings, or even inferred from one's "likes." Moreover, individuals post information or pictures of a variety of legal activities in which they participate, and which do not necessarily affect job conduct, which nonetheless might be viewed negatively by a hiring manager.

In the above discussion, we have focused on the possibility of disparate treatment (i.e., intentional discrimination) based on protected class membership. However, adverse impact is also a concern here. In particular, adverse impact can occur when there are group differences (based on protected class status) in the use of social media or in the use of certain SNW platforms. Adverse impact can also occur when there are group differences in the evaluations of candidates' SNW profiles. This topic will be discussed in greater detail later, when addressing the question of criterion-related validity.

Beyond the civil rights laws and Civil Service Reform Act, additional protections of the content of SNWs may be had under the National Labor Relations Act (NLRA). We see this as a particularly difficult area for employers when evaluating the content of social media for selection. Many employers assume that if they are not a unionized workplace, then they do not need to be concerned with the provisions of the NLRA. Nothing could be further from the truth. First, employers are prohibited from refusing to hire job applicants based on their membership in a union, or their union activities or sympathies under Section 8(a)(3) of the NLRA. Thus, if a job candidate posts information about union membership or even union sympathies on their SNW, evaluating such information in screening the candidate could violate the NLRA.

Moreover, the National Labor Relations Board (NLRB) has clearly stated that the NLRA "…protects the rights of employees to act together to address conditions at work, with or without a union. This protection extends to certain work-related conversations conducted on social media, such as Facebook and Twitter" (NLRB, 2015a). Specifically, if employees engage in protected concerted activity, then they are covered under the NLRA. However, not all speech meets the standards to be protected concerted activity. Specifically, "concerted" refer to whether multiple employees were involved in the activity; this could be "two or more employees acting together to improve wages or working conditions" or a single employee who "involves co-workers before acting, or acts on behalf of others" (NLRB, 2015b). "Protected" activity is activity that seeks to benefit other employees, such as improvements in pay, safety, working hours, workload, etc., and is not simply in the form of a "personal gripe." Protected activity also must not involve reckless or malicious behavior (e.g., sabotage, threats of violence) that can result in a concerted activity losing protection under the NLRA (NLRB, 2015b).

Most of the current issues surrounding protected concerted activity under the NLRA in social media involve terminations or discipline (as well as the legality of employer policies on social media use). However, insofar as employee postings on SNWs might also be used for determining who would receive a promotion (i.e., an internal selection decision), if the posting met the standards for protected concerted activity, then the organization might also run afoul of the NLRA. Thus, employers should take care to abide by the NLRA when considering social media in their hiring and promotion decisions.

2.3.3 Summary

Here we must acknowledge that managers may be tempted to search for job applicant information on SNWs, believing that such a search would not be detected by anyone, even though the search might lead to an illegal employment decision. However, we should make several important points. First, this issue is not unique to SNW screening, as oftentimes applicants have no way of knowing why they were turned down for a job. For example, applicants may be turned down for illegal, discriminatory reasons based solely on their resume content. Gender bias based on the applicant's name on the resume has been demonstrated (cf. Davison & Burke, 2000), and racial bias has been found based on names on resumes as well (e.g., Bertrand & Mullainathan, 2004). Thus, employers may use SNWs for screening and "get away with it," but this concern is not unique to SNW screening.

Second, we believe that it may become more difficult for employers to search for information on applicants anonymously. For example, Facebook users can set privacy settings to limit who sees their profiles, many LinkedIn users can see who has looked at their profiles, and Twitter lists a user's followers. Third, if an employer conducts a search without the applicant's knowledge, and the applicant subsequently sues for discrimination, there may still be records of the search in the computer system, such as in the browser's history, and possibly in servers and SNW systems, that could provide evidence of the web-based search.

Finally, our concern with the use of SNWs for screening goes beyond the question of whether they are legal to use—we consider the primary concern to be whether using these sites provides an employer with reliable and valid (i.e., job-relevant) information. In other words, we are not simply recommending that employers avoid using these sites for screening in order to avoid lawsuits. We assert that employers should not use these sites in order to avoid making bad business decisions, namely incorrect applicant selections and false applicant rejections, based on unreliable information that has not been proven valid.

Having cautioned the reader as to the various laws relevant to screening using social media, in the next section we address the question of whether useful (i.e., job-relevant) information can be obtained by evaluating social media. This question is of importance for two primary reasons: if job-relevant information cannot be obtained from a SNW, then (1) the employer has no defense against a charge of adverse impact, and (2) why is the employer evaluating social media at all if it is unhelpful for improving selection decisions?

2.4 Potential Usefulness of Social Media as a Selection Device

When investigating the potential value of any selection technique, several aspects should be of focus, including a sound theoretical rationale for why the technique may be relevant to the job, consistency of scoring, various forms of reliability, and various forms of validity (Binning & Barrett, 1989; Gatewood, Feild, & Barrick, 2008). It is likely, in most instances, that SNWs have been used for selection with little consideration of these factors. Here we explore what is known about the psychometric properties of SNW screening, with a focus on validity and related issues.

2.4.1 Standardization

Standardization is a key issue in understanding many aspects of how SNWs might be used in personnel selection. We first note the likely differences among platforms and uses as well as types and varying amounts of information available to personnel decision-makers. This key issue begins to shed light on many concerns related to the reliability and validity of SNW assessment.

Standardization is the extent to which the scoring, content, and administration of a selection measure are consistent across applicants, locations, and administrators (Gatewood et al., 2008). SNW screening likely lacks standardization on all of these aspects, as much screening is often performed in an unstructured manner. First, a lone screener (e.g., an individual manager or HR representative) typically reviews the applicant's SNW, *without* using established criteria for evaluating the webpage's content. Different screeners may be looking for different information and using their own idiosyncratic standards for evaluating applicants. Thus, *scoring* is unstandardized, and adequate measurement of the applicant's SNW is therefore likely lacking, preventing consistent, reliable, and valid evaluation of an applicant's SNW. In this respect, SNW screening is similar to a holistic approach to evaluating application forms or unstructured interviews, which have been criticized for lack of standardization, reliability, validity, and scientific rigor (Gatewood et al., 2008; Highhouse, 2002).

Moreover, as SNWs and their *content* differ among applicants in the type of information contained within a particular SNW and the differences in information across different SNW platforms, SNW content is therefore unstandardized. Users present what content they and their acquaintances choose, resulting in widely varying profiles. Although platforms such as Facebook and LinkedIn, for example, suggest new users include certain information on their webpages, these guides do not *require* the user to complete all sections. Twitter has no restrictions, except in terms of the character limit of 140 characters per "tweet." Thus, missing information is of particular concern in all of these platforms, but it seems particularly likely in Twitter and could therefore often generate selection criteria deficiencies (Gatewood et al., 2008).

SNW screening also lacks standardization in terms of its "*administration*." For example, a screener may examine various applicant SNWs and view LinkedIn pages for some applicants, Facebook for others, Twitter for still others, etc., which leads to further inconsistency in content among applicants. This is also legally problematic if there is protected class information within the SNW platforms, a concern that will be addressed later in more detail.

Other standardization concerns in SNW screening are that some applicants will not have a particular SNW that an employer uses for screening purposes, some applicants might apply security settings which limit access to the screener whereas other applicants do not, and still more applicants may include such a limited amount of information as to render the SNW useless for the purpose of evaluation. For example, if a screener examines applicant Facebook pages, some applicants may not have a Facebook account, some may restrict access, and some will have limited information available for evaluation, while still others may allow full access to a wide range of information. This variability in terms of not only the content but the amount of information available across applicants creates problems for employers from a psychometric perspective. Specifically, some applicants are being judged on a large sample of information, which should provide greater reliability, whereas others are being judged on a smaller sample of information. If we were to make an analogy to testing, we would be judging some applicants on a large number of items (or tests) and judging other applicants on just a few or no items (or tests). Thus, some applicants are being assessed with less error and others with much more.

One potential approach for enhancing the standardization of assessments of SNWs would involve the use of automated (i.e., computer-based) approaches, such as latent semantic analysis or other text analytic approaches. For example, Park et al. (2015) used a language-based assessment (i.e., an open-vocabulary method for language analysis) of Facebook posts to obtain assessments of personality. They found that these assessments correlated significantly with self-reports of the Big Five in the .30 to .46 range, as well as with informant reports of personality (r's in the .20–.30 range). Thus, it appears that personality may be measured using computer-based approaches in a more standardized manner than typically performed by a human screener, although we believe that more research is warranted given the relatively modest correlations found in the Park et al. study. We must also keep in mind that although the assessment would be standardized using such methods, the material being assessed (e.g., SNW posts) remains unstandardized as previously discussed, which can harm reliability and subsequent validity of the assessment.

In sum, the lack of standardization, measurement difficulties, and scoring differences in SNW screening are particularly problematic when used for employment selection purposes. Research on the aspects of SNWs that screeners generally attend to would be useful. Future research on SNWs should develop more effective ways to score content on SNWs. Additionally, although some SNW platforms share common elements and functional building blocks (Kietzmann, Hermkens, McCarthy, & Silvestre, 2011; Mayfield, 2008) such as conversations, user presence, and connectedness, they vary in the identity users employ on diverse SNW platforms, social motivations, openness to technology, and the platforms' reputation (Kluemper, Davison, Cao, & Wu, 2015), leading to additional unstandardization.

2.4.2 *Reliability*

Reliability represents various ways to demonstrate that a measure is consistent and, hopefully, not overly plagued with errors. Three methods of estimating reliability may be readily applied to SNW screening: internal consistency reliability—consistency of results across independent evaluations/items designed to measure the same thing within a test, test-retest reliability—consistency of scores from one test administration to the next, and interrater reliability—consistency of test scores when measurements are taken by different evaluators. Here we should note that to calculate reliability, empirical scoring of SNWs is necessary.

2.4.2.1 Internal Consistency Reliability

Evaluating internal consistency reliability with SNWs is more complex than with most established selection tests, in which answers on different test items measuring the same construct can be compared. Kluemper and Rosen (2009) and Kluemper, Rosen, and Mossholder (2012) demonstrated adequate internal consistency reliability for the Big Five personality traits assessed via SNWs using trained evaluators who viewed a user's entire profile, and then completed structured ratings of personality (i.e., a self-rated personality test was reworded so that the trained evaluator conducted ratings after viewing a SNW profile). However, the number of characteristics that could be assessed within and across posts is vast, as is potentially the content of a user's profile (e.g., Facebook has been around since 2004, thus over 10 years' worth of posts could potentially be viewed).

2.4.2.2 Test-retest Reliability

Test-retest reliability assesses the temporal consistency of a test at two or more time intervals. Test-retest reliability could be evaluated by examining SNWs users' ratings at different points in time to determine whether assessments of social networking website applicant characteristics remain consistent across time. However, one issue is in the determination of an appropriate time interval. With established selection tests, applicants take the same test on two different occasions. With SNWs, examining an applicants' SNWs at two different times may reflect either more or less change than has actually occurred. For example, imagine that a SNW was examined on two occasions, one month apart. The content posted on the SNWs could include pictures that were *taken* during that one-month period. However, it could also contain pictures taken years earlier but *posted* during that 1 month period. In this latter case, changes in behaviors across phases in one's life (Slovensky & Ross, 2012) could lead to inconsistent or masked SNW screening results over time, potentially distorting test-retest reliability. At present, there is very little research on the test-retest reliability of SNW screening. For example, Park et al. (2015) examined the test-retest reliability of language-based assessment (LBA) across four consecutive 6-month subsets (i.e., Time 1, Time 2, Time 3, and Time 4) of Facebook posts, and correlated the LBA's personality predictions across those four subsets. They found average test-retest correlations of .70 for consecutive subsets (e.g., Time 1 with Time 2, or Time 3 with Time 4), and the lowest average correlation of .61 for Time 1 correlated with Time 4. Thus, there is some evidence of test-retest reliability for measuring personality in SNWs using LBA. However, to our knowledge, no SNW studies address test-retest reliability using human raters.

2.4.2.3 Interrater Reliability

Interrater reliability in SNW screening is evaluated by comparing two or more rater evaluations of a set of SNWs. Although such comparisons can be based on the raters' holistic judgments (e.g., "acceptable" vs. "unacceptable"), more precise scoring can be advantageous for assessing interrater reliability. Such rigorous comparisons are rare, however, as only one screener likely screens the profiles, and likely without a standardized scoring rubric. Thus, little is known about the interrater reliability of SNW screening. Kluemper and Rosen (2009) conducted an interrater reliability study in which 63 raters from an undergraduate employment selection course assessed the personality traits and cognitive abilities of six Facebook profiles by spending 10 min evaluating all aspects of the Facebook profile. Intra-class correlation coefficients (ICCs) ranged from .93 for extraversion, to .99 for conscientiousness. Further, raters were generally able to distinguish those with high- versus low-grade point average. These results demonstrate that scholastic aptitude and the Big Five personality traits can be reliably assessed via Facebook, at least under certain conditions with a substantial number of trained raters using a structured approach (e.g., five raters). As noted above, the Park et al. (2015) study also examined the correlations between LBA and informant ratings of personality, which showed rather modest "interrater" reliabilities (i.e., *r*'s .20–.30) between the computer and human raters.

A major issue associated with interrater reliability is that ratings are potentially affected by what is being rated and rater characteristics (e.g., similarity with the ratee; see Turban & Jones, 1988), resulting in multiple sources of potential measurement error. Further, inconsistent and/or incomplete information across SNW profiles may lead to different rater attributions and resulting evaluations which could magnify problems in interrater reliability. For example, if an applicant has a SNW profile with limited information, one rater may attribute the information to the applicant's introverted nature, another might believe the applicant is hiding something, and yet another may assume the applicant is too lazy to complete the recommended profile information. Regardless of the rater's perception, it is likely that the rater will score the applicant with complete information more positively, all other things being held equal (cf. Jaccard & Wood, 1988).

In sum, there are various problems with assessing reliability in SNW ratings. There is some initial evidence that personality can be reliably assessed, specifically, interrater and internal consistency reliability, with the latter typically requiring a substantial number of raters. However, reliability has only been examined for a few personality traits, and whether other characteristics can be measured reliably warrants further investigation.

2.4.3 Validity of SNW Screening

Validity in personnel selection consists of "the degree to which available evidence supports inferences made from scores on selection measures" (Gatewood et al., 2008). Applied psychologists and HR researchers and practitioners often examine several types of evidence of validity, each of which we now address.

2.4.3.1 Content Validity

Content validity assesses whether (a) the content of the instrument is a representative sample of the content of the job performance domain and (b) the degree of fidelity of the measure relative to job performance is adequate (Gatewood et al., 2008). Implicit within these ideas is that content validity typically involves a process in which job analytic information is first considered to explicate the job performance domain and then the assessment device is developed to relate to that performance-based information (e.g., Section 14. C.1 of the *Uniform Guidelines on Employee Selection Procedures,* 1978). When SNWs are screened without careful consideration of the job analysis and the particular constructs, meaning the job-relevant knowledge, skills, abilities, and other characteristics (KSAOs) being measured, the measure may not reflect the content of the job. Further, the Equal Employment Opportunity Commission (EEOC, 1978) has indicated in the *Uniform Guidelines on Employee Selection Procedures* (1978) that content validation is inappropriate when measuring what they refer to as mental processes (e.g., intelligence, personality, judgment). Content validation might be more appropriate when assessing observable behaviors via SNWs. As an example, certain marketing or interior design jobs might involve creativity and artistic expression. Such factors might be assessed on SNWs via posted pictures of the applicant's previous work, and thus might relate to subsequent job performance.

Content validity may also be particularly problematic for assessing SNWs. Recall that most SNWs do not require individuals to post any standardized information and the purpose of many SNWs is not employment-related (e.g., Facebook, Twitter). These problems may manifest themselves in several ways. Content validity may require consideration of how much of the job content is being assessed. The *Guidelines* note that content validity should be based on critical work behaviors or important work behaviors that cover most of the job in question (14.C.2). Thus, job analyses supporting the use of SNWs may require careful consideration of critical work behaviors per se, which may or may not be typically assessed in an organization's job analysis procedures or cover a majority of the job performance space. This may be troublesome when there is no standard information required by the social media platform and when so much information is missing due to the factors noted above. That is, it may be difficult to make assessments when information is either posted inconsistently or not posted at all.

It is also unlikely that SNW posts have high fidelity with most jobs. Recall that the *Guidelines* (1978, p. 21) note "the closer the content and the context of the selection procedure are to work samples or work behaviors, the stronger the basis for showing content validity." The *Guidelines* (1978) go on to state that the less that a predictor resembles the work product or work setting, the greater the need for other types of evidence of validity (Section. 14.C.4). It is unclear how much fidelity a SNW will have with most jobs that do not involve web design or a few other areas that might involve high correspondence between the nature of the specific work in question and the nature of the SNW-based activities themselves.

Overall, the use of SNWs based on content validity will require careful job analysis, development of the SNW assessment, and, perhaps, how this assessment relates to other assessments to cover a substantial portion of the job. It would appear clear that a quick look at a SNW with no structured process by a manager with little background in selection could easily fail to show content validity. Thus, organizations wishing to use content validity to justify assessment of SNWs will need to do substantial work to justify such inferences or be faced with problematic results, such as low levels of content validity.

2.4.3.2 Construct Validity

Construct validity is present when a measurement assesses what it claims to be measuring. However, assessors may often have no specific construct in mind when screening SNWs, but instead often casually scan profiles to screen out potential new hires. Again, a key issue is to identify what job-relevant construct(s) might be measured via SNW profiles. Another issue is to show that what hiring managers are measuring via SNW profiles is in fact what they believe themselves to be measuring, assuming they have a set of constructs (i.e., KSAOs) in mind. Probably, the most common current approach to SNW screening is that of disqualifying information, as a type of background check. SNW information pertaining to illegal drug use, discriminatory comments, misrepresented qualifications, or shared confidential information about a current employer (CareerBuilder.com, 2009) might provide what appears to be a strong basis to reject an applicant. At present, little is known about the construct validity and accuracy of using SNW screening in this manner. Recent work by Becton, Walker, Schwager, and Gilstrap (2013) suggests that SNW screening may have some use for predicting alcohol use. However, in their study SNW screening failed to predict counterproductive workplace behaviors (CWBs); thus, it may be unclear how judgments of disqualifying information would be related to the job itself (see Section 14.D.2 of the *Uniform Guidelines on Employee Selection Procedures*, 1978). A study by Stoughton, Thompson, and Meade (2013) also examined self-reports of badmouthing and substance use postings in SNWs and found that agreeableness and conscientiousness were related to badmouthing, whereas extraversion was related to substance use. These findings suggest there may be some convergent validity in measuring such counterproductive behavior via SNW postings, but it is important to note that their study examined self-reported badmouthing and substance use, rather than measures of these counterproductive behaviors taken directly from actual SNW postings.

Empirical evidence has begun to emerge which suggests that traits such as the Big-five personality dimensions (Kluemper et al., 2012; Kluemper & Rosen, 2009), narcissism (Buffardi & Campbell, 2008), and cognitive ability (Kluemper & Rosen, 2009) can be measured with SNWs, assuming rater training, structured assessment, and the use of multiple raters are in place for the assessment. Further, a range of additional KSAOs have been suggested in the literature, including job-relevant background information, such as education, work history, and professional memberships (Davison et al., 2012), language fluency, certain technical proficiencies, creative outlets, teamwork skills (Smith & Kidder, 2010), network ability and social capital (e.g., Steinfield, Ellison, & Lampe, 2008), creativity (Davison et al., 2012), communication, interpersonal skills, leadership, persuasion, and negotiation skills (Roth, Bobko, Van Iddekinge, & Thatcher, in press). However, empirical work is needed to demonstrate whether these characteristics can be accurately assessed with SNW profiles. Hiring managers may also attempt to measure person-organization (P-O) fit via SNWs (Roth et al., in press; Slovensky & Ross, 2012). In this case, employers may search for similarities between the person and the organization (Kristof, 1996) in terms of interests, goals, values, and attitudes that may lead the applicant to fit well within the organization. However, assessors may not have specific P-O fit characteristics in mind when screening SNWs.

In sum, it is apparent that various constructs *might* be measured via SNW screening, but much scientific work is needed to provide empirical evidence as to whether each potential construct can be measured validly. Evidence is accumulating that certain personality traits might be measured successfully under the right circumstances. For example, all of the Facebook-rated (i.e., rated by humans) Big Five personality traits have been shown to demonstrate convergent validity with self-rated personality traits (Kluemper et al., 2012). There is also evidence that computer-based analysis of language and other SNW mechanisms (e.g., Facebook "Likes") can assess personality traits (e.g., Kosinski, Stillwell, & Graepel, 2013; Park et al., 2015). Beyond personality, little is known about whether other disqualifying information, KSAOs, P-O fit, or qualifications can be measured accurately via SNWs. Research could involve obtaining established measures of relevant KSAOs from participants, and then using standardized procedures to screen SNW profiles of those participants. This would provide an initial step of establishing convergent and discriminant validity of SNW screening. However, even if this evidence of construct validity were obtained, other and perhaps more important, meaning selection-relevant, aspects of validity (e.g., criterion-related and incremental validity) are also needed before SNWs should be used in applied settings for employment selection. In other words, a construct-valid measure is not inherently job-relevant because job-irrelevant constructs can also be reliably and validly measured. Ultimately, we also caution that individual organizations will likely have to go through a substantial process of construct validation for their SNW assessments, and such processes can take large amounts of time to satisfy the technical requirements of construct validity in the *Uniform Guidelines* (1978).

2.4.3.3 Criterion-related Validity

Criterion-related validity assesses whether test scores are correlated with scores on a job-relevant outcome such as a measure of job performance. This is particularly important given the *Uniform Guidelines* (1978) titles Section 9 "No assumption of validity." The *Guidelines* state that casual reports of validity, testimonials, and promotional literature are not acceptable substitutes for evidence of validity. Further, the *Guidelines* encourage the use of professional supervision of selection procedures. Such standards may be particularly important if untrained individuals or those with limited HR backgrounds are quickly performing an employment screen without thoughtful consideration of job analytic information.

Limited research has examined whether ratings of traits from SNW profiles correlate with job performance. Kluemper et al. (2012) provide initial evidence that Facebook-rated personality traits correlate with supervisor ratings of job performance (Study 1) and academic success (Study 2). However, SNWs were evaluated for a hypothetical position, while job performance was measured for the student's current job while they were a student. Thus, it is unclear if such a performance measure would satisfy the requirements for a criterion in the *Uniform Guidelines* (Section 14.B.3). Further, only roughly 10% of the originally rated student SNWs were able to be matched with a criterion. So, data loss was also substantial (see Roth et al., in press).

A more recent study by Van Iddekinge, Lanivich, Roth, and Junco (in press) found that Facebook ratings of KSAOs did not predict job performance. That is, the functional validity of actual recruiters looking at job applicant Facebook pages, using whatever process was typical of their organization, was empirically unrelated to subsequent measures of job performance by supervisors overseeing the jobs subsequently acquired by the students (i.e., criterion-validity was functionally zero). Although this study used college recruiters to rate student Facebook profiles and obtained supervisor ratings of job performance one year later, this study utilized only one untrained evaluator per profile, with different evaluators across profiles, which likely results in unstandardization against which we previously cautioned, and thus subsequent unreliability of assessment. Further, the 10 KSAOs measured were not necessarily relevant to each of the wide range of students' subsequent occupations, although other summary performance evaluations were also available.

A potentially troubling result of the Van Iddekinge et al. (in press) study was the presence of standardized group differences. Recall that the *Uniform Guidelines* explicitly address the issue of adverse impact (Section 4). That is, there is concern when a substantially smaller portion of one protected group is hired relative to the highest scoring group (often the "majority" group, as per section 4.D). We are not aware of any other studies addressing this issue. Van Iddekinge et al. found evidence of standardized group differences (*d*) in favor of Whites relative to Blacks and Hispanics in some cases. Thus, adverse impact could occur if such an approach was used for hiring, further necessitating evidence of validity for legal defensibility. Interestingly, females, on-the-average, scored somewhat higher than males. Thus, there was no evidence indicating adverse impact against females in their sample.

How one summarizes the evidence of criterion-related validity depends upon how one weighs the evidence. A more optimistic view is that taken together, the above studies provide initial evidence that Facebook information based on personality, but not on other KSAOs, can be used to identify individuals who are more successful in college and on-the-job. Thus, SNW screening has some limited evidence of criterion-related validity. However, we urge caution when interpreting these findings. Far more replication and extension in the peer-reviewed academic literature is needed before drawing firm conclusions about the potential criterion-related validity of personality measurement via SNW assessment, as well as in drawing firm conclusions about the lack of viability of measuring other KSAOs via SNW screening.

A less optimistic view is that there is little professionally acceptable evidence of validity at this time. The study by Kluemper et al. (2012) emphasizes the importance of assessor training, analyzing the job, and multiple raters as key issues for organizations to consider. Yet, the data based on actual recruiters, using whatever practices their organization currently supported, and with the measurement of actual subsequent job performance showed *no* evidence of validity (Van Iddekinge et al., in press). At the same time, there was evidence of standardized group differences against Hispanics and Blacks in some instances. Thus, use of SNW screening by actual recruiters may be associated with the worst of two worlds: no validity and adverse impact. This could be considered as discrimination in Section 3 of the *Uniform Guidelines* (1978) and according to legal precedent (e.g., *Griggs v. Duke Power Co,* 1971). The absence of validity and the presence of adverse impact would make it difficult to defend such procedures. Finally, at present we have *no* information about the criterion-related validity of personality (or other traits) measured via automated computer-based text analytic methods (e.g., language-based assessments).

2.4.3.4 Incremental Validity

Incremental validity, whether an additional test adds predictive value beyond existing methods, of SNW screening is also an important area of inquiry (cf. Davison, Maraist, & Bing, 2011). As such, SNW selection techniques should be evaluated to demonstrate if they add incremental validity beyond tests such as application blanks, biodata, personality tests, etc. (Roth et al., in press) to be considered value-added

(Cronbach & Gleser, 1957). Again, results here are somewhat mixed. The Kluemper, McLarty, and Rosen (2013) studies show incremental validity beyond self-rated personality (Study 1) and self-rated personality and ACT/SAT scores (Study 2). In contrast, the study by Van Iddekinge et al. (in press) shows little functional incremental validity beyond constructs such as personality and cognitive ability. Of course, such incremental validity results will depend upon what constructs the SNW assessment measures and what other selection procedures, and the constructs they assess, are present. Once again, relatively little is known about the incremental validity of this new type of information gathered from SNWs.

2.4.3.5 Generalizability Across Platforms

The question of generalizability deals with the issue of whether what works in one context also works in another context. In particular, there are numerous SNWs with divergent purposes and different user demographics, along with different access limits, and different amounts and types of information provided. For example, Facebook and LinkedIn differ substantially in terms of their intended purposes, including connections with friends vs. professionals, the number of users, and the amount and type of information provided, etc. The SNW platforms may also differ in demographic characteristics (e.g., age; Duggan & Brenner, 2013) and user occupational characteristics.

Furthermore, these applications are constantly changing. Therefore, issues regarding Facebook may not be relevant to LinkedIn or Twitter, and establishing reliability and validity with one set of constructs, one SNW platform, or at one time-point in the evolution of a particular SNW, does not mean that such psychometric properties will hold for others, or at different points in time. Research is needed to determine what constructs are measured most accurately using which SNW platform. For example, personality and negative traits might be more accurately measured via Facebook, which has a very flexible format (i.e., a weak situation) that may be conducive to expressing such traits (cf. Blackman & Funder, 2002). Alternatively, more traditional KSAOs (e.g., work experience, problem solving) might be better assessed via the more structured and work-oriented LinkedIn platform.

2.5 Directions for Future Research

As the previous sections have detailed, numerous questions remain unanswered in the existing literature. A traditional first step would be to determine what constructs can most easily be assessed via SNW-based information (e.g., work experience, personality, etc.), and of those constructs, which ones may consistently demonstrate criterion-related validity. For example, as has been previously discussed, automated computer-based text analysis of SNWs may generate assessments of personality. However, future research is needed to see if these particular assessments of personality, obtained on unstandardized SNW-based text, can be used to predict job performance.

In addition to the questions about what constructs (i.e., job-relevant KSAOs) can be measured reliably and validly via SNWs, other questions also bear addressing. For example, future research should investigate differences in user demographics (e.g., age, gender, ethnicity, cultural background, socioeconomic status) across platforms or across social media use in general. Also, are there behavioral differences (e.g., differences in information disclosure, identity presentation) across platforms, such that individuals are presenting different "selves" on different platforms? If this is the case, then that would make the choice of platform for screening more crucial.

On a related note, research is needed to determine to what extent individuals "fake" or engage in impression management on SNWs.[1] For example, to what extent does innate impression management (see Roulin & Levashina's Chap. 15 in this book), or self-deception enhancement, occur when one generates a profile on a SNW? Future research should assess job applicants on various measures indicative of test faking, such as overclaiming (e.g., Bing, Kluemper, Davison, Taylor, & Novicevic, 2011), bogus items (e.g., Levashina, Morgeson, & Campion, 2009), and the more traditional self-report measures of impression management and self-deception enhancement, and correlate these assessments with those obtained on construct scores (e.g., personality scores) obtained from SNW information to determine the extent to which such SNW-based assessments are tainted with faking attempts. Research is also needed to determine whether faking on SNWs is necessarily "faking good" (see Davison et al., 2011), such that SNW users are trying to present a more socially acceptable or desirable picture of themselves. Alternatively, some users may be "faking bad" by presenting a less socially desirable (e.g., reckless, irresponsible, "devil-may-care") picture of themselves, perhaps in order to attempt to appear outgoing, fun-loving, or cool to peers. Moreover, there may be age, racial, or gender differences in faking good vs. faking bad on SNWs that are worth investigating.

Furthermore, do patterns of connections across social networks different among SNW platforms (e.g., personal friends vs. colleagues, close friends vs. acquaintances or even strangers)? For example, many non-acquaintances are connected via Twitter, whereas acquaintances tend to be connected via Facebook. Investigations into such variations in social networks across SNW platforms will further our understanding of the amount and quality of information available.

2.6 Recommendations and Best Practices for Using Social Media as a Selection Device

In determining recommendations and best practices for using social media in selection, we first review the reasons why employers might want to avoid using social media based on the current state of the research and the legal environment. We then

[1] One of the authors has heard that some college fraternities encourage their graduating seniors entering the job market to delete their current Facebook profile, if showing certain parties and events over the years, and then creating a new, sanitized Facebook account that would be highly unlikely to offend any potential employer.

detail the reasons why employers might want to use social media for screening, and with the caveats that if employers do choose to use social media in this manner, there are various best practices that can help the employer to obtain more reliable and valid data while mitigating legal liability.

2.6.1 Reasons for Not Using Social Media

There are several reasons for not using social media assessments. First, published validity evidence is not supportive of its use. As noted above, the case for content validity will be difficult to make given the lack of SNW use by some applicants and the unlikelihood of having information on any one area uniformly posted by others. Further, assessment of SNWs is not likely to have high levels of fidelity with most jobs. The evidence for criterion-related validity in the published literature is also not encouraging. In particular, the results for predicting job performance by actual supervisors was essentially zero (Van Iddekinge et al., in press) as were the non-significant results for predicting counterproductive work behaviors (Becton et al., 2013).

Second, there is some evidence that social media assessments can be associated with standardized ethnic group differences that negatively impact Blacks and Hispanics (though not females). Van Iddekinge et al. found a number of instances in which the standardized group differences existed and could be associated with adverse impact, depending upon selection ratios. Again, this could represent a real liability as adverse impact without evidence of validity is typically viewed as illegal discrimination (e.g., *Uniform Guidelines on Employee Selection Procedures*, 1978). Additionally, there is the real possibility that adverse impact could occur simply by using SNWs for selection, or using certain platforms, given that there are racial differences in SNW platform use (Duggan, Ellison, Lampe, Lenhart, & Madden, 2014).

Third, it is not clear that applicants have a positive view of organizations that use assessments of social media information. While published studies in this area are rare, at least one study suggests that assessments from Facebook resulted in negative reactions from applicants (Stoughton et al., 2015). Students who understood that their Facebook pages had been accessed reported in one study that they felt their privacy had been violated, they had been unjustly treated, and their reactions toward an organization engaged in such efforts were negative. A second study found similar results and also noted that self-reported intentions to litigate were elevated. The findings should be interpreted in light of the fact that the participants were students applying for what they thought was a real, though short-term job.

2.6.2 Reasons for Using Social Media

We see two possible reasons to examine social media, though even these may be considered with great caution. Organizations may wish to avoid negligent hiring claims. For example, an organization hiring transportation workers may wish to look for examples of driving while intoxicated. Or they may infer that individual's with many posts involving alcohol and parties are a risk, though this is potentially a weak and unwarranted inference, as such posts may have more to do with extraversion than with conscientiousness (see Stoughton et al., 2013). Yet, this places organizations in a dilemma. Do they use a predictor of job performance that does not have a track record of validity, or might be considered as having a track record of no validity, and the potential for adverse impact, all in order to avoid negligent hiring claims? Or, do they risk a charge of negligent hiring for failing to thoroughly investigate the candidate's background? While we lean towards using some other predictor such as a structured verbal background interviews of former supervisors, this is a difficult managerial decision. Managers wrestling with this dilemma may wish to consult Davison et al.'s (2012) risk-benefit analysis for insight.

Organizations that wish to use assessments of social media for selection purposes should have internal, well-conducted, and well-documented evidence of social media assessments predicting job performance. Organizations should be careful to note that the rather small, published literature does not provide support for predicting job performance at this time. Some organizations may have the technical expertise to conduct well-thought-out validity studies and may find positive results (e.g., analysis of gaps in employment on LinkedIn predict future turnover). Again we caution organizations that the validity studies should be able to stand up to legal discovery, critiques by unfriendly expert witnesses, and also that the data will convince legal decision-makers that there is meaningful criterion-related validity. Specifically, a four-page technical report in which the consulting organization (sometimes) changes the name of the contracting organization with a shoddy cut-and-paste is not likely to suffice in these circumstances! Further, we predict some sort of class action lawsuit over the merits of social media in selection is likely to ensue in the coming years. Organizations should be ready.

2.6.3 Recommendations/Best Practices

2.6.3.1 Recommendation #1: Do Not Use Social Media for Selection

All joking aside, we urge most employers to refrain from using social media. The validity and adverse impact "landscape" is not conducive to enhancing the quality of the workforce while avoiding litigation. Additionally, applicant reactions may be negative regarding the use of social media for selection purposes.

However, some employers may determine that the risks are worth the benefits. There are various best practices for assessing SNWs that may help the employer to obtain job-relevant information on job candidates and to do so in a more legal manner. Nonetheless, we again believe that social media assessments should probably come with a surgeon general's warning on the side of the package. We recommend that organizations consider both the principles of procedural justice, such as voice in decision-making, consistency in applying rules, accurate use of information, opportunity to be heard, and safeguards against bias (see Greenberg, 2011; see also Folger, Konovsky, & Cropanzano's, 1992 due process metaphor), as well as professionally endorsed practices in test development and application.

2.6.3.2 Recommendation #2: Best Practices: Proceed with Great Caution or Not at All

If one is to use SNWs for selection purposes, then we highly recommend that the following guidelines are followed.

Guideline #1 Begin the process with job analysis (see Davison et al., 2012). That is, understand the job in question and the behaviors that are to be predicted by this "test" of social media website assessment. The job analysis may be particularly important if organizations wish to predict a relatively small portion of the job performance domain such as an individual counter-productive work behavior. In this case, the job analysis will have to be structured to allow subject matter experts to rate various behaviors not just on importance, but on criticality (*Uniform Guidelines on Employee Selection Procedures*, 1978). Related to this recommendation is our suggestion that screening be done selectively; do not simply screen SNWs for all jobs, but instead determine if the legal risks are worth the possible benefits obtained (see Davison et al., 2012). For example, if it is a job in which negligent hiring is a significant concern, then *perhaps* assessment of SNWs is appropriate.

Guideline #2 We suggest that organizations focus on employment-based websites. For example, it is likely that analyses of LinkedIn would have more work-related behaviors and be viewed more positively by legal decision-makers, although no published evidence directly supports this supposition at the present time.

Guideline #3 Provide safeguards against bias. One such safeguard might be to train social media assessors in what to search for (i.e., job-related information such as "employee of the month"). Such information is more likely to be considered judgment based on evidence than judgment based on demographic stereotypes. Similarly, train decision-makers about information not to consider such as ethnicity, gender, or other factors that might not be job-related. Another safeguard might be to have individuals who conduct the social media assessment separate from those individuals who conduct the interviews. Further, there should not be sharing of information between these separate assessors to avoid self-fulfilling prophecies, halo and horn effects, etc.

Guideline #4 Have the HR department do such checks given their familiarity with issues of validity, adverse impact, and disparate treatment. Practicing managers may not have these same sensitivities and expertise as the HR professionals and may be too tempted to examine non-job-related factors, particularly in such an interesting and technological environment (see Van Iddekinge et al., in press). There are also third-party consultants (e.g., Social Intelligence) that will screen SNWs for various characteristics and provide a report with demographic information omitted. However, in this case compliance with the requirements of the FCRA is absolutely necessary, as discussed previously.

Guideline #5 Organizations should consider getting written permission from job candidates before assessing SNW information, but should never ask for the candidates' usernames and passwords. Again, obtaining written permission is consistent with procedural fairness, and indeed required by the FCRA if the assessment is done by a third party. However, organizations may suffer negative reactions in the process of notifying applicants or applicants may "clean up" their SNWs (see Footnote 1). Similarly, organizations may wish to give applicants the chance to respond to negative information or assessments, again consistent with the FCRA. For example, an applicant may wish to respond to several pictures of him/her drinking beer in Bavaria on vacation as not being job-related or illegal (i.e., applicants should be given an opportunity to explain or be "heard"). Of course, this may also entail legal risks when organizations use job-related, or non-job-related information, to make reasonable or unreasonable inferences about job candidates, which they would often like to keep secret.

Guideline #6 Organizations should have evidence of criterion-related validity *before* they operationally use assessments of SNWs for selection decisions. That is, we suggest that organizations conduct a full-scale validity study of assessing SNW information before it is used in selection in order to develop evidence that judgments from assessments of these SNWs are valid. Within this effort, adverse impact analyses should be conducted and consistent with professional standards.

Guideline #7 Compare assessment of SNWs with alternative predictors, such as traditional personality tests, background checks, etc. This comparison should include both comparisons of validity and adverse impact/standardized ethnic group differences. Organizations should consider that predictors with higher validity are typically preferred, particularly when they have less adverse impact. The incremental validity of SNW assessments should also be evaluated.

Guideline #8 The entire procedure should be structured, meaning standardized. Standardization is designed to give all applicants the same and equal opportunity to "perform" well on a test. Standardization should pervade the assessment process from job analysis to documentation of which behaviors are to be predicted, to the process of which sites are to be examined, and how the examination proceeds to the ratings made by assessors. Such standardization has helped HR professionals for years to generate structured interviews, and we believe it will mitigate problems for social media assessors (Campion, Palmer, & Campion, 1997). Of course, the procedure should also be done consistently across candidates.

Guideline #9 We also believe that the SNW screening should be done later in the process, once visible protected class memberships are likely already known (see Segal, 2014). Whereas some managers may be inclined to use it early to weed out certain candidates in a quick and dirty manner, that practice clearly invites legal challenge. Thus, SNW screening should be conducted late in the selection process, as is recommended with other kinds of background checks, drug testing, medical screening, and other tests of a private nature (Gatewood et al., 2008).

Guideline #10 Again, we do *not* endorse the use of social media screening at this point. While some individuals may infer that we do, given our guidance immediately above, we reiterate our first piece of advice in not using these screens in the vast majority of instances. Thus, distilling our advice is "when in doubt, don't." If you proceed, proceed with an overabundance of caution. To paraphrase Gene Roddenberry's *Star Trek*, when using social media for screening, "Do NOT boldly go where no one has gone before," and, instead, do so very cautiously.

References

Becton, B., Walker, H. J., Schwager, P., & Gilstrap, B. (2013). *Predicting counterproductive work behaviors, alcohol consumption, and episodic heavy drinking using social media*. Paper presented at the Southern Management Association Annual Meeting, New Orleans, LA.

Bertrand, M., & Mullainathan, S. (2004). Are Emily and Greg more employable than Lakisha and Jamal? A field experiment on labor market discrimination. *American Economic Review, 94*, 991–1013.

Bing, M. N., Kluemper, D. H., Davison, H. K., Taylor, S. G., & Novicevic, M. (2011). Overclaiming as a measure of faking. *Organizational Behavior and Human Decision Processes, 116*, 148–162.

Binning, J. F., & Barrett, G. V. (1989). Validity of personnel decisions: A conceptual analysis of the inferential and evidential bases. *Journal of Applied Psychology, 74*, 478–494.

Blackman, M. C., & Funder, D. C. (2002). Effective interview practices for accurately assessing counterproductive traits. *International Journal of Selection and Assessment, 10*, 109–116.

Buffardi, L. E., & Campbell, W. K. (2008). Narcissism and social networking web sites. *Personality and Social Psychology Bulletin, 34*, 1303–1314.

Campion, M. A., Palmer, D. A., & Campion, J. E. (1997). A review of structure in the selection interview. *Personnel Psychology, 50*, 655–702.

CareerBuilder.com (2009). *Forty-five percent of employers use social networking sites to research job candidates, CareerBuilder survey finds: Career expert provides dos and don'ts for job seekers on social networking*. Retrieved from http://www.careerbuilder.com/share/aboutus/pressreleasesdetail.aspx?id=pr519&sd=8/19/2009&ed=12/31/2009. Accessed 16 Oct 2013.

Cronbach, L. J., & Gleser, G. C. (1957). *Psychological tests and personnel decisions*. Urbana, IL: University of Illinois Press.

Davison, H. K., & Burke, M. J. (2000). Sex discrimination in simulated employment contexts: A meta-analytic investigation. *Journal of Vocational Behavior, 56*, 225–248.

Davison, H. K., Maraist, C. C., & Bing, M. N. (2011). Friend or foe? The promise and pitfalls of using social networking sites for HR decisions. *Journal of Business and Psychology, 26*, 153–159.

Davison, H. K., Maraist, C. C., Hamilton, R., & Bing, M. N. (2012). To screen or not to screen? Using the internet for selection decisions. *Employee Responsibilities and Rights Journal, 24*, 1–21.

Disabled World. (2015). *List of health & disability awareness days, weeks & months*. Retrieved from http://www.disabled-world.com/disability/awareness/awareness-dates.php. Accessed 11 June 2015.

Dowling, D. (2009). Preparing to resolve U.S.-based employers' disputes under Europe's new data privacy law. *Journal of Alternative Dispute Resolution in Employment, 2*, 31–44.

Duggan, M., & Brenner, J. (2013). The demographics of social media users—2012. Retrieved from http://www.pewinternet.org/reports/2013/social-media-users.aspx/. Accessed 12 June 2015.

Duggan, M., Ellison, N. B., Lampe, C., Lenhart, A., & Madden, M. (2014). *Demographics of key social networking platforms*. Retrieved from http://www.pewinternet.org/2015/01/09/demographics-of-key-social-networking-platforms-2/. Accessed 12 June 2015.

Ebnet, N. J. (2012). It can do more than protect your credit score: Regulating social media pre-employment screening with the Fair Credit Reporting Act. *Minnesota Law Review, 97*, 306.

EEOC. (2015). *Genetic information discrimination*. Retrieved from http://eeoc.gov/laws/types/genetic.cfm. Accessed 11 June 2015.

Federal Trade Commission. (2012). *Fair Credit Reporting Act*. 15 U.S.C. §1681.

Federal Trade Commission. (2015). *A summary of your rights under the Fair Credit Reporting Act*. Retrieved from https://www.consumer.ftc.gov/articles/pdf-0096-fair-credit-reporting-act.pdf. Accessed 3 Sept 2015.

Feuer, L. S. (2011). Who is poking around your Facebook profile? The need to reform the Stored Communications Act to reflect a lack of privacy on social networking websites. *Hofstra L. Review 40*, 473.

Folger, R., Konovsky, M. A., & Cropanzano, R. (1992). A due process metaphor for performance appraisal. *Research in Organizational Behavior, 14*, 129–177.

Gatewood, R. D., Feild, H. S., & Barrick, M. (2008). *Human resource selection* (6th ed.). Mason, OH: South-Western.

Greenberg, J. (2011). Organizational justice: The dynamics of fairness in the workplace. In S. Zedeck (Ed.), *APA handbook of industrial and organizational psychology, Vol 3: Maintaining, expanding, and contracting the organization* (pp. 271–327). Washington, DC, US: American Psychological Association.

Griggs v. Duke Power Co. (1971). 401 U.S. 424.

Highhouse, S. (2002). Assessing the candidate as a whole: A historical and critical analysis of individual psychological assessment for personnel decision making. *Personnel Psychology, 55*, 363–396.

Jaccard, J., & Wood, G. (1988). The effects of incomplete information on the formation of attitudes toward behavioral alternatives. *Journal of Personality and Social Psychology, 54*, 580–591.

Juffras, D. (2010). Using the Internet to conduct background checks on applicants for employment. *University of North Carolina School of Government Public Employment Law Bulletin Number, 38*, 1–22.

Kietzmann, J. H., Hermkens, K., McCarthy, I. P., & Silvestre, B. S. (2011). Social media? Get serious! Understanding the functional building blocks of social media. *Business Horizons, 54*, 241–251.

Kluemper, D. H., Davison, H. K., Cao, A., & Wu, B. (2015). Social networking websites and personnel selection: A call for academic research. In I. Mikolaou & J. K. Oostrom's (Eds.), *Employee recruitment, selection, and assessment: Contemporary issues for theory and practice*. London: Psychology Press\Taylor & Francis.

Kluemper, D. H., McLarty, B., & Rosen, P. (2013). Exploring the relationship between individual characteristics and LinkedIn use. In R. F. Miguel, *The promise and perils of social media data for selection*. Symposium presented at the Society for Industrial and Organizational Psychology, Houston, TX.

Kluemper, D. H., & Rosen, P. (2009). Future employment selection methods: Evaluating social networking websites. *Journal of Managerial Psychology, 24*, 567–580.

Kluemper, D. H., Rosen, P., & Mossholder, K. (2012). Social networking websites, personality ratings, and the organizational context: More than meets the eye? *Journal of Applied Social Psychology, 42*, 1143–1172.

Kosinski, M., Stillwell, D., & Graepel, T. (2013). Private traits and attributes are predictable from digital records of human behavior. *PNAS, 110*, 5802–5805.

Kristof, A. L. (1996). Person-organization fit: An integrative review of its conceptualizations, measurement, and implications. *Personnel Psychology, 49*, 1–49.

Levashina, J., Morgeson, F. P., & Campion, M. A. (2009). They don't do it often, but they do it well: Exploring the relationship between applicant mental abilities and faking. *International Journal of Selection and Assessment, 17*, 271–281.

Lusk, R. E. (2014). Facebook's newest friend—Employers: Use of social networking in hiring challenges US Privacy constructs. *Capital University Law Review, 42*, 709.

Massey, R. (2009). Privacy and social networks: A European opinion. *Journal of Internet Law, 13*, 1–17.

Mayfield, A. (2008). *What is social media?* Retrieved from http://www.icrossing.com/sites/default/files/what-is-social-media-uk.pdf. Accessed 16 Oct 2013

Meinert, D. (2015). Heads up. *HR Magazine, 6*, 88–98.

Mgrditchian, G. (2015). Employment & social media privacy: Employer justifications for access to "private" material. *Rutgers Computer & Tech. L. J. 41*, 108.

Naito, A. (2012). A Fourth Amendment status update: Applying constitutional privacy protection to employees' social media use. *U. PA. J. Const. L. 14*, 849.

NLRB. (2015a). *The NLRB and social media*. Retrieved from http://www.nlrb.gov/news-outreach/fact-sheets/nlrb-and-social-media. Accessed 11 June 2015.

NLRB. (2015b). *Protected concerted activity*. Retrieved from http://www.nlrb.gov/rights-we-protect/protected-concerted-activity. Accessed 11 June 2015.

Park, G., Schwartz, H. A., Eichstaedt, J. C., Kern, M. L., Kosinski, M., Stillwell, D. J., et al. (2015). Automatic personality assessment through social media language. *Journal of Personality and Social Psychology, 108*, 934–952.

Petrone, P. (2015, May 12). *CEO revokes offer after candidate asks the internet if he should take the job*. Retrieved from http://talent.linkedin.com/blog/index.php/2015/05/ceo-revokes-offer-after-candidate-asks-the-internet-if-he-should-take-the-job. Accessed 19 May 2015.

Rogelberg, S. G. (2006). *Encyclopedia of industrial and organizational psychology*. Thousand Oaks, CA: Sage.

Roth, P. L., Bobko, P., Van Iddekinge, C. H., & Thatcher, J. B. (in press). Social media in employee selection: Research needs and reasons for caution in uncharted territory. *Journal of Management*.

Segal, J. A. (2014). The law and social media in hiring. *HR Magazine, 59*, 70–72.

Slovensky, R., & Ross, W. H. (2012). Should human resource managers use social media to screen job applicants? Managerial and legal issues in the USA. *Information, 14*, 55–69.

Smith, W. P., & Kidder, D. L. (2010). You've been tagged! (Then again, maybe not): Employers and Facebook. *Business Horizons, 53*, 491–499.

Society for Human Resource Management. (2013). *SHRM survey findings: Social Networking Websites and Recruiting/Selection*. Retrieved from http://www.slideshare.net/shrm/social-networkingwebsitesrecruitingselectingjobcandidatesshrm2013final. Accessed 10 June 2015.

Society for Industrial and Organizational Psychology (2001). *How Many U.S. Companies Use Employment Tests?* Retrieved from http://www.siop.org/workplace/employment%20testing/usingoftests.aspx. Accessed 14 June 2015.

Steinfield, C., Ellison, N. B., & Lampe, C. (2008). Social capital, self-esteem, and use of online social network sites: A longitudinal analysis. *Journal of Applied Developmental Psychology, 29*, 434–445.

Stoughton, J. W., Thompson, L. F., & Meade, A. W. (2013). Big Five personality traits reflected in job applicants' social media postings. *Cyberpsychology, Behavior and Social Networking, 16*, 800–805.

Stoughton, J. W., Thompson, L. F., & Meade, A. W. (2015). Examining applicant reactions to the use of social networking websites in pre-employment screening. *Journal of Business and Psychology, 30*, 73–88.

Sullivan, B. (2012). *Govt. agencies, colleges demand applicants' Facebook passwords*. Retrieved fromhttp://www.nbcnews.com/business/consumer/govt-agencies-colleges-demand-applicants-facebook-passwords-f328791. Accessed 12 June 2015.

Turban, D. B., & Jones, A. P. (1988). Supervisor-subordinate similarity: Types, effects, and mechanisms. *Journal of Applied Psychology, 73*, 228–234.

U. S. Securities and Exchange Commission. (2015). *Antidiscrimination (EEO) law information*. Retrieved from https://www.sec.gov/eeoinfo/antidiscrimination.htm. Accessed 11 June 2015.

Uniform Guidelines on Employee Selection Procedures. (1978). 43 FR 38295, Section 60-3, (August 25, 1978).

Van Iddekinge, C. H., Lanivich, S. E., Roth, P. L., & Junco, E. (in press). Social media for selection? Validity and adverse impact potential of a Facebook-based assessment. *Journal of Management*.

Wright, A. D. (2014). *More states ban social media snooping*. Retrieved from http://www.shrm.org/hrdisciplines/technology/articles/pages/social-media-snooping.aspx. Accessed 12 June 2015.

Chapter 3
Theoretical Propositions About Cybervetting: A Common Antecedents Model

Julia L. Berger and Michael J. Zickar

Abstract Increasingly, human resource professionals are starting to utilize the internet as a means of performing supplemental background checks in prescreening and selection by "Googling" job applicants and reviewing their profiles on Social Network Sites like Facebook. In this chapter, we advance a theoretical model, wherein online behavior and workplace behavior share common antecedents, namely general mental ability and personality. Concurrently, we advance a taxonomy of cyber-behavior. We derive propositions hoping that our model will serve as a stepping stone toward standardizing and systematizing research and practice of cybervetting. We conclude with the lessons learned and future directions.

Keywords Cybervetting • Social media • Personnel selection • Taxonomy • Facebook

3.1 Introduction

The practice of "Googling" job applicants and/or reviewing their profiles on Social Network Sites (SNS; Boyd & Ellison, 2007) like Facebook has been labeled as *cybervetting* (Mikkelson, 2010). Because this practice has received little empirical and theoretical scrutiny, organizations that cybervet their job applicants or plan on doing so in the future to inform personnel selection decisions may face legal and social setbacks due to possible misuse of the information (Brown & Vaughn, 2011).

Several authors have recently highlighted the necessity for a theoretical framework, wherein the antecedents and consequences of cybervetting would be estab-

J.L. Berger, Ph.D. (✉)
Human Resources—Organizational Development, ProMedica,
2109 Hughes Drive, Suite 950, Toledo, OH 43606, USA
e-mail: julia.berger@promedica.org

M.J. Zickar, Ph.D.
Department of Psychology, Bowling Green State University,
233 Psychology Building, Bowling Green, OH 43403, USA
e-mail: mzickar@bgsu.edu

R.N. Landers, G.B. Schmidt (eds.), *Social Media in Employee Selection and Recruitment*, DOI 10.1007/978-3-319-29989-1_3

lished (Brown & Vaughn, 2011; Davison, Maraist, & Bing, 2011). Although there has been a burgeoning research literature on the correlates of social media and computer usage (much of that research summarized in this edited volume), without a theoretical framework it is difficult to develop a cumulative knowledge. In the current chapter, we answer this call by merging two streams of literature: One on the association between personality, general mental ability (GMA), and online behaviors and the other one on the association between personality, General Mental Ability (GMA), and workplace behaviors. Additionally, we advance a taxonomy of cyber-behavior.

This chapter is organized as follows. First, we begin by presenting the common antecedents model and its components. Then, we present the preliminary empirical support for the model. Finally, we derive propositions based on the model and conclude with the lessons learned.

3.2 A Common Antecedents Model

Figure 3.1 illustrates the common antecedents model of cybervetting. Note that the model is multidisciplinary as it bridges the gap between two streams of literature: One that comes from communications and cyber-psychology journals and the other one that comes from the Industrial–Organizational (I-O) psychology journals. The model asserts that cyber-behavior (except for a limited number of jobs) is unlikely to predict job performance directly. However, it posits that workplace behavior and online behavior share common correlates, such as personality and GMA.

The right-hand side of the model (see Fig. 3.1) has received a lot of empirical attention. A common corollary of numerous primary studies and meta-analyses published in peer-reviewed I–O journals is that GMA, the overall ability to learn and process information (Huffcutt, Conway, Roth, & Stone, 2001), is positively related to task performance and OCBs and is negatively related to CWBs (Farr & Tippins, 2013). The predictive validity of GMA is higher for the in-role behaviors

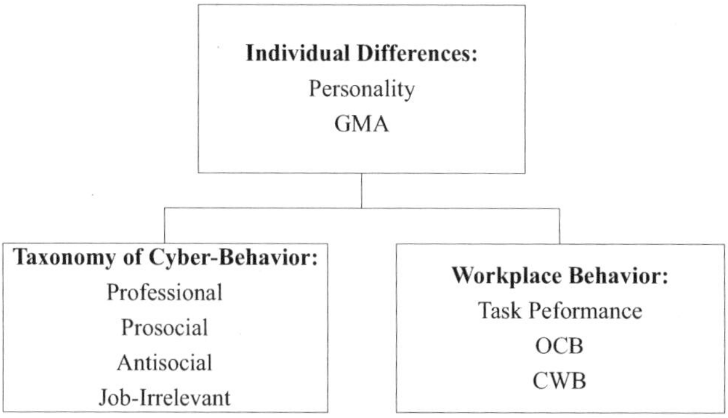

Fig. 3.1 A common antecedents model of cybervetting. This model predicts that personality and GMA serve as common correlates of both the cyber-behavior and workplace behavior

(i.e., task performance) than for the extra-role behaviors (i.e., OCB and CWB). This is due to the fact that task completion requires one to engage in a host of mental activities, including reasoning, abstract thinking, problem solving, decision-making, and planning (Farr & Tippins, 2013). Engagement in OCBs and CWBs, on the other hand, requires certain personality traits rather than cognitive abilities. In the field of I–O psychology, the most oft-researched personality taxonomy is the Five-Factor Model (FFM), which includes *conscientiousness* (the extent to which an individual is dutiful, organized, and careful), *extraversion* (the extent to which one is outgoing and sociable), *agreeableness* (the extent to which a person is cooperative and compliant), *neuroticism* (the extent to which one is reactive to stress), and *openness to experience* (one's willingness to explore new things; Costa & McCrae, 1992). Countless primary studies and meta-analyses have demonstrated criterion-related validity of the FFM with conscientiousness being the strongest correlate of job performance (r ranges from .20 to .23, Barrick & Mount, 1991; Outtz, 2002) followed by emotional stability, another name for neuroticism (r=.19; Judge & Bono, 2001). Openness to experience and extraversion have been linked to training proficiency (r=.25 and r=.26, respectively; Barrick & Mount, 1991). Agreeableness has been found to predict job performance when interacting with conscientiousness (Witt, Burke, Barrick, & Mount, 2002). Furthermore, conscientiousness and emotional stability have been found to correlate with OCBs (r=.24 and r=.24, respectively) and CWBs (r=-.23 and r=-.25, respectively; Le et al., 2011). It was also found that extraversion is a valid predictor of job performance for managers and sales representatives (r=.15 and r=.18, respectively; Barrick & Mount, 1991). In the interest of space, the current chapter will not delve into much detail regarding the association among personality, GMA, and the workplace behaviors.

Shifting gears toward the left-hand side of the common antecedents model, we will now review the literature and research germane to the taxonomy of cyber-behavior. Given that this area of empirical and theoretical inquiry is still at its infancy, few steps have been taken to develop a unified framework of online behavior (e.g., Landers & Callan, 2014). This is perhaps due to the fact that the very nature of online behavior is ever-changing and unstable. Therefore, orthodox methods for developing theories (that is, by proposing a theory *a priori*) may not prove useful in this area. We believe that a data-driven approach, which has been shown to be fruitful, especially in the area of personality research, may be more appropriate. We realize the limitations of this approach, yet we firmly believe that a rough start is better than no start at all!

A data-driven approach to studying the factor structure of online behavior was undertaken at Bowling Green State University and presented at the 28th annual conference of the Society for Industrial and Organizational Psychology (Berger, Zickar, Khosravi, Zhang, & King, 2014, May). The major purpose of the study was to explore the factor structure of SNS-based cyber-behavior. The study utilized a convenient sampling technique to obtain data from Facebook users by posting a study recruitment ad on the authors' Facebook walls. Additional data were collected from undergraduate students at a large mid-western university. The participants were asked to self-report their task performance, OCBs, CWBs, and the Big Five personality traits. They were also asked to share their Facebook links,[1] which were later cybervetted by 20 trained research assistants using the form designed specifically for this study (see Appendix A). To explore the factor structure of the cyber-behavior, exploratory factor analysis (EFA) was conducted using the Principal Component Extraction Method and Verimax Rotation with Kaiser Normalization. The results of the EFA are presented in Table 3.1. Four factors emerged that we later named professional, prosocial, antisocial, and job-irrelevant. Note that of the 50 cyber-behaviors listed in the cybervetting form, 25 behaviors with factor loading of less than .30 were omitted. Several items are cross-loaded on different factors (e.g., work-related and school-related behaviors). We decided to re-arrange these items into a more relevant category—professional cyber-behavior.

While we recognize the shortcomings of the exploratory factor analytic approach and encourage researchers to challenge these results, we believe that made a step closer toward furthering our understanding of cyber-behavior. Some question related to how behavior changes depending on the job being evaluated remain unanswered. For example, the behavior of posting updates related to one's particular sports team (e.g., the St. Louis Cardinals baseball team) might be viewed as job-irrelevant for most occupations, but there would be some for which the behavior might be extremely relevant, such as sportswriter. In addition, like any broad taxonomy, there are likely subdimensions within each of these broad categories. For example, within the antisocial dimension, there may be behaviors such as drug and alcohol usage that correlate more highly with each other than they would correlate with other negative behaviors such as excessive internet usage. Finally, another open question is the correspondence that individual raters would have in terms of assigning behaviors to similar dimensions. It may be that these dimensions are too broad to allow reasonable rater consensus. We fully expect future research to provide answers to these questions and to pit the proposed taxonomy against alternative models (e.g., Landers & Callan, 2014).

Now that we have reviewed the initial support for the taxonomy of cyber-behavior, we will discuss the research and theory that link personality and GMA to online behaviors.

Not surprisingly, the research investigating the relationships between GMA and online behavior is scarce. One study found that job candidates with positive posts on

[1] Note that the RAs cybervetted the content of the profiles that were set to public view only. To further ensure that the participants' privacy settings were not circumvented in any way, the RAs created brand new anonymous Facebook profiles specifically for the purposes of this study. This is due to ethical concerns as well as the fact that the majority of US states officially prohibited or restricted employers from soliciting the login information from their prospective employees in both private and public sector (National Conference of State Legislatures, 2014), which made it illegal to circumvent the privacy settings. The benefit of reviewing the profile information that is not restricted by the privacy settings is that the research process employed in this study maximally resembles "the real-world" practice, and therefore, improves the generalizability of the findings. Second, although some might argue that the use of non-professional hiring managers (i.e., RAs) may limit the external validity of the current study, there is evidence to suggest that professional and non-professional cybervetters yield fairly similar judgments about the employability of a particular job candidate (Frampton & Child, 2013).

Table 3.1 Pilot Study Results of Exploratory Factor Analysis

	Factor			
Variable	1	2	3	4
Recreation	.55			
Sports	.54			
Travel	.42			
Fitness	.52			
Volunteering	.36			
Family-oriented	.58			
Helpful	.38			
Humorous	.33			
Social	.53			
Cultural	.30			
Performing arts	.34			
Work-related		.30		
School-related		.65		
High School		.49		
College		.48		
Relationship status			.33	
Friends			.57	
Movies			.83	
Music			.81	
TV shows			.82	
Profanity				.55
Slang				.40
Spelling errors				.44
Alcohol				.39
Personal disclosure				.53

Note. All values were rounded to two decimal places. The behaviors with the loadings of less than .30 were dropped. Variance explained by the four factors was 37.29

their SNS profiles were rated as having higher GMA than their counterparts with negative profiles (Broeke, 2011). This is perhaps due to the fact that individuals with higher cognitive ability are more likely to be cautious about the information that gets posted on their profiles, because they realize that it may adversely influence their professional development. Furthermore, users with high-GMA may attempt to post information that may convey their job knowledge, skills, and abilities to the prospective employers. In other words, it is conceivable that high-GMA SNS users may be more likely to engage in cyber-behaviors that are self-complimentary in nature—professional and prosocial; whereas their low GMA counterparts may post self-discrediting information—thereby engaging in antisocial and job-irrelevant cyber-behavior. Therefore, we speculate that GMA predicts online behavior. Specifically, web-users with higher GMA would be more likely to engage in self-promoting online behaviors, such as professional and prosocial behaviors, whereas their counterparts with lower GMA would engage in antisocial and job-irrelevant behaviors.

The research on the association between personality and online behavior has yielded consistent findings. Specifically, a series of studies have reported a negative relationship between conscientiousness and the frequency of Facebook use, adding photos of oneself and others, commenting on one's own and other users' walls, and engaging in public self-disclosures, compulsive online shopping (Gosling, Augustine, Vazire, Holtzman, & Gaddis, 2011; Karl, Peluchette, & Schlaegel, 2010; Muscanell & Guadagno, 2012; Wang & Yang, 2008). This is likely due to the fact that highly conscientious people tend to engage in *impression management*, defined as an attempt to create and maintain favorable perceptions of themselves (Brown & Vaughn, 2011; Gardner & Martinko, 1988; Hill, 2004). That is, highly conscientious SNS users may attempt to modify their public accounts by posting professional and prosocial content and deleting or omitting problematic content to appear more attractive to prospective employers. Therefore, it is possible that conscientiousness may be inversely related to antisocial and job-irrelevant cyber-behaviors and positively related to professional and prosocial cyber-behaviors.

Extraversion has been associated with the frequency of internet use, such that highly extraverted SNS users tend to actively utilize SNSs by joining online groups, freely expressing their opinions, and sharing video- and audio-files (Acar, 2008; Jenkins-Guarnieri, Wright, & Johnson, 2013). This is likely due to the fact that individuals who are gregarious, talkative, and friendly tend to reach out to as many people as possible as a way to expand their social networks (Muscanell & Guadagno, 2012). Further, Zywica and Danowski (2008) showed that introverts tended to manipulate their SNSs to appear more popular and extraverted than they were in the real life. This speaks to a possibility that extraversion may predict both prosocial and antisocial cyber-behaviors. On one hand, it is likely that individuals low on this trait may engage in antisocial cyber-behavior to appear popular (Zywica & Danowski, 2008), create a hoped-for-identity (Leary & Kowalski, 1990; Zhao, Grasmuck, & Martin, 2008), conform to social norms (Smith & Kidder, 2010), and/or gain social approval (Marcus, Machilek, & Schultz, 2006). On the other hand, as previous research suggests, high levels of extraversion may predict self-promoting behaviors, such as posting self-enhancing information and omitting self-disparaging information (Bagby & Marshall, 2003; Kristof-Brown, Barrick, & Franke, 2002).

Albeit limited, the research on the neuroticism-cyber-behavior association is promising (e.g., Amichai-Hamburger & Vinitzky, 2010; Karl et al., 2010; Kluemper & Rosen, 2009). A study by Moore and McElroy (2012) showed that, although statistically nonsignificant, lower levels of neuroticism were negatively associated with the number of photos and self- and other-generated wall postings. Scholars explained these findings by speculating that users who are emotionally unstable are more likely to be anxious about the quality and quantity of posts and comments that they and their friends enter on their SNS walls and therefore exercise discretion when using publicly accessible profiles. In support, a study by Karl and associates (2010) found that high levels of neuroticism was related to lower propensity to post inappropriate material on their SNS pages. This reluctance to engage in antisocial cyber-behavior is not related to impression management, as several studies have shown (e.g., Davies, French, & Keogh, 1998; Hill, 2004). These findings suggest that neuroticism may be inversely related to job-irrelevant and antisocial cyber-behaviors due to the fact that individuals with low levels of this trait may be nervous about what image they convey to the viewers—therefore preferring not to engage in behaviors that may be misconstrued. Conversely, neuroticism may have a positive association with prosocial and professional behaviors, although empirical support for this is lacking.

Openness to experience has been shown to relate to online behaviors, such that individuals with a higher score on this trait tended to use SNSs for entertainment purposes (e.g., Muscanell & Guadagno, 2012; Wilson, Fornasier, & White, 2010). This may be explained by the fact that individuals with high levels of openness to experience may prefer engaging in job-irrelevant cyber-behaviors, such as game playing. Another study by Wang and Yang (2008) has demonstrated that individuals who are higher on openness and are innovative, creative, and open-minded tend to engage in online shopping more frequently than their counterparts who lower scores on this trait—again, suggesting a higher likelihood of accumulation of random, job-irrelevant information on their profiles. Marcus et al. (2006) have found that openness is positively associated with self-monitoring behavior, suggesting that individuals high on this trait may engage in self-enhancing and self-promoting behaviors on their SNS to appear more desirable as a job candidate. In another study by Gosling et al. (2011), openness predicted SNS users' propensity to adding and replacing profile photos, which may be viewed as an attempt to monitor the content of one's page. More research than not, however, shows no relationship between openness and SNS-based behavior.

3.3 Summary of Research and Theory of Personality and Online Behavior

Our common antecedents model, at its heart, is a very simple idea. It attempts to explain the link between online behavior and job performance. For most jobs, there is no direct link between the two, and so at best online behavior can be viewed as a potential indicator of traits, skills, and abilities that might or might not be related to job performance. According to this logic, the goal is to find online behaviors that have common antecedents with important job performance outcomes.

Future research will flesh out the specifics of this model, though we believe the model is useful for the purposes of deriving some principles related to cyber-behavior and job performance. We outline these propositions below. First, though, we believe future research should focus on refining our initial structure for the taxonomy of online behaviors, using different samples, and confirmatory techniques. In addition, better links need to be established with individual differences that have been found to be valid for typical job performance measures.

3.4 Propositions Derived from the Model

1. SNS-based online behaviors can be described in terms of four categories
2. Personality and GMA predict online and workplace behavior

3.5 Lessons Learned

This review and consideration of our model leads to some insights that we believe should be reiterated.

3.5.1 Cyber-Behavior Can Be Good or Bad

Reading much of the popular press literature about using the internet for cybervetting purposes, it is easy to conclude that the internet is a cesspool of negative information and that by digging for digital dirt, it will be possible to uncover negative information that will lead organizations to reject job candidates. Certainly cybervetting can be an effective tool for discovering negative information, but our model suggests that cybervetting can help companies discover positive information about candidates. Companies can get a better sense of the fit, learn about professional qualifications, and get a sense of whether an applicant would be a good organizational citizen. Cybervetting can be a tool for finding good employees, in addition to screening out bad apples!

3.5.2 View Cyber-Behavior as Indicators of Traits That You Might Care About in Your Selection Process

Our model suggests that you should not view online behavior as an end to itself, but that it should be viewed solely as an indicator of underlying traits that are viewed as important for the job. View the complex panoply of online behavior, focusing on traits that you may be interested in. For example, in most jobs, it would be desirable to see whether an applicant appears to be conscientious in his or her online behavior. Do not view the online behaviors as important in their own right, only as indicators of traits that matter most for the trait. The one exception is for jobs in which online behavior is part of the job description. In that case, the online behavior could be viewed as a work sample.

3.5.3 Managers Need to Understand Irrelevant Cyber-Behavior and Not Overreact

Social psychologists, I–O psychologists, and judgment and decision-making researchers have long known that humans are distracted by irrelevant information. For example, the research on employment interviews suggests that all candidates should be asked the same questions and that answers should be solicited that are job relevant. Interviewers might be likely to be swayed by knowing that candidates share the same political sensibilities or root for the same professional sports teams. In addition, research is quite clear that people are swayed by the physical attractiveness of applicants. In the old days, it was common for organizations to ask for a photograph to be attached with a job application. Because of concerns about biases, especially related to protected classes, this practice is rare now. However, with cybervetting, it is easy for decision makers to find out personal information that they would never ask during an interview. In addition, most web-users upload personal photos on their social media and so bias due to attractiveness is likely to happen. For these reasons, we think it would be best for a third-party to conduct cybervetting, and then provide recommendations to the decision makers.

3.6 Conclusions

We hope this review and proposed model stimulates research to test its propositions and some of its underlying assumptions. The practice of using social media and internet-related information in personnel decisions has exceeded research. We think theoretically based approaches can be useful in advancing both the research and practice in this area!

Appendix A: Cybervetting Form

Please review and rate the public Facebook profiles that have been provided to you by using the prompts presented in this survey. Use the prompts as well as other pertinent information (such as statuses, pictures, posts, likes, etc.) on the profile to answer the questions as fully as possible. I would like you to limit your review of the profiles to the year of 2014. Please rate the profiles to the best of your ability by using information visible on the page. If you cannot find the information that the prompts are asking, please leave that question or option blank.

WARNING: If for some reason you are presented with a profile of someone with whom you are acquainted, please DO NOT rate the profile and notify me. I will assign you a different profile. Failing to do so will result in a violation of the participants' privacy rights.

Enter YOUR first and last name:____________
Enter the FIRST name of the profile owner you are rating:__________
Enter the LAST name of the profile owner you are rating:__________
The following questions refer to the Facebook owner ONLY!

Gender:

- Male
- Female
- N/A

Education:

- Yes
- No
- N/A

Relationship status:

- Yes
- No
- N/A

Total number of groups:

- Enter the number below: ____________________
- N/A

Total number of photos:

- Enter the number below: ____________________
- N/A

Total number of friends:

- Enter the number below: ____________________
- N/A

Total number of movies:

- Enter the number below: ____________________
- N/A

Total number of musical artists/bands:

- Enter the number below: ____________________
- N/A

Total number of TV shows:

- Enter the number below: ____________________
- N/A

Total number of books:

- Enter the number below: ____________________
- N/A

Based on photos available, how physically attractive would you rate the owner of the profile?

- Very unattractive
- Unattractive
- Neither Attractive nor Unattractive
- Attractive
- Very Attractive

Please indicate how often the profile page contains each of the following:

Posts	Never	Rarely (1 or 2 posts)	Occasionally (3 or 4 posts)	Frequently (5 posts or more)
1. References to doing illegal drugs	○	○	○	○
2. Posts of a sexual nature	○	○	○	○
3. Use of profanity	○	○	○	○
4. Use of Internet slang	○	○	○	○
5. Improper grammar, spelling, and punctuation	○	○	○	○
6. References and photos related to alcohol consumption	○	○	○	○
7. Posts and photos related to volunteer work and charity donations	○	○	○	○
8. Family-oriented posts	○	○	○	○
9. Helpful posts	○	○	○	○
10. Criminal behavior	○	○	○	○
11. Gaming behavior	○	○	○	○
12. Rude or bullying posts and comments	○	○	○	○
13. Outdoor recreation	○	○	○	○
14. Sports	○	○	○	○
15. Travel	○	○	○	○

Please indicate how often the profile page contains each of the following and the appropriateness of the content. NOTE: If you checked NEVER for a post, please leave the appropriateness boxes empty.

Posts	Never	Rarely (1 or 2 posts)	Occasionally (3 or 4 posts)	Frequently (5 posts or more)	Completely Inappropriate	Somewhat Inappropriate	Somewhat Appropriate	Completely Appropriate
1. Political posts	☐	☐	☐	☐	☐	☐	☐	☐
2. Religious posts	☐	☐	☐	☐	☐	☐	☐	☐
3. Humorous posts	☐	☐	☐	☐	☐	☐	☐	☐
4. Posts about coworkers, supervisor, and/or job	☐	☐	☐	☐	☐	☐	☐	☐
5. Social activity	☐	☐	☐	☐	☐	☐	☐	☐
6. Personal/emotional disclosure	☐	☐	☐	☐	☐	☐	☐	☐
7. Intellectual posts	☐	☐	☐	☐	☐	☐	☐	☐
8. Posts about school, classes, and/or classmates	☐	☐	☐	☐	☐	☐	☐	☐
9. Cultural posts	☐	☐	☐	☐	☐	☐	☐	☐

Taking into account the entire Facebook profile as a whole, please answer the following questions.

What is your general impression of the owner of the Facebook profile?

- Highly Negative
- Moderately Negative
- Neutral
- Moderately Positive
- Highly Positive

How would this profile impact your evaluation of this person as a potential job candidate?

- To a very small extent
- To a small extent
- To a moderate extent
- To a large extent
- To a very large extent

If you were hiring for your company, how likely would you be willing to hire this candidate?

- Highly Unlikely
- Unlikely
- Neutral
- Likely
- Highly Likely

How likely is this a "top notch" candidate?

- Highly Unlikely
- Unlikely
- Neutral
- Likely
- Highly Likely

How would you rate the level of activity that this Facebook profile shows?

- Very low
- Low
- Neither high nor low
- High
- Very high

To what extent do you think the user of this Facebook profile utilizes privacy settings?

- Not at all
- Very little
- Somewhat
- To a great extent

References

Acar, A. (2008). Antecedents and consequences of online social networking behavior: The case of Facebook. *Journal of Website Promotion, 3*(1–2), 62–83.

Amichai-Hamburger, Y., & Vinitzky, G. (2010). Social network use and personality. *Computers in Human Behavior, 26*(6), 1289–1295.

Bagby, R. M., & Marshall, M. B. (2003). Positive impression management and its influence on the Revised NEO Personality Inventory: A comparison of analog and differential prevalence group designs. *Psychological Assessment, 15*(3), 333.

Barrick, M. R., & Mount, M. K. (1991). The big five personality dimensions and job performance: A meta-analysis. *Personnel Psychology, 44*(1), 1–26.

Berger, J. L., Zickar, M. J., Khosravi, J. Y., Zhang, D. C., & King, R. T. (2014, May). *Cybervetting: A Common Antecedents Model.* Poster presented at the annual meeting of the Society for Industrial and Organizational Psychology, Honolulu, HI.

Boyd, D., & Ellison, N. (2007). Social network sites: Definition, history, and scholarship. *Journal of Computer-Mediated Communication, 13*(1), 210–230.

Broeke, M. A. (2011). When two worlds meet, Hyves and recruitment: How recruiters' decision-making is influenced by content on adolescents' Hyves pages. University of Twente Student Theses.

Brown, V. R., & Vaughn, E. D. (2011). The writing on the (Facebook) wall: The use of social networking sites in hiring decisions. *Journal of Business and Psychology, 26*(2), 219–225.

Costa, P. T., & McCrae, R. R. (1992). Normal personality assessment in clinical practice: The NEO Personality Inventory. *Psychological Assessment, 4*(1), 5.

Davies, M., French, C., & Keogh, E. (1998). Self-deceptive enhancement and impression management correlates of EPQ-R dimensions. *Journal of Psychology, 132*, 401–406.

Davison, H. K., Maraist, C., & Bing, M. N. (2011). Friend or foe? The promise and pitfalls of using social networking sites for HR decisions. *Journal of Business and Psychology, 26*(2), 153–159.

Farr, J. L., & Tippins, N. T. (Eds.). (2013). *Handbook of employee selection*. New York: Routledge.

Frampton, B. D., & Child, J. T. (2013). Friend or not to friend: Coworker Facebook friend requests as an application of communication privacy management theory. *Computers in Human Behavior, 29*(6), 2257–2264.

Gardner, W. L., & Martinko, M. J. (1988). Impression management in organizations. *Journal of Management, 14*, 321–338.

Gosling, S. D., Augustine, A. A., Vazire, S., Holtzman, N., & Gaddis, S. (2011). Manifestations of personality in online social networks: Self-reported Facebook-related behaviors and observable profile information. *Cyberpsychology, Behavior, and Social Networking, 14*(9), 483–488.

Hill, S. (2004). Social desirability in the use of the five-factor model of employee selection. *Dissertation Abstracts International: Section B: The Sciences and Engineering, 64*(7-B), 3576.

Huffcutt, A. I., Conway, J. M., Roth, P. L., & Stone, N. J. (2001). Identification and meta-analytic assessment of psychological constructs measured in employment interviews. *Journal of Applied Psychology, 86*(5), 897.

Jenkins-Guarnieri, M. A., Wright, S. L., & Johnson, B. D. (2013). The interrelationships among attachment style, personality traits, interpersonal competency, and Facebook use. *Psychology of Popular Media Culture, 2*(2), 117.

Judge, T. A., & Bono, J. E. (2001). Relationship of core self-evaluations traits—Self-esteem, generalized self-efficacy, locus of control, and emotional stability—With job satisfaction and job performance: A meta-analysis. *Journal of Applied Psychology, 86*(1), 80.

Karl, K., Peluchette, J., & Schlaegel, C. (2010). Who's posting Facebook *Faux Pas*? A cross-cultural examination of personality differences. *International Journal of Selection and Assessment, 18*(2), 174–186.

Kluemper, D. H., & Rosen, P. A. (2009). Future employment selection methods: Evaluating social networking web sites. *Journal of Managerial Psychology, 24*(6), 567–580.

Kristof-Brown, A., Barrick, M. R., & Franke, M. (2002). Applicant impression management: Dispositional influences and consequences for recruiter perceptions of fit and similarity. *Journal of Management, 28*(1), 27–46.

Landers, R. N., & Callan, R. C. (2014). Validation of the beneficial and harmful work-related social media behavioral taxonomies: Development of the Work-related Social Media Questionnaire (WSMQ). *Social Science Computer Review, 32*, 628–646.

Le, H., Oh, I. S., Robbins, S. B., Ilies, R., Holland, E., & Westrick, P. (2011). Too much of a good thing: Curvilinear relationships between personality traits and job performance. *Journal of Applied Psychology, 96*(1), 113.

Leary, M. R., & Kowalski, R. M. (1990). Impression management: A literature review and two-component model. *Psychological Bulletin, 107*(1), 34.

Marcus, B., Machilek, F., & Schultz, A. (2006). Personality in Cyberspace: Personal web sites as media for personality expressions and impressions. *Journal of Personality and Social Psychology, 90*(6), 1014–1031.

Mikkelson, K. (2010). Cybervetting and monitoring employees' online activities: Assessing the legal risks for employers. *The Public Lawyer, 18*, 3.

Moore, K., & McElroy, J. C. (2012). The influence of personality on Facebook usage, wall postings, and regret. *Computers in Human Behavior, 28*(1), 267–274.

Muscanell, N. L., & Guadagno, R. E. (2012). Make new friends or keep the old: Gender and personality differences in social networking use. *Computers in Human Behavior, 28*(1), 107–112.

National Conference of State Legislatures (2014). Retrieved March 15, 2014, from http://www.ncsl.org/research/telecommunications-and-information-technology/employer-access-to-social-media-passwords-2013.aspx.

Outtz, J. L. (2002). The role of cognitive ability tests in employment selection. *Human Performance, 15*(1–2), 161–171.

Smith, W. P., & Kidder, D. L. (2010). You've been tagged! (Then again, maybe not): Employers and Facebook. *Business Horizons, 53*, 491–499.

Wang, C. C., & Yang, H. W. (2008). Passion for online shopping: The influence of personality and compulsive buying. *Social Behavior & Personality: An International Journal, 36*(5).

Wilson, K., Fornasier, S., & White, K. M. (2010). Psychological predictors of young adults' use of social networking sites. *Cyberpsychology, Behavior, and Social Networking, 13*(2), 173–177.

Witt, L. A., Burke, L. A., Barrick, M. A., & Mount, M. K. (2002). The interactive effects of conscientiousness and agreeableness on job performance. *Journal of Applied Psychology, 87*(1), 164.

Zhao, S., Grasmuck, S., & Martin, J. (2008). Identity construction on Facebook: Digital empowerment in anchored relationships. *Computers in Human Behavior, 24*(5), 1816–1836.

Zywica, J., & Danowski, J. (2008). The faces of Facebookers: Investigating social enhancement and social compensation hypotheses; predicting Facebook™ and offline popularity from sociability and self-esteem, and mapping the meanings of popularity with semantic networks. *Journal of Computer-Mediated Communication, 14*(1), 1–34.

Chapter 4
An Uncertainty Reduction Approach to Applicant Information-Seeking in Social Media: Effects on Attributions and Hiring

Caleb T. Carr

Abstract Increasingly social media are being used to learn about job applicants. Supplementing and sometimes replacing traditional materials (e.g., applications, cover letters, resumes), social media offer information of a unique nature to employers that can affect perceptions and attributions of applicants. This chapter approaches information seeking in employment through the lens of uncertainty reduction theory, exploring the affordances of extracting information from social media, the value of information therein, and the effects of the relational contexts, social media can isolate and span. With some noted limitations, social media reflect new tools for employers to obtain or supplement information to predict an individual's potential to perform job-related tasks and compliment the social structure of the organization.

Keywords Uncertainty reduction theory • Profiling • Information seeking • Social media

4.1 Introduction

Though reports vary from a substantive minority (33 %; SHRM, 2011) to near-ubiquity (91 %; Undercover Recruiter, 2009), employers' increasing integration of social media into hiring practices is demonstrable (see Carr, Klautke, Miller, & Walther, 2011; Kluemper, 2013; Landers & Schmidt, this volume). Around this growing practice are discussions of the legality of such searches (O'Connor & Schmidt, this volume), the ability for employers to correctly identify the intended applicant (Vaughn, Dudley, Ferrell, & Frantz, this volume), and individuals' and employers' means of using and circumventing, respectively, personal information privacy via system tools and social structures (Lehavot, 2009; Sprague, 2008).

C.T. Carr, Ph.D. (✉)
School of Communication, Illinois State University,
453 Fell Hall, Campus Box 4480, Normal, IL 61790-4480, USA
e-mail: ctcarr@ilstu.edu

R.N. Landers, G.B. Schmidt (eds.), *Social Media in Employee Selection and Recruitment*, DOI 10.1007/978-3-319-29989-1_4

Though these discussions are important for both scholars and practitioners to understand the processes and effects of this emergent practice—many of which occur in the chapters of this book—this chapter focuses on the intentions and outcomes of an employer seeking and obtaining information about an applicant via social media.

Taking an uncertainty reduction approach, this chapter explores the potential goals and outcomes of employers extracting information from social media tools, as compared to traditional sources (i.e., applications, resumes, cover letters, and references) or general online databases, as a means of increasing their attributional certainty regarding a job applicant. After first briefly presenting uncertainty reduction theory (URT) and its application in hiring, this chapter explicates the concept of social media and the unique properties they exhibit relative to other means of communication and information seeking, concluding by exploring the processes and effects of these properties on employers' attributions of job applicants. Ultimately, the purpose here is not necessarily to discuss the accessibility or fidelity of social media information for employers; but rather to develop the foundation of a discussion and future research regarding what happens with applicant information is extracted from social media. More specifically, consistent with prior uncertainty reduction research (e.g., Berger & Calabrese, 1975; Carr & Walther, 2014), this chapter focuses on the perceived certainty stemming from information which is related to actual attributional certainty and more readily assessed (see Clatterbuck, 1979).

4.2 An Uncertainty Reduction Approach to Hiring

Numerous types of uncertainty exist in organizations and for their members. Daft and Lengel (1986) noted *informational* uncertainty occurs when an employee (particularly a manager) does not have adequate knowledge or data to guide a future action. Alternately, *operational* uncertainty manifests when inputs to or outputs from the production process are unpredictable (Field, Ritzman, Safizadeh, & Downing, 2006). *Environmental* uncertainty is manifest when organizational members are unable to predict extraorganizational changes, such as in market forces, product demand, or the physical environment (Jauch & Kraft, 1986). Among this bevy of uncertainty in organizational contexts is *interpersonal* uncertainty—that which occurs in interactions between individuals, primarily anticipated future interactions but also including ongoing interactions—such as when an organization seeks to hire a new employee.

One of employers' primary motivations during the hiring process is to reduce their uncertainty about applicants. Managers, human resource personnel, and recruiters seek to lean about an applicant to predict how well the individual will fit to the available position. Uncertainty about future job performance is particularly high for new employees, with whom the organization or manager may have no experience. However, uncertainty exists even for known candidates (e.g., internal hires, former employees, well-known industry members) as an employer is unsure how the applicant with whom there is a preexisting relationship may perform in a different job role, as some employees may be capable in one job while not able to perform another. Thus, the hiring process can be effectively viewed as an uncertainty reduction process, making uncertainty reduction theory a utile lens to theorize employers' information seeking and subsequent gains in attributional certainty.

4.2.1 Uncertainty Reduction Theory

Uncertainty reduction theory (URT; Berger & Calabrese, 1975) was advanced to explain how individuals process information about those with whom they expect to interact. As the uncertainty of interacting with new people or in novel contexts is challenging and can lead to discomfort (Berger, 1979), individuals seek information to predict, anticipate, and guide future interactions, and in doing so reduce their own uncertainty (Rubin, 1977). Though prevalent in zero-history interactions amongst unacquainted strangers (Clatterbuck, 1979; Douglas, 1990; Kellermann, 1986), uncertainty can manifest even in established relationships (e.g., marriage, close friends) when an individual learns something new about the other party or must interact in an unusual or novel relational context (Afifi & Metts, 1998; Planalp, Rutherford, & Honeycutt, 1988; Siegert & Stamp, 1994).

URT has been extended to address uncertainty as it relates to organizational entry and exit. Individuals seeking to become a member of a new organization (exemplified by job applicants) often seek out information about their potential place of work to prepare themselves for both the job requirements and culture of their potential workplace environment (Kramer, 1993; Mignerey, Rubin, & Gorden, 1995). Likewise, information seeking is again high when an individual leaves an organization, and faces the uncertainty of new roles and demands following organizational exit (Kramer, 1993, 1994). An alternate manifestation of uncertainty in hiring is from the perspective of the hiring employer, seeking information to reduce uncertainty to predict job candidates' potential as employees.

4.2.1.1 Information-Seeking Strategies

When faced with uncertainty, individuals employ strategies to seek out information, thereby increasing their ability to predict future behaviors and exchanges (Rubin, 1977). Initially, Berger (1979, 1987) identified three information-seeking strategies by which a person could seek and obtain information about another to reduce relational uncertainty: Interactive, active, and passive information seeking. *Interactive* information seeking strategies are those in which an information seeker directly communicates with and receives feedback from a target individual. *Active* information seeking strategies are employed when an individual obtains information about a target from a second party who is more familiar with the target or when the individual manipulates the environment of the target to prompt and assess reactions to a novel stimulus. Finally, *passive* information seeking strategies are those in which the individual observes the target discretely. Later, acknowledging the increase of information archived and retrievable online, Ramirez, Walther, Burgoon, and Sunnafrank (2002) explicated *extractive* information seeking strategies, in which an individual, "draws upon a vast storehouse of written comments generated by targets" (p. 220) to obtain information and reduce uncertainty. Though research has generally noted that interactive strategies achieve the greatest reductions in uncertainty (or alternately the greatest gains in attribution certainty) relative to other strategies (e.g., Westerman & Tamborini, 2008), all four strategies have been demonstrated as effective means of obtaining information and reducing perceptions of uncertainty (e.g., Antheunis, Valkenburg, & Peter, 2010; Carr & Walther, 2014; Douglas, 1990; Gibbs, Ellison, & Lai, 2011; Knobloch & Solomon, 2005; Tong, 2013).

Organizationally, individuals engage in uncertainty-reduction strategies to reduce their uncertainty about the workplace, job requirements, and coworkers (Kramer, 1994, 2009). Applicants may engage in realistic job previews or questions to learn about job tasks and the work environment (interactive), inquire of current employees and their work experiences (active), engage in job shadowing to determine effective ways to accomplish job tasks or conform to workplace norms (passive), or look at online reviews from sites such as GlassDoor.com and GreatPlaceToWork.com to preview one's work environment (extractive).

A substantive amount of work, particularly in the fields of communication and management behavior, has addressed how job applicants and new employees engage in interactive, active, and passive uncertainty reduction strategies to better-predict their new job experiences and ease assimilation processes (see Kramer, 2009, 2010). An additional substantive literature exists—predominantly in the fields of human resources and personnel management—exploring the reverse: Traditional information-seeking strategies employers use to reduce uncertainty regarding job applicants (for review, see Van Iddekinge & Ployhart, 2008). Certainly, seeking to maximize the ability to predict how a specific applicant will be able to accomplish requisite job skills and integrate into the cultural fabric of the workplace are key goals of employers identifying and hiring a new employee (Kristof, 1996).

4.3 Seeking Information to Reduce Uncertainty About Job Applicants

To effectively anticipate how an individual applicant will perform should s/he be hired for a position, employers seek information to predict their potential fit should the applicant be hired, predominantly information to be able to assess an applicant's expected person–job (PJ) and person–organization (PO) fit. Person–job fit refers to the compatibility between an individual's knowledge, skills, and abilities

(KSAs) and the skill sets required to perform the job (Hedge & Teachout, 1992; Kristof-Brown, Zimmerman, & Johnson, 2005). Alternately, person–organization fit refers to the compatibility between an individual's and an organization's or workgroup's needs or characteristics (Kristof, 1996). Hiring employers make significant effort throughout the hiring process to reduce their uncertainty about applicants' PJ and PO fit as they attempt to predict their potential success in the available position and organization (Sekiguchi, 2007; Sekiguchi & Huber, 2011).

4.3.1 Tools for Reducing Uncertainty Regarding Applicants

4.3.1.1 Traditional Tools

Historically, employers have used three primary means to reduce uncertainty regarding job applicants: Documentation, references, and interviews. These three tools reflect various traditional information-seeking strategies through which employers have sought to reduce their uncertainty about how applicants would perform if hired. Documentation (including applications, resumes, and cover letters) provide applicants a means of allowing employers to passively obtain information about prior training, workplace accomplishments, certifications, and awards, primarily serving as tools to assess an applicant's KSAs, and thus potential PJ fit (Cable & Judge, 1996; Kristof-Brown, 2000). References, the statements of prior employers, colleagues, or clients of an applicant—are tools facilitating active information seeking strategies, whereby an employer can ask knowledgeable others about an applicant's prior workplace performance and personality, increasing attributional certainty regarding both PJ and PO fit (Knouse, 1989). Interviews represent tools facilitating an interactive strategy, and are often the final stage of a hiring process, allowing the employer an opportunity to follow-up on unclear, discrepant, or interesting items revealed in prior stages (Adams, Elacqua, & Colarelli, 1994), utilizing the dialogic format of an interpersonal exchange to make final assessments, primarily regarding an applicant's personality and thus PO fit (Rynes & Gerhart, 1990). Notable here is that these tools need not (and often do not) occur face-to-face: Applications are submitted online, interviews are held via telephone or Skype, and references can be emailed. Thus, there is a separation between the tool used to obtain information and the information-seeking strategy per URT.

4.3.1.2 Extractive Tools

Beyond these traditional tools for reducing uncertainty regarding job applicants, employers are increasingly turning to online tools to further obtain information to attempt to predict individual applicants' potential fit. However, relative to traditional informational tools in hiring, Kluemper (2013) notes employers' use of online tools to assess applicants has received relatively little attention. Information about individuals is increasingly available online, from which others may learn about an individual, her/his interests, personality, behaviors, and experiences.

Early online tools made available a modicum of information to interested parties seeking extractive information to reduce uncertainty about others. Web searches and tools can be used to conduct criminal background checks, credit histories, and knowledge screening. Beyond these, Internet sources such as archived news stories and personal web pages can serve as sources of information available online to reduce uncertainty about others (Papacharissi, 2002; Vazire & Gosling, 2004).

A 2007 *Harvard Business Review* case study (Coutu, 2007) explored the circumstances under which a multinational corporation, in the final phase of hiring for a position liaising with their Chinese division, discovered the personal webpage of a final candidate, noting her involvement in the 1999 World Trade Organization riots in Seattle and articulating her anti-China business policies. Though almost a decade had passed since the applicant's involvement in the riot and her perceptions toward trade with and in China had since moved away from her position in 1999, the employer was faced with a difficult decision: Given that Chinese trade was an integral component to the available position, could the employer hire a candidate who at one point had been severely opposed to the very nature of that job? As this example illustrates, the use of extractive strategies to seek and obtain uncertainty-reducing information is not necessarily new. However, social media has likely exacerbated the strategy's use, and moreover altered the nature of the information sought and obtained, the processes by which information is evaluated, and the subsequent attributional effects on employers' perceptions of applicants and subsequent hiring decisions.

4.4 Extractive Information Seeking Via Social Media in Hiring

The further expansion of online tools to include social media has exacerbated the ability to utilize extractive strategies to learn about an individual. Social network sites (SNSs) in particular have made identity displays in online common, constituting repositories of information about individuals. Individuals self-disclose abundant information about themselves and others on SNSs such as Facebook, LinkedIn, and Twitter—information that is archived, indexed, and searchable (Acquisti & Gross, 2006; Caverlee & Webb, 2008; Zimmer, 2008). Given the exponential growth of information about individuals' personal and professional lives available online, extractive information seeking is of increasing interest to hiring managers, recruiters, and human resource employees seeking to learn about job applicants to reduce uncertainty before hiring. Social media afford several unique opportunities for uncertainty reduction, both through the quantity and quality of information facilitated by their dynamic social and technical processes.

4.4.1 Social Media

Though a relatively new opportunity for reducing uncertainty about applicants, employers are increasingly turning to social media in the hiring process, in part to reduce uncertainty. But how are social media different from other online information sources such as news archives and web pages, particularly in regard to uncertainty reduction? Some common traits of social media have been identified that help distinguish extractive information seeking and subsequent attributions via these channels as compared to others, including other online tools.

Carr and Hayes (2015) define *social media* as, "Internet-based, disentrained, and persistent channels of masspersonal communication facilitating perceptions of interactions among users, deriving value primarily from user-generated content" (p. 49). Two elements of this definition are particularly relevant to information seeking and uncertainty reduction in social media. First, social media are *masspersonal*, in that interaction therein can be personalized or directed at an intended receiver, yet are broadcast to a large, mass audience (O'Sullivan, 2005). Thus, many of the interactions in social media are public and accessible to others—like employers. Second, social media must facilitate the *perception of interactivity* among users, but users must not necessarily interact. The perceived sociability of a medium, even if that socialness is not utilized, affects how information in that medium is perceived (Hayes & Carr, 2015). A final, though non-definitional element of social media is their diverse relational context, as some sites are developed for use in a particular context (e.g., professional, romantic, social) while others span multiple contexts. Taken together, these elements of social media afford novel opportunities for employers seeking to reduce uncertainty regarding job applicants as compared to other uncertainty-reduction tools and strategies.

4.4.2 Extracting Hiring Information Via Social Media

4.4.2.1 Obtaining Information to Predict Fit

Social media can be rife with extractable information about applicants. Unlike resumes or applications, social media are not constrained to single-page, predetermined fields, and thus may afford more robust information, as individuals can expand on items that may be mere line items or bullet points in a resume, include or link to rich content (e.g., video, websites, online portfolios), and generally provide deeper and broader information than may be initially requested of applicants by an employer. Further, information extracted from social media may supplement information from traditional hiring materials, either vetting claims made in traditional hiring tools or extending information about an applicant.

Assessing PJ Fit

Social media may be rich sources of information of an applicant's knowledge, skills, and abilities, which can increase employers' attributions regarding the applicant's PJ fit (Kristof-Brown, 2000). Professional networking sites (PNSs) like LinkedIn, Xing, and Zerply encourage users to post information about their own and others' professional skills, accomplishments, and experiences often serving as virtual resumes. However, PNSs can differ from traditional uncertainty-reducing tools in hiring in two ways: supplementing information from traditional materials and by allowing others to make or vet claims about an individual's KSAs. First, social media may be used to supplement claims made in traditional media by providing greater explication or detail regarding job skills. For example, Zerply hosts multimedia content to allow audiovisual producers an opportunity to display their work and outcomes, rather than just list a piece's title on an application, thereby giving an employer a richer look into the actual KSAs related to media production an individual possesses and can demonstrate. Second, as masspersonal for a social media can allow other users to make identity claims for a particular applicant, further helping add detail to an applicants' espoused KSAs. LinkedIn profiles include the "Skills & Endorsements" field, which allow other users to identify particular job-related abilities of an individual, even beyond those skills the individual may self-identify on an application. Similar to references, these other-generated claims can supplement and strengthen (or potentially challenge if discrepant with) the job-related skills and abilities claimed by an applicant. Thus, social media may either supplement or provide novel information relative to that available in other channels as well as providing a tool in which others may create and augment the KSAs claimed by an applicant, adding potentially either greater breadth or depth to an employers' knowledge regarding the applicant's skills, and thus increasing attributional certainty regarding PJ fit.

Assessing PO Fit

Additionally, and perhaps of even more importance to employers, social media can be used to reduce uncertainty regarding an applicant's personality, and thus PO fit. Though an individual's ability to perform required job tasks is important, recently the importance of PO fit has been highlighted as more essential for job applicants as, unlike job skills, an organization cannot train an individual's personality to compliment the organization and current employees (Rynes & Gerhart, 1993). Moreover, once hired, an individual's PO fit is more strongly linked to turnover and intent to leave than PJ fit (Cable & Judge, 1996; Lauver & Kristof-Brown, 2001).

Social media can be a rich source of information to reduce uncertainty regarding an individual's potential PO fit. SNSs are particularly rife with information about users' extracurricular interests, social interactions, and personalities (Gosling, Augustine, Vazire, Holtzman, & Gaddis, 2011; Stoughton, Thompson, & Meade, 2013), all of which can be relatively difficult to assess through other means in the hiring process (Chatman, 1991; Kristof, 1996). Moreover, individuals form robust and relatively accurate impressions of personality characteristics such as openness, agreeableness, conscientiousness, and extraversion based on diverse cues available via social media, including language use and structure, personal information, activities and interests, and publicly posted messages (Golbeck, Robles, & Turner, 2011). These personality attributions are typically accurate relative to both the individual's self-evaluation and the evaluations of their close friends (Gosling, Gaddis, & Vazire, 2007). Thus, unlike personality assessments from a job interview (which are often distorted to maximize a positive impression; Posthuma, Morgenson, & Campion, 2002), an applicant's personality as evidenced via social media is likely a rich and accurate information source as to whether the applicant is truly an affable, gregarious, and amenable individual who would be pleasant to work with.

4.4.2.2 High Warranting Value Within Social Media

An additional and novel affordance of social media is the presence of other-generated information, and the subsequent value of that information in shaping perceptions of the individual's offline characteristics. In earlier, static online content (e.g., webpages), most information about individuals was self-generated, as individuals provided claims and data about themselves (Papacharissi, 2002). Self-generated claims remain common in social media, as individuals often create profiles or content presenting themselves (Lampe, Ellison, & Steinfield, 2007), often accurately with respect to their offline attributes (Back et al., 2010). Yet a key affordance of social media is the collaborative generation of content: Other sources can contribute content and present or verify information about the individual. The mere opportunity for others to interact increases the credibility and uncertainty reduction of a self-generated claim, even if others do not utilize that affordance, by increasing the claim's warranting value (Hayes & Carr, 2015).

An online claim possesses *warranting value* if it is believed to accurately reflect the offline characteristics of the individual (Walther & Parks, 2002). For an identity claim to be high in warranting value, members of the individual's social network must be able to publicly comment on the claim in a way that information seekers are able to compare the claim and the comment (DeAndrea, 2014; Parks, 2011). Social media afford multiple opportunities both for individuals to make identity claims and for others to publicly comment on that claim via comments, replies, reposts, shares, and a myriad of other tools. For example, an individual may simply state that s/he has a particular skill set (a low-warrant claim); but making that claim on the professional network site LinkedIn would increase the warranting value—the belief that the individual possesses that skill set offline—of the claim as employers and coworkers can confirm or refute the individual possessing that skill.

This warranting effect has been borne out empirically, as observers' attitudes about the characteristics of a target (e.g., extroversion, attractiveness) are more strongly influenced by a third-party (e.g., family, friend, coworker) claiming the individual possesses that attribute than the target herself/himself making the same claim (Walther, Van Der Heide, Hamel, & Shulman, 2009). Within the hiring context, this finding can be readily parlayed into self- and other-generated claims of an applicant's KSAs. Whereas an applicant may merely claim a particular ability on a resume (a low-warrant claim), others' endorsement of the individual's same ability via the "Skills & Endorsements" section of LinkedIn or a previous employer's testimonials on Xing (both high-warrant claims) may more strongly reduce the employer's uncertainty that the individual possesses the professed ability.

Information in a social medium may also be generated by the system itself. System metrics such as the total number of connections, usage statistics, or network graphs are automatically created and available in many social media systems, and serve as a source of uncertainty-reducing information about an individual. For example, an individual may easily claim to be extroverted and socially popular, yet exploration of their social medium profile may reveal only a limited social network with few network connections—as computed and displayed automatically by the medium. In such cases, perceivers' attributions regarding a target are significantly more influenced by the system-generated cue than by the target's self-statements, strengthening perceptions if claims are supplementary and changing minds in favor of the system-generated information if the claims are discrepant (Tong, Van Der Heide, Langwell, & Walther, 2008; Utz, 2010). Thus, an applicant's claim that s/he is a diligent worker may be refuted by a potential employer discovering the applicant frequently engages in multiple social interactions on Facebook throughout the workday at her/his present job, as evidenced by the timestamps of the applicant's post to the social medium.

Taken together, whether applicant information obtained via social media is self- or other-generated, it likely possesses greater warranting value than traditional hiring materials (e.g., resumes, cover letters, interviews), as the public, masspersonal nature of social media content afford an opportunity for others to correct deceptive or inauthentic claims, even if this affordance is not used (Hayes & Carr, 2015). Thus, as employers seek to accurately learn whether an applicant possesses a specific job skill or truly determine how the individual interacts with others, social media may serve as a means of extracting veracious information about individuals on which to base a hiring decision by allowing other users to vet or refute claims, skills, and other information about an applicant.

4.4.2.3 Contexts for Information-Seeking

A final advantage of social media is the opportunity to obtain information about an applicant in an environment that spans multiple contexts. Berger and Douglas (1981) noted that observation of a target individual across multiple contexts reduces attribution uncertainty more than information-seeking strategies in a single relational context—particularly the one in which the information-seeker and target anticipate interaction. Whereas in a single, expected relational context a target individual can selectively and strategically present only those traits or attitudes of herself/himself perceived to be socially desirable, when forced to interact in other contexts the same individual may not be able to actively manger her/his identity as s/he seeks to interact with a more diverse and potentially disparate set of audiences. For example, within the context of an interview, an applicant may strategically highlight work skills, downplay or omit shortcomings, or deceive the recruiter regarding attributes the applicant perceives as undesirable to the company to maximize her/his chances of being hired. However, this level of strategic self-perception may not be possible when presenting across social contexts given the need to present herself/himself to an employer, but also to other social groups (e.g., grandma). Social media afford a ready opportunity for observation across relational contexts in two ways: By affording distinct alternate contexts for observation and through collapsing contexts.

Unique Contexts

Employers typically encounter applicants in a single, professional context. Particularly when applying to jobs, applicants try to strategically self-present themselves as they perceive to be most valued or desired by the employer within the workplace (Bolino, Kacmar, Turnley, & Gilstrap, 2008). Over time, this strategic self-presentation has led many employers to be concerned with the veracity of self-presented information in the hiring context (Ployhart, 2006; Posthuma, Morgenson, & Campion, 2002), as applicants feel incentivized to stretch or fabricate both their personality and skill set to maximize their chances of being hired. Thus, extracting information from an alternate relational context via the myriad of available social media tools may afford employers more faithful information about an applicant.

Preliminary studies already bear out this effect. Mere pictorial self-presentations on social network sites such as Facebook, CyWorld, and Hyves can affect perceptions of an individual's professionalism and employability. In one of the first such studies, Bohnert and Ross (2010) asked employers to look at applicants' purported Facebook profiles alongside traditional hiring materials. All contents were kept consistent, except for the manipulation of the Facebook profile photograph depicting the applicant either (a) studying, (b) with family, or (c) drinking alcohol. Though it is perhaps of little surprise that both the studying and familial contexts (not significantly different from each other) were perceived as more employable than the applicant in the drinking condition, Bonhert and Ross further found that, were the participant to offer the applicant a job, the starting salary offered to the target in the drinking condition was $3000 less than subjects in either of the other two experimental conditions.

Schouten, Antheunis, Abeele, and Van Lith (2015) extended this line, utilizing a 2 (professional vs. unprofessional profile photo) × 2 (grammatically correct vs. flawed resume) experimental design to explore the effects of [in]consistent self-presentation across contexts. Findings revealed that while congruent information did little to affect impressions of applicants, incongruent information resulted in impressions changing in the direction of the picture's valence. In other words, applicants with grammatically erred (i.e., unprofessional) resumes found employers' attributions raised by positive social profile pictures, while applicants with grammatically correct (i.e., professional) resumes found employers' attributions of them lowered by unprofessional social media photos.

Moreover, textual self-descriptions can affect employers' perceptions of an applicant. Carr and Walther (2014) exposed participants to applicants' Facebook positively-, neutrally-, or negatively valenced disclosures regarding their recent work performance. As hypothesized, participants perceived applicants more favorably when exposed to positive statuses, and more perceived applicants as less employable when exposed to negative statuses. However, the effect of positive information was greater than the effect of negative information, so that gains in perceived employability in the positive-status condition were greater than losses in perceived employability in the negative-status condition. Carr and Walther suggested this unexpected positivity effect may be an artifact of the non-normative nature of positive disclosure of work-related information on the socially oriented Facebook. Regardless of cause, this finding of the relatively stronger effect of positive information obtained via social media is more uplifting than the pessimism of many career centers and the popular press who suggest information from social media can only harm applicants.

A caveat is merited here to consider the role of contexts and subsequent attribution errors that may manifest. The fundamental attribution error refers to individuals attributing behavior to an individual's personality without consideration of the influence of the context or outside actions that may have guided such actions (Ross, 1977), and may affect attributions made from information extracted from social media. For example, an employer may see a photograph posted to a social network of an applicant engaging in drinking and partying behaviors, attributing those behaviors to the personality of the applicant as unprofessional and not a rigorous worker (see Bohnert & Ross, 2010). However, the photograph may actually be from a celebration party for the applicant's latest big sale or promotion, and the partying depicted is merely an artifact of the context in which it was taken: A party celebrating the applicant's professional and task-related accomplishments. Moreover, the likelihood of such attribution errors occurring are, in part, a function of the information-seeker's mood at the time the information was obtained (Forgas, 1998), so that an employer who is happy following a recent workplace success may be more likely to attribute the aforementioned picture to a workplace celebration or social outing showing the applicant as a sociable and personable candidate; while another employer in a bad mood following a recent workplace shortcoming may be more likely to attribute the picture to the applicant's personality as a partier with low regards for workplace values. Therefore, while information-seeking in the alternate contexts of social media can afford more diverse contexts in which to learn about the applicant's personality and KSAs, so too may these contexts result in attribution errors by observing the applicant in a context that may or may not be accurately reflective of her or his workplace persona.

Collapsed Contexts

In addition to their ability to allow employers to isolate specific alternate contexts in which to extract information about applicants, social media also represent an opportunity to see several typically disparate social contexts collapsed into one space. Social media have been noted for their ability to span contexts, bringing together disparate social groups into a single communicative medium (Marwick & boyd, 2011; Vitak, 2012). Thus, rather than merely allowing observation of a target in an alternate context, social media exemplify Berger and Douglas (1981) claim that observation in alternate contexts further reduces uncertainty by forcing individuals to interact not just in an alternate context, but across potentially disparate contexts.

Individuals typically seek to enact the personality or face they perceived to be valued in a specific context, hiding the facets of themselves that may not be utile (Goffman, 1959). However, when interacting across contexts, personality aspects valued by one social group may not be valued by another: You likely slightly modify your behavior when interacting with your boss as compared to your drinking buddies as compared to a clergy member. Yet in the rare circumstances an individual is confronted with members of these disparate social groups, what face should be presented? Hogan (2010) argues that, in social media where presenting to multiple audiences is common, individuals address this challenge by presenting their *least common denominator* self, or a minimalist self-presentation that should both (1) appeal to the broadest social groups and (2) present a self distilled down to the simplest essence of the individual. More simply: If you want to know who an individual really is, see how s/he acts when interacting simultaneously with their grandmother, boss, and college roommate.

Unlike prior channels and forms of information seeking, social media often afford this opportunity for employers to observe applicants interacting not only with coworkers, subordinates, and supervisors; but more importantly interacting simultaneously with family, friends, and a bevy of other social relations outside of the workplace. It has been argued that the collapse of relational contexts necessitate individuals to exhibit an authentic, verifiable, and singular identity (Hogan, 2010; Marwick & boyd, 2011), avoiding the multiplicity of identity performances addressed by Goffman (1959). Though applicants may seek to strategically present a self on context-collapsing social media like Twitter (Lair, Sullivan, & Cheney, 2005), such presentations are still constrained by the lowest-common denominator self that resonates with disparate audiences. Thus, social media that collapse relational contexts into a single communicative venue (e.g., Twitter, Facebook, YouTube) may not help an employer identify idiosyncrasies of an applicant (e.g., how s/he acts in stressful situations), but may serve to greatly reduce the general attributional certainty of an applicant by providing an impression of the applicant at her/his most basic level that could be expected to be maintained across the broadest swath of interactions.

4.5 Future Directions

An URT approach to social media in hiring provides several benefits, including a robust theoretical foundation, initial empirical support, and a parsimonious explanation regarding employers' motivations to utilize social media to learn about job applicants beyond what is available from traditional hiring tools. Yet this perspective also innately contains assumptions and several blind spots that future work should explore.

First, the use of social media for extractive information seeking assumes information is anathema to uncertainty. Though this assumption is neither novel nor unexpected (Clatterbuck, 1979), it is not ubiquitously accurate, as sometimes additional information can increase uncertainty about a target (Afifi & Metts, 1998; Planalp et al., 1988). As noted by Carr et al. (2011), discrepancies among information between sources may lead to greater uncertainty for an employer, resulting in either (a) subsequent information-seeking to resolve the dissonant information or (b) simply removing the applicant from further consideration for the position due to perceived deceptiveness. For example, an employer may read that an applicant has graduated from a prestigious university on a transcript; but exploration of the applicant's Facebook profile reveals the applicant attended a lower-status but geographically close to school based on school affiliations and the composition of the applicant's social network. In such a case, the employer may either (a) seek additional sources to determine whether the applicant really graduated from Harvard University and just had several friends from the nearby Bunker Hill Community College, or merely took a single Harvard course as a guest student while enrolled at Bunker Hill, or fabricated the degree on their resume entirely; or (b) take the opportunity to screen out the applicant from subsequent steps in the hiring process given the discovered inconsistency. Though the effects of photographs and self and others' statements on hiring-related attributions have been explored (Bohnert & Ross, 2010; Carr & Walther, 2014; Schouten, Antheunis, Abeele, & Van Lith, 2015), future work should seek to explore the boundaries of information type in the attenuation of attributional certainty in hiring, including the potential for uncertainty increasing information.

Second, it is unlikely that all information and all jobs are created equal. The first implication of this limitation is that the valence of information may be influenced by the nature of the job to which an individual applies. Recalling Bohnert and Ross (2010) findings, for most jobs it is understandable an individual may be perceived as less professional (PO fit) or employable (PJ fit) when a social media profile picture depicts the candidate engaging in drinking and heavy partying behaviors. Yet the same behaviors—debaucherous in one industry—may be viewed positively in another, such as a party promoter position which may view social drinking as a job-related skill or personality trait beneficial to successful applicants. Thus, future work should benefit by probing the compatibility of fit between the information obtained and the job's task and personality needs. The second implication of this limitation is that not all information salient to a hiring decision may be available via social media. For example, while social media may contain information that can help assess basic personality characteristics or fundamental job skills relevant to entry-level jobs, social media may be less utile at obtaining information relevant to upper-management hiring decisions. For example, a candidate for a CEO position may not frequently or publicly share her/his views on spot exchange rates or multinational expansions, either of which topic may be more germane to a CEO position than broader personality disclosures. Thus, while work is beginning to look at social media as a means of reducing information primarily for entry-level jobs, future work should delve into the processes and effects on more specialized jobs or those higher in the organizational hierarchy.

A third constraint to this approach is its presumption that employers can find information. The most popular social media services like Facebook and LinkedIn have been adopted nearly-ubiquitously, particularly among young adults and early-career job seekers (Ellison, Steinfield, & Lampe, 2007; Pew Research Internet Project, 2014). However, what about the small percentage of individuals who have not adopted social media? What attributions are made of a job applicant who does not have a Facebook, Twitter, or LinkedIn profile to be found? Some employers may feel the applicant is being surreptitious by not creating or hiding a social media presence, whereas other employers may find the novelty of such behaviors refreshing and intriguing. Such attributions may be mediated by the nature of the position for which the individual is being considered: Is an applicant for a job as social media manager highly qualified or utterly-incompetent if no personal social media profile can be found? Attributions in the absence of social media information are likely made, but research into such attributions will be challenged by the complex and subtle effects on employer's uncertainty about an applicant based on the *absence* of information, and thus should proceed very carefully.

Likewise, although the mere presence of a self-disclosure in a masspersonal social medium should increase the warranting value of information by nature of allowing individuals to comment and either validate or discredit the identity claim even if that feature is not used (Hayes & Carr, 2015), it is possible (and in some cases likely) that individuals or groups would not utilize that affordance to publicly correct or refute an errant claim. For example, a supervisor may claim on Xing that s/he possesses good management and leadership skills—a claim that her/his subordinates believe to be inaccurate. However, fearing potential repercussions from doing so, the subordinates may not publicly refute their boss' claim, providing a false impression of the individual online due to others' silence. Though atheoretical, this practical concern suggests another caveat to the present approach to uncertainty reduction, further suggesting that employers seeking to rigorously vet an applicant should not limit their information seeking to a single strategy or tool set.

4.6 Conclusion

Employers are increasingly turning to social media to learn about potential employees (Carr et al., 2011), attempting to predict applicants' behaviors and attitudes should they be hired for the available position. Uncertainty reduction strategies have long been used by employers, but traditional tools (i.e., resumes, cover letters, interviews, and references) are increasingly suspect to employers as applicants strategically self-present themselves via these tools in an attempt to maximize their chances of being hired (Posthuma et al., 2002). Social media afford new tools for reducing uncertainty about applicants, providing deeper and broader information that is higher in warranting value and illustrative of the applicant in a bevy of social contexts than traditional tools for reducing uncertainty in the hiring context. Thus, information extracted from social media may often better-reflect the applicant's actual KSAs and personality than information requested and obtained (and thus strategically self-presented) via traditional tools such as resumes and cover letters, thereby providing more predictive power for employers.

From profile pictures to others' statements about an applicant, information encountered via social media affects employers' attributions, including perceptions of an applicant's employability, credibility, professionalism, and starting salary. Employers and applicants alike should therefore be mindful of their use of social media: Employers to be aware of the effects—intentional and otherwise—of their integration of social media as an uncertainty reduction tool in the hiring process, and applicants cautious to present their professional selves across various social media platforms. Though they represent yet another blur between the personal and professional self, social media afford an opportunity for all parties to increase attributional certainty, helping to ensure the best applicant is hired.

References

Acquisti, A., & Gross, R. (2006, June). *Imagined communities: Awareness, information sharing, and privacy on the Facebook*. Paper presented at Privacy Enhancing Technologies, Cambridge, England.

Adams, G. A., Elacqua, T. C., & Colarelli, S. M. (1994). The employment interview as a sociometric selection technique. *Journal of Group Psychotherapy, Psychodrama and Sociometry, 47*, 99–114.

Afifi, W. A., & Metts, S. (1998). Characteristics and consequences of expectation violation in close relationships. *Journal of Social and Personal Relationships, 15*, 365–392. doi:10.1177/0265407598153004.

Antheunis, M., Valkenburg, P. M., & Peter, J. (2010). Getting acquainted through social network sites: Testing a model of online uncertainty reduction and social attraction. *Computers in Human Behavior, 26*, 100–109. doi:10.1016/j.chb.2009.07.005.

Back, M. D., Stopfer, J. M., Vazire, S., Gaddis, S., Schmukle, S. C., Egloff, B., et al. (2010). Facebook profiles reflect actual personality, not self-idealization. *Psychological Science, 21*, 372–375. doi:10.1177/0956797609360756.

Berger, C. R. (1979). Beyond initial interaction: Uncertainty, understanding, and the development of interpersonal relationships. In H. Giles & R. N. St. Clair (Eds.), *Language and social psychology* (pp. 122–144). Oxford, England: Basil-Blackwell.

Berger, C. R. (1987). Communicating under uncertainty. In M. E. Roloff & G. R. Miller (Eds.), *Interpersonal processes* (pp. 39–62). Newbury Park, CA: Sage.

Berger, C. R., & Calabrese, R. J. (1975). Some explorations in initial interaction and beyond: Toward a developmental theory of interpersonal communication. *Human Communication Research, 1*, 99–112. doi:10.1111/j.1468-2958.1975.tb00258.x.

Berger, C. R., & Douglas, W. (1981). Studies in interpersonal epistemology III: Anticipated interaction, self-monitoring, and observational context selection. *Communication Monographs, 48*, 183–196. doi:10.1080/03637758109376058.

Bohnert, D., & Ross, W. H. (2010). The influence of social networking web sites on the evaluation of job candidates. *Cyberpsychology, Behavior and Social Networking, 13*, 341–347. doi:10.1089/cyber.2009.0193.

Bolino, M. C., Kacmar, K. M., Turnley, W. H., & Gilstrap, J. B. (2008). A multi-level review of impression management motives and behaviors. *Journal of Management, 34*, 1080–1109. doi:10.1177/0149206308324325.

Cable, D. M., & Judge, T. A. (1996). Person-organization fit, job choice decisions, and organizational entry. *Organizational Behavior and Human Decision Process, 67*, 294–311. doi:10.1006/obhd.1996.0081.

Carr, C. T., & Hayes, R. A. (2015). Social media: Defining, developing, and divining. *Atlantic Journal of Communication, 23*, 46–65. doi:10.1080/15456870.2015.972282.

Carr, C. T., Klautke, H. A., Miller, V. D., & Walther, J. B. (2011, May). *Discovering online information about job applicants*. Paper presented at the annual meeting of the International Communication Association, Boston, MA.

Carr, C. T., & Walther, J. B. (2014). Increasing attributional certainty via social media: Learning about others one bit at a time. *Journal of Computer-Mediated Communication, 19*, 922–937. doi:10.1111/jcc4.12072.

Caverlee, J., & Webb, S. (2008, March). *A large-scale study of MySpace: Observations and implications for online social networks*. Paper presented at the International Conference on Weblogs and Social Media (ICWSM), Seattle, WA.

Chatman, J. A. (1991). Matching people and organizations: Selection and socialization in public accounting firms. *Administrative Science Quarterly, 36*, 459–484.

Clatterbuck, G. W. (1979). Attributional confidence and uncertainty in initial interaction. *Human Communication Research, 5*, 147–157. doi:10.1111/j.1468-2958.1979.tb00630.x.

Coutu, D. (2007). We Googled you. *Harvard Business Review, 85*(6), 37–47.

Daft, R. L., & Lengel, R. H. (1986). Organizational information requirements, media richness and structural design. *Management Science, 32*, 554–571.

DeAndrea, D. C. (2014). Advancing warranting theory. *Communication Theory, 24*, 186–204. doi:10.1111/comt.12033.

Douglas, W. (1990). Uncertainty, information seeking, and liking during initial interaction. *Western Journal of Speech Communication, 54*, 66–81. doi:10.1080/10570319009374325.

Ellison, N. B., Steinfield, C., & Lampe, C. (2007). The benefits of Facebook "friends:" Social capital and college students' use of online social network sites. *Journal of Computer-Mediated Communication, 12*, 1143–1168. doi:10.1111/j.1083-6101.2007.00367.x.

Field, J. M., Ritzman, L. P., Safizadeh, M. H., & Downing, C. E. (2006). Uncertainty reduction approaches, uncertainty coping approaches, and process performance in financial services. *Decision Sciences, 37*, 149–175. doi:10.1111/j.1540-5915.2006.00120.x.

Forgas, J. P. (1998). On being happy and mistaken: Mood effects on the fundamental attribution error. *Journal of Personality and Social Psychology, 75*, 318–331. doi:10.1037/0022-3514.75.2.318.

Gibbs, J. L., Ellison, N. B., & Lai, C.-H. (2011). First comes love, then comes Google: An investigation of uncertainty reduction strategies and self-disclosure in online dating. *Communication Research, 38*, 70–100. doi:10.1177/0093650210377091.

Goffman, E. (1959). *The presentation of self in everyday life*. New York, NY: Doubleday.

Golbeck, J., Robles, C., & Turner, K. (2011, May). *Predicting personality with social media*. Paper presented at the 2011 ACM CHI Conference on Human Factors in Computing Systems, Vancouver, BC

Gosling, S. D., Augustine, A. A., Vazire, S., Holtzman, N., & Gaddis, S. (2011). Manifestations of personality in online social networks: Self-reported Facebook-related behaviors and observable profile information. *Cyberpsychology, Behavior and Social Networking, 14*, 483–488. doi:10.1089/cyber.2010.0087.

Gosling, S. D., Gaddis, S., & Vazire, S. (2007, March). *Personality impressions based on Facebook profiles.* Paper presented at the International Conference on Weblogs and Social Media, Boulder, CO.

Hayes, R., & Carr, C. T. (2015). Does being social matter? The effect of enabled comments on credibility and brand attitude in social media. *Journal of Promotion Management, 21*, 371–390. doi:10.1080/10496491.2015.1039178.

Hedge, J. W., & Teachout, M. S. (1992). An interview approach to work sample criterion measurement. *Journal of Applied Psychology, 77*, 453–461. doi:10.1037/0021-9010.77.4.453.

Hogan, B. (2010). The presentation of self in the age of social media: Distinguishing performances and exhibitions online. *Bulletin of Science, Technology & Society, 30*, 377–386. doi:10.1177/0270467610385893.

Jauch, L. R., & Kraft, K. L. (1986). Strategic management of uncertainty. *Academy of Management Review, 11*, 777–790. doi:10.5465/AMR.1986.4283934.

Kellermann, K. (1986). Anticipation of future interaction and information exchange in initial interaction. *Human Communication Research, 13*, 41–75. doi:10.1111/j.1468-2958.1986.tb00095.x.

Kluemper, D. H. (2013). Social network screening: Pitfalls, possibilities, and parallels in employment selection. In M. R. Olivas-Lujan & T. Bondarouk (Eds.), *Social media in human resources management* (pp. 1–21). Bingly, England: Emerald Group.

Knobloch, L. K., & Solomon, D. H. (2005). Relational uncertainty and relational information processing: Questions without answers? *Communication Research, 32*, 349–388. doi:10.1177/0093650205275384.

Knouse, S. B. (1989). The role of attribution theory in personnel employment selection: A review of the recent literature. *The Journal of General Psychology, 116*, 183–196. doi:10.1080/00221309.1989.9711122.

Kramer, M. W. (1993). Communication and uncertainty reduction during job transfers: Leaving and joining processes. *Communication Monographs, 60*, 178–198. doi:10.1080/03637759309376307.

Kramer, M. W. (1994). Uncertainty reduction during job transitions: An exploratory study of the communication experiences of newcomers and transferees. *Management Communication Quarterly, 7*, 384–412. doi:10.1177/0893318994007004002.

Kramer, M. W. (2009). Managing uncertainty in work interactions. In T. D. Afifi & W. A. Afifi (Eds.), *Uncertainty, information management, and disclosure decisions* (pp. 164–181). New York: Routledge.

Kramer, M. W. (2010). *Organizational socialization: Joining and leaving organizations.* Malden, MA: Polity.

Kristof, A. L. (1996). Person-organization fit: An integrative review of its conceptualizations measurement, and implications. *Personnel Psychology, 49*, 1–49. doi:10.1111/j.1744-6570.1996.tb01790.x.

Kristof-Brown, A. L. (2000). Perceived applicant fit: Distinguishing between recruiters' perceptions of person-job and person-organization fit. *Personnel Psychology, 53*, 643–671. doi:10.1111/j.1744-6570.2000.tb00217.x.

Kristof-Brown, A. L., Zimmerman, R. D., & Johnson, E. C. (2005). Consequences of individuals' fit at work: A meta-analysis of person-job, person-organization, person-group, and person-supervisor fit. *Personnel Psychology, 58*, 281–342. doi:10.1111/j.1744-6570.2005.00672.x.

Lair, D., Sullivan, K., & Cheney, G. (2005). Marketization and the recasting of the professional self. *Management Communication Quarterly, 18*, 307–343. doi:10.1177/0893318904270744.

Lampe, C. A. C., Ellison, N., & Steinfield, C. (2007, April). *A familiar Face(book): Profile elements as signals in an online social network.* Paper presented at the SIGCHI conference on Human factors in computing systems, San Jose, CA.

Lauver, K. J., & Kristof-Brown, A. (2001). Distinguishing between employees' perceptions of person–job and person–organization fit. *Journal of Vocational Behavior, 59*, 454–470. doi:10.1006/jvbe.2001.1807.

Lehavot, K. (2009). "MySpace" or yours? The ethical dilemma of graduate students' personal lives on the internet. *Ethics & Behavior, 19*, 129–141. doi:10.1080/10508420902772728.

Marwick, A. E., & boyd, d. (2011). I tweet honestly, I tweet passionately: Twitter users, context collapse, and the imagined audience. *New Media & Society, 13*, 114–133. doi:10.1177/1461444810365313.

Mignerey, J. T., Rubin, R. B., & Gorden, W. I. (1995). Organizational entry: An investigation of newcomer communication behavior uncertainty. *Communication Research, 22*, 54–85. doi:10.1177/009365095022001003.

O'Sullivan, P. B. (2005, May). *Mass personal communication: Rethinking the mass interpersonal divide*. Paper presented at the annual meeting of the International Communication Association, New York, NY.

Papacharissi, Z. (2002). The self online: The utility of personal home pages. *Journal of Broadcasting & Electronic Media, 46*, 346–368. doi:10.1207/s15506878jobem4603_3.

Parks, M. R. (2011). Boundary conditions for the application of three theories of computer-mediated communication to MySpace. *Journal of Communication, 61*, 557–574. doi:10.1111/j.1460-2466.2011.01569.x.

Pew Research Internet Project. (2014). Social media networking fact sheet. *Internet & Technology.* Retrieved from http://www.pewinternet.org/fact-sheets/social-networking-fact-sheet/

Planalp, S., Rutherford, D. K., & Honeycutt, J. M. (1988). Events that increase uncertainty in personal relationships II: Replication and extension. *Human Communication Research, 14*, 516–547. doi:10.1111/j.1468-2958.1988.tb00166.x.

Ployhart, R. E. (2006). Staffing in the 21st century: New challenges and strategic opportunities. *Journal of Management, 32*, 868–897. doi:10.1177/0149206306293625.

Posthuma, R. A., Morgenson, F. P., & Campion, M. A. (2002). Beyond employment interview validity: A comprehensive narrative review of recent research and trends over time. *Personnel Psychology, 55*, 1–81. doi:10.1111/j.1744-6570.2002.tb00103.x.

Ramirez, A., Jr., Walther, J. B., Burgoon, J. K., & Sunnafrank, M. (2002). Information-seeking strategies, uncertainty, and computer-mediated communication: Toward a conceptual model. *Human Communication Research, 28*, 213–228. doi:10.1093/hcr/28.2.213.

Ross, L. (1977). The intuitive psychologist and his shortcomings: Distortions in the attribution process. In L. Berkowitz (Ed.), *Advances in experimental social psychology* (Vol. 10, pp. 173–220). New York: Academic.

Rubin, R. B. (1977). The role of context in information seeking and impression formation. *Communication Monographs, 44*, 81–90. doi:10.1080/03637757709390117.

Rynes, S. L., & Gerhart, B. (1990). Interviewer assessments of applicant "fit": An exploratory investigation. *Personnel Psychology, 43*, 13–35. doi:10.1111/j.1744-6570.1990.tb02004.x.

Rynes, S. L., & Gerhart, B. (1993). Recruiter perceptions of applicant fit: Implications for individual career preparation and job search behavior. *Journal of Vocational Behavior, 43*, 310–327. doi:10.1006/jvbe.1993.1050.

Schouten, A. P., Antheunis, M. L., Abeele, M. V., & Van Lith, V. (2015, May). *How online profile pictures affect recruiters' perceptions of job candidates*. Paper presented at the annual meeting of the International Communication Association, San Juan, PR.

Sekiguchi, T. (2007). A contingency perspective of the importance of PJ fit and PO fit in employee selection. *Journal of Managerial Psychology, 22*, 118–131. doi:10.1108/02683940710726384.

Sekiguchi, T., & Huber, V. L. (2011). The use of person–organization fit and person–job fit information in making selection decisions. *Organizational Behavior and Human Decision Processes, 116*, 203–216. doi:10.1016/j.obhdp.2011.04.001.

SHRM. (2011, August 25). The use of social networking websites and online search engines in screening job candidates. *Society for Human Resource Management.* Retrieved from http://www.shrm.org/research/surveyfindings/articles/pages/theuseofsocialnetworkingwebsitesandonlinesearchenginesinscreeningjobcandidates.aspx.

Siegert, J. R., & Stamp, G. H. (1994). "Our first big fight" as a milestone in the development of close relationships. *Communication Monographs, 61*, 345–360. doi:10.1080/03637759409376342.

Sprague, R. (2008). Rethinking information privacy in an age of online transparency. *Hofstra Labor & Employment Law Journal, 25*, 395–417.
Stoughton, J. W., Thompson, L. F., & Meade, A. W. (2013). Big five personality traits reflected in job applicants' social media postings. *Cyberpsychology, Behavior and Social Networking, 16*, 800–805. doi:10.1089/cyber.2012.0163.
Tong, S. T. (2013). Facebook use during relationship termination: Uncertainty reduction and surveillance. *Cyberpsychology, Behavior and Social Networking, 16*, 877–793. doi:10.1089/cyber.2012.0549.
Tong, S. T., Van Der Heide, B., Langwell, L., & Walther, J. B. (2008). Too much of a good thing? The relationship between number of friends and interpersonal impressions on Facebook. *Journal of Computer-Mediated Communication, 13*, 531–549. doi:10.1111/j.1083-6101.2008.00409.x.
Undercover Recruiter. (2009). How employers use social media to screen applicants. *Employer.* Retrieved from http://theundercoverrecruiter.com/infographic-how-recruiters-use-social-media-screen-applicants/.
Utz, S. (2010). Show me your friends and I will tell you what type of person you are: How one's profile, number of friends, and type of friends influence impression formation on social network sites. *Journal of Computer-Mediated Communication, 15*, 314–335. doi:10.1111/j.1083-6101.2010.01522.x.
Van Iddekinge, C. H., & Ployhart, R. W. (2008). Developments in the criterion-related validation of selection procedures: A critical review and recommendations for practice. *Personnel Psychology, 61*(4), 871–925.
Vazire, S., & Gosling, S. D. (2004). e-perceptions: Personality impressions based on personal websites. *Journal of Personality and Social Psychology, 87*, 123–132.
Vitak, J. (2012). The impact of context collapse and privacy on social network site disclosures. *Journal of Broadcasting & Electronic Media, 56*, 451–470. doi:10.1080/08838151.2012.732140.
Walther, J. B., & Parks, M. R. (2002). Cues filtered out, cues filtered in: Computer-mediated communication and relationships. In M. L. Knapp & J. A. Daly (Eds.), *Handbook of interpersonal communication* (3rd ed., pp. 529–563). Thousand Oaks, CA: Sage.
Walther, J. B., Van Der Heide, B., Hamel, L. M., & Shulman, H. C. (2009). Self-generated versus other-generated statements and impressions in computer-mediated communication: A test of warranting theory using Facebook. *Communication Research, 36*, 229–253. doi:10.1177/0093650208330251.
Westerman, D. K., & Tamborini, R. (2008, May). *Uncertainty reduction over time in initial stranger interactions: A Social Information Processing Theory approach.* Paper presented at the annual meeting of the International Communication Association, Montreal, QC, Canada.
Zimmer, M. (2008). The externalities of search 2.0: The emerging privacy threats when the drive for the perfect search engine meets Web 2.0. *First Monday, 13*(3). doi:10.5210/fm.v13i3.2136.

Chapter 5
Social Media Use: Antecedents and Outcomes of Sharing

Nathan Weidner, Kimberly E. O'Brien, and Kevin T. Wynne

Abstract This chapter addresses three major aspects of general and workplace social media usage. The first section briefly describes how people use social media, with specific attention given to social networking sites (SNS). The second section summarizes the motivations for why people and organizations use social media. The third section identifies the outcomes associated with the usage of social media for both the individual users and the workplace. The outcomes for individuals are often contradictory and include social aspects, such as building social capital versus perpetuating loneliness, and health aspects, such as improving well-being versus increased stress over privacy concerns. Similarly, conflicting positive and negative organizational outcomes associated with job performance, job attitudes, social capital, and privacy issues are discussed.

Keywords Antecedents • Positive Outcomes • Negative Outcomes • Psychological Needs • Privacy

N. Weidner, Ph.D. (✉)
Department of Psychological Science, Missouri S&T,
110 HSS 500. W. 14th Street, Rolla, MO 65409, USA
e-mail: weidnern@mst.edu

K.E. O'Brien, Ph.D.
Department of Psychology, Central Michigan University,
100 Sloan Hall, Mount Pleasant, MI 48858, USA
e-mail: obrie1ke@cmich.edu

K.T. Wynne, M.S.
Department of Psychology, Wayne State University,
5057 Woodward Avenue, 7th Floor, Detroit, MI 48202, USA
e-mail: k.wynne@wayne.edu

R.N. Landers, G.B. Schmidt (eds.), *Social Media in Employee Selection and Recruitment*, DOI 10.1007/978-3-319-29989-1_5

5.1 Types of Social Media Usage

5.1.1 How People and Organizations Use Social Media

When considering using social media for selection, it is important to first consider how and why social media is being used. Social media encompasses a wide variety of tools including wikis, blogs, social bookmarking, and social networking sites (SNS) all of which have seen an increase in usage over the past decade. Even within the specific domain of SNS, there exists a wide variety of sites each with varying purposes or orientations. Currently, some of the more popular SNS include Facebook, LinkedIn, and Twitter. Although the various SNS share the same basic functions, they significantly differ in their primary content, audience, and formats (Boyd & Ellison, 2007). Facebook, for example, began by targeting college students poised to start their professional careers, whereas LinkedIn has more directly focused on applications for professionals from its start (Skeels & Grudin, 2009). SNS sites such as LinkedIn are therefore more likely to contain job-specific and job-relevant information (job history, accomplishments, endorsed skills) than sites such as Facebook or Twitter.

Regardless of the specific medium of social media, it is clear that social media has reshaped the boundaries between our public and private lives (Mcdonald & Thompson, 2015). In addition to personal usage, social media has been rapidly gaining acceptance and use among organizations, which are seeking new and innovative ways to incorporate SNS into the workplace (Kaplan & Haenlein, 2010; Leftheriotis & Giannakos, 2014). This does, however, present concerns as social media users may view the typical type of social media information being shared (e.g., photos and comments) as being personal and private (Mohamed & Ahmad, 2012). As a result, individuals may react negatively when they perceive that organizations are misusing their private information (Smith, Milberg, & Burke, 1996).

Social media provides unique challenges and benefits for organizations in particular. These include more frequent contact with current employees and future job applicants, more targeted advertising, enhanced collaborative practices, and increased transparency (e.g., Kaplan & Haenlein, 2010). As such, researchers have sought to identify the strategies for social media use by companies. Nagendra (2014), for example, described how social media is influencing business through the five Cs: content, conversation, collaboration, community, and collective intelligence. More specifically, social media provides a variety of tools for organizations to share content that they generate either with customers or internally with employees. It provides an excellent set of tools to structure conversations, which can enhance problem solving and collaboration. Furthermore, social media helps to create communities of interest where ideas can be shared and pools of talent or collective intelligence can be targeted for recruitment. Nagendra (2014) also describes how social media can impact a variety of HR functions across the life cycle of an employee. In particular, social media influences attraction and recruitment of employees (Colao, 2012), onboarding (Willyerd, 2012), collaboration (Byrne, 2015), and employee retention (Coy, 2013). Social media is even being used by companies to help maintain alumni connections after employees leave (Gone but not forgotten, 2014). Maintaining and expanding these networks can offer organizations better access to highly skilled talent. This may also serve as a mechanism for organizations to openly convey their culture and values, perhaps leading to better fitting applicants as a function of the Attraction Selection Attrition (ASA) model (Schneider, 1987).

5.1.2 Types of Social Media Users

In order to properly understand how people use social media, it is important to first recognize that not all individuals use social media in the same way. Several different authors have proposed typologies of social media usage. One classification (Brandtzaeg & Heim, 2011) identified five types of social media users: sporadics, lurkers, socializers, debaters, and actives. *Sporadic* usage is typified by infrequent use of social media sites with very limited information sharing. *Lurkers*, in contrast, check their social media often, but rarely engage. *Socializers* use their social media sites more frequently for recreational connection with others. *Debaters* are also highly engaged on their social media sites, but tend to post more comments and use their sites for self-expression rather than connection. *Actives* are also engaged, but don't focus on a specific reason; rather they engage on all levels. Research still needs to examine how this may impact the validity of assessments made using information posted on SNS. For example, sporadics and lurkers, by definition, post less information. This in turn could make it much more difficult to make evaluative judgements based upon their SNS as compared to actives who likely have more personal information available on their sites.

Personality is also linked to differences in social media use (see Chap. 3, this volume, for a review). For example, Facebook users are more extraverted and less conscientious than non-users (Ghosh & Dasgupta, 2015). Additionally, Facebook users had higher levels of self-esteem and less social anxiety than non-users (Ghosh & Dasgupta, 2015). Narcissism is a personality trait that has been strongly and repeatedly linked to social media usage (e.g., Carpenter, 2012; Panek, Nardis, & Konrath, 2013; Ryan & Xenos, 2011). Narcissists are typified by their grandiosity, self-love, and inflated sense of self (Campbell, Hoffman, Campbell, & Marchisio, 2011). Narcissists view themselves as exceptional and desire power and esteem. These qualities, in turn, are associated with low levels of empathy and emotional intimacy. Consequently narcissists tend to foster numerous shallow relationships and seek out opportunities to self-promote, manipulate, or exploit. As such, it is no surprise that narcissists use social media differently than others. Specifically, narcissists were more likely to use SNS in order to have as many friends as possible, to keep those friends updated on what they were doing, and to project a positive self-image (Bergman, Fearrington, Davenport, & Bergman, 2011). As a note of caution, this suggests that narcissists are more engaged users of SNS and are more widely connected which may make them more appealing to organizations using SNS for selection.

Organizations, on the other hand, may have a much simpler classification of users. A cluster analysis designed to examine social media adoption and usage patterns for disclosing information about their companies (although limited in scope) identified two primary clusters representing high and low adopters of social media technology (Zhang, 2015). In addition, social media adoption related to higher levels of disclosure through social media, as opposed to more traditional sources such as websites. However, when controlling for adoption level, disclosure through social media and traditional sites were governed by the same factors such as firm performance, information environment, information asymmetry level, and debt structure (Zhang, 2015).

Future research should build upon this classification to examine whether or not organizations that more actively use social media are more likely to use it for recruitment and selection purposes specifically or if their usage is more strongly targeted at connecting with clients. Additionally, it may be worth examining if organizational usage of social media directly relates to the quality of outcomes from that usage. For example, organizations with a more active social media presence may both gain a wider range of applicants, as well as applicants who are more strongly attracted to their organization.

5.2 Motivations for Social Media Usage

5.2.1 Why Individuals Use Social Media

Researchers examining social media's potential for selection should also consider that the reasons that drive individuals to use social media may vary greatly. There have been several attempts to explain why individuals seek to use social media sites (e.g., Dogruer, Menevi§, & Eyyam, 2011; Lin, Le, Khalil, & Cheng, 2012; Nadkarni & Hofmann, 2012). For example, perceived encouragement and having a relationship orientation have been found to be important factors in predicting who chooses to use SNS (Kwon & Wen, 2010). Additionally, enjoyment has been found to be an important driver of social network usage (Lin & Lu, 2011). Other research has found that users may access social media regularly out of habit more than anything else (Khang, Han, & Ki, 2014).

Nadkarni and Hoffman (2012) suggest that there are two primary psychological needs that drive people to use SNS, including the need to belong and the need for self-presentation. Research has found that viewing and especially editing your Facebook profile as a type of selective self-presentation has a positive impact on self-esteem (Gonzales & Hancock, 2011). These differences in usage may in turn relate to the amount and content of posts. The reasons for which a person chooses to use social media may be a more meaningful predictor of the type of information being shared than other personality or selection-relevant variables.

Brandtzæg and Heim (2009) identified 11 specific reasons for using SNS. The most popular objectives included seeking out and meeting new people, maintaining contact with friends and acquaintances, general socializing behaviors, and seeking out information about various topics. Less frequent reasons included debating or discussing topics with others, sending free short messages, killing time, having fun, profile surfing, and keeping in contact with family. Other research has identified four major reasons for using Facebook groups in particular, including socializing, entertainment, self-promotion, and information seeking (Park, Kee, & Valenzuela, 2009). Furthermore, motivations for joining groups were related to students' involvement in voluntary political and charity organizations (Park et al., 2009). Although these lists of reasons are likely not exhaustive, they do represent the most common purposes for using SNS.

It should also be noted that different sites likely have very different purposes for use. The lists above represent some general reasons for SNS usage which are probably most applicable to sites such as Facebook and Twitter. Sites such as LinkedIn which have a much stronger career focus are likely much more focused in that people use them for career advancement. Some recent studies have, however, reported that individuals use Facebook (Burke & Kraut, 2013) to aid in job-seeking behaviors as well. This diversity of usage only speaks to the powerful impact that social media and SNS sites in particular are having on our lives.

Taken together, it becomes clear that people use social media in different ways and for very different purposes. Thus, identifying antecedents and outcomes of social media usage is a very complicated task. Ngai, Tao, and Moon (2015) summarized various psychological and behavioral theories that have been used to explain antecedents, outcomes, mediators, and moderators of social media usage. The review identified over 30 different psychological and behavioral theories across 46 articles that were being used to explain various aspects of social media usage. With such a surfeit of guiding theories, social media usage can be examined from a wide variety of contexts. Future research will need to emphasize integration across these theories in order to develop a more comprehensive model of social media usage.

Future research is also needed to help organizations better predict how people will use social media. Organizations that are attempting to engage current and future employees over social media must first acknowledge that even within a specific SNS, there is no one type of user. Thus, outgoing messages should be prepared for mixed audiences, including people who are looking to engage more highly with the organization, people who perceive attempts at connection as unwanted solicitation and invasions of privacy, and even those who may intentionally react with offense to benign interactions. In other words, outgoing messages designed to recruit potential job applicants and increase the reputation of the organization need to consider factors beyond the conventional demographics. Although it is standard practice to determine the target audience when delivering any organizational message, this becomes complicated when members of the same demographic (e.g., female heads of home or millennials) can interpret a message in multiple ways. This ambiguity is perhaps more relevant over social media than other methods of communication, given character limitations or lack of contextual information (e.g., tone of voice, nonverbal information).

To expand, there are many contextual factors within the message that have not been adequately researched, such as the effect of the social media platform (e.g., blog, LinkedIn), formality of language (e.g., text speak, emoticons), device/interface (e.g., phone, desktop computer), and when/where people are interacting with the information (e.g., during leisure time, at work). All of these factors and more can affect how organizational messages are interpreted. For example, the success of attempts to recruit might vary based on whether prospective applicants are engaging with the organization's message while at work on a desktop versus at the zoo with their children on a smartphone. Thus, Monday evening might be a good time for a formal message including a link to apply to the organization, whereas Sunday afternoon might be good time for a casual message about the organization's commitment to work-life balance.

The varying motivations for why individuals use social media will also affect selection not just through outgoing recruitment messages, but also, perhaps, when evaluating applicants. The differential reasons that people use social media may provide clues as to the quality and fit of the applicant. However, there is very little research on this area (thus very little information that will benefit the organization's hiring) or on the potential for harm (e.g., perceived privacy invasions) that may come from this type of contact.

At this point, recommendations to use social media to decide which applicants to select are done with great reservation. For one, there are potential legal issues such as allowing irrelevant information (e.g., photos showing the applicant volunteering with a political group that the hiring manager disagrees with) to interfere with an unbiased review. Also, evaluating an applicant's social media usage for selection purposes can lead to privacy concerns that can lower applicant test-taking motivation, organizational attraction, and intentions to apply to the organization (Bauer et al., 2006).

Furthermore, information about an applicant's protected class status (e.g., disability or religion) may become apparent over social media earlier than during a traditional application process, potentially increasing the vulnerability of an organization to adverse impact claims. Before social media sites can effectively contribute to selection, measures with high predictive ability that target job-relevant characteristics while ignoring irrelevant and potentially protected information need to be developed. For example, a potentially useful selection measure might be a software program that analyzes an applicant's SNS profile for personality information, such as narcissism (status updates that use "me" or "I") or negative emotional traits (e.g., status updates that use the word "hate"). A potential risk assessment tool could scan for troubling words or phrases such as sexist comments, racial slurs, or general posting of derogatory content which may present a candidate that is at a high risk of negatively representing the company or potentially causing a discrimination case. These tools could potentially keep interested hiring managers blind to the specific protected class information while offering a systematic evaluation of an applicant based on their publicly available social media information.

5.2.2 Why Organizations Use Social Media

Social media includes a variety of new tools that organizations can use to engage their employees and customers as well as to enhance internal processes. As such, organizations may have a wide variety of reasons for using social media beyond employee selection. Fundamentally, organizations are using social media tools to enhance the performance of their employees and business as a whole. Organizations primarily use social media for connecting with external contacts, and/or for internal communication amongst employees (Leonardi, Huysman, & Steinfield, 2013). For example, social media tools are being used to improve performance in service industries by enhancing contact with customers (Kim, Lim, & Brymer, 2015). Additionally, many organizations are using social media to augment a large variety of traditional HR processes, such as recruitment, to cut costs, and to increase effectiveness (Kaplan & Haenlein, 2010). However, internal uses of social media are popular as well. For example, social media usage has been linked to increased creativity amongst workers (Pigg, 2014; Sigala & Chalkiti, 2015). Many companies even implement their own internal SNS more commonly referred to as enterprise social media (ESM) sites (Leonardi et al., 2013). These sites may hold high potential for use when examining employees' potential for promotion.

In addition to engaging employees, social media also allows for a unique and powerful tool to connect with customers and future applicants. Social media facilitates customers' interactions with each other outside of the organization's control (Mangold & Faulds, 2009). Customers are now more capable than ever of being able to communicate with other people to share the details of their personal experiences and interactions with companies, both positive and negative, and these interactions may affect the reputation of the company for prospective employees. As an example, Ryan Block shared a recorded portion of his conversation with a Comcast representative in which he attempts to cancel his service (Eadicicco, 2014; Stampler, 2014). Ryan was able to share 8 min of his infuriating conversation through the social media site SoundCloud (Block, 2014). Ryan's frustrations with Comcast were reflective of many other users' experiences, which caused the recording to go viral. In response, Comcast issued an apology (Karinshak, 2014) and continues to submit statements to respond to complaints about their poor customer service (Herrin, 2015). Other authors have also noted the importance of properly framing social media and news releases when dealing with a corporate crisis (Etter & Vestergaard, 2015). Social media, for better or worse, has been found to be an effective tool to increase customer engagement (Dijkmans, Kerkhof, & Beukeboom, 2015) and thus, prospective employee perceptions.

Many organizations are using social media platforms to increase connectivity internally rather than externally. One common method for doing so involves creating enterprise social media (ESM) sites (Leonardi et al., 2013; McAfee, 2009; Treem, Dailey, Pierce, & Leonardi, 2015). These social media sites often mimic public social media sites such as Facebook. However they restrict usage only to members of a given organization (Leonardi et al., 2013). These ESM systems can create an internal record of social interaction and performance which could be particularly useful for evaluating current employees for promotion opportunities. However, relatively little is known about the actual usefulness of these ESM sites for selection purposes or in general.

Previous research has identified at least three possible advantages of ESM over traditional knowledge-sharing methods within organizations (Fulk & Yuan, 2013). First, ESM helps to locate experts and expertise that already exists within the organization. Second, ESM can increase the likelihood for employees to share their knowledge with each other by reducing the effort needed and increasing the recognition for doing so. Third, ESM helps to develop and maintain these knowledge-sharing connections. Interestingly, some research suggests that individuals who are older or less familiar with external social media sites may be more optimistic about the utility of implementing ESM within an organization (Treem et al., 2015). It remains unclear, however, if employees use external sites differently from internal sites. For example, employees might self-monitor more carefully on internal sites, such that external sites are subject to less faking. In general, although ESM may be a good option for many organizations to realize the benefits of social media while maintaining the privacy of their information, more research needs to examine how these sites specifically impact functioning within an organization. In particular, a more thorough understanding of how different types of users may choose to adopt and interact with ESM may be important, given that experience with social media may bias opinions about ESM systems even prior to implementation (Treem et al., 2015).

Dreher (2014) outlines eight key steps that organizations need to take when trying to engage their employees through social media. Specifically, organizations should first research their employees' comfort with and concerns about social media usage. Next, organizations need to ensure that their employees are allowed unrestricted access to social media sites. Although some organizations may be hesitant to allow unfettered access to social media sites while at work, this is a necessary step in order to enhance engagement. It is also important for organizations to have commitment from the CEO for social media usage, along with clear guidelines and policies for employee social media usage. Having a designated social media team and providing employees who are unsure of how to use social media with proper training can prevent negative social media experiences. Finally, organizations should integrate the social media strategy policies into the organization's overall communication policy and set social media communication goals to enhance employee engagement. If employers are using ESM as part of an internal selection process, it would be particularly important to inform the employees about this policy ahead of time.

In summary, the reasons why organizations use social media are broad and varied. This is not surprising because social media is simply a tool for communication, and thus can be used in a variety of ways, just like postal mail or face-to-face interactions. There are some key differences, of course, such as the longevity of the message and the public interaction that takes place, causing some unique concerns. As such, organizations are encouraged to closely follow established guidelines (e.g., Dreher, 2014) and use preexisting customer service guidelines, such as showing empathy (which can be quite difficult, given the anonymity of the internet and the resulting offensive behavior of some social media users), patience, and consistency (this is especially important over social media, when communications are stored indefinitely).

5.3 Outcomes of Social Media Usage

5.3.1 Personal Outcomes

Researchers are still exploring the many potential outcomes of social media usage. Numerous positive and negative effects have been noted already. For example, researchers have had mixed results when examining the impact of social media sites and internet usage in general on psychological well-being. Some researchers have stated that the use of social media for communication can reduce well-being by cutting off individuals from more enriched social interactions (Kraut et al., 1998). In support of this proposition, one study found that individuals who use Facebook more often were less satisfied with their lives in general (Kross et al., 2013). Contrary to these findings, other studies have found that having many connections through Facebook can increase social capital and lead to higher levels of psychological well-being (e.g., Ellison, Steinfield, & Lampe, 2007; Johnston, Tanner, Lalla, & Kawalski, 2013).

In part, these effects may depend on the way in which users are utilizing their social media sites to communicate with others. Most social media content focuses on positive and entertaining content (Bryant & Marmo, 2012, Reinecke & Trepte, 2014). This content has generally been found to relate to better relationships with friends and acquaintances (Bohn, Buchta, Hornik, & Mair, 2014; Valenzuela, Park, & Kee, 2009). In particular, authentic or honest communication through SNS has been linked to increased psychological well-being (Reinecke & Trepte, 2014). Users who demonstrate a high level of this type of communication may appear to be more attractive to organizations. Organizations should, however, also consider the possible downside of increased social media usage as well. In particular, this positive content bias may create an overly positive impression of others when viewing others' content pages. For example, passive Facebook usage has been found to lead to increases in envy, which results in a reduction in affective well-being (Verduyn et al., 2015).

These contradictory findings regarding well-being may depend on the rate of usage (Chan, 2014). Specifically, although Facebook may have some positive benefits at lower levels of usage by facilitating social interaction and well-being, for those high in neuroticism, Facebook was found to have negative impacts with higher levels of usage. Research has further found that using Facebook is often perceived as being a waste of time, which in turn leads to a decreased mood as a result of having used it (Sagioglou & Greitemeyer, 2014). The potential impact of mood changes as a result of SNS usage at work is an area that future researchers will need to address. Perhaps by using social media for selection purposes, hiring managers may avoid this negative mood change by perceiving their own action as useful rather than as a waste of time.

Using SNS has also been found to impact decision making (Sadovykh, Sundaram, & Piramuthu, 2015). In particular, individuals commonly use social media to enhance their decision making around a variety of topics including professional, consumer, educational, and health issues. Researchers found that social media may significantly contribute to many common biases in decision making, such as the illusion of transparency (the tendency to overestimate the ability for other people to understand your mental state), the bandwagon effect (the tendency to adopt trends more readily as more people have done so), and the false consensus effect (the tendency to overestimate the degree to which your opinions are shared by others) (Sadovykh et al., 2015). Hiring managers should be made aware of these biases in their perceptions when using social media for selection purposes. Future research should also further examine the effects that these particular biases may have when interpreting characteristics deemed relevant for selection from a prospective employee's SNS sites.

In general, these findings are often conflicting and do not offer the ability to draw clear implications. Future research identifying moderators of these relationships is pivotal in providing any sort of practical suggestions. For example, we have determined that people's reasons for using social media varies, but tests of whether certain motivations are associated with changes in social adjustment and well-being have yet to be conducted. In general, there are a variety of moderators that are promising, including the valence of message being shared (e.g., positive or negative), the traits of the person posting the message (e.g., personality, attributional style, demographics), the platform for the message (e.g., Instagram versus LinkedIn), and the content of the message (e.g., photograph, political article, status update). These characteristics are likely to be better predictors of social and health outcomes for individuals than simply usage of social media in general. In fact, it is possible that these characteristics will interact with motivation (e.g., self-promotion, information gathering, social support) to predict social adjustment and well-being. On that note, however, it is also important that researchers expand their criteria to include other outcomes, such as interpersonal skill, knowledge of current events, or other traits that can be applicable to the workplace.

5.3.2 *Workplace Outcomes*

5.3.2.1 Positive

There is a growing body of research linking social media to positive workplace outcomes, particularly regarding job attitudes, job performance, and enhancing the reputation of the organization. For example, one study found that employees will follow their employers on social media, provided that the employer is actively using social media to convey relevant information (Eren & Vardarlıer, 2013). Furthermore, this may result in increased levels of organizational commitment from these employees (Eren & Vardarlıer, 2013). However, other research suggests that the impact of social media usage on organizational commitment may be mediated through an increase in job satisfaction of the employees who use social media while at work (Moqbel, Nevo, & Kock, 2013).

In addition to improving job attitudes, SNS usage may also have value for workplace productivity. Some employees rely on social media tools to gather information about the environment or competitive market as well as to keep contact with customers (Leftheriotis & Giannakos, 2014). In particular, proper management of social media sites has been found to be an important element of organizational performance in service industries such as hotels (Kim et al., 2015). Furthermore, several studies have suggested that properly using social media can increase work productivity indirectly, as these tools help to improve job attitudes and communication among employees, which in turn leads to an increase in job performance (e.g., Cao, Vogel, Guo, Liu, & Gu, 2012; Charoensukmongkol, 2014). Collectively these studies suggest there are certainly positives to purposefully selecting employees with proficiency in the use of social media. In particular for service based industries, examining a job applicant's social media site may be a good predictor of their social media proficiency which in these industries would be directly related to performance.

Similarly, social media may help improve creativity and innovation processes. Specifically, social media may encourage networks of relationships at all phases, including access, creation, development, maintenance, and finally leveraging toward future action (Pigg, 2014). Research has suggested that employees use social media to engage in a form of knowledge management (Sigala & Chalkiti, 2015). By sharing, discussing, and creating information online through social media, individuals engage in cognitive processes that may lead to creativity. For example, employee creativity was positively correlated with levels of engagement on social media as well with the number of social media sites used (Sigala & Chalkiti, 2015). Although not causal in nature, these initial findings suggest that social media may provide important opportunities for creative expression and collaboration amongst employees. Researchers may therefore consider developing assessment methods to better predict which applicants will be able to use social media to their advantage when working on creative projects.

Social media, and SNS in particular, may also offer benefits through employee connectivity outside of the workplace. Recent research has identified how SNS can be used to accomplish both transactional and relationship-oriented work goals outside of the workplace (Mak & Chui, 2013). Specifically, Facebook creates an environment in which workplace relevant communication can be handled in a less formal way. This presents a situation in which the traditional organizational hierarchy and power relationships that regulate communication norms can be superseded (Mak & Chui, 2013). Allowing employees to opportunity to address workplace concerns in a less formal setting can provide a more open and honest dialogue between employees and generally enhance the social capital of the organization. Companies with strict social media policies that limit usage for work-related connection and communication may miss out on the potential benefits of this informal communication. These informal networks may provide opportunities for interested applicants to approach organizational members to get a better understanding of job requirements prior to applying, potentially increasing the selection pool or fit of applicants to the organization.

Social media offers a variety of ways in which it can enhance career development (Roman, 2014). For example, self-presentation through information posted on

LinkedIn has been linked to subsequent recommendations for hiring by recruiters (Chiang & Suen, 2015), acculturation (Li & Tsai, 2015), employee socialization (Mak, 2013), and an increase in voluntary on-the-job learning behaviors (Puijenbroek, Poell, Kroon, & Timmerman, 2013).

From a more macro perspective, social media may also enhance the sense of accountability within organizations (Treem, 2014). As a communication tool, social media allows people to consider and edit what they publicly post. This leads to an enhanced belief that the intention of a post may be more clearly understood by observers. Together with a digital record of what was posted, this creates a situation in which employees may feel a greater sense of accountability for what they choose to share through social media (Treem et al., 2015). In fact, one study showed that employees were less likely to use a social media system when implemented within an organization, due to the increased accountability (Treem et al., 2015). Researchers may need to develop ways to overcome accountability concerns in order to better reap the benefits of social media in the workplace.

5.3.2.2 Negative

Although some research shows positive workplace outcomes from SNS usage, much like with personal outcomes, other research indicates that SNS usage can be detrimental to job attitudes, job performance, and social capital. For example, the frequency of Facebook usage has been negatively related to how much participants liked their current job and positively related to their intentions to quit (Chou, Hammond, & Johnson, 2013). Likewise, the introduction of social media into the workplace may unintentionally create a more stressful working environment (Bucher, Fieseler, & Suphan, 2013). Social media presents a substantial amount of information and options for individuals to deal with which may result in information overload (Edmunds & Morris, 2000) or technology overload (Karr-Wisniewski & Lu, 2010) and eventually lead to social media fatigue (Bright, Kleiser, & Grau, 2015). Furthermore, social media can blur the boundaries between work and home life, resulting in more work–family conflict (e.g., Olson-Buchanan & Boswell, 2006). Another study found that in addition to relating to work attitudes such as lower happiness and higher stress, Facebook usage during work time may result in lower performance (Brooks, 2015).

Social media has also opened up new concerns over potential avenues for other harmful job activities, including counterproductive work behaviors (e.g., Brown, Weidner, Wynne, & O'Brien, 2015), sexual harassment (Mainiero & Jones, 2012, 2013), cyberbullying (Privitera & Campbell, 2009), and cyberstalking (Piotrowski, 2012). The proliferation of social media and ease of access can extend the boundaries of these behaviors outside of the workplace, creating an avenue for online posts and actions taken outside of the workplace to directly cause a hostile work environment. Legal professionals have recognized these claims (Moore, 2014) and have issued advice on how to best reshape policies to deal with these potential issues (Ponolly, 2014). For example, Mainero and Jones (2012) recommend legal agreements between two employees who are romantically linked to supplement companies' standard anti-sexual harassment policies. More specifically, they recommend that these contracts specify how and why behaviors on social media may constitute a form of sexual harassment to ensure that employees are aware of this and to limit company liabilities.

Another potential negative outcome of social media usage is known as social media addiction. Characterized by excessive monitoring of online social media sites and withdrawal from everyday activities, social media addiction has been linked to feelings of loneliness, generalized and social anxiety, depression, and insomnia (Koc & Gulyagci, 2013; Wang, Lee, & Hua, 2015; Yao & Zhong, 2014). Research has also linked social media addiction to decreased academic performance and reduced social capital among students (Huang, 2014). More generally, obsessive internet use has been related to having poorer interpersonal relationships (Milani, Osualdella, & Di Blasio, 2009). Not surprisingly social media use has also been implicated in developing an internet addiction (Kuss, van Rooij, Shorter, Griffiths, & van de Mheen, 2013), which has been linked to social anxiety (Weinstein et al., 2015), reduced social self-efficacy, and increased academic external locus of control (Iskender & Akin, 2010). Individuals who use social media may have more content from which they can be judged for selection purposes. On the other hand, it may be difficult to determine from a cursory examination of one's SNS whether or not they are suffering from this addiction. This too presents a problem for practitioners seeking to use social media for selection purposes as it may unintentionally appear more attractive to individuals with this affliction.

Social media use can also have negative effects on the social capital of the organization. For example, organizations have begun to openly use social media for employment decisions (Brown & Vaughn, 2011). This could potentially have a variety of negative impacts for these organizations, as several studies have found that younger adults tend to oppose these behaviors (e.g., Drouin, O'Connor, Schmidt, & Miller, 2015). Similarly, SNS-based selection criteria may cause negative applicant reactions (Schneider, Goffin, & Daljeet, 2015). The net impact of using social media for employment decisions could potentially result in a reduction of social capital or the development of a poor organizational image.

5.4 Privacy Issues

One concern inherent in the usage of social media is the issue of privacy. Traditionally, employees present themselves differently depending on the audience (e.g., supervisors vs. friends) and context (e.g., at work vs. at happy hour). When using social media, however, selective self-presentation can be difficult as people often choose to connect to a wide audience, including friends, family, and coworkers, sometimes on the same platform (Weidner, Earl, O'Brien, & Cooper, 2015). In fact, most individuals are willing to accept Facebook friend requests from coworkers, particularly if they had less privacy management concerns, better communication with coworkers, and worked in organizations with a lower privacy orientation

(Frampton & Child, 2013; Jiang, Hughes, & Pulice-Farrow, 2014). Additionally, most individuals (75 %) did so without feeling a need to revise their privacy settings or profile content (Frampton & Child, 2013). Similarly, most students indicated that they would accept a friend request from their boss (Karl & Peluchette, 2011). Other researchers note that this may not be a good idea for working adults, as friending the boss could cause negative employee reactions (Peluchette, Karl, & Fertig, 2013). In particular, women have been found to find friend requests from their supervisor as more inappropriate than men (Jiang et al., 2014).

Similarly, the traditional one-to-one pattern of dialogue is less represented via social media. Instead, social media favors a one-to-many distribution of information (Boyd, 2008). Furthermore, social media is highly searchable and there are repeated reports of publically accessible websites containing information that was not intended for the viewer to access (Ancken, 2015). This wide dissemination of information raises the issue of communication privacy (Houghton & Joinson, 2010; Vitak & Ellison, 2012).

There are a number of strategies that social media users can employ in order to deal with the invasion of privacy caused by this context collapse. Some users choose not to acknowledge context collapse as a problem, instead opting to treat public channels as being more private than they actually are. They often distribute content meant only for a few specific people to their entire network (Marwick & Boyd, 2011). Others try to maintain their privacy, taking a "lowest common denominator" approach, wherein they post only the amount of information that would be acceptable to share with individuals for whom the message is not intended but would nonetheless receive that message (Hogan, 2010).

Mohamed and Ahmad (2012) examined the antecedents of privacy concerns and subsequent privacy behaviors with regard to SNS usage. In particular, they found that perceived self-efficacy about their ability to protect their information on SNS, perceived severity about the loss of information, and perceived vulnerability about the security of SNS were all significantly related to concerns about the privacy of information shared over SNS and through that, to subsequent privacy behaviors. Interestingly, although Mohamed and Ahmad (2012) also found a greater concern for privacy amongst females, they note that other research (Lang & Barton, 2015; Milne, Rohm, & Bahl, 2004) has not found significant gender differences in the practice of other privacy protection behaviors.

Other researchers (Child & Agyeman-Budu, 2010) have found that individuals higher in self-monitoring displayed more privacy management practices when blogging. They also found that individuals with higher levels of concern for appropriateness were actually more open and sharing in their posts. Both self-monitoring and concern for appropriateness were positively related to time spent blogging indicating that regardless of their privacy rules, these traits were both related to increased sharing activities.

Higher levels of concern for privacy have been linked to what is known as *social media fatigue* (Bright et al., 2015). Social media fatigue is characterized by a withdrawal from social media. These individuals have previously used social media and consciously make a choice to withdraw from it. Results found that both confidence in social media usage and social media self-efficacy were inversely related to social media fatigue. Interestingly, social media self-efficacy was also positively related to social media usage, indicating that social media fatigue may occur as a form of burnout (Bright et al., 2015).

Despite these privacy concerns, individuals commonly post unprofessional or inappropriate material on social media sites (Miller, Parsons, & Lifer, 2010; Peluchette & Karl, 2009). This is a trend that has continued despite the wide publicity that surrounds many instances of this type of information leading to negative consequences for the individuals (Love, 2014), including losing one's job right after being hired (ESPN.go.com, 2015). Although individuals may choose to share information publicly on SNS and often regret sharing sensitive or inappropriate information (Wang et al., 2011), people still react negatively when they perceive organizations are misusing their private information (Smith, Milberg, & Burke, 1996). There are other complexities regarding the sharing of information from organizations, including legal boundaries that have yet to be clarified, issues of public perception of privacy protection, and use of publicly available information for selection and termination reasons.

Thus, future research should further examine issues associated with both sharing and disclosing information through social media. One promising theory that may be of help in determining self-disclosure behaviors may be *communication privacy management* (CPM) theory (Petronio, 2002, 2007). According to Petronio (2002), individuals feel that they own and have the right to control or distribute their private information. People develop rules that guide how they share their private information and expect others who have access to this information to respect those rules. Furthermore, people may experience conflict when they feel that these rules are violated. CPM theory has been used to explore self-disclosure and privacy management in a variety of situations including through social media and other online forms of communication (Metzger, 2007; Sanderson, 2011; Seung-A, 2012).

5.5 Practical Implications and Recommendations

This chapter described, broadly, how and why people and organizations use social media, as well as positive and negative outcomes associated with social media use. There seem to be varied and complex reasons for social media use, thus creating many uncertain outcomes for social media users.

Organizations seeking to increase their emphasis on social media usage for selection and other purposes should strongly consider the various broader impacts that this may have upon their organization. Additionally, careful thought about implementation of any formal social media policy is strongly advised.

5.5.1 Research Recommendations

There are several notable recommendations which can be made to researchers seeking to explore the impacts of social media on organizational processes and selection in particular.

First, standardized, validated, and broadly adopted measures of social media usage are absolutely essential for the continued growth of research into how social media impacts organizations. Numerous studies used independently developed and non-validated measures of social media usage. Research on social media cannot continue to grow without increased standardization of measurement to enhance replicability and generalizability. Landers and Callan (2014) WSMQ represents a good example of a scale developed for this type of research. This measure includes both positive and negative behaviors commonly performed by employees using social media for workplace-related purposes.

Second, many of these studies took an exploratory approach to workplace applications of social media. While social media has been around for over a decade, it has only recently caught the attention of researchers. As the number of social media users has grown, so too have the impacts and applications for the workplace. At this point in time, it is well established that social media has many different impacts on the modern workplace. However, there is too little evidence to show that our ability to evaluate the social media entries of applicants has strong enough predictive validity to be better than existing selection measures, such as personality or integrity tests. This is especially important considering the legal risks, such as adverse impact and privacy concerns associated with using social media for selection purposes. Future research emphasizing the unique contributions of social media, methods to avoid considering irrelevant information (such as protected class status) and cognitive biases, as well as effect sizes would greatly illuminate our understanding of how social media content can be applied for selection. Overall, at this point, social media might be better used for recruitment and building a brand than as a selection tool.

Thus, future studies need to put an increased emphasis on both theory and rigor to build upon established principles. There are two theories in particular that we draw from to guide future social media research. The first is *goal setting theory*. Goal setting is one of the most well-supported and understood theories in the workplace, and has been shown to increase productivity in a variety of settings (e.g., Locke & Latham, 2006). Thus, we expect that goal setting can be used to enhance productivity through ESM usage. Employees, for example, can be encouraged to post three challenging specific goals at the beginning of each week and then share their achievements online as they accomplish them. This can increase employee visibility, encourage positive thinking, and overall help employees to stay accountable and engaged.

Attribution theory (e.g., Martinko & Gardner, 1987) is also relevant here, as attributions are a bigger issue in virtual communications than face to face, as there is less context and therefore more opportunity for messages to be obfuscated. Media richness theory (Daft & Lengel, 1986) states that richer media (media which contains more characteristics of face-to-face communication, such as nonverbal cues) provides more clarity. Ambiguity lends itself to people relying on attributional tendencies and cognitive biases to make judgements about a situation (e.g., Martinko & Gardner, 1987), thus richer media (face to face versus text only) is expected to help provide clarity. This has implications for selection, as we expect to find that, for example, a SNS profile contains richer information than a Twitter feed (limited to 140 characters). Similarly, this theory suggests that EMS should allow for videos, images, and emoticons to include more contexts when evaluating messages.

Third, while social media is a global phenomenon, little is known about the generalizability of these findings, particularly to other cultures. Some nations limit the way in which social media is used (Tuysuz, 2015), and certain cultural norms or characteristics may affect the type of information that is considered appropriate to share on social media. Furthermore, many of the studies cited in this chapter would be difficult to replicate due to their highly specialized samples (e.g., qualitative observation of a single writer (Pigg, 2014)) or unique questionnaires. In order to demonstrate the robustness of these relationships, an increased emphasis should be placed on sampling broader, international populations using validated measures.

5.5.2 Practical Recommendations

The HR uses for social media are at least twofold. (1) Outgoing social media messages can enhance organizational attraction and recruit more and better applicants by sharing corporate values to increase the reputation and visibility of the organization. Social media might also be useful in terms of making it easier for potential applicants to find jobs within the company and submit an application. Additionally, current employees can serve as spokespersons by sharing positive messages about the organization and liaising between the organization and their network of colleagues. (2) ESM can be used to engage current employees. For example, information can be uploaded to ESM to facilitate knowledge sharing. Goals and accomplishments can be shared with group members to raise accountability and keep employees focused. In certain situations, ESM activity might be useful for promotion or development within the organization.

In general though, our knowledge of the antecedents and outcomes of sharing is still very limited because many studies do not report effect sizes or are otherwise limited by design or sample characteristics. While the benefits of using social media for selection are uncertain, the dangers are clear, including lower organizational attraction and legal issues. Thus, the costs of evaluating an applicant's social media usage for most selection purposes do not currently seem to outweigh the benefits. People are not required to be truthful in social media, and even simple background checks against social media postings cannot be trusted. Thus, we suggest that organizations using an applicant's social media for evaluation purposes do so late in the hiring process, after initial judgements are made, to limit the cognitive errors that may bias selection. Also, when possible, it might be best to rate social media for standardized, specific purposes, such as background checking, so that candidates are compared on the same dimensions.

References

Ancken, E. (2015). Nude pictures of students allegedly posted on social media. Retrieved June 3, 2015,fromhttp://www.clickorlando.com/news/nude-pictures-of-students-allegedly-posted-on-social-media/32799670.

Bauer, T. N., Truxillo, D. M., Tucker, J. S., Weathers, V., Bertolino, M., Erdogan, B., et al. (2006). Selection in the information age: The impact of privacy concerns and computer experience on applicant reactions. *Journal of Management, 32*, 601–621.

Bergman, S. M., Fearrington, M. E., Davenport, S. W., & Bergman, J. Z. (2011). Millennials narcissism, and social networking: What narcissists do on social networking sites and why. *Personality and Individual Differences, 50*, 706–711.

Block, R. (2014). *Comcastic service disconnection (recording starts 10 mins into call)*. Retrieved May 23, 2015, from https://soundcloud.com/ryan-block-10/comcastic-service.

Bohn, A., Buchta, C., Hornik, K., & Mair, P. (2014). Making friends and communicating on Facebook: Implications for the access to social capital. *Social Networks, 37*, 29–41.

Boyd, D. M. (2008). *Taken out of context: American teen sociality in networked publics*. Ph.D. dissertation. University of California, Berkeley, CA.

Boyd, D. M., & Ellison, N. B. (2007). Social network sites: Definition history, and scholarship. *Journal of Computer-Mediated Communication, 13*, 210–230.

Brandtzæg, P.B., & Heim, J. (2009). *Why people use social networking sites*. In A.A. Ozok and P. Zaphiris (Eds.): Proceedings of the HCI International. San Diego, CA. Online Communities, LNCS. Springer-Verlag Berlin Heidelberg, 143–152.

Brandtzæg, P.B., & Heim, J. (2011). A typology of social networking sites users. *International Journal of Web Based Communities, 7*, 28–51.

Bright, L. F., Kleiser, S. B., & Grau, S. L. (2015). Too much Facebook? An exploratory examination of social media fatigue. *Computers in Human Behavior, 44*, 148–155.

Brooks, S. (2015). Does personal social media usage affect efficiency and well-being? *Computers in Human Behavior, 46*, 26–37.

Brown, V. R., & Vaughn, E. D. (2011). The writing on the (Facebook) wall: The use of social networking sites in hiring decisions. *Journal of Business and Psychology, 26*, 219–225.

Brown, A., Weidner, N., Wynne, K. T., & O'Brien, K. E. (2015). *Social networking use as a counterproductive work behavior*. Poster presented at the 30th annual meeting of the Society for Industrial and Organizational Psychology, Philadelphia, PA.

Bryant, E. M., & Marmo, J. (2012). The rules ϙf Facebook friendship: A two-stage examination of interaction rules in close, casual, and acquaintance friendships. *Journal of Social and Personal Relationships, 29*, 1013–1035.

Bucher, E., Fieseler, C., & Suphan, A. (2013). The stress potential of social media in the workplace. *Information Communication and Society, 16*, 1639–1667.

Burke, M., & Kraut, R. (2013) *Using Facebook after losing a job: Differential benefits of strong and weak ties*. Paper presented at the Conference on Computer Supported Cooperative Work Companion (CSCW 2013), San Antonio, TX.

Byrne, T. (2015). *How to use internal collaboration and social networking technology*. Retrieved June 1, 2015, from http://www.inc.com/guides/2010/03/internal-collaboration-and-social-media-technology.html.

Campbell, W. K., Hoffman, B. J., Campbell, S. M., & Marchisio, G. (2011). Narcissism in organizational contexts. *Human Resource Management Review, 21*, 268–284.
Cao, X., Vogel, D. R., Guo, X., Liu, H., Gu, J. (2012). *Understanding the influence of social media in the workplace: An integration of media synchronicity and social capital theories*. Paper presented at the 45th Hawaii International Conference on System Sciences, Maui, HI.
Carpenter, C. J. (2012). Narcissism on Facebook: Self-promotional and anti-social behavior. *Personality and Individual Differences, 52*, 482–486.
Chan, T. H. (2014). Facebook and its effects on users' empathic social skills and life satisfaction: A double-edged sword effect. *Cyberpsychology, Behavior, and Social Networking, 17*, 276–280.
Charoensukmongkol, P. (2014). Effects of support and job demands on social media use and work outcomes. *Computers in Human Behavior, 36*, 340–349.
Chiang, J. K.-H., & Suen, H.-Y. (2015). Self-presentation and hiring recommendations in online communities: Lessons from LinkedIn. *Computers in Human Behavior, 48*, 516–524.
Child, J. T., & Agyeman-Budu, E. A. (2010). Blogging privacy management rule development: The impact of self-monitoring skills, concern for appropriateness, and blogging frequency. *Computers in Human Behavior, 26*, 957–963.
Chou, H.-T. G., Hammond, R. J., & Johnson, R. (2013). How Facebook might reveal users' attitudes toward work and relationships with coworkers. *Cyberpsychology, Behavior, and Social Networking, 16*, 136–139.
Colao, J. J. (2012). *The Facebook job board is here: Recruiting will never look the same*. Retrieved June 1, 2015, from http://www.forbes.com/sites/jjcolao/2012/11/14/the-facebook-job-board-is-here-recruiting-will-never-look-the-same.
Coy, C. (2013). *How building a 'Social Business' can boost employee retention*. Retrieved May 28, 2015, from http://www.cornerstoneondemand.com/blog/how-building-'social-business'-can-boost-employee-retention#.vxys10b8yio.
Daft, R. L., & Lengel, R. H. (1986). Organizational information requirements media richness and structural design. *Management Science, 32*, 554–571.
Dijkmans, C., Kerkhof, P., & Beukeboom, C. J. (2015). A stage to engage: Social media use and corporate reputation. *Tourism Management, 47*, 58–67.
Dogruer, N., Menevi§, I., & Eyyam, R. (2011). What is the motivation for using Facebook? *Procedia Social and Behavioral Sciences, 15*, 2642–2646.
Dreher, S. (2014). Social media and the world of work. *Corporate Communications: An International Journal, 19*, 344–356.
Drouin, M., O'Connor, K. W., Schmidt, G. B., & Miller, D. A. (2015). Facebook fired: Legal perspectives and young adults' opinions on the use of social media in hiring and firing decisions. *Computers in Human Behavior, 46*, 123–128.
Eadicicco, L. (2014). *A guy recorded his phone call when he tried to cancel cable, and it's a total nightmare*. Retrieved May 23, 2015, from http://www.businessinsider.com/ryan-block-comcast-phone-call-2014-7.
Edmunds, A., & Morris, A. (2000). The problem of information overload in business organisations: A review of the literature. *International Journal of Information Management, 20*, 17–28.
Ellison, N. B., Steinfield, C., & Lampe, C. (2007). The benefits of Facebook "Friends:" Social capital and college students' use of online social network sites. *Journal of Computer-Mediated Communication, 12*, 1143–1168.
Eren, E., & Vardarlıer, P. (2013). Social media's role in developing an employee's sense of belonging in the work place as an HRM strategy. *Procedia Social and Behavioral Sciences, 99*, 852–860.
ESPN.go.com. (2015). Facebook post costs newly hired Nebraska stadium announcer his job. Retrieved September, 2015, from http://espn.go.com/college-football/story/_/id/13559872/nebraska-cornhuskers-fire-pa-announcer-jon-schuetz-facebook-post-cited.
Etter, M. A., & Vestergaard, A. (2015). Facebook and the public framing of a corporate crisis. *Corporate Communications: An International Journal, 20*, 163–177.
Frampton, B. D., & Child, J. T. (2013). Friend or not to friend: Coworker Facebook friend requests as an application of communication privacy management theory. *Computers in Human Behavior, 29*, 2257–2264.

Fulk, J., & Yuan, Y. C. (2013). Location, motivation, and social capitalization via enterprise social networking. *Journal of Computer-Mediated Communication, 19*, 20–37.

Ghosh, A., & Dasgupta, S. (2015). Psychological predictors of Facebook use. *Journal of the Indian Academy of Applied Psychology, 41*, 101–109.

Gone but not forgotten. (2014). Retrieved June 1, 2015, from http://www.economist.com/news/business/21597935-more-firms-are-seeking-stay-touch-former-staff-gone-not-forgotten.

Gonzales, A. L., & Hancock, J. T. (2011). Mirror, mirror on my Facebook Wall: Effects of exposure to Facebook on self-esteem. *Cyberpsychology, Behavior, and Social Networking, 14*, 79–83.

Herrin, C. (2015) *Respecting our customers*. Retrieved May 23, 2015, from http://corporate.comcast.com/comcast-voices/respecting-our-customers.

Hogan, B. (2010). The presentation of self in the age of social media: Distinguishing performances and exhibitions online. *Bulletin of Science, Technology, and Society, 30*, 377–386.

Houghton, D. J., & Joinson, A. N. (2010). Privacy, social network sites, and social relations. *Journal of Technology in Human Services, 28*, 74–94.

Huang, H. (2014). *Social media generation in urban china: A study of social media use and addiction among adolescents*. New York: Springer.

Iskender, M., & Akin, A. (2010). Social self-efficacy, academic locus of control, and internet addiction. *Computers & Education, 54*, 1101–1106.

Jiang, Y., Hughes, J. L., & Pulice-Farrow, L. (2014). Coworkers and supervisors on Facebook? Effect of workplace friendship, trust, and sex. *Psi Chi Journal of Psychological Research, 19*, 144–153.

Jin, S.-A. A. (2012). "To disclose or not to disclose, that is the question": A structural equation modeling approach to communication privacy management in e-health. *Computers in Human Behavior, 28*, 69–77.

Johnston, K., Tanner, M., Lalla, N., & Kawalski, D. (2013). Social capital: The benefit of Facebook 'friends'. *Behaviour & Information Technology, 32*, 24–36.

Kaplan, A. M., & Haenlein, M. (2010). Users of the world unite! The challenges and opportunities of social media. *Business Horizons, 53*, 59–68.

Karinshak, T. (2014). *Comcast statement regarding customer service call*. Retrieved May 23, 2015,fromhttp://corporate.comcast.com/comcast-voices/comcast-statement-regarding-customer-service-call.

Karl, K. A., & Peluchette, J. V. (2011). "Friending" professors, parents and bosses: A Facebook connection conundrum. *Journal of Education for Business, 86*, 214–222.

Karr-Wisniewski, P., & Lu, Y. (2010). When more is too much: Operationalizing technology overload and exploring its impact on knowledge worker productivity. *Computers in Human Behavior, 26*, 1061–1072.

Khang, H., Han, E.-K., & Ki, E.-J. (2014). Exploring influential social cognitive determinants of social media use. *Computers in Human Behavior, 36*, 48–55.

Kim, W. G., Lim, H., & Brymer, R. A. (2015). The effectiveness of managing social media on hotel performance. *International Journal of Hospitality Management, 44*, 165–171.

Koc, M., & Gulyagci, S. (2013). Facebook addiction among Turkish college students: The role of psychological health, demographic, and usage characteristics. *Cyberpsychology, Behavior, and Social Networking, 16*, 279–284.

Kraut, R., Patterson, M., Lundmark, V., Kiesler, S., Mukophadhyay, T., & Scherlis, W. (1998). Internet paradox: A social technology that reduces social involvement and psychological well-being? *American Psychologist, 53*, 1017–1031.

Kross, E., Verduyn, P., Demiralp, E., Park, J., Lee, D. S., Lin, N., Shablack, H., Jonides, J., Ybarra, O. (2013). Facebook use predicts declines in subjective well-being in young adults. *PLoS One, 8*. Retrieved May 24, 2015, from http://journals.plos.org/plosone/article?id=10.1371/journal.pone.0069841.

Kuss, D. J., van Rooij, A. J., Shorter, G. W., Griffiths, M. D., & van de Mheen, D. (2013). Internet addiction in adolescents: Prevalence and risk factors. *Computers in Human Behavior, 29*, 1987–1996.

Kwon, O., & Wen, Y. (2010). An empirical study of the factors affecting social network service use. *Computers in Human Behavior, 26*, 254–263.
Landers, R. N., & Callan, R. C. (2014). Validation of the beneficial and harmful work-related social media behavioral taxonomies: Development of the Work-related Social Media Questionnaire (WSMQ). *Social Science Computer Review, 32*, 628–646.
Lang, C., & Barton, H. (2015). Just untag it: Exploring the management of undesirable Facebook photos. *Computers in Human Behavior, 43*, 147–155.
Leftheriotis, I., & Giannakos, M. N. (2014). Using social media for work: Losing your time or improving your work? *Computers in Human Behavior, 31*, 134–142.
Leonardi, P. M., Huysman, M., & Steinfield, C. (2013). Enterprise social media: Definition, history, and prospects for the study of social technologies in organizations. *Journal of Computer-Mediated Communication, 19*, 1–19.
Li, C., & Tsai, W.-H. S. (2015). Social media usage and acculturation: A test with Hispanics in the U.S. *Computers in Human Behavior, 45*, 204–212.
Lin, J. Y.-C., Le, A. N. H., Khalil, S., & Cheng, J. M.-S. (2012). Social media usage and work values: The example of Facebook in Taiwan. *Social Behavior and Personality, 40*, 195–200.
Lin, K.-Y., & Lu, H.-P. (2011). Why people use social networking sites: An empirical study integrating network externalities and motivation theory. *Computers in Human Behavior, 27*, 1152–1161.
Locke, E. A., & Latham, G. P. (2006). New directions in goal-setting theory. *Current Directions in Psychological Science, 15*, 265–268.
Love, D. (2014). *17 people who were fired for using Facebook*. Retrieved June 1, 2015, from http://www.businessinsider.com/17-people-who-were-fired-for-using-facebook-2014-7.
Mainiero, L. A., & Jones, K. J. (2012). Workplace Romance 2.0: Developing a communication ethics model to address potential sexual harassment from inappropriate social media contacts between coworkers. *Journal of Business Ethics, 114*, 367–379.
Mainiero, L. A., & Jones, K. J. (2013). Sexual harassment versus workplace romance: Social media spillover and textual harassment in the workplace. *Academy of Management Perspectives, 27*, 187–203.
Mak, B. C. N. (2013). Socialization into the workplace: A newcomer's chitchat with colleagues on Facebook status updates. *International Journal of English Linguistics, 3*(6), 1–16.
Mak, B. C. N., & Chui, H. L. (2013). Colleagues' talk and power after work hours: A community of practice in Facebook status updates? *Discourse, Context & Media, 2*, 94–102.
Mangold, W. G., & Faulds, D. J. (2009). Social media: The new hybrid element of the promotion mix. *Business Horizons, 52*, 357–365.
Martinko, M. J., & Gardner, W. L. (1987). The leader/member attribution process. *Academy of Management Review, 12*, 235–249.
Marwick, A. & Boyd, D. (2011). I tweet honestly, I tweet passionately: Twitter users, context collapse, and the imagined audience. *New media & society, 13*, 114–133.
McAfee, A. (2009). *Enterprise 2.0: New collaborative tools for your organization's toughest challenges*. Boston: Harvard Business Press.
Mcdonald, P., & Thompson, P. (2015). Social Media(tion) and the reshaping of public/private boundaries in employment relations. *International Journal of Management Reviews, 10*, 1–16.
Metzger, M. J. (2007). Communication privacy management in electronic commerce. *Journal of Computer-Mediated Communication, 12*, 335–361.
Milani, L., Osualdella, D., & Di Blasio, P. (2009). Quality of interpersonal relationships and problematic internet use in adolescence. *CyberPsychology & Behavior, 12*, 681–684.
Miller, R., Parsons, K., & Lifer, D. (2010). Students and social networking sites: The posting paradox. *Behaviour & Information Technology, 29*, 377–382.
Milne, G. R., Rohm, A. J., & Bahl, S. (2004). 'Consumers' protection of online privacy and identity. *Journal of Consumer Affairs, 38*, 217–232.
Mohamed, N., & Ahmad, I. H. (2012). Information privacy concerns, antecedents and privacy measure use in social networking sites: Evidence from Malaysia. *Computers in Human Behavior, 28*, 2366–2375.

Moore, J. (2014). *Think before you post: EEOC cases show pitfalls of social media in the workplace*. Retrieved June 1, 2015, from http://www.federalnewsradio.com/434/3580540/think-before-you-post-eeoc-cases-show-pitfalls-of-social-media-in-the-workplace.

Moqbel, M., Nevo, S., & Kock, N. (2013). Organizational members' use of social networking sites and job performance an exploratory study. *Information Technology & People, 26*, 240–264.

Nadkarni, A., & Hofmann, S. G. (2012). Why do people use Facebook? *Personality and Individual Differences, 52*, 243–249.

Nagendra, A. (2014). Paradigm shift in HR practices on employee life cycle due to influence of social media. *Procedia Economics and Finance, 11*, 197–207.

Ngai, E. W., Tao, S. S., & Moon, K. K. (2015). Social media research: Theories, constructs, and conceptual frameworks. *International Journal of Information Management, 35*, 33–44.

Olson, P. (2015). *Facebook was the Â one network people used less Â in 2014*. Retrieved June 1, 2015, from http://www.forbes.com/sites/parmyolson/2015/01/27/facebook-active-users-decline/.

Panek, E. T., Nardis, Y., & Konrath, S. (2013). Mirror or Megaphone?: How relationships between narcissism and social networking site use differ on Facebook and Twitter. *Computers in Human Behavior, 29*, 2004–2012.

Park, N., Kee, K. F., & Valenzuela, S. (2009). Being immersed in social networking environment: Facebook groups, uses and gratifications, and social outcomes. *CyberPsychology & Behavior, 12*, 729–733.

Peluchette, J., & Karl, K. (2009). 'Examining Students' intended image on Facebook: "What were they thinking?!". *Journal of Education for Business, 85*, 30–37.

Peluchette, J. V. E., Karl, K., & Fertig, J. (2013). A Facebook 'friend' request from the boss: Too close for comfort? *Business Horizons, 56*, 291–300.

Petronio, S. S. (2002). *Boundaries of privacy dialectics of disclosure*. Albany, NY: State University of New York Press.

Petronio, S. (2007). Translational research endeavors and the practices of communication privacy management. *Journal of Applied Communication Research, 35*, 218–222.

Pigg, S. (2014). Coordinating constant invention: Social media's role in distributed work. *Technical Communication Quarterly, 23*, 69–87.

Piotrowski, C. (2012). From workplace bullying to cyberbullying: The enigma of E-Harassment in modern organizations. *Organization Development Journal, 30*, 44–53.

Ponolly, M. H. (2014). *Smartphones, social media and sexual harassment: 5 steps to mitigate the risks of hostile work environment claims in the workplace*. Retrieved June 1, 2015, from http://www.laborandemploymentlawcounsel.com/2014/01/smartphones-social-media-and-sexual-harassment-5-steps-to-mitigate-the-risks-of-hostile-work-environment-claims-in-the-workplace/.

Privitera, C., & Campbell, M. A. (2009). Cyberbullying: The new face of workplace bullying? *CyberPsychology & Behavior, 12*, 395–400.

Puijenbroek, T. V., Poell, R., Kroon, B., & Timmerman, V. (2013). The effect of social media use on work-related learning. *Journal of Computer Assisted Learning, 30*, 159–172.

Reinecke, L. & Trepte, S. (2014). Authenticity and well-being on social network sites: A two-wave longitudinal study on the effects of online authenticity and the positivity bias in SNS communication. Computers in Human Behavior, 30, 95–102.

Roman, L. A. (2014). Using social media to enhance career development opportunities for health promotion professionals. *Health Promotion Practice, 15*, 471–475.

Ryan, T., & Xenos, S. (2011). Who uses Facebook? An investigation into the relationship between the Big Five, shyness, narcissism, loneliness, and Facebook usage. *Computers in Human Behavior, 27*, 1658–1664.

Sadovykh, V., Sundaram, D., & Piramuthu, S. (2015). Do online social networks support decision-making? *Decision Support Systems, 70*, 15–30.

Sagioglou, C., & Greitemeyer, T. (2014). Facebook's emotional consequences: Why Facebook causes a decrease in mood and why people still use it. *Computers in Human Behavior, 35*, 359–363.

Sanderson, J. (2011). To Tweet or not to Tweet: Exploring Division I athletic departments' social-media policies. *International Journal of Sports Communication, 4*, 492–513.

Schneider, B. (1987). The people make the place. *Personnel Psychology, 40*, 433–457.
Schneider, T. J., Goffin, R. D., & Daljeet, K. N. (2015). "Give us your social networking site passwords": Implications for personnel selection and personality. *Personality and Individual Differences, 73*, 78–83.
Sigala, M., & Chalkiti, K. (2015). Knowledge management, social media and employee creativity. *International Journal of Hospitality Management, 45*, 44–58.
Skeels, M. M., & Grudin, J. (2009). *When social networks cross boundaries*. Proceedings of the ACM 2009 international conference on Supporting group work. Sanibel Island, FL.
Smith, H., Milberg, S., & Burke, S. (1996). Information privacy: Measuring individuals' concerns about organizational practices. *MIS Quarterly, 20*, 167–196.
Stampler, L. (2014). *Recording of man's attempt to cancel comcast will drive you insane*. Retrieved May 23, 2015, from http://time.com/2985964/comcast-cancel-ryan-block/.
Treem, J. W. (2014). Social media as technologies of accountability: Explaining resistance to implementation within organizations. *American Behavioral Scientist, 59*, 53–74.
Treem, J. W., Dailey, S. L., Pierce, C. S., & Leonardi, P. M. (2015). Bringing technological frames to work: How previous experience with social media shapes the technology's meaning in an organization. *Journal of Communication, 65*, 396–422.
Tuysuz, G. (2015). *Turkey blocks social media websites*. Retrieved April, 2015, from http://www.cnn.com/2015/04/06/world/turkey-social-media-blocked/.
Valenzuela, S., Park, N., & Kee, K. F. (2009). Is there social capital in a social network site?: Facebook use and college students' life satisfaction, trust, and participation. *Journal of Computer-Mediated Communication, 14*, 875–901.
Verduyn, P., Lee, D. S., Park, J., Shablack, H., Orvell, A., Bayer, J., et al. (2015). Passive Facebook usage undermines affective well-being: Experimental and longitudinal evidence. *Journal of Experimental Psychology, 144*, 480–488.
Vitak, J., & Ellison, N. B. (2012). There's a network out there you might as well tap: Exploring the benefits of and barriers to exchanging informational and support-based resources on Facebook. *New Media & Society, 15*, 243–259.
Wang, C., Lee, M. K. O., & Hua, Z. (2015). A theory of social media dependence: Evidence from microblog users. *Decision Support Systems, 69*, 40–49.
Wang, Y., Norcie, G., Komanduri, S., Acquisti, A., Leon, P. G., Cranor, L. F. (2011). *I regretted the minute I pressed share*. Proceedings of the Seventh Symposium on Usable Privacy and Security, Pittsburgh PA.
Weidner, N., Earl, E. C., O'Brien, K. E., & Cooper, A.D. (2015). *Exploring workplace ego threat management through social media*. Poster presented at the 30th annual meeting of the Society for Industrial and Organizational Psychology, Philadelphia, PA.
Weinstein, A., Dorani, D., Elhadif, R., Bukovza, Y., Yarmulnik, A., & Dannon, P. (2015). Internet addiction is associated with social anxiety in young adults. *Annals of Clinical Psychiatry, 27*, 4–9.
Willyerd, K. (2012). *Social tools can improve employee onboarding*. Retrieved June 1, 2015, from https://hbr.org/2012/12/social-tools-can-improve-e.
Yao, M. Z., & Zhong, Z. (2014). Loneliness social contacts and internet addiction: A cross-lagged panel study. *Computers in Human Behavior, 30*, 164–170.
Zhang, J. (2015). Voluntary information disclosure on social media. *Decision Support System, 73*, 28–36.

Chapter 6
Game-Thinking Within Social Media to Recruit and Select Job Candidates

Andrew B. Collmus, Michael B. Armstrong, and Richard N. Landers

Abstract Social media and game-thinking are increasingly popular in society and in organizations. Together, they can become a powerful tool for recruitment and selection. Recruiting is about branding and communicating information, social media facilitate rapid dissemination of information, and game-thinking can encourage individuals to spend more time interacting with that information or to understand it more completely. As a result, more candidates can be reached and provided with better quality information about job vacancies in organizations, thus improving the applicant pool in two ways. Personnel selection depends on the ability to assess traits and behaviors that predict job performance and compare assessment results between candidates. Social media are replete with games, quizzes, surveys, and other tests that individuals take and share their results online, including skill endorsements, qualifications, and recommendations. Utilizing big-data techniques, organizations can tap into these habits to harvest data for assessing and comparing applicants. Several third-party companies are already connecting organizations to job seekers and vice versa by analyzing performance on social media games. We evaluate relevant theory related to game-thinking in social media (GSM) in recruitment and selection through the lens of applied and theoretical examples.

Keywords Gamification • Selection • Social media • Recruitment • Assessment • Person–organization fit • Brand equity • Organizational attraction

6.1 Introduction

The use of social media among individuals and organizations has grown rapidly in recent years. Researchers estimate 2.08 billion active social media accounts across the globe (Kemp, 2015), with projected growth to 2.44 by 2018 (eMarketer,

---

A.B. Collmus • M.B. Armstrong, M.S. • R.N. Landers, Ph.D. (✉)
Department of Psychology, Old Dominion University,
250 Mills Godwin Building, Norfolk, VA 23529, USA
e-mail: acollmus@odu.edu; marms018@odu.edu; rnlanders@odu.edu

R.N. Landers, G.B. Schmidt (eds.), *Social Media in Employee Selection and Recruitment*, DOI 10.1007/978-3-319-29989-1_6

American Marketing Association, 2015). In the early days of social media, organizations primarily used them as a tool to communicate with customers, clients, vendors, and the general public (Leonardi, Huysman, & Steinfield, 2013). More recently, social media have been increasingly used to enable internal processes such as knowledge sharing, role support, and collaboration (Ellison, Gibbs, & Weber, 2014). In the recruitment context, they have been used to identify both external job candidates and internal candidates for promotion. In the selection context, social media are often used to gather information about job candidates for consideration during the job selection process. Job seekers increasingly rely on social media to research organizations and job openings and to solicit their social networks for potential leads. Statistics from Jobvite (2015) indicated that when modern job seekers searched for new work opportunities, 67 % used Facebook, 45 % used Twitter, and 40 % used LinkedIn. Because of the relative ease with which information can be acquired and disseminated, social media are an ideal platform for organizations wishing to fill job vacancies and for individuals searching for new work opportunities.

Another rapidly developing trend is the use of game-thinking, the process of utilizing game-principles and elements in nongame contexts (e.g., work, education, sales), in organizations (Landers, Armstrong & Collmus, 2015). Organizational applications of game-thinking include, but are not limited to, marketing, training, onboarding, health and wellness, and sustainability (Seaborn & Fels, 2015). In part, the popularity of game-thinking among organizations and academics is due to the wild popularity of video games in general. For example, US consumers spent $22.4 billion on video games in 2014 (Entertainment Software Association, 2015), and in defiance of the stereotypical view that most gamers are teenaged males, data indicate that 74 % of video game players are over the age of 18 and 44 % are female (Entertainment Software Association, 2015). Because so many working-age adults spend a great deal of time and money on games, many organizations have recognized this as an opportunity to motivate current employees and to reach applicants.

Game-thinking in social media (GSM), the intersection point between these two trends, can become a powerful tool for employee recruitment and selection, because recruitment and selection are built on information sharing and testing, respectively. Games are fun, interactive, and engaging, which can make them an ideal platform for transferring information to job seekers and for motivating desirable applicant behaviors. Social media too are interactive and enable users to quickly share a variety of information but also represent an underlying wealth of behavioral data that can be collected and assessed. Social media quizzes and games are common on various social media platforms, enabling users to share scores, results, political information, and anything else that can be made into a quiz or a game. With clever applications of GSM, organizations can encourage people to share job vacancy information or participate in selection tests by encouraging people to engage in behaviors that mimic a portion of their existing social media habits.

Several third-party recruitment and assessment organizations have begun to capitalize on these unique benefits of GSM. One such company, Pymetrics®, maintains a suite of brief assessment games embedded within a social media platform that they developed as a social site for job seekers (Zeldovich, 2015). Applicants who play a sufficient number of games receive a detailed report on several traits such as personality, attention, cognitive speed, and emotional intelligence; a career report, which shows percentage of fit with various jobs; matches to specific companies; and a recruiting report, which matches them to specific job openings. By taking this approach, Pymetrics hopes to decrease costs for their clients by screening out poor-fitting employees early in the process and to improve retention rates by matching applicants on several fit indices (Zeldovich, 2015). Thus, a job seeker can play several games on this platform to be matched to an industry or specific job based on their personality traits and cognitive ability. Organizations looking for new applicants can seek out, screen, and rank job candidates based on their measured traits, performance, or fit indices. However, validity information surrounding this relatively new technique is very limited. As such, research is needed to assess the content, predictive, and construct validity of these and similar "games" (i.e., tests).

Pymetrics is not unique in their approach. Several websites and mobile applications now analyze game performance to provide applicants with career feedback and businesses with recruitment information (Noguchi, 2015). For example, Knack® has developed a series of mobile-device games that, ostensibly, can assess in-game performance to predict job-relevant behaviors (Moltz, 2013). Some third-party sites offer personality assessment as a means to facilitate social connectivity and self-exploration (Browne, 2014). Other companies combine elements of social media and game-thinking on career-matching websites, by making the assessment of knowledge skills and abilities interactive and game-like, and allowing job opportunities to be up-voted or shared with friends (Cohan, 2012).

These companies and the concepts they represent have generated a great deal of hype in media and in industry, although they generally remain empirically untested. Thus, to provide guidance to both researchers and practitioners in this domain, this chapter will explore theory relevant to GSM, providing empirical examples (when available) and theoretical applications.

6.2 Definitions and Scope

Social media is a dynamic concept, similarly, game-thinking encompasses several concepts without universal meaning. This section is intended to disambiguate these two terms and to provide the conceptual framework on which we base our analysis. In general, we favor broad, inclusive definitions of both. First, this is due to the nascence of research on GSM in selection. By providing one of the first theoretical explorations of this topic, we hope to provide a foundation for a wide range of research and applications. As the body of literature surrounding GSM grows, narrower definitions may become more appropriate. Second, the constructs of social media and game-thinking are themselves unstable. Ten years ago, social media included a few sites for people to share personal information on computers, and digital gameplay was mostly inhabited by dedicated gamers with gaming PCs or consoles (e.g., Nintendo or PlayStation systems). In contrast, most modern media are social media. For example, news sites have comment sections, direct links to share stories or comments across other social networks, and frequently maintain several social media accounts themselves to share and deliver information. Individuals are no longer limited to accessing social media from a desktop computer, or from one of only a few major websites; smartphones, televisions, tablets, and even watches can now be used socially.

Mirroring these trends, digital gameplay now occurs on multiple platforms, including mobile platforms, and digital games themselves are often a social experience, allowing users to post, share, compare, and compete, sometimes offering rewards or in-game bonuses for users who link their game performance to a social media account. To the extent that we can be futurists, we predict that this popularity will continue and increase. Lines will continue to blur and digital content will continue to expand in to a greater portion of our everyday lives. Given this continuing expansion, we contend that broader conceptualizations now are likely to have greater utility in the future, when social media and game-thinking have evolved in unforeseeable ways.

The term *social media* presently has many different definitions, some from a technical orientation (e.g., dynamic user generated content based on Web 2.0; Kaplan & Haenlein, 2010) and others from a behavioral orientation (e.g., somewhat unmediated, user generated, computer enabled; Lampe, 2014). We find it helpful to define social media by their affordances (i.e., the current or potential behaviors and processes they enable) rather than specific technical features. Common affordances in the social media literature include visibility (the ability to communicate beliefs, preferences, and behaviors), editability (the ability for users to modify and edit content before or after posting), persistence (the ability for content to remain over time, even after the user has logged out), association (the ability to connect with other people or organizations), and recombinability (the ability to borrow, build on, and combine others' contributions; Wagner, Vollmar, & Wagner, 2014; Treem & Leonardi, 2012). Other affordances, such as scalability, searchability, authoring, tagging, and sharing, are also commonly found in social media literature (Wagner et al., 2014). Indeed, one strength of the affordance approach is its robustness to the introduction of novel affordances for which technologies may not yet even exist.

The affordances approach to defining social media is appealing because specific technologies become obsolete, sometimes more quickly than scientific publishing occurs, rendering definitions based on those specific technologies obsolete. In contrast, as technologies emerge and evolve, yielding novel data capture opportunities (e.g., wearable devices; Zhang, Wang, Guo, & Yu, 2012), the affordances approach endures. By analogy, one could define a bench by describing the tools, materials, and process used to design and build benches currently, but this definition would exclude benches made from newly invented materials. A more effective way to describe the bench is to describe the behavior it enables; specifically, a bench enables sitting, with room for more than one person. This definition is robust to different locations, techniques, and materials. Similarly, it is better to define social media by describing the behaviors afforded by their existence. These behaviors represent different types of information that can be captured and evaluated. Behaviors on social media that elicit information useful to organizations can be encouraged with game-thinking. Further, game-thinking can be used to increase sharing or other behaviors that might communicate information from organizations to potential applicants. For these reasons, GSM can enhance recruitment and selection.

The term *game-thinking* encompasses the oft conflated (see Landers, 2015) but related concepts of gamification and serious games (Armstrong, Landers, & Collmus, 2015). Gamification has been defined as the use of game elements in non-game contexts (Deterding, Sicart, Nacke, O'Hara, & Dixon, 2011) and is typically developed in business applications to shape customer or employee behavior. In contrast, serious games are fully produced games whose main purpose is something other than entertainment (Michael & Chen, 2005) and in the organizational context are most commonly used for employee training. Despite important differences, these concepts do have much in common. Specifically, both involve the application of game elements, such as adaptation, assessment, conflict, challenge, immersion, rules/goals, feedback, and fantasy or fiction (Bedwell, Pavlas, Heyne, Lazzara, & Salas, 2012; Garris, Ahlers, & Driskell, 2002; Wilson et al., 2008), which may exist explicitly in the game's programming or implicitly in the mind of game players. The critical difference is that many game elements exist to varying degrees in serious games, whereas gamification involves the application of game elements individually. Thus, both approaches apply the same game element tool kit but in slightly different ways (Landers, 2015). For this chapter, the broader term game-thinking is used to describe the myriad applications of either complete games or the individual game elements that drove their design.

Taken together, GSM represents a unique intersection of domains in employee selection. Social media connects organizations to people and those people to other people. Game-thinking drives behavioral engagement, in this case, engagement with social media. Each domain separately provides opportunities for applicant assessment (e.g., personality ratings from social media sites, Gosling, Augustine, Vazire, Holtzman, & Gaddis, 2011; Stoughton, Thompson, & Meade, 2013; assessing behavior within games, Shute, Ventura, Bauer, & Zapata-Rivera, 2009). However, when these domains interact, new opportunities for staffing emerge. For example, game-thinking further engages applicants with social media such that they are increasingly motivated to interact with recruiting organizations and other potential applicants. Game-thinking thus provides new opportunities for behavioral observation and assessment in social media, increasing data quality and quantity for selection purposes. Game-thinking capitalizes on the affordances and behaviors of social media, such as association and interactivity, providing new opportunities and insights for recruiting, assessing, and selecting applicants.

6.3 GSM for Job Seeking and Recruitment

Broadly, recruitment refers to organizational acts that affect the amount or type of people willing to apply to or accept a job (Chapman, Uggerslev, Carroll, Piasentin, & Jones, 2005). Contemporary recruitment theory has drawn from the marketing research literature, likening the job-seeking process to that of a consumer comparing different options and ultimately making a choice (e.g., Cable & Turban, 2001; Collins, 2007; Collins & Han, 2004; Lievens & Highhouse, 2003). In order to attract the most applicants in a competitive market, the product should meet applicant expectations (Smither, Reilly, Millsap, Pearlman, & Stoffey, 1993).

Brand-equity theory describes the process by which various domains of knowledge affect application intentions and behaviors by modifying or reinforcing this organizational image (Cable & Turban, 2001). Thus, communicating information is key to shaping brand perceptions. The brand-equity conceptualization is particularly relevant to GSM for at least two reasons. First, word-of-mouth information, which is commonly spread via the affordances of social media (e.g., recombinability, sharing), is especially influential on a potential applicants' decision to apply (Collins & Stevens, 2002; Van Hoye & Lievens, 2009). Second, game-thinking can be used to communicate employer image and facilitate employer familiarity.

Organizations can use GSM to influence the number and quality of applicants, as well as their intentions to apply or proceed through the selection process. This can be achieved by shaping perceptions of person–environment (P-E) fit, the congruence between an individual's traits and some aspect of their work environment, such as personal and organizational values (Kristof-Brown & Guay, 2011). Moreover, organizations can affect candidate behaviors by influencing applicant reactions to selection procedures (Hausknecht, Day, & Thomas, 2004). Attributes of a selection procedure, such as subjective enjoyment or test anxiety, can influence offer-acceptance intentions and brand image. Incumbents too can be influenced by GSM to improve organizational recruitment. Since internal referrals tend to be higher quality applicants (Zottoli & Wanous, 2000), game-thinking can be used to motivate employees to seek out new recruits from their own social media networks.

GSM can increase applicant intentions within targeted populations by influencing applicant perceptions of organizational image, which in turn shape perceptions of P-E fit. Organizational image communicates key aspects of employment, and also transfers cultural information such as organizational personality and values, which affects attraction via social identity (Darnold & Rynes, 2013, p. 113). P-E fit has two major subcategories—person–job fit, the degree to which an individual's knowledge, skills, and abilities match those required by a job (Carless, 2005), and person–organization fit, the degree to which an individual's other characteristics (e.g., personality and values) align with an organization (Kristof-Brown, 2000)—each of which predicts application intentions (Resick, Baltes, & Shantz, 2007) as mediated by organizational attractiveness (Carless, 2005). Tsai and Yang (Study 1, 2010) found that product and service image, organizational citizenship image, and corporate credibility image were significantly and positively related to organizational attractiveness ($r=0.75$, $r=0.55$, and $r=0.80$, respectively). Thus, organizations can take advantage of GSM to better communicate organizational culture and job characteristics, improving the attractiveness of their organizations. For example, Microsoft created a job ad that could only be found by using web-developer tools to find and analyze a web programming error on the Bing® Homepage (Leonhard, 2013). This type of advertisement communicates several key aspects of the job that potential applicants can use to infer P-E fit. Job characteristics were inherently communicated by the technical and analytic skills required to find the advertisement. Additionally, game elements (e.g., puzzle, mystery, challenge) inherent to this advertisement signal cultural messages to potential applicants beyond what could be transferred through a traditional advertisement. Furthermore, information regarding this recruitment category was discussed and shared on various internet forums and webpage comment sections, amplifying the reach of the job ad.

Organizations can increase information transfer by adding game elements to existing social media recruitment sources. Ryan, Horvath, and Kriska (2005) found that recruitment source affected application intentions via informativeness and organizational familiarity, which can be fostered by GSM. Specifically, recruitment strategies and locations that provided more information elicited a higher level of application intentions. Feedback (Garris et al., 2002) in the form of a progress bar (i.e., an example of gamification) can inform applicants as to their progress through recruitment materials. Whereas a typical recruitment ad may be briefly scanned then dismissed, the inclusion of a progress bar sends the message that there is more information to be found. In turn, applicants are encouraged to spend more time interacting with the materials, which should lead to more information transfer. Enrichment of the information provided to each potential applicant will lead to more total applications within a given sample (Ryan et al., 2005).

GSM can increase intentions to accept job offers by increasing organizational attraction. From the applicant's perspective, organizational attractiveness is influenced by characteristics of the job and organization, perceptions of the recruitment process, and perceptions of fit (Chapman et al., 2005). Thus, organizations must communicate a positive and accurate image to attract and retain a desired population of employees. The use of games or game elements communicates symbolic attributes (i.e., associated human traits) about a given company or position. Organizational attraction is affected by symbolic attributes of a brand or image (Lievens & Highhouse, 2003). For example, a sophisticated interactive media experience may communicate a preference for technology, comfort with big data and statistics, or a desire for new ideas. Applicants who are seeking specific organizational traits will then be able to infer those traits from their GSM experience with an organization. Firm reputation, through organizational attraction, influences the likelihood of job-offer acceptance (Cable & Turban, 2001). To the extent that symbolic attributes are communicated to and align with the desires of applicants, job acceptance intentions will be increased. Selection procedures that are motivating or less likely to induce anxiety affect organizational attraction and in turn affect job acceptance intentions (Hausknecht et al., 2004).

GSM can increase the number of quality applicants and decrease the number of poor-fitting applicants. Organizational incumbents now commonly share vacancy information on existing social media. This sort of sharing can be considered a type of internal referral, which is often a better recruitment source than other common methods, such as walk-ins, third-party recruiters, and advertisements (Van Hoye & Lievens, 2009; Zottoli & Wanous, 2000), because employees recruited from internal referrals tend to have higher performance and lower turnover (Zottoli & Wanous, 2000). For organizations that maintain internal social media, referrals can be encouraged by using game-thinking to reward sharing of such information on social media. Several game elements are at play here, including competition, feedback, and rules/goals. GSM in this case can be used to remind incumbents to spend time and effort recruiting their peers. It also can inspire competition among employees who wish to stand out as high performers.

Customized feedback about fit during an online application process, which can be facilitated via GSM, can increase mean applicant fit while decreasing the total number of applicants (Dineen & Noe, 2009). Meta-analytic results suggest that P-J and P-O fit relate to job satisfaction ($\rho=0.56$, $\rho=0.44$), organizational commitment ($\rho=0.47$, $\rho=0.51$), and turnover intentions ($\rho=-0.46$, $\rho=-0.35$), respectively (Kristof-Brown, Zimmerman, & Johnson, 2005). By presenting fit information, poorer fitting recruits are more likely to self-select out of the application process when provided information by which to make that judgment (Dineen & Noe, 2009), ultimately lowering the number of poor-fitting applicants. In lieu of providing objective feedback information, game elements can be used to encourage user interaction with P-E fit information more organically, via implicit cues provided by a game. For example, a company might deploy a game on Facebook that allows job seekers to explore various aspects of company life.

In addition to applicant-related outcomes, there may be effects of GSM on non-applicants. Consistent with the marketing-branding approach to recruitment, it is helpful to think of applicants as consumers of not only recruitment materials, but of the organization in general. Branding not only affects organizational attraction but also affects individual's willingness to purchase goods or services from the organization (Macan, Avedon, Paese, & Smith, 1994). In 2004, Google posted a math puzzle on a billboard hoping to attract software engineers (Olsen, 2004); however, this action produced a great deal of discussion within both traditional and social media, increasing brand awareness more broadly. A more recent example is that of a computer science student who googled "python lambda function list comprehension." Upon entering those terms, the search engine interface asked him if he would like to solve a computer-programming puzzle. After the successful completion of several puzzles over the course of a few weeks, he was invited to apply at Google, where he was ultimately offered a job (Rosett, 2015). This applicant's story initially appeared in a blog post, but thanks to social media has since been reshared, retweeted, and rewritten several thousand times (Rosett, 2015). This demonstrates how the affordances of social media greatly enhance the visibility of game-thinking, thus broadening the recruitment audience.

Thus, game-thinking can influence organizational attractiveness, via branding, on social media. That is, GSM inherently communicates organizational traits and attributes. In addition, game-thinking can be used to encourage behaviors that are important for recruiting, such as internal referrals, time spent interacting with job vacancy information or other organizational materials, or a deeper understanding of the organization itself. These outcomes influence the applicant pool, such that accurate perceptions of P-J and P-O fit can encourage well-fitting candidates to apply while deterring candidates who may not be a great match for the position or organization. In turn, well-matched applicants become more satisfied employees who are less likely to quit.

6.4 GSM to Improve Selection

GSM can enhance several aspects of employee selection, the process of identifying and assessing determinants of job performance and other key organizational outcomes for use in hiring decisions (Cortina & Luchman, 2013; Schmitt, Cortina, Ingerick, & Wiechmann, 2003). By incorporating GSM into selection practices, the methods used become more game-like, which has potential for three improvements to the selection process. First, GSM allows the opportunity to collect applicant data on established selection predictors in new ways. Coupled with traditional selection methods, GSM can provide an additional perspective on individual differences across applicants. Second, GSM can be used to improve the quality of data gathered through the selection processes thereby enhancing the validity of selection assessments. GSM enables new predictors of job performance and can improve existing predictors. Third, GSM can increase the utility of the selection process through both increases in validity and decreases in overall costs.

GSM provides new methods to assess established job performance predictors, including cognitive ability, skills, personality, biodata, and person–environment fit. A common gamification implementation in recent years has been the use of points, levels, and leaderboards (Mekler et al., 2013). Within the context of social media, points, levels, and leaderboards are utilized as methods for rating users and their content. For example, on LinkedIn, users can endorse one another for different skills. The total number of endorsements a user receives for each skill can be likened to a score or rating indicating his or her experience level with that skill. This score would be considered an other-rating, which in personnel selection is a rating of the applicant given by family, friends, or strangers (Connolly, Boyle, MacArthur, Hainey, & Boyle, 2012) in contrast to self-ratings (Gaugler, Rosenthal, Thornton, & Bentson, 1987). Other-ratings of psychological traits demonstrate incremental validity over self-ratings when predicting future job performance (Connelly & Ones, 2010). However, empirical evidence for LinkedIn endorsements predicting job performance has not yet appeared in the literature. Despite this lack of empirical evidence, theory on other-ratings can be applied to GSM contexts in order to predict job performance.

The Realistic Accuracy Model, which describes how accurate personality judgment from an other-rater occurs (Funder, 2012), provides a framework for understanding ratings obtained via GSM. First, relevant behaviors representing the personality under judgment must occur. For example, if examining the trait of extraversion, some form of sociable, assertive, or active behavior must occur (Barrick & Mount, 1991). In the context of social media, extraverted behavior must occur on a social media platform, such as posting an open invitation to friends for a party. Second, relevant behavior must be available to the rater. For example, the social media profile on which the extraverted behavior occurs must be accessible by the rater. Third, the rater must detect the behavior, which depends upon the perceptiveness and attention of the rater (Funder, 2012). Of all the behaviors exhibited on a social media platform, the rater must see the behavior in question, such as the party invitation. Fourth, the rater must utilize the information gleaned from this detection correctly. The extraverted behavior, the party invitation, must be correctly interpreted as being a sincere, sociable invitation versus a narcissistic or self-absorbed post about the wild lifestyle of the person under judgment. Assuming that behavior relevant to a psychological construct will occur, the connectivity of job applicants to family, friends, and others through social media can be utilized to make those behaviors available to the other-raters. Once those behaviors are available, other-raters can detect and utilize those behaviors to make accurate judgments through the quality and quantity of information that is available to them. Raters who have known the applicant for years, such as friends or family, are more accurate in their judgments of personality than raters who have been acquainted with the applicant for a few weeks or months (Funder & Colvin, 1988). Further, raters make more accurate judgments from unstructured situations, such as home or social interactions, than from highly structured situations, such as work tasks (Letzring, Wells, & Funder, 2006). Social media may provide a new unstructured environment for ratings, facilitating the accuracy of other-ratings.

Another method for assessing established predictors with GSM is the use of serious assessment games to measure biodata, personality, or cognitive ability. A hiring organization will most typically utilize a game this way within an existing social media platform that incorporates games, like Facebook, as part of a consolidated recruitment-selection strategy. Simulated job behavior in such a game can be used to predict job performance. The fidelity of a simulation, or level of correspondence between that simulation and the task it is intended to represent (Tuzinski, 2013), influences its effectiveness at predicting performance. Simulation fidelity can vary in terms of physical fidelity (i.e., how much a test or simulation involves actual tasks performed on the job) and psychological fidelity (i.e., how much a test or simulation involves the knowledge, skills, and abilities needed for completing job tasks; Tuzinski, 2013). Each type of fidelity can be expressed as a continuum ranging from high fidelity, where simulations present job-relevant situations to applicants that require actual behavior responses, to low fidelity, where simulations might consist of a paper and pencil test based on hypothetical work situations (Lievens & Patterson, 2011; Tuzinski, 2013). Higher fidelity simulation typically yields incremental improvements in validity over lower fidelity simulations (Lievens &

Patterson, 2011). Serious games can be used to simulate a job with moderate to high fidelity (i.e., realism; Tuzinski, 2013). For example, a game simulating a job as a restaurant server might be used to assess time management skills. In such a game, players could attempt to balance various game goals with competing deadlines, such as taking orders, cleaning and setting tables, and hosting new customers. If an applicant can manage time and work priorities appropriately within the game, this level of performance may predict similar time management performance in the job context. A game like this would not simulate physical fidelity, as applicants would not perform actual server behaviors, but the psychological fidelity would be high, as the time management skills necessary to perform at the game would be necessary as a restaurant server (Tuzinski, 2013). Business simulation games may predict future career outcomes (Wolfe & Roberts, 1993), but empirical validity evidence for social media assessment games predicting job performance has not been thoroughly examined. However, because assessment games are currently used in hiring practice (Morgan, 2013), rigorous validity testing in future research is essential. Online assessment games can be considered a form of social media based on the affordance of association (Treem & Leonardi, 2012). These games become the media through which applicants associate and interact with hiring organizations or other potential applicants.

GSM can be used to improve the quality of data gathered through the selection processes by providing criterion-related and construct-related validity evidence for selection assessments. Criterion-related validity refers to evidence supporting how well a test can predict an outcome variable, like job performance (Furr & Bacharach, 2014). Armstrong et al. (2015) identified two ways that game-thinking can be used to improve the criterion-related validity of selection assessments, broadly, which can be applied to GSM as well. First, job-relevant applicant behavior within a gamified social media platform is directly observable in contrast to the inferred behavior captured by questionnaires. If behavior within a gamified social media platform simulates task performance on the job with high fidelity, it might be able to give a better representation of future work performance (Lievens & Patterson, 2011). For example, behavior on the question-and-answer website StackExchange might be predictive of future job performance in customer service. As users post questions and answers on this website regarding a variety of areas including computer science platforms, academic interests, and hobbies, other users can rate questions and answers as useful or not useful. StackExchange tracks ratings for each question and answer, but also tracks contributor ratings (i.e., how many people thought that contributor's answer was an excellent response). Users with high ratings for answering questions might perform well answering questions in a job context, such as in customer service, and extant research suggests that task-related motivation for those participating in such platforms is high (Deng, Liu, & Qi, 2011; Jin, Zhou, Lee, & Cheung, 2013; Morris, Teevan, & Panovich, 2010). In addition to task performance, GSM behavior might predict other organizational outcomes such as organizational citizenship behavior or counterproductive work behavior (Motowidlo & Kell, 2013). An applicant might display organizational citizenship behavior by helping another user within a gamified social media platform when they are not required to do so.

An applicant might display counterproductive work behavior by attempting to derail conversations in the gamified social media platform. Just as low-fidelity simulations like situational judgment tests (Landy, 2007) are often more predictive of future behavior than simple questionnaires, behavior elicited by games has the potential to be more predictive than situational judgment tests due to its increased fidelity (Lievens & Patterson, 2011).

The second reason that GSM may improve the criterion-related validity of selection assessments is because faking and cheating may be more difficult for applicants during game-like assessments (Armstrong et al., 2015). This is especially true if the gamified social media platform is well designed and the applicant does not know which behaviors employers are evaluating within the platform. The ability to identify selection criteria is considered a prerequisite to faking behavior (Konig, Melchers, Kleinmann, Richter, & Klehe, 2007). In noncognitive measures (e.g., personality surveys), many test-takers are susceptible to social desirability bias (Ganster, Hennessey, & Luthans, 1983) in their responses when they try to present themselves in a more positive way than what would reflect their true traits. Because much of the content that appears on social media is outside the direct control of the applicant, this bias may be reduced. For example, on LinkedIn, users provide a list of presumed skills on their profile, but professional connections choose whether to endorse the user on particular skills. Endorsements such as these can be likened to letters of recommendation. Although letters of recommendation as a whole might be poor predictors of job performance (Muchinsky, 1979), the extraction of certain traits from recommendations can be predictive of performance (Aamodt, Bryan, & Whitcomb, 1993). Ideally, if a user has demonstrated his or her skills to a variety of people, the user will receive more endorsements, crediting his or her ability at that skill. However, it should be noted that other forces might also be at play in these endorsements, such as one user endorsing another user's skills in the hope that the endorsed user will reciprocate with a favorable recommendation (Chamorro-Premuzic & Steinmetz, 2013). GSM should be designed carefully to account for extraneous influences on predictors in addition to faking behavior. To exclude extraneous effects, validity evidence is needed before GSM selection methods should be implemented. GSM methods should be designed to be as objective as possible and might incorporate standardized rating systems, with a focus on job-related behavior.

GSM also can improve construct validity, which refers to how well a test reflects a psychological construct such as personality (Furr & Bacharach, 2014). This improvement can be achieved in two ways. First, GSM can be used to motivate applicants to exert maximum effort during assessment. By motivating test-takers to use the gamified social media platform, more data can be obtained for making selection decisions. Self-determination theory (Deci & Ryan, 2000) provides a useful framework for examining motivation in games (Ryan, Rigby, & Przybylski, 2006; Przybylski, Rigby, & Ryan, 2010) as well as for examining motivation to use social media (Sjöklint, Constantiou, & Trier, 2013). Self-determination theory focuses on the innate psychological needs that are the basis for motivating one's self (Ryan & Deci, 2000). It proposes a continuum of motivational forces ranging from self-motivation (also called intrinsic motivation), where motivation is self-authored and endorsed, to external regulation, where motivation is controlled by a force external to the self. When individuals are self-motivated, they have more interest, excitement, and confidence, resulting in greater performance and well-being (Ryan & Deci, 2000). Cognitive evaluation theory, a component of self-determination theory, is useful for understanding the self-motivation, or intrinsic motivation (Ryan & Deci, 2000), associated with GSM.

GSM can satisfy the three psychological needs presented by cognitive evaluation theory that must be satisfied in order for humans to be intrinsically motivated: autonomy, competency, and relatedness (Deci & Ryan, 2000). GSM might satisfy the need for autonomy, or the need to experience one's behavior as self-determined (Ryan & Deci, 2000), by giving the player the power to make choices over goal pursuits or appearance within the social media platform. A potential applicant might pursue the goal of accruing the highest reputation score on a social media platform. GSM might satisfy the need for feelings of competence, through providing feedback toward the goals the user has decided to pursue. In the pursuit of a high score, this might be a gauge displaying point increases, such as a progress bar. Finally, GSM might satisfy the need for relatedness to others if the player had to collaborate with other players in order to improve an individual or group score. When people are self-directing their behavior, optimally challenged, and within a secure and socially supportive context, their motivation to behave will become more authentic and intrinsic in nature, with enhanced interest, excitement, and confidence (Ryan & Deci, 2000). The use of GSM can satisfy all three of these needs by giving the player the power to make choices over what goals to pursue, what strategies to use, who to befriend, or how to appear within the game while demonstrating increased skill progression through the game, all within the context of social media, alongside others (Przybylski et al., 2010).

The second way GSM can improve construct validity is by decreasing test anxiety, which otherwise might skew selection test results (Hausknecht et al., 2004) by making the test appear less intimidating or more fun. For example, adding a layer of fantasy can make unpleasant tasks more enjoyable (Downes-Le Guin, Baker, Mechling, & Ruyle, 2012) Alternatively, if score sharing is available within the social media context, applicants might be motivated by a challenge to earn the highest score in comparison to their peers or other applicants, such as in a leaderboard (Mekler et al., 2013). One GSM provider, Knelf®, employs gamification within its online assessments to reduce test anxiety. By introducing light-hearted elements such as a smiling, cartoon groundhog to relay assessment instructions and results, Knelf aims to create a fun, friendly, and approachable testing experience (Chow & Hu, 2015).

The face validity of selection procedures employing GSM might be affected in different ways for different people. Face validity refers to the perceptions of relatedness between a test and the construct it is intended to measure (Furr & Bacharach, 2014). Although face validity perceptions do not generally affect the construct or criterion-related validity of a test, they do play a role in applicant reactions to the selection process (Hausknecht et al., 2004). Because games are not "work-like" and social media is generally regarded as a personal activity, face validity may be poor for selection incorporating GSM. Cognitive load theory (Sweller, 1988) provides one explanation for understanding why people might not like either or both of these two technologies. Cognitive load theory states that an individual mind has a limitation on the amount of cognitive resources it can use at any given time. When a video game, social media platform, or other technology is complex (e.g., the game is complex in strategy or rules; a social media site is heavy in menus or unfamiliar terminology), users must spend more of their cognitive resources trying to learn the system in order to be successful (Krentler & Willis-Flurry, 2005; Piccoli, Ahmad, & Ives, 2001). If the technology is too new or is sufficiently dissimilar from the technology the applicant expects to encounter, users are more likely to see the technology as low in job relatedness and perceive the application to be unfair. In the broader organizational game-thinking literature, relationships have been found between pre-existing attitudes/experiences with games and the anticipated benefits and anticipated job-relevance of games used for organizational purposes (Landers & Armstrong, 2015). Thus, this problem is not unique to GSM but is highlighted by it.

Finally, GSM can be used to increase the utility of assessments, the amount of money saved by an organization by adopting a particular new selection system in contrast to their previous system (Schmidt, Hunter, McKenzie, & Muldrow, 1979). Some types of GSM can increase utility by reducing the overall costs associated with administering a test in the selection process. It is important to note the differences in cost across different implementations of GSM. The cost of developing a highly immersive, three-dimensional video game could be upwards of hundreds of thousands of dollars, whereas the addition of a few simple game elements to a pre-existing assessment might cost a few thousand dollars, mostly in development time. Thus, implementing a serious game into a social media platform for selection purposes is unlikely to have positive utility without a dramatic increase in criterion-related validity. In contrast, the gamification of an existing social media selection system has great potential to increase utility. The initial costs of different selection methods should be compared thoroughly before deciding to implement a GSM platform into the selection process.

6.5 Future Directions

Emerging technologies will enable new possibilities for both social media and game-thinking and in turn new possibilities for GSM in recruitment and selection. For example, as household appliances, clothing items, and cars become computerized and connected to the internet (i.e., the "internet of things"), new opportunities for social sharing and commentary become possible. Consequentially, organizations may gain access to behavioral data that have been traditionally difficult to capture or considered private. With the emergence of new data streams, new analytic techniques will be necessary. Presently, big data analytics are wildly popular in industry and in business journals. These new techniques are and will continue to be necessary to handle, organize, and analyze the copious amounts of new data. Although promising, these new variables should be thoroughly investigated before their use in measurement or prediction of key organizational outcomes such as job performance. Just because data are measured, does not mean they should be haphazardly used to make decisions about individuals. Game-thinking too is affected by evolving technology. Several efforts working to create, immersive user-friendly virtual and augmented reality experiences in medicine (Vera, Russo, Mohsin, & Tsuda, 2014), education (Ibáñez, Di Serio, Villarán, & Kloos, 2014), and other fields (Rosman, 2014). How these technologies will affect selection and recruitment remains to be seen, but there will be a plethora of research opportunities as enterprises will undoubtedly continue to adopt new technologies faster than researchers can thoroughly collect and evaluate empirical evidence.

The Internet of Things (IoT) refers to the interconnected network of everyday objects and appliances (Atzori, Iera, & Morabito, 2014)—cars, shoes, watches, refrigerators, clothing, wearable fitness devices, et cetera, comprise the IoT—and these data are becoming increasingly available to organizations, presenting new opportunities for personnel selection. The depth of data collection is difficult to fathom for many nonprogrammers; for example, many organizations can already examine historical data from IoT-connected weight scales, which could theoretically be used as an indicator of applicant health if a hiring manager was inclined to check. Taken a step further, data from fitness games (e.g., weight, heart rate, body temperature) could be gathered and used in hiring decisions. Similarly, "friend" information could be used to identify individuals who share the same game experiences, and thus may be similar. Additionally, research on stealth assessment indicates that Bayesian analytic strategies can be used to assess multidimensional individual traits, such as complex problem solving (Shute & Kim, 2014), by assessing performance in fully designed entertainment games. Such behaviors represent a wealth of new information that could potentially predict human performance in organizations, and we are only at the foremost edge of these possibilities.

Beyond game-thinking, behavioral metadata, such as "likes," shares, retweets, and follows, can be gathered and assessed using big data techniques to infer psychological traits that are traditionally assessed during the selection process. For example, Youyou, Kosinski, and Stillwell (2015) describe a machine learning methodology to assess Big Five personality traits from "likes" on Facebook. They were able to gather Facebook data from 70,000 participants who also took the 100-item International Personality Item Pool (IPIP) FFM survey. Then, a sophisticated multi-stage linear regression was used to predict FFM on 10% of the sample at a time. Further refinement and development of this methodology could be used to infer psychological variables from video game behavior. For example, data that indicate a player's social tendencies within a game (e.g., teamwork, leadership, communication) could be gathered and assessed. Consequently, it is possible that mainstream social games, in the future, could be used to conduct behind-the-scenes analyses of the players and then to provide that information to organizations. Big data techniques enable multisource, nontraditional data to be gathered, combined, and assessed, and will lead to powerful analytical tools for employee selection in the future.

6.6 Summary

As social media use continues to rise, affording new opportunities for information sharing, sociability, expression, and entertainment, organizations seek to leverage social media platforms as a tool for recruitment and selection. Several tech startups are capitalizing on game-thinking to connect applicants with organizations (Noguchi, 2015), despite a lack of empirical evidence. A review of pertinent theory indicates that game-thinking could enhance social media-based recruitment and selection in several ways:

1. *Game-thinking in social media (GSM) could increase the number and quality of job applicants.* Specifically, organizations could use game elements, such as competition or point-tracking to influence applicants to share information about job vacancies on various social media, thus increasing the number of potential applicants. Similarly, game elements can encourage sharing of organizational brand information and the use of game elements in and of itself communicates brand image. Accurate brand information can discourage poorly fitting applicants and encourage well-fitting applicants to apply, thus improving the quality of the applicant pool.
2. *GSM could improve organizational attraction, consequently increasing application and offer-acceptance intentions.* Tsai and Yang (Study 1, 2010) found that product and service image, organizational citizenship image, and corporate credibility image were significantly and positively related to organizational attractiveness. Carless (2005) found positive relationships between organizational attractiveness and intentions to accept a job-offer mid-selection process and at the end of the selection process, and a relationship between organizational attractiveness and job-offer acceptance. Thus, gamified advertisements on social media, game-thinking to encourage applicants to share information on social media, and gamified selection procedures that generate a buzz on social media can increase organizational attraction, intentions to accept a job offer, and actual job offer-acceptance.
3. *GSM could encourage incumbents to find and refer suitable applicants.* Employees recruited from internal referrals tend to have higher performance and lower turnover (Zottoli & Wanous, 2000), so game-thinking that increases incumbents' willingness to seek out and recruit applicants could benefit organizations. Points and leaderboards could inspire a sense of competition among certain employees; others might be motivated by reward or feedback regarding their referrals. Thus, multiple options exist for organizations to use game-thinking to facilitate or motivate employees to utilize their existing social media accounts or become more active in new ones, with the intention to find and attract new colleagues.
4. *GSM could yield novel data capture opportunities by encouraging or facilitating observable behaviors.* Research in assessment via social media has focused on behavior, typically behavioral indicators of personality (Gosling et al., 2011; Stoughton et al., 2013). Currently, GSM provides a form of other-ratings, which

have potential to be more valid than self-ratings of personality (Connelly & Ones, 2010). GSM in selection also offers new behavioral patterns to observe beyond typical social media behavior such as liking, commenting, or posting. Through serious assessment game integration with social media, opportunities for assessing behaviors like goal striving, problem solving, and human interaction will increase in number, producing more data and insight into each potential applicant.

5. *GSM could relieve some of the applicant tension commonly associated with selection tests and assessments.* Through the gamification of social media, applicants could become less anxious and more engaged during testing. Decreasing anxiety should improve the accuracy of assessments (Hausknecht et al., 2004), while improving engagement and motivation during testing may provide hiring organizations with more quality and quantity data.

In conclusion, this chapter has reviewed relevant theory and provided conceptual and empirical examples as a first step toward scholastic understanding of GSM to recruit and select employees. With affordances theory providing technological context, brand-equity theory and fit theory help to explain the potential benefits of GSM in the recruitment process. In the selection context, applicant reactions theory and the realistic accuracy model can be used to understand the potential impact of such systems on selection processes. Future research is needed to build an integrated theory related to GSM, toward the creation of a solid basis from which practitioners can draw to confidently recommend organizational practices.

GSM has a great deal of potential to improve both recruitment and selection, and extant theory suggests several mechanisms for this improvement. Many entertainment games are designed with sophisticated social capabilities, and some even have what would be considered a full-blown social media platform embedded within the game. Organizations are already beginning to take advantage of GSM like this for selection and recruitment purposes despite a lack of research in the organizational context. There are many lessons to be learned from existing research before building GSM-specific theory, and this chapter takes a first step toward this goal.

References

Aamodt, M. G., Bryan, D. A., & Whitcomb, A. J. (1993). Predicting performance with letters of recommendation. *Public Personnel Management, 22*(1), 81–90.

Armstrong, M. B., Landers, R. N., & Collmus, A. B. (2015). Gamifying recruitment, selection, training, and performance management: Game-thinking in human resource management. In D. Davis & H. Gangadharbatla (Eds.), *Handbook of research trends in gamification* (pp. 140–165). Hershey, PA: IGI Global.

Atzori, L., Iera, A., & Morabito, G. (2014). From "smart objects" to "social objects": The next evolutionary step of the internet of things. *IEEE Communications Magazine, 52*(1), 97–105.

Barrick, M. R., & Mount, M. K. (1991). The big five personality dimensions and job performance: A meta-analysis. *Personnel Psychology, 44*, 1–26.

Bedwell, W. L., Pavlas, D., Heyne, K., Lazzara, E. H., & Salas, E. (2012). Toward a taxonomy linking game attributes to learning: An empirical study. *Simulation & Gaming, 43*(6), 729–760. doi:10.1177/1046878112439444.

Browne, A. (2014, September 4). Knelf re-releases free personality test and character training games. *Startup Calgary*. Retrieved from http://startupcalgary.ca/knelf-re-releases-free-personality-test-and-character-training-games/.

Cable, D. M., & Turban, D. B. (2001). Establishing the dimensions, sources, and value of job seekers' employer knowledge during recruitment. In G. R. Ferris (Ed.), *Research in personnel and human resources management* (Vol. 20, pp. 115–163). Greenwich, CT: JAI Press.

Carless, S. A. (2005). Person-job fit versus person-organization fit as predictors of organizational attraction and job acceptance intentions: A longitudinal study. *Journal of Occupational and Organizational Psychology, 78*(3), 411–429. doi:10.1348/096317905x25995.

Chamorro-Premuzic, T., & Steinmetz, C. (2013). The perfect hire. *Scientific American Mind, 24*(3), 42–47.

Chapman, D. S., Uggerslev, K. L., Carroll, S. A., Piasentin, K. A., & Jones, D. A. (2005). Applicant attraction to organizations and job choice: A meta-analytic review of the correlates of recruiting outcomes. *Journal of Applied Psychology, 90*(5), 928–944. doi:10.1037/0021-9010.90.5.928.

Chow, S., & Hu, E. (2015). *Gamifying psychometric assessments: Driving engagement for more data.* Paper presented at the 30th Annual Conference of the Society for Industrial and Organizational Psychology, Philadelphia, PA.

Cohan, P. (2012, December 13). When it comes to talent, HireArt lets you try before you buy. *Forbes*. Retrieved from http://www.forbes.com/sites/petercohan/2015/06/12/pick-adam-bain-over-sheryl-sandberg-as-twitters-next-ceo/.

Collins, C. J. (2007). The interactive effects of recruitment practices and product awareness on job seekers' employer knowledge and application behaviors. *Journal of Applied Psychology, 92*(1), 180–190. doi:10.1037/0021-9010.92.1.180.

Collins, C. J., & Han, J. (2004). Exploring applicant pool quantity and quality: The effects of early recruitment practice strategies, corporate advertising, and firm reputation. *Personnel Psychology, 57*(3), 685–717. doi:10.1111/j.1744-6570.2004.00004.x.

Collins, C. J., & Stevens, C. K. (2002). The relationship between early recruitment-related activities and the application decisions of new labor-market entrants: A brand equity approach to recruitment. *Journal of Applied Psychology, 87*(6), 1121–1133. doi:10.1037/0021-9010.87.6.1121.

Connelly, B. S., & Ones, D. S. (2010). An other perspective on personality: meta-analytic integration of observers' accuracy and predictive validity. *Psychological Bulletin, 136*(6), 1092–1122. doi:10.1037/a0021212.

Connolly, T. M., Boyle, E. A., MacArthur, E., Hainey, T., & Boyle, J. M. (2012). A systematic literature review of empirical evidence on computer games and serious games. *Computers & Education, 59*(2), 661–686. doi:10.1016/j.compedu.2012.03.004.

Cortina, J. M., & Luchman, J. N. (2013). Personnel selection and employee performance. In N. W. Schmitt, S. Highhouse, & I. B. Weiner (Eds.), *Handbook of psychology* (Industrial and organizational psychology 2nd ed., Vol. 12, pp. 143–183). Hoboken, NJ: Wiley.

Darnold, T. C., & Rynes, S. L. (2013). Recruitment and job choice research: Same as it ever was? In *Handbook of psychology* (Industrial and organizational psychology 2nd ed., Vol. 12, pp. 104–142). Hoboken, NJ: Wiley.

Deci, E. L., & Ryan, R. M. (2000). The "what" and "why" of goal pursuits: Human needs and the self-determination of behavior. *Psychological Inquiry, 11*(4), 227–268. doi:10.2307/1449618.

Deng, S., Liu, Y., & Qi, Y. (2011). An empirical study on determinants of web based question-answer services adoption. *Online Information Review, 35*(5), 789–798. doi:10.1108/14684521111176507.

Deterding, S., Sicart, M., Nacke, L., O'Hara, K., & Dixon, D. (2011). *Gamification: Using game-design elements in non-gaming contexts.* Paper presented at the CHI '11 Extended Abstracts on Human Factors in Computing Systems, Vancouver, BC, Canada.

Dineen, B. R., & Noe, R. A. (2009). Effects of customization on application decisions and applicant pool characteristics in a web-based recruitment context. *Journal of Applied Psychology, 94*(1), 224–234. doi:10.1037/a0012832.

Downes-Le Guin, T., Baker, R., Mechling, J., & Ruyle, E. (2012). Myths and realities of respondent engagement in online surveys. *International Journal of Market Research, 54*(5), 613–633. doi:10.2501/IJMR-54-5-613-633.

Ellison, N. B., Gibbs, J. L., & Weber, M. S. (2014). The use of enterprise social network sites for knowledge sharing in distributed organizations: The role of organizational affordances. *American Behavioral Scientist, 59*(1), 103–123. doi:10.1177/0002764214540510.

eMarketer, & American Marketing Association. (2015). *Number of social network users worldwide from 2010 to 2018 (in billions)*. Retrieved June 3, 2015, from www.statista.com/statistics/278414/number-of-worldwide-social-network-users/.

Entertainment Software Association. (2015). 2015 Sales, demographic and usage data. *Essential facts about the computer and video game industry*. Retrieved from http://www.theesa.com/wp-content/uploads/2015/04/ESA-Essential-Facts-2015.pdf.

Funder, D. C. (2012). Accurate personality judgment. *Current Directions in Psychological Science, 21*(3), 177–182. doi:10.1177/0963721412445309.

Funder, D. C., & Colvin, C. R. (1988). Friends and strangers: Acquaintanceship, agreement, and the accuracy of personality judgment. *Journal of Personality and Social Psychology, 55*(1), 149–158. doi:10.1037/0022-3514.55.1.149.

Furr, R. M., & Bacharach, V. R. (2014). *Psychometrics: An introduction* (2nd ed.). Thousand Oaks, CA: Sage.

Ganster, D. C., Hennessey, H. W., & Luthans, F. (1983). Social desirability response effects: Three alternative models. *Academy of Management Journal, 26*(2), 321–331. doi:10.2307/255979.

Garris, R., Ahlers, R., & Driskell, J. E. (2002). Games, motivation, and learning: A research and practice model. *Simulation & Gaming, 33*(4), 441–467. doi:10.1177/1046878102238607.

Gaugler, B. B., Rosenthal, D. B., Thornton, G. C., & Bentson, C. (1987). Meta-analysis of assessment center validity. *Journal of Applied Psychology, 72*(3), 493–511. doi:10.1037/0021-9010.72.3.493.

Gosling, S. D., Augustine, A. A., Vazire, S., Holtzman, N., & Gaddis, S. (2011). Manifestations of personality in online social networks: Self-reported Facebook-related behaviors and observable profile information. *Cyberpsychology, Behavior and Social Networking, 14*(9), 483–488. doi:10.1089/cyber.2010.0087.

Hausknecht, J. P., Day, D. V., & Thomas, S. C. (2004). Applicant reactions to selection procedures: An updated model and meta-analysis. *Personnel Psychology, 57*(3), 639–683. doi:10.1111/j.1744-6570.2004.00003.x.

Ibáñez, M. B., Di Serio, Á., Villarán, D., & Kloos, C. D. (2014). Experimenting with electromagnetism using augmented reality: Impact on flow student experience and educational effectiveness. *Computers & Education, 71*, 1–13.

Jin, X.-L., Zhou, Z., Lee, M. K. O., & Cheung, C. M. K. (2013). Why users keep answering questions in online question answering communities: A theoretical and empirical investigation. *International Journal of Information Management, 33*(1), 93–104. doi:10.1016/j.ijinfomgt.2012.07.007.

Jobvite. (2015) *Job seeker nation study: Inside the mind of the modern job seeker* [Infographic]. Retrievedfromhttp://www.jobvite.com/resources/infographics/jobvite-infographic-the-2015-job-seeker-nation-study/.

Kaplan, A. M., & Haenlein, M. (2010). Users of the world, unite! The challenges and opportunities of social media. *Business Horizons, 53*(1), 59–68. doi:10.1016/j.bushor.2009.09.003.

Kemp, S. (2015). *Digital, social & mobile worldwide in 2015*. Retrieved from http://wearesocial.net/blog/2015/01/digital-social-mobile-worldwide-2015/.

Konig, C. J., Melchers, K. G., Kleinmann, M., Richter, G. M., & Klehe, U.-C. (2007). Candidates' ability to identify criteria in nontransparent selection procedures: Evidence from an assessment center and a structured interview. *International Journal of Selection and Assessment, 15*(3), 283–292.

Krentler, K. A., & Willis-Flurry, L. A. (2005). Does technology enhance actual student learning? The case of online discussion boards. *Journal of Education for Business, 80*(6), 316–321.

Kristof-Brown, A. L. (2000). Perceived applicant fit: Distinguishing between recruiters' perceptions of person-job and person-organization fit. *Personnel Psychology, 53*(3), 643–671. doi:10.1111/j.1744-6570.2000.tb00217.x.

Kristof-Brown, A. L., & Guay, R. P. (2011). Person–environment fit. In *APA handbook of industrial and organizational psychology, Vol 3: Maintaining, expanding, and contracting the organization* (pp. 3–50, APA Handbooks in Psychology.). Washington, DC: American Psychological Association.

Kristof-Brown, A. L., Zimmerman, R. D., & Johnson, E. C. (2005). Consequences of individuals' fit at work: A meta-analysis of person-job, person-organization, person-group, and person-supervisor fit. *Personnel Psychology, 58*(2), 281–342. doi:10.1111/j.1744-6570.2005.00672.x.

Lampe, C. (2014). Gamification and social media. In S. Deterding & S. P. Walz (Eds.), *The Gameful world: Approaches, issues, applications*. Cambridge, MA: MIT.

Landers, R. N. (2015). Developing a theory of gamified learning: Linking serious games and gamification of learning. *Simulation & Gaming*, doi:10.1177/1046878114563660.

Landers, R. N. & Armstrong, M. B. (2015). Enhancing instructional outcomes with gamification: An empirical test of the Technology-Enhanced Training Effectiveness Model. *Computers in Human Behavior*. doi:10.1016/j.chb.2015.07.031.

Landy, F. J. (2007). The validation of personnel decisions in the twenty-first century: Back to the future. In *Alternative validation strategies: Developing new and leveraging existing validity evidence* (pp. 409–426, The professional practice series.). Hoboken, NJ: Wiley.

Leonardi, P. M., Huysman, M., & Steinfield, C. (2013). Enterprise social media: Definition, history, and prospects for the study of social technologies in organizations. *Journal of Computer-Mediated Communication, 19*(1), 1–19. doi:10.1111/jcc4.12029.

Leonhard, W. (2013, May 17). Want to work on Bing? Have I got an Easter egg for you! *Infoworld*. Retrieved from http://www.infoworld.com/article/2614626/it-jobs/want-to-work-on-bing-have-i-got-an-easter-egg-for-you-.html.

Letzring, T. D., Wells, S. M., & Funder, D. C. (2006). Information quantity and quality affect the realistic accuracy of personality judgment. *Journal of Personality and Social Psychology, 91*(1), 111–123. doi:10.1037/0022-3514.91.1.111.

Lievens, F., & Highhouse, S. (2003). The relation of instrumental and symbolic attributes to a company's attractiveness as an employer. *Personnel Psychology, 56*(1), 75–102. doi:10.1111/j.1744-6570.2003.tb00144.x.

Lievens, F., & Patterson, F. (2011). The validity and incremental validity of knowledge tests, low-fidelity simulations, and high-fidelity simulations for predicting job performance in advanced-level high-stakes selection. *Journal of Applied Psychology, 96*(5), 927–940. doi:10.1037/a0023496.

Macan, T. H., Avedon, M. J., Paese, M., & Smith, D. E. (1994). The effects of applicants' reactions to cognitive ability tests and an assessment center. *Personnel Psychology, 47*(4), 715–738. doi:10.1111/j.1744-6570.1994.tb01573.x.

Mekler, E. D., Bruhlmann, F., Opwis, K., & Tuch, A. N. Do points, levels and leaderboards harm intrinsic motivation? An empirical analysis of common gamification elements. In *First International Conference on Gameful Design, Research, and Applications, Toronto, Ontario, Canada, 2013* (pp. 66–73). New York: ACM. doi:10.1145/2583008.2583017.

Michael, D. R., & Chen, S. L. (2005). *Serious games: Games that educate, train, and inform*. New York: Muska & Lipman/Premier-Trade.

Moltz, B. (2013). *Throw balloons, assess employee skills* [Web Article]. Your Business Unstuck. Retrieved from http://barrymoltz.com/2013/07/throw-balloons-assess-employee-skills/.

Morgan, J. (2013). *Want to work here? Play this game first!* Forbes. Retrieved from http://www.forbes.com/sites/jacobmorgan/2013/12/17/want-to-work-here-play-this-game-first/.

Morris, M. R., Teevan, J., & Panovich, K. (2010) What do people ask their social networks, and why? A survey study of status message Q&A behavior. In *Proceedings of the SIGCHI*

Conference on Human Factors in Computing Systems, Atlanta, GA, 2010 (pp. 1739–1748). doi:10.1145/1753326.1753587.

Motowidlo, S. J., & Kell, H. J. (2013). Job performance. In N. W. Schmitt, S. Highhouse, & I. B. Weiner (Eds.), *Handbook of psychology* (Industrial and organizational psychology 2nd ed., Vol. 12, pp. 82–103). Hoboken, NJ: Wiley.

Muchinsky, P. M. (1979). The use of reference reports in personnel selection: A review and evaluation. *Journal of Occupational Psychology, 52*(4), 287–297. doi:10.1111/j.2044-8325.1979.tb00463.x.

Noguchi, Y. (2015, February 25). Recruiting better talent with brain games and big data. *NPR*. Retrieved from http://www.npr.org/sections/alltechconsidered/2015/02/25/388698620/recruiting-better-talent-with-brain-games-and-big-data.

Olsen, S. (2004, July, 9). Google recruits eggheads with mystery billboard. *CNET*. Retrieved from http://news.cnet.com/Google-recruits-eggheads-with-mystery-billboard/2100-1023_3-5263941.html.

Piccoli, G., Ahmad, R., & Ives, B. (2001). Web-based learning environments: A research framework and a preliminary assessment of effectiveness in basic IT skills training. *MIS Quarterly, 25*(4), 401–426.

Przybylski, A. K., Rigby, C. S., & Ryan, R. M. (2010). A motivational model of video game engagement. *Review of General Psychology, 14*(2), 154–166. doi:10.1037/a0019440.

Resick, C. J., Baltes, B. B., & Shantz, C. W. (2007). Person-organization fit and work-related attitudes and decisions: examining interactive effects with job fit and conscientiousness. *Journal of Applied Psychology, 92*(5), 1446–1455. doi:10.1037/0021-9010.92.5.1446.

Rosett, M. (2015, August 24). Google has a secret interview process… And it landed me a job. *TheHustle*. Retrieved from http://thehustle.co/the-secret-google-interview-that-landed-me-a-job.

Rosman, K. (2014, March 3). Augmented reality finally starts to gain traction. *The Wall Street Journal*. Retrieved from http://www.wsj.com/news/articles/SB10001424052702304585004579417612087615766.

Ryan, R. M., & Deci, E. L. (2000). Self-determination theory and the facilitation of intrinsic motivation, social development, and well-being. *American Psychologist, 55*(1), 68–78. doi:10.1037/110003-066X.55.1.68.

Ryan, A. M., Horvath, M., & Kriska, D. K. (2005). The role of recruiting source informativeness and organizational perceptions in decisions to apply. *International Journal of Selection and Assessment, 13*, 235–249.

Ryan, R. M., Rigby, C. S., & Przybylski, A. (2006). The motivational pull of video games. A self-determination theory approach. *Motivation and Emotion, 30*(4), 344–360. doi:10.1007/s11031-006-9051-8.

Schmidt, F. L., Hunter, J. E., McKenzie, R. C., & Muldrow, T. W. (1979). Impact of valid selection procedures on work-force productivity. *Journal of Applied Psychology, 64*(6), 609–626. doi:10.1037/0021-9010.64.6.609.

Schmitt, N., Cortina, J. M., Ingerick, M. J., & Wiechmann, D. (2003). Personnel selection and employee performance. In W. C. Borman, D. R. Ilgen, & R. J. Klimoski (Eds.), *Handbook of psychology: Industrial and organizational psychology* (Vol. 12, pp. 77–105). Hoboken, NJ: Wiley.

Seaborn, K., & Fels, D. I. (2015). Gamification in theory and action: A survey. *International Journal of Human-Computer Studies, 74*(1), 14–31. doi:10.1016/j.ijhcs.2014.09.006.

Shute, V. J., & Kim, Y. J. (2014). Formative and stealth assessment. In J. M. Spector (Ed.), *Handbook of research on educational communications and technology* (pp. 311–321). New York: Springer.

Shute, V. J., Ventura, M., Bauer, M., & Zapata-Rivera, D. (2009). Melding the power of serious games and embedded assessment to monitor and foster learning: Flow and grow. In U. Ritterfeld, M. Cody, & P. Vorderer (Eds.), *Serious games: Mechanisms and effects* (pp. 295–321). New York: Routledge.

Sjöklint, M., Constantiou, I. D., & Trier, M. (2013). *Numerical representations and user behaviour in social networking sites: Towards a multi-theoretical research framework.* Paper presented at The European Conference on Information Systems, Utrecht, Netherlands.

Smither, J. W., Reilly, R. R., Millsap, R. E., Pearlman, K., & Stoffey, R. W. (1993). Applicant reactions to selection procedures. *Personnel Psychology, 46*(1), 49–76. doi:10.1111/j.1744-6570.1993.tb00867.x.

Stoughton, J. W., Thompson, L. F., & Meade, A. W. (2013). Big five personality traits reflected in job applicants' social media postings. *Cyberpsychology, Behavior and Social Networking, 16*(11), 800–805. doi:10.1089/cyber.2012.0163.

Sweller, J. (1988). Cognitive load during problem solving: Effects on learning. *Cognitive Science, 12*(2), 257–285. doi:10.1016/0364-0213(88)90023-7.

Treem, J. W., & Leonardi, P. M. (2012). Social media use in organizations: Exploring the affordances of visibility, editability, persistence, and association. *Communication Yearbook, 36*, 143–189. doi:10.2139/ssrn.2129853.

Tsai, W., & Yang, I. (2010). Does image matter to different job applicants? The influences of corporate image and applicant individual differences on organizational attractiveness. *International Journal of Selection and Assessment, 18*, 48–63.

Tuzinski, K. (2013). Simulations for personnel selection: An introduction. In M. Fetzer & K. Tuzinski (Eds.), *Simulations for personnel selection* (pp. 1–13). New York: Springer.

Van Hoye, G., & Lievens, F. (2009). Tapping the grapevine: A closer look at word-of-mouth as a recruitment source. *Journal of Applied Psychology, 94*(2), 341–352. doi:10.1037/a0014066.

Vera, A. M., Russo, M., Mohsin, A., & Tsuda, S. (2014). Augmented reality telementoring (ART) platform: A randomized controlled trial to assess the efficacy of a new surgical education technology. *Surgical Endoscopy, 28*(12), 3467–3472.

Wagner, D., Vollmar, G., & Wagner, H.-T. (2014). The impact of information technology on knowledge creation. *Journal of Enterprise Information Management, 27*(1), 31–44. doi:10.1108/jeim-09-2012-0063.

Wilson, K. A., Bedwell, W. L., Lazzara, E. H., Salas, E., Burke, C. S., Estock, J. L., et al. (2008). Relationships between game attributes and learning outcomes: Review and research proposals. *Simulation & Gaming, 40*(2), 217–266. doi:10.1177/1046878108321866.

Wolfe, J., & Roberts, C. R. (1993). A further study of the external validity of business games: Five-year peer group indicators. *Simulation & Gaming, 24*(1), 21–33.

Youyou, W., Kosinski, M., & Stillwell, D. (2015). Computer-based personality judgments are more accurate than those made by humans. *Proceedings of the National Academy of Sciences, 112*(4), 1036–1040. doi:10.1073/pnas.1418680112.

Zeldovich, L. (2015, April 14). Sick of your job? Pymetrics lets you play games to find your next career. *Digital Trends.* Retrieved from http://www.digitaltrends.com/cool-tech/pymetrics-games-point-you-to-the-right-job-or-career/

Zhang, D., Wang, Z., Guo, B., & Yu, Z. (2012). Social and community intelligence: Technologies and trends. *IEEE Software, 29*(4), 88–92.

Zottoli, M. A., & Wanous, J. P. (2000). Recruitment source research: Current status and future directions. *Human Resource Management Review, 10*(4), 353–382. doi:10.1016/s1053-4822(00)00032-2.

Part III
Practical Guidelines

Chapter 7
Social Media, Big Data, and Employment Decisions: Mo' Data, Mo' Problems?

Sarah Guilfoyle, Shawn M. Bergman, Christopher Hartwell, and Jonathan Powers

Abstract Big data and analytics are popular "buzzwords" gathering momentum in the academic literature and trade journals. While the exact definition of big data and analytics remains widely debated, it cannot be argued that the predictive power and obscure trends that big data and analytics can reveal have the potential to transform the field of human resources. Organizations, looking for new ways to collect and harness big data, are scouring the Internet in search of untapped outlets of information about job applicants and automated ways to use social media for recruiting and selection, and are using analytics on their internal big data generated by internal social media and intranets to improve their performance management systems and internal processes. However, there are a number of questions surrounding the accuracy, ethics, and legality of big data and analytics in human resources. This chapter will discuss the implications of using big data and analytics in making employment decisions, the potential they have to revolutionize the industry, and the possible unforeseen consequences of their use.

Keywords Big data • Community data • Self-quantification data • Structured data • Unstructured data • Semi-structured data • Analytics

Chapter Overview

- Overview of big data, analytics, and social media in selection.
- What are the implications for social media data and analytics in recruitment and selection?
- Do analytics and mo' data help human resource functions or cause mo' problems?

S. Guilfoyle, M.A. • S.M. Bergman, Ph.D. (✉) • J. Powers, M.A.
Department of Psychology, Appalachian State University,
222 Joyce Lawrence Ln, Boone, NC 28608, USA
e-mail: guilfoylese@appstate.edu; bergmans@appstate.edu; powersj1@email.appstate.edu

C. Hartwell, Ph.D.
Management Department, Jon M. Huntsman School of Business, Utah State University,
3555 Old Main Hill, Logan, UT 84341, USA
e-mail: chris.hartwell@gmail.com

R.N. Landers, G.B. Schmidt (eds.), *Social Media in Employee Selection and Recruitment*, DOI 10.1007/978-3-319-29989-1_7

7.1 Big Data, Analytics, and Social Media: Revolutionizing Human Resources?

A number of popular-press authors have claimed that big data and analytics will transform human resource (e.g., Clark, 2013; Galer, 2013; Sridharan, 2013). At the core of these claims is the idea that organizations can now collect vast amounts of data on job candidates and employees and, through the use of quantitative methods, make empirically based employment discussions. While the concept of employing evidence-based practices and the science-practitioner model to human resources has been around for decades (e.g., Baker, Benjamin, & Ludy, 2000; Muchinsky, 2011), a recent survey of 480 large organizations found that only 4 % of companies use predictive analytics to information decision about their workforce and only 14 % have conducted any statistical analytics of their employee data (Bersin, 2013). There are a number of reasons why human resource professionals have been slow to use data when making employment decisions. However, advances in technology are allowing companies to quickly and fairly inexpensively collect and analyze the digital signals that job candidates and employees leave behind. Information from e-mails, phone calls, and social media can now be captured and analyzed to get a richer picture of job candidates and determine how people work. This data capture and analysis allows for a wider application of data in human resource decisions (Lohr, 2013). As a result, big data and analytics are beginning to transform, and in many ways improve, human resource practice.

One way that the practice of human resource is being improved is by the simple collection and use of data when making employment decisions. While industrial–organizational psychologists have been advocating the use of data and quantitative analysis for some time (e.g., Katzell & Austin, 1992; Muchinsky, 2011), the increased availability of technology to aid in the capture and analysis of data makes the use of data much more practical. For example, practitioners can use text analytics to examine applicants' cover letters, resumes, and/or applications and help streamline the process of reviewing these application materials. Descriptive analytics can be used to deliver an immediate summary picture of a company's applicant pool that is continually updated. Diagnostic analytics can be used to mine data that human resource practitioners already collect to determine if patterns can be discovered that will improve operations. Predictive analytics can take this newly discovered insight and automate human resource processes, which can improve efficiency and potentially reduce human bias in employment decisions.

The social media revolution is technological advance that is transforming human resource activities. Social media is a set of Internet-based operations that are based on Web 2.0 technology, enabling users to interact and exchange the content or information (Kaplan & Haenlein, 2010). The exploding popularity of social media is well known, and it is quickly becoming the predominant medium by which individuals exchange information, share pictures, audio, videos, and messages with their fellow users. Whether it is an online blog or profile on popular platforms—such as Facebook, Twitter, LinkedIn, Snapchat, Instagram, or Google+—virtually everyone has a digital footprint (i.e., data which is left behind by using these online services).

Given the extraordinary popularity of social media, it is not surprising that organizations have moved to using it to help meet their business goals. Whether it is the way that organizations are building their customer base, managing their brand, or recruiting and selecting employees, social networking sites (SNSs), and other online social media platforms have changed the way that companies communicate with individuals outside of their organization (Axelson, 2014; Waxer, 2013). Social media technologies have also changed the way that businesses operate internally and allowed employees to share ideas quickly and efficiently using in-house social media platforms (Huertas, 2012; Mullaney, 2012).

In the area of human resources, social media and online resources have changed the way recruiters think about attracting applicants (Anders, 2011; O'Brien, 2014). Given the unfettered information that individuals voluntarily provide about themselves on social media, human resource professionals, and hiring managers use it as a way to improve their selection procedures. Indeed, the overwhelming majority of organizations, 93 %, currently use or are planning to use social media in their hiring process (Jobvite, 2014).

There is an overwhelming amount of information available online and on social media outlets that human resource researchers and professionals would need to sift through in order to effectively use these online sources for recruiting and selection. Technological advances in big data and analytics make the continual monitoring and processing of this information possible to help human resources departments make better hiring decisions. For example, information generated from job-seekers' online applications could be scanned and automatically combined with publically available information (e.g., criminal history) and/or gathered from social media to generate a richer applicant profile. This applicant information could then be added to other publically available data (e.g., economic data) and internal organizational financial and performance data. The results of previous analytic and statistical analyses could then use all of this data to automatically evaluate and rate each job applicant. This type of machine-learning system could be deployed and make employment decisions or recommendation about applicants without a human resource professional personally examining applications' materials.

These advances and benefits, however, also have new challenges and possible unforeseen consequences. The current chapter provides an overview of big data and analytics, how these concepts and practices can be used by organizations to help make employment decisions, and the logistic, ethical, and legal implications for doing so. In providing this overview, the authors hope to help human resource professionals and research decide if the "mo' data" they collect from social media is worth the "mo' problems" that potentially ensue.

7.2 What Is Big Data?

Although the term "big data" is discussed and used more today than ever before, a consensus regarding a universally accepted definition of term has yet to be met. While researchers and practitioners alike do not agree on a single definition of big data, the McKinsey Global Institute (2011) has suggested that big data involves handling "datasets whose size is beyond the ability of typical database software tools to capture, store, manage and analyze" the information. Yet this interpretation relies wholly on the capabilities of statistical software (which are constantly changing) and focuses only on amount of data. While data amount is certainly one agreed upon defining characteristic (hence the term "big" data), SAS (n.d.) focuses on the actual process of analyzing big data and suggests that one characteristic of such data is that it can "uncover hidden patterns, unknown correlations and other useful information that can be used to make better decisions." This definition, however, blurs together the information collected, the analyses conducted, and results ascertained into a single definition.

The current chapter takes the view that the information that is collected (i.e., big data), the processes that are used to make sense of that information (i.e., analytics), the results, their interpretation, and decisions made are separate concepts. While the these concepts are all strongly linked in the business world, we view them as separate processes that need to be understood before exploring how information from social media, or from any online source, can be harnessed and used to aid in employment decisions. Thus, the chapter first provides an overview of concepts of big data and analytics and before discussing how these concepts can be applied to information collective via social media and other online sources to be used in employment decisions.

7.2.1 Three Components of Big Data

While the broader definition of exactly what is "big data" is widely debated, there is much more of a consensus surrounding the components of big data. Big data is commonly discussed in terms of its "3 Vs:" Volume, Variety, and Velocity (Di Martino, Aversa, Cretella, Esposito, & Kołodziej, 2014; Dumbill, 2012). Volume, arguably big data's most obvious "V," refers to the enormous size of datasets. Specifically, this component of big data has to do with the amount of information or data that is collected. To get an idea of the volume of data that is generated and can be potentially captured on social media every minute, it is estimated that YouTube users upload 300 h of new videos, Facebook users share over 2.5 million pieces of content (e.g., status updates, pictures, likes), and Twitter users send at least 277,000 tweets every minute (Ahmad, 2014; YouTube, n.d.).

The different types of content that are posted and shared on Facebook might best embody the second the "V" of big data, Variety. Variety reflects the fact that data come in a variety of forms and formats and are not limited to the clean numeric information with which most researchers and human resource professionals are familiar. The variety component of big data means that information collected is now not just numeric but includes information such as text, video, and pictures posts, Facebook likes, Twitter re-tweets, and LinkedIn endorsements.

When scanning and collecting data from multiple sources, datasets can grow rapidly. The swift pace at which large amounts of information are collected from various sources is reflected in big data's third "V," Velocity. Velocity does not necessarily mean real-time information, but it does indicate the information is continually being collected, and continuous collection has important implications for both the technology needed to store the data and the quantitative methods used to make sense of the data. This is perhaps the most challenging component of big data, the ability to manage, and make sense out of information that is continually being collected.

Unlike the general definition of big data, the "3 Vs" of big data are generally agreed upon. And while the question remains as to whether these components fully represent all of the unique aspects of big data, what is not debated is that these three components influence one another and work together to create datasets that are unquestionably large, contain a diversity amount of information, and are continually being updated. These characteristics make big data an attractive source of information that can potentially be mined to help all departments in an organization, including HR, make business decisions.

7.2.2 Five Sources of Big Data

Today, big data is typically gathered from five major sources: public forums, private forums, data exhausts, community data, and self-quantification (George, Haas, & Pentland, 2014). Understanding different sources of data is important because each source of data can provide unique or untapped types of information that can assist human resource professionals in making employment decisions. These untapped sources of information can potentially be used to verify applicant information and could provide hiring managers information about applicant characteristics that are difficult to assess using traditional personnel selection measures and techniques.

Public data are held and organized by local, state, and federal governments or agencies. The publicly available information about individuals might or might not be confidential. Examples of anonymous publicly available information would be data on agriculture, consumer spending, education, finance, or public safety. There are also some forms of publicly available data that are not anonymous such as criminal records and voter registrations. Together there are a number of sources providing anonymous (e.g., Google Public Data and Data.gov) and non-anonymous (e.g., Publicdata.com and Searchsystems.net) data and numerous other companies that provide preemployment screening services that can assist in employment decisions.

While public data are held by public organizations and are typically available to the masses, private data are collected by private organizations for their own personal use. Large organizations often collect information regarding the purchasing habits of their customers to more effectively advertise their products. Organization also collect information on their employees in order to help make changes to their human resources practices. For example, Google analyzed data their own internal performance reviews and surveys data to develop help better understand what makes a manager effective. These lessons were then integrated into training, coaching, and performance reviews (Rafter, 2013). Bank of America used privately held data on their call-center employees to determine that they could lower workers stress (measured by analyzing worker's voices) and improve call-center their performance metrics by allowing more staff to take their breaks together (Marrs, 2014).

Data exhaust refers to data generated as a by-product of digital activities, such as web browsing histories, cookies, log files, or temporary Internet files. These data are not always analyzed and may even be blatantly ignored or discarded by the organizations that own it. However, in the context of big data, information amassed through data exhaust can translate to millions of dollars in revenue. For example, one marketing start-up began to collect the email addresses that accidentally sent to "parked" web domains (i.e., a domain name that is not associated with any services such as e-mail or a website). This start-up company then began to send email advertisements to the collected emails, generating $50 million in revenue (Williams, 2013). In the area of HR, the incidental statistics and information that accumulate when people interact with a company's job board or internal web-portal can help an organization assess the pattern of usage on the site and make improvements to better organize the information to make the site more efficient (e.g., Napper, 2014).

Community data refers to the unstructured information that can be found on numerous Web 2.0 Internet sites, including social media platforms, in which visitors to the sites provide input and information, rather than simply consuming data that is already posted. Social media feeds and comments sections are two such examples of community data. In the context of social media, every "like," status update, or picture posted on an SNS produces community data that has the potential to be analyzed to better understand human behavior. In the realm of HR, there are software platforms available that will scan and collect (or scrape) public information on social media and other online information that is publically available to help companies better understand their employees and candidates (Marrs, 2014).

Finally, self-quantification data are information that individuals produce through their personal actions and are captured by electronic devices. The market is awash with apps that count calories consumed or hours of sleep, and personal monitors, such as wristbands that track the wearer's heart rate or steps walked throughout the day. Organizations are increasingly implementing this type of technology and capturing this data to monitor their employees by placing sensors and name badges to monitor social interactions, requiring workers to install apps on their smart phone to monitor work hours, and placing sensors in office chairs to assess how long employees have been away from their workstations (Howley, 2015; Marrs, 2015).

Examining these various sources of data, it becomes easy to understand how organizations can begin to amass gigantic databases of information. The opportunities to collect information on people are practically endless. The difficulty comes in wading through such information to identify trends, make inferences about behavioral patterns, and make effective use this information when making employment decisions.

7.2.3 Three Types of Data

These five sources of information produce a wide variety of data. While the volume, velocity, and variety of data that is produced by these sources, the information they produce can be classified into three categories: structured, unstructured, and semi-structured data (McKinsey Global Institute, 2011).

Structured data refers to information that is formatted in fixed fields. This information can be in a variety of formats (e.g., numeric or text) and is typically characterized as information that can be easily split part from the rest of the information (Landers, Brusso, Cavanaugh, & Collmus, 2015). Information in spreadsheets and webforms and information produced by clicking on a given link are examples of structured data. Human resource researchers and professionals are probably most familiar with this form of data because it encompasses most contemporary personnel and performance information. For example, a human resource information system (HRIS) that automatically collects login information, hours spent per project, performance appraisal ratings, and engagement in professional development activities generates primarily structured information in the form of count and numeric rating scale information. Social media can also produce structured data that is useful to human resource professionals. For example, the number of postings and/or comments employees have made on a company's internal social media portal that are recorded in the company's database. Additionally, an organization's application portal has the potential to continually collect survey data on applicants, allowing human resource analysts to quickly and easily identify the most relevant predictors of future job success and inform the decisions of selection professionals. These are just two examples of the use of structured data within HR.

Unstructured data, by contrast, are information that are not organized in a pre-defined manner and do not reside in fixed fields (Landers et al., 2015). This type of information is estimated to represent 80% of big data that is being generated (Hurwitz, Nuget, Halper, & Kaufman, 2015). Commonly analyzed unstructured data include numeric, text, audio, visual, and location information that are presented on social media. Pictures uploaded on SNS or the comments posted on companies' websites also constitute unstructured data. While human resource and research professionals are aware of the potential insight that can be gleaned from these unstructured sources, traditional methods of organizing and making sense of this data are extraordinarily onerous. For example, in order to sift through and conduct any analysis on this type of information could require someone to go through this information and organize it into fixed fields (i.e., turn unstructured data into structured data). Computer programs can now help to automate this process and help to systematically organize the type of unstructured data. For example, SNSs profiles—both external (e.g., Twitter) and internal (e.g., company intranet)—present a rich source of unstructured data in the form of text posts. Analyzing unstructured data on social media can reveal users attitudes, emotions, and even enduring characteristics such as personality (e.g., Park et al., 2014; Schwartz et al., 2013). Adding the collection, organization, and analysis of social media profile unstructured information to an organization's human resource metrics can result in meaningful flags/correlates for existing personnel data, provide better predictors for important work outcomes such as employee attrition or satisfaction, or can be used to develop outcome measures such as employee engagement or organizational commitment.

Semi-structured data, unsurprisingly, involve a mix of features of both structured and unstructured data. McKinsey Global Institute (2011) defines semi-structured data as data that "do not conform to fixed fields but contain tags and other markers to separate data elements." One example of semi-structured data would be the skills appearing on job candidates' LinkedIn profiles. When a user begins to type in a skill or competency that they feel would be relevant to employers, LinkedIn provides suggestions of skills with similar names (e.g., if someone typed in "math," LinkedIn would suggest "Mathematics," "Mathematical Modeling," "Applied Mathematics"). This common tag language facilitates easier comparisons across individuals (an important feature of structured data) while still allowing for unique entry (an important feature of unstructured data). Resumes could also be thought of as semi-structured data because they typically contain elements that allow comparison across individuals (e.g., past job tenure) while also containing free-form, unstructured text information (e.g., past job descriptions), although keyword tagging within a software program can create more structure here (Inmon & Nesavich, 2007).

These three types of data are probably familiar to practitioners and researchers who are accustomed to collecting and using information tests, Likert-type rating scales, and open-ended comments. In this sense, the type of information big data being generated are not necessarily new, but a restatement of the types of qualitative and quantitative data that researchers and human resource professionals have been using to make employment decisions. What is unique about this type of information is that volume, variety, and velocity of information that is now being generated and the technology that allows for the collection, integration, and analysis of an amount of this data.

7.2.4 Analytics: Making Sense of Big Data

As noted earlier, the current chapter takes the view that collecting large amounts of information (i.e., big data) and making sense of that information (i.e., analytics) are separate concepts. As with the term "big data," there is no universally accepted definition of analytics. One popular definition that summarizes the main idea of data analytics is the *science of examining raw data with the purpose of drawing conclusions about that information* (e.g., Myerson, 2015; Vishal, 2013). While this definition is one that certainly allows users to make sense out of big data, its application is certainly not limited to big data, nor does it distinguish analytics from other quantitative methods, such as statistics, use to make sense of information.

As a solution, the authors of this chapter propose that analytics refers to a collection of computer-automated algorithms and methods that follow a set of parameters defined and monitored by the user that are used to interpret, describe, and identify patterns within and between structured and unstructured data. While many of the algorithms (e.g., ordinary least squares regression, maximum likelihood factor analysis, agglomerative cluster analysis) and methods (e.g., Q-sort, coding of narrative information) are essentially the same as those typically used by human resource researchers and professionals on "small" data (e.g., traditional test, survey, and performance appraisal data), the introduction of computer automation and machine learning allows for these algorithms and methods to handle the volume, velocity, and variety of big data. Thus, analytics, which can be applied to big and small data alike, allows human resource researchers and professionals to make use of their structured and unstructured data in ways that were previously too onerous for the typical quantitative and qualitative methods.

This section will provide a brief overview of four types of analytics (descriptive, diagnostic, predictive, and prescriptive) that can be applied to human resource data to help assist in employment decisions. These four types of analytics represent a continuum of techniques that can be applied to structured and unstructured data and are often integrated into an analytic maturation model, which begins with descriptive and ends with predictive analytics. This maturation model represents the manner in which an organization can use data to drive business decisions. Organizations are thought to reach maturity in this model when they can successfully leverage all four types of analytics capabilities in their decision-making processes (Cech, Spaulding, & Cazier, 2015a, 2015b).

Descriptive analytics essentially answers the question "what happened?" The goal of this type of analytics is to understand what happened in the past (Cech et al., 2015a, 2015b). This is the simplest form of analytics and is the most commonly used by organizations, with over 90 % of companies reporting some use and 35 % reporting consistent use (CI&T, 2014). It is most useful for summarizing information and when looking for patterns within the data. For example, human resource professionals who use HRIS systems encounter descriptive analytics in the form of dashboard reports that inform them of the number of applicants who have applied, the demographic breakdown of those applicants, and the number of those individuals who have moved through the selection process. Human resource professionals and researchers are likely familiar with this type of analysis as basic statistics such as measures of central tendency (e.g., mean and median) and dispersion (e.g., range and standard deviation). Techniques such as principal components and cluster analysis are included in this type of analytics. However, descriptive analytics are not limited to numeric data.

Descriptive analytics can also be conducted on text. Text analytics, which digests bodies of text and analyzes trends in writing, is a particularly salient example of descriptive analytics because it allows the summarization and presentation of a large body of text information (Powers, Bergman, & Cazier, 2015). There are a variety of open- and closed-vocabulary computational linguistics techniques that can be used to identify common themes or categories within a large body of text. As such, human resource professionals and researchers now stand to benefit from analyzing text because often the most telling information about a problem cannot always be captured by a numeric value or a 1–5 survey response. For example, in the course of reporting workplace safety violations, employees are often encouraged to write out open-ended comments that may do a better job of describing the issue than survey-style or checklist data (i.e., they can include contextual information about an issue). In the same vein, text analytic software can be used to examine case notes added to a database in call-centers, potentially allowing the early identification of employee detachment. Text analytics can also be used to identify if an overall positive or negative sentiment is being conveyed in the words that are used (e.g., Blei, Ng, & Jordan, 2003; Grimmer & Stewart, 2013; Thelwall, Buckley, Paltoglou, Cai, & Kappas, 2010). Recruiters can use text analytics to examine resumes to access relevant experience or identify grammar quality across a large number of cover letters and resumes. Some organizations are using text analytics to assess a variety of characteristics of job applicants and create profiles that assess applicants' skills, personality, interests, and attitudes (e.g., Axelson, 2014; Waxer, 2013).

When the goal is to go beyond summarization, and organizations want to understand why a certain event occurred or why a trend is showing up in the data, organizations move to diagnostic analytics (Cech et al., 2015a, 2015b). Diagnostic analytics essentially answer the question "why did this happen?" and look at patterns between variables to determine the strength of the relationship between various concepts. Used consistently by 5 % of organizations (CI&T, 2014), this form of analytics is one step higher in the analytic maturation model because it is concerned with understanding what is causing a pattern or trend to show up in the data (Banerjee, Bandvopadhyay, & Archarya, 2015). Results from descriptive analytics along with other forms of raw data are often used as input or as outcomes in diagnostic analytics. Diagnostic analytics might use statistical procedures such as multiple regression to determine what is predicting employee satisfaction, turnover, and/or performance in their organization. In another example, the incidence of worker's compensation claims could be analyzed through a diagnostic lens to indicate what factors most frequently lead to workplace injuries

While descriptive and diagnostic analytics examine what happened in the past, the goal of predictive analytics is to determine what's going to happen in the future using data from the past (Cech et al., 2015a, 2015b). Essentially, predictive analytics answers the question "what is going to happen?" Because these types of analyses often require more extensive resources and personnel with a higher level of expertise, less than 1 % of organizations regularly use predictive analytic methods (CI&T, 2014). Predictive analytics builds upon the ability of diagnostic analytics to identify causes and attempts to use that information to predict future outcomes. As an example, a company may first analyze its workforce to determine the most important qualities of a productive employee (diagnostic analytics), but they then take a step further and use those qualities to develop an algorithm to assign job applicants a "fit score" based on the extent to which the applicant displays those qualities on their social media profiles. Predictive analytics include a series of techniques with which many human resource professionals and researchers are familiar (i.e., regression forecasting models and propensity scoring), but can also include computer simulations which allows decision-makers to determine how various strategies will perform in the future through the examination of alternative simulated scenarios. This simulation analysis could be particularly helpful to human resource professionals in workforce planning.

The final stage in the analytic maturation model is prescriptive analytics. This stage is a synergy between descriptive, diagnostic, and predictive analytics and suggests an optimal way to handle a current situation (Bertolucci, 2013). That is, prescriptive analytics combines business rules with the results from the other three analytic types to compare the outcomes of various situations being encountered and proactively recommends or takes a course of action (Cech et al., 2015a, 2015b). This is the most advanced type of analytics with only 3 % of businesses reporting use (Ingram Micro, 2015). The primary advantage of prescriptive analytics is that it can render near real-time decisions based on previous trends, business rules, and the vast array of information that is available. For example, in the realm of personnel selection, prescriptive analytics can take all of the information from an applicant's selection battery, apply predetermined business rules, and the algorithms from the first three types of analytics, and make a decision if that individual should pass through to the next hurdle in a selection process.

An all-encompassing application of big data and analytics would be to use data from a variety of sources and all four analytic types to make employment decisions. For example, a job-seeker could complete an online application that consists of a weighted application blank, basic work history information, work sample, and a resume. This private data could be then combined with the data exhaust from the application portal (e.g., amount of time taken to complete the tasks in the work sample or answer-specific questions in the application blank) and data automatically requested from public sources (e.g., criminal history and driving record), and information scraped from community sources (e.g., Facebook, Twitter, and LinkedIn). Descriptive analytics could then be conducted on the unstructured data collected to identify applicant characteristics and qualities not captured by the structured data. This applicant information could then be combined with an organizations performance data and diagnostic analytics could be used to determine the predictive value of this information. Predictive analytics could then use these results combined with publicly available economic and forecast data to determine a likelihood of success for this job candidate and the predicted tenure with the company. Finally, prescriptive analytics could use all of this information and make an employment decision on this job-seeker without a human resource professional personally examining an individual's application materials.

While this potentially sounds like a distant future reality, these types of applications are currently happening in the area of human resources. The next section provide a more in-depth discussion some of these applications followed by a discussion of the challenges and potential unforeseen consequences of using big data and analytics when making employment decisions.

7.3 Social Media Data, Analytics, Recruiting, and Selection

7.3.1 Social Media and Recruiting

Social media has changed the way that recruiters find and attract applicants to their organizations. It used to be that recruiters worked their sources, made phone calls, sent emails, or looked through paper contacts in order to develop contact lists (O'Brien, 2014). Recruiters can now look through social media and SNS in particular (e.g., LinkedIn, Facebook, and Twitter) to find potential candidate pools from which to recruit. In fact, the majority of organizational recruiters indicate that they use LinkedIn (94 %), Facebook (66 %), and Twitter (52 %) for recruiting (Jobvite, 2014). The activities that recruiters engage in vary from platform to platform, but include activities such as searching for and contacting candidates, keeping tabs on potential candidates, and posting job openings.

While a number of recruiters report still looking through social media platforms in search of talent themselves, the combination of social media, big data, and analytics now offers a way to automate that process. This automation can be rather simplistic (e.g., just using descriptive analytics) or rather mature (e.g., using prescriptive analytics) and can combine structured and unstructured data from social media to help recruiters identify a viable pool of potential applicants. An example of a rather simple, yet effective, use of social media data and analytics is a large chain of US supermarkets that uses Facebook and Twitter to target recruiting campaigns to reach people in ZIP codes near stores that are hiring (Robb, 2014). Other organizations use a more sophisticated analytic strategy to identify potential applicants. For instance, in the recruitment of computer programmers, one recruiting company analyzes information regarding the skills that programmers report having on LinkedIn, and the language they use on professional networking sites in reference to different types of technology to identify, target, and recruit programmers for variety of clients (Anders, 2011; Richtel, 2013).

Some companies use a more mature analytic process and only pull data from one social media source (e.g., Facebook or LinkedIn). Other technology recruiting companies combine information from multiple SNS and online sources (Axelson, 2014; O'Brien, 2014; Waxer, 2013). For example, many companies scan multiple social media profiles, in some cases up to 50 profiles on different sites, and use descriptive analytics to compile a "super-profile" for thousands of job candidates. These "super-profiles" contain information such as individuals' job titles, skills, experience, and contact information and psychographic information such as attitudes and interests (Waxer, 2013). These companies then work with organizations and use diagnostic analytics to develop "fit" scores identify candidates with that have the background suitable to open positions and similar attributes to the current employees (Axelson, 2014; O'Brien, 2014). Other recruiting companies go a step further and use descriptive, diagnostic, and predictive analytics to examine over 70 variables from 300 million social profiles and flag candidates that are likely to change jobs in the next 3 months (Waxer, 2013). In analyzing this vast amount of information, these technology companies use prescriptive analytics to help automate the decision-making process and identify the best possible candidates for a job opening.

It is easy to see why organizations are beginning to embrace this use of big data, analytics, and social media to assist in their recruiting. The combination of these technologies and methods allow organizations to recruit from a wider applicant pool. Some technology and recruiting companies even explicitly promote the ability to recruit a diverse applicant pool and help employers increase their diversity. Once organizations have developed this rich applicant pool through automated recruiting techniques, social media data and analytics can also be used to help streamline and improve the selection process.

7.3.2 *Social Media and Selection*

Organizations are also turning to information posted by users on social media to help make better hiring decisions. It is well known that job candidates engage in a series of impression management techniques during the selection process. Research has shown that the use of different impression management techniques can have an influence on employment decisions and hiring recommendations (e.g., Kacmar, Delery, & Ferris, 1992; Rosenfeld, 1997). Thus, getting to know the "real" person is desirable when attempting to assess the extent to which an applicant will fit with the job and/or the company's organization culture. This is where hiring managers and some human resource professionals believe that information gleaned from social media can provide an enhanced and unfiltered look at individuals' background, personality, expertise, and attitude (e.g., Florentine, 2014; Urshel, 2012).

One of the larger concerns about personality and its use in selection revolves around the "fake-ability" of personality measures. When applying for a job, applicants may be highly aware of the organization's expectations for its employees and intentionally adjust their responses to be more favorable in the eyes of the organization in an effort to enhance their chances of being hired (Heggestad, Morrison, Reeve, & McCloy, 2006; Mueller-Hanson, Heggestad, & Thornton III, 2003; Ones & Viswesvaran, 1998). To offset these concerns, organizations are looking for alternative personality measures to confirm, or even replace, self-report personality questionnaires (e.g., measuring personality in a job interview; Van Iddekinge, Raymark, & Roth, 2005). One potential way organizations have found to gain additional information about job applicants' personality is through their surveillance of applicants' social media pages.

In essence, using social media information to assess individual attributes is simply an extension of previous work examining the validity of rating such attributes based on behavioral artifacts that require personal knowledge of, or interaction with, the person being rated. For example, observer ratings of personality have been obtained based on photographs (Naumann, Vazire, Rentfrow, & Gosling, 2009; Vazire, Naumann, Rentfrow, & Gosling, 2008), living and working spaces (Gosling, Ko, Mannarelli, & Morris, 2002), personal possessions (Burroughs, Drews, & Hallman, 1991), creative writing samples (Küfner, Back, Nestler, & Egloff, 2010), self-selected e-mail addresses (Back, Schmukle, & Egloff, 2008), e-mail messages (Gill, Oberlander, & Austin, 2006), visual online representations of the self (a.k.a. avatars; Bélisle & Bodur, 2010), and personal websites (Marcus, Machilek, & Schütz, 2006; Vazire & Gasling, 2004). These ratings have been shown to be reliable and to significantly correlate with self-report measures of personality. Behaviors on social media can be thought of as the same type of "behavioral residue" that is left behind in other situations. However, unlike the other situations in which this "residue" has been in observed, information on social media covers a wider variety of behaviors and is continually updated.

This unfettered and continual self-disclosure on social media has led many human resource professional to believe that social media may allow for accurate personality inference. This belief comes from the generally accepted premise that people project a more polished and positive portrait of themselves shine in the strong and more "professional" situations inherent to the selection process (e.g., interviews, resumes, self-rated assessments), but let the let their "real" persona out on "personal" SNS, such as Facebook or Twitter (Urshel, 2012). Indeed, some argue that information on social media, even information on "professional" SNS such as LinkedIn, accurately reflects the "real" person because users' social media network connections can challenge and/or correct inaccurate information (Davison, Maraist, & Bing, 2011) and because putting out fake information on social media run counter to the basic purpose of social media platforms (Kluemper, Rosen, & Mossholder, 2012). This perspective is supported by research showing that ratings of personality gleaned from users' social media profiles more closely aligned with the user's actual personality than with the user's self-reported "ideal" version of themselves (Back et al., 2010). Other studies have shown that users of "personal" SNS tend to engage in an unusually high level of self-disclosure (Naaman, Boase, & Lai, 2010).

It is easy to see why some human resource professionals believe that sites like Facebook, Twitter, and Google + allow employers to get a glimpse of their applicants outside the confines of the information they collect during the traditional selection process and provided valuable insight into what these individuals would be like to work with on the job. Indeed, a growing number of employers (52 %) are using social media to research job candidates (CareerBuilder, 2015). As with recruiting, the overwhelming number of social media profiles and online information available about a job applicant makes the union of big data and analytics to help making hiring decisions seem intuitive. However, a review of the industry revealed that, when compared to the number of companies that disclose the use of social media data for recruiting, there are fewer companies that publically disclose the use of social media data to assist with selection decisions. While the exact reason for this is not known, one possible explanation is the legal implications for using social media data in hiring decisions (e.g., Davison et al., 2011; Society for Human Resource Management, 2015).

However, social media data does not represent the bulk of the data that organizations use to inform decisions: the vast majority of technology companies that are using big data and analytics in the selection process use information from social media only as a part of the information they input into their predictive and prescriptive analytic algorithms. For example, one technology company offers a software tool that assesses candidates by examining half a billion data points on everything from gas prices to national and local unemployment rates in combination with their social media usage (Marrs, 2014). Big data and analytics are most often used in the hiring process with private, in-house data. Analytics are used on these data to help organizations select the best employees for open positions ranging from call-center operators to department store cosmetics department sales staff to information technology professionals (Bloomberg, 2011; Kutik, 2014; Pearlstein, 2014). While there are a number of issues surrounding hiring managers manually scanning social media profiles when making employment decisions (see Davison et al., 2011), it appears that this is the primary way social media data is being integrated into the selection process.

An emerging line of computational linguistics research could possibly automate and improve the scanning of social media profiles to extract information traditionally contained in an applicant's selection measures. This line of research uses extracts unstructured data in the form of the words and phrases that users post on SNS and other social media sites, more specifically Facebook, and then uses text analytics to examine this information. This line of research has steadily increased its accuracy in the assessment of the five factor model of personality (see Park et al., 2014; Schwartz et al., 2013). While this line of research looks promising and could be used to more accurately assess "fakeable" characteristics such as personality and attitudes, more research is needed before these techniques can be used in selection (see the section on Challenges and Unforeseen Consequences of Big Data and Analytics).

One of the most promising ways to integrate social media technology into the selection process is to use the information produced by an organization's internal social network platform. More and more companies, large and small, are turning to internal SNS to solve problems faster, share information more quickly and efficiently among internal and external employees, develop new and improved products more efficiently, and redesign organizational business processes using in-house software that often resembles Facebook's easy-to-learn style (Huertas, 2012; Mullaney, 2012). While this internal social networking platform can make work more effective and efficient for the employees, it also provides human resource researchers and professionals with structured and unstructured data to objectively assess work processes, employee engagement, performance, and job satisfaction.

Using big data collection techniques to capture this internal social networking information along with internal other data could give human resource professionals and researchers access to unprecedented objective process and performance metrics. Analyzing this type of data with modern analytic techniques will allow human resource researchers and practitioners to examine relationships in ways they have not been able to do in the past. In the area of selection, for example, traditional methods of validating selection batteries rely on a retrospective approach. That is, both traditional predictive and concurrent validation strategies require data to be collected and analyzed to determine how useful a selection system has been. This approach provides an extremely useful, albeit retrospective, examination of the validity of a company's selection system.

These traditional validation strategies can be improved through the implementation of big data and analytics. Specifically, companies capture structured and unstructured data from employees' emails, computer logs, internal social media and intranets, and project tracking timesheets. Descriptive and diagnostic analytics can then be run on this data to develop performance, engagement, and satisfaction metrics. Diagnostic and predictive analytics can then be used with these metrics and the company's traditional selection system data to continually validate the selection battery. Further, these engagement and performance metrics can be combined with traditional employee culture and job satisfaction survey data and, using diagnostic and predictive analytics, help develop a model of employee morale and retention. These data and analyses would even allow for a more valid assessment of person-environment fit during the hiring process. Prescriptive analytics could then be used to help identify, in near real-time, employees or departments that have low morale and are at risk to leave the company and propose interventions that could help improve the situation.

Finally, all this information can be combined with employee compensation data, HRIS project tracking information, and the financial data from the various internal and external projects on which employees spend their time. Linkage or path-analysis help can then be used to a return on investment model. This model would help quantify the financial return on a variety of human resource activities, including recruiting and selection. Given that only about one in five human resource professionals use data and analytics to assess return on investment (Chaudhary, Subramanian, Sinha, & Bhattacharya, 2012), using internal social media data in combination with existing company data and analytics can both improve human resources function and provide clear evidence for human resources' financial impact on an organization's bottom line.

7.4 Challenges and Unforeseen Consequences of Big Data and Analytics

Despite the potential upside of using big data, analytics, and social media for employment decisions, there are some logistical challenges that need to be considered and addressed before these benefits can be fully realized. There are also some extremely important, and potentially unforeseen, consequences of using social media information when making employment decisions that need to be carefully considered and thought through. This section highlights a few of the technical and logistical challenges and legal, ethical, and social implications of using big data, analytics, and social media when making human resource decisions.

7.4.1 Scale and Timeliness of Data

If an organization wishes to undertake the task of monitoring and assessing applicants' social media activity they will be continually faced with the issue of scale. That is, staying up-to-date on the ever-changing types and amounts of information being produced in the online environment is an uphill battle. Given that social media features are continually changing, the types of data being generated are also continually changing. These rapid changes mean that organizations that wish to incorporate social media data must constantly evolve, refine, and adapt to the types and amounts of information they are collecting, cleaning, and storing. Continuous changes also mean that these organizations need to continually validate and revalidate their analytic algorithms to ensure the accuracy and validity of the conclusions they are producing.

In addition to the scale of the data, the timeliness of the information is also equally important. Due to the frequency with which people use social media platforms and the subsequent speed with which data is generated on social media sites, timeliness is of particular concern when considering the use of big data. Organizations must be careful to ensure that any data collected from social media platforms that is used to make employment decisions is not only accurate, but up-to-date. Different SNS will vary in the rate at which information is generated and updated. For example, LinkedIn activity is fairly static, with users updating their pages with mastered skills and making connections with other professionals. LinkedIn users may also share business-relevant links with other users with whom they are connected. Unlike LinkedIn, data on Twitter and Facebook pages is often constantly being updated by users. By using such dynamic and fluctuating sources of information about their job candidates, organizations run the risk of not being able to efficiently organize and effectively analyze social media data in a timely manner. If organizations begin to fall behind on data collection and cleaning and start to make decisions with out-of-date information, the accuracy and validity of those employment decisions may falter.

7.4.2 Issues of Privacy, Consent, and Accountability

Privacy concerns surrounding big data and its use in human resources leave practitioners in a legal and ethical quagmire. While organizations currently use massive amounts of data simultaneously collected from a variety of different sources, including social media platforms, the ethicality and legality of such practice is unclear (Miller & Weckert, 2000). For example, using social media when making employment decisions may be considered an invasion of privacy (Brandenburg, 2008; Clark & Roberts, 2010), defamation (Davison, Maraist, Hamilton, & Bing, 2012), or a violation of the Fair Credit Reporting Act and/or the Stored Communications Act (Smith & Kidder, 2010). IBM recently identified several important factors to consider when collecting and using applicant data, including context, consent, and accountability (Chessell, 2014).

First, IBM highlights the importance of considering the original purpose for collecting the data, or the data's context (Chessell, 2014). For example, job-seekers who engage in social media often fail to consider the implications of their latest politically incorrect tweet or posted pictures of a particularly bacchanal evening, yet these same people carefully groom their LinkedIn page in the hopes of attracting a future employer. If job-seekers were aware that potential employers may view their Facebook profiles or activity on Twitter, hopeful employees would most assuredly take additional measures to censor behaviors or comments that would be unpopular (or illegal) in the workplace. While some people recognize the fact that employers are increasingly using social media to make employment decisions and, therefore, take care to limit controversial content on their social media pages (Florentine, 2014; Urshel, 2012), others are lulled into a false sense of security with platforms' security features.

On a similar vein, IBM also suggests examining the idea of consent and the options available to the generators of data. In the case of social media, users have moderate control over privacy settings and the access that outside entities have to social media users' personal information (Chessell, 2014). Despite security controls, organizations and outside individuals are able to gain access to individuals' data with relative ease through the use of security bypasses and the majority of users' lenient privacy settings. The Electronic Communications Privacy Act (ECPA) of 1986 prohibits the intentional interception of "any wire, oral or electronic communication"; however, the ECPA does include a business use exemption, which allows for the monitoring of email and phone calls provided that several elements, including consent, are present (Beesley, 2012). What is not known is how this act extends to social media. Thus, several legal questions remain: *Is there an implied lack of consent when users choose to attempt to protect their personal information? Or are lax security settings the equivalent of applicants' or employees' consent?*

While the issue of consent has potential legal and ethical implications, there are also social and cultural implications for using social media information when making employment decisions. Specifically, there is anecdotal evidence that employees have a negative reaction to having their digital footprints monitored and evaluated at the workplace. For example, one company used electronic monitoring, big data, and analytics to assess the extent to which employees' health and insurance rates could be improved by monitoring anonymous usage rates of the company gym. The reaction of the employees was so strong and negative the company abandons its plans to implement this strategy when the program was only in the pilot phase (Such & Tippins, 2015). Others suggest that by electronically looking over employees' shoulders, companies can stifle creativity and hurt the long-term viability of the business (Kumar, 2015). Finally, empirical research examining applicants' perceptions and reactions to employers using social media data for hiring decisions shows companies' usage of social media as a screening tool is related to increased perceptions of invasion of privacy (Stoughton, Thompson, & Meade, 2015). These invasions of privacy perceptions in turn link to higher intentions to litigation, lower perceptions of fairness, and lower organizational attraction.

Accountability is another important factor to consider when collecting applicant information (Chessell, 2014). When organizations gain access to individuals' personal information, data security, concerns develop. For example, it is currently unknown how the Fair Credit Reporting Act applies to information gleaned from publically available social media information. Questions involving organizations' obligations to explain decisions made on the basis of social media content also surface. *As with credit scores, are organizations required to provide applicants with any negative findings and give the applicants an opportunity to explain questionable behavior or comments posted on social media platforms?* Along with providing applicants with the opportunity to explain their social media activity, concerns about the protection of this data also arise. For instance, it is unknown the extent to which the Stored Communications Act is relevant to information scored from social media platforms. *When organizations collect or receive applicant data gathered from social media, do they assume responsibility for protecting this information?* The answers to these questions, and many more, remain largely unanswered.

7.4.3 Inconsistent and Incomplete Data

Due to the complex nature of big data, numerous challenges may present themselves throughout the process of collecting, cleaning, and analyzing big data. These issues become even more salient when scouring data from social media and include data heterogeneity and possible incomplete or inconsistent data. Structured and unstructured data in a variety of different forms from a variety of different social media platforms must be integrated and coded in some meaningful way before any analytics can be conducted. Integrating these various forms of data, even using computer automation, can be time-consuming and challenging.

The amount and types of data that organizations receive may be also inconsistent. Take, for instance, the example of using external social media data during employee recruitment or selection. If organizations wish to analyze information on the social media sites of their job candidates, they will likely run into incomplete or inconsistent data. For example, job candidates who do use social media likely have a different number of profiles across different platforms. Even in the unlikely event that all of an organization's candidates happen to use the same platform(s), they will likely use social media sites with varying frequencies. Applicants will also differ in the level of their activity on the sites, what kind of information they share, how much of that information is viewable to the organization due to varied privacy settings, and have different reasons for using these online services. Thus, direct comparisons across applicants may prove to be difficult, if not impossible.

The consistency of the information available and the ability to make direct comparisons across job candidates is an important issue. A recent review of federal and state employment litigation cases revealed that one of most legally risky employment practice were ones in which an inconsistent application of the selection process was utilized (Williams, Shaffer, & Ellis, 2013). While some companies scan multiple social media sites to produce a "super profile," it is currently not known how the absence of information from one or more social media profiles might impact the accuracy and consistency of the assessments that are being used in recruiting and employment decisions. With regard to the inconsistent use of the same social media sites, it is not known what impact this differential usage has on the selection process. For example, a number of recruiting and selection companies indicate that during their collection of social media information they eliminate any protected class information. This practice is done to ensure that information which is illegal to use in employment decisions is not directly used in the analytic algorithm. However, research has suggested that usage on social media sites co-vary with protected class information such as sex, age, and race/ethnicity (Bergman, Bergman, Whitaker, & Thompson, 2014; Van Iddekinge, Lanivich, Roth, & Junco, 2013). Thus, human resource professionals using social media, either by manual or computer-aided scanning, for applicant screening appear to be running an increased risk of litigation by using information and engaging in practices that could result in adverse impact.

7.4.4 Data and Information Accuracy

Beside issues of consent and responsibility, organizations can also run into issues with "dirty data," or misinformation (Hoovers.com, n.d.). In their quest to use all of the data available to them, organizations can fall prey to dirty data's trap, which is estimated to cost the US economy over $3 trillion per annum. Inaccurately measured or irrelevant data (i.e., dirty data) can result in erroneous interpretations, leaving organizations with a damaged reputation, wasted resources, and the potential for bad business decisions. As a response to the weakness of misinformation, or dirty data, proponents of big data analytics have suggested that factors other than big data's "3 Vs" need to be considered (Saporito, 2014). One popular proposed factor is "Veracity." "Veracity" refers to the accuracy and fidelity of the data (Paxata, n.d.)

The suggestion of this fourth "V" of big data draws users' attention to the importance of ensuring the quality of the data that is collected and used, especially if the data will be used to make important decisions.

"Veracity" is important for human resource professionals to consider is when algorithms are used to scrap social media to gather information about job candidates. Given the commonality of some names, organizations must be careful when gathering applicant social media profiles to ensure that they are gathering information from the correct profiles. Similar to the difficulty that individuals may have when their names are the same as someone on the government's "no fly" list, some applicants may be unfairly held accountable for the negative actions of a different person with the same name. For example, a quick search on Facebook for any of the authors of this chapter will return more than 25 profiles with matching names. This illuminates the arduous task of ensuring that the correct applicant's social media page is being assessed.

This fourth "V" of big data can also be applied to information gleaned from social media through manual ratings or text analytics. These types of assessments are thought to provide a picture of a job applicant that is not available in numerical data or from traditional selection assessment. However, there are conflicting views regarding the "Veracity," or what human resource professionals and researchers refer to as measurement validity, of social media as an assessment of personality. Research using both manual assessments (Kluemper & Rosen, 2009; Kluemper et al., 2012; Van Iddekinge et al., 2013) and text analytics (Park et al., 2014; Schwartz et al., 2013) have found significant correlations between self-rated and social-media-based personality measurements. However, the magnitude of the correlations between the self-report measures and the manual (correlations ranging from 0.19. to 0.44) and text analytics (correlations ranging from 0.38 to 0.46) assessment of personality indicate a non-zero, but weak, relationship between these measures. These relatively weak relationships could call into question the construct validity of these social-media-based personality assessments.

The empirical evidence of the criterion-related validity of manual and text analytic assessments of personality is mixed. One empirical study found that social-media-based assessment provide academic and job performance (Kluemper et al., 2012) and provide inconsistent incremental validity over self-report assessments. Other empirical studies found no incremental validity of manual (Van Iddekinge et al., 2013) or text analytic (Rupayana, Puchalski, & Hedricks, 2015) assessment of personality. Together, these results call into the question the predictive validity of assessments made from social media profiles. More research and psychometric work is needed to determine if these types of social-media-based assessments could meet the reliability and validity standards recommended by the Equal Employment Opportunity Commission's (EEOC) Uniform Guidelines on Employee Selection Procedures and Society for Industrial and Organizational Psychology's (SIOP) Principles for the Validation and Use of Personnel Selection and withstand legal scrutiny if challenged. Given the two most legally dangerous selection devices and employment practices were those in which the selection device was not job related and an inconsistent application of the selection processes was utilized (Williams et al., 2013) and the questions about the missing or inconsistent data on social media and the validity of the assessments garnered from social media, human resource professionals should be cautious when utilizing data collected from social media for employment decisions. In fact, the Society for Human Resource Management (2015) explicitly cautions employers about using social media information for job screening.

7.5 Conclusions and Implications

Some claim that big data and analytics will revolutionize human resources. In fact, there are those that claim technology will take the "human" out of human resource all together (e.g., Gaebler, 2012). Others, including the authors of this chapter, take a more tempered approach and believe that the increased use of data to assist in making employment decisions will, overall, improve the discipline. There is little doubt, however, that technological advances in the way that data are collected make it easier to collect information on current employees than ever before. The exploding popularity of social media combined with the computation advances in analytics has also made it easier to collect and make sense of data from job candidates before they ever formally apply to an organization. However, while the increased availability and use of data can help improve employment decisions, blind and unchecked use of this information could lead to poor employment decisions and have unintended consequences.

Many human resource professionals, industrial–organizational psychologists, and social scientists are often intimidated by big data and analytics. One of the goals of this chapter was to help educate these groups about the basics of big data and analytics and show that the majority of these techniques are extremely similar to the "small" data and the quantitative and qualitative methods with which they are familiar. In fact, we argue that instead of being threatened or intimidated, human resource professionals and researchers should embrace the increased reliance on technology, data, and analytics as this only emphasizes the importance of the skills and training that human resource professionals and researchers possess. While it is undeniable that technology has the capability to enhance human resource decision-making, the strong emphasis on technology also highlights the importance of asking the right questions, having the right measures, using the proper analyses, correctly interpreting the results, and knowing the business and legal environment in which results will be used. Human resource professionals, in particular industrial–organizational psychologists, are perfectly poised to address all of these issues.

Rather than being intimidated, we strongly encourage human resource professionals and researchers to partner with computer science, computer information systems, and information technology professionals and researchers to help guide and shape the future of human resource management. These technology experts know the technical and computational processes involved in data collection, storage, cleaning, and processing of large amounts of information. In addition, information technology professionals are well versed in data security and information technology regulatory issues. Human resource professionals and industrial–organizational psychologists, on the other hand, bring knowledge of the legal and ethical issues surrounding the use of big data in organizations, and they can help inform the information technology professionals regarding what data from current and prospective employees should and should not be collected and/or analyzed. Additionally, human resource professionals and industrial–organizational psychologists understand the broader implications that processes and procedures can have on an organization's culture and the powerful force that a negative or mistrustful work environment can have on productivity and a company's bottom line. Together, the combination of these disciplines is a formidable force that can appropriately leverage the structured and unstructured data being produced by the five sources of big data.

Human resource professionals and industrial–organizational psychologists also possess the methodology knowledge and skills necessary to analyze and interpret big data results in the "messy social and psychological reality" that workplace and social media information represent (Kobylinski, 2012). Due to the extremely large sample sizes often associated with big data, there is an increased likelihood of finding significant relationships that are spurious and/or not practically useful. To avoid falling into such traps, it is imperative that a carefully planned and deductive scientific process be used when applying big data and analytics to business decisions (Conlin, 2014). This is consistent with the science-practitioner approach advocated by industrial–organizational psychologists. This deductive approach suggests that the process should begin by defining the research questions that need to be answered. Starting with research questions, rather than blindly trying to make assumptions about the data in question, can help avoid spurious correlations and misinterpretation of the results.

After the research questions have been formulated, hypotheses based on prior and/or newly developed theories should be formulated, and the data should then be empirically tested against these hypotheses. Data from multiple sources should be collected and robust analyses conducted. Results should be examined only after the theoretical hypotheses have been developed to avoid misinterpreting meaningless relationships, and results should be cautiously interpreted within the context of the research questions and the legal and business environment in which decisions will be made. These steps follow the basic scientific methodology that social scientists use to understand employee attitudes and behavior.

Human resource professionals and researchers, social scientists, and industrial–organizational psychologists are also trained in the proper measurement of psychological and cognitive concepts. This knowledge is particularly relevant to the application of big data and analytics to employment decisions as assessments and tests used in this area need to adhere to the EEOC's Uniform Guidelines and SIOP's Principles. Computer science, computer information systems, and information technology professionals are extremely good at ensuring that results at which they arrive are replicable and predict the appropriate outcomes. However, these technology experts do not have as strong of a background in the application of the scientific method and are generally not as familiar with the psychometric concepts. Thus, technology professionals might be more apt to utilize data gleaned from a variety of social media outlets for employment decisions because these data have been shown to relate to business-related metrics or have produced results in the field of marketing. However, human resource professionals and researchers look at the unknown criterion and construct-related validity of these assessments and are rightly cautious about using them to make employment decisions.

While understanding psychometrics and adhering to the scientific method of collecting information and running analyses will protect against committing research methodological, big data errors, many of the potential pitfalls associated with using data from social media are ethical or legal in nature. Here again, human resource professionals and industrial–organizational psychologists are well suited to help effectively and appropriately implement data from social media into employment decisions. Specifically, these fields have a working knowledge of the legal environment in which employment decisions are made. They also better understand the damage that can occur to an organization's reputation and culture if job candidates or employees believe their privacy is being invaded and that information is being collected and used in an unethical manner.

It is undeniable that the technological revolution that is big data, analytics, and social media is not going away and its application in human resources is likely to continue to grow. The authors of this chapter encourage human resource professionals and researchers to partner up with technology experts to help guide and shape the future use of technology in analytics in human resource management. While the increased use of data in making employment decisions is a positive trend, it is quite possible that having access to mo' data on job applicants and employees may lead to mo' problems.

References

Ahmad, I. (2014). *How much data is generated on social media every minute—Infographic.* [online] Digital Information World. Retrieved June 2, 2015, from http://www.digitalinformationworld.com/2014/04/data-never-sleeps-60-seconds-on-internet-infographic.html.

Anders, G. (2011). *The rare find: Reinventing recruiting* [online]. Bloomberg Business. Retrieved September 15, 2015, from http://www.bloomberg.com/bw/magazine/the-rare-find-reinventing-recruiting-10132011.html.

Axelson, M. (2014). *The candidate selfie: How to evaluate job skills using social networks* [online]. Skilled Up. Retrieved June 12, 2015, from http://www.skilledup.com/insights/the-candidate-selfie-how-to-evaluate-job-skills-using-social-networks.

Back, M. D., Schmukle, S. C., & Egloff, B. (2008). How extraverted is honey.bunny77@hotmail.de? Inferring personality from e-mail addresses. *Journal of Research in Personality, 42*, 1116–1122. doi:10.1016/j.jrp.2008.02.001.

Back, M. D., Stopfer, J. M., Vazire, S., Gaddis, S., Schmukle, S. C., Egloff, B., et al. (2010). Facebook profiles reflect actual personality, not self-idealization. *Psychological Science, 21*, 372–374.

Baker, D. B., Benjamin, J., & Ludy, T. (2000). The affirmation of the scientists-practitioner: A look back at Boulder. *American Psychologist, 55*(2), 241–247. doi:10.1037/0003-066X.55.2.241.

Banerjee, A., Bandvopadhyay, T., & Archarya, P. (2015). *Data analytics: Hyped up aspirations or true potential?* [online]. Retrieved June 8, 2015, http://www.vikalpa.com/pdf/articles/2013/04-Perspectives.pdf.

Beesley, C. (2012). Email, phone and social media monitoring in the workplace—Know your rights as an employer [online]. *Small Business Administration.* Retrieved March 14, 2015, from https://www.sba.gov/blogs/email-phone-and-social-media-monitoring-workplace-know-your-rights-employer.

Bélisle, J., & Bodur, H. O. (2010). Avatars as information: Perception of consumers based on their avatars in virtual worlds. *Psychology and Marketing, 27*, 741–765. doi:10.1002/mar.20354.

Bergman, S. M., Bergman, J. Z., Whitaker, B. G., & Thompson, K. (2014, May). Social media use by protected classes: Implications for adverse impact. In R. Landers (Chair) & G. Schmidt (Chair), *Social media in selection: Validity, applicant reactions, and legality*. Symposium session conducted at the annual Society for Industrial and Organizational Psychology Conference, Honolulu, HI.

Bersin, J. (2013). *Big data in human resources: A world of haves and have-nots* [online]. Forbes. Retrieved June 12, 2015, from http://www.forbes.com/sites/joshbersin/2013/10/07/big-data-in-human-resources-a-world-of-haves-and-have-nots/.

Bertolucci, J. (2013). *Prescriptive analytics and big data: Next big thing?* [online]. Information Week. Retrieved June 12, 2015, from http://www.informationweek.com/big-data/big-data-analytics/prescriptive-analytics-and-big-data-next-big-thing/d/d-id/1109537.

Blei, D. M., Ng, A. Y., & Jordan, M. I. (2003). Latent dirichlet allocation. *Journal of Machine Learning Research, 3*, 993–1022.

Bloomberg. (2011). *Bon-ton stores achieve greater sales performance with Kenexa* [online]. Bloomberg. Retrieved Mar 12, 2015, from http://www.bloomberg.com/apps/news?pid=newsarchive&sid=aL7_iAUGbicc.

Brandenburg, C. (2008). The newest way to screen job applicants: A social networker's nightmare. *Federal Communications Law Journal, 60*, 597–626.

Burroughs, W. J., Drews, D. R., & Hallman, W. K. (1991). Predicting personality from personal possessions: A self-presentational analysis. *Journal of Social Behavior and Personality, 6*(6), 147–163.

CareerBuilder. (2015). *More employers checking out candidates on social media* [online]. CareerBuilder. Retrieved March 14, 2015, from http://thehiringsite.careerbuilder.com/2015/05/14/employers-checking-candidates-social-media/.

Cech, T. G., Spaulding, T. J., & Cazier, J. A. (2015). *Applying business analytic techniques to increase educational attainment in the public school system.* 21st Americas Conference on Information Systems, Puerto Rico.

Cech, T. G., Spaulding, T. J., & Cazier, J. A. (2015, June) The data maturity model and application to secondary education. *Working Paper.*

Chaudhary, K., Subramanian, K. S., Sinha, V., & Bhattacharya, S. (2012). The contemporary framework on social media analytics as an emerging tool for behavior informatics, HR analytics and business process. *Management-Journal of Contemporary Management Issues, 2*, 65–84.

Chessell, M. (2014). *Ethics for big data and analytics* [online]. IBM Big Data Hub. Retrieved May 12, 2015, from http://www.ibmbigdatahub.com/sites/default/files/whitepapers_reports_file/TCG%20Study%20Report%20-%20Ethics%20for%20BD%26A.pdf.

CI&T United States. (2014). *The four types of analytics* [online]. CI&T. Retrieved June 6, 2015, from http://www.ciandt.com/card/four-types-of-analytics-and-cognition.

Clark, D. (2013). *How big data is transforming the hunt for talent* [online]. Jobvite. Retrieved June 12, 2015, from http://www.jobvite.com/wp-content/uploads/2014/10/JobviteSocialRecruiting_Survey2014.pdf.

Clark, L. A., & Roberts, S. J. (2010). Employer's use of social networking sites: A socially irresponsible practice. *Journal of Business Ethics, 95*, 507–525. doi:10.1007/s10551-010-0436-y.

Conlin, M. (2014). *Big data is worthless without big questions* [online]. LinkedIn Pulse. Retrieved May 12, 2015, from https://www.linkedin.com/pulse/20140903164100-306988-big-data-is-worthless-without-big-questions.

Davison, H. K., Maraist, C. C., Hamilton, R. H., & Bing, M. N. (2012). To screen or not to screen? Using the internet for selection decisions. *Employee Rights and Responsibilities Journal, 24*, 1–21. doi:10.1007/s10672-011-9178.

Davison, H. K., Maraist, C., & Bing, M. N. (2011). Friend or Foe? The promise and pitfalls of using social networking sites for HR decisions. *Journal of Business and Psychology, 26*, 153–159.

Di Martino, B., Aversa, R., Cretella, G., Esposito, A., & Kołodziej, J. (2014). Big data (lost) in the cloud. *International Journal Big Data Intelligence, 1*(1/2), 3.

Dumbill, E. (2012). *Volume, velocity, variety: What you need to know about big data* [online]. Forbes. Retrieved May 12, 2015, from http://www.forbes.com/sites/oreillymedia/2012/01/19/volume-velocity-variety-what-you-need-to-know-about-big-data/.

Florentine, S. (2014). *3 Ways to use social media to recruit better tech talent* [online]. CIO.com. Retrieved March 13, 2015, from http://www.cio.com/article/2855173/careers-staffing/3-ways-to-use-social-media-to-recruit-better-tech-talent.html.

Gaebler, K. (2012). The future of hiring: human resources, without the humans [online]. The Atlantic. Retrieved June 14, 2015, from http://www.theatlantic.com/business/archive/2012/02/the-future-of-hiring-human-resources-without-the-humans/252518/.

Galer, S. (2013). *How analytics is transforming HR into a strategic business partner* [online]. Forbes. Retrieved June 12, 2015, from http://www.forbes.com/sites/sap/2013/08/15/how-analytics-is-transforming-hr-into-a-strategic-business-partner/.

George, G., Haas, M., & Pentland, A. (2014). From the editors: Big data and management. *Academy of Management Journal, 57*, 321–326.

Gill, A. J., Oberlander, J., & Austin, E. (2006). Rating e-mail personality at zero acquaintance. *Personality and Individual Differences, 40*, 497–507. doi:10.1016/j.paid.2005.06.027.

Gosling, S. D., Ko, S. J., Mannarelli, T., & Morris, M. E. (2002). A room with a cue: Personality judgments based on offices and bedrooms. *Journal of Personality and Social Psychology, 82*, 379–398. doi:10.1037//0022-3514.82.3.379.

Grimmer, J., & Stewart, B. M. (2013). Text as data: The promise and pitfalls of automatic content analysis methods for political texts. *Political Analysis, 21*, 267–297. Retrieved from http://dx.doi.org/10.1093/pan/mps028.

Heggestad, E. D., Morrison, M., Reeve, C. L., & McCloy, R. A. (2006). Forced-choice assessments of personality for selection: Evaluating issues of normative assessment and faking resistance. *Journal of Applied Psychology, 91*, 9–24. doi:10.1037/0021-9010.91.1.9.

Hoovers.com. (n.d.). *The cost of dirty data* [online]. Hoover's. Retrieved May 12, 2015, from http://www.hoovers.com/lc/sales-marketing-education/cost-of-dirty-data.html.

Howley, D. (2015). *Woman allegedly fired for deleting app that let her boss track her movements 24/7* [online]. Yahoo. Retrieved Junev, 2015, from https://www.yahoo.com/tech/a-california-woman-claims-she-was-fired-for-118711413499.html.

Huertas, E. (2012). *Internal social networks: The return of new and improved intranets* [online]. Social Media Today. Retrieved March 6, 2015, from http://www.socialmediatoday.com/content/internal-social-networks-return-new-and-improved-intranets.

Hurwitz, J., Nuget, A. L., Halper, F., & Kaufman, M. (2015). *Unstructured data in a big data environment* [online]. Books for Dummies. Retrieved June 12, 2015, from http://www.dummies.com/how-to/content/unstructured-data-in-a-big-data-environment.html.

Ingram Micro. (2015). *Four types of big data analytics and examples of their use* [online]. Retrieved June 8, 2015, from http://www.ingrammicroadvisor.com/big-data/four-types-of-big-data-analytics-and-examples-of-their-use.

Inmon, W. H., & Nesavich, A. (2007). *Tapping into unstructured data: Integrating unstructured data and textual analytics into business intelligence*. Crawfordsville, IN: Prentice Hall.

Jobvite. (2014). *Social recruiting survey 2014* [online]. Jobvite. Retrieved February 26, 2015, from http://www.jobvite.com/wp-content/uploads/2014/10/JobviteSocialRecruiting_Survey2014.pdf.

Kacmar, K. M., Delery, J. E., & Ferris, G. R. (1992). Differential effectiveness of applicant impression management tactics on employment interview decisions. *Journal of Applied Social Psychology, 22*(16), 1250–1272.

Kaplan, A. M., & Haenlein, M. (2010). Users of the world, unite! The challenges and opportunities of Social Media. *Business Horizons, 53*, 59–68.

Katzell, R. A., & Austin, J. T. (1992). From then to now: The development of industrial-organizational psychology in the United States. *Journal of Applied Psychology, 77*(6), 803.

Kluemper, D. H., & Rosen, P. A. (2009). Future employment selection methods: Evaluating social networking web sites. *Journal of Managerial Psychology, 24*, 567–580.

Kluemper, D. H., Rosen, P. A., & Mossholder, K. W. (2012). Social networking websites, personality ratings, and the organizational context: More than meets the eye? *Journal of Applied Social Psychology, 42*, 1143–1172.

Kobylinski, P. (2012). *Why data science needs social science. And vice versa!* [online]. Persontyle. Retrieved May 12, 2015, from http://www.persontyle.com/datascienceandsoicalscience/.

Küfner, A. C. P., Back, M. D., Nestler, S., & Egloff, B. (2010). Tell me a story and I will tell you who you are! Lens model analyses of personality and creative writing. *Journal of Research in Personality, 44*, 427–435. doi:10.1016/j.jrp.2010.05.003.

Kumar, S. (2015). *Why monitoring employees' social media is a bad idea* [online]. Time. Retrieved March 14, 2015, from http://time.com/3894276/social-media-monitoring-work/.

Kutik, B. (2014). *Predictive analytics dominates my first HR tech conference* [online]. www.HREOnline.com. Retrieved May 12, 2015, from http://www.hreonline.com/HRE/view/story.jhtml?id=534357731.

Landers, R. N., Brusso, R. C., Cavanaugh, K. J., & Collmus, A. B. (2015). *A primer on theory-driven web scraping: Automatic extraction of big data from the internet for use in psychological research.* Unpublished manuscript.

Lohr, S. (2013). *Big data, trying to build better workers* [online]. NY Times. Retrieved June 12, 2015, from http://www.nytimes.com/2013/04/21/technology/big-data-trying-to-build-better-workers.html?pagewanted=all&_r=1.

Marcus, B., Machilek, F., & Schütz, A. (2006). Personality in cyberspace: Personal Web sites as media for personality expressions and impressions. *Journal of Personality and Social Psychology, 90*, 1014–1031. doi:10.1037/0022-3514.90.6.1014.

Marrs, B. (2014). *The amazing ways big data is now used in HR* [online]. Smart Data. Retrieved June 2, 2015, from http://smartdatacollective.com/bernardmarr/212431/how-big-data-changing-hr-forever.

Marrs, B. (2015). *The quantified workplace: Big data or big brother?* [online]. Forbes. Retrieved June 2, 2015, from http://www.forbes.com/sites/bernardmarr/2015/05/11/the-nanny-state-meets-the-quantified-workplace/.

McKinsey Global Institute. (2011). *Big data: The next frontier for innovation, competition, and productivity*. 1st ed. [ebook] McKinsey & Company. Retrieved May 7, 2015, from http://www.mckinsey.com/insights/business_technology/big_data_the_next_frontier_for_innovation.

Miller, S., & Weckert, J. (2000). Privacy, the workplace, and the internet. *Journal of Business Ethics, 28*(3), 255–265.

Muchinsky, P. M. (2011). *Psychology applied to work* (10th ed.). Summerfield, NC: Hypergraphic Press.

Mueller-Hanson, R., Heggestad, E. D., & Thornton, G. C., III. (2003). Faking and selection: Considering the use of personality from select-in and select-out perspectives. *Journal of Applied Psychology, 88*, 348–355. doi:10.1037/0021-9010.88.2.348.

Mullaney, T. (2012). *Social media is reinventing how business is done* [online]. USA Today. Retrieved March 6, 2015, from http://usatoday30.usatoday.com/money/economy/story/2012-05-14/social-media-economy-companies/55029088/1.

Myerson, P. A. (2015). *Supply chain and logistics management made easy: methods and applications for planning, operations, integration, control and improvement, and network design.* Upper Saddle River, NJ: FT Press. ISBN 0133994252.

Naaman, M., Boase, J., & Lai, C. H. (2010, February). *Is it really about me?: Message content in social awareness streams*. In Proceedings of the 2010 ACM conference on Computer Supported Cooperative Work (pp. 189–192). Retrieved June 14, 2015, from http://infolab.stanford.edu/~mor/research/naamanCSCW10.pdf.

Napper, C. (2014, May). *It's not you, it's me: Candidate selection process drop-out rates.* Symposium session conducted at the annual Society for Industrial and Organizational Psychology Conference, Honolulu, HI.

Naumann, L. P., Vazire, S., Rentfrow, P. J., & Gosling, S. D. (2009). Personality judgments based on physical appearance. *Personality and Social Psychology Bulletin, 35*, 1661–1671. doi:10.1177/0146167209346309.

O'Brien, J. (2014). *Big data is changing the game for recruiters* [online]. Mashable. Retrieved June 12, 2015, from http://mashable.com/2014/06/11/big-data-recruiting/.

Ones, D. S., & Viswesvaran, C. (1998). The effects of social desirability and faking on personality and integrity assessment for personnel selection. *Human Performance, 11*, 245–269. doi:10.1080/08959285.1998.9668033.

Park, G., Schwartz, H. A., Eichstaedt, J. C., Kern, M. L., Kosinski, M., Stillwell, D. J., et al. (2014, November 3). Automatic personality assessment through social media language. *Journal of Personality and Social Psychology*. Retrieved from http://dx.doi.org/10.1037/pspp0000020.

Paxata. (n.d.). *The missing V in big data—Data veracity* [online]. Paxata. Retrieved May 12, 2015, from http://www.paxata.com/missing-v-data-veracity.

Pearlstein, S. (2014). *People analytics: 'Moneyball' for human resources* [online]. Washington Post. Retrieved May 12, 2015, from http://www.washingtonpost.com/business/people-analytics-moneyball-for-human-resources/2014/08/01/3a8fb6ac-1749-11e4-9e3b-7f2f110c6265_story.html.

Powers, J., Bergman, S. M., & Cazier, J. A. (2015). *Analytics for good: Predicting secondary education attainment with text analytics*. 21st Americas Conference on Information Systems, Puerto Rico.

Rafter, M. V. (2013). *Companies making HR big data work* [online]. Workforce. Retrieved June 3, 2015, from http://www.workforce.com/articles/companies-making-hr-big-data-work.

Richtel, M. (2013). *How big data is playing recruiter for specialized workers* [online]. NY Times. Retrieved May 12, 2015, from http://www.nytimes.com/2013/04/28/technology/how-big-data-is-playing-recruiter-for-specialized-workers.html?_r=0.

Robb, D. (2014). *How three companies went social with recruiting* [online]. Society for Human Resource Management. Retrieved February 7, 2015, from http://www.shrm.org/publications/hrmagazine/editorialcontent/2014/0914/pages/0914-social-media-recruiting.aspx.

Rosenfeld, P. (1997). Impression management, fairness, and the employment interview. *Journal of Business Ethics, 16*(8), 801–808.

Rupayana, D., Puchalski, L., & Hedricks, C. A. (2015, April). Qualitative vs. Quantitative data for predicting outcome: Focus on conscientiousness. In D. Rupayana (Chair), *Beyond mining: Harnessing the power of text data*. Symposium session conducted at the annual Society for Industrial and Organizational Psychology Conference, Philadelphia, PA.

Saporito, P. (2014). *2 More big data V's—Value and veracity* [online]. Innovation. Retrieved May 10, 2015, from http://blogs.sap.com/innovation/big-data/2-more-big-data-vs-value-and-veracity-01242817.

SAS. (n.d.). *Big data analytics: What it is and why it matters.* [online] SAS. Retrieved May 11, 2015, from http://www.sas.com/en_us/insights/analytics/big-data-analytics.html.

Schwartz, H. A., Eichstaedt, J. C., Kern, M. L., Dziurzynski, L., Ramones, S. M., Agrawal, M., et al. (2013). Personality, gender, and age in the language of social media: The open-vocabulary approach. *PLoS One, 8*(9), e73791. doi:10.1371/journal.pone.0073791.

Smith, W. P., & Kidder, D. L. (2010). You've been tagged! (Then again, maybe not): Employers and Facebook. *Business Horizons, 53*, 491–499. doi:10.1016/j.bushor.2010.04.004.

Society for Human Resource Management. (2015). *Know before you hire: 2015 Employment screening trends* [online]. Society for Human Resource Management. Retrieved September 2, 2015, from http://www.shrm.org/hrdisciplines/staffingmanagement/articles/pages/2015-employment-screening-trends.aspx#sthash.XM8kUVAv.dpuf.

Sridharan, M. (2013). *Transforming HR recruitment practices with big data* [online]. Smart Data. Retrieved June 12, 2015, from http://smartdatacollective.com/mithunsridharan/173976/transforming-hr-recruitment-practices-big-data.

Stoughton, J. W., Thompson, L. F., & Meade, A. W. (2015). Examining applicant reactions to the use of social networking websites in pre-employment screening. *Journal of Business and Psychology, 30*(1), 73–88. doi:10.1007/s10869-013-9333-6.

Such, M., & Tippins, N. (2015, April). *Using big data for employment decisions*. Community of interest session conducted at the annual Society for Industrial and Organizational Psychology Conference, Philadelphia, PA.

Thelwall, M., Buckley, K., Paltoglou, G., Cai, D., & Kappas, A. (2010). Sentiment strength detection in short informal text. *Journal of the American Society for Information Science and Technology, 61*(12), 2544–2558. doi:10.1002/asi.21416.

Urshel, H. (2012). *How employers view your online presence.* [online] Career Rocketeer. Retrieved March 13, 2015, from http://careerrocketeer.com/2012/01/how-employers-view-your-online--presence.html.

Van Iddekinge, C. H., Lanivich, S. E., Roth, P. L., & Junco, E. (2013). Social media for selection? Validity and adverse impact potential of a Facebook-based assessment. *Journal of Management*, 0149206313515524.

Van Iddekinge, C. H., Raymark, P. H., & Roth, P. L. (2005). Assessing personality with a structured employment interview: Construct-related validity and susceptibility to response inflation. *Journal of Applied Psychology, 90*, 536–552. doi:10.1037/0021-9010.90.3.536.

Vazire, S., & Gasling, S. D. (2004). e-Perceptions: Personality impressions based on personal websites. *Journal of Personality and Social Psychology, 87*, 123–132. doi:10.1037/0022-3514.87.1.123.

Vazire, S., Naumann, L. P., Rentfrow, P. J., & Gosling, S. D. (2008). Portrait of a narcissist: Manifestations of narcissism in physical appearance. *Journal of Research in Personality, 42*, 1439–1447. doi:10.1016/j.jrp.2008.06.007.

Vishal, B. (2013). *Data mining in dynamic social networks and fuzzy systems.* Hershey, PA: IGI Global. ISBN 1466642149, 9781466642140.

Waxer, C. (2013). *Subscribe to data informed HR recruiters turn to social media as data quality challenges persist.* [online] Data informed. Retrieved February 26, 2015, from http://data-informed.com/hr-recruiters-turn-to-social-media-as-data-quality-challenges-persist/.

Williams, A. (2013). *The power of data exhaust.* [online] TechCrunch. Retrieved May 9, 2015, http://techcrunch.com/2013/05/26/the-power-of-data-exhaust/.

Williams, K. Z., Shaffer, M. M., & Ellis, L. E. (2013). Legal risk in selection: An analysis of processes and tools. *Journal of Business and Psychology, 28*(4), 401–410.

YouTube.com. (n.d.). *Statistics.* [online] Youtube. Retrieved June 2, 2015, http://www.youtube.com/yt/press/statistics.html.

Chapter 8
Comparing the Social Media in the United States and BRIC Nations, and the Challenges Faced in International Selection

Brandon Shields and Julia Levashina

Abstract This chapter examines social network sites (SNSs) common in the United States and compares them to popular social media platforms in BRIC countries. Based on the Information Systems research (e.g., Kane & Alavi (MIS Quarterly 38(1), 275–304, 2014), we propose a social media features framework in order to enhance our understanding and accumulate knowledge of SNSs. The framework includes dynamic and static profile content, authenticity, third-party contributions, and privacy. Throughout the chapter, we examine the impact of SNSs features on the selection process. In order to stimulate future research on this topic, we state 13 research questions. We hope that this chapter will enhance understanding of how US companies can use BRIC SNSs during the international selection process.

Keywords BRIC nations • International selection • Social network sites • Social media features • Brazil • Russia • India • China

8.1 Introduction

Employers are increasingly using social network sites (SNSs) during the selection process (Jacobs, 2009; Jobvite, 2012; McDonnell, 2012). The proliferation of SNSs means people are no longer using just one SNS. Moreover, multiplatform adoption has increased from 42 % in 2013 to 54 % in 2014 (Duggan, Ellison, Lampe, Lenhart, & Madden, 2015). The increased adoption of social media platforms and the increased amount of public, personal information available to employers indicate that companies have more information than ever about applicants during the hiring process. It is possible that SNSs could provide information that helps assess

B. Shields (✉) • J. Levashina, Ph.D. (✉)
College of Business Administration, Kent State University,
475 Terrace Drive, Kent, OH 44242-0001, USA
e-mail: bshield6@kent.edu; jlevashi@kent.edu

R.N. Landers, G.B. Schmidt (eds.), *Social Media in Employee Selection and Recruitment*, DOI 10.1007/978-3-319-29989-1_8

applicant's organizational fit (Grasz, 2012), personality (Back et al., 2010), skills, and abilities (Black, Johnson, Takach, & Stone, 2012).

Much of what is known about social media during the selection process looks specifically at Facebook and LinkedIn, but there has been little insight into how specific dimensions of social media impact the selection process. Furthermore, many developing countries have created their own social networks that have their own set of unique features and are different from the US-based SNSs. Understanding the features, and obstacles related to foreign SNSs is extremely important for US firms looking to expand international selection efforts. By assessing both US and foreign SNSs, we will highlight some of the challenges facing firms involved in international selection.

8.2 SNS and BRIC Countries

Social media usage in the United States has steadily increased since 2008 where only 24 % of Americans had social media profile. Today, that number is about 75 % with many Americans having multiple profiles on multiple platforms (Statista, 2015a, 2015b). There are many SNSs that are ubiquitous in American culture today such as Facebook (www.facebook.com), Google+ (www.plus.google.com), Twitter (www.twitter.com), LinkedIn (www.linkedin.com), Instagram (www.instagram.com), Pinterest (www.pinterest.com), and Tumblr (www.tumblr.com). However, while these sites are both popular in the United States and around the world, these are not the only sites used in foreign countries, some of which have specific SNSs.

While SNSs are extremely popular in the developed western economies, these platforms are increasingly used by developing countries whose population and economic growth make them an integral part of the future of the international selection process. The developing countries with the most global influence are Brazil, Russia, India, and China, commonly referred to as the BRIC nations (BRICS Ministry of External Relations, n.d.). The name was coined by the chief economist for Goldman Sachs, Jim O'Neill (Tett, 2010). He identified these countries as having the capability of becoming the largest global economies in the world, replacing the six largest western economies (Tett, 2010). Today, the BRIC countries exceed for three billion people (IBGE 2014) and it is estimated that by 2020, the economies of Brazil, China, and India combined will be larger than the output of Canada, France, Germany, Italy, the United Kingdom, and the United States (United Nations Development Program, 2013). Essentially, BRIC has come to represent the ushering in of a new era; an era where the West looks towards Brazil, Russia, India, and China for international economic growth and stability.

Along with population and economic growth, the BRIC nations are also where social media is growing the quickest. It is estimated that by 2018, four of the top six countries in terms of social media users will be BRIC nations (Statista, 2015a, 2015b). Both Brazil and India have social media platform preferences similar to those of the United States. More people in India have a Facebook account (94 %)

than any other SNS (Kemp, 2014). Other popular social media platforms include Google+ (81 %), Twitter (66 %), and finally LinkedIn (53 %; Kemp, 2014). A survey in Brazil also found Facebook to be the most widely adopted SNS (92 %), followed by Google+ (78 %), Twitter (59 %), and LinkedIn (41 %; Kemp, 2014). While these figures demonstrate that social media platforms are similar in between these two countries and the United States, it does not mean that the information is used in the same and for the same purposes in the selection process.

Russia and China, on the other hand, have popular social media sites that are not used in the United States. The top two social media sites in Russia, as measured by a penetration rate, are in fact Russian. Vkontakte (www.vk.com) is the most popular social media site in Russia with a penetration of 28 % and Odnoklassniki (www.ok.ru) has penetration rate of 24 % (Statista, 2015a, 2015b). Vkontakte (VK) has a striking similarity to Facebook; in fact one can even login using their Facebook credentials and link content posted on Facebook to their VK profile. This means the user would make the same post on both profiles. In China, the most popular SNS, excluding exclusive messaging services, are RenRen (www.renren.com) and Sina Weibo (www.weibo.com; Zhang & Pentina, 2012). The former is a service similar to Facebook while the latter is a microblog similar to Twitter. Reviewing the features of these foreign platforms is important in understanding how firms engaging in international selection can leverage these SNSs during the hiring process.

8.3 Framework of Social Media Features

Our analysis of the features of SNSs is grounded in Information Systems research. Based on the work by Kane and Alavi (2014), we propose SNSs features framework in order to enhance our understanding and accumulate knowledge of SNSs and their use in selection. Kane and Alavi developed a litmus test of four main components that all SNSs must possess in order to be accurately labeled as SNSs, including a unique digital profile created by the user on the platform, various privacy settings on the profile, the ability to connect with other users on the platform, and the capability to view the profiles of others.

We modified these SNSs features and identified five main components that are relevant to the selection process, including dynamic profile content, static profile content, authenticity, third-party contributions, and privacy. Content refers to any information that the owner of the profile publishes on their various social media platforms. For our purposes, content has been further divided into dynamic profile content (content that is regularly added by the user) and static profile content (prompted background information about the user). Authenticity refers to both the ability to identify the correct profile, as well as the accuracy of the information on the profile. Third-party contributions refer to how others interact and impact the user's profile. Finally, privacy refers to the degree of visibility of the user's information.

Combined, these aspects may have significant impact on the selection process. To best understand the differences between popular SNSs in the United States and those in BRIC nations, we will compare the SNSs in accordance with the aforementioned features. This will reveal a continuum for each feature, showing how the SNS design influences the type of information shared, and thus the behavior of the user.

8.3.1 Dynamic Profile Content

SNSs allow users to post different types of media content on their respective profiles, which can include text, pictures, multimedia media files, hyperlinks, and connections. Many social media sites allow users to interact and publish with all of the aforementioned types of media; however, every platform has limits and restrictions that actually shape the behavior of the user and dictate the type of content on the profile. This will affect the type of information that can be obtained when viewing applicant's profiles on different social media websites. We can begin to understand how differences in SNSs are rooted in restrictions established by the platform.

8.3.2 Text

Tumblr is a social media site that is centered on blogging and therefore, allows an unlimited amount of characters per post. While not unlimited, Facebook and Google+ both allow for lengthy posts of 60,000 and 100,000 characters, respectively (Constine, 2011). VK, Odnoklassniki, and RenRen also offer similar spaces for large amounts of text in individual posts. LinkedIn has two different types of text posts. Users can "share an update" which is limited by 700 characters or they can also "publish a post" which is lengthier and acts more like a blog post. The difference then between "share an update" and "publish a post" is that the content of the former is about the user and the latter about a topic. These five platforms all permit users to make text posts that stand alone, whereas Instagram and Pinterest, only allow users to provide text in conjunction with another type of media. Twitter famously, limits "tweets" to 140 characters in order to accomplish their vision where users "communicate and stay connected through the exchange of quick, frequent messages" (Twitter, n.d.). Sina Weibo, China's Twitter alternative, is very similar with a few nuanced differences. The character restriction on Sina Weibo is limited to 140 characters along with direct uploads of outside links, photos, etc. However, a post on Sina Weibo's microblog has richer content that those posts of Western countries. This is because each character in the Chinese language is one word (Zhang & Pentina, 2012). Therefore, while those using Twitter only receive 140 characters including spaces, Sina Weibo effectively allows for 70 words (a space between every word) per post. In some ways, this can make the richness of content more similar to Facebook and Google+ as opposed to Twitter.

8.3.3 Photos

Photos are another popular form of media found on social networking sites. Facebook and Google+ give users a wide variety options when dealing with photos; like many other social media sites such as VK, Odnoklassniki, and RenRen they allow users to create posts involving photos, but they also allow for uploading multiple photos at once onto the platforms, creating "photo albums." Instagram is the most prominent social media platform for pictures due to the wide range of tools given to users such as filters and balancing effects. Twitter has also positioned itself towards those wanting to share photos by offering a few filters as well as some basic editing tools for users. Tumblr, LinkedIn, and Sina Weibo also permit photo posts.

8.3.4 Videos

Video is another popular form of media where the biggest area of differentiation between platforms is the length of the video supported. Facebook and Google+ both support videos up to 20 min in length and Tumblr permits video files up to 100 MB in size as indicated by their websites. Instagram and Twitter on the other hand only allow short video clips of up to 15 s (Instagram, n.d.) and 30 s, respectively (Twitter, n.d.). While difficult to determine the exact time limits for videos on VK, Odnoklassniki, RenRen, and Sina Weibo, they all support video uploads in some capacity. The divide in time represents a divide in function and purpose. Instagram and Twitter are optimal for videos that represent spontaneous moments and brief snippets of life while Facebook and Google+ give users a place to post videos of events in their entirety. LinkedIn does not support video uploads, but does permit videos from other sites to be embedded in the post.

8.3.5 Hyperlinks and Hashtags

Finally, most every social media platform is equipped for users to use hyperlinks to news articles, audio files, and videos. Another form of hypermedia includes hashtags, which are used on Facebook, Twitter, Tumblr, Instagram, Google+, LinkedIn, and Pinterest. Hashtags aggregate similar content on the platform and are assigned by the user. Clicking on the hashtag takes users to an online storage center of all media, by all users, who have used an identical hashtag. Hashtags are often used as a source of emphasis, underlining summary points or phrases that users use as a gateway to similar content. These hashtags also "tag" the post and make it searchable within the social media platform. This is a very powerful function, especially for blogging sites such as Tumblr, which uses hashtags as means to target material towards relevant readers.

8.3.6 Number of Connections

The number of connections refers to the amount of other users on the SNS who initiated the offer to connect or agreed to be connected to a person. This variable may characterize a job applicant's capacity to influence other people, authority, respectability, or social hierarchical standing. Thus, it can indicate the job applicant's social skills or accumulated social capital. The amount of connections may have implication related to other aspects of social media. For example, a user with more connections is likely to have more third-party contributions on their profile than those who have fewer. Furthermore, the number of connections may also indicate additional information to employers. The number of connections may also be reflective personality traits, where users with more connections my have more outgoing personalities. More connections may also be indicative of user's who possess certain qualities that others are interested in. There may also be a link between the number of connections and authenticity, although this may be dependent on the type of SNS. For example, users with more connections on LinkedIn have more people with the ability to view the user's profile; this may encourage a higher level of authenticity of the information than profiles with only a few connections. This may not be the case on platforms such as Twitter and Instagram where the authenticity of the profile content is less likely to be influenced by the number of connections.

The amount of connections a user has may also be considered dynamic content, as it is common to add and delete connections throughout time. The general process of adding and deleting connections is pretty standard among all of the social media platforms. A majority of connections will be made upon the creation of the profile. It's in this stage that the platform will suggest connections based on email contacts, groups you are involved with, and your geographical location. Beyond the initial setup, connections may be established or terminated on a less frequent basis. However, it is also not uncommon for people to "purge" or "prune" their connections. A quick search on the Internet provides many articles articulating how often users should go through and eliminate connections and how to make those decisions. There can be a variety of reasons users decide to eliminate people from their network ranging from privacy concerns to a lack of a relationship to a connection. The Pew Research Center conducted a survey that asked questions related to pruning social media connections (Madden, 2012). The results indicated that 63 % of social media users engaged in this behavior, up from 56 % in 2009. The study also found that this behavior was more common in women, and more common among younger users (Madden, 2012).

It is this type of "dynamic" profile information that may be most useful to employers when attempting to assess the personality or organizational fit. Employers are interested in applicant's personality, their creativity, and well roundness (Reppler, 2011). Therefore, when attempting to determine the organizational fit, creativity or personality of an applicant, their dynamic profile content seems like the best place to start. This is enhanced not only by the content posted on their page but also through pages they have "liked," and how they interact with other users. This is supported by Back et al. (2010) who found that Facebook profile can accurately depict the personality of users. However, this is also the part of the profile that may be most likely to have a negative impact on the applicant during the selection process. According to Reppler (2011), an applicant's online reputation can be damaged by posting about drug or alcoholic use, proactive pictures, and discriminatory comments.

The different types of dynamic profile content serve to demonstrate the multiple ways applicants can express themselves on SNSs. With that in mind, different mediums may represent different information about the applicants, and therefore may be used for specific purposes by employers. Furthermore, each SNS is constructed in a way that guides users towards specific behavior, i.e., Instagram for pictures and LinkedIn for employment history. The opportunities and limitations that each SNS grants users in regard to the type of dynamic profile content mean that SNSs exist in a multidimensional spectrum. Employers may move along this spectrum and use different SNSs for different selection purposes. What is not clear though is if employers in BRIC countries use dynamic content in a similar way as American companies for selection. This is important for companies involved in international selection who use this dynamic profile content to ascertain organizational fit.

American companies involved in international selection may also be challenged by a lack of dynamic profile content due censorship restrictions. Carnegie Mellon conducted a study specifically on the Chinese SNS Sine Weibo, monitoring deletion rates and the subsequent content of those posts. The results suggested that the Chinese government was actively involved in censoring posts on that were political in nature, as well as nonpolitical posts that may have propagated misinformation or rumors (Carnegie Melon, 2012). It's not clear if the information suppressed through censorship inhibits employers from using dynamic profile content in the aforementioned ways. In other words, does the type of information being suppressed inhibit the employer's ability to assess the applicants organizational fit, personality, and creativity? The subject of censorship in conjunction with understanding how to use foreign applicants' dynamic profile content for selection purposes, highlights the challenges US employers face.

Research Question 1: What type of dynamic profile content is used by employers in different countries during the selection process?

Research Question 2: What constitutes inappropriate dynamic profile content for employers in various parts of the world?

Research Question 3: (a) How does dynamic profile content impact the selection decision? (b) How does inappropriate dynamic profile content impact the selection decision?

Research Question 4: How does a country's censorship policies impact the type of dynamic profile content posted by users?

Research Question 5: How does the number of connections impact the authenticity of the profile?

8.3.7 Static Profile Content

So far we have looked only at dynamic profile content, or content that is regularly updated, altered, and changed by the user. However, profiles also provide static profile content, or content that is not regularly changed by the user. This information provides background information or a summary on the user. As a means for comparison, we will look at how social media sites are compared to Facebook since Facebook prompts the user for the most information.

Facebook's "About" section provides six different categories of information: Overview, Work and Education, Places You've Lived, Contact and Basic Info, Family and Relationships, Details About You, and Life Events. Under "Work and Education," Facebook prompts users to disclose past high schools and universities attended along with past and current employers. Facebook allows for further detail here by allowing the user to list specific projects completed at each place of employment, as well as the ability to list any professional skills. The "Contact and Basic Info" page prompts users for contact information, along with birthday, gender, sexual orientation, languages, religious views, and political affiliations. "Family Relationships" is where users can post relationship statuses and detail other family members on Facebook. Finally, "Details About You" is a place for miscellaneous information and "Life Event" details major life events. When you scroll down on the "About" page, it shows your interests categorized by media type including but not limited to favorite movies, TV shows, books, and video games.

The closest platform to Facebook in terms of static profile content is Google+. Google+ has sections for education and work, although they are separate. Like Facebook, Google+ prompts users for information on last educational institutions attended and for employment, provides fields for employers, job descriptions, and skill set. It also has two distinct fields for "Contact Information" and "Basic Information." With Google+, however, "Basic information" is not as personal as Facebook and has fields only for gender, relationship, birthday, and "what are you looking for." Unlike Facebook it does not ask such personal questions as sexual orientation, political affiliation, or religious beliefs. Two unique sections that Google+ offers as compared to Facebook include "Links" and "Story." Under "Links" the user can link to other social media profiles such as Facebook and Twitter, or links to another website of their choosing. The "Storyline" section provides the user an empty space where they can write a unique biography about themselves. This is the only place on the Google+ "About" section where the user is not limited by prompts and categories.

Interestingly, some social media platforms only provide an open-ended area for a short bibliography as static profile content. This is true for Pinterest, Twitter, and Instagram which provide a space for a bibliography consisting of only 160, 160, and 150 characters, respectively. While the user has the ability to provide background information on themselves free of restrictions and prompts, they are limited to a few key choice words and phrases. Tumblr similarly offers a "description" and while this could be a place where the author describes who they are, it also functions as place to describe the blog. So while Pinterest, Twitter, and Instagram offer bios specific to information about the user, Tumblr offers a "description" specific to user, but also the blog.

Perhaps the platform with the most detailed and well-known profile content is LinkedIn. LinkedIn differentiates itself from other platforms in that "posting" is not the main function of this platform, as its purpose centers around static profile content, specifically related to employment. While LinkedIn prompts the users for information in specific fields, it gives the user plenty of space to provide detailed information in each category heading. The main sections of a LinkedIn profile include Background, Education, Experience, Projects, Honors and Awards, Languages, Contact Info, Skills, and Interests. LinkedIn profiles are a more in-depth virtual resume. The main fields on LinkedIn match many of the fields in the aforementioned platforms, but more space provides more room for the user to elaborate and be specific.

For example, the "Background" section on LinkedIn is similar in function to the "Story" in Google+ and the "Bio" on Instagram and Twitter except that it is not restrained by severe character limits and is specific to employment. LinkedIn provides an "Experience" section, which is used for delineating places of employment and accomplishments. This varies from Facebook and Google+ in that there are no individual fields for the user to fill in. Most platforms "About" section acts as a type of virtual form, but LinkedIn, in most cases, provides an organic and individualistic approach that allows each user to determine the best way to convey information. This is supported by the fact that unlike any other social media platforms mentioned, LinkedIn allows for the inclusion of media files and links in certain sections of the static profile content. Some sections specifically require additional media, such as the "Projects" section, which requires users to provide a link to past projects completed. However, many other sections offer the option to include photos, videos, links, and presentations to enhance each individual section. The variety of media options available in the profile section is unique to LinkedIn.

Being that the Russian VK is essentially a Facebook derivative, its static information varies in no meaningful way from Facebook. While RenRen also provides similar static content information on users, unlike Facebook RenRen centers on specific background information: school and colleges attended. RenRen is organized and categorized based on this information, and consequently RenRen has a much younger user base than Facebook (Niu, Peng, Shu, Tong, & Liao, 2013). This categorization is also a key feature of Odnoklassniki's static profile content. Odnoklassniki prompts the user only for information that would categorize the user in a particular group (work, university, military, etc.). Furthermore, the user can only enter group information that the site recognizes as an already created group. Therefore, the focus of Odnoklassniki is not as much on the individual, but on groups. This focus is also demonstrated by highlighted features such as group messaging, group chatting, and showing the number of groups the user is "in." It is unclear what type of static profile content is available for Sina Weibo users, although it can be assumed that at the minimum they are allotted a short space for biographical information.

The static profile content perhaps provides the most valuable information for employers, but also puts them at the most risk for violating sections of the Equal Employment Opportunity Act. This is the most cited reason in a survey conducted by SHRM why companies have never used, or no longer use SNSs during the selection process (SHRM, 2013). Naturally, only US firms are required to follow the EEOC and it is out of the scope of this chapter to examine the laws of BRIC nations and how they apply it during the selection process. However, it is important that the US companies must follow EEOC guidelines when they select international applicants (United States Equal Employment Opportunity Commission, 2003).

Static profile information can reveal an applicant's age, race, national origin, sex, and religious affiliations. Knowledge of all of these could create a bias in hiring decisions and such could lead to discrimination on the part of the employer. Research in the field has found that when using SNSs to determine an applicant's KSAOs, KSAOs varied based on particular subgroups such as color and gender. For examples, Whites tended to score higher on cognitive-based skills than others and women scored higher in consciousness than men (Van Iddekinge, Lanivich, Roth, & Junco, 2013).

Using static profile content during the hiring process is also limited if applicants do not post information relevant to the selection process. Therefore, a mismatch exists between the users of SNSs and the employers and the resulting difference is that the information may not be relevant for determining applicants' KSAOs (Roth, Bobko, Van Iddekinge, & Thatcher, 2016). Research has shown that the connection between this content and KSAO may be only indirectly related at best (Black et al., 2012). Another issue with using static profile content for hiring decisions is that users are not required to fill out this information; it is optional. It has been proposed that applicants who have missing information will receive more negative assessments than those who have completed most of the information (Roth et al., 2016). This may lead to skewed results, resulting in more favorable assessments merely by higher levels of completion and not more applicable KSAOs.

The main difference regarding static profile information that arises between the US social media sites and BRIC social media sites is individual vs group. US social media sites are centered around unique information about the user, while those of China and Russia are inclined to show static information related to group involvement. While this could be attributed to cultural differences between East and West, it does provide different and perhaps limited information of US employers during the selection process. Understanding how companies in China and Russia use group centric static profile information for selection will help US firms determine how to interpret this type of information from these foreign SNSs.

Research Question 6: What type of static profile information is used by employers in different countries during the selection process?

Research Question 7: What constitutes inappropriate static profile information for employers in different countries?

Research Question 8: How does static profile content information impact the selection decision?

Research Question 9: (a) Do employers in different countries place a different emphasis on dynamic and static profile information during the selection process? (b) What KSAOs are measured with dynamic and static content across countries?

8.3.8 Authenticity

The profile content is very much related to the component of authenticity. Kane and Alavi (2014) describe authenticity as the degree to which the online profile reflects the identity of the user. Naturally, some platforms make it easier for users to have online identities that do not match their offline identities. SNSs that require more background information, or static profile content, may be more likely to have authentic users than profiles that require less information. Less requirements or fields for background information give the user a greater sense of anonymity and thus can promote the divide between online and offline identities. As we explained, Facebook, Google+, and LinkedIn can provide large amounts of background information, while Tumblr, Pinterest, Instagram, and Twitter have much less.

This would explain in part why LinkedIn is such a popular SNS more than other social media platforms during the selection process. Of those employer's who use social media during the selection process, 92 % referenced applicants LinkedIn profiles, higher than any other SNSs (SHRM, 2013). LinkedIn provides the most space for objectively verifiable information about the user. Research has shown that users on LinkedIn are less likely to engage in deception regarding verifiably objective information than as compared with unverifiable information (Guillory & Hancock, 2012). Therefore, virtual impression management is limited because the public aspect of the professional profile means any deceptions may at some point have to be detected. While LinkedIn does not provide a way to flag deception, it does allow users to "endorse" the skills of others, and allow them to write recommendations for others. Thus, LinkedIn should have the highest degree of authenticity because by design it mitigates deception in areas most related to KSAOs and allows for third-party endorsement and thus some verification of the listed KSAOs.

One of the more striking differences between US SNSs and those of Russia and China is how latter are designed to promote more authentic profiles. VK authenticity is similar to Facebook since it asks for similar background information, which if filled out should help employers determine if the offline profile matches the online profile. The group function of Odnoklassniki enhances authenticity because users can only join formed groups. Users who join groups, are very likely to join groups that they actually belong to otherwise, the functionality of the social media site is limited. RenRen does not allow users to create aliases on its website, which means the name connected with the profile is without question authentic. RenRen is able to do this by requiring specific registration requirements issued by the Chinese government (Niu et al., 2013). While this does not guarantee that the material posted in necessarily authentic, it greatly improves the odds. Sina Weibo, unlike RenRen, does allow users to have a display name or alias. Users can provide their identification number to Sina Weibo in order to become a verified user but this is optional (Zhang & Pentina, 2012).

Providing such detailed information also makes it possible for employers to match the applicant with their profile. While, social media platforms do provide valuable information to the employer, it is not useful if the employer cannot determine if the online profile is owned by the applicant. One way around this has been to request from the applicant links to their specific social media sites during the online application process. This ensures certainty on behalf of the employer and recruiter that the profile belongs to the applicant. From there, online profiles can then be cross-referenced with identity and information supplied by the applicant to ensure authenticity. Based on these conclusions, we would expect LinkedIn to be used more than Facebook and Twitter during the hiring process due to its high degree of authenticity which is echoed by research showing that recruiters around the world relied on LinkedIn more than both Facebook and Twitter (Bullhorn Reach, 2015).

US firms engaging in international selection in China and Russia may have a reason to believe that the information posted on their SNS is more accurate than that of the United States. In China, for example, sites where the identity number is required for registration can allow for quickly matching the online and offline profile, while group centric SNSs in Russia may help to generate a more accurate and authentic profile of the candidate. It's important to therefore determine the impact of this increased authenticity in terms of selection, and if international candidates using SNSs that are deemed to create more authentic profiles have an advantage in the selection process. Understanding the role of authenticity in all areas of selection is important, as it determines what applicant information can accurately be accessed during the selection process.

Research Question 10: Do international social media platforms promote more authentic profiles through their features than those in the United States?

Research Question 11: How does authenticity impact selection decisions across countries? What do companies do to increase authenticity of applicant's social media profiles across countries?

8.3.9 Third-Party Contributions

Another aspect of social media that is used by employers during the selection process is third-party contributions to a user's profile. Third-party contributions are when one user interacts with another user's social media platform. Facebook has both unique and generic ways to interact with other user's profiles. A unique contribution would be commenting on a post, or posting a message, article, or video on another user's wall. This type of contribution has significant implications during the selection process. When reviewing a social media profile, recruiters will not only see content from the owner of the profile but the "contribution" or comments, posts, and pictures posted by other users. Employers should not find it difficult to discern the difference between the applicant's contribution and the third-party contributions. However, even if recognized that questionable content is the result of other's posting, employers are then left with a judgment call. For example, an employer is reviewing an applicant's social media profile, when a racist comment posted by third-party on the applicant's profile. The employer now must determine if the questionable content is a reflection of the applicant, and does the applicant support the spirit of the content.

This can be tricky and often the easiest thing to do in this situation is to simply no longer consider the applicant. Therefore, these third-party comments may have a powerful impact on the reviewer; one study even found that comments posted by third parties left a more powerful impact on those viewing the profile than comments by the owner of the profile (Walther, Van Der Heide, Kim, Westerman, & Tong, 2008). The other type of contribution is much more general and certainly less problematic for recruiters. On Facebook, this would be the "like" button denoted by a thumbs-up. Third parties can lend their support by "liking" posts by the owner of the profile.

Facebook is not the only platform with these two types of third-party contribution. Third-party contributions on VK include commenting on others' posts (unique contributions) and "liking" posts and photo uploads (generic contributions). On Odnoklassniki, others can comment on posts, as well as like and repost content of the user. RenRen also permits third-party contributions in the form of liking content, and uploading original content on to the user's personal homepage. Google+ works in a similar fashion with ways to comment and post on other profiles and has a "+" for simply endorsing content published by the profile owner.

Twitter has three main ways to interact with other profiles. The general contributions include "favoriting" and "retweeting" which both act as clear endorsements of the statements of others on twitter; the difference between the two exists in how they are stored on Twitter. Retweeting republishes someone else's tweet on your feed or profile, while "favoriting" a tweet does not publish the tweet but stores it in a "favorites" list on the user's profile. Sina Weibo also allows for third-party contributions, which are identical to Twitter's "retweeting" and "favorting." However, Sina Weibo has added certain gamification aspects to third-party contributions where the user can earn Weibo medals by retweeting particular content (Zhang & Pentina, 2012). Unlike Facebook, these endorsements are not demonstrated on the original owner's profile, but rather appear on the third party's profile. The unique contribution aspect of Twitter occurs through mentions. Any Twitter user can mention someone in a tweet by using another user's twitter handle.

Instagram allows users to like others' photos (general contribution), and also comment on other posts (unique). Furthermore, a fundamental aspect of Instagram that exists in all social media platforms where photos can be uploaded is "tagging." "Tagging" is the act of digitally marking individuals in a photo. On Facebook, for example, tagging someone in a photo will cause the photo to be published on the tagged person's profile if security settings are not altered from the default settings. On Instagram, when someone is tagged in a photo it is not published but stored on their profile under the menu option "Photos of Username." These can be viewed by anyone who can view the user's Instagram account. Tagged photos of job seekers can be problematic if they depict behavior not considered appropriate such as drinking, substance abuse, or improper dress/behavior. While users can generally delete, remove, or hide the photo from their profile, or "untag" themselves, this can be burdensome given the amount of photos published. Other sites like Tumblr permit "reblogging," which is similar to retweeting and commenting on others' posts, and LinkedIn has both a feature to comment on posts and "tag" people in updates as well as the function to like posts and updates. Third-party contributions on social media websites can create a gray area for recruiters that may cause ineffective hiring decisions.

How third-party contributions are assessed is completely up to the employer reviewing the applicants' profile. Inappropriate profile content seems to be the biggest issue in this area, whether it is from connected third-party users or spamming. It is also important to note for US companies that while it may be easy to determine who has posted content on US SNSs, it may in fact be more difficult with foreign platforms which are set up differently, and often in other languages. Companies need to determine how to handle inappropriate third-party content when accessing applicants, and US firms in particular should look at other countries and determine if their unique SNSs provide any insight to this question.

Research Question 12: (a) What is the impact of the inappropriate content posted on the applicant's profile by another user on the selection decision? (b) Does this impact vary by country?

8.3.10 Privacy

Finally, all SNSs have some sort of privacy settings, as it's a core requirement in the aforementioned framework, that the user can use to control who sees their profile and how others interact with their profile. Facebook splits their privacy setting into three core groups: Privacy, Timeline and Tagging, and Blocking. The privacy category determines who can see the user's profile. The main options include either friends, or public, but clicking more options reveals additional, albeit less popular options. These include only users in a certain geographical location, and certain groups the user belongs to. Tagging and Timeline provides restrictions on third-party contributions. Here, the user can limit who is able to post on their timeline as well as the option to review all posts the user has been tagged in before they appear on their profile. Finally, the Blocking Tab allows for blocking of specific pages, events, apps, and even users. Facebook provides many options and customization when it comes to privacy. They allow for viewing privacy and contributing privacy as well as targeted blocking.

VK has an array of privacy settings that again mirror the spectrum created by Facebook. RenRen also provides users with similar privacy settings to Facebook such as settings that make it so that only a user's friends can view their profile. RenRen also gives users the ability to make it so that anyone who is not a friend, but lives within a certain geographical area can view their page. They can also make it so that users from outside school networks cannot view their content either (Niu et al., 2013).

Twitter's security and privacy setting are less detailed than those of Facebook. By default anyone can view a user's twitter profile, regardless of whether or not they follow the user. Twitter does provide the ability to have restricted account, where only those you accept as followers will be able to view your tweets. This is similar to Sina Weibo whose profiles are public and can be seen by anyone. Every user has a feed that displays posts only from those they are a "fan" of or following. The major downside of this feature is that it prevents others from "retweeting" your content, which is the major way users interact with one another on the platform. Other basic privacy settings for Twitter include limiting photo tagging to only your followers, as well limiting direct messaging to only twitter followers, which is the default setting.

Twitter provides privacy settings that are more along the lines of all or nothing, which is also similar to Odnoklassniki. The two main functions of Odnoklassniki's privacy settings include blocking and making the private profile. While blocking prevents individuals from seeing the user's profile, the private setting prevents everyone from seeing the user's profile. Interestingly in order to make a profile private, the user must pay a small fee. Instagram's main privacy feature is the establishment of a private account, which means the user must approve every other person who wishes to follow them. Like Twitter, by default the account is public and anyone can see any other person. Users also have the option to manually select photos they are tagged in. This is similar to Facebook; every time the user is tagged in a photo they must accept it before it is posted to their profile. Instagram also allows users to hide photos they have been tagged in from their profile, and can even remove the tag altogether.

LinkedIn has security settings that are both similar to other social media platforms and some that are unique to LinkedIn. LinkedIn users can either make their profile public or completely private. Even when users choose to have a public profile that can still customize which parts of the profile is visible, i.e., profile picture, educations, and recommendations. A unique aspect of LinkedIn is that unlike other platforms it automatically will post user behavior to the user's activity field, which can be seen by others. The user can eliminate these activity updates, which may be beneficial if the user is looking for a job while currently employed. LinkedIn provides further privacy customization in relation to the activity feed, where the user can decide who can view the feed (Your Connections, Everyone, Your Network, and Only You). The most interesting area of privacy on LinkedIn is related to the ability for a user to be anonymous. Other social media platforms do not notify users of who has viewed their profiles, but this is not the case with LinkedIn. By default each time a user views a profile, the owner of that profile is notified of the name of the user who viewed it.

The main implication of privacy as it relates to social media in the selection process is how the employer responds to profiles that are private. All SNSs offer a spectrum of privacy settings that limits visibility to the employer. Therefore, every profile can fall into one of the three categories: public, semi-private, and completely private. An employer benefits from a profile that is completely public, as it gives them access to the information they use to make selection decisions. The question arises as to how the employer reacts to applicants who have private or semi-private profiles. Employers can always ask for the applicant to connect with them, or in some states even ask for the password of the applicant. The more important question is how the employer interprets the reason for an applicant's use of privacy settings. It's hard not to consider that the applicant may be attempting to hide information that could hurt them in the selection process. In fact, this idea may be more prevalent in profiles that are semi-private because the natural question is why is some information deemed acceptable to share, while the other is not. Employers, weary of possible deception, may then decide to eliminate the applicant from the pool of applicants. A semi-private profile may seem more deceptive than a completely private one which comes across as more precautionary than deceptive. The result for the applicant is that privacy settings may inadvertently be sending a negative message to employers and hurting them in the selection process.

It is unclear if all countries respond similarly to variations in privacy settings by applicants. While the option exists to merely attempt to connect with them on the given platform, this is challenged during international selection, especially for US companies. It is unlikely that American companies selecting talent from China have a Sina Weibo account, and they cannot even obtain a RenRen account because they do not have a Chinese identification number. In this case, there is no alternative option besides determining the likelihood of deception given the privacy settings. Understanding how foreign companies interpret privacy settings on their own SNSs may provide useful guidance to US firms that are looking for a solution.

Research Question 13: What is the impact of semi-private and private profiles on selection decisions in different countries?

8.4 Final Thoughts

Social Networking Sites have changed the landscape of the selection process by giving employers vast amount of applicant information that can be used. Every SNS presents this information in different ways and in turn suggests that employers can use different SNSs to meet their individual needs during the selection process. Some companies may find that Facebook gives them the best idea about an applicants' organizational fit, while the static profile information on LinkedIn is best at accessing a candidate's KSAOs. When applicants have enacted certain privacy features, employers can use others' SNSs to create a better picture of the candidate. Employers need to carefully look at the information they want about applicants and then strategically use the features of the SNSs in order to accomplish this. This will become more difficult overtime as more SNSs are becoming popular every year, especially with younger users. Some of these include the likes of Vine and Snapchat.

However, companies involved in international selection face complications in using SNSs strategically for hiring decisions. They need to be familiar with popular foreign SNSs especially in countries like Russia and China. It is not clear that people in these countries use SNSs in the same way as their American counterparts which may mean it is more difficult to make use of dynamic and static profile content. In cases of privacy, US firms may find it challenging or even impossible to create accounts on these SNSs and request a connection with applicants. Therefore, it is even more crucial that employers understand the features and components of foreign SNSs in order to leverage them properly. But beyond that, US companies cannot expect that methods used for selection purposes regarding SNSs will be effective with foreign SNSs. Thus, there needs to be an understanding of how foreign companies use their SNSs during selection. There are many questions left to be answered, but their importance is paramount to having effective selection process that cross national borders.

References

Back, M., Stopfer, J., Vazire, S., Gaddis, S., Schmukle, S., Egloff, B., et al. (2010). Facebook profiles reflect actual personality, not self-idealization. *Psychological Science, 21*, 372–374. Retrieved April 16, 2015, from Scopus.

Black, S., Johnson, A., Takach, S., & Stone, D. (2012). Factors affecting applicants' reaction to the collection of data in social network website. *Paper Presented at the Annual Meeting of the Academy of Management*. Retrieved April 1, 2015.

BRICS Ministry of External relations. (n.d.). *Information about BRICS*. Retrieved September 19, 2015, from http://brics.itamaraty.gov.br/about-brics/information-about-brics.

Bullhorn Reach. (2015). *Understanding social media in recruiting*. 2014 Social Global Activity Report. Retrieved April 12, 2015.

Carnegie Melon. (2012). *Carnegie Melon performs first-large scale analysis of soft censorship of social media in China*. Retrieved September 19, 2015, from http://www.cmu.edu/news/stories/archives/2012/march/march7_censorshipinchina.html.

Constine, J. (2011). *Facebook ups character limit to 60,000, Google's is still bigger*. Retrieved April 16, 2015, from http://techcrunch.com/2011/11/30/status-update-character-limit/.

Duggan, M., Ellison, N., Lampe, C., Lenhart, A., & Madden, M. (2015). *Social media update 2014*. Retrieved April 15, 2015, from http://www.pewinternet.org/2015/01/09/social-media-update-2014/.

Grasz, J. (2012). *Thirty-six percent of employers plan to hire full-time, permanent employees in the new year, CareerBuilder's annual forecast finds—CareerBuilder*. Retrieved April 12, 2015, from http://www.careerbuilder.com/share/aboutus/pressreleasesdetail.aspx?id=pr691&sd=4/18/2012&ed=4/18/2099.

Guillory, J., & Hancock, J. (2012). The effect of Linkedin on deception in resumes. *Cyberpsychology, Behavior, and Social Networking, 15*(3). Retrieved March 23, 2015, from Scopus.

IBGE. (2014). *Joint statistical publication 2014*. Retrieved September 1, 2015, from http://brics.ibge.gov.br/downloads/BRICS_Joint_Statistical_Publication_2014.pdf.

Instagram. (n.d.). *Instagram help center*. Retrieved April 3, 2015, from https://help.instagram.com/270963803047681.

Jacobs, P. (2009). What is social recruiting. *Human Resource Magazine, 14*(15), 2–3. Retrieved September 17, 2015.

Jobvite. (2012). *2012 Social recruiting survey*. Retrieved September 18, 2015, from http://web.jobvite.com/Social_Recruiting_Survey-2012-13.html.

Kane, G., & Alavi, M. (2014). What's different about social media networks? A framework and research agenda. *MIS Quarterly, 38*(1), 275–304. Retrieved February 1, 2015, from Business Source Premier.

Kemp, S. (2014). *We are social*. Retrieved March 3, 2015, from http://wearesocial.net/.

Madden, M. (2012). Privacy management on social media sites. *The Pew Research Center.* Retrieved September 18, 2018, from http://www.pewinternet.org/2012/02/24/privacy-management-on-social-media-sites/.

McDonnell, A. (2012). *What are employers discovering about candidates through Social Media.* Retrieved September 17, 2015, from http://thehiringsite.careerbuilder.com/2012/04/20/what-are-employers-seeking-and-finding-out-about-candidates-through-social-media/.

Niu, J., Peng, J., Shu, L., Tong, C., & Liao, W. (2013). An empirical study of a chinese online social network—RenRen. *Computer, 46*(9), 78–84. Retrieved April 9, 2015, from Inspec.

Reppler. (2011). *Job screening with social networks.* Retrieved September 18, 2015, from http://theundercoverrecruiter.com/infographic-how-recruiters-use-social-media-screen-applicants/.

Roth, P., Bobko, P., Van Iddekinge, C., & Thatcher J. B. (2016). Social media in employee-selection-related-decisions: A research agenda for uncharted territory. *Journal of Management. 42*(1), 269–298. Retrieved March 14, 2016, from General OneFile.

SHRM. (2013). *SHRM survey findings: Social network websites and recruiting/selection.* Retrieved September 17, 2015, from http://www.slideshare.net/shrm/social-networkingwebsitesrecruiting selectingjobcandidatesshrm2013final.

Statista. (2015). *Russia: Social network penetration 2014.* Retrieved March 27, 2015, from http://www.statista.com/statistics/284447/russia-social-network-penetration/.

Statista. (2015). *Social network users in 2014 and 2018.* Retrieved March 27, 2015, from http://www.statista.com/statistics/278341/number-of-social-network-users-in-selected-countries/.

Tett, G. (2010). *The story of the brics.* Retrieved September 1, 2015, from http://www.ft.com/intl/cms/s/0/112ca932-00ab-11df-ae8d-00144feabdc0.html.

Twitter. (n.d.). *New user FAQs.* Retrieved March 27, 2015, from https://support.twitter.com/articles/13920-new-user-faqs.

United Nations Development Program. (2013). *Human development report.* Retrieved December 18, 2014, from http://hdr.undp.org/sites/default/files/reports/14/hdr2013_en_complete.pdf.

United States Equal Employment Opportunity Commission. (2003). *Employee rights when working for multinational employers.* Retrieved September 19, 2015, from http://www.eeoc.gov/facts/multi-employees.html.

Van Iddekinge, C., Lanivich, S., Roth, P., & Junco, E. (2013). Social media for selection? Validity and adverse impact potential of a Facebook-based assessment. *Journal of Management.* DOI: 10.1177/0149206313515524. Retrieved April 2, 2015, from Sage Publishing http://jom.sagepub.com/content/early/2013/12/13/0149206313515524.full.pdf+html.

Walther, J., Van Der Heide, B., Kim, S., Westerman, D., & Tong, S. (2008). The role of friends' appearance and behavior on evaluations of individuals on Facebook: Are we known by the company we keep? *Human Communication Research, 34*, 28–49. Retrieved April 10, 2015, from Scopus.

Zhang, L., & Pentina, I. (2012). Motivations and usage patterns of Weibo. *Cyberpsychology', Behavior, and Social Networking, 15*(6), 312–317. Retrieved April 11, 2105 from Scopus.

Chapter 9
Social Media and Employee Recruitment: Chasing the Run Away Bandwagon

Yalcin Acikgoz and Shawn M. Bergman

Abstract One particular area for which organizations have turned to social media is employee recruitment. Common uses of social media for recruiting include searching for candidates and screening job applicants; with 73 % of recruiters reporting to have hired through social networking sites (SNSs) and 93 % reporting intentions to review candidates' social profiles. However, common as they are, the effectiveness of these practices in terms of delivering the intended results and recommendations regarding best practices are largely lacking from the literature. There is also a gap in the literature regarding how the addressees of these applications, namely candidates, view social media recruiting. This chapter will begin to fill this gap by discussing what recruiters are attempting to accomplish on SNSs, their perceptions regarding best practices, and whether or not these alleged best practices align with candidates' perceptions about the utility of various SNSs in the job search process.

Keywords Employee recruitment • Social media • Recruitment source • Social networking sites • Credibility

9.1 Introduction

Over the past decade, a new online environment has emerged which consists of various tools, websites, and mobile applications that allow individuals to create content and share it with the general public. In what has become to be known as social media, this new environment has given every individual the opportunity to have an online presence, connect to a wide number and variety of people, and have ones'

Y. Acikgoz, M.A. (✉)
Department of Psychology, Middle East Technical University, Cankaya, Ankara, Turkey
e-mail: acikgoz.yalcin@metu.edu.tr

S.M. Bergman, Ph.D.
Department of Psychology, Appalachian State University,
222 Joyce Lawrence Ln., Boone, NC 28608, USA
e-mail: bergmans@appstate.edu

R.N. Landers, G.B. Schmidt (eds.), *Social Media in Employee Selection and Recruitment*, DOI 10.1007/978-3-319-29989-1_9

content and voice delivered all over the world (Edosomwan, Prakasan, Kouame, Watson, & Seymour, 2011). This privilege, which was once held almost exclusively by corporate media outlets, is now a possibility for almost every individual owning a computer or a mobile device with access to the Internet.

This access has resulted in an exploitation of social networking sites (SNSs). While there are some similarities between outlets (i.e., content creation and connecting with others), each SNS has unique features or a specific purpose. Facebook, for example, has evolved into an environment where people build a community of friends, share latest news about themselves, and follow what their friends, family, and acquaintances are doing. Twitter, on the other hand, has become a platform where people express themselves, share updates with anyone who chooses to follow them, and follow others without the expectation that other users will reciprocally follow them. Instagram is similar to Twitter, with pictures replacing the 140 characters. Not all SNSs are intended to be social, as LinkedIn evolved into a platform where people join and interact with a network of professionals and users' profiles are actually online versions of their resumes.

Given the popularity of SNSs, it did not take long before organizations realized the potential offered by this new medium (Barnes, Lescault, & Andonian, 2014). They realized, for example, that they could create and/or expand their customer base by sharing content about their products, services, or organization on Facebook. Similarly, organizations realized they could increase corporate and product visibility and cultivate brand awareness by having a large number of Twitter followers and actively sending out tweets. Unlike traditional outreach or advertisement efforts, SNSs allow organizations to engage their customer base like never before (Treem & Leonardi, 2012) by allowing the company to get almost immediate feedback through the use of Facebook "likes," Twitter "re-tweets," and "hashtags." Organizations can also increase their visibility exponentially by having their shared content persist as their customers recirculate and recreate content. In short, SNSs have made it possible for organizations to create two-way connections between themselves and their stakeholders that were difficult or impossible to achieve before the mainstream availability of social media (Treem & Leonardi, 2012).

The ability to market products and sell goods or services is not the only motivation for organizations to be on social media today. With SNSs providing organizations with the tools needed to interact with the general public, there are a variety of different functions for which organizations can utilize them to accomplish organizational goals. One particular area for which organizations have increasingly turned to SNSs is employee recruitment (HR Focus, 2010). According to the latest yearly Social Recruiting Survey by the online recruitment services company Jobvite, 93 % of organizations were using or planning to use SNSs for recruitment in 2014, with 73 % planning to increase their investment in SNSs recruiting in 2015 (Jobvite, 2014).

Despite this mainstream adoption of SNSs for employee recruitment by organizations, there is dearth of empirical research investigating the benefits and pitfalls of using SNSs for employee recruitment. With SNSs being a relatively new medium for employee recruitment, research has fallen behind practice in terms of how to best to utilize these tools in order to attract the type of applicants desired by organizations. Most recruitment studies examining the effectiveness of traditional recruitment sources (e.g., newspaper ads, online ads, job fairs) provide information regarding best practices for how to use these traditionally available sources (e.g., Allen, Mahto, & Otondo, 2007; Birgelen, Wetzels, & Dolen, 2008). However, as the use of SNSs as a recruitment source is at its infancy, empirical research is lacking and little is known about how to best use SNSs for recruiting purposes and how this use is viewed by job applicants. Accordingly, by comparing and contrasting SNSs against organizational websites and online job boards, this chapter examines how recruiters are using SNSs for employee recruiting and whether or not SNSs are used by job seekers when looking for job information. In addition, factors potentially contributing to this usage preference are examined.

9.2 Recruiting on Social Networking Sites

More than a decade ago, Michaels and colleagues envisioned a "war for talent" in which recruiting qualified applicants would become increasingly difficult due to demographic and economic factors (Michaels, Handfield-Jones, & Axelrod, 2001). Organizations now operate in this environment with the importance of human capital increasingly being recognized (Phillips & Gully, 2015). Consequently, learning how to attract top talent has become critical for most organizations to thrive, prosper, and even survive (Beechler & Woodward, 2009). Employee recruitment, which is defined as activities that influence the number and types of applicants who apply for and accept a job offer (Breaugh, 1992), has become a critical factor for organizational success and viability.

There are a variety of traditional and new recruiting sources available to organizations today. Traditional recruitment sources include print, radio, and television advertisements, employee/friend/relative referrals, employment agencies, internal job postings, walk-ins, campus visits, and job fairs (Zottoli & Wanous, 2000). Internet recruiting was introduced as a new recruiting outlet with the proliferation of the Internet in the mid-1990s. Online employee recruitment is now an established practice for organizational recruiters and organizations typically engage in online external recruitment through posting job and company information on their corporate websites (e.g., Microsoft.com) and online job boards (e.g., Monster.com). In 2011, a total of 30 % of all hires came from either online job boards or company career sites (CareerXroads, 2012). Similarly, based on a survey of 1140 companies, it was found that in 2014, 61 % of all external hires (25 % of all hires) came from online job boards, while 15 % of all hires came from company career websites (SilkRoad, 2014). These results suggest that number of hires through online job boards and company websites has increased from 30 to 40 % between 2011 and 2014. Online recruiting has generally been preferred over traditional methods as online sources tend to generate a large number of applicants at a relatively low cost (Breaugh, 2008).

Organizations added another option to the recruiter toolbox with the explosion of SNSs in the mid-2000s (Edosomwan et al., 2011). There are different ways in which organizations can use SNSs to recruit their employees. An organization which has high visibility through a large follower base on Twitter or Facebook, for example, can tweet or post about available positions and may ask their followers to retweet or share the news, increasing the circulation and availability of the message. Organizations can also utilize the associations they establish with their followers to recruit from among them. Actively searching for job seekers is another option available to organizations, with tens of thousands of profiles publicly available on SNSs such as LinkedIn or Facebook. Using one or more of these methods, many organizations are in fact using SNSs for employee recruitment (Hunt, 2010).

According to Social Recruiting Survey results by Jobvite (2014), the SNS most frequently used by recruiters around the world is LinkedIn, which is being used by a 94 % of the recruiters. This is followed by Facebook (66 %) and Twitter (52 %). Recruiters report using LinkedIn to search for (95 %) and contact (95 %) candidates, keep tabs on potential candidates (93 %), vet candidates pre-interview (93 %), and post jobs (92 %). Facebook is mostly used to showcase employer brand (59 %), generate employee referrals (51 %), and post jobs (48 %). Finally, Twitter is mostly used to showcase employer brand (44 %), post jobs (39 %), and generate employee referrals (32 %).

Another survey which reports results from mostly European recruiters reports similar results in terms of SNS usage by recruiters (Zanella & Pais, 2014). First, Zanella and Pais found that LinkedIn and Facebook both were being used by 53 % of companies for employee recruiting, followed by Twitter (31 %). These authors also examined active company presence on SNSs by sector and found that the most active companies on SNSs were recruiting agencies with 92 % of these companies using SNSs for professional purposes. Zanella and Pais also reported that the recruitment activity most often pursued through SNSs was advertising jobs with 65 % of recruiters reporting to have engaged in this activity. This is followed by sourcing passive candidates (60 %) and vetting candidates (53 %). When examined by the type of job candidate targeted through SNSs, most recruiters (66 %) reported searching for individuals for nonmanagerial positions, but still a substantial proportion (41 %) reported using SNSs to search for senior management candidates. Top reasons for using SNSs for recruitment include diversifying recruitment channels (58 %), reaching targeted applicant demographics (56 %), and increasing the quantity of applications (56 %) (Zanella & Pais, 2014).

The survey results reported above suggest that the use of SNSs by recruiters include both active and passive recruiting activities. And while recruiters still prefer to contact the most qualified candidates through traditional channels or face-to-face networking (Zanella & Pais, 2014), the use of SNSs for active recruiting is growing. Active recruiting refers to recruiters directly contacting a potential applicant about a job opening. Passive recruiting activities, on the other hand, refer to companies placing job or company brand information on recruiting sources in the hopes that job seekers and candidates will find this information and apply for a position or leave with a positive view of the organization. The distinction between the two methods is important because different criteria may predict success of active and passive recruiting efforts.

In order for active recruiting efforts to succeed, it is enough for job seekers to maintain a presence on a recruiting platform (e.g., any specific SNS). This is because as long as a potential candidate has presence on an SNS, organizational recruiters can proactively review the candidate's credentials and contact that individual directly. While there are a number of factors that predict the effectiveness of recruiting efforts, such as job and organizational characteristics and recruiting process characteristics (see Uggerslev, Fassina and Kraichy 2012 for an excellent meta-analysis), recruiters need to ensure that they are "hunting in the right waters" before they start proactively looking for qualified job candidates on SNSs.

The literature on social media usage provides some clues regarding the types of job candidates that might be available on various SNSs for these active recruiting efforts. For example, a national survey of 2003 individuals conducted in the United States by Pew Research Center (Duggan, Ellison, Lampe, Lenhart, & Madden, 2014) indicated that the vast majority of adults in the United States use Facebook while a substantial, but still minority adults, report using Twitter and LinkedIn, see Fig. 9.1. This same study also outlined the reported frequency of use on these SNSs and found that 70 % of adult Facebook users use the site daily, compared with 36 % daily use by adult Twitter users and 13 % daily use by LinkedIn users.

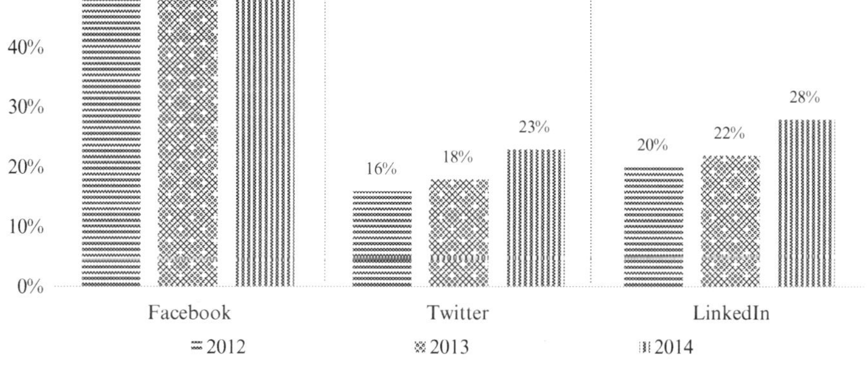

Fig. 9.1 Percent of online adults who use Facebook, Twitter, and LinkedIn by year *Source*: Duggan et al. (2014)

Table 9.1 Percent of online adults who use Facebook, Twitter, and LinkedIn

	Facebook	Twitter	LinkedIn
Age			
18–29 (%)	87	37	23
30–49 (%)	73	25	31
50–64 (%)	63	12	30
65+ (%)	56	10	21
Educational attainment			
High school graduate or less (%)	70	16	12
Some college (%)	71	24	22
College + (%)	74	30	50
Income level			
<$30,000/year (%)	77	20	15
$30,000–$49,999/year (%)	69	21	21
$50,000–$74,999/year (%)	74	27	31
>$75,000/year (%)	72	27	44

Source: Duggan et al. (2014)

Perhaps more telling than the frequency in which adult users engage with specific SNSs are the characteristics of these users. Duggan et al. (2014) found noticeable differences in educational attainment, reported income level, and age, see Table 9.1. Their results show that the majority of online adults in the United States with college degrees are active on Facebook and half of online adults with college degrees are active on LinkedIn. When looking across the three SNSs in the report, it appears that the majority of online adults have a Facebook account with these percentages not drastically varying across user characteristics. However, user characteristics are not stable on LinkedIn and Twitter. For instance, a larger percentage of college educated online adults use LinkedIn compared to the percent of online adults who use LinkedIn who do not have a college degree. These results paint an interesting picture for recruiters who are actively recruiting on SNSs for nonmanagerial and senior management positions. For example, while a larger percent of online adults with a college degree have a profile on Facebook (74 %) compared with LinkedIn (50 %) and Twitter (30 %), a larger ratio of individuals on LinkedIn might be qualified for certain positions based on the relative percentages of relevant characteristics on these SNSs.

Studies conducted outside the United States suggest that the SNS usage patterns found in the United States are similar to those patterns found across the globe. For example, a study conducted in Greece examined how SNSs are used by job seekers and recruiters and found that 90 % of job seekers reported using either Facebook or LinkedIn, with participants indicating a higher usage of Facebook than LinkedIn (Nikolaou, 2014). The Nikolaou study also found that higher levels of education tend to associate with LinkedIn engagement. Similarly, a study examining Facebook and LinkedIn usage in Israel found that 97 % of participants reported using Facebook and 54 % reported using LinkedIn (Zhitomirsky-Geffet & Bratspiess, 2015) and that their frequency of use was much higher on Facebook compared to LinkedIn. Zhitomirsky-Geffet and Bratspiess participants with LinkedIn profiles were more educated and wealthier compared to participants without LinkedIn profiles.

This wide adoption of SNSs by adults indicates that these platforms have the potential to become effective tools for actively recruiting employees. This is partly due to the overwhelming majority of adults who are using at least one SNS and the frequency in which they are contributing content to these sites. This presence and active use of SNSs make it possible for recruiters to proactively search for and find job candidates. Given the popularity of Facebook, it would seem reasonable that active recruiting efforts would be more successful on this platform. However, given the fact that Facebook is a socially oriented SNS and encourages users to post content that very likely is irrelevant or unrelated to job performance, it is likely that a professionally oriented SNS (e.g., LinkedIn) may be more fruitful for actively searching for employees.

The limited empirical evidence on the effectiveness of SNSs in recruiting supports the notion that professionally oriented SNSs are more effective than socially oriented SNSs. Specifically, Jobvite (2014) found that LinkedIn was the most effective SNS recruiting source with 74 % of recruiters reporting hiring through LinkedIn, 26 % through Facebook, and 14 % through Twitter. After beginning to use social media for recruitment, recruiters experience an increase in the quality (44 %) and quantity (44 %) of candidates and a decrease in the time to hire (34 %; Jobvite, 2014). However, the usage patterns of different SNSs seem to suggest that different types of job candidates could be recruited actively from socially oriented SNSs (e.g., Facebook) and professionally oriented SNSs (e.g., LinkedIn). The data are less clear about the types of job candidates that could be recruited from microblogging sites such as Twitter.

The evidence presented thus far does not consider job seekers' use and perceptions of usefulness of these platforms when looking for jobs and does not examine the nuanced differences between the various social media platforms that are available. Accordingly, not much can be said about the potential effectiveness of passive recruitment efforts carried on over SNSs or the potential antecedents of recruiting effectiveness on these platforms. When it comes to passive recruitment, the effectiveness of any recruitment source is influenced by the extent to which potential applicants choose to utilize that source for job-seeking purposes. For example, the circulation rate of a newspaper may be used as a metric for determining its potential efficacy as a recruitment source. However, if potential applicants do not look for employment information in that newspaper, it is unlikely to be an effective recruitment source regardless of the circulation rate. Similarly, the overwhelming popularity of Facebook may not guarantee that it is used to look for employment information by potential applicants. In order for organizations to use SNSs as a viable means for passively attracting potential applicants, organizations first need to know if job seekers are likely to look for and use the information on a wide variety of online recruitment sources when making employment decisions.

Accordingly, the remainder of this chapter is organized around empirically investigating three issues. First, in order to determine the potential chances of success when engaging in passive recruiting on these online sources, the extent to which job seekers prefer to get information from SNSs, company websites, and online job boards when making employment decisions is examined. Second, which recruitment sources are more likely to be preferred at different stages of the recruitment process will be examined. Finally, to gain additional insight regarding the antecedents of this recruitment source preference, the extent to which job seekers perceive the content posted on an organization's SNSs, its official website, and online job boards as credible and as providing a realistic job preview will be examined. However, before we move on to the findings, we believe it is necessary to provide the readers with a description of the sample, some information about each recruitment source we examined, and the measures we utilized to examine job seekers' perceptions of those recruitment sources.

9.3 Recruitment Sources, Measures, and Sample

9.3.1 Recruitment Sources

In order to examine the extent to which job seekers were using social media when looking for jobs, we asked a sample of 456 job seekers questions about their use of Facebook, Twitter, and LinkedIn when looking for jobs. We also asked the same questions regarding two other online job boards, Monster.com and CareerBuilder.com, and company websites to put their SNS usage into perspective.

Facebook is a social networking platform on which users can create profiles, share text, images, videos, or web links on their timelines, connect with other users by adding them as "friends," and react to what other users have posted by liking them or sharing them on their profiles. Depending on the privacy settings chosen by the user, only his or her friends or everyone can view the content shared by an individual. Facebook also allows organizations to create and run pages similar to profile pages of individuals, and individual users can subscribe to the content shared on those pages by "liking" the page.

Twitter, another social networking service, allows users to post short messages, called "tweets," which cannot exceed 140 characters. Messages can contain links to web pages. Every individual can browse tweets posted by users through the web or mobile interfaces; but only users with Twitter accounts can post tweets or subscribe to other Twitter feeds by "following" them. Organizations can also become Twitter users and share content with their followers.

LinkedIn is a large network of professionals from various sectors. Users can create their profiles on which they share their professional credentials and backgrounds, similar to the way on a resume. It is also possible to connect with other individual users, similar to a real-life professional network. Organizations can become

LinkedIn users, create profile pages that individual users can follow, and share content with their followers.

Finally, Monster.com and CareerBuilder.com are online job boards where recruiters can post basic information about job openings and job seekers can browse through the available job postings by conducting searches based on criteria such as sector, location, and keywords.

9.3.2 Measures

Job seekers were asked a variety of questions about which of the above online sources they used when looking for a job and reasons for using or not using each online source. Specifically, through an online survey we asked 456 individuals who were actively searching for jobs questions about how often they used specific online sources when they were looking for jobs. We also examined this usage for each stage of the job search process by asking job seekers which recruitment sources they were likely to prefer (a) when looking for job openings, (b) after finding a job posting to learn more about a job, and (c) to learn more about the company before an interview. Response options ranged from 1-Never to 5-All of the time.

In addition, to get a better understanding of what was related to usage or non-usage of certain sources by job seekers, we examined the extent to which each recruitment source was perceived to be a credible source of employment information. We measured credibility by asking the participants whether or not they agreed with the following statements: "the information on… (recruitment source) is accurate," "the information on… is credible," "the information on… is trustworthy," and "the information on… is legitimate." The response options ranged from 1-Strongly Disagree to 6-Strongly Agree.

In order to examine perceptions regarding whether or not each recruitment source provided job seekers with a realistic job preview (RJP), we asked participants the extent to which they agreed with the statements "… (recruitment source) gives me a good idea of what would be expected of me in a potential job," "… gives me an idea of what it would be like to work for a company," "… gives me a good idea of the kind of people with which I would work," and "… helps me decide if the job would be a good fit for me." The response options ranged from 1-Strongly Disagree to 6-Strongly Agree.

9.3.3 Job Seeker Sample

In order to empirically examine the previously described issues, 456 active American job seekers were recruited via MTURK (Buhrmester, Kwang, & Gosling, 2011) to complete an online survey. These individuals reported applying for at least one job in the past month (Mean = 9.30, SD = 15.34, Median = 5.00) and the final sample had a mean age of 32.81 (SD = 10.29, Median = 31.00); was 52.2 % female, 72.1 % White, 11.4 % Black, and 7.0 % Hispanic; 37.8 % possessed a high school degree, 14.1 % possessed a 2-year college degree; and 48.1 % possessed a bachelor's degree or greater.

9.4 Findings

9.4.1 How Does Social Networking Sites Compare to Other Online Recruitment Sources?

Employee recruitment and selection is costly. For instance, one estimate is that companies in the United States spend an average of $3500 per hire (O'Leonard, 2011). Thus, the question of which recruitment sources are more likely to be preferred by job seekers, and therefore produce a larger pool of applicants, has important practical and financial implications. One way to help maximize the return on passive recruiting efforts and expenditures is to use outlets that job seekers are most likely to use when looking for job information. Recruiting via online resources such as SNSs is no different. While most organizations are recruiting on SNSs such as LinkedIn, Facebook, and Twitter, there is little to no empirical research that asks active job seekers their preferences about online recruiting resources such as company websites, SNSs, and online job boards. The results presented in this chapter represent an important first step in helping to empirically answer this question from the job seekers' perspective.

Figure 9.2 shows the extent to which job seekers reported using various online sources when looking for job information. In contrast to the figures presented previously, these results can help recruiters engaged in passive recruiting efforts. As can be seen in the graph, Facebook and Twitter were among the sources that were the least likely to be preferred by job seekers. A statistical analysis that compared the usage results against one another revealed that Twitter was the online source that was the least used of all the sources, all p-values < 0.001. While used more than Twitter, Facebook was used less by job seekers compared with all other sources, all p-values < 0.001.

LinkedIn, the only other SNS in the study, was found to be used substantially more frequently than Facebook, $p < 0.001$, and Twitter, $p < 0.001$, but slightly less than Monster, $p = 0.035$, and CareerBuilder, $p = 0.038$. Similar to Facebook and Twitter, LinkedIn was found to be substantially less frequently used by job seekers when looking for job information, $p < 0.001$, compared to company websites.

When comparing the more typical online job boards Monster and CareerBuilder against one another, results showed that job seekers reported similar frequencies of usage with neither source being preferred over the other, $p = 0.972$. However, both of these online job boards were strongly preferred over Twitter, $p_{\text{Monster}} < 0.001$ and $p_{\text{CareerBuilder}} < 0.001$, and Facebook, $p_{\text{Monster}} < 0.001$ and $p_{\text{CareerBuilder}} < 0.001$, and slightly

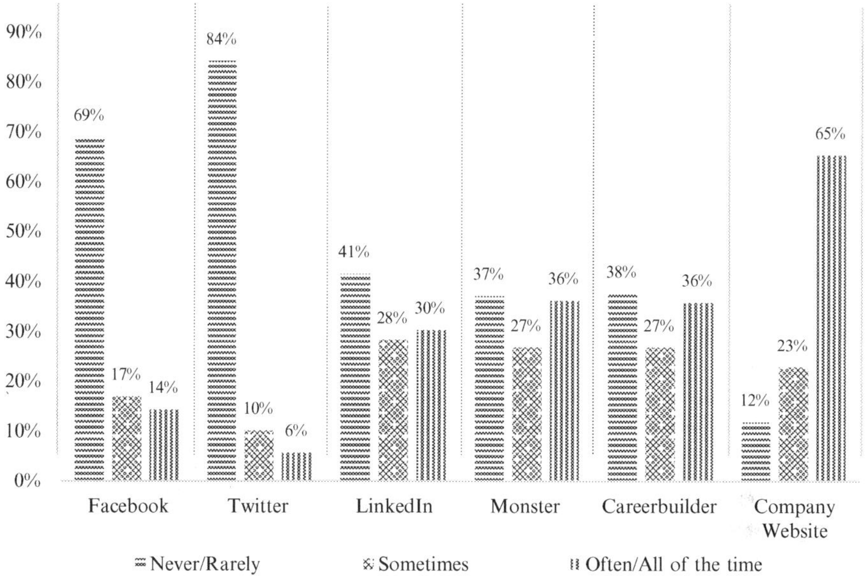

Fig. 9.2 Proportion of job seekers who report using each recruitment source

preferred over LinkedIn, $p_{\text{Monster}} = 0.035$ and $p_{\text{CareerBuilder}} = 0.038$. Company websites were strongly preferred as sources of job information over both Monster, $p < 0.001$, and CareerBuilder, $p < 0.001$.

These results indicate that job seekers use a variety of different sources when looking for information about a job. While job seekers tend to prefer going to the company's website to learn more about the job opportunity, they also report using the more typical online job boards and the professional SNS LinkedIn when looking for a job or learning about a place they want to work. Together, these results suggest that job seekers use SNSs Facebook and Twitter for personal communication, but that they do not rely on these platforms when looking for job information. Rather, our results indicate that job seekers prefer to use the company's website and online job boards during the job search process. This information will help organizations engaging in passive recruitment place job information where active job seekers are most likely to encounter it.

9.4.2 How Are Online Recruitment Sources Being Used?

Previous results provide an indication as to what online sources job seekers generally use when looking for job information, but they do not examine how or when in the recruitment process job seekers use these online sources. Given that job seekers report using a variety of online sources, including SNSs, it is possible that potential applicants prefer different recruitment sources at different stages of the recruitment process because they may wish to get different types of information at different recruitment phases (Phillips, 1998). Knowing when job seekers are looking for specific types of information can help recruiters get those individuals the right type of information and in time, and in doing so, potentially attract a larger applicant pool.

From a job seeker's perspective, the process of job search can be broken down into two phases (Barber, Daly, Giannantonio, & Phillips, 1994). First, job seekers look for jobs which generally fit their hard criteria such as location, hours, and job type. Second, after finding one or more jobs which seem to be good fits, job seekers go deeper into the available information to learn more about the job and the company in order to make the decision to apply or not. It can be argued that different types of information at different levels of specificity are needed to get through each of these phases. For example, in the first phase in which the job seeker only wants to learn if a job opening is available, recruitment sources in which a large number of jobs are available such as online job boards may be more useful. However, job seekers who have clear ideas regarding where they want to work may utilize company websites in this phase. After a pool of job postings are found, other recruitment sources with more detailed and rich information regarding the job and the organization may be more useful. For example, job seekers may want to utilize social media to reach current employees in that organization regarding working conditions or occupational growth opportunities. Similarly, job seekers may want to examine the available information on company websites to learn more about the organization. To the extent that a recruitment source is perceived as giving the desired information when needed, it can be expected that potential applicants will choose to utilize that source at that stage. To date little is known about how social media is used by job seekers when collecting job information at various phases of the job search process.

Figure 9.3 shows how job seekers that report looking at particular sources for job information use each of the online sources. Results for the SNSs indicate that job seekers who indicated using Facebook to look for job information tend to increasingly use it later in the job search process. Specifically, only about one-third of those that used Facebook reported using it during the first phase, when looking for job postings. However, a significantly higher relative percentage use Facebook to learn more about the company after they learn of the job listing, $p = 0.006$ and to prepare for an upcoming interview, $p < 0.001$.

This relative usage pattern was found to be different than that of those who reported using Twitter when looking for job information. Job seekers who reported using Twitter to learn about job openings reported extremely similar usage patterns during different phases of the job search process. That is, comparing to the percentage of respondents who reported using Twitter to look for job postings, a similar percentage reported using it to learn more about the company, $p = 0.169$, and to prepare for an upcoming interview, $p = 0.217$. These results indicate that job seekers who use Twitter during their job search tend to use it equally throughout the recruitment process.

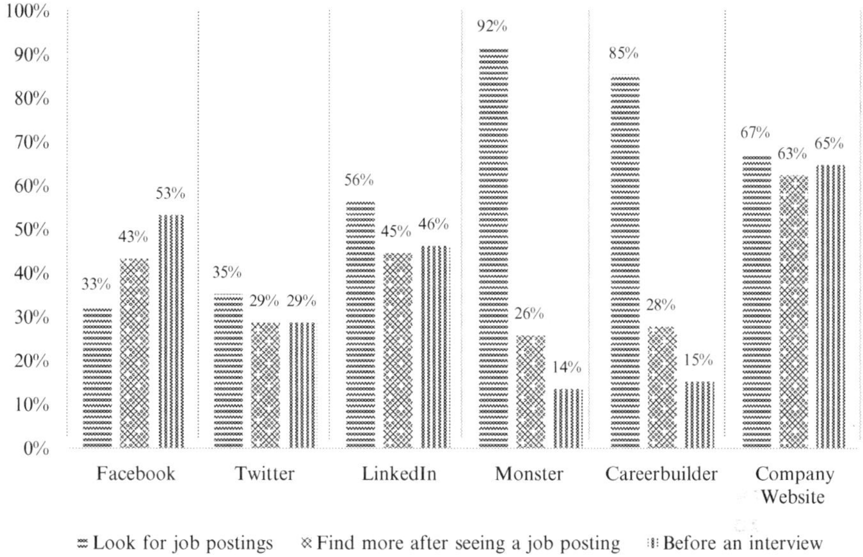

Fig. 9.3 How job seekers use each recruitment source (Percentages are of respondents who indicated using the recruitment source)

Both the Facebook and Twitter usage patterns differ from those of LinkedIn. Job seekers utilizing this SNS tend to use it most during the first stage of the job search process. Specifically, more than half of job seekers who use LinkedIn to learn about job information use it to find job postings, while a significantly few percentage use it to learn more about a job, $p=0.001$, and when preparing for an interview, $p=0.007$. While these relative percentages on LinkedIn do decrease throughout the process, it should be noted that the two later-phase percentages are statistically similar to those found for Facebook, $p_{\mathrm{Learn}}=0.745$, $p_{\mathrm{Interview}}=0.074$. Together, these results suggest that organizations should consider having a presence on Facebook and LinkedIn, and this presence is particularly important during the later phases of recruiting.

Results also suggest that organizations need to maintain a presence on online job boards, such as Monster and CareerBuilder, but this presence is most important during the first phase of the process. Specifically, an overwhelming majority of job seekers that use either Monster or CareerBuilder to look for job information use these online sources when looking for job postings. However, substantially fewer use these online sources when either trying to learn more about a job that has already been posted, $p_{\mathrm{Monster}}<0.001$; $p_{\mathrm{CareerBuilder}}<0.001$, and even fewer use these job boards to prepare for an interview, $p_{\mathrm{Monster}}<0.001$; $p_{\mathrm{CareerBuilder}}<0.001$.

Results suggest that company websites are the most important online recruiting sources that need to be maintained. As shown in Fig. 9.2, company websites are still the preferred method that jobs seekers use when learning about job opportunities, and the results shown in Fig. 9.3 indicate that the majority of job seekers that use company websites when looking for a job or learning about a place they want to work use it equally throughout the process. Specifically, compared to the percentage of job seekers who use company websites to look for postings, a similar percentage report using them to learn more about the company, $p = 0.083$, and to prepare for an upcoming interview, $p = 0.417$. These results indicate that the vast majority of job seekers that use a company's website during their job search use it equally throughout the recruitment process.

Interestingly, there were a percentage of job seekers that reported not using any of the online sources during the three phases of the job search process. The largest percentages were noticed within the SNSs with 17 % of job seekers not using Facebook for these three job search activities, 30 % not using Twitter, and 15 % not using LinkedIn. A substantially smaller percentage of job seekers did not use Monster.com (4 %), Careerbuilder.com (8 %), and the company website (8 %) for any of these three job search activities. The most likely explanation for this finding is that the three job search activities broadly represented the general phases of the job search process, but were not intended to be an exhaustive list. Adding other activities, such as learning about the company before submitting an application or further investigating the company before accepting a position to this list would likely reduce this percentage of non-usage to practically zero. While not an exhaustive list, the finding that certain online resources were preferred by job seekers throughout the job search process provides insight into the types of information that recruiters engaged in passive recruiting efforts should offer on these resources.

9.4.3 Factors Affecting the Recruitment Source Preference

It is not enough to only know which among the currently available recruitment sources are used by job seekers when looking for employment information in order to be able to make policy decisions regarding in which recruitment sources to invest and maintain. Equally important are the factors influencing the extent to which one recruitment source is used by job seekers to get employment information. This is especially true in today's fast-paced business environment where innovation and technology change is the norm.

Even though recruitment literature is replete with studies regarding which recruitment sources are superior to others (e.g., Breaugh, 1981; Reid, 1972), there is a gap in this literature when it comes to explaining why each source works (Breaugh & Starke, 2000). Knowing the factors that lead one potential applicant to use a specific recruitment source over another can help organizations make informed choices regarding which recruitment sources to utilize. This knowledge will also help organizations ensure that recruitment sources which are not currently available, but are developed in the future, are appealing to job seekers so that they can develop a deep applicant pool. Fortunately, the recruiting literature offers some guidelines for why some recruitment sources are superior to others (e.g., Zottoli & Wanous, 2000) and may be more likely to be preferred by potential applicants.

9.4.3.1 Credibility

One of the most common explanations for why some sources are preferred over others is the realism hypothesis (Breaugh & Starke, 2000). This hypothesis suggests that providing more accurate information about the job and the organization will lead to more effective recruiting outcomes (Breaugh & Mann, 1984). While providing accurate information about a job is likely to be beneficial for organizations (Mumford, 2012), it is reasonable to assume that those benefits also extend to job seekers as possessing accurate information should enable potential applicants to make more informed choices regarding pursuing employment in an organization (Breaugh & Starke, 2000). From job seekers' perspective, getting accurate information about a job opportunity is likely to be in their best interest because applying for a job with limited or inaccurate information will likely lead to unmet expectations, which have been found to be related with lower levels of job satisfaction (Moser, 2005).

Two ways to gauge the perceived accuracy of a recruiting source is to assess the extent to which job seekers believe the information on a source is credible and the recruitment source provides them with a realistic preview of the job and the company in which they would work. Credibility can be defined as the perceived believability of a source of information (Tseng & Fogg, 1999). RJPs, on the other hand, can be defined as the presentation of unfavorable information along with favorable information about a job (ed. Dunnette, 1991). RJPs are based on the notion that many job applicants have inflated expectations regarding the job, and this may potentially lead them to be dissatisfied with the job if they are hired (Breaugh, 2008).

There is evidence from other online applications suggesting that sources that are perceived as more credible are utilized more frequently when looking for information (e.g., Johnson & Kaye, 2000; Ridings, Gefen, & Arinze, 2002; Stavrositu & Sundar, 2008). Thus, it is reasonable to assume that this tendency extends to the situations in which job seekers are looking for information about employment options. Support for this notion comes from research that found the perceived credibility of recruiting sources and messages were positively related with job search outcomes and behaviors (Allen, Van Scooter, & Otondo, 2004; Ryan, Horvath, & Kriska, 2005). Credibility concerns may appear to be especially salient for SNSs because the content of an SNS is at least partly generated by users outside of the organization that may provide their opinions or feelings rather than accurate information.

The basic idea of the realism hypothesis is similar to the idea of an RJP in which if job applicants' expectations are not fulfilled, they become dissatisfied and more likely to quit than applicants with more accurate expectations (Breaugh & Starke, 2000). This notion is supported by three meta-analytic investigations regarding the effectiveness of RJPs (Earnest, Allen, & Landis, 2011; Phillips, 1998; Premack & Wanous, 1985), which found that RJPs have a positive effect on reducing turnover. While these are benefits to the organization, no empirical research has examined the relationship between RJPs and online recruiting source preference. Given the

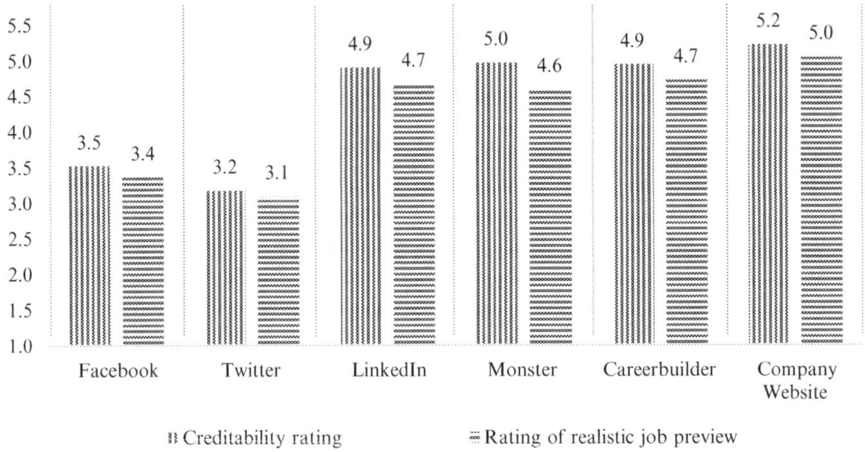

Fig. 9.4 Job seekers' ratings of source credibility and realistic job preview (Ratings were provided on a 6-point scale)

importance of providing applicants with an RJP, and that company websites, online job boards, and social media can all provide RJPs, knowing the extent to which these two concepts are related is important in developing more effective recruiting sources.

Figure 9.4 shows the extent to which job seekers rated each source as providing credible information and an RJP. Social networking sites, Facebook and Twitter, were among the sources that were thought to provide the least accurate information. Statistical analyses comparing Twitter's ratings against all other online sources revealed that it had the lowest ratings of credibility, all p-values < 0.001, and RJP, all p-values < 0.001. While seen as more accurate than Twitter, Facebook had lower credibility ratings, all p-values < 0.001, and RJP ratings, all p-values < 0.001, compared with the remaining sources. These results are consistent with the relatively low usage statistics reported in Fig. 9.2 and suggest that one reason Facebook and Twitter are not used by job seekers when looking for job information may be that they are perceived to lack accurate information about the job and the company.

In contrast, the SNS LinkedIn was found to have a credibility rating that was higher than both Facebook and Twitter, but had credibility and RJP ratings that were statistically equivalent to Monster, $p_{\text{Credibility}} = 0.352$; $p_{\text{RJP}} = 0.256$, and CareerBuilder, $p_{\text{Credibility}} = 0.579$; $p_{\text{RJP}} = 0.421$. These accuracy perceptions also reflect the overall usage patterns reported in Fig. 9.2. LinkedIn, a professional SNS, and the job boards of Monster and CareerBuilder were not found to be different in regard to job seekers accuracy perceptions and were found to have relatively similar usages levels. Together, these results suggest that one reason that LinkedIn is preferred over Facebook and Twitter when gathering information about a job is that LinkedIn is seen as providing more accurate and useful information compared to these personal SNSs

Results suggest that company websites were viewed as the source that provided the most accurate information as they were rated as the most credible, all p-values < 0.001, and provide the most RJP, all p-values < 0.001. Unlike company websites, in which the content is solely generated by the organization, the content in social media is generated collaboratively by the organization and by non-corporate users. Previous research has compared content generated by the organization to user-generated content in the context of online advertising, but not in the context of employee recruitment. The online advertising line of research (e.g., Cheong & Morrison, 2008; Jonas, 2010) has found evidence that user-generated content is preferred by product consumers over company-generated content. The inconsistency between this finding and the findings of this study suggests that the information gathering practice people use to learn about a product may be different from the process in which they engage in when looking for a job. Specifically, trustworthiness is domain specific (Mayer, Davis, & Schoorman, 1995), and there is some evidence suggesting that one necessary condition of trust is competence in the specific area (Butler, 1991). Accordingly, individuals may form different perceptions regarding the most knowledgeable party in each area, and this difference may explain the contradiction between this study's findings and previous research examining online advertising. It may be that individuals trust organizations when looking for employment information, but they do not trust when looking for product information because they perceive that users of the same product are more capable than the organization to give accurate information.

These perceptions can provide a partial explanation as to why company websites are preferred over other sources. It should be noted, however, that when the differences between accuracy ratings and the reports of general usage are compared, the credibility gap between company websites and LinkedIn, Monster, and CareerBuilder is less than the usage gap. This suggest that the lower usage patterns seen on professional SNSs and online job boards are due, at least in part, to other unmeasured factors, rather than only because they are seen as not providing accurate information.

Regardless, the fact that the official lines of communication, such as the company's website, are seen as trusted and valued sources of job information is good news for recruiters. The results of the current study suggest that recruiters, engaged in active or passive recruiting efforts, do not have to compete with sources that might have content about their organization or brand that are beyond their control (i.e., social networking sites). Rather, these results suggest that job seekers inherently trust the information on company's website and having this initial trust is an important first step in helping recruiters attract and retain the best possible applicants. Another reason for why the findings reported in this chapter should come as good news is that in addition to being under the recruiters' sole control, recruiting on an already built and maintained company website is also much less costly than recruiting on other platforms through paid advertising. Given the increased cost of filling each individual position (O'Leonard, 2011), recruiters are well advised to invest more time on recruiting through their company websites as compared to online job boards and SNSs.

9.5 Conclusion

In this chapter, we aimed at answering three major questions regarding the use of social media for employee recruitment. First, we examined the extent to which individuals preferred to get information from SNSs, online job boards, and company websites when looking for jobs. Second, we examined which recruitment sources were more likely to be preferred at different stages of the recruitment process. And finally, we examined the extent to which SNSs, online job boards, and company websites were seen as credible sources of employment information and as providing job seekers with an RJP.

The results of the study indicate a strong preference by job seekers towards company websites when looking for jobs, which are followed by online job boards and LinkedIn. Facebook and Twitter, on the other hand, are not seen as useful sources of information when looking for jobs. We also examined which sources are more likely to be preferred at different stages of the job search process. We found that online job boards were the most likely utilized recruitment sources in the first stage, followed by official company websites. However, when job seekers want to learn more about a company before they apply or while preparing for an interview, official company websites are more likely to be consulted. These results suggest that organizations should be smart about what information they post on which recruitment source at which stage of the recruitment process. Organizations should also better utilize multiple recruitment sources to support their recruiting efforts.

Information regarding which sources are utilized by job seekers at which phases of the job-seeking process is valuable to recruiters. Using this information, recruiters engaged in active and passive recruiting efforts may design recruitment strategies in such a way that they make the right information available on the right recruitment source at the right time, saving resources which otherwise would be wasted. For example, based on the results reported in this chapter, sharing only the basic information about the job opening on online job boards and making more information available about the job and the organization on the company websites seems like the most cost-effective approach to passive employee recruitment.

As two of the potential antecedents of recruitment source preference, we examined the credibility of the information and the extent to which the source is perceived to be providing an RJP. As Breaugh and Starke (2000) note, recruitment studies mainly focus on "what" of the recruitment (e.g., which sources are more effective than others) instead of why these source effects are occurring. These authors propose that more work needs to be done in order to discover the theoretical mechanisms leading to these source effects. In this chapter, we found that the credibility perceptions and whether or not the recruitment source is perceived to be providing job seekers with an RJP were likely to be related with the extent to which recruitment sources were utilized during job search. These are possibly among the many factors leading to recruitment source preference, and clearly more research is needed in this area. For example, most large organizations today are using formal applicant tracking systems to manage their hiring processes, and these systems are generally accessed through their recruiting websites. Accordingly, another explanation for why company websites are more likely to be preferred over other sources may be that job seekers are funneled to these applicant tracking systems, which are accessed over company websites, through recruiting ads or other means.

Recruitment efforts are aimed at achieving the pre-hire objectives of the broader process of creating a qualified workforce. Once the applicant pool is generated, it is selection, not recruitment, which is more effective in determining the overall quality of the workforce. Accordingly, utilizing selected employees as the subject pool and post-hire outcomes as the criteria in recruitment studies may become problematic as it may not be possible to isolate the effects of the recruitment from other processes the employees have gone through during their selection and entry to the organization. However, most recruitment studies have focused on post-hire outcomes and used recently hired employees as their samples (e.g., Evers, Anderson, & Smit-Voskuijil, 2005). Breaugh (2008) calls for more studies examining pre-hire outcomes and using applicants and job seekers as the sample.

This chapter is an effort in that direction as we examined the reactions of job seekers to SNSs, online job boards, and company websites as recruitment sources. The results explained in this chapter suggest that, despite the claims that corporate website is dead (Mainwaring, 2010; Shankland, 2011), it is a little early to announce the demise of the corporate website just yet. This is because even though organizations maintain presence on Facebook and Twitter for some time now, these social media channels are not yet seen as credible sources of information. However, it is possible that as people get used to the use of Facebook and Twitter by organizations for business issues like recruitment, the perceptions regarding the credibility of these recruitment sources may change and people may begin to see SNSs as places to search for job information. Until that time, companies are well advised to maintain a strong company website along with their social media presence.

References

Allen, D. G., Mahto, R. V., & Otondo, R. F. (2007). Web-based recruitment: Effects of information, organizational brand, and attitudes toward a website on applicant attraction. *Journal of Applied Psychology, 92*, 1696–1708.

Allen, D. G., Van Scooter, J. R., & Otondo, R. F. (2004). Recruitment communication media: Impact on prehire outcomes. *Personnel Psychology, 57*, 143–171.

Barber, A. E., Daly, C. L., Giannantonio, C. M., & Phillips, J. M. (1994). Job search activities: An examination of changes over time. *Personnel Psychology, 47*(4), 739–766.

Barnes, N. G., Lescault, A. M., & Andonian, J. (2014). *The 2014 Fortune 500 and social media: LinkedIn dominates as use of newer tools explodes*. Retrieved May 24, 2015, from http://www.umassd.edu/cmr/socialmediaresearch/2014fortune500andsocialmedia/.

Beechler, S., & Woodward, I. C. (2009). The global war for talent. *Journal of International Management, 15*, 273–285.

Birgelen, M. J. H., Wetzels, M. G. M., & Dolen, W. M. (2008). Effectiveness of official employment web sites: How content and form influence intentions to apply. *International Journal of Manpower, 29*(8), 731–751.

Breaugh, J. A. (1981). Relationships between recruiting sources and employee performance, absenteeism, and work attitudes. *Academy of Management Journal, 24*(1), 142–147.

Breaugh, J. A. (1992). *Recruitment: Science and practice*. Boston: PWSKent.

Breaugh, J. A. (2008). Employee recruitment: Current knowledge and important areas for future research. *Human Resource Management Review, 18*, 103–118.

Breaugh, J. A., & Mann, R. B. (1984). Recruiting source effects: A test of two alternative explanations. *Journal of Occupational Psychology, 57*, 261–267.

Breaugh, J. A., & Starke, M. (2000). Research on employee recruitment: So many studies, so many remaining questions. *Journal of Management, 26*, 405–434.

Buhrmester, M., Kwang, T., & Gosling, S. D. (2011). Amazon's mechanical turk: A new source of inexpensive, yet high-quality, data? *Perspectives on Psychological Science, 6*(1), 3–5.

Butler, J. K. (1991). Toward understanding and measuring conditions of trust: Evolution of a conditions of trust inventory. *Journal of Management, 17*, 643–663.

CareerXroads. (2012). *2012 Sources of hire: Channels that influence*. Retrieved May 22, 2015, from http://www.slideshare.net/gerrycrispin/2012-careerxroads-source-of-hire-channels-of-influence.

Cheong, H. J., & Morrison, M. A. (2008). Consumers' reliance on product information and recommendations found in UCG. *Journal of Interactive Advertising, 8*(2), 38–49.

Duggan, M., Ellison, N. B., Lampe, C., Lenhart, A., & Madden, M. (2014). *Social media update 2014*. Retrieved August 25, 2015, from http://www.pewinternet.org/2015/01/09/social-media-update-2014/.

Dunnette, M. D. (Ed.). (1991). *Handbook of industrial and organizational psychology*. Palo Alto, CA: Consulting Psychologists Press.

Earnest, D. R., Allen, D. G., & Landis, R. S. (2011). Mechanisms linking realistic job previews with turnover: A meta-analytic path analysis. *Personnel Psychology, 64*, 865–897.

Edosomwan, S., Prakasan, S. K., Kouame, D., Watson, J., & Seymour, T. (2011). The history of social media and its impact on business. *Journal of Applied Management and Entrepreneurship, 16*(3), 79–91.

Evers, A., Anderson, N., & Smit-Voskuijil, O. (Eds.). (2005). *Handbook of personnel selection*. Malden, MA: Blackwell.

HR Focus. (2010). *Recruiting and marketing are top benefits of social media*. Retrieved May 25, 2015, from http://hrpeople.monster.com/news/articles/3247-recruiting-and-marketing-are-top-benefits-of-social-media.

Hunt, K. G. (2010). Finders keepers: Social media strategies help find top talent. *Journal of Property Management, 75*(6), 36–40.

Jobvite. (2014). *Social recruiting survey 2014*. Retrieved February 26, 2015, from http://www.jobvite.com/wp-content/uploads/2014/10/JobviteSocialRecruiting_Survey2014.pdf.

Johnson, T. J., & Kaye, B. K. (2000). Using is believing: The influence of reliance on the credibility of online political information among politically interested internet users. *Journalism and Mass Communication Quarterly, 77*, 865–879.

Jonas, J. R. O. (2010). Source credibility of company-produced and user-generated content on the internet: An exploratory study on the Filipino youth. *Philippine Management Review, 17*, 121–132.

Mainwaring, S. (2010). *The death of corporate websites: Top 10 ways they will change*. Retrieved April 27, 2015, from http://wefirstbranding.com/brands/the-death-of-corporate-websites-top-10-ways-they-will-change/.

Mayer, R. C., Davis, J. H., & Schoorman, F. D. (1995). An integrative model of organizational trust. *The Academy of Management Review, 20*, 709–734.

Michaels, E., Handfield-Jones, H., & Axelrod, B. (2001). *The war for talent*. Boston: Harvard Business School Press.

Moser, K. (2005). Recruitment sources and post-hire outcomes: The mediating role of unmet expectations. *International Journal of Selection and Assessment, 13*(3), 188–197.

Mumford, T. V. (2012). Whom to believe: Recruiting information source credibility and organizational attractiveness. *Business and Management Research, 1*(4), 63–80.

Nikolaou, I. (2014). Social networking web sites in job search and employee recruitment. *International Journal of Selection and Assessment, 22*(2), 179–189.

O'Leonard, K. (2011). *Talent Acquisition Factbook 2011: Benchmarks and trends of spending, staffing and key talent metrics*. Retrieved April 30, 2015, from http://www.bersin.com/News/Content.aspx?id=14998.

Phillips, J. M. (1998). Effects of realistic job previews on multiple organizational outcomes. A meta-analysis. *Academy of Management Journal, 41*(6), 673–690.

Phillips, J. M., & Gully, S. M. (2015). Multilevel and strategic recruiting: Where have we been, where can we go from here? *Journal of Management, 41*(5), 1416–1445.

Premack, S. L., & Wanous, J. P. (1985). A meta-analysis of realistic job preview experiments. *Journal of Applied Psychology, 70*, 706–719.

Reid, G. L. (1972). Job search and the effectiveness of job-finding methods. *Industrial and Labor Relations Review, 25*, 479–495.

Ridings, C. M., Gefen, D., & Arinze, B. (2002). Some antecedents and effects of trust in virtual communities. *Journal of Strategic Information Systems, 11*, 271–295.

Ryan, A. M., Horvath, M., & Kriska, S. D. (2005). The role of recruiting source informativeness and organizational perceptions in decisions to apply. *International Journal of Selection and Assessment, 13*(4), 235–249.

Shankland, S. (2011). *Will Facebook replace company web sites?* Retrieved April 15, 2015, from http://news.cnet.com/8301-30685_3-20038242-264.html.

SilkRoad. (2014) *Top sources for hires 2014*. Retrieved May 24, 2015, from http://hr1.silkroad.com/Source-of-Hire-Resource-Center.

Stavrositu, C., & Sundar, S. (2008). If internet credibility is so iffy, why the heavy use? The relationship between medium use and credibility. *Cyberpsychology and Behavior, 11*, 65–68.

Treem, J. W., & Leonardi, P. M. (2012). Social media use in organizations: Exploring the affordances of visibility, editability, persistence, and association. *Communication Yearbook, 36*, 143–189.

Tseng, S., & Fogg, B. J. (1999). Credibility and computing technology. *Communications of the ACM, 42*, 39–44.

Zanella, S., & Pais, I. (2014). *#Social recruiting: A global study*. Retrieved May 27, 2015, from http://www.adecco.com/en-US/Industry-Insights/Documents/social-recruiting/adecco-global-social-recruiting-survey-global-report.pdf.

Zhitomirsky-Geffet, M., & Bratspiess, Y. (2015). Perceived effectiveness of social networks for job search. *International Journal of Libraries and Information Services, 65*(2), 105–118.

Zottoli, M. A., & Wanous, J. P. (2000). Recruitment source research: Current status and future directions. *Human Resource Management Review, 10*(4), 353–382.

Chapter 10
How to Stay Current in Social Media to Be Competitive in Recruitment and Selection

Stephanie L. Black, Montressa L. Washington, and Gordon B. Schmidt

Abstract With social media currently being used in employee recruitment and selection, organizations need to make sure they are looking at and engaging with the right social media sites. This issue is complicated by the fact that technology advances rapidly and the social media sites people use can change significantly over time. This chapter helps practitioners to deal with these issues by offering processes and criteria to be used to keep current on social media. It is discussed how organizations can keep current on social media sites used, existing practice, existing laws, and existing research related to social media use. Processes organizations can use to keep current and use appropriate social media data is discussed, as well as how organizations can create audits of social media use. The chapter concludes by highlighting developing technologies and other developments that could have significant impact on how social media is best used by organizations.

Keywords Social media • Selection • Recruitment • Credibility • Mobile • Tablets • Innovation • Big data

S.L. Black, M.B.A. (✉)
Department of Management, School of Business, University at Albany, BB 349, 1400 Washington Avenue, Albany, NY 12222, USA
e-mail: slblack@albany.edu

M.L. Washington, Ph.D.
Weatherhead School of Management, Case Western Reserve University, 10900 Euclid Avenue, Cleveland, OH 44106-7235, USA
e-mail: mlw41@case.edu

G.B. Schmidt, Ph.D.
Division of Organizational Leadership and Supervision, Indiana University-Purdue University Fort Wayne, Neff 288D, 2101 East Coliseum Blvd., Fort Wayne, IN 46805, USA
e-mail: schmidtg@ipfw.edu

R.N. Landers, G.B. Schmidt (eds.), *Social Media in Employee Selection and Recruitment*, DOI 10.1007/978-3-319-29989-1_10

10.1 Introduction

Since 1991, when the Web was first made available to the public, its usage has readily expanded to create a globally networked computing environment. The expansion of this technology and the growth of social media in particular have helped foster the emergence of many new selection and recruitment practices with both hiring managers and human resource managers placing more emphasis on the utilization of social media for recruiting and selection of candidates both outside and within the organization. Although this new means of communication was initially used by organizations primarily for job postings, online testing, and other practices, it has readily expanded. Currently, it is used as a tool by organizations in the recruitment and selection of applicants, and its adoption in the workplace has influenced all areas of employment (Gregory, Meade, & Thompson, 2013).

The rapid diffusion of social media adoption by organizations provides many new possibilities for organizations in the manner in which this technology is used and directed at potential and existing employees. The standard use of viewing a pool of resumes has become outdated as potential candidates can be selected and specifically targeted from a global population through the use of new and more innovative practices. However, with the ever increasing changes in technology, human resource managers and recruiters also have the challenge of keeping current with the latest trends in social media usage as well as advances in technologies in order to ensure that their organizations continue to attract, recruit, and retain the best individuals that fit their job specifications.

At present, most of the extant research has focused on the current methods of social media adoption within organizations, and paid little attention to looking forward to what will appear next on the horizon. However, with companies increasingly competing for highly skilled labor, it is not enough for organizations to just maintain the status quo. Instead, organizations must become more proactive in adapting to the swift technological changes in recruiting and selection practices.

One of the primary purposes of the Internet was to ease global communication, but the paths that individuals take to communicate through technology and social media are ever changing. The history of social media shows us that even popular social media sites can rise and fall in short periods of time. Examples of this can be seen with the social media site Friendster, founded in 2002, which is considered to be one of the original social networks to have relatively widespread use but by 2006 was essentially finished in the United States market (McMillian, 2013). MySpace is another example, which was launched in the United States in 2003 and held a dominant position as a social network platform from 2006 to 2009, but was surpassed in popularity by Facebook and shed users, quickly falling into insignificance (Gillette, 2011). How people communicate and the social media that is used can and does change rapidly as new technology and different preferences develop.

Today, Facebook appears to have established a strong foothold as a social networking platform, but it too is evolving from a website which was originally intended for students within a particular university to communicate with each other (originally just at Harvard University), to a site where individuals communicate with their friends and family, and to now a site that has expanded to include professional web pages, online job postings, and has a significant proportion of users who only access the site through mobile devices (Ha, 2015). However, while Facebook may have 1.49 billion users today (Facebook 2015), nothing can ensure that its usage is sustainable. In fact, in comparing the amount of US adults online using social media sites, Facebook was flat in growth from 2013 to 2014 while sites like Twitter, Instagram, and Pinterest grew significantly (Duggan, Ellison, Lampe, Lenhart, & Madden, 2015). The rapid adoption of new technology has shown us that the emergence of new technologies often is the demise of older ones.

The fact that the future is likely to have significant differences from the present is a concern for organizations and academics. Best practice and academic research is predominately focused on the present state of affairs, and in fact with the time that can pass between the creation of material and ultimate dissemination to the public it could be fair to categorize such research and practice as actually reporting on the recent past, not the present. Lord and Dinh (2014) and Lord, Dinh, and Hoffman (2015) discuss the problems of looking backward and planning for the past rather than the future with regard to the areas of leadership and organizational change, respectively. Schmidt (2014) highlights that social media changes rapidly as to how employees and leaders use it. In a changing world, looking forward and preparing for change is essential.

With the rapid technological innovations and emergence of new social media platforms everyday, it is critical that human resource managers start developing a more future-focused orientation with regard to recruitment and selection to ensure that they are able to continue to attract, hire, and retain individuals now and in the future. Organizations must be proactive in developing practices to not only ensure that they are using the most current and accurate information to screen applicants, but also utilize the best platforms to inform and attract potential employees. To date, research has provided us little information on how to keep current and develop a sustained competitive advantage in the use of social media. We take up this task in the chapter by offering potential answers to the following questions:

1. How does a company keep current with social media trends?
2. How does a company keep up on practice, research, and the law on social media in recruiting and selection?
3. What processes can organizations create and sustain over time in order to keep updated?
4. What systems can organizations put into place to ensure that the most current information is being utilized?

These specific questions will be examined by examining organizational structures and procedures to update and keep current on social media, developing auditing methods to check the content and quality of the information gleaned from social media platforms, and providing suggestions for developing a proactive approach to the adoption of new technologies.

10.2 Social Media Adoption by Organizations

Since the inception of the Web and expansion of the use of the Internet, social media platforms have allowed individuals to generate and share information and experiences online (Tussyadiah & Fesenmaier, 2009). The large audience and the extensive amount of information that is readily available have also made social networking sites (SNS) an ideal potential medium for organizations to utilize for both recruitment and selection purposes. However, along with the rapid diffusion of this technology, we have also witnessed a shift in the usage of various platforms overtime. A recent study by Barnes, Lescault, and Augusto (2014) of Inc. 500 companies and their usage of social media showed that although Facebook is extremely popular among organizations, its usage has dropped. For example, in 2014 the usage dropped 4 % (Barnes et al., 2014). In this same time period, the company usage of Twitter rose 5 %, Foursquare 6 %, and Instagram 7 %.

There has also been a shift in the technology used to access social media. According to Jobvite (2014), 43 % of job seekers use mobile cell phones in their job searches, but at present there appears to be a lag in organizations' adoption of this technology as only 59 % of organizations are currently investing in mobile career sites (Jobvite, 2014). These studies show that while social media has penetrated many aspects of the business community with tremendous speed, organizations need to become more agile in determining which social media platforms best fit their needs and are currently relevant so that they can incorporate the use of new platforms and tools while discarding the use of others that become obsolete (Barnes et al., 2014).

10.3 Current Practices

The socialization of the Web has created significant changes to how and when we choose to communicate with each other over the Internet, and organizations have readily adopted the use of the Internet to hire new staff using online software, social networks, and other platforms to conduct what is now called "social recruiting" (Wauters, 2011). According to Jobvite (2014), 89 % of US companies said they recruit through social media, which is up from 83 % in 2013. In fact, social media ranked fourth in terms of the quality of applicants, behind referrals, internal transfers, and direct sourcing, but before a company's own career site (Jobvite, 2014). Another study showed that 93 % of the Inc. 500 organizations are using some type of social media tool within their companies, and LinkedIn, Facebook, and Twitter are currently among the more popular platforms (Barnes, Lescault, & Augusto, 2014).

For organizations, LinkedIn provides an abundance of information about the qualifications of various jobseekers, and organizations can effectively use LinkedIn to leverage their own networks (and those of their employees) in order to find potential candidates. LinkedIn also allows organizations to create company profiles as well as set-up feeds of information for those whom would like to follow them and be contacted about new job postings (Heathfield, 2015). LinkedIn also offers organizations a fee-based solution which enables human resource managers to more readily find potential job candidates that best fit the qualifications of the job they want to fill. Facebook has more recently also become a popular platform for organizations to develop a brand presence, target potential job applicants, and post jobs. Using Facebook organizations may also interact with job applicants and create an online community. In contrast, Twitter is effective at increasing exposure and communicating with groups of individuals who want to follow organizations, and it is also popular among jobseekers viewing new job postings. In fact, some organizations have created job channels on Twitter in order to communicate and attract new talents (Heathfield, 2015).

10.4 Organization Recruitment Via Social Media

Over the years, we have also seen organizations expand their usage of SNS for sourcing and recruiting potential employees, and social media has emerged as a tool for how employers recruit talent to their organizations. Social media enables organizations to build their employment brand, expand their network, target their audience, and attract employees that fit with the company culture and core values.

Organizations are using SNS to collect data because they want to maximize dependable role behavior, avoid negligent hiring lawsuits, and screen out applicants who might be untrustworthy (Framingham, 2008; Roth, Bobko, Van Iddekinge, & Thatcher, 2016; Shea & Wesley, 2006; Taylor, 2007). According to Herd Wisdom (Akiode, 2013) 89 % of all recruiters reported having hired someone through LinkedIn or chosen not to hire someone based on their online content. Approximately three-quarters (73 %) of recruiters in a study indicated that they have made successful hires through social media and, conversely, one-third of employers rejected candidates because of something that they found in their social media profiles (Bennet, 2014).

10.5 Applicant Screening and Selection

In addition to organizations utilizing SNS to attract applicants, many human resource managers are using SNS in order to screen applicants in the selection and recruitment process.

Through the use of social media platforms, organizations are now potentially able to target a wider audience in their recruiting and gather more information that traditional resumes provide (Brown & Vaughn, 2011), and potentially significantly lower their costs (Anderson, 2003; Brady, Thompson, Wuensch, & Grossnickle, 2003; Hull, 2011).

Presently, LinkedIn is among the most popular professional SNS used by organizations, but there are other social media platforms targeted at specific industries that are also utilized by human resource managers and job recruiters. Examples of some of these communities include Dice.com, which is a community for tech careers; eFinancialCareers, which is a global career site for professionals looking for work in the banking and finance industry; FinancialJobBank, which is for job seekers and employers in the accounting and finance industry; and CollegeRecruiter.com, which is a leading job board for students seeking internships as well as recent graduates looking for entry-level positions. Sites like these allow employers to target specific jobs and place job postings on these sites. Moreover, the amount of information that is readily available online and the ability to specifically target the potential candidates from global talent provides organizations with a potentially effective tool for evaluating candidates.

10.6 Keeping Current on Social Media

Social media sites such as LinkedIn, Twitter, and Facebook are currently valuable resources for identifying qualified candidates and communicating with and recruiting applicants to fill positions. However, the social media space is very large, and new platforms such as Pinterest or Highlight, are continually launching. Social media sites rapidly appear, disappear, and morph into other entities and as a result some are popular one year and fall off the radar the next. In order for organizations to stay current on social media and know the most relevant recruiting and selection SNS, HR professionals need to think partly like an angel investor (keeping abreast of current developments in a particular business arena), curator (compiling digital data, images, web links), futurist (systematically exploring predictions and possibilities about the future) and technologist (practical application of knowledge especially in the particular area of social media technology).

In addition to organizations developing current social strategies to attract the best talent, they must continuously work on listing and regularly monitoring rising sites to determine if a site is becoming an important site or just a fad. For instance, between 2014 and 2015 a newer social media site Ello received increased media coverage because of its seemingly more privacy friendly polices versus that of Facebook. Ello created a buzz as the new "Anti-Facebook" and hoped that fed-up Facebook users would switch to the Ello. Despite their efforts to gain market share, however, in this instance Ello did not surpass Facebook. "As quickly as it appeared, Ello faded from the spotlight. Now, only a year later, Ello is nearly forgotten" (Finley, 2015). If an organization had a social media site monitoring procedure in place, they would have known that Ello did not have a significant impact on disrupting the Facebook user base. At the same time, as blogging has decreased, Twitter usage has increased. Thus, keeping current on social media will require HR professionals to strategically reference social media site traffic statistics, technology press, research organizations, and the use of customized internal and external surveys.

Social Media Sites Traffic Statistics. HR managers should take advantage of the ability to gather information not only about their target audience but also social media trends. HR managers can utilize statistics to help provide feedback on relevant sites. The volume of traffic experienced by a social media site is often a good indicator of users' perceived popularity and usefulness of a site. Presently, there are several companies that monitor and track social media traffic and publish the statistics. This information can be useful for recruiting and selection because social media site traffic stats provide insight into the sites that are the most popular and utilized. Please note our DISCLAIMER, the examples provided may not exist in the future. This is why this chapter matters, organizations need to be thoughtful on current and future social media sites and must be ready to make quick changes to keep current.

For example, Alexa.com provides analytical insights to benchmark, compare, and optimize businesses on the Internet. Alexa provides traffic data, global rankings, and other information on 30 million websites, and as of 2015 its website is visited by over 6.5 million people monthly (http://www.alexa.com/siteinfo/alexa.com). According to Alexa.com, their tools allow users to narrow search of relevant web content to that which meets specific criteria, benchmark any site to know if it is gaining audiences and attention compared to similar sites, understand how much traffic is getting and from where, and then use such information related to users own use of such sites.

Another company that provides social media reporting for organizations is Sproutsocial (sproutsocial.com). This company provides organizations with analytics on the content that resonates best with the targeted audience. Sproutsocial also tracks trends and usage across various platforms so that organizations can gain efficiencies with their social media strategies.

Google's Display Planner (https://adwords.google.com/da/DisplayPlanner/Home) is another good resource for HR managers, because it provides information about the sites the target audience or prospective employee is likely to visit and suggests new ways to connect with them. This resource uses all of the targeting options available on the Google Display Network. For example, once demographic and sites associated with your target audience is entered into the tool then new websites, mobile applications, and video channels for your ads are suggested. Organizations can follow recruitment-related sites to help to determine where advertising is best.

Technology Press. Online and print publications dedicated to technology are also viable resources to help determine new and more popular social media sites. TechCrunch (http://techcrunch.com/) and Mashable (http://mashable.com) are examples of two websites dedicated to providing current information about social media trends. These sites cover new technology and have specific content about social media. Organizations can use these sites to learn about technology on the horizon. TechCrunch is an online publisher of information technology news, which primarily covers businesses, ranging in size from startups to established NASDAQ-100 firms. Presently, TechCrunch is the highest-read technology startup news source on the Web, with over 35 million readers per month (http://www.similarweb.com/website/techcrunch.com).

Another example, Mashable (http://mashable.com) has a site dedicated to social media and is considered to be a leading global media company. Mashable tracks technology trends and new social media sites and uses. This site provides in-depth social media guides and resources. Mashable allows users to set-up various channels and feds to follow current content using services such as Facebook, Twitter, LinkedIn, and daily emails.

Webtrends (www.webtrends.com) tracks Internet and technology trends in addition to offering website analytics to understand new ways to reach customers. Webtrends monitors, tracks, and documents users' meaningful experiences with digital interactions on websites, apps, and social media.

Wired (wired.com) and Fast Company (fastcompany.com) are magazines published in both print and online editions that report on how emerging technologies affect culture, the economy, and politics. These sources highlight and provide subject matter expertise from leading creative thought leaders who are actively involved in creating the future of business.

Research Organizations. Organizations may also take advantage of using research entities that generate intellectual capital regarding technology trends and specifically social media. For example, the Pew Research Center (http://www.pewinternet.org/) regularly publishes current statistics and data on how social media is being used by the general population. This center also provides statistics on social media site usage over time segmented by demographics. It examines such issues both within the United States and internationally.

Other research organizations that provide content related to social media statistics and trends are—Society for Human Resource Management (www.shrm.org), Nielson (www.nielsen.com), Gallup (www.gallup.com), Forrester (www.forrester.com), and Gartner (www.gartner.com). Consulting firms have research divisions that publish white papers and other content related to trends in technology, which may be helpful to human resource managers. Some of the more popular resources are: McKinsey (www.mckinsey.com), Accenture (www.accenture.com), and IBM (www.ibm.com/services/us/gbs/thoughtleadership).

Surveys. The use of surveys is an effective tool for gathering data on the current most popular social media sites. This can be accomplished using a few methods, (1) issuing a survey to your current employees to determine which social media sites they use the most, (2) asking applicants which social media sites they frequent the most, and (3) using panels to obtain information on most frequently used social media sites. When using employees as the subjects for a survey a decision must be made upfront if the responses will be anonymous or non-anonymous which will be influenced by an organization's internal culture.

Social media sites are forever changing and it is important to create a routine of frequent monitoring to identify new sites for consideration. Conducting surveys with current employees and potential applicants is one way to learn which sites should be used for future screening or recruiting. When developing the questions for the survey, compile information on the most promising sites and examine how those sites work. Once the survey data is collected, use the results to determine which sites should be kept monitored and which sites are no longer relevant and can be deleted as some sites may become defunct or some sites may just lose active users and no longer be relevant. Next, determine how to integrate new sites into existing processes for social media use in recruiting and selection. Lastly, disseminate the findings to appropriate HR personnel with your organization.

Amazon Mechanical Turk (https://www.mturk.com/mturk/welcome) is a viable resource for obtaining panel data. Mechanical Turk allows you to target specific groups and you can even choose groups where current selection/recruitment is lacking in effectiveness. Using samples from Mechanical Turk provides information from samples that do not have an incentive to be untruthful to protect their own interests and privacy since they are anonymous.

10.6.1 Keeping Current with Practice

There are also resources available from a practitioner perspective in order to keep current with social media sites related to recruitment and selection. Some of the traditional trade journals are: *Human Resource Management*, *Human Resource Management Review*, *Journal of Human Resources*, *HRM The Journal*, *Workforce Magazine*, *International Public Management Association Publications*, *The HR Direct*, and *The International Journal of Human Resource*. These journals all provide valid information from research and top analysts on human resource topics and cover a variety of topics. Organizations may want to monitor such journals for content relevant to social media selection and recruitment. This can be done by having HR staff scan table of contents of issues, and most such trade journals offer the ability to get table of content alerts as new issues come out.

In addition to the journals listed above, there are also other applied practice journals available to HR managers and HR recruiters that can be of significant value. Business Horizons (http://www.journals.elsevier.com/business-horizons/) is published by Indiana University and has a general goal of getting its readers to consider business practice in new ways, often through articles discussing new innovations in the workplace. The journal has been home to many important articles on the developing use of social media in organizations and is potentially a key place for HR professionals to keep abreast of social media-related developments in the academic literature.

The MIT Sloan Management Review (http://sloanreview.mit.edu/) and the Harvard Business Review (https://hbr.org/) are long running journals that have a focus on helping those in practice to understand important innovations and research. The California Management Review (cmr.berkeley.edu) and the Thunderbird International Business Review (http://tibr.thunderbird.edu/) fill a similar purpose as management journals featuring practitioner-oriented research. HR professional can monitor the table of contents of all these journals for articles relevant to social media usage in recruitment and selection. HR practitioners may want to monitor indicators of journal quality such as impact factors in deciding what practice-orientated journals they want to start following or want to continue following over time.

10.7 Associations

Human resource managers may also want to stay current by participating in associations and attending relevant conferences. For one example, the Society for Human Resource Management (http://www.shrm.org/pages/default.aspx) is one of the largest current HR management associations and has over 27,500 members in over 160 countries members in 140 countries. They also hold an annual conference and provide resources to members and the public through their website. The Academy of Management (http://aom.org/) has 20,000 members in 115 countries and is made up of management scholars, students, and practitioners. They publish five academic journals and have an annual conference. There are also many industry, field, and profession-based organizations such as the America Society for Healthcare Human Resource Administration (http://www.ashhra.org/). HR professionals need to determine which such groups are relevant to their own industry and determine if they might provide useful information related to social media use in recruitment and selection.

10.7.1 Keeping Current with the Law

It is critical that human resource managers keep well-informed of current legislation at the state, federal, and international level. Legislation in many states and countries have lagged behind the rapid adoption of the technology and new legislation is still being enacted. A later chapter in this book by Schmidt and O'Connor (2016) goes into detail of the existing state of the law in the United States and globally so we will not make such a summary here.

What is relevant related to the law and this chapter's focus is how to keep current over time on legal issues related to social media usage in recruitment and selection. The websites and journals discussed above will help organizations to gain relevant information about new laws and legal rulings. Other online sources can provide useful information as well, so for instance the National Labor Relations Board posts all rulings on their website (https://www.nlrb.gov/) as does the United States Supreme Court (http://www.supremecourt.gov/). HR staff members could collect relevant rulings as they come out and have internal or external legal counsel analyze such results as to how they impact the organization's use of social media in the recruitment and selection processes.

We also recommend that organizations consider retaining legal counsel to keep abreast of new rulings as they arise. Organizations could hire counsel to give yearly updates exclusively on social media use in recruitment and selection or have such duties added to existing lawyers on retainer. Keeping legally compliant is crucial for avoiding lawsuits and maintaining an ethical environment.

10.7.2 Example Procedure for Keeping Current Regarding Social Media

In order to be most effective in the use of social media and keep current with recruiting and social networking sites, we recommend that organizations develop a routine of performing certain functions. These behaviors include finding, tagging, rating commenting, updating, and contextualizing information.

Step 1. Finding refers to locating relevant information on recruiting and selection-related social media sites. This information can start being located via simple search engine searches of Google and other search engines. HR staff can also ask peers in other organizations or conduct surveys to discover what sites others are looking at for information related to recruiting and selection through social media. Once information is located, the HR staff member can set-up Google alerts or equivalent alerts to be notified when and if the selected site is updated.

Step 2. Tagging involves identifying images or text within a site which are categories or topics that relate to recruiting and selection. Web pages and blogs with identical tags can then be linked together allowing users to search for similar or related content. If the tags are made public, online pages that act as a Web-based bookmark service are able to index them. Tags can be created using words, acronyms, or numbers (Webopedia, 2015).

Step 3. Rating involves developing a system to rank social media sites based on their content relevance and usability. Such ratings would then inform how information gained from a site is weighted compared to other information gained from other sites.

Step 4. Commenting is where organizational representatives express opinions or reactions about particular social media sites. Engaging with the community will keep you relevant to your audience and keep you current about important topics. The organization may also gain new sources of information as users of sites might bring information to the organization's attention. The community can be a powerful resource and the company as active partner in the community is likely to gain more valuable information about relevant social media sites (Breakenridge, 2012).

Step 5. Updating is having an online library and bookmarks with the most current social media recruiting and selection information. This would involve using the resources noted above to keep current with relevant information. New information learned needs to be stored and integrated into existing systems.

Step 6. Contextualizing involves placing in context the information on social media as it relates to recruiting and selection. Often times the most popular social media used are not specifically designed for recruiting and selection (e.g., Facebook). The norms and behaviors of users may create alternative uses for a social media site. The organization needs to develop a good

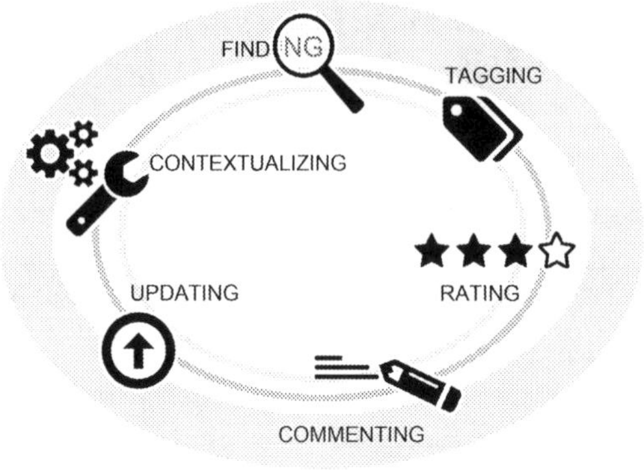

Fig. 10.1 Important behaviors to stay current on social media

understanding of the context that the content is being posted in. This will help the organization to draw accurate conclusions from content for the organization's purposes (Fig. 10.1).

Staying current with relevant recruiting and selection-related social media sites could involve setting up automated systems as well as incorporating elements of human review into such systems. An automated data mining system can be set up to include RSS, Twitter, and Facebook feeds to provide updates about relevant social media content for the organization. An actual person needs to review the data on a schedule, monthly is a good cadence to review automatically generated content. Information collected on relevant sites can be filed into a shared folder among colleagues on an organization's shared internal network. The data needs to be organized to make sure only relevant and useful information is included. An organization will need to assign dedicated staff members to make judgement calls regarding irrelevant off-topic content that needs to be removed. Organizations will need to ensure relevant data is moved to the correct folders for examination and consideration.

10.8 Social Credibility and Effectiveness

As human resource professionals continue to use the Internet and SNSs for recruiting purposes, it is important that they have a framework in place for evaluating these sites. A criteria used to filter information is credibility or believability (Fogg, 1999; Tseng & Fogg, 1999). Credibility is often defined as the degree a person believes that a particular piece of information is in fact true and trustworthy in nature (Jensen, Lowry, & Jenkins, 2011; Self, Salwen, & Stacks, 1996). Sources are judged as credible based on factors such as perceived competence, character, composure, dynamism, and sociability (Burgoon et al., 2000). One of the more difficult aspects when using social media is how to understand the context in which the social media content was originally shared (SHRM 2014) and determining if the source is credible. For example, when employers view an individual's social media presence, they need to understand that they may not be looking at the entire conversation, history, or other factors. Moreover, they may be utilizing an individual's personal site, such as Facebook, where the individual makes posts primarily to friends and family, but the person may also have another site, such as LinkedIn where he/she wishes to present his/her professional attributes. When an employer does not utilize the correct site for evaluating an applicant it may create an undue bias or cause incorrect conclusions to be drawn.

At present, there is limited research about the best method to determine credible and professional social networking site content to use for recruiting and selection efforts. However, we propose using the framework in Fig. 10.2 as a plausible model for human resource professionals to guide their decision process in examining and applying social media information in selection and recruitment. This model was adapted from Wathen and Burkell's (2002) proposed model for how users judge the credibility of online information.

The initial part of the process is the determination of what process social media data will be examined in and obtaining such social media content. What will be

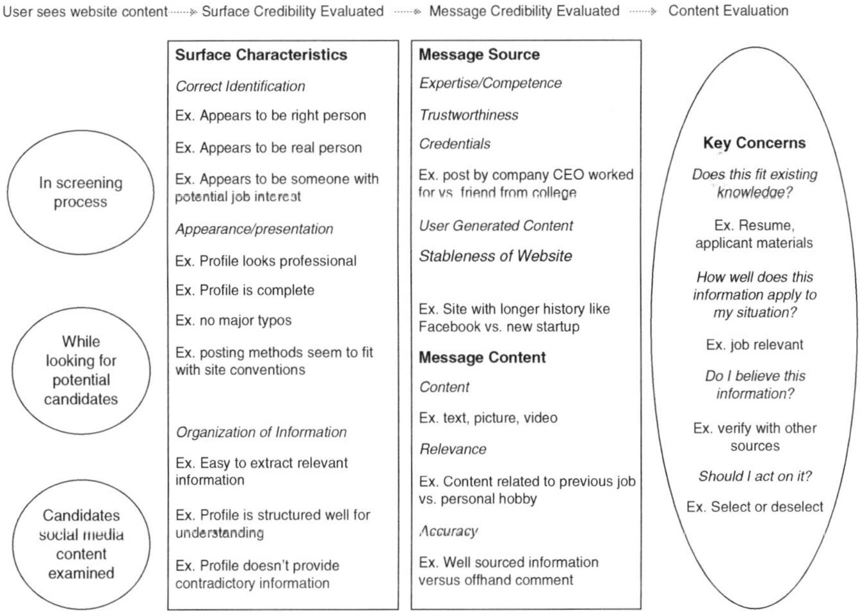

Fig. 10.2 Judging credibility of social media information for selection and recruitment (Adapted from Wathen & Burkell, 2002, p. 141)

looked at will vary based on the organization, the position, and the potential candidate pool.

The first step in evaluating the credibility of social media information obtained is to examine the surface characteristics. This initial examination will help in determining the nature of the social media content and the general trustworthiness of the social media site examined. A key aspect here will be determining if a correct identification has been made. Is this social media profile or content actually connected to the right candidate or potential candidate? For applicants with common names it may be difficult just determining if the social media content is from the right person to evaluate. For recruitment purposes, an evaluator may need to determine if the social media profile seems to represent a real person versus a bot, a masked identity or persona of a user. Users may create social media account where they claim to be someone they are not, like a recent case of a person who was arrested for having a Twitter account that said he was the mayor of Peoria (Burris, 2015).

When examining surface characteristics an evaluator will also want to look at the appearance/presentation of the profile and the organization of information on the profile. For appearance the evaluator may want to consider if the profile looks professional, well-proofed, and is complete in nature. This can help the evaluator to determine if the site should be taken as a reflection of the applicant's professional nature or is a more personal source. Complete profiles can offer clues to how much the applicant has actually engaged with the site as well as help in the determination that the profile is for the correct person. Evaluators may also look at the organization of content. For profiles that are confusing in organization it may be difficult to find and extract information. Profiles can also have contradictory information and in such cases evaluators will need to determine which information they look at and how they deal with such contradictions.

In the second step the evaluator goes beyond the surface characteristics of the profile and looks at the actual social media content and messages presented. The evaluator will then look at individual social media content and judge whether particular pieces of content seem relevant. One major area of credibility to judge will be the message source. Some content will seem more or less credible based on the source. A social media post on an applicant's Facebook wall by the CEO of a company that an applicant had worked for is likely to be more trustworthy and relevant than a post by a gym buddy of the applicant. The social media site itself might be used as a characteristic for judging message source credibility. A Facebook comment might be weighted more strongly than a post made about the user on a smaller or more disreputable social media site.

An evaluator will also want to judge the credibility of the message content. This can include whether the content is a text comment, a video, a picture, or a recording. An allegation that a user is a "drunk" is less believable as an offhand text comment on a single post than if there is a video documenting problem drinking behavior or that there is detailed accounts of such behaviors from multiple other users. Content may also vary in relevance. A comment related to a previous job might be very relevant in the recruiting/selection context while a comment related to a user's fantasy baseball team may be completely irrelevant.

The final step of the credibility judgement process is the ultimate content evaluation. In this last step the evaluator needs to determine how credible overall they find the social media content and how that information will actually be used. Some comments that seem not credible or are irrelevant may be ignored or discarded. Evaluators will also want to compare social media content to other sources of data they have such as resumes or personal interactions with the applicant. Evaluators could also look for additional data sources such as contacting references or people mentioned in allegations. Thus the evaluator can engage in verification of social media information. These judgments will lead to the evaluator ultimately weighing the information gained from social media content and how it may impact the selection of a candidate for a position or recruitment activities.

10.8.1 Credible Data for Selection

Presently, there is relatively little evidence that employers are making valid inferences about applicants' job performance based on SNS data and generally limited research on social media use in selection and recruitment (Brown & Vaughn, 2011; Davison, Maraist, & Bing, 2011; Kluemper, Rosen, & Mossholder, 2012; Van Iddekinge, Lanivich, Roth, & Junco, 2013). With the increased use of SNS to gather information on applicants (Grasz, 2009), it is important that human resource managers consider how this practice will affect various human resource decisions pertaining to hiring, promotion, and termination (Black, Stone, & Johnson, 2015). The information gleaned from SNS has the potential to increase or decrease the likelihood of that applicant being considered for further consideration.

Researchers have argued that the validity of SNS data needs to be established before they are used in the selection process (Brown & Vaughn, 2011; Davison et al., 2011; Lucero, Allen, & Elzweig, 2013; Roth et al., 2016). Therefore, organizations should take precautions to make certain that they are making valid inferences about applicants' job performance before using SNS data in the selection process (Black et al., 2015).

10.8.2 Credible Social Media Use for Recruitment

As organizations and recruiters use SNS to make hiring decisions, they must become cognizant that applicants may utilize different SNS, and where they place their professional content may vary. Globally, 91 % of Internet users between the ages of 16–64 have one have at least one social media account, but many individuals belong to more than one site. In fact, the average Internet user accesses five different social media platforms (Bennet, 2014). For example, although LinkedIn is considered to be a very popular professional networking site and often utilized by recruiters, Facebook is often more readily utilized by applicants. In fact, many job seekers prefer to use Facebook, with 83 % reporting they are active on this site (Jobvite, 2014).

Therefore, when accessing applicant's social media presence, it is important that organizations validate the information to ensure that it is accurate (Black et al., 2015) as well as relevant to the job posting. The spread of false information through social media is among the emerging risks identified by the World Economic Forum in its Global Risks 2013 report, and such false information can have negative ramifications (Black et al., 2015). Organizational policies should ensure that the data collected from these systems are accurate, and require that decision makers verify the information from multiple sources prior to using it to make hiring decisions.

Moreover, organizations need to take an active role to insure that the content they provide to candidates is accurate as well. For example, if they are using online communities and have their own form whereby existing employees are used to recruit candidates, they may want to train the employees to make sure that they are presenting an accurate picture and what the company wants them to portray in order to be perceived as credible with applicants. Thus, it is important that organizations develop consistent and accurate methods of utilizing social media and the information it provides to ensure that they are evaluating the correct applicant, appropriate content, and making better and more informed hiring decisions.

10.9 Auditing Social Media Data Use

Once an organization understands how to best use social media for recruiting and selection and implements a social strategy, it is also important to conduct an audit of current processes to validate overall effectiveness. The purpose of the audit is to compare effectiveness over time, and make sure existing processes are still best. Performing a routine social media audit could lead to new procedures, new sources of information or different task divisions with a company based on strengths and weaknesses found. A social media audit procedure and relevant questions are listed below:

1. Determine which department within an organization will be completing the social media audit.
2. Set a schedule for performing a social media audit. Will it be performed yearly? quarterly? other?
3. List the social media platforms that your company uses for recruiting and selection. Do the sites still exist? Is traffic to these sites increasing or decreasing?
4. Revisit your goals for each social media site. Ask yourself what are you trying to achieve by using a particular social media site. What are your objectives for each site?

5. Benchmark your metrics against desired and actual results from year to year. Did the social media sites used yield your desired outcomes?
6. Determine what changes and updates are needed for each social media site used.
7. Potentially create an audit document for managers to examine now and for those creating future audits to refer back to if needed.

10.10 Developing Processes

In order to be successful, organizations must be proactive in the development of their social recruiting and selection processes. With the rapid changes in technology and ever changing trends in social media usage, HR managers must be timely in evaluating their social recruiting and selection strategies.

We recommend developing a monthly schedule to evaluate the social media recruitment and selection process in order to determine which sites are currently used, which ones are up and coming, and which ones have become obsolete. Moreover, organizations need to also determine which technologies have been implemented and ensure that their selection and recruiting practices incorporate the latest technologies, for example usage on mobile devices.

However, each HR department needs to determine the most effective means of keeping current for themselves. For example, it may be better for one organization to contract an outside entity and have them provide analytics on current trends and overall social media effectiveness of the firm on a weekly basis, and another firm may want to track the information in house and have scheduled meetings on a monthly or quarterly basis. Some firms will also want to appoint a particular individual or team to manage the social media plan. Team composition could be crucial to the success of such teams and the organization's social media plan (Breakenridge, 2012). The organization must also determine what type of information is relevant for them to collect and how they will choose to disseminate it. Furthermore, the organization will need to assign an individual or a team that will monitor social media and technology applications and determine how to utilize and communicate this information within the firm as well as outside to the community. Thus, the organization must determine who will be utilized to communicate the information as well as the best method for others to receive feedback. Breakenridge (2012) discusses some of these concerns and potential solutions with respect to public relations professionals.

For one example, it may be useful for an organization to train multiple employees in how to present company information to potential employees. In this manner organizations can try to attract better candidates and get good referrals. We suggest that it will be beneficial for each organization to set goals and regularly schedule meetings to receive feedback to ensure that everyone is staying current on the application of technology and utilizing the most appropriate social media platforms.

From an organizational perspective, we also believe that organizations should proactively establish fair information policies that address the use of SNS information as part of their overall Internet usage policy (see Paschal, Stone-Romero, & Stone, 2009 for examples). The use of SNS in hiring decisions is simply one part of a vast revolution in the use of Internet data. Organizational policies should address Internet and SNS use by employers, and clarify applicants' expectations of privacy (Black et al., 2015). Although this work is focused on SNS data, many other types of information may be posted on the Internet through social media (such as Instagram pictures, YouTube videos, Wikipedia edits), and the use of these new systems pose unique challenges for managing information in the workplace. As such, it is suggested that organizations establish practices to verify the social media used by the applicant to ensure that they are not screening the wrong applicant and making recommendations based on false information.

Moreover, it is recommended that organizations notify and ask permission of the applicant to screen the individual's SNS of choice. This will ensure that the employee will be presenting the organization with the desired content that he/she chooses to present. This will allow organizations to make inferences based on content that is related to the job as opposed to personal content that the applicant may ideally not wish to divulge to the organization. Some organizations, however, may resist such ideas because they want information that is unguarded and not subject to impression management techniques, fearing prior warning will lead to relevant information being deleted or hidden. This is an issue that organizations will need to determine what seems best for their own interest.

Furthermore, fair information policies might require that organizations voluntarily limit the amount and types of data collected from SNS. This practice would ensure that data about protected classes are not shared with decision makers Black et al. (2015) suggest that fair information policies may be used to increase individuals' perceived control over information, and decrease their negative reactions to these practices. For example, organizational policies might provide advanced notice to applicants that SNS data will be collected during the selection process. Advanced notice of the SNS data collection should allow individuals to take steps to control information on these sites and protect their privacy. Moreover, it is suggested that human resource managers and recruiters access professional sites first before viewing more personal SNS of applicants. Similarly, fair information policies might dictate that organizations should gain permission from applicants prior to collecting data from SNS or elsewhere on the Internet. Some experts say that for a number of reasons, it is not a best practice to either ask for personal login information or read anyone's private social media postings with or without their knowledge (SHRM 2014). In practice, employers could provide a disclosure form to applicants requesting a release of information, and specifically refer to the company's policy regarding access to SNS.

10.11 New Trends in Technology Adoption and Suggestions for the Future

New information technologies are being developed and implemented everyday, and organizations should strive to keep pace with such changes. Presently, we see a lag in adoption rates of normal site users and organizations adopting sites for recruitment and selection purposes. For example, given the present popularity of Facebook among users, there appears to be a disconnect between the social platforms being used by employers and recruiters to find talent and where candidates are actually looking for jobs. Facebook is currently the preferred social network for job searches across all income levels, yet LinkedIn remains the primary social channel for recruiters (Scrimshaw 2014). With up to two-thirds of job seekers using Facebook for their job search (Scrimshaw 2014), it is increasingly more important that organizations keep up to date with changes in the use of technology as well as trends in the use of social media platforms.

According to Scrimshaw (2014) younger job applicants have expressed the need for a mobile-friendly application process, more than half of Millennials want the ability to see job listings without being required to register, and a third want to apply for jobs directly from their mobile device (JobviteMore 2014). An Industry View (2015) study indicates that organizations are not effectively utilizing Twitter. For example, more job openings are posted to Twitter than any other social media site, and Twitter has more job seekers than the more professionally minded LinkedIn. However, only 15% of recruiters have actually hired someone through Twitter. Their research also showed that 58 % percent of job seekers use Twitter in their job search to look primarily at company profiles for opportunities (76 %), and that 47 % of Millennials now consider a prospective employer's online reputation matters as much as the job it offers (Spherion Staffing, 2013). However, nearly half of respondents say companies are "ineffective" at using Twitter to post frequent job openings (47 %), communicate with job seekers (43 %), and in effectively marketing themselves as a great place to work. Taken as a whole, these results suggest significant concerns for how effectively organizations are using social media in selection and recruitment.

10.12 Tablet and Smartphone Application

Organizations also need to take into consideration the adoption and use of new technologies and adapt their recruitment strategies accordingly. For example, presently applicants show a preference for viewing new job postings on their tablets, as well as learning and collaborating with others on their smartphones. According to a study of Fortune 500 companies conducted by Careerbuilder (Gaspary, 2013), 39 % of the US population uses tablet devices, and 43 % of job candidates research their prospective employer and read the job description on their mobile device prior to their interviews

(Glassdoor.com 2014). However, only 20 % of Fortune 500 companies have a mobile-optimized career site. Thus, 80 % of companies have still not incorporated their job listings and information to be appealing to tablet and smartphone users.

More corporations need to develop both a mobile-optimized career site and a smartphone app to pull together all the information about the company's recruiting efforts into one easy-to-access place. In this way, potential employees can utilize a mobile app in order to search and apply for jobs, join a talent community, receive job alerts, and get an insider's perspective about what it's like to work for the organization.

An example of this can be seen in corporations such as the food-services corporation Sodexo, which has currently utilized technology in this manner. According to Arie Ball, VP Talent Acquisition at Sodexo, "17 % of job traffic from potential new hires now comes from the mobile app versus just 2 % of mobile traffic in early 2012. In the first year, mobile app downloads totaled 15,000, leading to over 2000 new job candidates and 141 actual new hires, all while saving the company $300,000 in job board postings" (Meister, 2014).

10.13 Social Media and the Use of Big Data

Given the rapid changes in application of various technologies, HR departments need to strategically develop a plan for how their organizations market themselves to applicants as well as provide the appropriate technology in order to enable employees to apply for available postings. The ability to attract highly skilled talent is a growing concern among organizations. According to PWC's global CEO Study (2014), 66 % of CEOs say that the absence of necessary skills is their biggest talent challenge. Eighty-three percent say they're working to change their recruiting strategies to address that fact.

Big data analysis is being used in order to identify and attract new talents before the prospective employees even know they are in the job market. For example, companies such as Entelo, Gild, TalentBin, and the UK's thesocialCV analyze not just a job candidate's LinkedIn profile, Twitter feed, and Facebook postings, but also their activity on specialty sites specific to their professions, such as the open-source community forums StackOverflow and GitHub (for coders) Proformative (for accountants), and Dribbble (for designers) (Meister, 2014). This method is a technical means of finding candidates and evaluating them through their social media based on their merits and contributions prior to them actually physically interviewing. The application of Big Data for recruiting purposes has enabled organizations to better identify "hard-to-find" talent.

Other companies, such as Entelo and TalentBin utilize various tools to evaluate not just the experience and history mentioned in users' profiles, but also their *use* of social networks. These companies can identify users who have updated their bios, how frequently, as well as other information in order to determine which candidates are getting ready to enter the job market. Through this method, these companies seek to gain a competitive advantage over other organizations by finding talent that is not readily visible on more popular social media platforms. This can offer an head start in the search for top candidates (Meister, 2014).

10.14 Conclusion

In this chapter we discussed the importance of companies keeping current with social media trends in order to be competitive in their recruitment and selection processes and have success in attracting applicants that fit their organizational criteria. Current research and practice regarding social media has been focused on the present. Although there is value in understanding the current landscape, social media and its use is constantly changing and evolving. Therefore, we contend that HR managers and recruiters need to have good planning for the present but prepare for the future rather than reflecting on the past (Lord et al., 2015; Lord & Dinh, 2014). For organizations to stay current and prepare for the future in the utilization of social media platforms, we have provided guidance on how to stay ahead on the best uses and resources for social media information. We have also outlined how organizations should formulate and adopt best practices that will incorporate measures for staying current on social media trends and track adoption of new platforms and technologies that can be utilized by organizations.

A company can keep up on practice, research, and the law on social media in recruiting and selection by incorporating a routine to monitor social media sites and web resources dedicated to reporting current trends in social media. Some of the processes that organizations can create and sustain over time in order to keep updated include establishing governance that clearly identifies the department within an organization responsible for harvesting social media trend data and making judgments about what sites to use and discontinue. Systems organizations can be put into place to ensure that the most current information is being utilized include data mining of relevant social media sites and industry periodicals and archiving this information into shared folders within the organization.

By proactively managing their use of social media platforms and implementing proper protocols, HR managers can stay connected to their target audience and be more successful in attracting and selecting a talented workforce.

References

Akiode, S. (2013, June 19). *[INFOGRAPHIC] The social recruiting pocket guide*. Retrieved October 22, 2015, from http://socialmeep.com/infographic-the-social-recruiting-pocket-guide/

Anderson, N. (2003). Applicant and recruiter reactions to new technology in selection: A critical review and agenda for future research. *International Journal of Selection and Assessment, 11*(2–3), 121–136.

Barnes, N. G., Lescault, A. M., & Augusto, K. D. (2014). LinkedIn dominates, Twitter trends and Facebook falls: The 2014 Inc. 500 and social media. Center for Marketing Research. Retrieved March 17, 2016, from http://www.umassd.edu/cmr/socialmediaresearch/2014inc500/.

Bennet, S. (2014). *The average Internet user has 5 social media accounts*. Retrieved September 25, 2015, from http://www.adweek.com/socialtimes/social-media-accounts/502588

Black, S. L., Stone, D. L., & Johnson, A. F. (2015). Use of social networking websites on applicants' privacy. *Employee Responsibilities and Rights Journal, 27*(2), 115–159.

Brady, P. W., Thompson, L. F., Wuensch, K. L., & Grossnickle, W. F. (2003). Internet recruiting. The effects of webpage design features. *Social Science Computer Review, 21*(3), 374–385.

Breakenridge, D. K. (2012). *Social media and public relations*. Upper Saddle River, NJ: FT Press.

Brown, V. R., & Vaughn, E. D. (2011). The writing on the (Facebook) wall: The use of social networking sites in hiring decisions. *Journal of Business and Psychology, 26*(2), 219–225.

Burgoon, J. K., Bonito, J. A., Bengtsson, B., Cederberg, C., Lundeberg, M., & Allspach, L. (2000). Interactivity in human–computer interaction: A study of credibility, understanding, and influence. *Computers in Human Behavior, 16*, 553–574.

Burris, S. (2015, October 16). *"The Daily Show" unravels America's dumbest mayor: This pol sent the cops to shut down parody Twitter account*. Retrieved October 20, 2015, from http://www.salon.com/2015/10/16/the_daily_show_unravels_americas_dumbest_mayor_this_pol_sent_the_cops_to_shut_down_parody_twitter_account/

Davison, H. K., Maraist, C., & Bing, M. N. (2011). Friend or foe? The promise and pitfalls of using social networking sites for HR decisions. *Journal of Business and Psychology, 26*, 153–159.

Duggan, M., Ellison, N.B., Lampe, C., Lenhart, A., & Madden, R. (2015, January 9). *Social media update 2014*. Pew Research Center. Retrieved September 23, 2015, from http://www.pewinternet.org/2015/01/09/social-media-update-2014/

Finley, K. (2015, September 25). *Sorry Ello, the Real Ant-Facebook is Good Old Email*. Retrieved September 23, 2015, from http://www.wired.com/2015/09/sorry-ello-real-anti-facebook-good-old-email/

Fogg, B. J. (1999). Persuasive technologies—Now is your chance to decide what they will persuade us to do—And how they'll do it. *Communications of the ACM, 42*, 26–29.

Framingham, H. H. (2008, October 16). Employers use social networks in hiring process. *Computerworld*. Retrieved September 23, 2015, from http://computerworld.co.nz/news.nsf/care/63C6E9BE6A2CD920CC2574C90003ADDD

Gaspary, S. (2013). New study: Trends in mobile recruitment adoption. The Hiring Site Blog. Retrieved March 19, 2016, from http://thehiringsite.careerbuilder.com/2013/08/14/mobile-recruitment-adoption/

Gillette, F. (2011, June 22). *The rise and inglorious fall of myspace*. Retrieved September 23, 2015, from http://www.bloomberg.com/bw/magazine/content/11_27/b4235053917570.htm

Grasz, J. (2009). Forty-five percent of employers use social networking sites to research job candidates, CareerBuilder survey find. CareerBuilder. Retrieved March 18, 2016, from http://www.careerbuilder.com/share/aboutus/pressreleasesdetail.aspx? id=pr519&sd=8/19/2009&ed=12/31/2009

Gregory, C. K., Meade, A. W., & Thompson, L. F. (2013). Understanding internet recruitment via signaling theory and the elaboration likelihood model. *Computers in Human Behavior, 29*(5), 1949–1959.

Ha, A. (2015, January 28). More than half a billion people access Facebook solely from mobile. *TechCrunch*. Retrieved September 15, 2015, from http://techcrunch.com/2015/01/28/facebookmobileonly2/

Heathfield, S. (2015). *Use social media for recruiting, screening, and background checks?* Retrieved September 22, 2015, from http://humanresources.about.com/od/selectemployees/qt/why-use-social-media-for-recruiting-and-screening.htm

Hull, J. (2011, April 27). 50% reduction on recruitment costs: How social media became my best friend. *HR Magazine Online*. Retrieved March 15, 2015, from http://www.hrmagazine.co.uk/hro/features/1019381/-reduction-recruitment-costs-social-media-friend.

Jobvite. (2014). *2014 social recruiting survey*. Retrieved May 24, 2015, from https://www.jobvite.com/…/2014/…/Jobvite_SocialRecruiting_Survey2014.pdf

Jensen, M. L., Lowry, P. B., & Jenkins, J.L. (2011). Effects of automated and participative support in computer-aided credibility assessment. *Journal of Management Information System, 28*(1), 201–234.

Kluemper, D. H., Rosen, P. A., & Mossholder, K. W. (2012). Social networking websites, personality ratings and the organizational context: More than meets the eye? *Journal of Applied Psychology, 22*(2), 1143–1172.

Lord, R. G., & Dinh, J. E. (2014). What have we learned that is critical in understanding leadership perceptions and leader-performance relations? *Industrial and Organizational Psychology: Perspectives on Science and Practice, 7*(2), 155–177.

Lord, R. G., Dinh, J. E., & Hoffman, E. L. (2015). A quantum approach to time and organization change. *Academy of Management Review, 40*(2), 263–290.

Lucero, M. A., Allen, R. E., & Elzweig, B. (2013). Managing employee social networking: Evolving views from the National Labor Relations Board. *Employee Responsibilities and Rights Journal, 25*(3), 143–158.

McMillian, R. (2013, February 27). The Friendster autopsy: How a network dies. *Wired*. Retrieved August 10, 2015, http://www.wired.com/2013/02/friendsterautopsy/

Meister, J. (2014). The year social HR matters. *Forbes*. Retrieved August 10, 2015, from http://www.forbes.com/sites/jeannemeister/2014/01/06/2014-the-year-social-hr-matters/

Paschal, J., Stone-Romero, E. F., & Stone, D. L. (2009). Effects of electronic mail policies on invasiveness and fairness. *Journal of Managerial Psychology, 24*(6), 502–525.

PWC. (2014). *17th CEO survey*. Retrieved August 20, 2015, from http://www.pwc.com/gx/en/ceo-survey/

Roth, P. L., Bobko, P., Van Iddekinge, C. H., & Thatcher, J. B. (2016). Social media in employee-selection-related decisions: A research agenda for uncharted territory. *Journal of Management, 42*(1) 1–30.

Schmidt, G. B. (2014). Virtual leadership: An important leadership context. *Industrial and Organizational Psychology: Perspectives on Science and Practice, 7*(2), 182–187.

Schmidt, G. B., & O'Connor, K. W. (2016). Legal concerns when considering social media data in selection. In R. N. Landers & G. B. Schmidt (Eds.), *Social media in employee selection and recruitment*. Cham: Springer.

Self, C. S., Salwen, M., & Stacks, D. (Eds.). (1996). *An integrated approach to communication theory and research*. Mahwah, NJ: Erlbaum.

Shea, K., & Wesley, J. (2006). How social networking sites affect employers, students, and career services. *Nace Journal, 66*(4), 26–32.

Spherion Staffing. (2013). *Latest emerging workforce study discovers new workplace realities and significant employer/employee disconnects*. Retrieved September 20, 2015, from http://www.spherion.com/Documents/2013EWSQ1_FINAL.pdf

Taylor, S. (2007). Creating social capital in MNCs: The international human resource management challenge. *Human Resource Management Journal, 17*(4), 336–354.

Tseng, S., & Fogg, B. J. (1999). Credibility and computing technology. *Communications of the ACM, 42*, 39–44.

Tussyadiah, I. P., & Fesenmaier, D. R. (2009). Mediating tourist experiences: Access to places via shared videos. *Annals of Tourism Research, 36*(1), 24–40.

Van Iddekinge, C. H., Lanivich, S. H., Roth, P. L., & Junco, E. (2013). Social media for selection? Validity and adverse impact potential of a Facebook-based assessment. *Journal of Management*, 1–25. doi:10.1177/0149206313515524

Wathen, C. N., & Burkell, J. (2002). Believe it or not: Factors influencing credibility on the Web. *Journal of the American Society for Information Science and Technology, 52*(2), 134–144.

Wauters, R. (2011). *Exclusive: Jobvite recruits $15 million in funding for social hiring application*. Retrieved September 20, 2015, from http://techcrunch.com/2011/05/17/exclusive-jobvite-recruits-15-million-in-funding-for-social-hiring-applications/

Webopedia. (2015). *Tagging*. Retrieved October 20, 2015, from http://www.webopedia.com/TERM/T/tagging.html

Part IV
Challenges and Limitations

Chapter 11
Impression Management and Social Media Profiles

Nicolas Roulin and Julia Levashina

Abstract There is ample evidence from the selection literature that job applicants engage in various forms of impression management (IM), for instance when completing personality tests or answering employment interview questions. Such behaviors can impact the selection process outcome and threaten its validity, particularly if applicants use deceptive IM. In parallel, research in cyberpsychology has examined how social media users engage in IM to create specific impressions on friends or family members, and achieve a positive online identity. However, with organizations increasingly relying on cyber-vetting, job applicants are also likely to engage in IM tactics oriented towards employers in their social media profiles. This chapter thus brings those two literatures together and proposes a framework of job applicants' IM on social media.

Keywords Impression management • Deception • Online tactics • Personal vs. professional social media • Cyber-vetting

11.1 Introduction

Social media platforms such as Facebook, Instagram, or LinkedIn have been described as a new way for organizations to obtain information about applicants' qualifications (Roth, Bobko, Van Iddekinge, & Thatcher, 2016; Roulin & Bangerter, 2013). Some early findings have suggested that applicants' characteristics, such as personality traits, could be reliably assessed based on social media content (Kluemper, Rosen, & Mossholder, 2012). Many organizations have already started

N. Roulin, Ph.D. (✉)
Asper School of Business, University of Manitoba,
181 Freedman Crescent, Winnipeg, MB, Canada, R3T 5V4
e-mail: nicolas.roulin@umanitoba.ca

J. Levashina, Ph.D.
College of Business Administration, Kent State University,
475 Terrace Drive, Kent, OH 44242-0001, USA
e-mail: jlevashi@kent.edu

R.N. Landers, G.B. Schmidt (eds.), *Social Media in Employee Selection and Recruitment*, DOI 10.1007/978-3-319-29989-1_11

relying on assessments of applicants through social media to make initial screening decisions. Yet, potential issues with such practices have been highlighted, including legal challenges (Brown & Vaughn, 2011) or lack of validity (Van Iddekinge, Lanivich, Roth, & Junco, in press). In this chapter, we discuss another potential challenge associated with using social media to assess and select job applicants: impression management (IM).

Existing research on personnel selection has clearly highlighted that job applicants can (and do) engage in IM during the selection process, for instance when completing personality tests (Barrick & Mount, 1996) or answering employment interview questions (Levashina & Campion, 2007; Stevens & Kristof, 1995). Although some forms of IM are expected from applicants and can even be a valuable source of information for organizations (Kleinmann & Klehe, 2010), some deceptive forms of IM can be more problematic and are often an important source of concerns for organizations (Stewart, Darnold, Zimmerman, Parks, & Dustin, 2010). Indeed, there is evidence that IM can influence the ranking of applicants (Stewart et al., 2010) and potentially the validity of selection instruments (Komar, Brown, Komar, & Robie, 2008; Peterson, Griffith, Isaacson, O'Connell, & Mangos, 2011). However, both conceptual and empirical research on applicants' use of IM on their social media profiles is lacking. This chapter thus aims at proposing a framework for applicant IM on social media based on the existing literature on IM.

The chapter is structured as follows: First, we provide a brief review of the existing research on applicant IM in the selection process, discussing the various forms of IM tactics, the important difference between honest and deceptive IM (or faking), the frequency of such behaviors, and their antecedents and impact on selection and job-related outcomes. Then, we review the existing literature surrounding the use of IM by individuals on social media, including honest and deceptive IM, to create a positive impression on other social media users (e.g.,*friends*). We then propose to bring together those two literatures and describe a framework for applicant IM on social media. We discuss which IM tactics that applicants use in traditional selection situations (e.g., interviews) also apply to social media, what could be the antecedents of such behaviors, and what could be the impact for applicants and for organizations. Finally, we conclude with some suggestions for future research as well as practical recommendations for organizations using social media as part of their selection process.

11.2 Impression Management in Selection

The research on applicant IM on social media is still extremely scarce. Therefore, in this first section, we briefly review the existing literature on IM with more established selection instruments like interviews or personality measures. We will use the types of tactics, antecedents, and outcomes from this literature (together with research on IM in online interactions) as the foundations on which we will build our framework of applicant IM on social media.

11.2.1 What Is IM?

IM can be defined as a "desire to create particular impressions in others' minds" (Leary & Kowalski, 1990, p. 35). Such behaviors are particularly pertinent in evaluative situations, such as the selection process. Indeed, the objective of job applicants is to be perceived as qualified for the job and be hired. Engaging in IM during the selection process is one strategy that applicants can use to achieve this objective. It is therefore not surprising that applicant IM has received extensive attention in the selection literature in the last few decades.

In the selection literature, various labels and terminologies have been used to discuss applicant IM, and IM has sometimes been assimilated with other concepts. For instance, in the testing literature, IM has been often labeled faking or socially desirable responding, and measured using social desirability scales (Griffith & Peterson, 2008; Levashina & Campion, 2006). Therefore, it seems important to understand the similarities and differences between those constructs before exploring further applicant's use of IM. First, IM and social desirability differ in scope. Social desirability involves voluntary response distortion as well as involuntary self-deception, whereas IM only captures a voluntary, job- or organization-specific response strategy (Barrick & Mount, 1996; Burns & Christiansen, 2011). Moreover, faking represents deceptive tactics used by applicants to influence the outcome of the selection process, whereas IM involves both honest and deceptive forms of influence tactics. In other words, applicant faking has been described as a deceptive form of IM (Leary & Kowalski, 1990; Levashina & Campion, 2006). In summary, IM should be considered as the voluntary facet of social desirability, and can take both honest and deceptive forms.

Research has shown that applicants can use IM in multiple selection situations, including interviews (Levashina, Hartwell, Morgeson, & Campion, 2014; Roulin, Bangerter, & Levashina, 2014), personality tests (Barrick & Mount, 1996; Griffith & McDaniel, 2006), biodata inventories (Levashina, Morgeson, & Campion, 2009), or assessment centers (Klehe, Kleinmann, Nieß, & Grazi, 2014; McFarland, Yun, Harold, Viera, & Moore, 2005). However, the forms of IM that applicants use depend on the selection instrument (McFarland, Ryan, & Kriska, 2003). In selection situations involving interpersonal interactions, like employment interviews and assessment center exercises, applicants can use a variety of IM tactics. They can use assertive tactics oriented towards themselves, such as honestly highlighting job-related skills or past accomplishments (i.e., self-promotion; Stevens & Kristof, 1995), but also deceptively exaggerating or inventing such qualifications or experiences (i.e., image creation; Levashina & Campion, 2007). Alternatively, IM tactics can be oriented towards the interviewer or the hiring organization, through honest or deceptive forms of ingratiation to create a perception of similarity or person–organization fit (Chen, Lee, & Yeh, 2008; Levashina & Campion, 2007). For instance, applicants might emphasize values or hobbies that they share (or pretend to share) with the interviewer. Finally, applicants can use defensive tactics to repair or protect their image of good applicant, for instance by providing excuses or justifications for negative past experiences or simply hiding them (Tsai, Huang, Wu, & Lo, 2010).

Applicant can also use IM in testing (e.g., when completing personality tests). In such situations, the choice of IM tactics available is more limited. Most of the time, the best strategy involves identifying the ideal personality profile for the position, deriving the expected or correct responses, and adjusting one's answer to fit the ideal profile (Klehe et al., 2012). For instance, applicants engaging in IM tend to use the extreme points of the scales more often (Levashina, Weekley, Roulin, & Hauck, 2014). IM allows applicants to obtain higher scores on personality traits deemed valuable by the organization (Zickar & Robie, 1999). As an example, in experimental studies participants instructed to use IM scored 0.5 standard deviations higher than participants instructed to respond honestly (Viswesvaran & Ones, 1999). Meta-analytical results also highlight larger differences between applicants and non-applicants on personality trait scores for conscientiousness or emotional stability (Birkeland, Manson, Kisamore, Brannick, & Smith, 2006).

11.2.2 Do Applicants Use IM in Selection?

To have a better understanding of the impact of IM in selection (and later on in the specific context of assessing applicants on social media), it is important to first examine how prevalent such tactics are among job applicants. Although field studies on applicant IM are still limited, research has accumulated evidence about the frequency of IM use in various selection settings and across different countries. We discuss below the use of IM with two selection instruments: employment interviews and tests.

In the interview context, it has been reported that up to 97.5 % of job applicants used at least one IM tactic per interview, with self-promotion and ingratiation being more prevalent than defensive tactics (Ellis, West, Ryan, & DeShon, 2002). When looking at honest vs. deceptive IM, a study highlighted that 81 % of applicants used at least one deceptive IM tactic in their last interview (Weiss & Feldman, 2006). Levashina and Campion (2007) examined deceptive IM of undergraduate job applicants in three studies and found that 65–99 % of them used various types of deceptive IM. The prevalence of these tactics was smaller in a sample of experienced Swiss job applicants, with only 21–70 % of them using deceptive IM (Roulin et al., 2014). Further evidence of country-to-country difference was provided by König, Wong, and Cen (2012) who compared the use of deceptive IM in the United States, Europe (Iceland and Switzerland), and China. They found such behaviors to be particularly frequent in United States and Chinese applicants (e.g., about 40 % of applicants in both countries reported exaggerating their past work experience and about 50 % reported exaggerating their skills).

Obtaining frequencies of faking in tests using field studies can be difficult, mostly because of the difficulty to reliably capture IM (Burns & Christiansen, 2011). This is why many studies have focused on comparing applicant in a selection vs. non-selection context (Birkeland et al., 2006). Yet, some studies have demonstrated that a large number of applicants engaged in IM (Griffith & Converse, 2011).

For instance, Griffith, Chmielowski, and Yoshita (2007) compared personality test scores of individuals in a selection situation (i.e., where they were expected to put their best foot forward) vs. an honest condition (i.e., where participants were told to respond truthfully) and found that between 30 and 50 % used deceptive IM. Levashina et al. (2009) examined applicants' use of deceptive IM when completing biodata inventories using bogus items. They found that 24 % of applicants for entry-level US government jobs used such tactics.

11.2.3 What Are the Antecedents of Applicant IM?

We showed above that a large proportion of applicants engage in IM. Yet, not all of them do (or do it to the same extent). The next logical step in our review of applicant IM thus involves understanding what factors make some individuals engage in IM when applying for jobs. Numerous theoretical models and frameworks have discussed potential antecedents of applicant IM, and especially its deceptive form (e.g., Levashina & Campion, 2006; Marcus, 2009; McFarland & Ryan, 2006; Roulin, Krings, & Binggeli, in press). Most models agree that applicants engage in IM if they have the motivation, the ability, and the opportunity to do so. The extent to which applicants are motivated, capable, and perceived the opportunity to use IM then depends on their individual differences (e.g., personality traits, values, and beliefs), the type or format of selection instruments used by organizations, or the competition for jobs.

Some of those antecedents have been empirically examined as well. For instance, job applicants who are low in conscientiousness, agreeableness, or honesty, and high in extraversion, neuroticism, narcissism, or Machiavellianism are described as being more likely to be motivated to engage in IM (e.g., Hogue, Levashina, & Hang, 2013; Kristof-Brown, Barrick, & Franke, 2002; Levashina & Campion, 2007; O'Neill et al., 2013). Applicants with more interpersonal skills and able to identify what selection criteria are used by employers are more capable to use IM (Ellingson & McFarland, 2011; Klehe et al., 2012). Finally, applicants have more opportunities to use IM when specific selection instruments or formats are employed. For instance, applicants use more IM in unstructured vs. structured interviews or when the interviewer is asking situational vs. past-behavior questions (Levashina & Campion, 2007; Levashina, Hartwell, et al., 2014), but also when the organization is relying on tests where answers are easier to falsify, such as personality vs. cognitive ability tests (Converse, Peterson, & Griffith, 2009; Lievens & Burke, 2011).

11.2.4 What Are the Outcomes of Applicant IM?

The impact of applicant IM can be examined in two ways. First, one can look at how IM influences the selection process for applicants, for instance by examining the relationship between IM use and selection outcomes. In interviews, there is ample evidence that applicants engaging in IM tend to obtain higher evaluations from interviewers (Barrick, Shaffer, & Degrassi, 2009; Levashina, Hartwell, et al., 2014). Interestingly, such results are not limited to honest forms of IM, but applicants using deceptive IM can also benefit from such a strategy (Levashina & Campion, 2007). One reason for why deceptive IM can lead to high interview evaluations is that interviewers cannot effectively detect when applicants use such tactics (Roulin, Bangerter, & Levashina, 2015). Similarly, applicants using IM in personality tests adapt their responses to items measuring valuable traits and thus tend to obtain higher scores overall (Birkeland et al., 2006; Levashina, Weekley, et al., 2014). As a result, IM can significantly impact the ranking of applicants and their chances to obtain the job (Stewart et al., 2010). Altogether, using IM can help job applicants reaching more positive outcomes.

The other way to examine the impact of applicant IM is to evaluate how it affects organizations. First, IM can negatively impact the reliability of selection instruments like personality tests (MacCann, 2013). Relatedly, IM has often been described as potentially attenuating the validity of selection instruments (e.g., Gilmore, Stevens, Harrell-Cook, & Ferris, 1999; Marcus, 2006) although some researchers disagree with this statement (e.g., Hogan, Barrett, & Hogan, 2007; Ones & Viswesvaran, 1998). In theory, if some applicants used deceptive IM in the selection process, organizations risk hiring less qualified applicants who may end up being lower performers (Roulin et al., in press). And there is indeed some evidence of a negative relationship between (mostly deceptive) IM and job performance (Donovan, Dwight, & Schneider, 2014; Komar et al., 2008), although some researchers have also found positive relationships between (honest) IM and performance (Ingold, Kleinmann, König, & Melchers, 2015; Kleinmann & Klehe, 2010). Applicants using deceptive IM in the selection process are also more likely to engage in counterproductive work behaviors once hired (O'Neill et al., 2013). Taken together, the literature thus suggests that applicant IM, and especially its deceptive forms, can have negative consequences for organizations.

In summary, the selection literature (a) describes IM as tactics or response strategies used by applicants to increase their chances of obtaining a job, (b) highlights that IM can take various forms and can be honest or deceptive, (c) demonstrates that a large proportion of job applicants use IM, (d) describes IM as caused by a combination of individual differences and opportunities created by the selection instruments used by organizations, and (e) emphasize that IM usually leads to positive outcomes for applicants but potentially negative ones for employers. In the next section, we turn to the literatures on cyberpsychology and computer science to better understand the role and impact of IM on social media.

11.3 Impression Management on Social Media

Industrial–organizational psychology researchers have yet to examine how job applicants use IM on social media to influence selection decisions. Yet, researchers in computer-mediated communication and online psychology have already started to explore the IM tactics people used while interacting with other members of their online social network. In this section, we briefly review this (growing) literature, which we will later use to adapt our knowledge of applicant IM to the specific context of social media to build our framework.

11.3.1 Do People Use IM on Their Social Media Profiles?

Social media have been described as an ideal platform for IM because they allow people to easily control or manipulate information and content (Krämer & Winter, 2008; Siibak, 2009). Contrary to interpersonal interactions where one has to quickly adapt one's behavior (e.g., decide what to say) to create a positive impression, one usually has plenty of time to do so on social media. Of course, some people can spontaneously post content on their profile, such as an impulsive comment on Facebook or tweets. Yet, in most situations, users can take their time to choose, adapt, and present information in order to create the desired impression.

Social media users can rely on a variety of IM tactics to achieve positive outcomes. While job applicants must generally rely on the responses they choose or the stories they tell in the selection process, social media users have the opportunity to use visual or multimedia content, including text, pictures, or videos. For instance, posting only very positive photos is a very popular online IM tactic to obtain social recognition (i.e., *likes*) from others (Dorethy, Fiebert, & Warren, 2014). More specifically, users can spend time editing the pictures they post by cutting or cropping parts of the picture, using photographic filters, or editing pictures with software and applications (Fox & Rooney, 2015). IM tactics also involve how users present themselves in their profile's main page or the types of updates or comments they post (Mehdizadeh, 2010). Pictures tend to have a larger impact than textual information on perceivers' judgments about the profile user (Van der Heide, D'Angelo, & Schumaker, 2012). For instance, if pictures suggest that the user is an extrovert, adding verbal disclosure suggesting introversion does not change perceivers' evaluations of the user.

When engaging in IM, users' objective is to create a particular impression on the members of their network. Yet, the type of IM used and the target of IM is different on personal vs. professional social media, where users want to present their social vs. their professional selves respectively (Van Dijck, 2013). For instance, on personal social media like Facebook the goal of IM tactics is usually to impress their *friends* (Rosenberg & Egbert, 2011). The overarching goal of IM is to increase the number of *friends* in one's online social network, obtain higher status and social support, and indirectly increasing one's well-being (Kim & Lee, 2011). Growing a large social network is not only the outcome of online IM, but can also contribute to creating an online impression. Indeed the number of *friends* and what they look like or say about the user contribute to an online impression (Utz, 2010; Walther, Van Der Heide, Kim, Westerman, & Tong, 2008). For instance, if the user's *friends* make an extroverted and outgoing (vs. introverted) impression, the user is also perceived as more (vs. less) popular. Yet, because the main target of online IM on personal social media are *friends*, such tactics may lead to undesirable impressions on unintended targets. For example, users' willingness to impress friends may increase the likelihood of posting information or pictures that can be perceived negatively by employers, such as *faux pas* (e.g., self-photos drinking alcohol; Roulin, 2014) or badmouthing (e.g., criticisms and disparaging remarks; Stoughton, Thompson, & Meade, 2013). On professional social media like LinkedIn however, users tend to engage in more professional IM, for instance by building a narrative of competence and past job performance (Van Dijck, 2013).

11.3.2 Do People Use Deceptive IM on Their Social Media Profiles?

We described in the previous paragraphs how social media users engage in IM to create a positive impression. However, similar to IM in the selection context, such tactics could be honest or deceptive. Recent studies have compared assessment of users based on their social media to both honest and exaggerated self-descriptions, and found stronger relationships with the honest self-description (e.g., Sievers, Wodzicki, Aberle, Keckeisen, & Cress, 2015). There is also evidence that social media profile can depict the true personality (Kluemper et al., 2012) and real-life activities (Van Hoof, Bekkers, & Van Vuuren, 2014) of their owners. This suggests that social media profiles may mostly reflect the true characteristics of their users, and not an idealized profiles boosted by deceptive IM. One reason for this is the ability of other users (i.e., one's online connections) to comment on someone's profile and sometimes even edit its content. Such a verification process can make social media profiles more likely to limit falsifications (Back et al., 2010; Walther et al., 2008).

Beyond verifying the veracity of information posted on social media profiles, some professional social media platforms such as LinkedIn allow users to list skills or areas of expertise. Members of their network, such as colleagues, supervisors, or classmates, can then endorse the user for those skills. This endorsement feature works like the reputation system in commercial websites (e.g., eBay) or the reviews function on hotel booking websites. In the context of personnel selection, this feature can be comparable to recommendation letters from previous employers who would highlight the skills of their previous employee. It could also be used as a type of background checking, which is usually performed in addition to selection tests or interviews (Levashina & Campion, 2009). In part because of these endorsement mechanisms, some researchers have argued that deception on LinkedIn profiles is more likely to be caught than on a traditional resume (Guillory & Hancock, 2012).

Although IM on social media appears to be mostly honest, some people still engage in deception. People can engage in deception in online group discussions, for instance, to hide their real age, gender, or marital status (Caspi & Gorsky, 2006). Yet, only 29 % of respondents in this particular study reported using deception online. Similarly, some people exaggerate or hide their physical attributes (e.g., height, weight, and age) on dating websites (Toma, Hancock, & Ellison, 2008). Moreover, individuals may engage in deception to "look better" on social media. On personal websites like Facebook, users engage in deceptive IM in order to portray some personality traits more positively (e.g., being more outgoing that they truly are; Toma & Carlson, 2015). In some situations, extreme forms of deceptive IM can be used. For instance, in the case of *farcing attacks* people have created completely phony profiles to *friend* victims, communicate with them, and then steal information from them (Vishwanath, 2014).

11.3.3 Who Uses More IM on Their Social Media Profiles?

Not all social media users engage in IM or do it to the same extent. For instance, online IM tactics are mostly used by individuals high on neuroticism, extroversion, and Narcissism, and low on conscientiousness or self-esteem (Fox & Rooney, 2015; Krämer & Winter, 2008; Mehdizadeh, 2010; Seidman, 2013). For instance, users higher on Narcissism tend to spend more time on social media, post more *selfies*, and engage in more photo editing. More extroverted social media users tend to post pictures of them that have a more original or artistic style. Users who are higher on neuroticism engage in more IM on their profile, including deceptive forms of IM. Interestingly, most of these personality traits are similar to those associated with applicant IM in the selection context. Yet, no research has investigated individual differences associated with deceptive IM on social media.

11.4 A Framework of Applicant IM on Social Media

In this section, we propose a general framework of applicant IM on social media. This theory-driven framework builds on the previously reviewed literatures on IM in selection and social media. It describes the reasons why social media becomes a natural medium for applicant IM, the types of IM they can use, the impact of social media platforms, and the antecedents and potential outcomes of IM. This framework is visually summarized in Fig. 11.1.

To illustrate some of the key elements of our framework, we also conducted a small-scale survey with 31 senior students and recent graduates from various Canadian business schools. All our respondents were either recently hired ($n = 14$) or actively looking for (full-time, part-time, or summer) jobs at the time of the survey ($n = 17$), thus representing how (young) applicants may behave on social media. A research assistant contacted them by email and asked them to respond to three open-ended questions online. The first question measured if (and how) they considered the impression they would make on potential employers when posting or updating something on their social media profile. The second question asked them

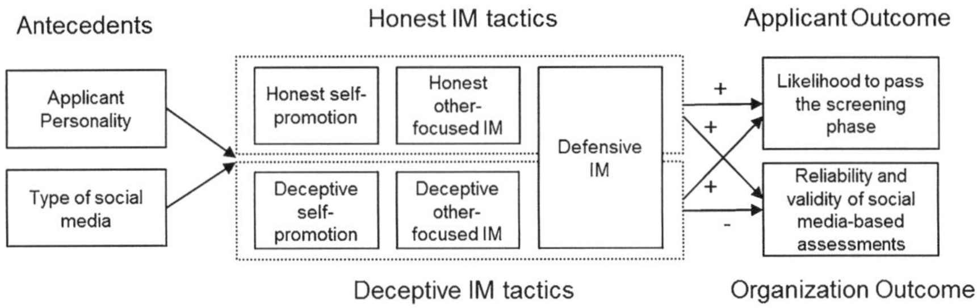

Fig. 11.1 Framework of applicant IM on social media

if (and if so, how) they ever posted, changed, updated, removed, or hidden something strategically from their profile, that is, with the specific objective to make a good impression on potential employers. Finally, we asked them if their strategy was specific to one social media or similar across all social media.

We present a number of examples of responses throughout this section, for instance to illustrate some of the IM tactics that applicants can use. We note that these examples are based on a short survey and a small sample and thus should only be considered as an illustration to our theory-driven framework.

11.4.1 Why Applicants Should Engage in IM on Social Media

As discussed above, job applicants extensively engage in honest but also deceptive forms of IM in the selection process. Applicants' motivation to engage in IM is related to their expectations about the potential benefits associated with such behaviors (Ellingson & McFarland, 2011). In other words, applicants use IM because they believe that it will improve their score or evaluation during the selection process, and thus increase their chances of obtaining the job. Or they may believe that using IM is one (or the only) way to outperform other applicants competing for the same job (Roulin et al., in press).

Recent studies have highlighted how cyber-vetting can become a new norm in the personnel selection process (Roth et al., in press), with HR managers reviewing applicants' profiles as part of the initial screening phase. As such, the logical reaction for applicants would be to adapt to this changing norm and apply the techniques they have been using in tests or interviews to social media, in order to pass the first hurdle of the screening process. Indeed, changing one's behaviors has been described as an adaptive mechanism used by applicants to meet organizations' changing expectations, as well as obtain a competitive advantage over other job seekers (Bangerter, Roulin, & König, 2012). As social media become a new way for applicants to signal their qualities to employers (Roulin & Bangerter, 2013), they also become a new platform for them to use IM.

As a first exploration of how much job applicants value the image they portray on their social media profiles, we present below a few illustrative examples from our survey:

> "I consistently think of how I am shaping my *personal brand* to employers. For example, through Twitter I make sure there is a healthy balance between *professional tweets* (such as posting business articles I find interesting) and *fun/personal tweets* (such as tweeting about local sports or the woes of being a student)."
>
> "I often try to look at my online profiles from a third party perspective and try to imagine what they would see, what judgments they would make and what conclusions they would come to about my personality, work ethic, etc."
>
> "I am aware that recruiters and company representatives may view my public profile and information so I make sure that what I post reflects how I would like to portray myself. I view social media to be an extension of my portfolio."
>
> "Potential employers will always look you up when deciding if you are the right fit for their company, so it's a way of creating a positive image in the employers' eyes."
>
> "I always consider that potential employers could or will see what I am posting, and make sure I never post anything that would be compromising to my future or disrespectful to my future employers and their company reputations. In some situations, most particularly with LinkedIn and Twitter, I actually use social media with the hopes they will be seen by potential employers."

11.4.2 Forms of Applicant IM Relevant on Social Media

We have described the various forms of IM that people use on their social media profiles, such as selecting or editing text and pictures to create a positive impression, in the previous section. Yet, most of these tactics were oriented towards friends and not potential employers. And no research has yet examined how such tactics could be adapted to the selection context. Below, we propose to describe possible applicant IM on social media building on the three general types of IM tactics from the interview literature (Levashina & Campion, 2007; Stevens & Kristof, 1995): self-focused assertive tactics (i.e., honest or deceptive self-promotion), other-focused tactics (i.e., honest and deceptive ingratiation), and defensive tactics (i.e., image repair and image protection). We also highlight similarities with specific IM tactics within each of these categories, based on the more detailed typologies described by Bolino, Kacmar, Turnley, and Gilstrap (2008) or Levashina and Campion (2007).

Yet, before describing specific IM tactics, it is important to understand the fundamental difference between employment interviews or tests and social media profiles. Applicants may participate in multiple interviews (or complete multiple tests) for different jobs and organizations. In each selection process, they can thus use different IM tactics that are adapted to the particular job requirements or the organizations' values. By doing so, they can resemble the ideal applicant (Klehe et al., 2012), and indirectly increase perceptions of person–job or person–organization fit (Kristof-Brown et al., 2002). However, applicants will likely create only one social media profile (or one per platform) that will be potentially consulted by multiple employers or hiring managers. This particularity forces applicants to decide on a generic IM strategy to apply to their social media profile(s) that should be effective across all jobs/organizations they may apply for/to.

We describe below which IM types are more likely to be used by applicants on social media and how the specificities of social media can potentially impact those tactics. We also illustrate those IM types with concrete examples of tactics used by the senior Canadian business students and graduates we surveyed, when asked about situations where they posted, changed, updated, removed, or hid something strategically on/from their profile. We present some of their responses aligned with the three types of IM. Interestingly, the majority of responses highlighted defensive IM tactics, but only a handful of them described the assertive tactics they use. Although those responses represent only a small group of applicants, they suggest that defensive IM are easier to use, whereas assertive IM tactics may be more complex to implement on social media, especially for less-experienced applicants.

11.4.2.1 Self-Promotion on Social Media

Self-promotion in selection involves using positive statements to describe one's qualities, past accomplishments, or future plans (Stevens & Kristof, 1995). Its deceptive equivalent, image creation, involves embellishing, exaggerating, or inventing such qualities or accomplishments to create a (falsified) image of a good applicant for the job (Levashina & Campion, 2007). Both types are very similar to the IM tactics used by social media users to present themselves in favorable ways online (Rosenberg & Egbert, 2011). Because self-promotion is the most frequent form of IM in both the selection context and on social media in general, we can also expect these tactics to be a prominent form of applicant IM on social media.

Yet, it remains unclear how frequently applicants would engage in deceptive self-focused IM (i.e., image creation) on social media, or how frequent it is in comparison to other selection methods, like interviews or tests. On the one hand, earlier studies suggest that deception is as frequent on social media as in resumes (Guillory & Hancock, 2012). On the other hand, because profiles can be reviewed by friends or past employers (who can comment, endorse, etc.), deception can be flagged by others and is thus more risky for applicants (Back et al., 2010). We note that existing studies have not directly tested how friends, co-workers, or past employers engage in such a verification process, or its effectiveness. Altogether, we expect applicants to engage mostly in less severe forms of image creation (e.g., exaggeration, embellishment) because more severe forms (e.g., inventions of fact or borrowing experiences from others) are likely to trigger reactions by other members of one's online network. As an example, NBC anchor Brian Williams' largely exaggerated experience in the Iraq war in 2003 (i.e., he pretended to be in a helicopter hit by a rocket) was publicly exposed on social media by veterans involved in the mission. Although Williams' deceptive behavior was not social media-based, the online reactions illustrate how social media communities can act as a verification mechanism.

Social media users may selectively post information or pictures about themselves to increase their popularity (Fox & Rooney, 2015). In the IM literature, such self-promotion tactics refer to *self-enhancement*, that is, making one's best characteristics salient to potential targets (Bolino et al., 2008). Applicants could thus strategically post information, comments, or pictures allowing them to highlight personality traits that are universally valued by organizations (e.g., conscientiousness, emotional stability) or required for jobs they may apply to (e.g., extroversion for job involving interpersonal interactions). They could also illustrate their knowledge, skills, and abilities by posting information about their past professional and personal accomplishments (e.g., degrees earned, work experience, volunteering activities). If deceptive IM is used, it is likely to be oriented towards information that is less widely known to network members and therefore less verifiable. For instance, when instructed to create a LinkedIn profile to position themselves as applicants for an attractive job, students used on average 2.87 deceptive IM tactics. Although, they engage in deception to improve their abilities (e.g., language, software), they mostly exaggerated their interest and involvement in job or other activities, which is more difficult to verify (Guillory & Hancock, 2012).

Social media users can build a large network of connections, ideally with a profile that corresponds to the image they want to create, to boost their social attractiveness (Utz, 2010). In the IM literature, such self-promotion tactics could be assimilated to *boasting* about one's positive connections with favorable others (Bolino et al., 2008). Job applicants could therefore try to accumulate connections to appear agreeable and extroverted, or more generally to signal social or interpersonal skills. Similarly, they could try to obtain positive comments or endorsements from their connections for activities or areas of expertise, to highlight knowledge, skills, or abilities that are likely to be required for future jobs.

Below are some examples of self-promotion tactics used by our surveyed business students and graduates on their social media profiles:

> "I definitely post about academic accomplishments whenever possible. Or anything that shows I am helping out in the community."
>
> "My LinkedIn profile is solely used with the idea of impression potential employers with past work and volunteer experience."
>
> "On LinkedIn, I use quite a bit of strategy and try different things to showcase different abilities I have. I think it has worked well, I get head hunters asking me about various roles every now and then… so I have a feeling that it is working."
>
> "I like to post both personal and academic accomplishments with potential employers in mind. Hopefully it will impress them!"
>
> "On LinkedIn I will really invite anyone that I would have free connection to within my network."

11.4.2.2 Other-Focused IM on Social Media

Ingratiation in the selection context involves tactics designed to evoke interpersonal attraction or liking, such as praising the target, conforming with their opinion, or highlighting similarities between one's and the target's values (Bolino et al., 2008; Stevens & Kristof, 1995). Applicants can also insincerely praise the target or express values similar to those of the target (Levashina & Campion, 2007). Social media users can use similar ingratiation tactics to create an impression of similarity with members of their network and gain popularity (Hong, Tandoc, Kim, Kim, & Wise, 2012). Yet, because applicants' profiles are not organization- or job-specific, there are less opportunities for other-focused IM aimed at enhancing the perceived fit between the applicant and a particular organization (or their representative) than in an interview for example.

Social media users can post comments about their *friends*' online activities (or use *likes*) to create an impression of similarity and gain popularity (Hong et al., 2012). Applicants can thus engage in ingratiation by directly *following* or *liking* companies they are interested in on social media or try to connect with employees of those organizations. Moreover, they could highlight specific interests, hobbies, or beliefs in their profiles through comments, pictures, etc. to create an impression of similarity with the values of organizations they are interested in. This can be done honestly, but also deceptively. For instance, students instructed to create a LinkedIn profile for a job did exaggerate their involvement in activities or societies to appear more attractive to the organization (Guillory & Hancock, 2012). As a more advanced strategy, applicants can join interest groups that match the values of those organizations, participate in the group's discussion, and eventually become a top contributor in the group.

As expected, other-focused IM tactics were mentioned far less often than the other two forms of IM by our surveyed business students and graduates. We present below some rare examples of other-focused IM tactics that they used on their social media profiles:

> "On Twitter, I *follow* many companies and professionals I would like to work with."
> "I make sure I am *following* all sorts of potential employers' social networking sites."

11.4.2.3 Defensive IM on Social Media

Defensive IM can be used by applicants to repair their image when it has been damaged either by their own behavior or by information made available to the organization, such as a recently lost job (Stevens & Kristof, 1995). Justifications, excuses, or burying are examples of such tactics (Bolino et al., 2008). Applicants can also proactively protect their image by hiding or omitting negative information or distancing themselves from negative events in their past (Levashina & Campion, 2007). Because social media allow users to select what information they post vs. do not post on their profile (Krämer & Winter, 2008; Siibak, 2009), similar defensive tactics are readily available.

There is an important difference between defensive IM on social media and selection situations like an interview: In interviews, applicants may use defensive IM as a reactive strategy, for instance when asked to talk about something negative in their past. In such situations, the applicant can decide to use honest IM (e.g., justify what happened or apologize for it) or deceptive IM (e.g., intentionally hide what really happened). However, on social media, applicants are not asked to provide specific information about undesirable traits they possess or negative events in their past, but they decide what to post (or not post) on their profile. It is therefore more difficult to draw a clear line between honest and deceptive defensive IM. As a result we describe below examples of defensive IM on social media, but do not define them as being honest or deceptive tactics.

As a general defensive IM strategy, applicants can use restrictive privacy settings, selecting what sections of their profile (if any) would be visible to the public, thus preventing organizations to access the information (Schneider, Goffin, & Daljeet, 2015). Similarly, they could use an online alias or create two profiles, one *clean* profile for professional purposes and one with accurate information to interact with friends using slightly different names (e.g., their middle name instead of their first name). Such tactics would prevent organizations' searches using their real name to access their real profile.

Applicants can also engage in more specific types of defensive IM tactics on social media. For instance, omissions can involve purposely not including information that could potentially hurt the impression applicants are trying to make online. Although, incomplete profiles could be viewed negatively by HR managers as compared to complete profiles (Zide, Elman, & Shahani-Denning, 2014), some information could be more risky to include than to omit or remove from one's profile. For instance, comments or pictures that involve drugs or alcohol consumption, sexual, or rule violations could be considered as *faux pas* by employers, and could strategically be removed from profiles (Roulin, 2014). Similarly, people can be judged by the company they keep on social media (Walther et al., 2008), suggesting that employers can assess applicants based on the number of friends an applicant has, who those friends are, and how they interact with applicant on social media (e.g., what they post on the applicant's Facebook wall or Timeline). As such, applicants can also decide to distance themselves from members of their network whose posts can damage their impression. For instance, they may realize that a friend's posts (or comment on their own posts) they once found fun could actually be perceived negatively by potential employers. The short-term defensive tactic involves deleting or hiding that particular post. The more long-term (and drastic) tactic would be to decide to *unfriend* people who regularly post comments threatening the image the applicant wants to create. In a similar way, applicants could also decide to leave groups they don't want to be perceived as being affiliated with.

As mentioned above, defensive IM tactics were cited extensively by our surveyed business students and graduates. Below are some examples of defensive IM tactics they used on their social media profiles:

"I make it as difficult as I can for employers to find me on my social media platforms, i.e., not using my last name, enhanced privacy settings, etc."

"I deleted an entire Facebook profile from when I was in high school. It was too much of a chronicle of any mischievous thing I had said or done before I was 18."

"I have gone through my Facebook account and deleted pictures and posts that involve a lot of alcohol and partying. The pictures were old, from a few years prior, but it can still leave the impression that you don't take your work seriously when you are out drinking many nights of the week."

"I have hidden photos from my [Facebook] timeline that I did not want seen by others, and deleted past tweets and status updates that I posted from when I was young and lacked better judgement."

"I have deleted photos where I have been intoxicated from Facebook to prevent them from being seen by potential employers. I have also limited my privacy settings. I have deleted tweets that contained inappropriate comments or language."

"I have hidden/untagged myself in images where I was with individuals who were partaking in excessive partying, even if I was not. I have also removed friends from my pages who I went to high-school with but no longer want to be acquainted with because of their current actions."

"I have removed old photos or posts which at the time I thought were funny or appropriate but now see how others could find them offensive or inappropriate. You never know who will be looking at your social media and the earlier you get the embarrassing or inappropriate posts hidden away, the more likely someone will not have saved a screenshot or have memory of that particular post. It is especially crucial if in future I ever find myself in a position where I am in the public eye."

"I also updated or removed past experiences that I did not want employers to think about when they evaluate me. For example, I removed my experience as a manager at a fast-food restaurant on my LinkedIn profile. It was a great experience and I learned a lot, but it was a long time ago and isn't extremely transferable to my desired line of work."

11.4.3 Differences in Applicant IM Between Social Media Platforms

As we have highlighted above, job applicants can engage in a variety of IM tactics on their social media profiles. Yet, it is possible that they engage in different forms of IM (or to a different extent) on different social media. Indeed, social media could be positioned on a continuum with primarily personal ones (e.g., Facebook, Instagram, Google+, Tumblr, Snapchat) at one end, and primarily professional ones (e.g., LinkedIn, GitHub, ResearchGate) at the other. Other social media, such as Twitter, fall somehow in the middle as they can be used to achieve both personal and professional goals. It is also possible that some individuals use primarily personal social media like Facebook mostly in a professional way, for instance artists or entrepreneurs building a Facebook presence to advertise their activities. However, from an applicant's perspective, taking into account the type or role of different social media is important to understand what types of IM tactics can be used.

To illustrate how job applicants may perceive different social media as ways to achieve different IM objectives, we asked our sample of business students and graduates if their overall IM strategy was platform-specific or not. Although many students reported using a broad approach across social media, some described different strategies they used depending on the platform. Below are some examples:

"I would consider my LinkedIn profile my primary social media for employer evaluation, but knowing that recruiters often do a social media background check, I consider Twitter to be my secondary social media for employers to evaluate me. I see my LinkedIn as a means to establish my credibility, and my Twitter as a glimpse into my personality and interests. However, my Instagram and Facebook is entirely personal (but publicly accessible), and my Snapchat is entirely private."

"On LinkedIn, I log on once in a while and look at posts on my news feed and update my profile every now and then. On my Instagram account, I usually post pictures that I think my followers would find interesting such as vacation pictures and pictures of my dogs. On Facebook, that is where I can play around a little bit more and post random stuff such as music I like and have conversations with friends."

"On LinkedIn obviously I do very little, as that is viewed much more by current or future employers and colleagues in the business community. That is the social media platform that I care about my image the most. But Facebook and Twitter are expected to have a bit of your personal life on them and they are less frequently checked by employers."

"I only update my LinkedIn profile to accurately capture recent achievements and job placements. I rarely use Facebook, as it's mostly a communication tool for me."

Employers and applicants alike recognize that some social media are primarily personal and others primarily professional, and perceive each type of social media to highlight different pieces of information about applicants (Roulin & Bangerter, 2013). For instance, personal social media are a potential antecedent of Person–Organization fit information about applicants, such as personality traits, values, or interests. Professional social media are a potential antecedent of Person–Job fit information, such as skills, competencies, or job experiences. Similarly, we can expect applicants to use different forms of IM on personal vs. professional social media. We describe those differences below and summarize them in Table 11.1.

Personal and professional social media profiles have different primary objectives, which influences what self-promotion IM job applicants can use. Personal social media profiles are generally created to interact with friends and family. They are extensively used for self-presentation tactics oriented towards *friends* to increase one's online popularity (Rosenberg & Egbert, 2011). It is therefore easy to use similar self-promotion tactics aiming at creating an image of sociability in the eyes of potential employers, for instance by highlighting or exaggerating personality traits like extroversion, agreeableness, or openness to experience through one's main profile, comments, or pictures. Moreover, on personal social media, accumulating a large number of connections is often seen as a good way to demonstrate social skills. In contrast, professional social media profiles are built like extended online resumes for career-related purposes (Guillory & Hancock, 2012). Self-promotion tactics will thus be oriented towards creating an image of competence or expertise, for instance by highlighting or exaggerating one's skills, past experiences, and accomplishments, or by creating an impression of being conscientious through a professional-looking profile pictures and written statements. Applicants engaging in IM are not likely to blindly accumulate connections on professional social media, but instead decide to selectively connect with individuals that may help them in their career and/or job search. For instance, they may connect with individuals likely to endorse their skills.

Other-focused IM tactics used by applicants are likely to be quite similar across personal and professional social media. In both cases, applicants can show their interest in specific organizations by *following* their activities on the network and *liking* their news post. Indeed, most large organizations have profiles on both personal and professional social media to describe their activities, present their new products, or job opportunities. Applicants can also join groups to highlight the values that

Table 11.1 Summary of potential IM tactics per social media platform

IM tactic	Personal social media	Professional social media
Honest self-promotion	• Highlighting one's true positive personality traits and values through one's main profile, posts, and pictures	• Highlighting one's true knowledge, skills, and abilities through education and past experiences
	• Accumulating *friends* to appear more social	• Connecting with professionals and getting one's skills endorsed by them
Deceptive self-promotion (i.e., image creation)	• Selectively posting information and comments that would enhance one's image of a good applicant	• Exaggerating one's skills or areas of expertise
	• Using photo editing software before posting pictures to enhance attractiveness or positive personality traits	• Embellishing one's past academic or professional accomplishments
Honest other-focused IM	• Liking organizations' posts	• Following organizations
	• Joining interest groups to highlight one's core values	• Joining professional groups
Deceptive other-focused IM	• Liking posts or comments by (or related to) organizations only because one plans to apply there	• Trying to create an impression of similarity by connecting with employees one does not know in organizations one plans to apply to
	• Exaggerating one's interest in causes or topics viewed positively by employers (e.g., ecology, a new technology)	• Joining professional groups only to appear interested in issues valued by potential employers
Defensive IM	• Changing privacy settings so that one's profile (or parts of it) is accessible to friends only	• Justifying negative professional experiences in the past or highlight how one's learning from it
	• Removing comments or pictures that could be seen as *faux pas* by employers	• Intentionally omitting or removing past job experiences or associations with organizations having a negative reputation from one's profile
	• Unfriending close friends whose online activities may have a negative impact on one's image	
	• Creating separate profiles for potential employers and friends using different names	

organizations they like (or their members) have in common with them and create a perception of similarity. The type of groups may differ by platform, focusing more on interest groups on personal social media vs. on professional groups or associations on professional social media, but the mechanism will be similar.

The type of defensive IM tactics is also likely to vary by platform. On personal social media, *friends* are the main target of the information posted. Employers or HR managers trying to access their information can be perceived as privacy invaders (Stoughton, Thompson, & Meade, 2015). To protect their personal information, most of the defensive IM tactics described above can be used. This may include changing one's privacy settings so that employers cannot access their profile or creating two separate profiles, one that looks professional for employers to see and one being kept secret to employers using another name. Yet, some job applicants may want to strategically use their personal profile to create a good impression on employers, which would be incompatible with a *no-access* strategy. Job applicants can thus decide to protect their image by cleaning their profile, that is, proactively decide to remove pictures or comments that were oriented towards their friends but that could be perceived negatively by employers. For instance, job applicants informed that personal social media profiles are frequently visited by employers are more likely to limit their *faux pas* postings (Roulin, 2014).

On professional social media, individuals actively looking for jobs want their profile to be visited by employers. Restricting access to their profile is thus not a pertinent strategy. Yet, applicants can control or justify the information published to defend their image of a good applicant. Like in a job interview, they can try to justify negative events in their past, such as losing a job or staying unemployed for some time, or describe how they benefited from this experience, for instance by taking classes or simply learning from the past. Alternatively, they can decide to voluntarily leave such negative experiences off their profile.

11.4.4 Antecedents and Outcomes of Applicant IM on Social Media

Are all job applicants likely to use IM on their social media profiles? If not, then what are the characteristics of job applicants likely to engage in IM on social media? Although this particular research question has not yet been examined empirically, we have described earlier the extensive literature discussing the antecedents on applicant IM in selection and the initial attempts to identify the characteristics of social media users engaging in IM. We propose that some of the individual characteristics of applicants identified as antecedents on IM in the selection process (e.g.,in interviews or tests) will also predict who will use IM on social media. We rely on two pieces of evidence for this assertion. First, studies comparing applicant IM across selection methods have highlighted some levels of consistency in IM use, especially for other-focused tactics (McFarland et al., 2003, 2005). Second, many personality traits associated with honest or deceptive IM in selection (e.g., Hogue et al., 2013; O'Neill et al., 2013) have also been described as predicting users' IM on social media (e.g., Fox & Rooney, 2015; Seidman, 2013). These traits include some of the Big-5 personality traits (e.g., extroversion, neuroticism, conscientiousness) as well as some of the dark traits (e.g., narcissism, Machiavellianism). We thus expect those traits to be predictors of applicant IM on social media, such as applicants high on neuroticism, extroversion, Narcissism, and Machiavellianism but low on conscientiousness being more likely to engage in more IM.

What is the impact of IM on social media for applicants and organizations? Recruiters and HR managers increasingly rely on social media cyber-vetting to screen job applicants. For instance, recruiters can make inferences about applicants' person–job fit and person–organization fit based on how they present themselves on LinkedIn, which influences their hiring recommendations (Chiang & Suen, 2015). Such inferences are similar to those made in employment interviews, where applicant IM tactics impact evaluations (e.g., Kristof-Brown et al., 2002; Levashina & Campion, 2007). Overall, we can thus expect applicant-assertive IM on social media to have similar effects as in interviews. Using IM will improve applicants' chances to move forward in the selection process. For organizations, the impact on applicant IM on the quality of hiring (or screening) decisions will depend on the veracity of the tactics used. Similarly to the interview context (Ingold et al., 2015; Levashina & Campion, 2006), honest IM can potentially improve decisions by making the true qualities of applicants available to evaluators, but deceptive IM can bias decisions by manipulating the information provided.

The effect of some defensive IM tactics on social media can have a quite different impact for applicants and organizations. Most importantly, privacy settings or aliases preventing employers to access their profile can potentially eliminate applicants if organizations have cyber-vetting as a required step of their selection process. For instance, a recent study showed that 57.87 % of applicants would refuse to provide full access to their profile to recruiters (i.e., provide their password), thereby removing themselves from the applicant pool (Schneider et al., 2015). This could obviously have negative consequences for both applicants (i.e., being eliminated) and organizations (i.e., overlooking potentially qualified applicants). Fortunately, legislation is evolving and some US states (e.g., California, Maryland, Michigan, Oregon, etc.) have passed new laws prohibiting organizations to ask applicants for their password of social media access. It is likely that more states will pass similar laws in the near future. Yet, it is unclear what would happen if an organization includes cyber-vetting as a formal step in the selection process but cannot find anything about an applicant on social media, for instance because the applicant uses another name (or alias) online.

Other defensive IM tactics, such as *cleaning* one's profile of content that may be perceived negatively by employers can also impact the validity of social media-based assessments, and thus the quality of hiring decisions. For instance, studies suggesting that Facebook profiles can potentially provide reliable information about users' personality (e.g., Kluemper et al., 2012) have used students' (and not applicants') profiles. Such profiles were arguably free from defensive IM, and it is likely that removing (negative) information will reduce the reliability of personality assessment and, indirectly, their potential predictive validity.

11.5 Conclusion

The antecedents, types, mechanisms, and outcomes of applicant IM in the selection process have been extensively examined in the past decades. But there are still a number of unknowns that future research should explore (e.g., Levashina, Hartwell, et al., 2014). In parallel, research on social media is still in its infancy. Studies on using social media profiles for assessing job applicants' qualities or users IM have only begun to scratch the surface. Bringing those two literatures together, this chapter suggests that examining applicant use of IM on social media and the potential impact of such tactics on organizations' assessments needs to be part of the agenda for future research. We therefore present below some suggestions for researchers to generate novel studies in this area. Moreover, we outline some practical recommendations for organizations, recruiters, or managers already using (or planning to use) social media as part of their selection process.

11.5.1 Future Research Directions

We described above the types of IM tactics that job applicants can potentially use on their social media profiles to influence recruiters' evaluations. We also presented some illustrative examples based on the experiences of a small group of senior business students or graduates. But there are multiple ways to continue exploring this in future studies. For instance, one could empirically examine the extent to which applicants engage in self-promotion, other-focused, and defensive IM on their social media profile, and what specific tactics they use. Moreover, studies could differentiate honest from deceptive IM tactics or compare IM use across social media platforms (e.g., personal vs. professional sites).

Furthermore, research could empirically examine the antecedents and outcomes of applicants' use of honest vs. deceptive IM on social media. For instance, our review of the literature on IM on social media and in selection pointed towards some of the Big-5 and dark personality traits as potential predictors of IM. Previous models of IM have also highlighted the importance of situational factors, such as interview formats, on applicants' opportunity to use IM (e.g., Levashina & Campion, 2006). Similarly, some social media platforms may favor vs. impede the use of specific IM tactics. For job applicants, studies could test if using IM can positively influence recruiters' assessments and increase their chances to pass the first hurdle of the selection process. We suggest examining the impact of various IM types separately, as assertive (i.e., self-focused and other focused) and defensive tactics could have quite different consequences for example. For organizations, studies could explore how honest and deceptive IM tactics influence assessments of applicants' qualities. For instance, although research suggests that one can reliably assess personality through a Facebook profile (Kluemper et al., 2012), the actual validity of such assessments appears to be minuscule (Van Iddekinge et al., in press). Maybe applicants' assertive IM does bias recruiters' evaluations and thus reduces the potential validity of social media assessments. It is also possible that some profiles have limited information, possibly because of defensive IM tactics that prevent recruiters from making a comprehensive assessment of applicants.

11.5.2 Practical Recommendations

Cyber-vetting applicants using their social media presence can be seen as a valuable screening tool for organizations because of its low costs and potentially extensive amount of information about applicants available. Yet, beyond the legal or ethical issues associated with such practices (e.g., Brown & Vaughn, 2011), this chapter suggests that organizations should also consider the potential impact of applicant IM. If applicants realize that organizations are checking their social media profiles, the logical reaction would be to start to proactively using social media to create a positive impression (Roulin, 2014). This can involve honest self-promotion tactics allowing applicants to showcase their true personality, skills, or past accomplishments. Such tactics would likely benefit organizations, by providing them valuable information to assess applicants. But applicant IM can also involve deceptive tactics aimed at manipulating their online image to appear a better fit with the job or organization. Moreover, defensive tactics could include hiding or omitting negative information, possibly biasing recruiters' evaluations. Or, perhaps even more damaging, strategies to prevent organization to access applicants' information such as changing one's privacy settings or using an alias online. In conclusions, organizations may want to carefully weigh the pros and cons of relying on social media assessments to make decisions about job applicants.

References

Back, M. D., Stopfer, J. M., Vazire, S., Gaddis, S., Schmukle, S. C., Egloff, B., et al. (2010). Facebook profiles reflect actual personality, not self-idealization. *Psychological Science, 21*, 372–374.

Bangerter, A., Roulin, N., & König, C. J. (2012). Personnel selection as a signaling game. *Journal of Applied Psychology, 97*, 719–738.

Barrick, M. R., & Mount, M. K. (1996). Effects of impression management and self-deception on the predictive validity of personality constructs. *Journal of Applied Psychology, 81*, 261–272.

Barrick, M. R., Shaffer, J. A., & Degrassi, S. W. (2009). What you see may not be what you get: Relationships among self-presentation tactics and ratings of interview and job performance. *Journal of Applied Psychology, 94*, 1394–1411.

Birkeland, S. A., Manson, T. M., Kisamore, J. L., Brannick, M. T., & Smith, M. A. (2006). A meta-analytic investigation of job applicant faking on personality measures. *International Journal of Selection and Assessment, 14*, 317–335.

Bolino, M. C., Kacmar, K. M., Turnley, W. H., & Gilstrap, J. B. (2008). A multi-level review of impression management motives and behaviors. *Journal of Management, 34*, 1080–1109.

Brown, V., & Vaughn, E. (2011). The writing on the (Facebook) wall: The use of social networking sites in hiring decisions. *Journal of Business and Psychology, 26*, 219–225.

Burns, G. N., & Christiansen, N. D. (2011). Methods of measuring faking behavior. *Human Performance, 24*, 358–372.

Caspi, A., & Gorsky, P. (2006). Online deception: Prevalence, motivation, and emotion. *CyberPsychology and Behavior, 9*, 54–59.

Chen, C.-H. V., Lee, H.-M., & Yeh, Y.-J. Y. (2008). The antecedent and consequence of person-organization fit: Ingratiation, similarity, hiring recommendations and job offer. *International Journal of Selection and Assessment, 16*, 210–219.

Chiang, J. K.-H., & Suen, H.-Y. (2015). Self-presentation and hiring recommendations in online communities: Lessons from LinkedIn. *Computers in Human Behavior, 48*, 516–524.

Converse, P. D., Peterson, M. H., & Griffith, R. L. (2009). Faking on personality measures: Implications for selection involving multiple predictors. *International Journal of Selection and Assessment, 17*, 47–60.

Donovan, J. J., Dwight, S. A., & Schneider, D. (2014). The impact of applicant faking on selection measures, hiring decisions, and employee performance. *Journal of Business and Psychology, 29*, 479–493.

Dorethy, M. D., Fiebert, M. S., & Warren, C. R. (2014). Examining social networking site behaviors: Photo sharing and impression management on Facebook. *International Review of Social Sciences and Humanities, 6*, 111–116.

Ellingson, J. E., & McFarland, L. A. (2011). Understanding faking behavior through the lens of motivation: An application of VIE theory. *Human Performance, 24*, 322–337.

Ellis, A. P. J., West, B. J., Ryan, A. M., & DeShon, R. P. (2002). The use of impression management tactics in structured interviews: A function of question type? *Journal of Applied Psychology, 87*, 1200–1208.

Fox, J., & Rooney, M. C. (2015). The Dark Triad and trait self-objectification as predictors of men's use and self-presentation behaviors on social networking sites. *Personality and Individual Differences, 76*, 161–165.

Gilmore, D. C., Stevens, C. K., Harrell-Cook, G., & Ferris, G. R. (1999). Impression management tactics. In R. W. Eder & M. M. Harris (Eds.), *The employment interview handbook*. Thousand Oaks, CA: Sage.

Griffith, R. L., Chmielowski, T., & Yoshita, Y. (2007). Do applicants fake? An examination of the frequency of applicant faking behaviour. *Personnel Review, 36*, 341–355.

Griffith, R. L., & Converse, P. (2011). The rules of evidence and the prevalence of applicant faking. In M. Ziegler, C. MacCann, & R. D. Roberts (Eds.), *New perspectives on faking in personality assessment*. New York: Oxford University Press.

Griffith, R. L., & McDaniel, M. (2006). The nature of deception and applicant faking behavior. In R. L. Griffith & M. H. Peterson (Eds.), *A closer examination of applicant faking behavior*. Greenwich, NC: Information Age Publishing.

Griffith, R. L., & Peterson, M. H. (2008). The failure of social desirability measures to capture applicant faking behavior. *Industrial and Organizational Psychology, 1*, 308–311.

Guillory, J., & Hancock, J. T. (2012). The effect of Linkedin on deception in resumes. *Cyberpsychology, Behavior and Social Networking, 15*, 135–140.

Hogan, J., Barrett, P., & Hogan, R. (2007). Personality measurement, faking, and employment selection. *Journal of Applied Psychology, 92*, 1270–1985.

Hogue, M., Levashina, J., & Hang, H. (2013). Will I fake it? The interplay of gender, Machiavellianism, and self-monitoring on strategies for honesty in job interviews. *Journal of Business Ethics, 117*, 399–411.

Hong, S., Tandoc, E., Kim, E. A., Kim, B., & Wise, K. (2012). The real you? The role of visual cues and comment congruence in perceptions of social attractiveness from Facebook profiles. *Cyberpsychology, Behavior, and Social Networking, 15*, 339–344.

Ingold, P. V., Kleinmann, M., König, C. J., & Melchers, K. G. (2015). Shall we continue or stop disapproving of self-presentation? Evidence on impression management and faking in a selection context and their relation to job performance. *European Journal of Work and Organizational Psychology, 24*, 420–432.

Kim, J., & Lee, J. E. R. (2011). The Facebook paths to happiness: Effects of the number of Facebook friends and self-presentation on subjective well-being. *Cyberpsychology, Behavior and Social Networking, 14*, 359–364.

Klehe, U.-C., Kleinmann, M., Hartstein, T., Melchers, K. G., König, C. J., Heslin, P. A., et al. (2012). Responding to personality tests in a selection context: The role of the ability to identify criteria and the ideal-employee factor. *Human Performance, 25*, 273–302.

Klehe, U.-C., Kleinmann, M., Nieß, C., & Grazi, J. (2014). Impression management behavior in assessment centers: Artificial behavior or much ado about nothing? *Human Performance, 27*, 1–24.

Kleinmann, M., & Klehe, U. C. (2010). Selling oneself: Construct and criterion-related validity of impression management in structured interviews. *Human Performance, 24*, 29–46.

Kluemper, D. H., Rosen, P. A., & Mossholder, K. W. (2012). Social networking websites, personality ratings, and the organizational context: More than meets the eye? *Journal of Applied Social Psychology, 42*, 1143–1172.

Komar, S., Brown, D. J., Komar, J. A., & Robie, C. (2008). Faking and the validity of conscientiousness: A Monte Carlo investigation. *Journal of Applied Psychology, 93*, 140–154.

König, C. J., Wong, J., & Cen, G. (2012). How much do Chinese applicants fake? *International Journal of Selection and Assessment, 20*, 247–250.

Krämer, N. C., & Winter, S. (2008). Impression management 2.0. *Journal of Media Psychology: Theories, Methods, and Applications, 20*, 106–116.

Kristof-Brown, A. L., Barrick, M. R., & Franke, M. (2002). Applicant impression management: Dispositional influences and consequences for recruiter perceptions of fit and similarity. *Journal of Management, 28*, 27–46.

Leary, M. R., & Kowalski, R. M. (1990). Impression management: A literature review and two-component model. *Psychological Bulletin, 107*, 34–47.

Levashina, J., & Campion, M. A. (2006). A model of faking likelihood in the employment interview. *International Journal of Selection and Assessment, 14*, 299–316.

Levashina, J., & Campion, M. A. (2007). Measuring faking in the employment interview: Development and validation of an interview faking behavior scale. *Journal of Applied Psychology, 92*, 1638–1656.

Levashina, J., & Campion, M. A. (2009). Expected practices in background checking: Review of the human resource management literature. *Employee Responsibilities and Rights Journal, 21*, 231–249.

Levashina, J., Hartwell, C. J., Morgeson, F. P., & Campion, M. A. (2014). The structured employment interview: Narrative and quantitative review of the research literature. *Personnel Psychology, 67*, 241–293.

Levashina, J., Morgeson, F. P., & Campion, M. A. (2009). They don't do It often, but they do it well: Exploring the relationship between applicant mental abilities and faking. *International Journal of Selection and Assessment, 17*, 271–281.

Levashina, J., Weekley, J. A., Roulin, N., & Hauck, E. (2014). Using blatant extreme responding for detecting faking in high-stakes selection: Construct validity, relationship with general mental ability, and subgroup differences. *International Journal of Selection and Assessment, 22*, 371–383.

Lievens, F., & Burke, E. (2011). Dealing with the threats inherent in unproctored Internet testing of cognitive ability: Results from a large scale operational test program. *Journal of Occupational and Organizational Psychology, 84*, 817–824.

MacCann, C. (2013). Instructed faking of the HEXACO reduces facet reliability and involves more Gc than Gf. *Personality and Individual Differences, 55*, 828–833.

Marcus, B. (2006). Relationships between faking, validity, and decision criteria in personnel selection. *Psychology Science, 48*, 226–246.

Marcus, B. (2009). 'Faking' from the applicant's perspective: A theory of self-presentation in personnel selection settings. *International Journal of Selection and Assessment, 17*, 417–430.

McFarland, L. A., & Ryan, A. M. (2006). Toward an integrated model of applicant faking behavior. *Journal of Applied Social Psychology, 36*, 979–1016.

McFarland, L. A., Ryan, A. M., & Kriska, S. D. (2003). Impression management use and effectiveness across assessment methods. *Journal of Management, 29*, 641–661.
McFarland, L. A., Yun, G., Harold, C. M., Viera, L. J., & Moore, L. G. (2005). An examination of impression management use and effectiveness across assessment center exercises: The role of competency demands. *Personnel Psychology, 58*, 949–980.
Mehdizadeh, S. (2010). Self-presentation 2.0: Narcissism and self-esteem on Facebook. *Cyberpsychology, Behavior and Social Networking, 13*, 357–364.
O'Neill, T. A., Lee, N. M., Radan, J., Law, S. J., Lewis, R. J., & Carswell, J. J. (2013). The impact of "non-targeted traits" on personality test faking, hiring, and workplace deviance. *Personality and Individual Differences, 55*, 162–168.
Ones, D. S., & Viswesvaran, C. (1998). The effects of social desirability and faking on personality and integrity assessment for personnel selection. *Human Performance, 11*, 245–269.
Peterson, M. H., Griffith, R. L., Isaacson, J. A., O'Connell, M. S., & Mangos, P. M. (2011). Applicant faking, social desirability, and the prediction of counterproductive work behaviors. *Human Performance, 24*, 270–290.
Rosenberg, J., & Egbert, N. (2011). Online impression management: Personality traits and concerns for secondary goals as predictors of self-presentation tactics on Facebook. *Journal of Computer-Mediated Communication, 17*, 1–18.
Roth, P. L., Bobko, P., Van Iddekinge, C. H., & Thatcher, J. B. (2016). Social media in employee-selection-related decisions: A research agenda for uncharted territory. *Journal of Management, 42*, 269–298.
Roulin, N. (2014). The influence of employers' use of social networking websites in selection, online self-promotion, and personality on the likelihood of faux pas postings. *International Journal of Selection and Assessment, 22*, 81–88.
Roulin, N., & Bangerter, A. (2013). Social networking websites in personnel selection: A signaling perspective on recruiters' and applicants' perceptions. *Journal of Personnel Psychology, 12*, 143–151.
Roulin, N., Bangerter, A., & Levashina, J. (2014). Interviewers' perceptions of impression management in employment interviews. *Journal of Managerial Psychology, 29*, 141–163.
Roulin, N., Bangerter, A., & Levashina, J. (2015). Honest and deceptive impression management in the employment interview: Can it be detected and how does it impact evaluations? *Personnel Psychology, 68*, 395–444.
Roulin, N., Krings, F., & Binggeli, S. (in press). A dynamic model of applicant faking. *Organizational Psychology Review*.
Schneider, T. J., Goffin, R. D., & Daljeet, K. N. (2015). "Give us your social networking site passwords": Implications for personnel selection and personality. *Personality and Individual Differences, 73*, 78–83.
Seidman, G. (2013). Self-presentation and belonging on Facebook: How personality influences social media use and motivations. *Personality and Individual Differences, 54*, 402–407.
Sievers, K., Wodzicki, K., Aberle, I., Keckeisen, M., & Cress, U. (2015). Self-presentation in professional networks: More than just window dressing. *Computers in Human Behavior, 50*, 25–30.
Siibak, A. (2009). Constructing the self through the photo selection-Visual impression management on social networking websites. *Cyberpsychology: Journal of Psychosocial Research on Cyberspace, 3*, Article 1.
Stevens, C. K., & Kristof, A. L. (1995). Making the right impression: A field study of applicant impression management during job interviews. *Journal of Applied Psychology, 80*, 587–606.
Stewart, G. L., Darnold, T. C., Zimmerman, R. D., Parks, L., & Dustin, S. L. (2010). Exploring how response distortion of personality measures affects individuals. *Personality and Individual Differences, 49*, 622–628.
Stoughton, J. W., Thompson, L. F., & Meade, A. W. (2013). Big Five personality traits reflected in job applicants' social media postings. *Cyberpsychology, Behavior and Social Networking, 16*, 800–805.

Stoughton, J. W., Thompson, L. F., & Meade, A. W. (2015). Examining applicant reactions to the use of social networking websites in pre-employment screening. *Journal of Business and Psychology, 30*, 73–88.

Toma, C. L., & Carlson, C. L. (2015). How do Facebook users believe they come across in their profiles?: A meta-perception approach to investigating Facebook self-presentation. *Communication Research Reports, 32*, 93–101.

Toma, C. L., Hancock, J. T., & Ellison, N. B. (2008). Separating fact from fiction: An examination of deceptive self-presentation in online dating profiles. *Personality and Social Psychology Bulletin, 34*, 1023–1036.

Tsai, W.-C., Huang, T.-C., Wu, C.-Y., & Lo, I.-H. (2010). Disentangling the effects of applicant defensive impression management tactics in job interviews. *International Journal of Selection and Assessment, 18*, 131–140.

Utz, S. (2010). Show me your friends and I will tell you what type of person you are: How one's profile, number of friends, and type of friends influence impression formation on social network sites. *Journal of Computer Mediated Communication, 15*, 314–335.

Van der Heide, B., D'Angelo, J. D., & Schumaker, E. M. (2012). The effects of verbal versus photographic self-presentation on impression formation in Facebook. *Journal of Communication, 62*, 98–116.

Van Dijck, J. (2013). 'You have one identity': Performing the self on Facebook and LinkedIn. *Media, Culture and Society, 35*, 199–215.

Van Hoof, J. J., Bekkers, J., & Van Vuuren, M. (2014). Son, you're smoking on Facebook! College students' disclosures on social networking sites as indicators of real-life risk behaviors. *Computers in Human Behavior, 34*, 249–257.

Van Iddekinge, C. H., Lanivich, S. E., Roth, P. L., & Junco, E. (in press). Social media for selection? Validity and adverse impact potential of a Facebook-based assessment. *Journal of Management*.

Vishwanath, A. (2015). Diffusion of deception in social media: Social contagion effects and its antecedents. *Information Systems Frontiers, 17*, 1353–1367.

Viswesvaran, C., & Ones, D. S. (1999). Meta-analysis of fakability estimates: Implications for personality measurement. *Educational and Psychological Measurement, 59*, 197–210.

Walther, J. B., Van Der Heide, B., Kim, S. Y., Westerman, D., & Tong, S. T. (2008). The role of friends' appearance and behavior on evaluations of individuals on Facebook: Are we known by the company we keep? *Human Communication Research, 34*, 28–49.

Weiss, B., & Feldman, R. S. (2006). Looking good and lying to do it: Deception as an impression management strategy in job interviews. *Journal of Applied Social Psychology, 36*, 1070–1086.

Zickar, M. J., & Robie, C. (1999). Modeling faking good on personality items: An item-level analysis. *Journal of Applied Psychology, 84*, 551–563.

Zide, J., Elman, B., & Shahani-Denning, C. (2014). LinkedIn and recruitment: How profiles differ across occupations. *Employee Relations, 36*, 583–604.

Chapter 12
Applicant Reactions to Social Media in Selection: Early Returns and Future Directions

J. William Stoughton

Abstract The current chapter focuses on the effect of social networking websites (SNS) on applicant reactions to selection procedures. Accordingly, the theoretical framework for evaluating the fairness of selection procedures and subsequent applicant reactions for social media use in selection was introduced by Stoughton et al. (J. Bus. Psychol. 30(1):73–78, 2015) are reviewed. The model proposed by Stoughton et al. (J. Bus. Psychol. 30(1):73–78, 2015) builds off the dominant model in the field, the Gilliland (Acad. Manage. Rev. 18(4):694–734, 1993) organizational justice model, and attention is paid to the theoretical underpinnings of the Gilliland (Acad. Manage. Rev. 18(4):694–734, 1993)) model and the evolution of that model into the more recently introduced Stoughton et al. (J. Bus. Psychol. 30(1):73–78, 2015) model. I then discuss the research on the topic to date, which has slowly moved from strictly conference papers and calls for research to peer-reviewed journals with wider dissemination. Key takeaways from this research are surfaced as well as significant findings that help organize recommendations for practitioners. Finally, I discuss proposed future directions for research on the use of social media in selection with a focus on both SNS designed for the workplace and those like Facebook, which were not designed with employer review in mind.

Keywords Applicant reactions • Social networking • Selection • Organizational justice • Fairness • Privacy invasion • Personality • Individual differences

J.W. Stoughton, Ph.D. (✉)
CEB, SHL Talent Measurement, 650 Third Ave South, Suite 1700, Minneapolis, MN 55402, USA
e-mail: will.stoughton@cebglobal.com

R.N. Landers, G.B. Schmidt (eds.), *Social Media in Employee Selection and Recruitment*, DOI 10.1007/978-3-319-29989-1_12

12.1 Applicant Reactions to Social Media in Selection: Early Returns and Future Directions

Over the years, psychological and organizational researchers have developed a variety of methods for assessing job-relevant knowledge, skills, abilities, and other attributes (KSAOs; Arthur & Villado, 2008). The primary focus of this research has been for the benefit of organizations. Ultimately the goal has been to devise the most effective means of assessing applicant and incumbent populations on job-relevant traits in hopes of increasing employee and organizational performance. As other chapters in this book illustrate, social networking websites (SNS) are a new such method of assessing individuals' KSAOs that present a wealth of user information allowing researchers and practitioners an abundance of phenomena to investigate (Ellison, Steinfield, & Lampe, 2007; Roth, Bobko, Van Iddekinge, & Thatcher, 2013). Moreover, because users view SNS as private forums for their own consumption, they may represent an environment free from the high stakes of work-related evaluation (Stoughton, Thompson, & Meade, 2013). However, it is this perspective of users, that some SNS are private forums for their own consumption, that has led to the negative reaction of applicants to various uses of these websites in organizational selection processes (Schneider, Goffin, & Daljeet, 2015; Stoughton et al., 2015).

Research concerning applicant reactions to organizational selection processes is not new. In 1980 Leventhal introduced ten procedural justice "rules" or dimensions that affect the degree to which applicants perceive a selection procedure to be fair, which was operationalized by Gilliland in (1993). The Gilliland (1993) model has been particularly dominant over the years and served as the primary outcome model of applicant reactions. As social media screening practices received greater attention in the popular press Stoughton et al. (2015) proposed a new model to guide future investigations of applicant reactions to the use of SNS in employee selection.

Interest in applicant reactions to the use of SNS in selection is not surprising. SNS are unique in that they give applicants a voice for their opinions about an organization's selection process and that voice has the ability to reach a sizeable audience. The effect of a soured applicant can be great in light of the applicant's newfound ability to widely disseminate their opinion. Additionally, some organizations recognize applicants are also customers and the negative reaction of an applicant to an organization's selection system risks that organization losing more than a potential employee; the organization risks losing a customer (Ott, Blacksmith, & Royal, 2008). Accordingly, the current chapter focuses on the effect of SNS on applicant reactions to selection procedures.

This chapter includes a review of the theoretical framework introduced by Stoughton et al. (2015), which builds off the Gilliland (1993) organizational justice model. The Stoughton et al. (2015) model provides a means of evaluating the fairness of selection procedures and applicant reactions in the context of social media in selection. Additionally, there is a discussion of the research on the topic to date, which is slowly moving from strictly conference papers and calls for research to peer-reviewed journals with wider dissemination. Finally, future directions for research on the use of social media in selection are proposed with a focus on both SNS designed for the workplace and those like Facebook, which were not designed with employer review in mind.

12.1.1 A Model for Applicant Reactions to SNS

As noted above the Gilliland (1993) model for procedural justice has been the primary model of applicant reactions within the broader employee selection literature. Procedural justice is defined by the impartiality of the process that results in decision outcomes (Colquitt, 2001). In effect, applicants' negative procedural justice perceptions represent their disapproval of an organization's hiring process. As part of his model, Gilliland (1993) operationalized ten dimensions of procedural justice as follows: job relatedness, opportunity to perform, reconsideration opportunity, consistency, explanation feedback, selection information, honesty [Bauer et al. (2001) refer to this as "openness"], interpersonal treatment/interpersonal effectiveness, two-way communication, and propriety of questions.

Job relatedness concerns the degree to which a selection procedure assesses the content that appears to be job relevant or valid (Gilliland, 1993). Opportunity to perform refers to an applicant's perception of adequate opportunity to demonstrate one's KSAOs throughout the selection process (Schleicher, Venkataramani, Morgeson, & Campion, 2006). Reconsideration opportunity can be operationalized as the ability to appeal screening decisions (Dineen, Noe, & Wang, 2004). Consistency of administration concerns both consistencies over time and consistencies across people with respect to the administration of the selection system (Stanton, 2000). Due to the public forum permitted by SNS, and increased ability of applicants to reach a wider audience, consistency across applicants becomes more readily verifiable, permitting participants of a given selection system to search social media to corroborate their experiences. Feedback can be defined as a given response to an action that provides information on a person's situation and either encourages or discourages a relevant behavior (Schinkel, Van Dierendonck, & Anderson, 2004). Selection information refers to justifications, if any, for a selection decision (Gilliland, 1993). Honesty or openness concerns the extent to which communications with the potential employer are perceived as sincere, truthful, and open (Bauer et al., 2001). Interpersonal treatment refers to the interpersonal effectiveness of the selection administrator when dealing with applicants (Gilliland, 1993). The move from proctored to unproctored Internet testing made this rule less salient; however, as organizations contemplate giving feedback in the selection process as a reaction to the increase of millennials in the applicant pool, this rule may become quite relevant again. Two-way communication concerns applicants' ability to have a voice in the selection process (Gilliland, 1993). Finally, propriety of questions refers to the fairness of the questions asked during selection (Gilliland, 1993; Stone-Romero, Stone, & Hyatt, 2003).

In 2001, Bauer and colleagues operationalized and extended Gilliland's (1993) model by developing the Selection Procedural Justice Scale (SPJS). This effort resulted in the addition of an eleventh factor, called job-relatedness content, which is defined as the extent to which a selection system appears to assess content relevant to the job situation. Bauer et al. (2001) organized these eleven dimensions into three higher-order factors known as structure, social, and job-relatedness content.

Researchers consider justice perceptions important because of their documented relationship with applicant reactions and attitudes towards an organization (Bauer et al., 2001, 2006; Lind & Tyler, 1988). Procedural justice outcomes range from organizational attraction to attitudes towards recommending others to apply to the hiring organization (Bauer, Dolen, Maertz, & Campion, 1998; Macan et al., 1994). Moreover, applicants may make decisions about an organization with incomplete information, so selection procedures provide the first information that an individual receives concerning how an organization treats its employees; this is important because signaling theory suggests the ambiguity and/or incomplete information available to applicants during the hiring process forces applicants to use available information as signals about the job and organization (Allen, Mahto, & Otondo, 2007; Gilliland, 1993; Rynes, Bretz, & Gerhart, 1991). Accordingly, poor perceptions of organizational hiring practices may be interpreted as an indication of how the organization treats employees and thus how the individual may be treated in the future (Gilliland, 1993). For instance, if an organization uses SNS in the pre-employment process, applicants may believe that the organization may subject them to various forms of electronic performance monitoring as incumbents. This particular example is especially poignant with respect to social media in light of numerous reports of individuals losing their jobs because of social media activity (Stoughton et al., 2013).

The preceding discussion implies that procedural justice would lie at the heart of a model for applicant reactions to the use of SNS screening in the pre-employment process. Applicants tend to favor procedures that are job-related and applicants view their SNS as a non-work-related arena of their lives (Berkelaar, 2014; Ployhart & Ryan, 1997; Rynes, 1993). To date a moderate to strong negative relationship between privacy invasion and procedural justice is demonstrated by empirical research on the topic (Alge, 2001; Eddy, Stone, & Stone-Romero, 1999; Raciot & Williams, 1993). For example, Bauer et al. (2006) showed that procedural justice mediated the effect of privacy concerns and organizational attraction. Moreover, Gilliland and Steiner (2012) point to the model proposed by Bauer et al. (2006) as a supplement to the generally supported Gilliland (1993) model and believe that the two models can be integrated as the outcomes are largely similar. Accordingly, Stoughton et al. (2015) place privacy at the center of the model they introduced for the evaluation of the fairness of SNS evaluation in selection systems.

The model proposed by Stoughton et al. (2015), presented in Fig. 12.1 integrates research from the electronic performance monitoring, privacy, and procedural justice literature sets. Stoughton et al. (2015) suggest that screening SNS affects perceptions of privacy, while individual differences, characteristics of the job, properties of the screening, and outcomes of the hiring process moderate the affect of

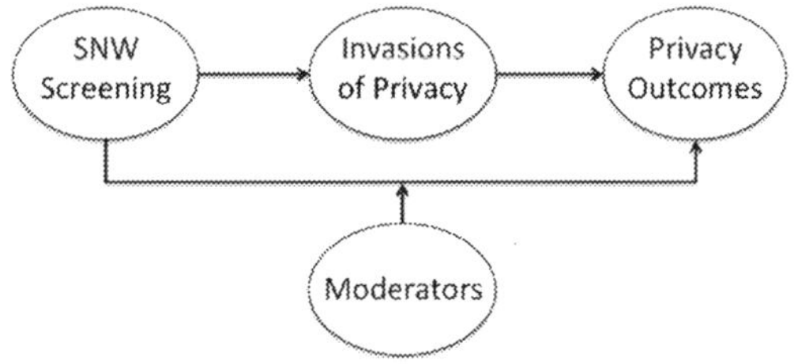

Fig. 12.1 Proposed model of applicant reactions to social network screening practices

SNS screening on privacy outcomes. Individual differences include constructs such as the level of Internet knowledge, conscientiousness, or familiarity with and use of social media. Characteristics of the job include the job-level (i.e., professional vs. hourly), the desirability of the position, industry segment, or competition for the role. Properties of the screening include type of SNS (i.e., one designed with perspective employers in mind; LinkedIn for example), which inherently implies content of an individual's SNS will moderate this relationship as well. Furthermore, prior knowledge of screening, consistency of the screening, and justification for the selection decision are some additional properties of screening practices proposed to moderate the effect on privacy outcomes. Privacy outcomes are wide ranging, including perceptions of procedural justice to the devaluation of the self as individuals perceive the invasion of privacy to disrupt the boundary between themselves and the environment in which they function (Alge, 2001; Altman, 1975; Margulis, 2003; Westin, 1967). Stoughton et al. (2015) provide two initial tests of aspects of their model, with early returns largely supporting the relationships proposed. That is, utilizing SNS in the pre-employment process was seen as a violation of the privacy of applicants, which in-turn caused lower perceptions of organizational justice. Applicants subjected to SNS screening reported lower levels of organizational attraction and higher intentions to pursue litigation against an organization engaged in SNS screening. Applicants low in agreeableness were found to have the most negative reaction to the screening practices. And, regardless of whether or not applicants received a job offer, they perceived the use of SNS in the hiring process to violate their privacy.

An example may be helpful to illustrate how the model works in practice. An applicant applies to an organization and through the course of the hiring process discovers that the organization uses social media to determine the "professionalism" of job candidates. Upon learning that the potential employer uses SNS like Facebook and Twitter for screening the applicant feels that their privacy is violated because they believe their Facebook and Twitter pages to be a private forums and not for employer consumption. This violation of privacy causes the applicant to feel that the hiring process of the organization is not procedurally just. As a result of their belief that the hiring system is not just the applicant chooses to withdraw from the hiring process and tells other friends and colleagues about the practices of the organization and the low opinion the applicant now has of the organization as a possible place to work. For researchers, it would be worth investigating whether or not this applicant had content on their Facebook and Twitter pages that could be perceived negatively by employers (i.e., moderators). Or, whether the candidate made attempts to hide the content of their Facebook and Twitter pages through privacy settings that the employer could bypass through a variety of different means (e.g., friending the would be employee).

The findings of Stoughton et al. (2015) and other researchers' exploration of applicant reactions to the use of SNS in the hiring process are reviewed subsequently. And, it is worth noting that Stoughton et al. (2015) urge psychological and organizational researchers to continue to test the broader concepts within their model. The model was created to organize research in the field and serve to ground future study in a common framework for exploration.

12.2 Research on Reactions to SNS to Date

The research on applicant reactions to the use of SNS in the pre-employment process is limited. However, there is evidence that the literature is maturing, as studies begin to emerge in peer-reviewed journals moving from exclusively being disseminated through conference presentations and proceedings. The current section of this chapter focuses on the existing body of research on applicant opinions to SNS use in the hiring process, drawing themes across studies and highlighting additional work that may be relevant to future researchers investigating these topics.

Madera (2012) provided one of the earliest published works on the use of social networking websites in the employment process by investigating the reactions of career fair participants to a hospitality company that either used or did not use SNS in the selection process. Madera (2012) used a 2 (SNS used as a selection tool) × 2 (SNS used for hiring or promotion) experimental design, which asked current job seekers to rate their perceptions of a selection system described by the authors through a job advertisement. After reading the description of the job, participants completed a survey containing the variables of interest. Madera (2012) found that organizational use of SNS in selection lowered both applicant perceptions of fairness and intentions to pursue employment. However, the population assessed (i.e., applicant vs. incumbent) did not moderate the relationships between screening practices and the outcomes of interest. This finding is especially interesting as it appears that irrespective of whether the organization is applying the screening practices to new hires or incumbents up-for-promotion and applicant population universally reacts poorly to the practice.

There are several limitations to the Madera (2012) work that should be addressed. First, the manipulation of social media screening practices was double-barreled; that is, the manipulation highlighted that the hiring organization used SNS to "recruit and assess" job candidates. Therefore, the study's manipulation leaves open the question of whether the negative reaction was to the recruitment or assessment practices, where the author highlights that hospitality organizations were commonly encouraging applicants to "friend" the company during the hiring process, a practice that could be perceived as an invasion of the applicant's personal space, but may be undertaken by the applicant if they believe that they would be disadvantaged in the hiring process by not "friending" the company. Another limitation of the study was the industry specificity. While the use of a specific industry undoubtedly added to the salience of the selection scenario for the participants, the idiosyncrasies of SNS use during the hiring process in the hospitality industry (i.e., actively encouraging applicants to friend the company) may serve to limit the findings from broader organizational contexts. Additionally, the manipulation itself was limited to a specific role (sales), which could have shaped participant perceptions of the job relatedness of the SNS assessment. For example, the participants may believe that the ability to view pictures of job applicants allowed for accurate assessment of traits relevant to sales roles (e.g., extraversion).

Early studies of SNS use in pre-employment screening within the management and psychology literature base first appeared in the form of conference proceedings and presentations. Sanchez et al. (2012) provided one of the first investigations of social networking presence checks in a college student population by soliciting opinions to a simulated selection scenario. Sanchez et al. (2012) found that social networking presence checks resulted in lower organizational attraction and decreased job pursuit intentions over those not subjected to social networking presence checks. However, Sanchez et al. (2012) did not find differences between the experimental and control conditions with respect to overall perceptions of the selection process. Again, we see the common practice in this literature of the use of a student population, which serves to limit the generalizability of a number of these studies.

Another conference presentation by Hartwell (2014) is noteworthy as it is one of the early works investigating the differences between reactions to job-relevant social media (e.g., LinkedIn) and social media not intended for various job-contexts like Facebook. Hartwell (2014) found the use of Facebook to be more invasive, less job-relevant, and ultimately less procedurally just than the use of LinkedIn in the hiring process. However, there were some study limitations; the study used a small sample of undergraduate students with a low response rate (10 %). Additionally, the study failed to investigate any outcomes of the procedural justice perceptions, leaving the tests of the Stoughton et al. (2015) model incomplete.

As stated above, this research domain is beginning to mature and the most recent research in the field is appearing in peer-reviewed journals. For example, Drouin, O'Connor, Schmidt, and Miller (2015) assessed applicant opinions on the use of Facebook and Twitter for hiring and firing decisions in a sample of undergraduate students. Results of the study indicated there was a significant relationship between openness to experience and disapproval of using social media for employment decisions. Additionally, those who were older were much more likely to disapprove of the use of social media use for selection decisions.

While this study was purely exploratory in nature making use of an undergraduate sample and a one-item measure of applicant opinion, the results concerning age were particularly noteworthy. Undergraduate populations, especially young undergraduate populations, have grown-up with social media websites as a pervasive part of their lives for more than half a lifetime (Facebook was launched in 2004). The results indicated that older populations are more likely to have an adverse reaction to social media screening and thus the use of undergraduate populations, already noted to be a common sampling source, may actually underestimate the effect of SNS screening on applicant perceptions of invasions of privacy and associated outcomes given the older nature of most applicant pools found in organizations today.

Stoughton et al. (2015) evaluated their model of the use of SNS in selection by utilizing a Study 1/Study 2 design. In their first study Stoughton et al. (2015) solicited applicants to a temporary position (fictitious) that would require a short-term commitment for compensation from the applicants. The applicants were solicited to the position from a larger data collection effort. Upon applying for the position, applicants completed a selection battery that was said to be created for a firm affiliated with the university and was partnering with the university's Industrial–Organizational psychology program to select individuals for the temporary position. Participants were randomly assigned to one of three conditions: (a) no screening, (b) consistent screening, and (c) inconsistent screening, which directly manipulated the procedural justice of the applicants and contacted them within 2 weeks informing them of the details of the screening procedure.

Applicants felt that screening based on their SNS represented an invasion of their privacy. This invasion of privacy resulted in lower perceptions of organizational justice, which ultimately lowered perceptions of organizational attraction. Additionally, the authors found that agreeableness moderated the relationship between screening practices and justice perceptions; individuals low in agreeableness were found to have the most adverse reaction to screening practices as represented by their resultant justice scores.

Study 1 was unique in that participants truly believed themselves to be applying for a position; so, while the participants were students, the manipulations were particularly salient as the participants believed themselves to be applicants engaged in a hiring process hoping to land a temporary position. It should be noted that the temporary nature of the position could serve to limit the generalizability of the study, however it seems reasonable that the findings would extend to higher stakes settings and that only the magnitude of the relationships between the variables of interest remains to be seen.

For Study 2 Stoughton et al. (2015) used a simulated selection scenario to solicit opinions from an older sample of full-time employees. Furthermore, the manipulation of procedural justice incorporated an additional moderator, a hiring decision. Again, the results demonstrated that the use of SNS for pre-employment screening increased applicants' perceptions of privacy violations. Moreover, like the first study invasions of privacy resulted in decreased organizational attraction as well as increased intentions to litigate (i.e., sue the hiring organization). The organization's hiring decision, which was hypothesized to moderate the effect of social media screening practices, did not appear to affect privacy outcomes. Instead the authors found that applying SNS practices affects privacy outcomes regardless of the hiring decision made by the employer. The results of this study were replicated by

Stoughton and Van Overberghe (2015) where again perceptions of a violation of privacy resulted in increased intentions to pursue litigation in the authors' study.

Outside of the applicant reactions literature, there have been a number of studies investigating myriad implications of social media in selection. One study by Schneider et al. (2015) is particularly remarkable and pertinent to this discussion because the authors reviewed the practice of organizations requiring applicants to give up their SNS passwords during the hiring process. The expressed purpose of the study was to investigate the implications of requests for SNS passwords on the make-up of the applicant pool. Schneider et al. (2015) supposed applicants refusing to give their SNS passwords to a hiring organization would affect the organization's applicant pool, such that those candidates that remained would have different mean levels on a number of traits. Such information however, can also inform which individuals are most likely to have an adverse reaction to the practice of SNS use in the pre-employment process (i.e., it informs organizational researchers of relevant moderators). One such finding emerged, Schneider et al. (2015) found participants high in agreeableness and conscientiousness more likely to divulge their SNS passwords during the hiring process.

The results of Schneider et al. (2015) bolsters the findings of Stoughton et al. (2015), in that study participants low in agreeableness have the most unfavorable reaction to a variety of SNS practices used in the hiring process. Moreover, the results of the study demonstrated that individuals high on mean levels of conscientiousness also disclose their SNS passwords more readily than those low in conscientiousness. While other personality variables commonly associated with selection batteries (e.g., extraversion and openness to experience) did not demonstrate a significant relationship with participants' willingness to divulge their SNS passwords, the study did uncover additional personality variables (i.e., conscientiousness) that may affect perceptions of particular practices of SNS screening in pre-employment, as well as highlight the condemnation of the practice of requesting passwords from applicants.

12.3 Key Takeaways for Practitioners

There are a number of critical takeaways from the preceding section. At this point a number of studies demonstrate that utilizing SNS to screen applicants will lower applicant perceptions of procedural justice (e.g., Madera, 2012; Sanchez et al., 2012; Stoughton et al., 2015; etc.) and ultimately affect outcomes of interest for organizations, such as: intentions to pursue employment, organizational attractiveness, or intentions to litigate (i.e., pursue legal action). The findings of Madera (2012) and Stoughton et al. (2015) highlight how pernicious applicants find this practice. For Madera (2012) it did not matter if the practice was used for internal or external candidates for a job, applicants disapproved of the use of SNS for employment decisions, while Stoughton et al. (2015) demonstrated it did not matter if applicants received a positive hiring outcome (i.e., a job offer), job candidates found the practice invasive and unjust. Additionally, Hartwell (2014) demonstrated that utilizing less job-relevant SNS (i.e., Facebook, Twitter, etc.) in the hiring process is perceived as more unjust. This should guide future research about SNS in selection, and for practitioners point to applicants being more permissive of the use of job-relevant SNS like LinkedIn. Moreover, a number of personality traits were found to moderate applicant perceptions of employer use of SNS (i.e., agreeableness, openness to experience, and conscientiousness) in studies to date. A number of these traits have explanation grounded in theory, for example agreeableness, which was shown to affect applicant perceptions such that those lower in agreeableness had the most adverse reaction to SNS use; these findings encourage future exploration of SNS moderators and serve to highlight who is most likely to react to various SNS pre-employment screening practices. Finally, the Drouin et al. (2015) study finding that older applicants have a greater reaction to the practice of SNS screening than younger applicants highlights that most studies to date may underestimate the magnitude of the effect of SNS practices in pre-employment, which should serve as strong caution to organizations looking to institute such practices in their hiring process.

Taking these findings as a whole, strong caution must be urged of practitioners looking to institute SNS screening practices in their hiring process. Practitioners should take care to weigh the perceived benefits gained by these screening practices (cf. Stoughton et al., 2013) and the reactions of applicants if practices are known or if clandestine screening is discovered. It was mentioned previously, but the ability of an applicant to broadly disseminate a negative message about a hiring organization is very real with the platform permitted by social media and findings like those of Stoughton et al. (2015) that applicants have greater intentions to sue an organization engaged in SNS screening suggest a willingness to follow-up on a negative experience. In the event that the hiring organization offers some good or service, it is possible that the organization would lose a customer in the soured applicant. Moreover, if an organization does choose to engage in SNS screening it is likely they would receive a greater negative reaction from older subsets of their applicant pool. This is not to suggest that these screening practices are best directed at a graduate recruitment program, but only meant to highlight that most of the studies to date have been on young college students and when these practices are employed within a broader subset of the workforce the research suggests a more acute negative reaction.

12.4 Avenues for Future Research

While the uptick of peer-reviewed literature summarized in the previous section is encouraging, the brevity of the section highlights the need for future research. Stoughton et al. (2015) provides a comprehensive review for future research on applicant reactions to the use of SNS in the pre-employment process grounded in the model outlined previously. Additionally, in a piece meant to direct management and psychology research about social media Roth et al. (2013) provide a number of valuable suggestions for future research some which will be highlighted in addition to novel areas for exploration.

First, Stoughton et al. (2015) were unable to successfully demonstrate that consistency of administration affects procedural justice perceptions as would be indicated by their model, this is likely due to their inability to effectively communicate the salience of the manipulation; a manuscript note confirms this supposition, as the manipulation appeared to be ineffective based on the results of manipulation checks. Future research should look for ways to ensure that consistency/inconsistency of screening is salient to job seekers. Doing so would enable more decisive conclusions regarding the effects of consistency, and may yield the results predicted by Stoughton et al. (2015). Research that makes that manipulation salient could extend the procedural justice literature toward pre-employment website screening in important new ways.

Hartwell (2014) provided an early first exploration of the differences between the reactions of applicants to social media perceived as job-relevant (e.g., LinkedIn) and those perceived as personal (e.g., Facebook). It would be fruitful to continue this line of investigation, as there are myriad job-relevant SNS on which to explore the reactions of applicants to various screening practices. Researchers could explore any number of concepts; for example, reactions of applicants to hiring organizations checking LinkedIn presence and the levels of activity or influence an individual has in their network. This may be especially interesting as metrics around an individual's activity/influence are starting to emerge, which could be utilized for hiring decisions.

Additionally, the characteristics of screening methods used can be very different. For example, Kluemper and Rosen (2009) outlined a process for using social media in the selection process that included training and subsequent evaluator ratings that correlated with successive supervisor performance ratings, whereas Van Iddekinge, Lanivich, Roth, and Junco (2013) evaluated the ratings of (untrained) recruiters' reviews of the social media profiles of job applicants and found no correlation with subsequent performance ratings. Alternatively, a study by Kosinski, Stillwell, and Graepel (2013) demonstrated the viability of using "likes" and profile information to predict personality and cognitive ability. Future research would do well to examine if there are differing reactions to the various methods identified to date aimed at predicting future performance through social media websites.

Future research would do well to examine the content of applicants' SNS. Researchers can determine whether the effects of the screening practices depend on whether the applicant's social media contains information generally regarded as inappropriate or unprofessional (e.g., bad mouthing or other so called Facebook faux pas). Also, exploring whether an applicant finds social media screening particularly pernicious when he or she attempted to make their social media profiles private (i.e., inaccessible to the general public) would be worthwhile. As mentioned above in reference to the study by Madera (2012), the nature of industry specific norms associated with SNS use in the pre-employment process could affect these attempts by applicants to make their profiles private if organizations encourage the "friending" of the organization in the recruitment process.

The increasingly global nature of the working world is reflected in the increase in international samples, in the applicant reactions literature the interest in reactions in different contexts is growing (see McCarthy et al., 2013). Roulin (2014) proposes similar research for SNS and suggests that social media use in pre-employment is different across national borders. This line of inquiry would be fruitful to pursue.

Finally, while generally agreeing that the procedural justice models of the broader applicant reactions literature, especially that proposed by Hausknecht, Day, and Thomas (2004), can guide future research on SNS use for selection, Roth et al. (2013) propose an alternative avenue for future research suggesting that applicants may react favorably to social media use in the hiring process. Citing studies that younger populations may be more amenable to social media use in the hiring process (i.e., Davison, Maraist, & Bing, 2011), a proposition bolstered by the findings of Drouin et al. (2015), Roth et al. (2013) assert that favorable reactions for young applicants may result from younger applicants assuming technology will permeate their lives (see also Berkelaar, 2014; Turkle, 2011).

12.5 Conclusions

Recent surveys of human resource practitioners reveal that a full 40% believe that social networking websites are a useful method for determining applicant fit with their organization (Kantrowitz, 2014). Survey results such as these as well as other chapters in this book highlight that SNS use in pre-employment is not going away. It is productive for researchers and practitioners alike to be fully aware of the likely reactions of applicants to different social networking practices and uncover those yet to be found. The results of the accumulated studies to date indicate that utilizing SNS to screen applicants is perceived as a violation of privacy that lowers applicant perceptions of procedural justice. The effects of low justice perceptions are numerous for organizations and should caution practitioners from engaging in SNS screening. At the very least, practitioners should account for the benefits they believe they will accrue from engaging in SNS screening with the likely negative reaction of the applicant pool.

References

Alge, B. J. (2001). Effects of computer surveillance on perceptions of privacy and procedural justice. *Journal of Applied Psychology, 86*(4),797–804. Retrieved April 24, 2011, from http://doi.apa.org/getdoi.cfm?doi=10.1037/0021-9010.86.4.797

Allen, D. G., Mahto, R. V., & Otondo, R. F., 2007. Web-based recruitment: Effects of information, organizational brand, and attitudes toward a Web site on applicant attraction. *Journal of Applied Psychology, 92*(6), 1696–1708. Retrieved August 16, 2011, from http://www.ncbi.nlm.nih.gov/pubmed/18020806

Altman, I. (1975). *The environment and social behavior: Privacy, personal space, territory, crowding*. Monterey, CA: Brooks/Cole.

Arthur, W., & Villado, A. J. (2008). The importance of distinguishing between constructs and methods when comparing predictors in personnel selection research and practice. *Journal of Applied Psychology, 93*(2), 435–442. Retrieved July 12, 2011, from http://www.ncbi.nlm.nih.gov/pubmed/18361642

Bauer, T. N., Dolen, M. R., Maertz, C. P., & Campion, M. A. (1998). Longitudinal assessment of applicant reactions to employment testing and test outcome feedback. *Journal of Applied Psychology, 83*(6), 892–903. Retrieved September 10, 2013, from http://doi.apa.org/getdoi.cfm?doi=10.1037/0021-9010.83.6.892

Bauer, T. N., Truxillo, D. M., Sanchez, R. J., Craig, J. M., Ferrara, P., & Campion, M. A. (2001). Applicant reactions to selection: Development of the Selection Procedural Justice Scale (SPJS). *Personnel Psychology, 54*(2), 387–419. Retrieved August 16, 2011, from http://doi.wiley.com/10.1111/j.1744-6570.2001.tb00097.x

Bauer, T. N., Truxillo, D. M., Tucker, J. S., Weathers, V., Bertolino, M., Erdogan, B., et al. (2006). Selection in the Information Age: The impact of privacy concerns and computer experience on applicant reactions. *Journal of Management, 32*(5), 601–621. Retrieved May 24, 2011, from http://jom.sagepub.com/cgi/doi/10.1177/0149206306289829

Berkelaar, B. L. (2014). Cybervetting, online information, and personnel selection: New transparency expectations and the emergence of a digital social contract. *Management Communication Quarterly, 28*(4), 479–506. Retrieved from http://mcq.sagepub.com/cgi/doi/10.1177/0893318914541966

Colquitt, J. (2001). On the dimensionality of organizational justice: A construct validation of a measure. *Journal of Applied Psychology, 86*, 386–400.

Davison, H. K., Maraist, C., & Bing, M. N. (2011). Friend or foe? The promise and pitfalls of using social networking sites for HR decisions. *Journal of Business and Psychology, 26*(2), 153–159. Retrieved May 24, 2011, from http://www.springerlink.com/index/10.1007/s10869-011-9215-8

Dineen, B. R., Noe, R. A., & Wang, C. (2004). Perceived fairness of web-based applicant screening procedures: Weighing the rules of justice and the role of individual differences. *Human Resource Management, 43*(2–3), 127–145.

Drouin, M., O'Connor, K. W., Schmidt, G. B., & Miller, D. A. (2015). Facebook fired: Legal perspectives and young adults' opinions on the use of social media in hiring and firing decisions. *Computers in Human Behavior, 46*, 123–128. Retrieved from http://linkinghub.elsevier.com/retrieve/pii/S0747563215000230

Eddy, E. R., Stone, D. L., & Stone-Romero, E. E. (1999). The effects of information management policies on reactions to human resource information systems: An integration of privacy and procedural justice perspectives. *Personnel Psychology, 52*(2), 335–358. Retrieved from April 8, 2013, from http://doi.wiley.com/10.1111/j.1744-6570.1999.tb00164.x

Ellison, N. B., Steinfield, C., & Lampe, C. (2007). The benefits of Facebook "friends:" Social capital and college students' use of online social network sites. *Journal of Computer-Mediated Communication, 12*(4), 1143–1168. Retrieved from http://jcmc.indiana.edu/vol12/issue4/ellison.html

Gilliland, S. W. (1993). The perceived fairness of selection systems: An organizational perspective. *Academy of Management Review, 18*(4), 694–734.

Gilliland, S. W., & Steiner, D. D. (2012). Applicant reactions to testing and selection. In N. Schmitt (Ed.), *The Oxford handbook of personnel assessment and selection* (pp. 629–666). Oxford, England: Oxford University Press.

Hartwell, C. J. (2014). In R. N. Landers & G. B. Schmidt (Eds.), *Applicant reactions to social media screens in employee selection*. Paper presented at the 29th annual meeting of the Society for Industrial and Organizational Psychology, Honolulu, HI.

Hausknecht, J. P., Day, D. V., & Thomas, S. C. (2004). Applicant reactions to selection procedures: An updated model and meta-analysis. *Personnel Psychology, 57*(3), 639–683. Retrieved June 20, 2011, from http://doi.wiley.com/10.1111/j.1744-6570.2004.00003.x

Kantrowitz, T. M. (2014). 2014 global assessment trends report, Alpharetta, GA. Retrieved from http://ceb.shl.com/images/uploads/GATR-042014v2-USeng.pdf

Kluemper, D. H., & Rosen, P. A. (2009). Future employment selection methods: Evaluating social networking web sites. *Journal of Managerial Psychology, 24*(6), 567–580. Retrieved June 16, 2011, from http://www.emeraldinsight.com/10.1108/02683940910974134

Kosinski, M., Stillwell, D., & Graepel, T. (2013). Private traits and attributes are predictable from digital records of human behavior. *Proceedings of the National Academy of Sciences of the United States of America, 110*(15), 5802–5805. Retrieved from http://www.pubmedcentral.nih.gov/articlerender.fcgi?artid=3625324&tool=pmcentrez&rendertype=abstract

Leventhal, G. S. (1980). What should be done with equity theory? New approaches to the study of fairness in social relationships. In K. Gergen, M. Greenberg, & R. Willis (Eds.), *Social exchange: Advances in theory and research* (pp. 27–88). New York: Plenum Press.

Lind, E. A., & Tyler, T. (1988). *The social psychology of procedural justice*. New York: Plenum Press.

Macan, T. H., Avedon, M. J., Paese, M., & Smith, D. E. (1994). The effects of applicants' reactions to cognitive ability tests and an assessment center. *Personnel Psychology, 47*, 715–739.

Madera, J. M. (2012). Using social networking websites as a selection tool: The role of selection process fairness and job pursuit intentions. *International Journal of Hospitality Management, 31*(4), 1276–1282.

Margulis, S. T. (2003). Privacy as a social issue and behavioral concept. *Journal of Social Issues, 59*(2), 243–261. Retrieved September 14, 2013, from http://doi.wiley.com/10.1111/1540-4560.00063

McCarthy, J. M., Van Iddekinge, C. H., Lievens, F., Kung, M. C., Sinar, E. F., & Campion, M. A. (2013). Do candidate reactions relate to job performance or affect criterion-related validity? A multistudy investigation of relations among reactions, selection test scores, and job performance. *Journal of Applied Psychology, 98*(5), 701–719. Retrieved October 24, 2013, from http://www.ncbi.nlm.nih.gov/pubmed/23937298

Ott, B., Blacksmith, N., & Royal, K. (2008). Job applicants are customers too. *Gallup Business Journal*. Retrieved from http://www.gallup.com/businessjournal/103546/job-candidates-customers-too.aspx

Ployhart, R. E., & Ryan, A. M. (1997). Toward an explanation of applicant reactions: An examination of organizational justice and attribution frameworks. *Organizational Behavior and Human Decision Processes, 72*(3), 308–335. Retrieved September 15, 2013, from http://www.ncbi.nlm.nih.gov/pubmed/21435355

Raciot, B. M., & Williams, K. J. (1993). Perceived invasiveness and fairness of drug-testing procedures for current employees. *Journal of Applied Social Psychology, 23*(22), 1879–1891. Retrieved April 8, 2013, from http://doi.wiley.com/10.1111/j.1559-1816.1993.tb01070.x

Roth, P. L., Bobko, P., Van Iddekinge, C. H., & Thatcher, J. B. (2013). Social Media in employee-selection-related decisions: A research agenda for uncharted territory. *Journal of Management*. Retrieved August 20, 2014, from http://jom.sagepub.com/cgi/doi/10.1177/0149206313503018

Roulin, N. (2014). The influence of employers' use of social networking websites in selection, online self-promotion, and personality on the likelihood of faux pas postings. *International Journal of Selection and Assessment, 22*(1), 80–87.

Rynes, S. L. (1993). Who's selecting whom? Effects of selection practices on applicant attitudes and behavior. In N. Schmitt, W. C. Borman, & Associates (Eds.), *Personnel selection in organizations* (pp. 240–274). San Francisco: Jossey-Bass.

Rynes, S. L., Bretz, R. D., & Gerhart, B. (1991). The importance of recruitment in job choice: A different way of looking. *Personnel Psychology, 44*, 487–521.

Sanchez, R. J, Roberts, K., Freeman, M., & Clayton, A. C. (2012). *Does it matter? Applicant reactions to online social networking presence checks*. Paper presented at the 72nd annual meeting of the Academy of Management. Boston, MA.

Schinkel, S., Van Dierendonck, D., & Anderson, N. R. (2004). The impact of selection encounters on applicants: An experimental study into feedback effects after a negative selection decision. *International Journal of Selection and Assessment, 12*(1–2), 197–205.

Schleicher, D. J., Venkataramani, V., Morgeson, F. P., & Campion, M. A. (2006). So you didn't get the job … Now what do you think? Examining opportunity-to-perform fairness perceptions.

Personnel Psychology, 59(3), 559–590. Retrieved August 13, 2011, from http://doi.wiley.com/10.1111/j.1744-6570.2006.00047.x

Schneider, T. J., Goffin, R. D., & Daljeet, K. N. (2015). "Give us your social networking site passwords": Implications for personnel selection and personality. *Personality and Individual Differences, 73*, 78–83. Retrieved from http://linkinghub.elsevier.com/retrieve/pii/S0191886914005285

Stanton, J. (2000). Reactions to employee performance monitoring: Framework, review, and research directions. *Human Performance, 13*(1), 85–113. Retrieved from http://www.informaworld.com/openurl?genre=article&doi=10.1207/S15327043HUP1301_4&magic=crossref||D404A21C5BB053405B1A640AFFD44AE3

Stone-Romero, E. F., Stone, D. L., & Hyatt, D. (2003). Personnel selection procedures and invasion of privacy. *Journal of Social Issues, 59*(2), 343–368. Retrieved September 15, 2013, from http://doi.wiley.com/10.1111/1540-4560.00068

Stoughton, J. W., Thompson, L. F., & Meade, A. W. (2013). Big Five personality traits reflected in job applicants' social media postings. *Cyberpsychology, behavior and social networking, 16*(11), 800–805. Retrieved November 12, 2013, from http://www.ncbi.nlm.nih.gov/pubmed/23790360

Stoughton, J. W., Thompson, L. F., & Meade, A. W. (2015). Examining applicant reactions to the use of social networking websites in pre-employment screening. *Journal of Business and Psychology, 30*(1), 73–78. Retrieved November 23, 2013, from http://link.springer.com/article/10.1007/s10869-013-9333-6

Stoughton, J. W., & Van Overberghe, C. T. (2015). In T. M. Kantrowitz (Ed.), *Social media in selection: Different pictures for research and practice*. Paper presented at the 30th annual meeting of the Society for Industrial and Organizational Psychologists. Philadelphia, PA.

Turkle, S. (2011). *Alone together: Why we expect more from technology and less from each other*. New York: Basic Books.

Van Iddekinge, C. H., Lanivich, S. E., Roth, P. L., & Junco, E. (2013). Social media for selection? Validity and adverse impact potential of a Facebook-based assessment. *Journal of Management*. Retrieved August 31, 2014, from http://jom.sagepub.com/cgi/doi/10.1177/0149206313515524

Westin, A. F. (1967). *Privacy and freedom*. New York: Atheneum.

Chapter 13
Legal Concerns When Considering Social Media Data in Selection

Gordon B. Schmidt and Kimberly W. O'Connor

Abstract This chapter examines the current state of the law in the United States on the use of social media data in the employee selection process. We begin by reviewing existing legal protections that could be violated when organizations use social media data, and we discuss recent case law involving social media and selection. We highlight various federal laws that have been used by the courts in social media selection cases, and we examine state laws that ban employers from asking applicants to provide social media user names and passwords as a condition of employment. We then review three examples of laws in other countries that could impact the use of social media data in selection both practically and legally. We conclude by suggesting practical guidelines for employers in their use of social media data in selection.

Keywords Social media • Selection • Title VII • Protected classes • Discrimination • Wrongful discharge • Case law • International law • Right to be forgotten • Social media passwords

Online social media has become a major part of the employment screening process, with a 2011 study by Reppler reporting that 91 % of surveyed employers have used social media websites to screen applicants. Sixty-nine percent of employers say they have declined an applicant based on the information they found on social media (Reppler, 2011). A Jobvite (2013) study found similar results, with 93 % of recruiters indicating they are likely to look at a candidate's social media profile and 42 % saying they have assessed a candidate in a positive or negative way after looking at the candidate's social media profile. The overall picture seems clear that many organizations are using social media in the screening and selection process in various ways. For example, employers could use social media to read candidates' status

G.B. Schmidt, Ph.D. (✉) • K.W. O'Connor
Division of Organizational Leadership and Supervision, Indiana University-Purdue University Fort Wayne, Neff 288D, 2101 East Coliseum Blvd., Fort Wayne, IN 46805, USA
e-mail: schmidtg@ipfw.edu; oconnok@ipfw.edu

R.N. Landers, G.B. Schmidt (eds.), *Social Media in Employee Selection and Recruitment*, DOI 10.1007/978-3-319-29989-1_13

updates and posts, look at their pictures, review their friends list, see what pages they "like," and view the groups they belong to, among many other uses. Any of these methods might yield information that employers could use to disqualify candidates. Such behavior poses potential legal issues when the information gleaned by employers is legally protected or is used in a way that discriminates against protected classes.

With the prevalence of social media use by organizations continuing to grow, many questions arise about the potential legal impact of such use. While viewing social media data during applicant screening is not illegal in the United States, it is possible that the information gathered and/or the methods used by an organization to screen applicants may violate the law (Davison, Maraist, Hamilton, & Bing, 2012). This has led scholars to call for the need for in-depth legal analysis of the use of social media in selection (Brown & Vaughn, 2011; Davison, Maraist, & Bing, 2011). This chapter answers those calls.

This chapter will review existing United States laws and legal rulings related to employee selection and discuss how social media selection processes could lead to potential legal problems for organizations. We will discuss the existing US case law on social media use in the selection processes, as well as existing laws aimed at protecting applicants and/or employees. We will then turn to the international legal context for social media use in selection, highlighting three examples that could have significant impact. Finally, we will discuss what we still need to learn to better understand the legal context of social media use in selection.

13.1 Existing Legal Standards/Laws for Selection Decisions

There are many potential reasons that organizational selection processes could result in conflicts which would lead to legal action. Williams, Schaffer, and Ellis (2013) examined all legal cases from 1998 to 2010 related to selection in Bloomberg Bureau of National Affairs ("BNA") case briefs, which resulted in a final sample of 312. They coded the cases as to the selection tools used in the company involved in the suit and the selection process issues alleged. The selection tools included: biographical information blank, interview, cognitive ability test, and psychomotor tests. The selection process issues alleged included: use of problematic criteria, violations of the Four-fifths Rule, administrative inconsistencies, personal bias or favoritism, lack of documentation, quota or unlawful affirmative action programs, unfair recruiting source, and failure to provide accommodations. In many cases, the selection tools used by the organizations caused one or more legal issues (Williams et al., 2013).

While social media use in the selection process was not studied by Williams et al. (2013), its use can also lead to legal issues for an organization. For example, if an organization is using social media screening, but the organization lacks a consistent selection (or de-selection) process, it could be the basis for a discrimination claim. Another example that could lead to a discrimination claim might be if different organizational representatives are screening candidates via social media and weighting data differently. To date, there has been sparse published academic work on the validity of using social media in selection decisions (Kleumper, Rosen, & Mossholder, 2012; Van Iddekinge, Lanivich, Roth, & Junco, 2013). Validation studies within an organization might be a crucial factor when litigating social media selection cases and could potentially convince a court that the methods used by the organization are, in fact, valid and job-related.

13.2 Reasons Why Organizations Might Have a Legal Duty to Access Applicant Social Media

While much of the existing social media selection research has focused on whether social media has helped the quality of candidate selection, there are circumstances where reviewing an applicant or employee's social media page may constitute a legal necessity. For example, employer responsibility for an employee's actions may fall under one of a handful of potential employer liability doctrines. First, under respondent superior, if an employee commits a tort (which is a wrongful act which leads to civil liability) while in the course and scope of employment, the employer can be held liable. Second, under the doctrine of negligence (or failure to exercise reasonable care), an employer may be liable for negligent hiring, negligent retention, or negligent supervision of an employee. Third, employer liability may arise for violations of anti-harassment laws.

For example, in Howard v. Hertz (2014), a customer sued Hertz for Facebook comments that a Hertz employee posted about the customer's race, sexual orientation, and financial status. The key to the customer's negligence case was the legal standard of foreseeability. In other words, was it foreseeable to Hertz that their employee would post such comments about a customer? The court held yes. The Hertz employee's Facebook posts were indeed foreseeable to the organization because the employee had already had two previous incidents involving posts about other customers. The district court allowed the case to proceed because the employer should have been on notice that this employee needed better training/supervision.

As this case illustrates, employers can be held liable for the actions of employees that the employer knows about or should know about, even when it comes to the employees' personal social media usage (Morgan & Davis, 2013). Employers screening out applicants based on social media posts in this regard may not just help to avoid hiring potentially bad employees, but also help in avoiding hiring candidates that lead to potential legal liability.

Employers also have to be aware that liability may arise for a hostile work environment that exists via social media. For example, in Blakely v. Continental Airlines, the issue was whether Continental Airlines could be held liable for the harassment of a female employee who alleged that defamatory statements about her were posted on social media by her coworkers. The social media site in question was an electronic bulletin board that was not maintained by Continental Airlines; however, its employees were required to log on to access work assignments. The court held that, even though the employer may not have an affirmative duty to monitor the online site in the case, employers may have liability related to the harassment if the employer had direct or constructive knowledge of the content posted online. Moreover, if the employer derives a benefit from the social media use by employees, then the court can consider it to be part of the employee's work environment. Thus, employer liability may attach (Desnlow, 2015).

13.3 Areas of Potential United States Legal Concerns When Accessing Applicant Social Media Data

We will now explore areas related to social media use in selection that are impacted by existing laws and court rulings. The goal of the following sections is to describe these general areas that can have legal implications when an organization uses social media data in selection. Existing laws and rulings related to social media use in selection will be discussed, but importantly existing laws that could be applied will be described as well as their implications. The two main areas we will look at are employment discrimination and applicant privacy. After this section, international implications will be discussed.

13.4 Employment Discrimination

When viewing social media sites, an employer may potentially view characteristics of applicants, such as gender, disability, age, nationality, race, pregnancy, or sexual orientation, among others. The employer may also discover information that the employer would never have known about the applicant without it being available on social media. Information the employer may obtain therefore affords a potential opportunity for unlawful discrimination. In other words, the employer can discriminate against the applicant, without their knowledge, by reviewing the applicant's social media sites and ultimately deny the applicant an opportunity for an interview and subsequent employment (Pate, 2012). The question is therefore raised, what legal protections are available to employees to protect them from unlawful discrimination through the use of social media? Though no federal statute specifically prohibits employers from obtaining or utilizing information gathered from social media sites, courts have been using already existing legal protections to decide social media cases.

13.4.1 *Title VII of the Civil Rights Act of 1964*

Title VII of the Civil Rights Act of 1964 and its subsequent amendments prohibit discrimination in employment against applicants, employees, and union members on the basis of protected class characteristics. These protected classes include race, color, national origin, religion, and sex. Every aspect of the hiring process, including promotion, employee benefits, discipline, and discharge, is covered by Title VII (Civil Rights Act, 1964).

Title VII applies to organizations with 15 or more employees. However, the Supreme Court has ruled that smaller employers might be subject to lawsuits filed under Title VII under some circumstances (e.g., Arbaugh v. Y & H Corp., d/b/a The Moonlight Café). The Act also prohibits discrimination in most federal government places of employment, labor unions with 15 or more members, as well as discrimination against undocumented workers (Civil Rights Act, 1964).

13.4.1.1 Who Enforces Title VII's Provisions?

The Equal Employment Opportunity Commission (EEOC) is the federal agency that monitors compliance with Title VII. Employees that allege discrimination must file the claim with the EEOC before a lawsuit can be brought against the employer. The EEOC may investigate the dispute, initiate a lawsuit, consent to an out-of-court settlement, or may issue a right to sue letter to the employee. The right to sue letter allows an employee to bring his or her own lawsuit against the employer. The EEOC also oversees complaints involving violations of the Americans with Disabilities Act of 1990 (ADA) and The Age Discrimination in Employment Act of 1967 (ADEA) (Cross & Miller, 2014).

13.4.1.2 Title VII Issues in Selection

The selection process has historically been a primary source of legal violations involving discrimination (Williams et al., 2013). Social media discrimination in selection is a new application of the long-standing legal principles found under Title VII. In the case of Gaskell v. Univ. of Kentucky (2010), Gaskell was a leading candidate for a position as the founding director of a new observatory at the University of Kentucky. The university's search committee, however, found Gaskell's personal website in which he expressed his religious views in an article called "Modern Astronomy, the Bible, and Creation." The committee, which included physics professor, Sally Shafer, voiced concern, in writing, over the plaintiff's reconciling of the Bible with the theory of evolution.

"Clearly this man is complex and likely fascinating to talk with," Shafer wrote, "but potentially evangelical. If we hire him, we should expect similar content to be posted on or directly linked from the department Web site" (Oppenheimer, 2010).

As a result of this information, they chose another, less qualified candidate. Gaskell sued, claiming a violation of his Title VII protections against religious discrimination. Prior to trial, the University of Kentucky settled the case with Gaskell for $125,000 (National Center for Science Education, 2011).

Title VII prohibits discrimination on the basis of religion, and every other protected class characteristic, so interviewers generally avoid asking such types of questions during interviews. This case shows that discrimination, however, can and does result from online searches. It also shows that search committees need to be trained in what constitutes discrimination and to avoid using online searches in such a manner. Organizations could also advise against search committees looking online at all. As the Gaskell case shows, there is an inherent risk of employer liability for organizations when searching for candidate information online.

13.4.2 Americans with Disabilities Act

The Americans with Disabilities Act ("ADA") of 1990 prohibits employment discrimination on the basis of an individual's disability. It applies to all workplaces with 15 or more employees. The ADA requires employers to reasonably accommodate disabled applicants and employees unless it would create an undue hardship to the employer. The ADA's recent amendment broadens the class definitions of disability. To prevail under the ADA, a plaintiff must show that he or she (1) has a disability, (2) is otherwise qualified for the employment in question, and (3) was excluded from the employment because of a disability (ADA, 1990). Plaintiffs may seek the same remedies that are available under Title VII. These include compensatory and punitive damages, reinstatement to the employee's position within the organization, and back pay. Repeat violators may be fined up to $100,000 (ADA, 1990).

Disabilities may include health conditions and physical or mental impairments, and the law protects the confidentiality of such conditions. Under section 102 of the ADA, employers are required to treat information related to the disability as a confidential medical record (Wright, 2014). The ADA also prevents employers from taking adverse employment action based upon assumptions about individuals who associate with people who have disabilities. For example, an employer may not refuse to hire an applicant whose spouse has a disability based upon the assumption that the applicant will miss work (ADA, 1990; Cross & Miller, 2014).

The ADA, however, does not require that employers accommodate the needs of applicants or employees with disabilities who are otherwise not qualified for the work. Rather, if the individual with the disability can perform the essential functions of the job, with reasonable accommodation, the employer must make the accommodation. Only if making the accommodation would cause the employer undue hardship, meaning significant difficulty or expense on the part of the employer, will courts allow the employer to prevail (Cross & Miller, 2014).

In Shoun v. Best Formed Plastics (2016), George Shoun brought an action under the ADA against his employer alleging that an individual acting on behalf of his employer disclosed confidential information about his medical condition to other people via a Facebook post. The plaintiff, while employed by Best Formed Plastics, suffered a workplace injury to the shoulder. Shoun spent several months away from work recovering. Jane Stewart processed Shoun's workers compensation claim for the company. She posted the following statement on her Facebook page, "Isn't it amazing that Jimmy experienced a 5 way heart bypass just one month ago and is back to work, especially when you consider George Shoun's shoulder injury kept him away from work for 11 months and now he is trying to sue us." The post stayed on Facebook for 76 days and, according to Shoun, was viewable by the surrounding business community. The court refused to grant Best Formed Plastic's motion to dismiss the claim and instead held that Shoun set forth sufficient facts to allege a violation of the confidentiality provisions of the ADA. The jury awarded Shoun $412,680 in compensatory and punitive damages (Shoun v. Best Formed Plastics, 2016).

The Shoun case stands for some important principles. First, this case shows that there is potential employer liability for violating the confidentiality provisions of the ADA through social media posts. Second, this case is a good illustration of some bad practices (i.e., mocking an employee online) which employee training could beneficially address. Comparing the health issues of employees, as well as public shaming of an employee, can also lead to serious problems with future employee trust and morale within the organization (Goldman, 2014). It is best to train employees to refrain from publicly commenting about one another on social media, especially where the law already mandates strict confidentiality.

The ADA is another example of existing laws used in the new realm of social media cases. With regard to selection of candidates, the ADA's protection begins at the moment the applicant applies for the job in question. Thus, employers who are looking at social media profiles and pages to gain information about candidates must be aware that excluding candidates based upon information gleaned from social media about a physical or mental impairment or condition would be a violation of federal law.

13.4.3 The Age Discrimination in Employment Act

The Age Discrimination in Employment Act (ADEA) prohibits employment discrimination against individuals who are 40 years old and older. The Act also prohibits mandatory retirement for nonmanagerial workers. The ADEA protects federal and private-sector workers from age discrimination and claims of retaliation for complaining about age discrimination. For the Act to apply, an employer must have at least 20 employees and the employer's business activities must affect interstate commerce (ADEA, 1967).

To establish the case, the plaintiff must show that he or she was (1) a member of the protected age group, (2) qualified for the position from which he or she was discharged, and (3) was discharged because of age discrimination. If the employer can offer a legitimate reason for terminating the employee, which is not pretextual in nature, then the employer has a valid legal defense (ADEA, 1967).

Like the other federal protections discussed in this chapter, the ADEA also protects job applicants. In Nieman v. Grange Mutual Casualty Co. (2012) ("Grange"), the plaintiff, Jason Nieman, applied for a job with Grange affiliate Integrity Mutual Insurance Company ("Integrity"). Nieman claimed that he was passed over for the job based upon his age, in violation of the ADEA. He alleged that Integrity was aware of his age, which was over age 40, because the year he graduated from college (1989) was on Linkedin. The court concluded that there were sufficient facts established by the plaintiff to deny Integrity's motion to dismiss the case. This case ended in 2014, when a subsequent court held that Nieman's ADEA claim failed because the candidate that Integrity did hire was not significantly younger than Nieman (2013 U.S. Dist. LEXIS 47685).

Though the employer ultimately prevailed in Neiman v. Granger, this case illustrates how precarious ADEA claims can be for employers. Specifically, LinkedIn and other similar sites are tailored to professionals and job applicants, and many users list information which can reveal their actual ages. Employers must be aware that the ADEA will protect candidates and employees of age 40 and over who are passed over for hiring and promotion, or those who are ultimately terminated due to their ages. Having access to this information creates an extra layer of concern for employers, so effort should be made to make sure that personnel decisions are not based on, or appear to be based on, age for workers who are 40 years old and older.

13.4.4 Pregnancy Discrimination Act

The Pregnancy Discrimination Act of 1978 (PDA) amends Title VII to prohibit sex discrimination on the basis of pregnancy. It is an area of the law that is constantly developing, as pregnancy discrimination claims are on the rise and recent cases are being considered by high courts, such as the US Supreme Court. In 2014, sex and pregnancy discrimination lawsuits accounted for 55 % of all Title VII claims filed (McGowan, 2015).

The PDA prohibits discrimination on the basis of pregnancy, childbirth, or related medical conditions and applies to employers with 15 or more employees, including state and local governments. The Act states that women who are pregnant or affected by pregnancy-related conditions must be treated in the same manner as other applicants or employees with similar abilities or limitations.

In 2012, the EEOC issued a warning against pregnancy discrimination to employers who screen job applicants' social media profiles. This warning reminded employers that if an employer learns that a job applicant is in the early stages of pregnancy from that applicant's social media, then does not hire that applicant, the applicant could plausibly accuse the employer of discriminating based on her pregnancy (Phillips & Associates, 2012). By the same token, the EEOC reminded employees to be aware what information they are voluntarily posting on social media. Announcing pregnancies, posting ultrasound pictures, or posting pictures from pregnancy photo shoots are all common occurrences and are easily discoverable by employers.

So in the social media data screening process, HR professionals are likely to encounter information that may inform them that a candidate is pregnant or likely pregnant. This can be through posts made by the applicant, or by the applicant's social media connections. Organizations need to make sure that those who do the screening do not use pregnancy status as a negative factor or as a reason to remove a candidate from a search. If a candidate is de-selected due to pregnancy, violating the PDA may result in significant penalties for the organization.

13.4.5 Sexual Orientation Legal Protections

There is currently a limited amount of protection at the federal level for private employers for discrimination based upon sexual orientation, though governmental workers are protected from sexual orientation or gender identity discrimination under the Civil Service Reform Act of 1978. A July 15, 2015 ruling by the EEOC "recognize[d] that elements of the following issues are emerging and developing… coverage of lesbian, gay, bisexual, and transgender individuals under Title VII's sex discrimination provisions, as they may apply." The EEOC went on to reason that sexual orientation discrimination is linked to sex discrimination, which is protected under Title VII (National Law Review, 2015). At this time, it is unclear whether the courts will ultimately agree with the EEOC; however, a significant number of states already do provide sexual orientation protection for workers at the state and local level.

When using social media sites for information about candidates and employees, it is important for employers to know the laws of the states that they do business in. For multi-state corporations, it is entirely possible that workers may not be considered to have been discriminated against in one state, but the same set of facts will be considered discrimination in another. An example of a state where sexual orientation is a protected class is New York. New York bars discrimination based on sexual orientation in employment, housing, and public accommodations (The Sexual Orientation Non-Discrimination Act, 2003).

Some states go even further and also protect gender identity as a protected class. By including gender identity in their state statute, transgender individuals may not be discriminated against in employment, beginning at the time the potential employee applies for a position. This protection continues throughout employment (ACLU, 2015).

In Macy v. Holder (2010), the EEOC held that discrimination against a transgender employee is akin to sex discrimination. In this case, Mia Macy, a transgender woman, was employed as a police detective by the city of Phoenix. Her supervisor informed her that the federal Bureau of Alcohol, Tobacco, Firearms and Explosives ("ATF") was accepting applications for a ballistics expert in a crime laboratory near San Francisco, and that she had the right qualifications for the position. While in Phoenix, Macy was still presenting as a man, but Macy had plans to soon transition to a female identity.

In 2010, she relocated to San Francisco and applied for this job. Macy spoke with the Director of the ATF about the position, and she was given details about the position's salary and benefits. According to Macy, the Director told her that she would get the position so long as she passed her background check. Macy subsequently told the San Francisco office via e-mail that she was in the process of transitioning from male to female. Five days later, Macy received an e-mail from the office stating that the position in the ATF lab no longer existed due to federal budget reductions. However, Macy later learned that the position was actually not cut and was filled by someone else. In 2011, Macy filed a discrimination claim and won, establishing the legal precedent that discriminating against individuals who present non-conforming expressions of gender also violates Title VII (Grossman, 2012; Macy, 2010).

From the selection perspective, organizations need to make sure that the personal views of employees related to sexual orientation and gender identity do not result in social media data on sexual orientation or gender identity factors being used to disqualify candidates. This is legally crucial in states where existing legal protections for discrimination based on sexual orientation and gender identity exist. So organizations need to be up to date on such laws in all states where they employ workers.

13.5 Privacy Rights

Facebook, Google, Yahoo, etc. have all been accused of violating user's right to privacy (Cross & Miller, 2014). This is due to a common misperception that there is an inherent right to privacy for US citizens in all matters. In addition, many social media users believe that setting one's privacy settings on a social media site ensures that they have the site's assurances of privacy when they post. However, this is not the case.

Instead, courts have held that the legal standard in privacy cases is whether or not an individual has a "reasonable expectation" under the circumstances. In social media cases involving privacy arguments, courts have consistently held that users do not have a reasonable expectation of privacy because social media websites are publicly available. Moreover, social media users are voluntarily giving up their privacy by posting their personal information online (Carlson, 2014).

For example, in Nucci v. Target (2015), Target employee Maria Nucci suffered a slip and fall at work. After a lawsuit was filed against Target, Target requested Nucci's Facebook pictures. Target argued that the photographs were directly relevant to the lawsuit and would show Nucci's physical state prior to and following the accident. Nucci argued that she had a reasonable expectation of privacy in her Facebook photographs because she had her privacy settings set. Nucci even deleted three dozen pictures from her account following Target's request. The court ordered Nucci to produce and give all of her Facebook pictures to Target from a 2-year period surrounding her fall, including those that she had deleted. The court went on to emphatically hold that there can be no reasonable expectation of privacy in social media accounts.

So while workers may express concerns about their employer viewing their social media data and feel they should have privacy protections to what they post, to date there is little existing legal protection or case law that has been applied to such privacy concerns. In the next section, we will raise exceptions to this, which involves state laws that address employers that request applicant and employee social media username and password information.

13.5.1 Laws on Asking for Applicant Social Media Passwords

While general privacy protections on social media are nonexistent, a developing employer practice of requesting applicants' social media password as a condition of employment or as part of the hiring process has led to legislation being proposed and passed in many states banning the practice. As this practice gained ground, state legislatures began drafting laws to protect applicants, and in 2015, alone 23 states introduced legislation on this matter. These laws have mostly been argued as protection of privacy rights for applicants and current workers in organizations (National Conference of State Legislatures, 2015).

Approximately, 20 states currently have laws prohibiting employers from requiring applicants and employees to disclose their passwords (Drouin, O'Connor, Schmidt, & Miller, 2015; Pate, 2012). For example, Illinois' password protection law provides that "it shall be unlawful for any employer to ask any prospective employee to provide any username, password, or other related account information in order to gain access to a social networking website where that prospective employee maintains an account or profile." A handful of other states also extend this protection to prohibit academic institutions from requesting that a student or applicant log onto a personal social media account (National Conference of State Legislatures, 2015).

There are some elements that appear in the majority of these laws. The first element found almost universally is that it is illegal for employers to require applicants or current employees to disclose to the organization social media user names and passwords. Disclosing such information cannot be required. Another common element is that organizations cannot require applicants or current employees to add the organization, a supervisor, or an administrator as a social media contact (National Conference of State Legislatures, 2015). In such a case, this mandatory connection could be a way for the organization to access the applicant's social media content that is available to connections. Another element commonly found in such legislation is making it illegal to require applicants or current employees to change social media privacy settings. In this case, it could be removing all privacy settings, so the organization could see all content posted or even requiring workers to only have extremely strict privacy settings. A final common element is banning retaliation against applicants or employees who refuse to share password or user name information with an employer (National Conference of State Legislatures, 2015).

Some state laws will have unique elements, as well. For one example, the law passed in June 2015 in Oregon makes it illegal for the organization to require applicants and employees to create or maintain personal social media accounts or to require that the employer has the right to advertise on persons' personal social media account (National Conference of State Legislatures, 2015). Organizations located in multiple states will need to become familiar with the intricacies of laws in all states they have employees in.

There certainly are additional limitations. For example, employees in states where there is no existing legislative protection have no safeguard for social media data or other information that is openly available on the Internet (Pate, 2012). The existing password protection laws also typically do not protect an employee who is logging onto social media using an employer-provided device or sometimes even an employer-provided Internet service. Employer monitoring under these circumstances is mostly unregulated. Organizations need to know well what the laws cover (and do not cover) to be legally compliant. Such password laws also, of course, do not stop an employer from viewing social media content that can be found in google searches and content that was posted publicly.

Worth noting here is that from an organizational perspective, having applicant user names and passwords would most likely result in the organization acquiring the most accurate and encompassing social media data to use in the selection process. In such a case, the organization would have great confidence that they are looking at the right person's account(s) and be able to see all content that is relevant to inform the selection process. This assumes, of course, that some applicants don't have multiple accounts at the same site and the one whose password is shared isn't the one that is sanitized with regard to its content and/or is set up for impression management purposes. Such a possibility does exist, and in such cases, having applicant passwords may not be practically useful since the social media data gained is potentially inaccurate.

Having all applicants' social media user names and passwords would also avoid the difference in information found between applicants with different privacy settings. The employer could see all content from all applicants as opposed to just the content posted publicly. One might think this greater amount of information could help overall predictive quality of social media data. So here we see a law that puts applicant privacy rights above potential business interests. The question of the effectiveness of social media use in selection is dealt with in other places in this book, but such password laws do restrict how organizations can engage in obtaining social media data on candidates. Different governments may put the balance at different levels, as we will show in our next section on international differences in laws related to selection in social media.

13.6 International Differences in Laws Related to Selection Use in Social Media

While this chapter has focused so far on the US legal context with regard to social media use in employee selection, many such decisions will be made in other country and international legal contexts. For multinational organizations, the legal context business is done in is not one country, but many different countries with different and potentially conflicting legal standards. We will shortly examine three examples of laws in non-US countries that can impact social media screening from both legality and practicality standpoints.

In 2010, the German Parliament discussed a part of a general law about workplace privacy with a particular provision that would restrict the use of social media for selection screening. The bill would allow employers to search for publicly available data about a client and view applicant information on professional social networking sites like LinkedIn, but would specifically ban employers from using personal social media sites like Facebook. So the German law would have significantly limited what employers in Germany could look at (Jolly, 2010). While this bill did not pass the German Parliament, future bills that may pass could have huge impact on how social media screening can be done in particular country contexts. We will now look at three existing laws that could potentially impact social media selection.

13.6.1 European Union "Right to Be Forgotten"

Recent court rulings in the European Union have potentially serious impact on the type of information that organizations might find while using social media data for selection. A court ruling in May 2014 from the European Union's highest court held that EU citizens have the "right to be forgotten" online for their past behaviors that have been already resolved or are currently out of date (Strietfeld, 2014). The ruling held that citizens of the European Union have the right (in particular circumstances) to ask Internet search engines to remove links with personal information about them when that information is "inaccurate, inadequate, irrelevant, or excessive" (European Commission, 2014, p. 2). They note that the right to be forgotten is not absolute and would need to be balanced with other personal rights and thus decisions need to be made on a case-by-case basis for requests. Important to note here is that the information is not itself removed from the Internet, rather it no longer shows up in search results from search engines like Google.

Citizens of the European Union file a petition to have such content removed from search engine results from a search engine provider. Currently, the search engine providers themselves are making such determinations on a case-by-case basis, although the European Union privacy regulators can be involved in such decisions as deemed warranted (European Commission, 2014). Google reports that so far there have been requests for more than 733,000 URLs to be removed, and Google has agreed to the removal of approximately 238,000 URLs of the requested URLs from search results (Lomas, 2015a). Data analysis by Reputation VIP, a reputation management company that offers a service to help European citizens make such requests, found that requests made through their service were rejected by Google approximately 70 % of the time (Lomas, 2015b). So, currently it would seem the majority of requests are being refused.

Reputation VIP recently released a report on what types of content links have been removed from the 61,500 requests they have administered through their application. The most common categories of reasons for requests was "invasion of privacy" (58.7 %), which involves sites sharing things like personal addresses, religious affiliations, or political party membership (Lomas, 2015b). From the selection perspective, some of this information would be irrelevant and other information could lead to finding out individual characteristics that might run afoul of equal employment opportunities laws in the United States and elsewhere. The second most common category of reasons was "damage to reputation," (11.2 %) which depending on why it is damaging might be useful for organizations in screening out processes (Lomas, 2015b). For example, an applicant being delinquent in payments for previous business dealings might be information an organization would want if it was hiring someone to be responsible for a financial position.

The report also has categories of what types of sites the material was present on when the request was accepted. The largest specific category was social media sites/communities (20 %) with 6552 URL links removed from search engines (Lomas, 2015b). For organizations using search engines to find candidate information on social media, these removals might be material that would have led to the candidate being screened out.

One point of contention so far between Google and the European Union privacy regulators has been whether web content search links should be deleted from only European Union country-specific Google search engines sites or from the general search engine site Google.com. The European Union regulators are currently arguing that removal needs to be for the general Google.com domain as well, otherwise people in the European Union can circumvent the ruling by going to the general Google.com domain for search (Lomas, 2015a). Google has refused to do so. Removal from general Google.com search could have significant implications for employers and individuals worldwide who are being able to access such information. So for now, on a practical level, organizations using search engines to find social media material can use the general domains over country-specific domains but the European Union's stance is that this is a loophole that should be closed.

The "right to be forgotten" has clear implications for social media use in the screening of candidates. If past indiscretions are removed from search results, they likely will not appear in the screening processes done by organizations. For now, loopholes exist through using other country-specific sites or international sites and the majority of removal requests are being rejected by Google. This could certainly change, however, and the intent of the European Union regulators seems so far to be that these "loopholes" need to be closed. As currently applied, there has not been any discussion of whether organizations should be able to use such removed material if they use a loophole. Making use illegal regardless of how it is discovered could certainly be a future way the "right to be forgotten" would be applied.

While this European Union ruling has not been applied to international social media cases, it could certainly have future implications as well as potentially act as a model for laws passed in other countries or even in states in the United States. The ruling is likely to have more far-reaching consequence as time passes and more content is created and requested to be removed.

13.6.2 China Internet Censorship Laws

In the case of China, the biggest challenge to using social media data in the selection process is the significant legal restrictions related to Internet use and what sites can be visited. Starting in July 2009, Facebook and Twitter have been permanently blocked within China's borders and use by Chinese nationals elsewhere is also illegal (The Economist, 2013). The overall program of censorship and Internet restrictions has been called by some "The Great Firewall," although China has a complex web of laws and tools that involve both public and private sector operations (The Economist, 2013).

In 2010, a white paper from the Chinese government offered an idea of "Internet sovereignty" that all Internet users in China, both citizens and foreigners, were required to abide by Chinese laws and regulations. Chinese Internet companies have also been required to sign a pledge of self-regulation and professional ethics that built off the ideas of the white paper (Xu, 2015).

Much of the enforcement and censorship is done through what is called the "Golden Shield Project." Through the Golden Shield project, the Chinese government takes actions like restricting bandwidth, filtering search results by keywords that are seen as not in the best interest of China, and blocking access to certain websites such as the previously mentioned Facebook and Twitter (Xu, 2015). Site access can also be blocked for short-term periods such as during politically sensitive events and anniversaries. Chinese Internet users can attempt to use various circumvention applications and other means (ex. virtual private networks) to view blocked websites, although the Chinese censorship enforcers are consistently working to shut down any such workarounds (The Economist, 2013).

A more recent believed addition to China's censorship program has been dubbed "The Great Cannon." The Great Cannon acts as a middle man for web traffic such that, when a user in China tries to go to or search for a website, the program hijacks traffic to that individual website IP address and replaces normal benign web content with malicious malware content (Weaver, 2015). The malware installed then is used to make that user's computer an unwilling participant of denial of service attacks against a website. The websites attacked to date have both been websites with pages related to getting around the Chinese governments censorship applications, the New York Times' Chinese mirror site, and the anti-censorship organization

GreatFire.org. The Chinese government has not publicly acknowledged the existence of the Great Cannon or their use of it, although the analysis of Marzak et al. (2015) shows strong support for such a connection, including evidence of its co-location with the Great Shield Project servers.

Marzak et al. (2015) looked at the nature of the Great Cannon soon after its first identified action in March 2015. Their technical report goes into great detail on the technical aspects of this firewall application and evidence that it originates from the Chinese government. One of the most serious aspects of their report is describing how the Great Cannon could be deployed in powerful ways with small technical and software changes. Instead of targeting Internet users going to particular websites, the program could be used to target particular Internet users. In such a case, the Great Canon could target particular users who access even one unencrypted site that uses a server in China for the website or the ads on that site and deliver malicious malware to that person's computer. A user very well might not realize they are accessing a site using a server in China (Marczak et al., 2015). For a person within China, it would be very difficult to get on the Internet without interacting in some way with an unencrypted website or web content that would be vulnerable to the Great Cannon.

Another potential application noted by Marzak et al. (2015) is the widespread interception of all unencrypted emails within and to those in China or using China-based servers and the potential addition of malicious attachments to such emails. Email could be manipulated using the Great Cannon to spread malware to support future Denial of Service attacks or other actions. While there is no evidence of such use currently, Marzak et al. (2015) suggest that the existing architecture of the Great Cannon could support such uses with relatively small technological modifications.

China's extensive censorship system has major implications for organizations using social media in selection. One of the most basic logistic issues is that Chinese citizens who are applicants are unlikely to have common social media presences with Facebook and Twitter blocked and LinkedIn available but open to government censorship (Newman, 2014). This means that organizations will need to look at Chinese social media sites instead for information, potentially hurting comparability to candidates in others parts of the world. With the extensive censorship laws and enforcement, Chinese citizen workers are less likely to openly share information through social media sites, which means social media data may not exist for the type of behaviors organizations are using for screening out procedures.

The use of social media in the selection processes is even more complicated if the evaluator is located in China, which could certainly happen with multinational organizations. The Internet restrictions apply to all people in China regardless of citizenship (The Economist, 2013). This means that, from a practical perspective, accessing applicant's social media profiles on major sites like Facebook or Twitter while the evaluator is located in China would be extremely difficult. Even with workaround methods, the examination of social media content on such banned sites would be illegal and could result in legal consequences for the employee who uses them and the company that has asked him or her to do so. Thus, in the China context, social media use in selection processes might not be practical due to the existing censor-related laws and enforcement.

The Great Cannon offers a different challenge to organizations operating in China or interacting with individuals in China. The security of organizational data could be compromised by The Great Cannon. Searches for relevant candidate information could lead to malware being downloaded on organization's computers and networks, spreading beyond computers in China to other countries and users. In theory, this could lead to confidential information being spread in a way similar to what was seen in the Sony Pictures hack (Elkind, 2015). Confidential information release could also lead to lawsuits and lost customers. To deal with such potential threats, organizations need to consider implementing measures that make basic online practices and email systems encrypted and improve the overall security of their online systems. Unfortunately, there are currently no easy solutions to implement to resolve all the issues inherent in programs such as the Great Cannon.

13.6.3 United Arab Emirates Defamation Laws

The severity of United Arab Emirates defamation laws and how they are applied to social media content was highlighted internationally in the legal case of Ryan Pate, an American working for an UAE company who posted on Facebook criticism about his company. While the Facebook post was made, Pate was in the United States; upon returning to the UAE, Pate was arrested and faced a criminal charge of defamation against his employer punishable by up to 5 years in jail and a fifty thousand dollar fine (Altman, 2015). He ultimately was able to get the charges dropped due to intervention by his United States Congressman and the US State Department (Ingles, 2015). Most workers, and certainly those who are citizens of the UAE, are unlikely to be that lucky.

This criminal charge was due to existing severe defamation rules within the United Arab Emirates. Defamation that causes harm to the person the statement is about in any oral or written form is a criminal offense. This is quite broadly defined and just the presence of criticism may be enough to violate these laws (Kelly & Proctor, 2012). If the person's statements are given on behalf of or seen to represent the organization, the person's manager could be similarly charged. Company computers or devices can also be accessed in the investigation of such charges (Kelly & Proctor, 2012).

These strict and broad defamation laws offer both practical and legal consequences for organizations using social media in the selection processes. From a practical standpoint, more strict standards for screening out candidates may be warranted. An applicant who defames a previous employer, complains about an experience as a customer, or even makes a political statement may be in danger of defamation charges and the accompanying imprisonment. Such defamation behavior by an employee could lead to authorities accessing company devices and the person's manager potentially being arrested as well. Organizations may want to take extra efforts to avoid such situations and rigorous social media screening could help this goal. Of course, making generally more strict standards of social media screening may be more likely to lead to lawsuits or perceived unfairness by candidates in other countries without such defamation laws.

13.6.4 Overall Practical Legal Guidelines for Social Media Selection Internationally

When considering social media selection internationally, deep understanding of current national and international laws and how they are applied is essential. We highlighted three examples above, but there are many other examples that could at least potentially impact the social media selection process. Organizations need to review existing social media-related case law and existing selection-related case law for all nations they have workers in.

It must be noted that it is possible, and perhaps even likely, that laws of one nation will conflict with those of others with regard to how social media use in selection could proceed. Different countries can make different decisions on how privacy, national interests, and business interests should be balanced. As such, universal procedures and implementation for using social media data in selection internationally may not be practical or legally possible. Such a state of affairs may mean organizations need general guidelines for social media data use that can be modified by each particular country's legal context.

13.7 Overall Practical Legal Guidelines for Social Media Data Use in Selection

For organizations, it is important to consider how they can reduce legal risks related to using social media data in selection. Based on existing laws, there are some general actions organizations can take in engaging in social media date use for selection that should help reduce legal risks. One of the most importance aspects is to create clear procedures, standards, and criteria for how social media data will be considered. As noted in Williams et al. (2013), inconsistent hiring processes accounted for 22 % of legal cases and problematic criteria for 17 % of legal cases in their sample. Clear procedures for use are crucial for those in HR doing the searches to engage in them in a consistent manner. If they are inconsistent, there is potential for the use to not only be ineffective but also to allow the biases of the employee doing the search to effect decisions, leaving the organization open to lawsuits related to bias or favoritism.

Organizations need to clearly define what criteria they are using and why they are being used. This is especially true as social media and online-related matters are generally new territory for the United State legal system. As such, judges and juries may not have significant experience with this selection method and could see it as potentially suspect. The tool of social media data itself may be seen by some (i.e., judges or applicants) as unfair in the selection context. As such, organizations need to clearly define what criteria they have in examining social media, and in the best case scenario, have validation study data on its effectiveness in predicting workplace outcomes. To date, validation data on the effectiveness of social media use for selection in the academic realm has been mixed (Kleumper et al., 2012; Stoughton, Thompson, & Meade, 2013; Van Iddekinge, Lanivich, Roth, & Junco, 2013). We recommend that organizations perform validation studies for their own use of social media data in screening processes and the employee outcomes the social media data predicts.

With potential concerns that examining applicant's social media data will reveal protected class information that could lead to charges of discrimination against organizations, organizations may consider measures to limit such risks. One such way to do this would be to decouple who collects social media screening information from who makes employment decisions. In this case, one person would be in charge of collecting social media data and then handing over only relevant information to the person making the selection decision, removing all protected class information found in social media content.

LinkedIn allows user profiles to be downloaded in pdf form in a stripped-down version that does not include pictures or post history. Having one HR worker download the profiles to pdf and provide them to the person making employment decisions would remove potential protected class information that could be discovered through the profile picture and an examination of individual LinkedIn posts. This may not help for age-related discrimination claims, however, as information is provided about college years and years in the workplace. While no actual birth date is provided, an approximate one could be estimated using employment and education dates. This ability to estimate the age of candidate was part of the Shoun v. Best Formed Plastics (2016) case mentioned earlier in this chapter. LinkedIn profile pdf download would not have alleviated the issue alleged in that case. Thus, downloading pdfs of LinkedIn profiles would alleviate some, not all concerns. Also important is that other sites that might be looked at, such as Facebook or Twitter, lack this feature and thus would need more manual (or application based) scrubbing of protected class information. Organizations might consider creating in-depth and clear procedures of how social media data from sites examined would have protected class information removed before the relevant social media data is passed onto evaluators.

Companies may also consider having a third party vendor do the social media data collection process. One example of a company doing this is Inquirehire (http://inquirehire.com/services/social-media-screening). As noted by Morgan and Davis (2013), however, third party vendors doing such screening might be considered "consumer reporting agencies" under the Fair Credit Reporting Act and be subject to restrictions based on that law and other consumer protection laws. Regardless of choices made here, procedures used should be well-specified and followed consistently to avoid lawsuits and negative legal judgments.

13.8 Future Considerations

There are still a number of important issues related to the legality of social media data use in selection processes that will need to be examined in the future. One particularly important issue is that laws and court rulings related to social media use can change over time. Higher court rulings, such as those of the US Supreme Court, could have huge impact on the legality of elements of social media data use in selection. Federal laws would also have major impact and state laws have the potential to contradict each other as states balance businesses interests and individual privacy interests differently from state to state. Human Resource professionals need to keep abreast of new laws and rulings as they happen. Organizations may want to have staff or retain legal counsel to keep up to date on how new rulings may potentially impact the legality of current social media selection processes.

The international legal environment for social media data in selection is an area ripe for future examination. This chapter focused on the US legal context and gave three examples of other national laws that may impact social media data use in selection, but a systematic review across nations would be beneficial. Such legal analysis could help organizations to determine how to structure social media data using selection systems that could pass legal standards across all countries an organization has existing employees.

In-depth examinations of laws relevant to social media selection methods at the country level would be extremely helpful as well. One example is the recent book of Scaife (2014) on Internet-related law in the United Kingdom, which doesn't examine social media data use in selection directly, but does offer a comprehensive review of the existing UK laws relevant to social media. Examinations of law relevant to selection could be done at the country or region level. This would be especially crucial if organizations followed a strategy of having unique social media selection processes in each country, with such processes tailored to each country's unique set of laws. Such a system could lead to the highest levels of successful compliance with individual country laws, with the potential downside being a lack of consistency in selection procedures across countries. Such tradeoffs might be needed in the current legal environment where there is significant legal variance between countries.

13.9 Conclusion

This chapter begins the examination of existing case law in the United States related to social media data use in the applicant selection process. To date, only a handful of cases have directly dealt with this area, but there is a significant body of law and rulings that can have significant impact on social media data use in selection. This chapter also discussed examples of laws in countries outside the United States that could have significant impact on how social media data use in selection proceeds both practically and legally within those country contexts. Social media data use for selection is prevalent in organizational practice (Jobvite, 2013) and we would expect such major use will lead to more legal cases in the future. This chapter begins to build understanding of existing law so that organizations can be prepared for the current legal environment and have some forewarning of other areas that might ultimately be relevant.

References

ACLU. (2015). *Non-discrimination laws: State by state information—Map*. Retrieved June 10, 2015, from https://www.aclu.org/map/non-discrimination-laws-state-state-information-map

Altman, H. (2015). *March 2 Facebook posts from U.S. land Pinellas contractor in Arab jail*. Retrieved June 6, 2015, from http://tbo.com/list/military-news/anti-arab-facebook-remarks-land-pinellas-contractor-in-uae-jail-20150302/?page=1

Americans with Disabilities Act of 1990. (1991). Pub. L. No. 101–336, §2, 104 Stat. 328.

Arbaugh v. Y & H Corp., dba The Moonlight Café. (2006). 546 U.S. 500.

Brown, V. R., & Vaughn, E. D. (2011). The writing on the (Facebook) wall: The use of social networking sites in hiring decisions. *Journal of Business and Psychology, 26*, 219–225.

Carlson, K. (2014, January). Social media and the workplace: How I learned to stop worrying and love privacy settings and the NLRB. *66(1) Fla. L. Rev*. 479–509.

Civil Rights Act of 1964. (1964). § 7, 42 U.S.C. § 2000e et seq.

Cross, F., & Miller, R. (2014). *The legal environment of business: Text and cases*. Mason, OH: South-Western Cengage Learning.

Davison, H. K., Maraist, C., Hamilton, R. H., & Bing, M. N. (2012). To screen or not to screen? Using the Internet for selection decisions. *Employee Rights and Responsibilities Journal, 24*, 1–21.

Davison, H. K., Maraist, C., & Bing, M. N. (2011). Friend or foe? The promise and pitfalls of using social networking sites for HR decisions. *Journal of Business & Psychology, 26*, 153–159.

Desnlow, D. (2015, February 16). *The new four walls of the workplace*. Retrieved September 8, 2015, from http://jolt.richmond.edu/index.php/blog-the-new-four-walls-of-the-workplace

Drouin, M., O'Connor, K. W., Schmidt, G. B., & Miller, D. A. (2015). Facebook fired: Legal per spectives and young adults' opinions on the use of social media in employment decisions. *Computers in Human Behavior, 46*, 123–128.

Elkind, P. (2015, July 1). Inside the hack of the century. *Fortune*. Retrieved September 13, 2015, from http://fortune.com/sony-hack-part-1/

European Commission. (2014). *Factsheet on the "Right to be Forgotten" ruling C-131/12*. Retrieved June 7, 2015, from http://ec.europa.eu/justice/data-protection/files/factsheets/factsheet_data_protection_en.pdf

Gaskell v. Univ. of Kentucky. (2010). Civil Action No. 09-244-KSF. (E.D. KY Jan. 12, 2010).

Goldman, E. (2014, June 27). Bad idea: Shaming an employee on Facebook for health issues—Shoun v. best formed plastics. *Technology and Marketing Law Blog*. Retrieved June 10, 2015, from http://blog.ericgoldman.org/archives/2014/06/bad-idea-shaming-an-employee-on-facebook-for-health-issues-shoun-v-best-formed-plastics.htm

Grossman, J. (2012, May 1). The EEOC rules that transgender discrimination is sex discrimination: The reasoning behind that decision. *Justia.com*. Retrieved June 11, 2015, from https://verdict.justia.com/2012/05/01/the-eeoc-rules-that-transgender-discrimination-is-sex-discrimination

Howard v. Hertz. (2014). 3-00645 (D. Hawaii Oct. 23, 2014).

Ingles, J. (2015, March 24). Ryan Pate, who was accused of cyber slander by Abu Dhabi authorities, is back home in Tampa Bay. *WFTS Tampa Bay*. Retrieved June 6, 2015, from http://www.abcactionnews.com/news/region-tampa/ryan-pate-who-was-accused-of-cyber-slander-by-abu-dhabi-authorities-is-back-home-in-tampa

Jobvite. (2013). *Social recruiting survey results*. Retrieved June 1, 2015, from http://web.jobvite.com/Q313_SocialRecruitingSurvey_LandingPage.htm

Jolly, D. (2010, August 25). Germany plans limits on Facebook use in hiring. *The New York Times*. Retrieved June 4, 2015, from http://www.nytimes.com/2010/08/26/business/global/26fbook.html?_r=0

Kelly, R., & Proctor, S. (2012, September 25). Defamation and social media in the UAE. *Clyde & Co*. Retrieved June 7, 2015, from http://www.clydeco.com/insight/updates/view/defamation-and-social-media-in-the-uae

Kleumper, D. H., Rosen, P. A., & Mossholder, K. W. (2012). Social networking websites, personality ratings, and the organizational context: More than meets the eye? *Journal of Applied Social Psychology, 42*, 1143–1172.

Lomas, N. (2015a, January 20). Google-led report on Europe's right to be forgotten coming this month. *TechCrunch*. Retrieved June 1, 2015, from http://techcrunch.com/2015/01/20/rtbf-advisory-council-report-due-soon/

Lomas, N. (2015b, May 13). Europe's search de-listing ruling is mostly about social media privacy invasions. *TechCrunch*. Retrieved June 6, 2015, from http://techcrunch.com/2015/05/13/europes-search-delisting-ruling-is-mostly-about-social-media-privacy-invasions/?ncid=rss

Macy v. Holder, WL 1435995 (E.E.O.C. Apr. 20, 2012).

Marczak, B., Weaver, N., Dalek, J., Ensafi, R., Fifield, D., McKune, S., et al. (2015, April 10). *China's Great Cannon*. Retrieved September 13, 2015, from https://citizenlab.org/2015/04/chinas-great-cannon/

McGowan, K. (2015, January 20). EEOC focus on systemic bias likely to persist, firm says. *Answer Source*. Retrieved June 8, 2015, from http://www.firstdoor.com/AnswerSource/%283z3yqoazxpiwqwv1i3qh352u%29/Site/Content/ContentDefault.aspx?DocId=399927

Morgan, H. A., & Davis, F. A. (2013, March). Social media and employment law summary of key cases and legal issues. *Paul Hastings*. Retrieved June 7, 2015, from www.americanbar.org/content/dam/aba/events/labor_law/2013/04/aba_national_symposiumontechnologyinlaboremploymentlaw/10_socialmedia.authcheckdam.pdf

National Center for Science Education. (2011, January 11). *Settlement in the Gaskell case*. Retrieved June 10, 2015, from http://ncse.com/news/2011/01/settlement-gaskell-case-006427

National Conference of State Legislatures. (2015, June 4). *Employer access to user names and passwords*. Retrieved June 11, 2015, from http://www.ncsl.org/research/telecommunications-and-information-technology/employer-access-to-social-media-passwords-2013.aspx

National Law Review. (2015, August 10). *EEOC declares that Title VII covers discrimination based on an individual's sexual orientation*. Retrieved September 8, 2015, from www.natlawreview.com/article/eeoc-declares-title-vii-covers-discrimination-based-individual-s-sexual-orientation

Newman, L. H. (2014, February 25). Surprising no one, LinkedIn for China will be subject to government censorship. *Slate*. Retrieved June 7, 2015, from http://www.slate.com/blogs/future_tense/2014/02/25/linkedin_for_china_will_be_censored_a_chinese_language_site_in_simplified.html

Nieman v. Grange Mutual Casualty Co. 2012, 2013 U.S. Dist. LEXIS 47685.

Nucci v. Target, No. 4D14-138 (4th Dist. Fla. 2015).

Oppenheimer, M. (2010, December 18). Astronomer sues the University of Kentucky, claiming his faith cost him a job. *The NY Times*. Retrieved September 13, 2015, from http://www.nytimes.com/2010/12/19/us/19kentucky.html?_r=0

Pate, R. (2012). *Invisible discrimination: Employers & social media sites*. WCOB working papers. Paper 12. Retrieved June 11, 2015, from http://digitalcommons.sacredheart.edu/wcob_wp/12

Phillips & Associates. (2012, October 19). EEOC issues pregnancy discrimination warning to employers who screen job applicants' social media profiles. *New York Employment Attorney Blog*. Retrieved June 10, 2015, from http://www.newyorkemploymentattorney-blog.com/2012/10/eeoc-issues-pregnancy-discrimination-warning-to-employers-who-screen-job-applicants-social-media-pro.html

Reppler. (2011). Managing your online image across social networks. *REPPLER EFFECT*. Retrieved June 10, 2015, from http://blog.reppler.com/2011/09/27/managing-your-online-image-across-social-network

Scaife, L. (2014). *Handbook of social media and the law*. Abingdon, England: Taylor & Francis.

Shoun v. Best Formed Plastics. (2016) Ind. App. LEXIS 41 (Ind. Ct. App. 2016)

Stoughton, J. W., Thompson, L. F., & Meade, A. W. (2013). Big Five personality traits reflected in job applicants' social media postings. *Cyberpsychology, Behavior, and Social Networking, 16*(11), 800–805.

Strietfeld, D. (2014, May 13). European court lets users erase records on web. *The New York Times*. Retrieved June 4, 2015, from http://www.nytimes.com/2014/05/14/technology/google-should-erase-web-links-to-some-personal-data-europes-highest-court-says.html

The Age Discrimination in Employment Act of 1967. *U.S. Equal Employment Opportunity Commission (EEOC)*. N.p., n.d. Web. [11 June 2015].

The Economist. (2013, April 6). The art of concealment. *The Economist*. Retrieved June 8, 2015, from http://www.economist.com/news/special-report/21574631-chinese-screening-online-material-abroad-becoming-ever-more-sophisticated

The Pregnancy Discrimination Act of 1978 (PDA).

The Sexual Orientation Non-discrimination Act. (2003). Retrieved June 10, 2015, from http://www.ag.ny.gov/civil-rights/sonda-brochure

Van Iddekinge, C. H., Lanivich, S. H., Roth, P. L., & Junco, E. (2013, Dec 16). Social media for selection? Validity and adverse impact potential of a Facebook-based assessment. *Journal of Management*, 1–25. doi:10.1177/0149206313515524

Weaver, N. (2015, June 5). How China's 'Great Cannon' works—And why we should be worried. *CNN*. Retrieved from http://www.cnn.com/2015/06/04/opinions/china-great-cannon/

Williams, K. Z., Schaffer, M. M., & Ellis, L. E. (2013). Legal risk in selection: An analysis of processes and tools. *Journal of Business & Psychology, 28*, 401–410.

Wright, P. (2014, June 30). *Federal court finds employer may be liable under the ADA for employee's snarky Facebook comments about another employee's medical condition*. Retrieved June 1,2015,fromhttp://www.employerlawreport.com/2014/06/articles/uncategorized/federal-court-finds-employer-may-be-liable-under-the-ada-for-employees-snarky-facebook-comments-about-another-employees-medical-condition/

Xu, B. (2015, April 7). Media censorship in China *CFR. Backgrounders*. Retrieved June 5, 2015, from http://www.cfr.org/china/media-censorship-china/p11515

Chapter 14
Online Exclusion: Biases That May Arise When Using Social Media in Talent Acquisition

Enrica N. Ruggs, Sarah Singletary Walker, Anita Blanchard, and Shahar Gur

Abstract Some organizations have begun to use social media during the talent acquisition process as a way to attract, recruit, and screen job applicants. Although this method may provide ease and allow decision-makers to gain additional information about candidates, it may also lead to negative biases, particularly against minority applicants. In this chapter we discuss why minorities may be at an increased risk for exclusion when social media is used in attraction and recruitment as well as why they may experience greater amounts of negative bias when social media are used in screening in selection processes. We offer recommendations regarding avoiding potential biases for organizations using or considering the use of social media in talent acquisition. Additionally, we discuss avenues for future research related to the manifestation of bias when using social media tools to attract, recruit, and select employees.

Keywords Talent acquisition • Bias • Exclusion • Discrimination • Social media

E.N. Ruggs, Ph.D. (✉) • A. Blanchard, Ph.D.
Department of Psychology, University of North Carolina at Charlotte,
9201 University City Blvd., Charlotte, NC 28223, USA
e-mail: eruggs@uncc.edu; ablanch@uncc.edu

S.S. Walker, Ph.D.
Department of Management and Marketing, University of Houston Downtown,
One Main Street, Houston, TX 77002, USA
e-mail: walkersa@uhd.edu

S. Gur
Organizational Science, University of North Carolina at Charlotte,
9201 University City Blvd., Charlotte, NC 28223, USA
e-mail: sgur@uncc.edu

R.N. Landers, G.B. Schmidt (eds.), *Social Media in Employee Selection and Recruitment*, DOI 10.1007/978-3-319-29989-1_14

14.1 Introduction

As social networking sites (SNS) such as LinkedIn, Twitter, Facebook continue to become more central to our society, many individuals and organizations have begun to use it as a tool in various aspects of the employment cycle. Over the course of the last 5–10 years, there has been a steady increase in the number of organizations that use SNS, a type of social media, in some capacity for the purposes of talent acquisition. Talent acquisition includes attracting, recruiting, screening, and selecting individuals for positions within an organization.

A series of surveys conducted by the Society for Human Resource Management (SHRM) show that the percent of organizations reporting the use of SNS to recruit potential job applicants increased over 40 % between 2008 and 2013 (SHRM, 2013). Specifically, a review of SHRM studies during this period showed a steady linear trend across time such that only 34 % of organizations surveyed in 2008 reported using SNS in recruitment. This rate increased to 56 % in 2011 and 77 % in 2013 (SHRM, 2013). A more recent SHRM study found that 65 % of organizations survey in 2015 reported using SNS during recruitment over the past year (SHRM, 2015). In addition, there has been an increase in the percent of organizations reporting the use of SNS to screen job applicants, with 20 % reporting using some SNS during the screening phase in 2013 compared to just 13 % in 2008 (SHRM, 2013). Although the percentage of organizations in the SHRM survey that reported using social media for screening is relatively lower than those using it for recruitment, there is still evidence of the use of such media during the phase that directly precedes decision-making (i.e., selection). Furthermore, the percentage of organizations that uses social media for screening may be higher depending on the industry, as one study found that as many as 50 % of recruiters in the hospitality industry reported using SNS to screen job applicants (Chang & Madera, 2012).

For organizations, social media may help to streamline the talent acquisition process as a human resource (HR) personnel can use the organization's social media to attract and recruit individuals. They also can examine an applicant's SNS profile to gather information about potential applicants, which can be used to make preliminary assessments about individuals based on the available information. For individuals, SNS can aid in networking, marketing of skills, acquiring information about an organization's culture and climate, and as a resource for seeking new positions. Job seekers can examine the organization's reputation and culture through their SNS posts (Ployhart, 2012), which allows recruits the ability to assess how well they would match the organization's culture. Social media has streamlined the employment search process for job seekers (Jobvite, 2014), as they can quickly gain information about and market themselves to several organizations in one place. Because organizations advertise on SNS that potential employees are already using, recruits do not have to go to online job boards (e.g., Career Builder, Monster.com) to look for jobs (although active job seekers may still prefer this method over using SNS; Acikgoz & Bergman, 2015). In this way, organizations can more easily reach passive potential applicants who are engaged on SNS in which the organization advertises.

Despite the benefits, the use of social media in the talent acquisition process may have paradoxical effects on some individuals, particularly minorities or individuals from traditionally marginalized groups (e.g., racial minorities, women, older workers, low-income; Brown & Vaughn, 2011; Ruggs, Speights, & Walker, 2013). In this chapter, we discuss why minority job applicants may experience being at a greater disadvantage than non-minorities when using social media in the talent acquisition. We begin by discussing how potential differences in SNS presence may occur and how this in turn influences talent acquisition, then move to discuss how negative bias also plays a role in disadvantaging minority applicants.

We draw on Stigma Theory (Goffman, 1963), Attraction–Selection–Attrition (Schneider, 1987), and Social Information Processing Theory (Walther, 1995) to explain why minority job applicants may experience heightened negative bias in talent acquisition processes that use SNS. We define negative bias as factors that can have a negative influence on job applicants regardless of the intent behind those factors. Thus, negative bias includes forms of exclusion, which may be unintentional, expressions of prejudicial attitudes, and displays of discrimination, or behaviors that are engaged in by members within an organization that differentially disadvantage minority job applicants and lead to negative outcomes. Discrimination can manifest in overt explicit behaviors or more subtle behaviors that may or may not be intentional (for a review see Hebl, Foster, Mannix, & Dovidio, 2002). In this chapter we use the term negative bias to refer to any of these factors that may lead to differential treatment or outcomes between minority and non-minority job applicants. We propose a conceptual model (see Fig. 14.1) that explains how factors related to potential applicants and factors related to the organization may negatively impact minorities when social media is used in talent acquisition.

Our chapter makes several important contributions to research and practice. First, we illustrate how differences in actual SNS participation and perceptions of one's participation can influence job applicants in the early stages of talent acquisition and potentially exclude minority applicants from even having the opportunity to apply for positions. Second, although the patterns of negative bias toward

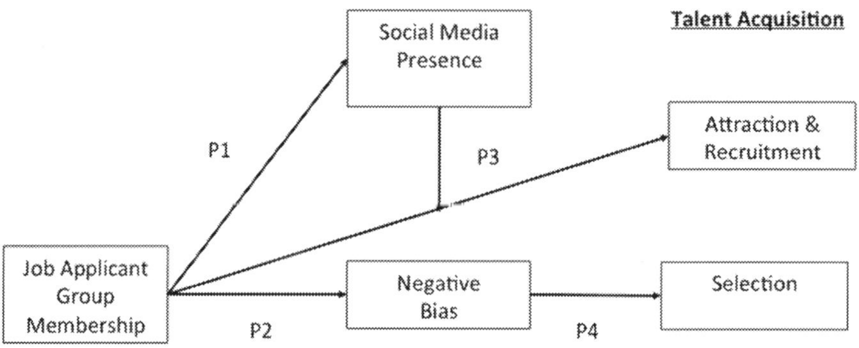

Fig. 14.1 The effect of job applicant group membership on talent acquisition processes that use social media

individuals from minority groups has been well-documented in offline employment situations, our chapter highlights mechanisms for why such biases may be heightened when using social media in the talent acquisition process. We specifically explore factors that may contribute to a disproportional amount of negative bias against individuals based on their group membership within traditionally marginalized groups. Third, we discuss individual and organizational consequences that may be associated with using social media in talent acquisition. That is, we explore how unintended bias against minority applicants has implications beyond those directly related to the applicant. Fourth, we have developed a model that we believe can serve as a basis for empirical research examining the impacts of social media in talent acquisition for minority applicants, and the information gleaned can be used as a guide for developing and implementing organizational policies in this area.

We begin this chapter by providing an overview of why minorities may be negatively affected when social media is introduced into talent acquisition, and then we move forward in discussing how applicants and organizations are affected at various stages of the talent acquisition process. Finally, we offer recommendations for future research and practice concerning bias implications of the use of social media in talent acquisition.

14.1.1 Effects of Social Media in Talent Acquisition on Minority Individuals

Individuals belonging to traditionally marginalized groups may be at a disadvantage in the talent acquisition process when social media is used for several reasons. In particular, these media may introduce additional negative biases into the talent acquisition process. These biases can arise due to the ways in which SNS are used by job seekers and organizations and may be influenced by a variety of factors such as job seeker demographics and the composition of an organization.

One factor that can negatively bias minority job applicants is differences in SNS presence based on group membership. We define SNS presence as not only having an account but also establishing an image that attracts and retains positive (or negative) attention. The percentage of individuals belonging to traditionally marginalized versus non-marginalized groups use some SNS at similar rates. Facebook for instance, has an equitable distribution across ethnicities in popularity (Pew Research Center, 2015). This SNS is more casual than sites such as LinkedIn, focusing on non-work issues (e.g., politics, entertainment, pictures, social topics). LinkedIn, however, which is primarily focused on employment issues, is primarily populated by older, more educated, more established employees (Duggan, Ellison, Lampe, Lenhart, & Madden, 2014). Organizations that have reported using SNS in recruiting use LinkedIn more often (94%) than Facebook (54%; SHRM, 2013, 2015). Furthermore, potential applicants report using LinkedIn more so than Facebook and Twitter when actively seeking jobs (Acikgoz & Bergman, 2015). Although SNS are generally not the sole recruitment tool for many organizations, the differences in applicant presence and organization recruitment on SNS may put older, educated, male applicants at an advantage during the early stages of talent acquisition, as there are more of these individuals receiving information about job openings at a quicker rate and being directly targeted for specific positions.

At their core, social media and SNS are media that allow individuals to connect with other individuals within their network. Networking partners can provide access to employment opportunities by providing recommendations and referrals of individuals to their own and other organizations to which they are connected. Such processes are important in talent acquisition as some research suggests that referrals lead to a higher probability of receiving a job offer than other recruitment methods such as job fairs and college placement officers (Breaugh, Greising, Taggart, & Chen, 2003). To the extent that individuals are differentially provided access to or are not engaged with networks that have access to resources such as job and advancement opportunities (whether this is through intentional targeting of certain groups through SNS or through unintentional passing of information within homogeneous networks on SNS), then some individuals may be at a greater disadvantage from the beginning of the talent acquisition process.

We posit that individuals' online social networks will mimic their offline social networks in that networks are often fairly homogenous in terms of demographic characteristics (Mollica, Gray, & Trevino, 2003). When looking specifically at online social networks on Facebook, research supports this notion as studies have shown high levels of racial homogeneity and race-based in-group favoritism in social networks (Hebl, Williams, Sundermann, Kell, & Davies, 2012; Wimmer & Lewis, 2010). This may particularly put job applicants from marginalized groups at a disadvantage in the talent acquisition process as White males traditionally belong to higher status networks than women, Hispanics, and Blacks (McDonald, 2011). Individuals who belong to higher status groups will have more access to resources including information about positions and connections to individuals who can help place someone in a position. Having a network that includes key connectors can be instrumental in helping applicants not only locate openings during recruitment processes, but also help them be recommended for positions during selection processes.

Overall, both the actual use of certain SNS and the type of networks established on these sites will likely negatively affect marginalized individuals' SNS presence. Particularly on LinkedIn where most recruiters start, minority applicants are likely to have less of a presence. Further, because we anticipate offline and online social networks look similar, we expect that the connection between recruiters and minority applicants will be more distant than the connection between recruiters and non-minority applicants.

Proposition 1: Minority job applicants will have less of a SNS presence than non-minority job applicants.

As seen in Fig. 14.1, another factor that may effect minority applicants when using SNS in talent acquisition is the presence of negative bias, which may manifest in the form of discrimination. This is based on Stigma Theory (Goffman, 1963), which states that individuals who possess a stigma characteristic, which is any characteristic that is devalued in society, may experience prejudice and discrimination based on this stigma. Stigma Theory has been used to explain why individuals belonging to groups such as minority racial and ethnic groups and women are marginalized and experience discrimination and other forms of bias across a variety of settings. Indeed, as individuals from marginalized groups already experience higher levels of negative bias than those in non-marginalized groups in traditional talent acquisition processes (for examples see Agerström & Rooth, 2011; Derous, Ryan, & Nguyen, 2012; Ruggs, Hebl, Walker, & Fa-Kaji, 2014), these negative biases are likely to be exacerbated when using SNS in talent acquisition. Thus, it is not the case that the use of social media leads to a new problem for minority applicants; rather, the use of social media may further promote the biases already seen in more traditional talent acquisition processes as the structures of and interactions within online networks are likely similar to those of offline networks (Ruggs et al., 2013). Therefore, the pattern of bias seen in offline processes will be intensified when using online SNS because people tend to use even fewer cues to make decisions about individuals online versus offline.

This is in line with the theory of Social Information Processing ([SIP]; Walther, 1995; Walther, Van Der Heide, Ramirez, Burgoon, & Peña, 2015), which states that people receive fewer cues about others online than they do in person, and they over-interpret the few cues that are received. In Walther's (1995) classic example, when people identified with their communication group, they rated their online communicators as smarter, kinder, and better looking than the people they interacted with over the phone or face-to-face. Walther called this "hyper-personalizing" of online relationships and is the effect of sharing group identifications (or not) and the over-interpretation of a few personal cues. This overinterpretation can lead to biased perceptions as people often use stereotypes about characteristics with which they are familiar when there is a lack of information available (Fiske & Neuberg, 1990).

When using factors presented on SNS such as pictures and personal preferences, decision-makers may be inviting bias into the decision-making process that may be more harmful to members of marginalized groups versus those of non-marginalized groups due to the bias that already occurs against individuals in these groups. Also, stereotypes related to culture and cultural differences may be increased when using SNS in talent acquisition as one study found that Black and Hispanics are more likely than Whites to express cultural tastes such as music and movie preferences on Facebook (Grasmuck et al., 2009). Indeed, Grasmuck and colleagues found that minorities make their racial identities salient on Facebook, which can be taken out of context and lead to stereotyped judgments when viewed in isolation by a recruiter or hiring manager. Some evidence of such biases were seen in a recent study that showed that recruiters evaluating SNS provided higher assessments of suitability (e.g., extent to which they thought the person was an attractive applicant) for White applicants than Black or Hispanic applicants (Van Iddekinge, Lanivich, Roth, & Junco, 2013).

The use of cultural, racial, and other demographic information by organizational decision-makers may be conscious and due to prejudicial attitudes about others;

however, research that suggests that such biases are also often implicit and automatic (c.f., Rooth, 2010). The use of stereotypes against minorities when viewing applicants' SNS also may be increased due to the lack of other job-relevant individuating information—information that allows decision-makers to view the applicant beyond the stereotype related to their minority group in that moment. Although decision-makers will have other, more job-relevant information collected during the talent acquisition process, the influence of biases raised by stereotypes from information on SNS may lead decision-makers to be more hesitant about or to discount minorities more so than individuals for whom negative stereotypes do not relate. Therefore, we believe that the use of SNS will increase biased decisions about minority applicants more so than non-minority applicants.

Proposition 2: Minority job applicants will experience greater amounts of subtle discrimination and bias than non-minority job applicants when SNS are used in talent acquisition.

Next, we explore how the factors mentioned above may lead to a disadvantage in talent acquisition for minority (versus non-minority) job applicants. As seen in Fig. 14.1, we believe that SNS presence and negative bias help explain negative consequences for minority applicants at various stages of the talent acquisition process, with SNS presence having more of an influence during earlier stages of the process (i.e., attraction and recruitment stages) and negative bias having an influence at both early and late stages (i.e., selection) of the process. We examine this process from both the perspective of job applicants and the organization throughout each stage.

14.1.2 Attraction and Recruitment

Attraction is the process by which organizations present an image to the public and potential applicants assess it. Recruitment is the process by which organizations solicit applications and potential employees apply for a job. Organizations that rely on SNS as one of their primary attraction and/or recruitment tools may unknowingly isolate potential applicants who do not have access to or do not keep up with the organizations via SNS. This may be in part due to the fact that SNS can be considered passive recruitment methods because they are meant to exist in the background (Dery, Tansley, & Hafermalz, 2014) and increase the appeal of the company (e.g., sharing the company's recent activities, especially if they are aligned with social trends). For example, posting on a SNS about a company sport tournament is a passive way to indirectly show that the company is promoting and values employee well-being, which may be attractive to potential applicants as it signals the organizations' concern for employees (Papakonstantinidis, 2014). Passive advertisements also may provide insight about the organizational culture, which is something that is important to recruiters who use SNS (Jobvite, 2014). For instance, organizations may provide information about awards and accolades they have received for being a leader in their industry as well as for working with traditionally marginalized groups (e.g., National Association of Female Executives Best 50 Companies for Women; DiversityInc Top 50 Companies for Diversity). Such awards signal excellence (e.g., industry awards) or an inclusive organizational culture (e.g., diversity-related recognition). Yet, such passive recruiting may only appeal to individuals who were initially interested in and/or had access to the organization for other reasons and may leave out those who the organization does not target.

Organizations also use SNS to project an image of an open and exciting organizational culture, thus increasing an individual's desire to work in the organization. An organization may post information on SNS about both its organizational and employment brand as a tool to not only conduct outreach to the public but also to attract potential applicants. For example, Bank of America uses its Facebook page (which has over two million likes) to post about "Community. News. Service and support." Although it also provides links to make appointments, find ATMs, and receive help, its actual posts provide information about the community (e.g., posts about the Special Olympics), and guidance on ways to save money on everyday things such as shopping for groceries and car maintenance. Following the ASA model (Schneider, 1987), individuals who value civic engagement may be more interested in working at Bank of America as a result of its social media presence.

However, there is some risk that using SNS can also have deleterious impacts. For example, Apple recently launched a new set of emojis including the first that included black and brown faces. In response, Clorox posted a picture of a bleach bottle covered in transparent emojis on Twitter which stated: "New emojis are alright but where's the bleach?" Many of their followers were offended (Goldman, 2015) and Clorox removed the post shortly after receiving the negative feedback. Such cultural offenses may not only decrease an individual's likelihood to purchase the organization's goods and services but may also deter potential minority applicants from pursuing an organization such as this as they may feel that the 180 character (potential) faux pas is representative of the organization's culture and values. Ineffect, individuals, and individuals in minority groups in particular, may be less attracted to organizations that violate social norms of political correctness. Thus, they may be less likely to follow such organizations on SNS.

Organizations can use SNS more actively during the recruitment process as well (Joos, 2008). Active recruitment methods employ strategies that display a need for a new hire (e.g., posting a job opening or search-engine optimization). Following the ASA model (Schneider, 1987), which suggests that individuals are attracted to organizations that have values they view as congruent with their own, such information may signal to potential employees what it will be like to work in the organization and whether or not they will "fit in" at a given organization (Jackson et al., 1991). In a survey of nearly 2000 recruitment and HR professionals, Jobvite (2014), a recruiting consulting company reported that 95 % of those surveyed planned on using SNS for recruiting with recruiters planning to use LinkedIn (94 %), Facebook (66 %), and Twitter (52 %) as a sourcing mechanism. However, organizations may still run into the problem of differential SNS presence if their followers (versus non-followers) tend to be people who find more similarities between themselves and the organization.

In addition to allowing applicants to assess organizations during attraction and recruitment, organizational recruiters may examine potential applicants' SNS during these stages. It is during this phase that applicants' SNS presence has the most potential to help or harm them in attraction and recruitment. LinkedIn is very popular because it allows organizations to search a wide group of people for particular skill sets like education and employment history (Zide, Elman, & Shahani-Denning, 2014). Recruiters who use LinkedIn report that they look for college information and years of experience to recruit potential employees. They also consider a larger number of connections and a significant number of diverse recommendations as positive, passive indicators of a person's abilities. Personal recommendations and referrals are an important part of the recruitment process, as such methods have been shown to lead to a higher chance of receiving a job offer than other recruitment methods such as job fairs and college placement officers (Breaugh et al., 2003). In online recruitment using LinkedIn, in particular, may put women at a greater disadvantage than men as evidence suggests that men receive more online recommendations on LinkedIn profiles than women (Zide et al., 2014).

Thus, using SNS in attraction and recruitment may present a twofold problem. First, minority applicants may be less attracted to passive online recruitment strategies and may be less targeted with more active recruitment strategies. Second, when recruiters are examining potential applicants' SNS they may perceive less of a SNS presence from minority applicants based on the size and composition of their networks, as well as the presence of recommendations from others. As seen in the model, this perception of SNS presence (or lack thereof) will further harm minorities during the attraction and recruitment phases.

Proposition 3: Minority (versus non-minority) job applicants will be less likely to be the targets during the attraction and recruitment phase when using (3a). SNS presence will moderate the relation between group membership and attraction and recruitment to organizations, such that minority (versus non-minority) job applicants will be less likely to be targets during these phases when SNS presence is low (versus high).

14.1.3 Screening and Selection

The second phase of the ASA model moves beyond individuals to suggest that organizations hire (i.e., select) individuals for employment because they possess attributes that the organization values. Selection is defined as the process of identifying individuals with the requisite knowledge, skills, and abilities (KSAs) required to perform a given job (Gatewood, Field, & Barrick, 2015). Selection methods vary with respect to the types of activities job applicants engage in (e.g., interviews, assessment centers, work samples). During the selection process, most job applicants seek to portray an image of themselves that enables an organization to develop a favorable impression in the hopes of securing employment. Organizations are examining the SNS profiles of job applicants as a mechanism for obtaining a more accurate picture of potential incumbents. The information obtained on SNS may reinforce an organization's decision to hire (or not hire) an individual. In addition, information gleaned through SNS may provide additional evidence used to justify selection decisions. For instance, in the case of Bank of America, individuals possessing volunteer experience with special needs population may be preferable to individuals who do not engage in service activities.

Social media is used to a lesser degree in the actual selection process than in the attraction and recruitment processes (SHRM, 2013). One aspect of the selection process for which social media may be particularly relevant is during the job applicant screening phase (i.e., background check). A recent examination of HR departments revealed that social media is used by some organizations (20 % of the organizations that responded to a survey by SHRM in 2013) in the applicant screening process with some organizations reporting the use of social media to verify information obtained from resumes or job applications, with the vast majority of organizations reporting that SNS is a way to acquire information quickly and easily (SHRM, 2013).

In addition to speed and ease of use, social media is also attractive in the screening phase of the selection process because it may provide information about job candidates that is not readily available from other sources (e.g., resumes, biodata; Brown & Vaughn, 2011). Specifically, SNS may provide additional information about an applicant's behaviors, preferences, and tendencies which some believe may be relevant for determining job suitability (Bohnert & Ross, 2010). A recent survey commissioned by Careerbuilder.com of over 2000 employers revealed that organizations using SNS in the screening process often review both the images and content of postings on SNS. The employers reported eliminating job candidates on the basis of a variety of factors including: provocative or inappropriate pictures (50 %), alcohol or drug use (38 %), disparage of a previous employer (33 %), poor online communication skills (30 %), discriminatory comments directed at protected classes (28 %), and falsified information about qualifications (24 %).

Such a review may be particularly problematic for minority applicants, as it may lead to an activation of negative biases (via stereotypes) that have negative consequences for selection processes (as seen in Fig. 14.1). Specifically, given that racio-ethnic minorities are more likely to use casual SNS (e.g., Facebook, Instagram) as opposed to professional SNS (i.e., LinkedIn), their SNS presence may likely consist of more casual images and language which in turn may eliminate them from further consideration compared to their majority-group counterparts with a more professional SNS presence. Furthermore, in instances where there are few differences in the nature of the general content of SNS profiles, the attributions for the content of a SNS may vary based upon the job applicant's demographic group membership. For instance, White individuals whose SNS contain slang and other casual vernacular may be viewed differently than the same word choice from Black individuals. For the White individual, the word choice may be attributed to the casual nature of an online account, whereas for a Black or Hispanic individual, the word choice may be attributed to a lack of intelligence or knowledge of appropriate grammar, which is more consistent with racial stereotypes about competence and intelligence.

Although such errors and unprofessionalism impacts all applicants, it may do more damage to minorities during the recruitment process, as individuals with ethnic sounding names experience greater levels of bias and discrimination in talent acquisition processes (Cotton, O'Neill, & Griffin, 2008). Additionally, spelling and grammatical errors may be more problematic for racial minorities such as Blacks and Hispanics, as these mistakes support stereotypes about these groups being low on competence (c.f., Fiske, Xu, Cuddy, & Glick, 1999). The effect of these and similar stereotypes about other marginalized groups have been shown to lead to greater negative bias toward members of minority (versus majority) groups when they do make mistakes. For instance, in one study Black managers who made aggressive mistakes (i.e., were too hostile with coworkers and subordinates) received lower salary recommendations than White managers who made similar mistakes (Walker, Madera, & Hebl, 2013).

There is a paucity of research pertaining to the effects of social media in the talent acquisition process and most of the extant literature focuses primarily on Facebook (the most widely used SNS). The literature is further limited by the reliance upon college students in the selection process and neglects a large segment of the working population (Peluchette & Karl, 2010; Zide et al., 2014). Some research shows that college students on Facebook are aware that potential employers are reviewing their information. However, some of these students believe they present professional and intelligent information about themselves on Facebook. A different study found that students do seem to realize that their posts are viewed as inappropriate by potential employers (Miller et al., 2010). This view is more aligned with reality, as recruiters believe their information is frequently inappropriate. More recently, Root and McKay (2014) report that students are aware that pictures and drunken posts may have a negative effect on their employability but do not realize that other content on their SNS pages will be viewed negatively (e.g., spelling errors; Zide et al., 2014). When factors such as grammatical errors or pictures of partying intersect with demographic characteristics such as race, minorities may be at a particular disadvantage due to the activation of greater negative stereotypes.

We base this assertion on Social Information Processing ([SIP]; Walther, 1995) and the effects of hyper-personalization. With so few cues available online compared to face-to-face, recruiters might seize upon the few that highlight acknowledged or unacknowledged biases. So although minority candidates who are on SNS may have greater knowledge about a variety of jobs, they may be judged more harshly because of the limited information available on their SNS. Furthermore, given the limited (and maybe even non-existent) oversight that is in place with regard to systematically evaluating SNS profiles in a standardized manner, decision-makers may be even more inclined to use biases based on stereotype-relevant information.

In addition to identifying instances where individuals were less likely to be hired, the employers reported several characteristics that were related to an increased likelihood of hire including: professional image (57 %), wide-ranging interests (50 %), creativity (46 %), great online communication skills (43 %), and references (38 %). In sum, organizations are using SNS to obtain more accurate information about an individual's character as well as to verify information obtained from resumes and job applications.

Beyond a background check or social media "prescreening," information about other KSAs may also be gleaned from an applicant's SNS presence. For instance, Kluemper, Rosen, and Mossholder (2012) examined the suitability of using social media as a proxy for measuring personality characteristics. Results indicated that trained raters could "provide reasonably reliable estimates of the Big Five personality traits" using information obtained on SNS. Given that personality measures are less likely to result in adverse impact (Ones & Anderson, 2002), using social media for this purpose may be beneficial for organizations. However, it is important to note that more research is needed to determine whether or not differences emerge with respect to the personality ratings of minority groups and their majority-group counterparts. This may be particularly true if individuals are differentially rating similar images and messages conveyed by majority and minority group members to determine personality.

Taken together, we posit that minority (versus non-minority) applicants may be at a particular disadvantage when SNS profiles are examined in the screening and selection phases of talent acquisition. As illustrated in Fig. 14.1, we believe that the use of SNS in screening and selection leads to greater negative bias toward minority (versus non-minority) job applicants, which then leads to lower rates of selection.

Proposition 4: Minority (versus non-minority) job applicants experience higher levels of negative bias when SNS is used in talent acquisition, which will lead to less favorable outcomes in selection.

14.2 Discussion

Social media have changed the way in which organizations interact with job applicants and employees (Roth, Bobko, Van Iddekinge, & Thatcher, 2016). Over the past decade, applicants have become increasingly aware that SNS accounts are being used by organizations in the talent acquisition process. When organizations solicit private information from SNS accounts, applicants typically react more negatively as many individuals (both job seekers and employees alike) believe that their online presence should be protected by privacy laws (Davison, Maraist, & Bing, 2011). In line with these beliefs, a total of 18 states have enacted state legislation preventing employers from requesting or requiring individuals to provide passwords or access to their personal social media and SNS accounts (Wright, 2014). It is important to note however that the state legislation does not prevent organizations from using social media as an aspect of the talent acquisition process. As discussed in this chapter and illustrated through our conceptual model, the use of social media and SNS in talent acquisition may lead to an increase in negative biases against minority applicants that are difficult to detect and in some cases unintentional on the part of organizations.

Some SNS, including LinkedIn, permit individuals to see who has viewed their profiles. This information can be used to develop a number of inferences about why an individual is, or is not, selected for a position. Saylin and Horrocks (2013) present an interesting challenge facing organizations by discussing a discrimination lawsuit filed by an older worker who believed that his age could be discerned from his LinkedIn profile. The individual filed an EEOC claim alleging age discrimination. Job applicants may have information on their SNS profiles that cannot be readily obtained through interviews or other mechanisms. Thus, when using SNS, organizations need to make sure that individuals who are making selection decisions are not unduly influenced by information that may result in discrimination.

As the use of such tools is becoming commonplace, organizational scientists need to know how these tools may differentially impact majority group members and their marginalized counterparts. In this chapter, we outline some of the ways in which employment biases against job applicants from traditionally marginalized groups may be enhanced when using social media in talent acquisition. Given that some organizations are using or considering the use of social media in talent acquisition, we offer recommendations to scholars and practitioners to help guide decision-making and policies in this area.

When considering the use of social media in attraction and recruitment phases, organizations should carefully consider the accessibility and target audience that will be reached with this method. Organizations can do research on the demographic makeup of its followers on various SNS to gain insight into who they are passively reaching when advertising through SNS. Such market research will not only provide information on who is being reached, but it also can provide information concerning how often potential applicants of various demographic backgrounds are perusing their sites as well as using the information found here to follow up on job postings. If there are discrepancies in the proportion of minorities compared to non-minorities that are using SNS to find out information about organizations that are hiring, then organizations can use this information to develop plans to broaden their target audience.

Organizations may be able to broaden their target audience by using campaigns or recruitment strategies that highlight diversity even on their SNS. Indeed, research indicates that racial minorities are more attracted to organizations that highlight diversity in their recruitment materials than those who do not (Avery, Hernandez, & Hebl, 2004). In doing so, organizations should consider how SNS marketing aligns with the organization's overall vision and mission and how this will be perceived by all potential applicants.

One way that organizations can track who is engaging in their SNS during the attraction and recruitment phases is through the use of gathering information in the form of big data. Organizations can collect some demographic information about types of individuals who are interacting with them on SNS (e.g., following their sites, reposting information) as well as who is actively engaging with them on SNS (e.g., active engagement may include sending correspondence about recruitment ads posted through SNS). Organizations can use these data to examine relations between the proportion of minorities who engage via SNS and the proportion who apply for positions posted via SNS. Although not all organizations may be at the place that they are able to gather and analyze big data, those that are can use such techniques to gain more fine grained information concerning not only who is attracted through SNS, but whether individuals from different groups interact with the organization's websites differently (e.g., spend differential amounts of time on the site, accessing additional information through provided links).

In addition to posting information on their own SNS pages, organizations may examine job applicants' SNS during the talent acquisition process. This is likely more often to occur during the selection phase of talent acquisition as decision-makers are trying to determine which applicant is the best fit for a position. At this phase, the use of social media may differentially impact minority versus non-minority applicants in the selection process because it may lead to discrimination against minority applicants due to the increased use of stereotypes and biases that can occur when browsing on job applicants' SNS pages. This may lead to adverse impact in selection, which can create legal turmoil for organizations in addition to the inherent negative consequences for minority applicants.

If organizations want to use social media in talent acquisition, they should first ensure that the use of examining job applicants' SNS pages is a valid predictor of future job performance. That is, organizations must be able to show that the information gained from applicants' SNS provides valid useful information about how that person will perform as an employee. Brown and Vaughn (2011) provide more in depth discussion of establishing validity as outlined by the Uniform Guidelines for Employee Selection for the purposes of using social media for hiring procedures. In addition, organizations should ensure that the use of such selection methods does not create adverse impact such that minority applicants are selected at significantly lower rates than non-minority applicants.

Researchers can shed light on this validity issue by thinking about what types of factors information from SNS may predict and examining the validity and associated adverse impact associated with such methods in controlled experiments. For instance, it may be the case the information gained from applicants' SNS pages provides useful information concerning traits such as creativity and personality characteristics such as openness to experience. These traits are needed in some jobs; however, it is important to determine if this method of testing for these traits is not only valid, but also more valid than other measures that can provide similar information. Some researchers have started to examine this, although the literature in this area is still sparse. One study found that evaluations of information from SNS did not predict job performance (Van Iddekinge et al., 2013). In this study, the authors used evaluations of suitability and KSAs from SNS as predictors of performance. Any organization that uses SNS in screening and selection would want to check the validity of what is being assessed with the job criteria for the position in question.

In addition to determining the validity of such methods, organizations that are considering the use of examining applicant SNS during the selection process should make sure that the decision-makers who are viewing candidate sites are trained to accurately assess the traits of interest in an objective and non-biased manner. One of the current dangers and real problems with using SNS in screening and selection is the lack of structure concerning how profiles are evaluated and the extent to which they are evaluated in a standardized manner. Research from traditional talent acquisition methods shows that the use of unstructured measures (e.g., unstructured interviews) leads to greater negative bias toward minority (versus non-minority) applicants than structured interviews (Huffcutt & Roth, 1998). The consequences of unstructured measures for minority applicants are likely to also be seen in the social media realm as people are more likely to use stereotypes and other biases in these situations. Thus, if SNS profiles are used as a screening measure, training should include making people to be aware of implicit biases that people have due to stereotypes as this has been shown to be an effective method of reducing bias in more traditional selection processes (Devine, Forscher, Austin, & Cox, 2012).

Prior to using social media in selection processes, organizations should develop clear communication with applicants to make them aware that this method will be used for decision-making purposes. Organizations should be transparent and upfront about the process and include information such as who will be evaluating SNS pages and how the information will be used. This is similar to the type of information provided to job applicants when background checks are needed to establish security-related information.

References

Acikgoz, Y., & Bergman, S. M. (2015). Social media and employee recruitment: Chasing the run away bandwagon. In R. N. Landers & G. B. Schmidt (Eds.), *Social media in employee selection and recruitment: Theory, practice, and current challenges*. Cham, Switzerland: Springer.

Agerström, J., & Rooth, D.-O. (2011). The role of automatic obesity stereotypes in real hiring discrimination. *Journal of Applied Psychology, 96*(4), 790–805.

Avery, D. R., Hernandez, M., & Hebl, M. R. (2004). Who's watching the race? Racial salience in recruiting advertising. *Journal of Applied Social Psychology, 34*(1), 146–161.

Bohnert, D., & Ross, H. R. (2010). The influence of social networking web sites on the evaluation of job candidates. *Cyberpsychology, Behavior and Social Networking, 13*(3), 341–347.

Breaugh, J. A., Greising, L. A., Taggart, J. W., & Chen, H. (2003). The relationship of recruiting sources and pre-hire outcomes: Examination of yield ratios and applicant quality. *Journal of Applied Social Psychology, 33*(11), 2267–2287.

Brown, V. R., & Vaughn, E. D. (2011). The writing on the (Facebook) wall: The use of social networking sites in hiring decisions. *Journal of Business and Psychology, 26*(2), 219–225.

Chang, W., & Madera, J. M. (2012). Using social network sites for selection purposes: An investigation of hospitality recruiters. *Journal of Human Resources in Hospitality and Tourism, 11*(3), 138–196.

Cotton, J. L., O'Neill, B. S., & Griffin, A. (2008). The "name game": Affective and hiring reactions to first names. *Journal of Managerial Psychology, 23*(1), 18–39.

Davison, H. K., Maraist, C., & Bing, M. N. (2011). Friend or foe? The promise and pitfalls of using social networking sites for HR decisions. *Journal of Business and Psychology, 26*(2), 153–159.

Derous, E., Ryan, A. M., & Nguyen, H. D. (2012). Multiple categorization in resume screening: Examining effects on hiring discrimination against Arab applicant in field and lab settings. *Journal of Organizational Behavior, 33*(4), 544–570.

Dery, K., Tansley, C., & Hafermalz, E. (2014). Hiring in the age of social media: New rules, new game. *University of Auckland Business Review, 17*(1), 44–51.

Devine, P. G., Forscher, P. S., Austin, A. J., & Cox, W. T. L. (2012). Long-term reduction in implicit race bias: A prejudice habit-breaking intervention. *Journal of Experimental Social Psychology, 48*(6), 1267–1278.

Duggan, M., Ellison, N. B., Lampe, C., Lenhart, A., & Madden, M. (2014). *Social media update 2014*. Pew Research Center. Retrieved March 31, 2015, from http://www.pewinternet.org/2015/01/09/social-media-update-2014/

Fiske, S. T., & Neuberg, S. L. (1990). A continuum of impression formation, from category-based to individuating processes: Influences of information and motivation on attention and interpretation. In M. P. Zanna (Ed.), *Advances in experimental social psychology* (Vol. 23, pp. 1–74). San Diego, CA: Academic.

Fiske, S. T., Xu, J., Cuddy, A. C., & Glick, P. (1999). (Dis)respecting versus (dis)liking: Status and interdependence predict ambivalent stereotypes of competence and warmth. *Journal of Social Issues, 55*(3), 473–489.

Gatewood, R., Field, H. S., & Barrick, M. (2015). *Human resource selection* (8th ed.). Boston: Cengage Learning.

Goffman, E. (1963). *Stigma: Notes on the management of spoiled identity*. Englewood Cliffs, NJ: Prentice Hall.

Goldman, D. (2015). *Clorox apologizes, deletes tweet after racial uproar*. Retrieved June 8, 2015, from http://money.cnn.com/2015/04/09/technology/clorox-emoji-tweet/

Grasmuck, S., Martin, J., & Zhao, S. (2009). Ethno-racial identity displays on Facebook. *Journal of Computer-Mediated Communication, 15*, 158–188. doi:10.1111/j.1083-6101.2009.01498.x.

Hebl, M. R., Foster, J. B., Mannix, L. M., & Dovidio, J. F. (2002). Formal and interpersonal discrimination: A field study of bias toward homosexual applicants. *Personality and Social Psychology Bulletin, 28*(6), 815–825.

Hebl, M. R., Williams, M. J., Sundermann, J. M., Kell, H. J., & Davies, P. G. (2012). Selectively friending: Racial stereotypicality and social rejection. *Journal of Experimental Social Psychology, 48*(6), 1329–1335.

Huffcutt, A. I., & Roth, P. L. (1998). Racial group differences in employment interview evaluations. *Journal of Applied Psychology, 83*(2), 179–189.

Jackson, S. E., Brett, J. F., Sessa, V. I., Cooper, D. M., Julin, J. A., & Peyronnin, K. (1991). Some differences make a difference: Individual dissimilarity and group heterogeneity as correlates of recruitment, promotions, and turnover. *Journal of Applied Psychology, 76*(5), 675–689.

Jobvite. (2014). *Jobvite 2014 social recruiting survey*. Retrieved March 31, 2015, from http://web.jobvite.com/Q414_Website_SocialRecruitingSurvey_LP.html

Joos, J. G. (2008). Social media: New frontiers in hiring and recruiting. *Employment Relations Today, 35*(1), 51–59.

Kluemper, D. H., Rosen, P. A., & Mossholder, K. (2012). Social networking websites, personality ratings, and the organizational context: More than meets the eye. *Journal of Applied Social Psychology, 42*(5), 1143–1172.

McDonald, S. (2011). What's in the "old boys" network? Accessing social capital in gendered and racialized networks. *Social Networks, 33*(4), 317–330.

Miller, R., Parsons, K., & Lifer, D. (2010). Students and social networking sites: The posting paradox. *Behaviour & Information Technology, 29*, 377–382. doi:10.1080/01449290903042491.

Mollica, K. A., Gray, B., & Trevino, L. K. (2003). Racial homophily and its persistence in newcomers' social networks. *Organization Science, 14*(2), 123–136.

Ones, D. S., & Anderson, N. (2002). Gender and ethnic group differences on personality scales in selection: Some British data. *Journal of Occupational and Organizational Psychology, 75*(3), 255–276.

Papakonstantinidis, S. (2014). *Social recruiting: Exploring the impact of social networking sites on digital natives' occupational opportunities*. Doctoral dissertation, Centre for Labour Market Studies.

Peluchette, J., & Karl, K. (2010). Examining students' intended image on Facebook: "What were they thinking?!". *Journal of Education for Business, 85*(1), 30–37.

Pew Research Center. (2015). *Social media preferences vary by race and ethnicity*. Retrieved September 20, 2015, from http://www.pewresearch.org/fact-tank/2015/02/03/social-media-preferences-vary-by-race-and-ethnicity/

Ployhart, R. E. (2012). The psychology of competitive advantage: An adjacent possibility. *Industrial and Organizational Psychology, 5*(1), 62–81.

Root, T., & McKay, S. (2014). Student awareness of the use of social media screening by prospective employers. *Journal of Education for Business, 89*(4), 202–206.

Rooth, D.-O. (2010). Automatic associations and discrimination in hiring: Real world evidence. *Labour Economics, 17*(3), 523–534.

Roth, P. L., Bobko, P., Van Iddekinge, C. H., & Thatcher, J. B. (2016). Social media in employee-selection-related decisions: A research agenda for uncharted territory. *Journal of Management, 45*, 269–298.

Ruggs, E. N., Hebl, M. R., Walker, S. S., & Fa-Kaji, N. (2014). Selection biases that emerge when age meets gender. *Journal of Managerial Psychology, 29*(8), 1028–1043.

Ruggs, E. N., Speights, S., & Walker, S. S. (2013). Are you in or out? Employment discrimination in online and offline networks. *Industrial and Organizational Psychology Perspectives on Science and Practice, 6*(4), 466–471.

Saylin, G. M., & Horrocks, T. C. (2013). *The risks of pre-employment social media screening*. Retrieved May 28, 2015, from http://www.shrm.org/hrdisciplines/staffingmanagement/articles/pages/preemployment-social-media-screening.aspx

Schneider, B. (1987). The people make the place. *Personnel Psychology, 40*(3), 437–453.

Society for Human Resource Management (SHRM). (2013). *Social networking websites and recruiting/selecting*. Retrieved from http://www.shrm.org/research/surveyfindings/articles/pages/shrm-social-networking-websites-recruiting-job-candidates.aspx

Society for Human Resource Management (SHRM). (2015). *The importance of social media for recruiters and job seekers*. Retrieved from http://www.shrm.org/Research/SurveyFindings/Documents/SHRM-Ascendo-Resources-Social-Media-Recruitment.pdf

Van Iddekinge, C. H., Lanivich, S. E., Roth, P. L., & Junco, E. (2013). Social media for selection? Validity and adverse impact potential of a Facebook-based assessment. *Journal of Management*, Online.

Walker, S. S., Madera, J. M., & Hebl, M. R. (2013). Effects of leader race and leader mistake on patronizing behaviors. *Journal of Business Diversity, 13*(1/2), 52–64.

Walther, J. B. (1995). Relational aspects of computer-mediated communication: Experimental observations over time. *Organization Science, 6*(2), 186–203.

Walther, J. B., Van Der Heide, B., Ramirez, A., Burgoon, J. K., & Peña, J. (2015). Interpersonal and hyperpersonal dimensions of computer-mediated communication. In S. Shyam Sundar (Ed.), *The handbook of the psychology of communication technology* (pp. 3–22). New York: Wiley.

Wimmer, A., & Lewis, K. (2010). Beyond and below racial homophily: ERG models of a friend ship network documented on Facebook. *American Journal of Sociology, 116*(2), 583–642.

Wright, A. D. (2014). *More states ban social media snooping*. Retrieved May 11, 2015, from http://www.shrm.org/hrdisciplines/technology/articles/pages/social-media-snooping.aspx

Zide, J., Elman, B., & Shahani-Denning, C. (2014). LinkedIn and recruitment: How profiles differ across occupations. *Employee Relations, 36*(5), 583–604.

Chapter 15
Is John Smith *Really* John Smith? Misrepresentations and Misattributions of Candidates Using Social Media and Social Networking Sites

Noelle B. Frantz, Elizabeth S. Pears, E. Daly Vaughn, Jared Z. Ferrell, and Nikki M. Dudley

Abstract In this chapter, we explore psychological factors which impact how social networking site (SNS) users may project themselves, as well as how users may be perceived by others on SNSs. The first section discusses research related to SNS users' projections and misrepresentations of the self, sometimes unknowingly as in the case of self-deception, and other times knowingly, as with impression management. Next, research reviewing the psychological mechanisms underlying potential misattributions by SNS data consumers will be discussed. The authors delve into possible biases held by those responsible for making hiring decisions, and explore how those biases may impact the candidate, as well as the interpretations of job candidate SNS data. More recent social psychology research on implicit biases, attitudes, and stereotypes is discussed throughout.

Keywords Misrepresentation • Impression management • Self-deception • Misattributions • Bias • Attitudes • Stereotypes • Social networking sites • Selection

N.B. Frantz, M.A. (✉) • E.S. Pears, M.A. • E.D. Vaughn, Ph.D. • J.Z. Ferrell, M.A.
N.M. Dudley, Ph.D.
SHAKER, 3201 Enterprise Parkway, Suite 360, Beachwood, OH 44122, USA
e-mail: Noelle.frantz@shakercg.com; Elizabeth.Pears@shakercg.com; dalyvaughn@gmail.com; Jared.Ferrell@shakercg.com; Nikki.Dudley@shakercg.com

R.N. Landers, G.B. Schmidt (eds.), *Social Media in Employee Selection and Recruitment*, DOI 10.1007/978-3-319-29989-1_15

15.1 Introduction

The question isn't, 'What do we want to know about people?', It's, 'What do people want to tell about themselves?'—Mark Zuckerberg

With any distribution of information there are at least two parties involved: the presenter and the consumer. When a presenter enters an online environment and provides user generated content (UGC) via a social networking site (SNS), the number of possible consumers of that information becomes exponentially larger than typically conceivable in a face-to-face or paper format. Users of SNSs are characteristically both presenters and consumers, sharing and consuming information with a large network of individuals.

According to Pew Research Center in January of 2014, 74 % of adult internet users (18 years and older) are SNS users (Pew Research Center, 2014). Also in 2014, it was reported that 52 % of adult internet users utilized two or more SNSs (Duggan, Ellison, Lampe, Lenhart, & Madden, 2015). With 2.1 billion active social media accounts (Kemp, 2015), an SNS user generating and presenting content can reach an astronomical number of other SNS users.

With social networking at the forefront of our daily lives, we can easily forget the differences between face-to-face communication and online self-presentation. When interacting in person, individuals have to react in real time, forming immediate responses while trying to maintain the image they wish to project. Online interactions are more ambiguous, allowing one to form a calculated response before sharing it. Presenters of SNS data are able to manipulate, filter, and control exactly what they share and the "self" they portray on SNSs. Therefore, we must consider if employers who are using SNSs to "learn" more about candidates are actually gathering accurate information.

Many employers argue that SNSs allow them to gather more authentic information about job applicants and thus make better informed hiring decisions. A May 2015 Harris Poll reported that 52 % of US employers are using SNSs to research candidates which is up from 43 % in 2014 and 39 % in 2013 (CareerBuilder, 2015). However, research has long suggested that even though employers tend to think they are good judges of applicants' potential, when left to their own devices, and utilizing an unstructured screening format, employers are not very effective at predicting future performance of candidates (Highhouse, 2008; Thorndike, 1920).

Whether or not a candidate misrepresents themselves on social media or SNSs is just one concern when considering the use of online information to aid in the selection process. Another concern is the effect of potential biases held by employers using this information for organizational hiring decisions. Literature has continued to show that explicit and implicit biases toward members of specific groups impact organizations (Adams, 2012; Budig, 2002; Finkelstein & Burke, 1998; Perry & Finkelstein, 1999; Schneider, Swan, & Fitzgerald, 1997; Wittenbrink, Judd, & Park, 1997). The use of social media and SNSs for cyber-vetting opens the door for employers to exercise more biases than ever before, providing access to information about candidates that is not pertinent to the job which might invoke other personal biases that are not typically present in traditional selection processes.

With increasing numbers of employers using SNSs to aide selection processes, and a paucity of research on the legitimacy of information provided via online profiles, the effect of consumer biases, and the validity of SNS use for selection purposes, it behooves researchers and practitioners alike to pause and evaluate the possible risks of such practices. Although research on SNSs as selection tools is slim, there is a long-standing history of research on selection processes and issues that may arise such as candidate misrepresentations of the self and employer misattributions of candidates. Throughout this chapter, we provide evidence illustrating how self-deception and impression management by SNS users, along with employers' implicit and explicit biases, are very real concerns when using SNS for selection purposes.

15.2 The Presenter: *Projections and Misrepresentations of the Self*

Social media and SNSs provide users with ample time to choose exactly the type of personal information they wish to share and how they wish to present that information. Users of SNSs, whether knowingly or not, project a certain image of themselves through their online aliases. Research suggests that these projections are not always accurate representations of one's true self, but instead, a manufactured idealized version of the self (Michikyan, Subrahmanyam, & Dennis, 2014). In these cases, "idealized self" is not necessarily the best version of oneself, but rather, the identity one wishes to portray to others.

Research has continually shown that a presenter of information can both unintentionally (self-deception) and intentionally (impression management) misrepresent themselves. Self-deception and impression management have been compared and contrasted in the literature with some researchers supporting the notion that self-deception is a nonpurposive dimension of impression management (e.g., Gardner & Martinko, 1988). For example, Jones et al. (1962) found that participants who were instructed to create purposely enhanced self-descriptions and subsequently received positive feedback concerning those descriptions, later reported believing the embellished self-descriptions were accurate self-portrayals (Gardner & Martinko, 1988). Thus, what may have been an exercise in impression management proved to also be self-deceiving. However, other researchers support the idea that self-deception and impression management are distinctly different processes (Paulhus, 1984, 1988, 1989; Paulhus & Reid, 1991; Zerbe & Paulhus, 1987). Whether related or not, both forms of misrepresentation manifest in social media and SNSs.

15.2.1 Self-Deception

Above all, don't lie to yourself. The man who lies to himself and listens to his own lie comes to a point that he cannot distinguish the truth within him, or around him, and so loses all respect for himself and others.—Fyodor Dostoyevsky

Not all faking is intentional. It has largely been assumed within the realm of selection that candidate response distortion is an entirely volitional, conscious occurrence. However, research has revealed that social desirability is not a unitary construct, and in many cases is far from consciously motivated (Farrow, Burgess, Wilkinson, & Hunter, 2014). Paulhus and colleagues (e.g., Paulhus, 1984, 1988, 1989; Paulhus & Reid, 1991; Zerbe & Paulhus, 1987) have shown that response distortion, or motivated social desirability, comprises two separate constructs, self-deception and impression management (which involves intention to deceive others). Self-deception is defined as a dispositional tendency to think of oneself in a favorable light (Barrick & Mount, 1996). It is the process of ignoring, rationalizing, or manipulating one's own thoughts or behaviors in order to maintain consistency between the ideal self and actual self (Balcetis, 2008). Self-deception is thought of as an unintentional tendency to present positively biased, but honestly believed, self-descriptions (Li & Bagger, 2006). Self-deception is not the same as simply being wrong or holding false beliefs, self-deception requires that an individual hold a belief that is in direct contradiction with a reality or truth to which that individual has been consciously or subconsciously exposed (Lynn, Pipitone, & Keenan, 2014). Farrow et al. (2014) note that when it comes to self-deception, the word "unintentional" most closely means habitual, automatic, and without forethought. Impression-management focuses on the desire to create specific, and oftentimes favorable, impressions on others, while self-deception is much more self-oriented and related to defensiveness toward unconscious personal threats (Farrow et al., 2014; Kroner & Weekes, 1996). In fact, research has shown that individuals who engage in self-deception are less likely to become depressed (Surbey, 2011).

Those who deceive others or themselves frequently do so unwittingly, without conscious awareness of personal motives (Peck, 1983). According to Gur and Sackeim (1979), to be self-deceived, an individual must hold two contradictory beliefs simultaneously, one of which remains in the subconscious. Much of self-deception is believed to stem from an unconscious desire to minimize anxiety. Particularly, individuals attempt to avoid the discomfort that accompanies information which is in conflict with their preferred view of themselves, others, or the world around them (Smith, 2003). In an attempt to avoid this discomfort and reduce anxiety, individuals may engage in forms of self-deception. In this way, self-deception is a tool employed by what has been called our "psychological immune system" which is responsible for defending against threats to emotional well-being (Balcetis, 2008; Gilbert, Pinel, Wilson, Blumberg, & Wheatley, 1998). Self-deception is thought to occur in three steps: (1) individuals attempt to protect themselves from potential anxiety inducing experiences and information by limiting their own awareness; (2) this action in turn creates "blind spots" in perceptions of reality; (3) these blind spots influence behavior as well as psychological functioning, to create a version of reality that reduces anxiety (Goleman, 1985; Litz, 2003).

In a classic study of self-deception, researchers either told participants that high pain tolerance was indicative of cardiac health or that high pain tolerance was a sign of possible cardiac issues. Participants who were told that high tolerance indicated a healthier heart actually endured pain longer than those told that high pain tolerance was indicative of poor heart health. Most noteworthy is that participants largely denied that the faulty information they had received concerning the correlation between pain tolerance and heart health had effected their subsequent behavior. Some participants even became more confident about the health of their hearts after enduring pain (Quattrone & Tversky, 1984). Those who tend to self-deceive are also found to have greater confidence in memory judgments, have greater illusion of control, and are even more likely to claim they are familiar with made-up products (Paulhus, 1988; Paulhus & Reid, 1991). Additionally, competitive swimmers who are better at self-deception are found to be faster and more successful swimmers than their peers who are less likely to self-deceive (Starek & Keating, 1991).

Interestingly, the majority of people believe that they are more intelligent (Paulhus & John, 1998), thinner (Taylor, Funk, & Craighill, 2006), and more popular (Zuckerman & Jost, 2001) than the average person (Balcetis, 2008). It is clearly a statistical improbability that the vast majority of individuals are "better than average" in any particular area, yet admitting the absurdity and illegitimacy of these common conclusions would necessitate that self-deceivers acknowledge their overly positive self-images (Balcetis, 2008). Psychologists have struggled for decades to completely understand how we are able to remain unaware that we change our behavior, or alter our perceptions such that the outcome is more desirable, while we know that in order to generate a desirable behavior or self-image we must somehow process and determine what a desirable behavior or self-image is (Fernbach, Hagmayer, & Sloman, 2014). Therefore, one would assume that this processing and illusion manufacturing must necessitate conscious awareness. Quattrone and Tversky (1984) describe the conundrum as follows, "people select actions to infer a [...] cause, then, to accept the inference as valid, they often render themselves unaware of their having selected the action just to infer the cause (p. 239)." Using the analogy of magic, when it comes to self-deception the individual is both the magician, tirelessly perfecting illusions, and guarding the secret behind each trick, as well as the audience member, completely blind to the slight-of-hand deception (Balcetis, 2008).

15.2.2 Why We Self-Deceive

Higgins' (1987) Self-Discrepancy Theory provides a framework within which we may better understand the motivations of self-deception. According to self-discrepancy theory, individuals will experience psychological distress when they perceive discrepancies between their ideal and actual selves and will thus be motivated to reduce this discrepancy as a means of lowering stress levels. The humanist Carl Rogers went as far as to claim that the ultimate need of all humans was to experience congruence between their ideal self and actual self, in what he called a process of "self-actualization" (Rogers, 1951, 1961). While one way to reduce discrepancies between the ideal and actual self is to change one's behavior such that the actual self more closely resembles the ideal self, another way one might reduce this perceived discrepancy is through a form of self-deception. Specifically, individuals may convince themselves that their actual and ideal selves are indeed not so different after all, thus reducing the perceived discrepancy and associated discomfort.

According to evolutionary biologist Robert Trivers, self-deception evolved as a means of helping humans to better deceive others (Trivers, 2011). Self-deception reduces the cognitive load of deceivers by making them less nervous about being discovered and guilt-ridden about their deception. Specifically, self-deceived liars are harder to detect as they are unaware that they are engaging in deception (Trivers, 2011). Self-deception can clearly be beneficial, but only up to a point. While deceiving oneself is found to increase self-confidence and make us appear more positively to others, too much self-deception can lead to overconfidence in combination with an underestimation of others' abilities leading to negative outcomes or failures (Trivers, 2011). Additionally, self-deception has been linked to elevated blood pressure and heart rates in men (Linden, Chambers, Maurice, & Lenz, 1993).

The most famous and extreme type of self-deceivers are narcissists. Narcissists have inflated grandiose self-concepts but are often thought to be consciously masking implicit self-loathing (Campbell, Bosson, Goheen, Lakey, & Kernis, 2007). Many believe that narcissists "deep down" have many insecurities and negative self-perceptions for which they are overcompensating. In other words, it has been argued that it is impossible for anyone to be truly unaware of a glaring self-truth, and thus narcissists, and non-narcissists for that matter, must be aware of their flaws despite their apparent blindness to it. This belief highlights a widespread misconception concerning self-deception. Specifically that we are really never truly blind to aspects of ourselves, rather we just consciously are choosing to ignore negative self-perceptions. However, extant research firmly contradicts the belief that we are consciously aware of our self-deception. For example, narcissists are found to have both highly positive implicit and explicit self-views, and thus appear to be just as self-deceived "deep down" as they seem on the surface (Campbell et al., 2007).

It should be noted that while narcissists likely are engaging in some form of self-deception, those who self-deceive are by no means necessarily narcissists, rather certain dimensions of the narcissism construct are reminiscent of certain aspects of self-deception. For instance, Panek, Nardis, and Konrath (2013) identify the superiority component of the narcissism construct as the state of feeling better than others, which is also indicative of a positively biased self-deceiver. The authors found that number of posts to certain SNSs, and the number of times individuals check SNS were both positively related to the superiority dimension of narcissism. Additionally, researchers have found that narcissism is positively related to the conscious importance individuals place on portraying a positive image through SNSs (Bergman, Fearrington, Davenport, & Bergman, 2011). These findings suggest that the fundamental belief that an individual is superior to others is impacting the way in which that individual uses SNSs (Panek et al., 2013).

15.2.3 Self-Deception and Selection

The role of self-deception in selection should not be underestimated. In fact, researchers were arguing more than 50 years ago that respondents' self-deception contributes more to lack of validity of self-report personality inventories than do other forms of deception or conscious lying (Anastasi, 1961; Meehl & Hathaway, 1946), yet we remain overly focused on intentional faking. Self-deception as well as intentional deception should be major concerns for those hoping to use social media to aid selection decisions. No area of our lives appears to be immune to the influence of self-deceptive presentation. There is no evidence to suggest that personal information discovered through SNS is any less distorted by motivated self-deception than more traditional presentations of personal information for selection purposes. Having access to an applicant's various SNSs is hardly a panacea for selection process ills. In fact, all evidence concerning what we know about conscious and unconscious personality distortions suggests that using SNSs to gain insights into the "authentic" nature of a candidate is just as problematic as any other traditional personality assessment.

Also worth noting, while self-deceptive behavior and thoughts are typically positively biased, they do not always have to be. For example, Farrow and colleagues (2014) argued that depressive, neurotic, or otherwise maladjusted individuals may instead experience negatively biased self-deception (Judge, Erez, & Thoresen, 2000). This further complicates the issue of controlling for self-deception as it appears as though individuals vary in the extent to which they self-deceive just as they vary on any other personality trait. Therefore, downwardly adjusting all evaluations gleaned from information identified on SNSs to account for the effect of self-deception may unfairly impact those users who engage in less self-deception or negative self-deception. In terms of understanding the role of self-deception within selection, it is important to note that self-deception is extremely difficult to detect. Unlike with impression management, individuals who engage in self-deception are not more likely to be detected on "lie" scales (e.g., Eysenck's lie scale, the MMPI lie scale) or other commonly used scales of overt impression management, making self-deception difficult to assess. Additionally, scores of self-deception are not significantly influenced by social demands while impression management activities are (Paulhus, 1984), thus manipulating the nature of external demands in an attempt to assess the extent of distortion is not an effective means of identifying self-deception. For example, the classic "evidence" for faking has been comparing incumbent self-reports to applicant self-reports with the assumption that because applicants are more motivated to lie and positively distort responses as they are competing for jobs, incumbent scores should be lower than applicant scores on various self-report assessments. However, because self-deception is a form of response distortion that is not conscious, and not impacted by external demands, incumbents are just as likely to engage in self-deception as applicants, thus comparing incumbent and applicant responses is an ineffective strategy in revealing and accounting for this type of distortion.

15.2.4 Self-Deception and SNS Usage

While on the surface looking into a job applicant's personal SNS profile may sound abundantly useful for uncovering the "true" personality of a candidate, this is hardly the case. One way that individuals are able to explore their ideal selves, or the person they want others to see them as, is through SNSs. SNSs are likely to be presentations of our ideal selves, thus when we interact with these social mediums our real and ideal selves intersect and the ideal self in many ways may feel actualized, perpetuating self-deception (Green, 2013). Personality and accomplishment distortions found within traditional assessments, interviews, or written application materials (e.g., resumes, cover letters) are likely just as prevalent within the SNS arena, and are very likely to be unintentionally distorted. As many users would likely attest following a perusal of social media postings from family members, classmates, and colleagues, SNS users as a whole tend to focus and broadcast successes and personal accomplishments from their lives, while posts of negative life events and failures may be less likely to be widely publicized. Indeed, extant research has found that SNS users are far more likely to display positively biased flattering images in general and disclose positive relative to negative emotional experiences on SNSs than they are in their "off-line" lives (Qiu, Lin, Leung, & Tov, 2012; Siibak, 2009). In fact, the extent of positively valenced information disclosed on some SNSs has actually lead users to perceive others on SNSs as happier and leading better lives than themselves (Chou & Edge, 2012). This may not be such a calculated form of deception and self-marketing as we so often think, but a deeply rooted positively biased series of misrepresentations which are honestly believed by the SNS user.

The online medium allows for more exaggerated distortions as the internet creates the perfect breeding ground for self-deceptive reflection. Additionally, self-deception may be even harder to detect on SNSs given the absence of cues and corroborating information often available in face-to-face interactions. Another reason for employers to be cautious when using SNSs to supplement the hiring process is the tendency for individuals to misrepresent themselves intentionally or knowingly, much like face-to-face communications. Candidates may, and likely will engage in impression management in an online environment which can have implications on the selection process.

15.2.5 Impression Management

Impression management is defined as the behaviors people engage in to create, manipulate, and maintain other's perceptions of themselves (Schneider, 1981) or more simply, "the process by which individuals attempt to control the impressions others form of them" (Leary & Kowalski, 1990). Impression management has also been referred to as self-presentation in the literature. Although some have argued that impression management is more than self-presentation because it can be managed by an outside party (i.e., a publicist) (Schneider, 1981), all references to impression management in this chapter refer to impressions managed by the self and, therefore synonymous with self-presentation (Rosenberg & Egbert, 2011).

Research has linked impression management to the employee selection process since the 1980s (Gardner & Martinko, 1988). Candidates use many impression management tactics to manipulate employers' perceptions of them including those covered in Chap. 11 of this book: honest self-promotion, deceptive self-promotion, honest other-focused impression management, deceptive other-focused impression management, and defensive impression management. Many of these impression management behaviors have been related to job interview success and performance on noncognitive selection measures such as personality inventories and biodata assessments (Baron, 1986; Gardner & Martinko, 1988; Schlenker, 1980), suggesting that impression management tactics can be effective.

While research on uses of impression management specifically by SNS users is slim, the literature on impression management in social and professional environments provides a strong foundation for expanding our knowledge and understanding of managing impression in an online environment. Recent research has investigated the uses of impression management tactics by SNS users and how these tactics affect the selection process, also leveraging the extensive impression management literature.

15.2.6 Use of Impression Management by SNS Users

For every SNS, a user creates a personal profile unique to him or her. As Sunden (2003) described it, a user can literally "type oneself into being" (p. 3). When creating a profile, SNS users have the opportunity to put their best foot forward, portraying themselves in a positive light, and many usually take advantage of this (Dunne, Lawlor, & Rowley, 2010). Users can actually live vicariously through their own SNS profiles which often depict idealized versions of themselves (Dunne et al., 2010). For example, Zhao, Grasmuck, and Martin (2008) found that Facebook users create highly socially desirable identities online that they aspire to project in real life, rather than present identities that reflect their "real" selves.

Users may choose to impression-manage on SNSs to a greater extent because of how public an environment it is. The publicity of one's behavior refers to the possible audience of that behavior, whether through firsthand observation or through a secondhand source (Leary, 1996). Individuals are more likely to engage in impression management when they perceive their image to be public (Schlenker & Weigold, 1992). Since the nature of an SNS is an online public forum, users should perceive their online behaviors as public and consequently, manage their impressions more carefully (Lampe, Ellison, & Steinfield, 2008; Rosenberg & Egbert, 2011).

Although it may seem easy to create an ideal self on an SNS, one must then maintain and manage the impression they set for their online audience (Zhao et al., 2008) as well as the relationships fostered with the members of that audience.

Research on SNS relationships has suggested that SNS users maintain certain relationships with the hope that these relationships may provide professional or social opportunities in the future (Ellison, Steinfield, & Lampe, 2007). SNS relationships can easily be maintained with occasional wall posts, requiring little effort but carrying potentially high payoff (Smock, Ellison, Lampe, & Wohn, 2011) 2011). In addition, research has found that we are more motivated to manage impressions for people we perceive as powerful, of high status, attractive, or likeable (Leary & Kowalski, 1990; Schlenker, 1980). Those who foresee a high likelihood of future interactions with powerful or higher status connections on SNSs are more likely to use impression management tactics as a user.

We as humans display our connections with others in various ways. Research suggests that strategies exist for determining and displaying one's online audience or "network." We decorate our offices and homes with photographs, cover our refrigerators in party invitations and announcements, we hold social gatherings to introduce strangers to one another, and name-drop well-known connections (Donath & Boyd, 2004). The reason behind displays of connections can vary from pride, love, friendship, and reputation to gaining social capital or getting ahead. On SNSs, displaying our connections is very easy, organized, and highly visible allowing consumers of SNSs to make inferences about users based on the data they present including political beliefs, taste in music, and social status by the connections they maintain (Boyd & Ellison, 2008; Donath & Boyd, 2004). Users can cater their SNS profiles to not only display connections that support their online image, but also to attract a certain type of SNS consumer, including potential employers.

In the modern world, it is not uncommon for relationships to begin and foster online. These connections can start over a common interest or information seeking. For example, someone who wants to be seen as a fitness expert on SNSs may hope to attract consumers looking for fitness advice, inspiration, or even training with the image they present. If that person is successful, the connections they have could easily lead to stronger or new connections through posts, comments, personal messaging, or other SNS tools (Lampe, Vitak, Gray, & Ellison, 2012).

15.2.7 Impression Management on SNSs and Selection Decisions

As with traditional selection procedures, impression management has implications for employers using SNSs to obtain information on candidates. As we mature, we learn to present ourselves differently based on who we perceive to be the audience (Marwick & Boyd, 2010). Whereas individuals applying for a job know their audience during the application process will be a potential employer, users of SNSs may not know who their audiences are.

Many popular SNSs collapse multiple audiences into a single audience, making it difficult to cater specific information to various groups (Marwick & Boyd, 2010). SNS users aware of this "context collapse" will often engage in self-censorship, assuming the consumer of their SNS data contains a variety of audience members including friends, family, clients, an employer, or a potential employer (Marwick & Boyd, 2010). With self-censorship, individuals consciously choose to display as much or as little information as personally deemed appropriated.

SNS users often self-censor to avoid negative consequences such as misinterpretation of SNS data that could arise from an employer hoping to obtain a fuller picture of who a candidate is. If a user does not censor what is demonstrated on his or her SNS profile, or if content made available online contradicts in some fashion the image the candidate has portrayed via other interactions with the employer, the recruiter, or hiring manager may form a negative impression of that candidate. For example, an employer may deem SNS content presented by a job candidate inappropriate or misaligned with company or personal values, and consequently, may choose to remove the candidate from further consideration regardless of job relevancy or performance on other job-related data available (Rosenberg & Egbert, 2011).

Employer misinterpretations of censorship can take many forms. An employer could assume the candidate is censoring their online content and make judgments accordingly. Alternatively, an employer may not pick up on the self-censorship and assume the candidate is a very professional person and therefore may be a good candidate. However, the employer could also assume the self-censored candidate is boring and uptight rather than professional. This example of how employers could interpret one act of impression management in various ways presents a potential problem. With no social cues that may allude to impression management in a face-to-face interaction, an employer's own conclusions and biases may interfere with their ability to fairly compare and consider candidates.

Individuals who do not want to self-censor or want to censor less of their UGC can manage their online presence by enacting strict privacy settings. It has been shown that SNS users believe they have a right to privacy with what they post online and take full advantage of the privacy settings provided by SNSs (Smith & Kitter, 2010). If a job candidate suspects potential employers may be looking them up online, they may choose to manage the impression they make by making their information difficult to access by those not connected to their SNS profiles.

The implications of privacy settings for employers who are looking to cyber-vet could be troublesome. Researchers and practitioners alike strongly advise against attempts to get around privacy settings (Smith & Kitter, 2010). As SNSs begin to provide more and more ways to show secondary connections to an SNS user, or connections two people have in common, it may be tempting for employers to reach out to those common connections for information on the candidate without the candidate's consent. Aside from the legal implications of invading someone's perceived privacy, it is unfair of employers to ask candidates' connections to do their dirty work for them.

Another complication for employers who are cyber-vetting job candidates with enabled privacy settings is the inconsistent amount of information they can gather about candidates. If three of five job applicants have no privacy settings while the other two applicants have strict privacy settings, an employer may not be able to fairly compare all five applicants based on the varying amount of information collected. Without policies in place to address these issues, employers may be walking a thin line between fair and unfair selection processes if any form of decision is made based on the information obtained from SNSs.

Employers may also walk the fine line of fairness when they take information posted on social media and SNSs at face value. Smith and Kitter (2010) suggest that employers try to verify information they gather from Social media and SNSs, particularly when the information gleaned may be potentially disqualifying. Making quick assumptions about something seen on an SNS could not only disqualify a worthy candidate, but it can also unfairly qualify a subpar candidate.

Job candidates can display socially desirable versions of themselves in a variety of ways. Additionally, SNS users may tailor their profiles to specific audiences to meet their personal, social, and professional needs. However, while many people may be misrepresenting themselves by managing their online impressions, not all SNS users impression manage online and these individuals, particularly younger individuals, may not understand the risks and subsequent ramifications of self-disclosure on SNSs (Smith & Kitter, 2010, p. 496). Someone may assume their profile is private and willingly share personal information on an SNS that they would not willingly disclose to an employer or potential employer (Smith & Kitter, 2010, p. 496). This decision to share personal information on SNSs may be substantially impacted by the user's age and online experience. For example, if you have two candidates, a millennial that grew up sharing their life on SNSs and a candidate from generation X who did not have internet access until college, their online presence is likely to be very different. The millennial may not be as cautious with what they post on SNSs or may manage an impression that is less than desirable by employer standards, while the generation Xer may be more likely to carefully manager their online image.

SNS users may also become victims of misrepresentations at the hands of others as it is easy for others to post unfavorable or inaccurate information about someone else online without consequence (Latham, Butzer, & Brown, 2008). In some cases, it could be a practical joke among friends while in other cases, individuals may not be aware of said information (Smith & Kitter, 2010). In both of these situations, a consumer, such as an employer looking up job candidates, could misconstrue the information presented and possibly make misattributions about said candidates.

In summary, since the information presented on SNSs is not necessarily accurate, job relevant, or clearly interpretable, we recommend employers be cautious when considering the use of SNS data in the hiring process, just as employers should be cautious when considering other more traditional selection tools. Job seekers may be more inclined to manage the impressions they present on SNSs, presenting information that is socially desirable as one would on a resume, biodata inventories, or self-report employment measures that may already be utilized in the selection process (Brown & Vaughn, 2011). Therefore, information gathered about a candidate from SNSs may not provide the kind of authentic picture hiring managers may hope for, and worse yet, gathering information in this way can open the door to a whole host of factors which may threaten the validity of the selection process

Research on using SNSs for selection purposes has not yet suggested how to detect or interpret impression management by SNS users, making the use of these practices for selection purposes potentially risky business. It may also be risky business due to the different forms of impression management used on social media and SNSs and the subsequent varying interpretations of candidate information made by consumers. However, for those who have already adopted this practice, it is critical they are aware that misrepresentations and distortions of information online are inevitable. In order to gain insights into the potential benefits and pitfalls of SNS screening in the selection process, we must consider the effects of both producer misrepresentations and consumer misattributions.

15.3 The Consumer: *Psychological Mechanisms Underlying Potential Misattributions*

Substantial bias literature has revealed that employers are known to engage in biased evaluations as consumers of SNS data. These biased evaluations appear to be even more harmful to a valid selection process and more vulnerable to legal action than misrepresentations expressed by the presenter of information. Social media allows for ease of access to work and non-work-related information about candidates in a way which was never possible before. While these insights potentially offer a great deal of promise for practitioners at low incurred monetary costs, they also expose the organization to larger opportunities for intentional or unintentional biases. When SNSs are being used for selection purposes, these biases could lead to discrimination that is more difficult to prevent, track, or defend (Brown & Vaughn, 2011).

15.3.1 Overview of Biases and Discrimination

Intergroup conflict, the source of explicit and implicit biases, occurs when people perceive themselves and others to be members of distinct groups (Fiske & Taylor, 2013). This occurs at both a conscious and subconscious level, leading to the development of numerous group identities, supported by theories in the social and cognitive psychology literatures, including: Social Identity Theory (Tajfel, 1981), Self-categorization Theory (Turner, 1985), and Optimal Distinctiveness Theory (Brewer, 1991), among others. In the United States, society and government have defined specific groups, prescribed to by most Americans, within the categories of race, ethnicity, gender, age, sexual orientation, and religion, with all people theoretically fitting into a specific group in each category. With the classification of these groups as societal norms, discrimination based on group membership is nearly inevitable.

As our daily lives are so intertwined with work, biases against specific groups and subsequent discrimination are also issues that arise in the workplace. Workplace discrimination has been extensively studied in the areas of race, ethnicity, and gender. These forms of discrimination have received significant attention from lawmakers, researchers, human resource managers, civil rights activists, and the public. This continued attention is justifiable, as researchers have supported that these forms of discrimination are evident in organizations (Budig, 2002; Schneider et al., 1997; Wittenbrink et al., 1997). Researchers are beginning to explore biases as antecedents to intolerance and discrimination against other less commonly studied target groups. Evidence also supports the notion that discriminatory practices exist in the present day based on age (e.g., Finkelstein & Burke, 1998; Perry & Finkelstein, 1999), sexual orientation (e.g., Clain & Leppel, 2001; Hebl, Foster, Mannix, & Dovidio, 2002), level of physical attractiveness (and/or unattractiveness) (e.g., Hosoda, Stone-Romero, & Coats, 2003; Stone, Stone, & Dipboye, 1992), and disability status (e.g., Ravaud, Madiot, & Ville, 1992; Vaughn, Thomas, & Doyle, 2011).

Social and cognitive psychology research has extensively focused on attitudes, stereotypes, and prejudices, all psychological constructs believed to be vulnerable to serving as antecedents to discriminatory practices. An attitude can be defined as "a psychological tendency that is expressed by evaluating a particular entity with some degree of favor or disfavor" (Eagly & Chaiken, 1993, p. 1). As defined by psychological research, attitudes typically involve some affective component. It is well established that an individual's attitude toward a target object or concept is a possible determinant of behavior toward that object or concept (Brehm, Kassin, & Fein, 2005; Kraus, 1995). Stereotypes are defined as generalized psychological representations of the characteristics shared by members of a particular group (McGarty, Yzerbyt, & Spears, 2002). Stereotypes pertain to inherent or learned beliefs about a certain group, while attitudes refer to the affective components or reactions to a group. Lastly, prejudice is most commonly defined within the academic literature as pertaining to hostile or negative attitude toward, or a negative evaluation of, a particular group (Greenwald & Pettigrew, 2014). Collectively, we refer to attitudes, stereotypes, and prejudices as biases moving forward.

15.3.2 Potential Gap in the Existing Workplace Discrimination Literature

Where we see a potential gap in the existing research is how discrimination relates to workplace decisions based on the use of SNSs in hiring and recruitment contexts. Social media and SNS use by organizations may be impacted by the biases previously discussed, resulting in intentional or unintentional discrimination.

Researchers have noted that under certain conditions, biases might strongly influence subsequent behavior (Antonak & Livneh, 1988). For example, in cases in which the holder of a given bias is presented with the opportunity to act with fewer normative constraints, the actor is more inclined toward behaving in a manor congruent with the attitude held (Fazio & Williams, 1986). In these weaker environmental conditions, more subjectivity and discretion is left to the individual. As an example within the area of human resources, highly structured interviews can mitigate the manifestation of discriminatory behaviors as little room is left for subjectivity in interpretation or discretion in judgment on the part of the interviewer (Heilman & Haynes, 2008). In contrast, when a consumer is presented with varying levels of information without strong environmental cues to direct appropriate use of said information, this unstructured environment may foster outcomes that are more heavily influenced by the consumer's personal attitudes and stereotypes (Greenwald & Pettigrew, 2014).

In thinking about a typical context in which a recruiter or hiring manager performs a search of candidates' SNS presence, this online environment presents a prime opportunity for a more subjective context, as these searches are often done informally, in private, and without any formal documentation, and often with few, if any, organizational policies in place to guide or direct practice.

Further, empirical research is just beginning to form around how SNSs are associated with potentially work-related constructs, such as the Big 5 personality characteristics (Măgurean, Vîrgă, & Sava, 2014). With such limited available research, it is perhaps even less likely that practitioners have data backed resources or guidelines available which they can use to make informed decisions based on best practices. In addition, although attitude, stereotype, and prejudice research has a long-standing history, measurement techniques have become increasingly complex theoretically (Antonak & Livneh, 2000), further challenging the forward progress of empirical research on the effect of using SNSs for hiring purposes.

Individuals' attitudes and the composite organizational and societal climate that these attitudes produce are barriers linked to discriminatory behavior (Antonak & Livneh, 1988; Colella & Stone, 2005). When considering these barriers, it is important to evaluate both explicit and implicit biases which may differentially impact consumer interpretations of SNS information.

15.3.3 Explicit Bias

Since the Civil Rights Act (CRA) of 1964, a societal revolution has taken place in the United States, with overt and explicit forms of discrimination steadily declining. We have also seen a significant decline in overt discrimination by employers due to the CRA and its Title VII mandate against selection procedures that result in disparate impact on, or disproportionally impacting members of, a protected class (race, color, religion, sex, or national origin). This important mandate means that it is imperative employers or organizations treat all people fairly, not providing any advantages to one group over another, protected group. However, it is well known that explicit biases still exist in today's society and in our workplaces.

The potential for explicit biases to negatively impact certain demographic groups was the initial reason for the implementation of the Uniform Guidelines on Employee Selection Procedures (Equal Employment Opportunity Commission, 1978), a set of guidelines focused on ensuring the fair treatment of certain protected demographic classes during the employment application process. As research has shown, both implicit and explicit biases can impact the hiring process, but the courts have been much harsher when discrimination is due to more blatantly explicit discrimination, originating from more overt stereotypes (Swim, Scott, Sechrist, Campbell, & Stangor, 2003).

15.3.4 Types of Explicit Bias and Their Implications for Selection

Explicit, or overt, biases against members of certain demographic groups can take many different forms. While not all explicit biases are hostile in nature, all do hold the potential to unfairly impact a job candidate.

In order for intergroup conflict, the source of explicit and implicit biases, to occur, people must perceive themselves and others as members of distinct groups (Fiske & Taylor, 2013). This occurs at both a conscious and subconscious level, leading to the development of numerous group identity theories in the social and cognitive psychology literatures, including: Social Identity Theory (Tajfel, 1981), Self-categorization Theory (Turner, 1985), and Optimal Distinctiveness Theory (Brewer, 1991), among others.

Once people have created their perceptions of group memberships, there are various ways in which group membership can lead to explicit biases against members of other groups. These explicit biases can be either more cognitively loaded stereotypes, or more emotionally loaded prejudice (Fiske & Taylor, 2013). While both types of explicit biases can drive discriminatory practices, the emotionally loaded prejudices have been found to drive discrimination more than cognitively loaded stereotypes (Dovidio, Brigham, Johnson, & Gaertner, 1996; Talaska, Fiske, & Chaiken, 2008, Tropp & Pettigrew, 2005).

Explicit stereotypes are cognitively loaded and can be extremely impactful in the hiring process. It is currently estimated that about 10 % of people hold extreme, blatant stereotypes (Fiske & Taylor, 2013). While 10 % of the population seems like a relatively low percentage, as Fiske and Taylor (2007) mention, this is an extremely impactful 10 %. These biases can become increasingly dangerous when they result from competition for scarce resources, such as jobs. Moreover, people typically believe others have stronger biases against out-groups than they themselves do, which can be especially troublesome for those who do hold blatant stereotypes against specific demographic groups. Affective prejudices, on the other hand, can potentially drive discrimination in hiring practices more because they are more immediate, often stronger, and can be less easily noticed by the person holding the affective bias.

Confirmation bias is one form of bias that can impact the ways a decision maker leverages SNSs during the selection process (Snyder & Swann, 1978). Confirmation bias is the tendency for people to search for information that confirms their preexisting beliefs. This type of bias becomes potentially detrimental if hiring managers hold negative preexisting beliefs regarding members of certain protected classes.

The kind of SNSs leveraged during the hiring process may have an impact on the extent to which confirmation bias plays a role. With the sheer amount of information available to consume on certain SNSs, such as Facebook, explicit biases have the potential to be much more impactful than they do on other SNSs, such as LinkedIn, that are strictly for professional networking. If an ill-meaning decision maker is using an SNS with a plethora of information presented, then it is a simple task to find information that would confirm negative stereotypes about a job applicant.

Confirmation bias can also benefit members of a decision maker's in-group. If a decision maker positively views a candidate based on demographic group membership, then it stands to reason the decision maker will seek out information to confirm positive biases he or she may hold regarding that job applicant. This shows the double-edged danger of explicit biases acting through confirmation bias to negatively impact certain demographic groups.

15.3.5 Implications of Explicit Biases on Cyber-Vetting

When leveraging SNSs in the hiring process, we must consider the more overt beliefs regarding races that SNS consumers may hold. Although explicit biases are likely to be less pervasive than implicit biases, they hold the power to be much more impactful. If even one decision maker within an organization holds explicit discriminatory beliefs regarding a specific group, then the potential ramifications could very easily lead to litigation against the organization for discriminatory hiring practices.

Although laws have been passed, procedures are in place, and court cases have been won in the effort to eliminate acted-upon bias in organizations, members of protected classes, including race, gender, and age, continue to be targets of explicit biases. When thinking of stereotypes and prejudice, race is generally the first defining characteristic that comes to mind. Indeed, racial prejudice has been studied by social psychologists since the 1920s (e.g., Allport, 1935; Thurstone, 1928). Numerous findings have stemmed from this research, and typically center around in-group versus out-group thinking that influences behaviors and actions. Racial biases have been a continual issue in employee selection and while holding strong, negative explicit biases based on race may be declining in modern times, the use of SNSs may offer a low-structure environment through which explicit racial biases can be engaged and acted upon to manifest in the form of intentional discrimination. However, it is important to note that many of the issues arising with race biases are due to less overt or intentional mechanisms as detailed later in this chapter, or as a result of disparate impact resulting from employment testing and procedures, rather than manifestations of strong, negative explicit biases.

In addition to racial biases, gender biases have a significant impact on hiring practices. Gender bias is thought to be an important antecedent in explaining males holding more positions of power in both business and government (Chen, Vanek,

Lund, & Heintz, 2005). Research has found that both cognitive and emotional explicit biases can result in gender discrimination when utilizing SNSs during the hiring process.

One discriminatory and enduring stereotype that continues to impact females in the workplace is the notion that they will have difficulty balancing work and family. It is still all too common for interviewers to ask the inappropriate, and illegal, question of whether or not a female candidate will be able to handle long hours if she has children. This is an example of something that could plague female job candidates if an employer uses SNSs, such as Facebook, to cyber-vet a female applicant and finds pictures indicating she has young children.

Other examples of the negative impact of explicit biases on gender discrimination during the hiring process stem from common stereotypes. For example, leadership is more congruous with stereotypically masculine behaviors and the male gender, than with stereotypically feminine behaviors and females. Moreover, leadership behaviors exhibited by males are viewed more favorably than those exhibited by females (Eagly & Karau, 2002). This could, for example, result in hiring managers, depending on the explicit gender biases they hold toward one gender, whom make gender-based assumptions about a candidate's skills and experiences outlined on SNSs like LinkedIn.

Age-related biases and discrimination in employment contexts led to the development of the Age Discrimination in Employment Act (ADEA; 1967). Age is an interesting demographic categorization in that the utilization of SNSs in the hiring process could potentially have a negative impact on both younger and older adults, depending on the context. Take, for example, a job opening for a leadership role. If two candidates are similarly qualified in terms of their resumes, but one looks a bit older in their SNS profile picture, and more mature in the eyes of the decision maker, then this could be a deciding factor that is non-job relevant in nature.

Conversely, meta-analyses have shown that older adults are often categorized through the lenses of a variety of negative stereotypes (Kite & Johnson, 1988). Interestingly, Cuddy and Fiske (2002) found that people often have feelings of condescension and compassion for older adults. Indeed, other researchers have found older adults to be perceived as socially, cognitively, and physically incompetent (Nelson, 2002).

All of these potential biases against different age groups become significantly confounded when considered in light of research showing that different age groups use SNSs differently. Information posted by older and younger job applicants is likely to be different, leading to more freedom of interpretation by the SNS consumer.

In addition to classes protected under federal employment laws, explicit biases present in selection procedures also affect unprotected classes such as sexual orientation. Currently, there is no national equal employment law regarding the treatment of job applicants based on sexual orientation, though individual states have begun implementing equal employment acts pertaining specifically to sexual orientation. These state laws regarding discrimination based on sexual orientation may impact selection practices which rely on SNS screenings in several ways. Numerous SNSs allow users to join virtual groups which identify its members based on sexual orientation

Additionally, some SNSs allow users to publically post their sexual orientation in the form of declaring the gender to which they are attracted. An SNS user's sexual orientation can be discovered in numerous other ways as well, such as in personal posts and pictures. The selection decisions of a hiring manager biased against individuals with a particular sexual orientation may easily be influenced should that hiring manager see a candidate's group membership or profile information identifying that candidate's sexual orientation. While it is conceivable that a biased hiring manager could learn the sexual orientation of a candidate screened using more traditional methods, we believe that the use of SNSs to screen applicants makes this event much more likely to occur. Although in many states this is not technically an illegal criterion to use in removing a candidate from consideration in the hiring process, it is an important area of consideration when discussing potential explicit biases that can unfairly disadvantage job candidates with different sexual orientations.

While the Uniform Guidelines long predate the development of SNSs and their subsequent usage in making hiring decisions, they can still lend guidance to practitioners regarding potentially troublesome issues in utilizing SNSs in selection decisions. Explicit biases regarding specific demographic groups still exist today, and the proliferation of potential information regarding a job candidate's membership in a variety of demographic groups should give pause to practitioners considering leveraging SNSs to cyber-vet candidates for employment.

While common explicit biases pertaining to specific demographic classes are discussed in this chapter, an exhaustive discussion of the legal ramifications of utilizing SNSs in selection is beyond the scope of our discussion. For a more in-depth understanding of the potential legal issues surrounding the utilization of SNSs in selection decisions, please see Chap. 14.

15.3.6 Implicit Bias

Title VII under the CRA of 1964 helped drastically decrease overt and hostile discriminatory practices toward members of protected classes. Although explicit biases are much less common today, individuals still make harmful implicit associations. Implicit biases and implicit associations refer to associations or evaluations that one makes without having knowledge of making them. Research in this area suggests that many people may engage in some form of discrimination due to held implicit associations without necessarily having the intent or awareness of doing so (Greenwald, Banaji, & Nosek, 2015; Greenwald, Poehlman, Uhlmann, & Banaji, 2009). Over the course of the past two decades, the study of implicit bias measurement has increased substantially (Antonak & Livneh, 2000; Greenwald et al., 2015; Greenwald, McGhee, & Schwartz, 1998; Greenwald, Nosek, & Banaji, 2003; Nosek & Banaji, 2001).

Implicit bias research draws heavily from literature on social and cognitive memory, and many of the most commonly used measures of implicit bias involve individuals making rapid classifications of stimuli representing two contrasted categories (Greenwald & Pettigrew, 2014). Greenwald and his colleagues (e.g., Greenwald et al., 1998, 2003; Greenwald & Banaji, 1995) provided much of the framework for the most commonly adopted measure of implicit associations (Fazio & Olson, 2003), the implicit association test (IAT) (Greenwald et al., 1998). Greenwald and Banaji (1995) described implicit measures as concerned with measuring the more automatic, and sometimes unconscious, associations that individuals hold. In their review of implicit measures, Fazio and Olson (2003) suggest that implicit measures "provide estimates of individuals' attitudes without our having to directly ask them for such information (p. 303)."

The IAT is a latency-based measure which operates on the premise that it will be cognitively less difficult for an individual to match two congruent ideas compared to two incongruent ideas. Introspective access to the associations is believed to be prevented by having participants respond to the task in as timely a fashion as possible while still eliciting the correct responses. Thus, the techniques "automatic evaluation" component is derived from the prevention of introspective access to the association strength being measured. Since the measure's introduction (Greenwald et al., 1998), the IAT has been used to classify various forms of implicit cognitions beyond implicit attitudes such as self-esteem, stereotypes, political views, and consumer preferences (Greenwald et al., 2009; Hofmann, Gawronski, Gschwendner, Le, & Schmitt, 2005). The ability to adapt the IAT for a variety of target groups is due to the flexibility of its methodology.

Researchers refer to implicit bias scores from measures such as the IAT to be relative scores of favorability toward one group in comparison to the other (e.g., Greenwald & Pettigrew, 2014). Further, it is believed that these more automatic and unconscious implicit cognitions feed into the higher levels of consciously controlled and mediated explicit cognitions.

More recently, researchers have turned attention to discriminatory behaviors as a result of favoritism toward the in-group, rather than necessitating hostility toward an out-group (Greenwald & Pettigrew, 2014). While not a completely new idea, attitude and stereotype researchers have increased attention to the impact of in-group favoritism as an important predecessor of discriminatory practices, much like out-group hostility (Greenwald & Pettigrew, 2014). Thus, discrimination may not only result from intentional hostility or malice toward a member of an out-group, but may also result from differential favoring and support for members of one's own group.

15.3.7 How Implicit Bias Can Affect SNS Consumers

The process of receiving and reacting to visual context in making judgements and evaluations about a prospective candidate based on demographic features is more easily enabled and happens much sooner via information presented on many SNSs compared to more traditional staffing procedures (e.g., determining who to invite for a first round interview on the basis of a traditional resume). Implicit processes based on demographic context (disability status, religious affiliation, age, sexual orientation, community groups, etc.) have been shown to impact conscious judgments about a person and can be powerful as the basis for more deliberate or intentional judgment and action.

As an example, two separately conducted meta-analyses on Black-White racial attitudes and stereotypes have found evidence of predictive validity correlations and racially discriminatory behavior (Greenwald et al., 2009; Oswald, Mitchell, Blanton, Jaccard, & Tetlock, 2013). While the effects found in these studies by Greenwald et al. (2009) and Oswald et al. (2013) were modest ($r=.236$ and $r=.117$, respectively), Greenwald et al. (2015) have argued that the magnitude of the relationships found in these sets of studies are societally impactful due to both the pure volume of individuals affected at one time, and the fact that these biases can repeatedly affect one individual over time.

Making matters more difficult, individuals with implicit biases that result in intergroup favoritism often do not believe their actions are discriminatory, as in-group favoritism is often perceived to be legitimate, normative, and procedurally fair (Greenwald & Pettigrew, 2014). These shifts in focus toward examining the impact of in-group favoritism are not only being acknowledged within the halls of the ivory towers, but many popular press outlets have also highlighted this phenomenon in organizational settings. For example, *Forbes* featured an article highlighting empirical research which suggested hiring managers at professional firms (lawyers, investment bankers, and consultants) would weight factors such as a candidate's perceived similarity to them in relation to experiences, leisure pursuits, and self-presentation styles over other qualifications such as evidence of productivity potential (Adams, 2012). This finding is in line with much of the historical research conducted in the area of similarity increasing or enhancing liking (Byrne, 1961; Byrne, Ervin, & Lamberth, 1970). Byrne and colleagues established and demonstrated that the similarity-attraction principle is robust, and can apply to various types of similarities including attitudes, personality traits, behaviors, beliefs, and values (Byrne, 1961; Byrne et al., 1970). As this applies to an SNS context, the similarity-attraction principle has been presented as an explanation for findings in workplace contexts where evaluations were found to be more favorable when the evaluator (e.g., hiring manager) and the evaluatee (e.g., candidate) are of the same race and gender (e.g., Riordan, 2000).

Researchers suggest that it is difficult to prevent unintended discrimination due to implicit biases or associations, but there are some things that one can do to lessen the impact of implicit bias in the context of SNS usage (Devine, Forscher, Austin, & Cox, 2012). As an example, Devine et al. (2012) demonstrated in a longitudinal study of Black-White implicit race bias, that biases could be dramatically reduced in a sample of non-Black participants via the use of a habit-breaking intervention which included both education and training components. Within a 45-min training session, participants in Devine et al.'s (2012) intervention group were first informed about the pervasiveness and impact of biases, and then viewed five common strategies, culled from the literature, that could be used in everyday situations to counteract the implicit biases formed. These authors found that those participating in the training intervention group reduced their levels of implicit bias in the Black-White race IAT in comparison to the control group. In addition, those participants receiving the intervention showed a sustained change in implicit bias over a period of 2 months.

Further, as the development and use of the structured interview process has enhanced the validity of the traditional interview process, and as rater training has been shown to reduce bias in the performance appraisal process, one recommendation posited herein for those using SNSs in selection and staffing functions would be to study, identify, and train end users on the elements of SNS content that have been found to be of most value in predicting future job success (i.e., focus attention toward the job-relevant information). This training would be based on applied research which links certain types of SNS content to subsequent job success in various roles. This recommendation is predicated on continued advancement of applied research in this area, expanding our knowledge of the most effective information gleaned from SNS in the prediction of job success. As an example, Back et al. (2010) evidenced convergence between actual personality and ratings of personality provided by consumers of users' SNS profiles on four of the Big 5 dimensions of personality (no relationship was found with emotional stability). The magnitude of the aggregated independent ratings were moderate, with extraversion and openness being most strongly predicted (Back et al., 2010).

In addition to identifying and sharing training and implementing policies that coach hiring managers and recruiters on the types of information that should be attended to when reviewing SNS profiles, awareness, and diversity training covering implicit associations, such as that conducted in the intervention used in Devine et al.'s (2012) research described earlier, may be beneficial. The manifestation of commonly held automatic associations into conscious discriminatory behaviors or actions may be decreased for hiring managers and recruiters with increased awareness of their presence, and conscious efforts and strategies to deploy to reduce their impact on decision-making. Various demonstrations related to the impact of implicit associations are available online, including the ability to take different versions of IATs for free, and many other valuable resources available at the *Project Implicit* website (https://implicit.harvard.edu/implicit/).

15.4 The Producer and Consumer: How Biases Can Simultaneously Affect Both and Potential Solutions for Decreasing Bias

As with more traditional application process materials, certain applicant information available through SNSs may allude to applicants' membership to specific groups (Smith & Kitter, 2010). For example, a hiring manager may look at the name Thomas on a resume and can safely assume the candidate is male. However, if the name on the resume was something more gender neutral like Taylor, the hiring manager would likely not be able to determine the gender of the candidate. If that same hiring manager were to look Taylor up on social media or an SNS, there would likely be several more obvious clues pointing to the gender of Taylor, such as pictures, family posts, or even the gender label itself.

The following lists provide a visual for the additional information employers or organizations may be able to glean from a candidate's SNS profiles during the screening process, above that provided in application materials prior to face-to-face contact.

- Information Available in Traditional Screening Methods:
  - Name
  - Pronouns used in resumes, cover letters, and letters of recommendation
  - Activities list
  - Scholarships
  - Year of graduation/degree earned
  - Years of experience
  - Work history
- Additional Available Information on Social Media/SNSs:
  - Pictures
  - Birthdate
  - Family/children
  - Membership to specific groups
  - Relationship status
  - Sexual Orientation
  - Group-related posts

We believe there is greater potential for individual biases to impact the selection process when hiring managers have access to candidates' more personal information on SNSs. Among the information readily available to hiring managers on SNSs are group-related posts, pictures, and comments that may lead to assumptions about group membership, support of a particular group, or provoke personal biases. SNS users often demonstrate their support for social, economic, political, or environmental causes by adopting common publically displayed symbols on their SNS profiles. For example, in June of 2015, following the US Supreme Court's ruling in *Obergefell v. Hodges,* that state-level bans on same-sex marriage were unconstitutional, over one million Facebook users applied a rainbow-colored filter to their individual profile pictures as a show of support. This visible show of support could have negative ramifications for job applicants if hiring managers with particular sexual orientation biases access applicants' SNS information.

Also in 2015, the #HeForShe campaign was launched, aiming to inspire men to become advocates for ending the inequalities females face throughout the world. This campaign sparked heated discussions on social media about gender equality, feminism, and male superiority globally. If a social media or SNS user partook in these public discussions or used the hashtag for the campaign, #HeForShe, they may have been subject to gender or other biases of employers examining their online presence.

It is important to note that the biases outlined above can have both positive and negative effects on a candidate's employment opportunities. For example, a hiring manager could view a rainbow-filtered profile picture positively, as a show of openness and support for equality of all humans, or a hiring manager could view the filter negatively, as supporting a decision that tarnishes the sanctity of marriage, two of the very common arguments surrounding the Supreme Court's ruling in 2015.

With one simple, seemingly harmless act of support, an individual could be helping or hurting their employment chances. A simple conclusion for job applicants fearful of exposing themselves to selection bias through SNSs may be to remove all online profiles while on the job market. However, not having an online presence at all may be riskier than having a less than pristine digital dossier. A 2015 Harris Poll reported that 35 % of US employers said they were less likely to consider a job candidate who does not have a "digital footprint" (CareerBuilder, 2015). Depending on the type of job one is applying for, participation in SNSs may be seen as desirable, showing a candidate is familiar with and proficient in differing and new types of media (Mattioli, 2007; Smith & Kitter, 2010).

In addition, the consumer of the SNS information is exposed to more opportunities for biases to influence their selection decisions, particularly early on in the process. For these reasons, the methods in which key decision makers leverage SNS data during the hiring process should be carefully considered. Fortunately, organizations do have options for reducing the potential risks associated with leveraging SNS data for selection purposes.

Organizations should set formal guidelines concerning how SNSs should be leveraged in the hiring process. Formal guidelines regarding which sites to use and what information to consider should help standardize the practice of cyber-vetting across organizational decision makers, and reduce the potential impact of decision makers who hold negative beliefs regarding one demographic group or another.

In addition to creating a formalized set of guidelines for social media or SNS use, a formal training for all key decision makers on the potential biases they hold and the consequences of these biases could be an important avenue for organizations to consider. Indeed, formal trainings have been shown to reduce explicit (Kawakami, Dovidio, Moll, Hermsen, & Russin, 2000) and implicit (Devine et al., 2012) biases held against specific demographic groups. The downside being that, to date, the training for reducing explicit biases against one demographic group have not been found to generalize to other demographic groups. This could result in the need for a variety of formal bias reduction trainings, but it is definitely better than the alternative of choosing not to deal with potential biases held by decision makers that could result in discriminatory hiring practices when utilizing SNSs in the hiring process. As an added bonus, trainings such as these will likely have positive implications across other areas of decision-making during the hiring process, including resume screening and interviews.

Organizations may also reduce the risks associated with leveraging SNS data for selection purposes by putting significant effort into detecting, and subsequently removing, individuals with discriminatory beliefs regarding any protected classes from decision-making processes. This action is not always as easy as it sounds. As described above, the number of individuals who carry and share blatant stereotypes is decreasing rapidly, which has led to the need to understand the potential impact of implicit biases.

In addressing the need to reduce more resistant and automatic implicit associations, a number of promising factors are available for consideration. For instance, Devine et al. (2012) evidenced that when presented with training about implicit biases, and strategies for counteracting biases, the participants that reported being more concerned about possible discrimination and those that expressed exerting more effort in implementing the strategies trained showed the largest reductions in implicit biases toward Blacks relative to Whites. Thus, identifying and training conscientious human resource professionals concerned about potential biases they may hold and how to improve those biases may be step one in mitigating the increased risks and exposure brought about by utilizing SNSs for recruiting and hiring purposes.

In addition, Devine et al. (2012) elaborated on five research-backed strategies which were influential in conjuring sustained lower levels of implicit bias in participants. A brief description of each of these strategies follows. Stereotype replacement (Monteith, 1993) involves recognizing and labeling a stereotyped response, reflecting on why it occurred, and considering how it could be avoided in the future by replacing a response with a non-stereotyped response. Counter-stereotypic imaging (Blair, Ma, & Lenton, 2001) entails imagining in detail counter-stereotypic others to have positive exemplars readily accessible when faced with an opportunity to challenge a stereotype's validity. Individuation (Brewer, 1988; Fiske & Neuberg, 2000) involves learning specific information about stereotyped group members so as to evaluate members of the out-group upon personal, rather than group-based, attributes. Perspective taking (Galinsky & Moskowitz, 2000) uses the strategy of taking the first person perspective of a member of a stereotyped group to experience enhanced psychological closeness with the stigmatized group. Lastly, increasing opportunities for contact (Pettigrew, 1998; Pettigrew & Tropp, 2006) is a strategy which encourages increased seeking out of opportunities to encounter and engage in positive interactions with members of the target group which can lead to a variety of positive effects such as enhanced evaluations of the group and altering the cognitive representations of that group.

15.4.1 Addressing Biases in the Twenty-First Century

As the evolution and use of SNSs continues, particularly in the area of selection, we do not advocate for burying our head in the sand and being left behind. The use of such resources by both producers and consumers will likely continue, with or without the involvement of industrial–organizational psychology researchers and practitioners. We see a need for applied research to contribute to the development of interventions aimed at reducing the impact of certain attitudes, stereotypes, and other biases in the use of SNSs for selection purposes. While ease of access to SNSs present a weak environment in which information is obtainable from anywhere a connection to the internet is possible (including the comfort and privacy of one's own home or office), focused efforts by researchers and practitioners may lessen these concerns, and enhance the utility of reviewing SNS data. Such research and practice could culminate in training seminars about how to avoid common biases. Awareness about the usage of SNSs, and the exposure that this usage provides to recruiters and hiring managers may also serve as a catalyst for adopting or increasing organizational diversity and awareness training. As supported by the strategy of increasing opportunities for contact discussed above, research has indicated that increased exposure to protected class groups can result in advancements toward reducing the negative attitudes and stereotypes held by the trainee.

As an example, Fichten, Schipper, and Cutler (2005) found that working with children with disabilities diminished social distance from persons with disabilities and improved certain attitudes, thoughts, and feelings. We believe this area is prime for innovative research that examines the interplay of attitudes and stereotypes in staffing and selection decisions, including those in which SNSs are utilized early in the hiring process.

Advancements might also include continued development and dissemination of knowledge through peer-reviewed and popular publications about how to recognize and focus on the types of SNS information that is likely to be most relevant to whether the candidate is likely to be successful in the job, and what types of work-relevant information is predicted by SNS data. Practical advancements could also include instruction on what practices have been shown to be most effective in gathering, documenting, and making evaluations about information available on SNSs.

15.5 Conclusion

SNSs are the wild west of the selection frontier. It is hard to determine *how* employers are actually using SNSs to research or screen candidates, or the extent to which online profiles are accurate representations of the applicants portrayed in them, and how conscious and unconscious impression management tactics on the part of applicants may be interacting with employer biases to impact assessments of SNSs. In light of these concerns, we see the need for *considerable* research to explore these and the myriad of other factors at play within the domain of SNS usage in selection contexts. Reminiscent of when Sherman and Freas (2004) wrote about the "largely unexplored, and fraught with risk, yet immensely promising" chaotic landscape of executive coaching for the Harvard Business Journal in 2004, the world of SNSs in selection is certainly the field's new frontier.

While other chapters contained in this collection discuss, in detail, the legal risks and ramifications of SNSs' use in selection and staffing decisions, this chapter reviewed some of the known psychological mechanisms that have a high likelihood to influence usage and interpretation of SNS data, but that to date have not received much empirical examination. The studies cited herein largely drew upon existing social psychology research. The authors encourage researchers to continue to find new and innovative ways to examine the influence that these known factors might have on behaviors, beliefs, and outcomes, on the part of either the presenter or the consumer of SNS information. Survey data suggests that usage of SNSs on the part of candidates and consumers is likely to continue to grow and expand in practice. Thus, researchers are also encouraged to develop and refine state-of-the-art methods and procedures for using information readily available from SNSs to increase or enhance the efficacy and fairness of this practice.

Provided the quick adoption of SNSs, it may be unrealistic to expect that organizations will be able to completely eliminate or heavily restrict individual recruiters and hiring managers' access to SNSs for the purpose of evaluating or learning more about potential candidates. It is unclear whether this would be best practice, as there may be valid and useful data available via these means of data gathering. However, practitioners are encouraged to continue to seek out, study, and adopt data-driven developments in this area to inform their own policies, training, interventions, and so forth. By doing so, practitioners can mitigate the risks associated with having consumers or end-users misinterpret, overestimate, or otherwise improperly utilize information made available from candidates via SNSs. In conclusion, with the relative absence of legal and professional standards to govern SNSs' use, employers are encouraged to proceed with the utmost caution in establishing policies and procedures for using SNSs to recruit and evaluate candidates, just as they should if considering using any other selection tool lacking legal or professional standards.

References

Adams, S. (2012, December 3). Employers hire potential drinking buddies ahead of top candidates. *Forbes*. Retrieved March 1, 2015, from http://www.forbes.com/sites/susanadams/2012/12/03/employers-hire-potential drinking-buddies-ahead-of-top-candidates.

Age Discrimination in Employment Act of 1967. (1967). Pub. L. No. 90-202, 81 Stat. 602, Dec. 15.

Allport, G. W. (1935). Attitudes. In C. Murchison (Ed.), *Handbook of social psychology* (Vol. 2, pp. 798–844). Worchester, MA: Clark University Press.

Anastasi, A. (1961). *Psychological testing*. New York: Macmillan.

Antonak, R. F., & Livneh, H. (1988). *The measurement of attitudes toward people with disabilities: Methods, psychometrics and scales*. Springfield, IL: Charles C. Thomas.

Antonak, R. F., & Livneh, H. (2000). Measurement of attitudes towards persons with disabilities. *Disability and Rehabilitation, 22*, 211–224.

Back, M. D., Stopfer, J. M., Vazire, S., Gaddis, S., Schmukle, S. C., Egloff, B., et al. (2010). Facebook profiles reflect actual personality, not self-idealization. *Psychological Science, 21*(3), 372–374.

Balcetis, E. (2008). Where the motivation resides and self-deception hides: How motivated cognition accomplishes self-deception. *Social and Personality Psychology Compass, 2*(1), 361–381.

Baron, R. A. (1986). Self-Presentation in job interviews: When there can be "too much of a good thing". *Journal of Applied Social Psychology, 16*(1), 16–28.

Barrick, M. R., & Mount, M. K. (1996). Effects of impression management and self-deception on the predictive validity of personality constructs. *Journal of Applied Psychology, 81*(3), 261–272.

Bergman, S. M., Fearrington, M. E., Davenport, S. W., & Bergman, J. Z. (2011). Millennials narcissism, and social networking: What narcissists do on social networking sites and why. *Personality and Individual Differences, 50*, 706–711.

Blair, I. V., Ma, J. E., & Lenton, A. P. (2001). Imagining stereotypes away: The moderation of implicit stereotypes through mental imagery. *Journal of Personality and Social Psychology, 81*, 828–841.

Boyd, D.M., & Ellison, N.B. (2008). Social network sites: Definition, history, and scholarship. *Journal of Computer-Mediated Communication, 13*(1), 210–230.

Brehm, S. S., Kassin, S., & Fein, S. (2005). *Social psychology* (6th ed.). Boston: Houghton Mifflin Company.

Brewer, M. B. (1988). A dual process model of impression formation. In R.S. Wyer & T.K. Srull (Eds.), *Advances in social cognition* (Vol. 1, pp. 1–36). Hillsdale, NJ: Lawrence Erlbaum Associates, Inc..

Brewer, M. B. (1991). The social self: On being the same and different at the same time. *Personality and Social Psychology Bulletin, 17*(5), 475–482.

Brown, V. R., & Vaughn, E. D. (2011). The writing on the (Facebook) wall: The use of social networking sites in hiring decisions. *Journal of Business and Psychology, 26*(2), 219–225.

Budig, M. J. (2002). Male advantage and the gender composition of jobs: Who rides the glass escalator. *Social Problems, 49*, 258–277.

Byrne, D. (1961). Interpersonal attraction and attitude similarity. *The Journal of Abnormal and Social Psychology, 62*, 713–715.

Byrne, D., Ervin, C. R., & Lamberth, J. (1970). Continuity between the experimental study of attraction and real-life computer dating. *Journal of Personality and Social Psychology, 16*, 157–165.

Campbell, W. K., Bosson, J. K., Goheen, T. W., Lakey, C. E., & Kernis, M. H. (2007). Do narcissists dislike themselves "deep down inside"? *Psychological Science, 18*(3), 227–229.

CareerBuilder. (2015). *Number of employers passing on applicants due to social media posts continues to rise, according to new CareerBuilder survey*. Retrieved May 25, 2015, from http://www.careerbuilder.com/share/aboutus/pressreleasesdetail.aspx?sd=6%2F26%2F2014&id=pr829&ed=12%2F31%2F2014.

Chen, M., Vanek, J., Lund, F., & Heintz, J. (2005). *Progress of the world's women 2005: Women, work and poverty*. United Nations Development Fund for Women. Retrieved March 14, 2007, from http://www.unifem.org/attachments/products/PoWW2005_eng.pd.

Chou, H., & Edge, N. (2012). "They are happier and having better lives than I am": The impact of using Facebook on perceptions of others' lives. *Cyberpsychology, Behavior, and Social Networking, 15*(2), 117–121.

Clain, S. H., & Leppel, K. (2001). An investigation into sexual orientation discrimination as an explanation for wage differences. *Applied Economics, 33*, 37–47.

Colella, A., & Stone, D. L. (2005). Workplace discrimination toward persons with disabilities: A call for some new research directions. In R. L. Dipboye & A. Colella (Eds.), *Discrimination at work: The psychological and organizational bases* (pp. 227–253). New Jersey: Lawrence Erlbaum Associates.

Cuddy, A. J. C., & Fiske, S. T. (2002). Doddering but dear: Process, content, and function in stereotyping of older persons. In T. D. Nelson (Ed.), *Ageism: Stereotyping and prejudice against older persons* (pp. 3–26). Cambridge: The MIT Press.

Devine, P. G., Forscher, P. S., Austin, A. J., & Cox, W. T. L. (2012). Long-term reduction in implicit race bias: A prejudice habit-breaking intervention. *Journal of Experimental Social Psychology, 48*(6), 1267–1278.

Donath, J., & Boyd, D. (2004). Public displays of connection. *BT Technology Journal, 22*(4), 71-82.

Dovidio, J. F., Brigham, J. C., Johnson, B. T., & Gaertner, S. L. (1996). Stereotyping, prejudice, and discrimination: Another look. *Stereotypes and Stereotyping, 276*, 319.

Duggan, M., Ellison, N. B., Lampe, C., Lenhart, A., & Madden, M. (2015). Social media update 2014. *Pew Research Center*. Retrieved February 12, 2015, from http://www.pewinternet.org/2015/01/09/social-media-update-2014/.

Dunne, Á., Lawlor, M. A., & Rowley, J. (2010). Young people's use of online social networking sites A uses and gratifications perspective. *Journal of Research in Interactive Marketing, 4*(2), 46–58.

Eagly, A. H., & Chaiken, S. (1993). *The psychology of attitudes*. Fort Worth: Harcourt, Brace, Jovanovich.

Eagly, A. H., & Karau, S. J. (2002). Role congruity theory of prejudice toward female leaders. *Psychological Review, 109*(3), 573–598.

Ellison, N. B. (2007). Social network sites: Definition, history, and scholarship. *Journal of Computer-Mediated Communication, 13*(1), 210–230.

Ellison, N. B., Steinfield, C., & Lampe, C. (2007). The benefits of Facebook "friends:" Social capital and college students' use of online social network sites. *Journal of Computer-Mediated Communication, 12*(4), 1143–1168.

Equal Employment Opportunity Commission C. S. C., Department of Labor, & Department of Justice. (1978). Uniform guidelines on employee selection procedures. *Federal Register, 43*(166), 38295–38309.

Farrow, T. F. D., Burgess, J., Wilkinson, I. D., & Hunter, M. D. (2014). Neural correlates of self-deception and impression-management. *Neuropsychologia, 67*, 159–174.

Fazio, R. H., & Olson, M. A. (2003). Implicit measures in social cognition research: Their meaning and use. *Annual Review of Psychology, 54*, 297–327.

Fazio, R. H., & Williams, C. J. (1986). Attitude accessibility as a moderator of the attitude–perception and attitude–behavior relations: An investigation of the 1984 presidential election. *Journal of Personality and Social Psychology, 51*(3), 505.

Fernbach, P. M., Hagmayer, Y., & Sloman, S. A. (2014). Effort denial in self-deception. *Organizational Behavior and Human Decision Processes, 123*(1), 1–8.

Fichten, C. S., Schipper, F., & Cutler, N. (2005). Does volunteering with children affect attitudes toward adults with disabilities? A prospective study of unequal contact. *Rehabilitation Psychology, 50*(2), 164.

Finkelstein, L. M., & Burke, M. J. (1998). Age stereotyping at work: The role of rater and contextual factors on evaluations of job applicants. *The Journal of General Psychology, 125*(4), 317–345.

Fiske, S. T., & Taylor, S. E. (2013). *Social cognition: From brains to culture*. London: Sage.

Galinsky, A. D., & Moskowitz, G. B. (2000). Perspective-taking: Decreasing stereotype expression stereotype accessibility, and in-group favoritism. *Journal of Personality and Social Psychology, 78*, 708–724.

Gardner, W. L., & Martinko, M. J. (1988). Impression management in organizations. *Journal of Management, 14*(2), 321–338.

Gilbert, D. T., Pinel, E. C., Wilson, T., Blumberg, S. J., & Wheatley, T. P. (1998). Immune neglect: A source of durability bias in affective forecasting. *Journal of Personality and Social Psychology, 75*, 617–638.

Goleman, D. (1985). *Vital lies, simple truths: The psychology of self-deception*. New York: Touchstone.

Green, R. K. (2013, August 7). The social media effect: Are you really who you portray online? *Huffington Post*. Retrieved March 1, 2015, from http://www.huffingtonpost.com/r-kay-green/the-social-media-effect-a_b_3721029.html.

Greenwald, A. G., & Banaji, M. R. (1995). Implicit social cognition: Attitudes self-esteem, and stereotypes. *Psychological Review, 102*, 4–27.

Greenwald, A. G., Banaji, M. R., & Nosek, B. A. (2015). Statistically small effects of the Implicit Association Test can have societally large effects. *Journal of Personality and Social Psychology, 108*(4), 553–561.

Greenwald, A. G., McGhee, D. E., & Schwartz, J. L. K. (1998). Measuring individual differences in implicit cognition: The implicit association test. *Journal of Personality and Social Psychology, 74*, 1464–1480.

Greenwald, A. G., Nosek, B. A., & Banaji, M. R. (2003). Understanding and using the implicit association test: I. An improved scoring algorithm. *Journal of Personality and Social Psychology, 85*, 197–216.

Greenwald, A. G., & Pettigrew, T. F. (2014). With malice toward none and charity for some: In-group favoritism enables discrimination. *American Psychologist, 69*, 669–684.

Greenwald, A. G., Poehlman, T. A., Uhlmann, E. L., & Banaji, M. R. (2009). Understanding and using the Implicit Association Test: III. Meta-analysis of predictive validity. *Journal of Personality and Social Psychology, 97*, 17–41.

Gur, R. C., & Sackeim, H. A. (1979). Self-deception: A concept in search of a phenomenon. *Journal of Personality and Social Psychology, 37*(2), 147–169.

Hebl, M. R., Foster, J. B., Mannix, L. M., & Dovidio, J. F. (2002). Formal and interpersonal discrimination: A field study of bias toward homosexual applicants. *Personality and Social Psychology Bulletin, 28*, 815–825.

Heilman, M. E., & Haynes, M. C. (2008). Subjectivity in the appraisal process: A facilitator of gender bias in work settings. In E. Borgida & S. T. Fiske (Eds.), *Beyond common sense: Psychological science in the courtroom* (pp. 127–155). Oxford: Blackwell.

Higgins, E. T. (1987). Self-discrepancy: A theory relating self and affect. *Psychological Review, 94*(3), 19–40.

Highhouse, S. (2008). Stubborn reliance on intuition and subjectivity in employee selection. *Industrial and Organizational Psychology, 1*(3), 333–342.

Hofmann, W., Gawronski, B., Gschwendner, T., Le, H., & Schmitt, M. (2005). A meta-analysis on the correlation between the Implicit Association Test and explicit self-report measures. *Personality and Social Psychology Bulletin, 31*, 1369–1385.

Hosoda, M., Stone-Romero, E. F., & Coats, G. (2003). The effects of physical attractiveness on job-related outcomes: A meta-analysis of experimental studies. *Personnel Psychology, 56*, 431–462.

Jones, E. E., Gergen, K. J., & Davis, K. E. (1962). Some determinants of reactions to being approved or disapproved as a person. *Psychological Monographs: General and Applied, 76*(2), 17.

Judge, T. A., Erez, A., & Thoresen, C. J. (2000). Why negative affectivity (and self-deception) should be included in job stress research: Bathing the baby with the bath water. *Journal of Organizational Behavior, 21*(1), 101–111.

Kawakami, K., Dovidio, J. F., Moll, J., Hermsen, S., & Russin, A. (2000). Just say no (to stereotyping): Effects of training in the negation of stereotypic associations on stereotype activation. *Journal of Personality and Social Psychology, 78*(5), 871–888.

Kemp, S. (2015). *Digital, social, and mobile worldwide in 2015*. Retrieved March 1, 2015, from http://wearesocial.net/blog/2015/01/digital-social-mobile-worldwide-2015/.

Kite, M. E., & Johnson, B. T. (1988). Attitudes toward older and younger adults: A meta-analysis. *Psychology and Aging, 3*(3), 233–244.

Kraus, S. J. (1995). Attitudes and the prediction of behavior: A meta-analysis of the empirical literature. *Personality and Social Psychology Bulletin, 21*, 58–75.

Kroner, D. G., & Weekes, J. R. (1996). Balanced inventory of desirable responding: Factor structure, reliability and validity with an offender sample. *Personality and Individual Differences, 21*(3), 323–333.

Lampe, C., Ellison, N. B., & Steinfield, C. (2008). Changes in use and perception of Facebook. In *Proceedings of the 2008 ACM Conference on Computer Supported Cooperative Work* (pp. 721–730). Retrieved March 1, 2015, from ACM Portal: ACM Digital Library.

Lampe, C., Vitak, J., Gray, R., & Ellison, N. (2012). Perceptions of Facebook's value as an information source. In *Proceedings of the SIGCHI Conference on Human Factors in Computing Systems* (pp. 3195–3204). Retrieved March 1, 2015, from ACM Portal: ACM Digital Library.

Latham, R. P., Butzer, C. C., & Brown, J. T. (2008). Legal implications of user-generated content: YouTube, MySpace, Facebook. *Intellectual Property & Technology Law Journal, 20*(5), 1–12.

Leary, M. R. (1996). *Self-Presentation: Impression Management and Interpersonal Behavior*. Boulder, CO: Westview.

Leary, M. R., & Kowalski, R. M. (1990). Impression management: A literature review and two-component model. *Psychological Bulletin, 107*(1), 34.

Li, A., & Bagger, J. (2006). Using the BIDR to distinguish the effects of impression management and self-deception on the criterion validity of personal measures: A meta-analysis. *International Journal of Selection and Assessment, 14*(2), 131–141.

Linden, W., Chambers, L., Maurice, J., & Lenz, J. W. (1993). Sex differences in social support, self-deception, hostility, and ambulatory cardiovascular activity. *Health Psychology, 12*(5), 376–380.

Litz, R. A. (2003). Cheating at solitaire: Self-deception, executive mental health, and organizational performance. *Business & Society Review, 108*(2), 235–261.

Lynn, C. D., Pipitone, R. N., & Keenan, J. P. (2014). To thine own self be false: Self-deceptive enhancement and sexual awareness influences on mating success. *Evolutionary Behavioral Sciences, 8*(2), 109–122.

Măgurean, S., Vîrgă, D., & Sava, F. A. (2014). Implicit and explicit personality assessment in the context of personnel selection. *Psihologia Resurselor Umane, 12*(1), 24.

Marwick, A. E., & Boyd, D. (2010). I tweet honestly, I tweet passionately: Twitter users, context collapse, and the imagined audience. *New Media & Society, 13*(1), 114–133.

Mattioli, D. (2007, May 15). Hard sell on 'soft' skills can primp a resume. *The Wall Street Journal.* p. B6.

McGarty, C., Yzerbyt, V. Y., & Spears, R. (2002). *Stereotypes as explanations: The information of meaningful beliefs about social groups*. Cambridge: Cambridge University Press.

Meehl, P. E., & Hathaway, S. R. (1946). The K factor as a suppressor variable in the Minnesota Multiphasic Personality Inventory. *Journal of Applied Psychology, 30*, 525–564.

Michikyan, M., Subrahmanyam, K., & Dennis, J. (2014). Can you tell who I am? Neuroticism, extraversion, and online self-presentation among young adults. *Computers in Human Behavior, 33*, 179–183.

Monteith, M. J. (1993). Self-regulation of prejudiced responses: Implications for progress in prejudice-reduction efforts. *Journal of Personality and Social Psychology, 65*, 469–485.

Nelson, T. D. (2002). *Ageism: Stereotyping and prejudice against older persons*. Cambridge, MA: The MIT Press.

Nosek, B. A., & Banaji, M. R. (2001). The go/no-go association task. *Social Cognition, 19*, 625–666.

Oswald, F. L., Mitchell, G., Blanton, H., Jaccard, J., & Tetlock, P. E. (2013). Predicting ethnic and racial discrimination: A meta-analysis of IAT criterion studies. *Journal of Personality and Social Psychology, 105*, 171–192.

Panek, E. T., Nardis, Y., & Konrath, S. (2013). Mirror or megaphone?: How relationships between narcissism and social networking site use differ on Facebook and Twitter. *Computers in Human Behavior, 29*, 2004–2012.

Paulhus, D. L. (1984). Two component models of socially desirable responding. *Journal of Personality & Social Psychology, 46*, 598–609.

Paulhus, D. L. (1988). Measurement and control of response bias. In J. P. Robinson, P. Shaver, & L. Wrightsman (Eds.), *Measures of personality and social psychological attitudes* (Vol. 1, pp. 17–60). New York: Academic.

Paulhus, D. L. (1989). Socially desirable responding: Some new solutions to old problems. In D. M. Buss & N. Cantor (Eds.), *Personality psychology: Recent trends and emerging direction* (pp. 201–209). New York: Springer.

Paulhus, D. L., & John, O. P. (1998). Egoistic and moralistic biases in self-perception: The interplay of self-deceptive styles with basic traits and motives. *Journal of Personality, 66*, 1025–1060.

Paulhus, D. L., & Reid, D. B. (1991). Enhancement and denial in socially desirable responding. *Journal of Personality and Social Psychology, 60*, 307–371.

Peck, M. S. (1983). *People of the lie: The hope for healing human evil*. New York: Touchstone.

Perry, E. L., & Finkelstein, L. M. (1999). Toward a broader view of age discrimination in employment-related decisions: A joint consideration of organizational factors and cognitive processes. *Human Resource Management Review, 9*(1), 21–49.

Pettigrew, T. F. (1998). Integroup contact theory. *Annual Review of Psychology, 49*, 65–85.

Pettigrew, T. F., & Tropp, L. R. (2006). A meta-analytic test of intergroup contact theory. *Journal of Personality and Social Psychology, 90*, 751–783.

Pew Research Center. (2014). Social networking fact sheet. *Per Research Center: Internet, Science & Tech.* Retrieved March 1, 2015, from http://www.pewinternet.org/fact-sheets/social-networking-fact-sheet/.

Qiu, L., Lin, H., Leung, A. K., & Tov, W. (2012). Putting their best foot forward: Emotional disclosure on facebook. *Cyberpsychology, Behavior, and Social Networking, 15*(10), 569–572.

Quattrone, G., & Tversky, A. (1984). Causal versus diagnostic contingencies: On self-deception and on the voter's illusion. *Journal of Personality and Social Psychology, 46*, 237–248.

Ravaud, J., Madiot, B., & Ville, I. (1992). Discrimination towards disabled people seeking employment. *Social Science & Medicine, 35*, 951–958.

Riordan, C. M. (2000). Relational demography within groups: Past developments, contradictions, and new directions. In G. R. Ferris (Ed.), *Research in personnel and human resources management* (Vol. 19, pp. 131–173). Greenwich: JAI Press.

Rogers, C. R. (1951). *Client-centered therapy: Its current practice, implications, and theory.* Boston: Houghton Mifflin.

Rogers, C. R. (1961). *On becoming a person.* Boston: Houghton Mifflin.

Rosenberg, J., & Egbert, N. (2011). Online impression management: Personality traits and concerns for secondary goals as predictors of self-presentation tactics on Facebook. *Journal of Computer-Mediated Communication, 17*(1), 1–18.

Schlenker, B. R. (1980). *Impression management: The self-concept, social identity, and interpersonal relations.* Monterey: Brooks/Cole Publishing Company.

Schlenker, B. R., & Weigold, M. F. (1992). Interpersonal processes involving impression regulation and management. *Annual review of psychology, 43*(1), 133–168.

Schneider, D. J. (1981). Tactical self-presentations: Toward a broader conception. In J. T. Tedeschi (Ed.), *Impression management theory and social psychological research* (pp. 23–40). New York: Academic.

Schneider, K. T., Swan, S., & Fitzgerald, L. F. (1997). Job-related and psychological effects of sexual harassment in the workplace: Empirical evidence from two organizations. *Journal of Applied Psychology, 82*, 401–415.

Sherman, S., & Freas, A. (2004). The wild west of executive coaching. *Harvard Business Review, 82*(11), 82–93.

Siibak, A. (2009). Constructing the self through the photo selection-visual impression management on social networking websites. *Cyberpsychology: Journal of Psychosocial Research on Cyberspace, 3*(1). Retrieved September 15, 2015, from http://www.cyberpsychology.eu/view.php?cisloclanku=2009061501.

Smith, T. (2003). The metaphysical case for honesty. *Journal of Value Inquiry, 37*(4), 517–532.

Smith, W. P., & Kitter, D. L. (2010). You've been tagged! (Then again, maybe not): Employers and Facebook. *Business Horizons, 53*(5), 491–499.

Smock, A. D., Ellison, N. B., Lampe, C., & Wohn, D. Y. (2011). Facebook as a toolkit: A uses and gratification approach to unbundling feature use. *Computers in Human Behavior, 27*(6), 2322–2329.

Snyder, M., & Swann, W. B. (1978). Hypothesis-testing processes in social interaction. *Journal of Personality and Social Psychology, 36*(11), 1202.

Starek, J. E., & Keating, C. F. (1991). Self-deception and its relationship to success in competition. *Basic and Applied Social Psychology, 12*(2), 145–155.

Stone, E. F., Stone, D. L., & Dipboye, R. L. (1992). Stigmas in organizations: Race, handicaps, and physical attractiveness. In K. Kelley (Ed.), *Issues, theory, and research in industrial and organizational psychology* (pp. 385–457). New York: Elsevier Science.

Sunden, J. (2003). *Material Virtualities.* New York: Peter Lang.

Surbey, M. K. (2011). Adaptive significance of low levels of self-deception and cooperation in depression. *Evolution and Human Behavior, 32*, 29–40.

Swim, J. K., Scott, E. D., Sechrist, G. B., Campbell, B., & Stangor, C. (2003). The role of intent and harm in judgments of prejudice and discrimination. *Journal of Personality and Social Psychology, 84*(5), 944–959.

Tajfel, H. (1981). *Human groups and social categories: Studies in social psychology*. New York: Cambridge University Press.

Talaska, C. A., Fiske, S. T., & Chaiken, S. (2008). Legitimating racial discrimination: Emotions, not beliefs, best predict discrimination in a meta-analysis. *Social Justice Research, 21*(3), 263–296.

Taylor, P., Funk, C., & Craighill, P. (2006). Americans see weight problems everywhere but in the mirror. *Pew Research Center: A Social Trends Report.* Retrieved September 15, 2015, from: http://www.pewsocialtrends.org/files/2010/10/Obesity.pdf.

Thorndike, E. L. (1920). A constant error in psychological ratings. *Journal of Applied Psychology, 4*(1), 25–29.

Thurstone, L. L. (1928). Attitudes can be measured. *American Journal of Sociology, 33*, 529–554.

Trivers, R. (2011). *The folly of fools: The logic of deceit and self-deception in human life*. New York: Basic Books.

Tropp, L. R., & Pettigrew, T. F. (2005). Relationships between intergroup contact and prejudice among minority and majority status groups. *Psychological Science, 16*(12), 951–957.

Turner, J. C. (1985). Social categorization and the self-concept: A social cognitive theory of group behavior. *Advances in Group Processes, 2*, 77–122.

Vaughn, E. D., Thomas, A., & Doyle, A. L. (2011). The multiple disability implicit association test: Psychometric analysis of a multiple administration IAT measure. *Rehabilitation Counseling Bulletin, 54*, 223–235.

Wittenbrink, B., Judd, C., & Park, B. (1997). Evidence for racial prejudice at the implicit level and its relationship with questionnaire measures. *Journal of Personality and Social Psychology, 72*, 262–274.

Zerbe, W. J., & Paulhus, D. L. (1987). Socially desirable responding in organizational behavior: A reconception. *Academy of Management Review, 12*, 250–264.

Zhao, S., Grasmuck, S., & Martin, J. (2008). Identity construction on Facebook: Digital empowerment in anchored relationships. *Computer in Human Behavior, 24*, 1816–1836.

Zuckerman, E. W., & Jost, J. T. (2001). What makes you think you're so popular? Self-evaluation maintenance and the subjective side of the 'friendship paradox'. *Social Psychology Quarterly, 64*, 207–223.

Part V
Future Directions

Chapter 16
Social Media in Employee Selection and Recruitment: Current Knowledge, Unanswered Questions, and Future Directions

Richard N. Landers and Gordon B. Schmidt

Abstract There is disagreement in the academic literature regarding the use of social media in selection and recruitment. To get a sense of the degree of disagreement, we conducted a qualitative survey of 13 experts in this domain. Results of the survey revealed four principle challenges for researchers and three principal challenges for practitioners in this area. Almost all experts recommended against the use of social media in selection at this time due to measurement issues, legal issues, and others, but approximately half stated that their recommendation could change in the future depending upon pending research. Several experts stated that the use of social media in recruitment was less risky than in selection and recommended it explicitly. All but one expert recommended adopting an interdisciplinary approach. From our results, we highlight four priorities for future research, involving the identification of useful information from social media, strategies for acting on that information, fairness and ethicality, and international implications.

Keywords Social media • Social network sites • Personnel selection • Selection • Recruitment • Reliability • Validity • Practical • Ethical • Legal

R.N. Landers, Ph.D. (✉)
Department of Psychology, Old Dominion University,
250 Mills Godwin Building, Norfolk, VA 23529, USA
e-mail: rnlanders@odu.edu

G.B. Schmidt, Ph.D.
Division of Organizational Leadership and Supervision, Indiana University-Purdue University Fort Wayne, Neff 288D, 2101 East Coliseum Blvd., Fort Wayne, IN 46805, USA
e-mail: schmidtg@ipfw.edu

R.N. Landers, G.B. Schmidt (eds.), *Social Media in Employee Selection and Recruitment*, DOI 10.1007/978-3-319-29989-1_16

16.1 Introduction

Social media are playing an increasingly important role in employee selection and recruitment, yet many unanswered questions remain (Landers & Schmidt, 2016). A majority of employers now report the rejection of some job applicants due to information found on social media (Grasz, 2014), but researchers have not yet provided clear, empirically driven guidelines or best practices to make such decisions effectively and legally. This is not a new realization of the science-practice gap. Instead, there has simply been an insufficient quantity of research conducted on the use of social media in selection and recruitment to form recommendations. As can be commonly observed throughout the chapters of this text, conclusions about what is likely to occur as a result of decision-making from information found on social media must be instead inferred from related research areas.

To a degree, this is to be expected. Although social media in selection and recruitment is a new research area for those in the organizational sciences, including industrial/organizational psychology, human resources, and organizational behavior, social media as a subject area has been studied extensively in a variety of disciplines for at least a decade (e.g., Oravec, 2003). The organizational sciences are often quite resistant to studying what could be considered fads, fashion, or folderol (Dunnette, 1966). Although it is difficult to remember now, there was a time when many organizational psychologists questioned whether this newfangled "Internet" thing would even become relevant to organizations. From that perspective, we have adapted fairly well.

Furthermore, many of the problems faced when social media were considered as selection tools are already familiar. Making evaluations of people with relatively little information on which to base judgments is the basis of interviewing, which has a robust and complex research literature (e.g., Salgado & Moscoso, 2002). In the United States and elsewhere, there is also already a significant amount of statutory and case law influencing current practices for selection procedures (Dunleavy, Morris, & Howard, 2015) and even articulated and well-accepted guidelines for designing systems that meet these requirements (Society for Industrial and Organizational Psychology [SIOP], 2003).

Thus, a major goal of this text and this chapter in particular was to identify where gaps remain when considering this prior work. Although broader literatures exist, questions unique to the social media context certainly linger. To identify these gaps, we took a two-pronged approach. First, we surveyed key experts in social media in selection and recruitment to determine to what extent consensus has been reached on a variety of key issues. Second, we integrated these results with an in-depth review of the chapters of this text to develop specific recommendations for both research and practice given the current state of the literature.

16.2 Survey of Experts in Social Media in Selection and Recruitment

To get a sense of remaining gaps and important issues in the domain of social media in selection, the authors of chapters within this text were anonymously surveyed to gain their opinions on several key issues. All corresponding authors were invited directly, and they were asked to forward to their coauthors or respond as a group based upon their preference. Thirteen responses were collected, which is approximately the number of chapters in the book that we (i.e., the editors) did not author. If only authors responded, this would represent approximately a 93 % response rate, whereas if every coauthor received an invitation from their authors, this would represent approximately a 46 % response rate. Thus, the true response rate is somewhere between these two values.

Once the data were collected, we conducted a content analysis of responses to each of the six open-ended questions presented in the survey in order to extract and summarize major themes where feasible. We present the results of these content analyses and other supplemental analyses alongside illustrative quotes from the experts surveyed across the next few sections.

16.2.1 The Most Significant Challenges Facing Researchers

The first question read, "Considering both your chapter and the chapter(s) that you reviewed, what do you see as the biggest challenge for researchers of social media in selection moving forward?" The results of our content analysis appear in Table 16.1.

Table 16.1 Expert perspectives on the most significant challenges for researchers

Category	Count	Prototypical quote
Establishment of a shared science	7	"For something that's such a big part of the conversation around current hiring practices, academia is still surprisingly fragmented and foundational, just now beginning to build the theoretical bones and conceptual frameworks to drive scholarship into the area. As academics, we're sometimes talking past each other (with one taking one perspective and another scholar taking a disparate perspective) or ignoring related fields (e.g., business, communication, psychology)."
Speed of technological progress	3	"As we just begin uncovering some of the mechanisms through which a type of social media is linked to selection, another type emerges...these new types of social media will just keep coming and we will never be able to close the gap."
Improving measurement	2	"Many of the studies we read and reviewed suffered from poor measurement tools."
Research-to-practice gap	1	"Convincing HR Professionals that unstandardized and unrecorded social media searches on job candidates are likely to be lacking in both reliability and validity."

$N=13$

The primary comment category in this content analysis was "Establishment of a Shared Science." Comments within this category generally focused upon the lack of prior research within this domain on which to build. Specifically, they noted the fragmented nature of prior research literature, suggesting that this fragmentation was slowing current progress. Authors disagreed on the best way to solve this problem. For example, one expert noted that the literature was only just now beginning to finish "foundational" development work, establishing conceptual frameworks on which to base further investigations. However, two other experts stated that the highest priority is empirical validation, suggesting that if such evidence cannot be found, there is little value in pursuing other research avenues.

We concluded from this that there are two dramatically different perspectives on display here. Some experts are approaching social media in selection as an existing practice. From this perspective, it is the responsibility of researchers to identify what is currently being done and work to understand it before attempting to influence it. Other experts are approaching social media as a potential selection tool, regardless of its current use in hiring, wishing to establish its value from a utility or prediction standpoint before worrying about contextual issues. Both of these views have merit. If no one can develop a way to get reliable and valid information from social media, the primary researcher perspective should be "don't use social media in selection," and such evidence is currently limited (e.g., Kluemper, Rosen, & Mossholder, 2012) or discouraging (e.g., Van Iddekinge, Lanivich, Roth, & Junco, 2013). However, if social media are going to be used by hiring managers *regardless of research findings*, and there is evidence of this already, there is still value in understanding how they are being used in order to direct it in more useful directions as much as possible. For example, even if evidence ultimately shows ratings from social media profiles cannot be practically used to predict job performance, they might still be used to predict person–organization fit.

The second comment category was "Speed of Technological Progress." Experts lamented the pace at which specific social media technologies are introduced, noting that the speed of academic publishing cannot generally keep up. It is important to note that this is a limitation of only certain research literatures, although that list includes the organizational sciences. In computer science, increased speed of technological progress is the purpose and direct result of research. For this and other historical reasons, computer science academic conferences (and the resulting proceedings) generally have higher publication standards and are more respected than journal articles (Ernst, 2006; Patterson, Snyder, & Ullman, 1999). Although the organizational sciences do not need to shift their publication model to conference in order to solve this problem, there are alternatives that could help, such as the often much shorter turnaround time and higher citation rates of publications in online open-access journals (Antelman, 2004).

The third comment category was "Improving Measurement." Both experts making comments in this category noted that while conducting their own literature reviews in the area of social media in selection, they repeatedly encountered studies with poor measurement methods and research designs.

The fourth comment category, which consisted of only one comment, was the "Research-to-Practice Gap." This expert suggested that regardless of the extent of research conducted highlighting problems associated with incorporating social media into selection, people will continue to do so because of its ease and attractiveness. In any area of organizational science, measurement issues and the translation of research into practice are difficult tasks. Although certainly significant challenges for researchers, we do not see either of these categories as unique to social media in selection.

16.2.2 The Most Significant Challenges Facing Practitioners

The second question read, "What do you see as the biggest challenge for practitioners working in this area currently?" The results of our content analysis appear in Table 16.2.

The first emergent category, "Supporting Decisions Already Made," contains comments related to existing use of social media in selection. Specifically, the tone from experts indicated that they believe practitioners are likely already incorporating social media into their decision-making process, but without much if any evidence to support that incorporation. The quote highlighted in Table 16.2 reflects many of the themes we identified in Chap. 1 (Landers & Schmidt, 2016) and summarizes the other comments in this category well: reliability/validity, fairness and legality emerged as dominant themes within this category. However, it is important to note that this reaction may be evidence of the practice–research gap; specifically, practitioners may have collected more promising evidence in support of social media-based selection than is currently available in the research literature, held from public scrutiny as proprietary intellectual property and thus a competitive advantage for the organization. Given the lack of data available in the research literature, any organization finding a way to incorporate social media into selection decisions that was reliable, valid, fair, and legal would likely have developed a highly profitable selection tool.

Table 16.2 Expert perspectives on the most significant challenges for practitioners

Category	Count	Prototypical quote
Supporting decisions already made	8	"Developing effective ways to use social media in selection in ways that are consistent across individuals, fair, do not invade privacy, and provide practical lawful value to the selection process."
Feeling pressure to adopt	4	"Practitioners will have to balance the desire of their clients to use social media for selection with the lack of evidence for its validity (and the accompanying legal issues). They will need to be able to tell clients, 'OK, I recommend against using it, but if you are going to do so, let's do the screening in a way that will give us the most useful and defensible data.'"
Speed of technological progress	1	"I think the challenge is roughly the same as academics, keeping up with pace of technology. Different than academics, however, practitioners need to figure out what is out there and figure out how to employ it in their workplace."

$N = 13$

Comments in the second category, "Feeling Pressure to Adopt," suggested that among those not currently using social media for selection decisions, the pressure to do so is high. One expert specifically noted pressure from clients to incorporate social media information into selection systems, presumably from the perspective of sales. Although not noted by the expert, we suspect this pressure comes from the current faddishness of big data, which is often associated with social media. For example, researchers outside of the organizational sciences have claimed that big data techniques enable the extraction of personality information from Facebook profiles that is more accurate and valid than personality judgments made by other people, even those closely related to them (Youyou, Kosinski, & Stillwell, 2015). Given the lack of evidence applying such findings to the organizational sciences, these experts have highlighted an important disconnect; in a number of cases, highly visible research in other disciplines is driving the desire for social media in the selection process.

Finally, one expert made a comment we labeled "Speed of Technological Progress," in parallel to the category displayed in Table 16.1. However, rather than the worry that researchers cannot keep up with progress, this expert noted that practitioners must worry about the specific technologies themselves. We agree that this is a significant challenge for practitioners, and one chapter in the present book is intended to provide exactly this type of guidance (Black, Washington, & Schmidt, 2016).

16.2.3 Overall Recommendations for Use of Social Media

The third question read, "Should the use of social media in selection be encouraged or discouraged? Why?" The results of our content analysis appear in Table 16.3.

Table 16.3 Expert recommendations for using social media in selection

Recommendation	Count	Prototypical quote
Mixed	6	"It should be encouraged but only if it becomes more standardized, targeted, and objective."
No	7	"Based on what we know currently about the potential risks and biases that could be more readily acted upon via social media use, and what we do not know in regard to fairness, validity, and job relevance, we would discourage employers from the use of social media content in screening potential candidates. Until more is known about what elements of social media and social networking sites (SNSs) should be attended to, and how to successfully encourage review of candidate data to focus on job-relevant information that also enhances validity of the overall selection process, we would recommend extreme caution in the use of this approach in the selection process."

$N = 13$

Responses to this question were universally negative. Experts making both Mixed and No recommendations, which constituted all experts we surveyed, were in consensus that as the current research literature stands, there are too many risks and too few demonstrated gains to adopt the examination of social media data as a selection method. Among the majority providing a clear "no," experts were quite consistent with this message.

Among the second largest group of experts, who provided more nuanced and mixed recommendations, two groupings emerged. One group of experts identified recruitment as a currently valid application of social media in the selection process. Specifically, by using social media channels, particular groups of potential applicants can be targeted and encouraged to apply. In the United States in particular, recruitment has been a common tactic used when pursuing affirmative action policies and diversity programs within the boundaries of federal law and most state laws (Kelly & Dobbin, 1998). These experts generally view the active use of social media to approach potential job applicants as much safer than the passive use of social media to collect information about existing job applicants. Importantly, there is little research in this domain as well. Social media used this way is bi-directional; employers and potential job applicants exchange information (Landers & Goldberg, 2014). It is currently unclear precisely how applicants incorporate information obtained via social media into their judgments about organizations, although it is clear that they do play an important role (Henderson & Bowley, 2010) and that organizations are trying to influence this process (Doherty, 2010).

The second group of experts noted that although it is probably unwise to adopt a social media-based hiring strategy currently, evidence reversing that recommendation could be coming in the near future. The only way to remain open to the new possibilities enabled by a new technology is to consider these possibilities as they appear, rather than dismissing the technology simply because it is new and untested. One expert noted this hopefulness by stating, "The use of social media in selection should be encouraged, because social media behaviors provide a novel opportunity that could better match employees and employers, thus making both happier." Despite the relatively poor state of the current literature, we thus recommend organizational scholars watch the technology closely as it develops, as such developments can change the social media landscape, and thus the information that can be obtained from social media, dramatically.

16.2.4 Overall Recommendations for Use of Social Media

The fourth question read, "Would this area benefit from an interdisciplinary perspective (e.g., bringing in technologists or data scientists), or do the organizational sciences (IO, OB, HRM) have it covered? Why?" The results of our content analysis appear in Table 16.4.

Responses to this question were almost universally positive. Eleven of the 12 respondents to this question (92 %) suggested an interdisciplinary perspective would

Table 16.4 Expert perspectives on the contribution of an interdisciplinary perspective

Recommendation	Count	Prototypical quote
Yes	11	"Most org science people are not as technically savvy and they need the help to more efficiently understand how the emerging technologies work. The tech and data science people don't always understand the discipline in which they are applying their skills. Blending the two together has the potential to help researchers and practitioners product a beneficial line of research and in a more efficient manner."
No	1	"I believe the organizational sciences pretty much have the potential to have it covered, but the pace with which it evolves is overwhelming. Technologists or data scientist may examine the issue from a systems perspective, but without bringing in the human aspect I do not believe they have much to contribute."

$N = 12$

Table 16.5 Expert recommendations for complimentary disciplines

Discipline	Count
Psychology	6
Data science	4
Computer science	3
Technology studies	3
Communication	3
Linguistics	1
Business	1
Sociology	1

$N = 12$

be helpful, and most suggested specific fields. We extracted the names of these fields and list them in Table 16.5. Importantly, these counts will not sum to the sample size, because most experts suggested multiple fields. Within this list, psychology emerged as dominant, with data science second. Importantly, this list has been influenced by the disciplines of those responding to this question. Our pool of experts included psychologists, sociologists, business researchers, and other interdisciplinary perspectives already; thus, a person's interpretation of "interdisciplinary" is likely based upon their own area. For example, a psychologist would be unlikely to say that increased interdisciplinary collaboration with psychologists would be useful. This list is also based upon the existing familiarity of the experts with the potential contributions of other disciplines, which varies by expert. Thus, the number of mentions of each of these disciplines should not be interpreted as their relative importance or promise to this area. Instead, this list provides guidance on which areas come to the minds of experts in the organizational sciences when asked whose perspective would be useful to understanding social media in selection.

With those caveats, psychology emerged as most mentioned discipline. Comments from experts emphasized the inclusion of complimentary areas of psychology, such as social psychology and personality psychology. Mentions of data science generally focused upon bringing analytic techniques and technological expertise. For example, one expert noted that data scientists have greater expertise with the types and formatting of data available on social media websites; many organizational scientists do not even know what type of data capture is theoretically possible on such sites. Researchers describing data scientists, computer scientists, and technology researchers commonly described those people as possessing skill-sets that would account for weaknesses in the expertise of current organizational scholars.

Interestingly, most researchers did not consider that people in these fields might bring content expertise, and several openly questioned their value for anything other than adding a technical perspective to existing efforts in the organizational sciences. For example, one expert stated, "Conferring with individuals who understand the technology and how to develop and manipulate it would almost certainly be helpful in partnering for the purposes of programming or developing content for research studies or in developing software to capture pertinent participant data." Most negative was the lone expert expressing that an interdisciplinary perspective would not be particularly useful, stating (as shown in Table 16.4), "I do not believe they have much to contribute."

From this, we conclude that organizational scientists are in general comfortable with the conclusions that can be drawn using traditional organizational science methods but are open to the contributions of other fields. Although these experts recognized the potential collaborative opportunities, there was no significant enthusiasm for seeking it out proactively. This is one of many common problems faced when pursuing interdisciplinary research (Morse, Nielsen-Pincus, Force, & Wulfhorst, 2007). It will likely require a dedicated and pointed effort by a particular expert or experts within the organizational sciences to bridge any of the gaps to other disciplines.

16.2.5 Best and Worst Practices

The fifth and sixth questions read, "Imagine an organization incorporating social media in its selection process in a way you would describe as 'could not be better/worse'. What is that organization doing?" With these two prompts, we hoped to get a clearer picture of expert-supported best practices and most harmful mistakes. Answers to these two questions varied widely and typically mentioned multiple themes, so we will summarize these content analyses narratively rather than in a tabular format.

Three practices appeared multiple times as answers to the best practices questions: First, much as observed among answers to the first and second questions, the most commonly mentioned best practice was the use of social media as an early step in the selection process: recruitment. As described above, social media offers an excellent opportunity to reach out to specific target audiences to invite to apply. Many social network sites even provide the ability to input unique combinations of demographic characteristics to whom to deliver advertisements. Organizations that are using social media in their selection pipeline effectively will be using social media to reach out to desirable job candidates.

Second, standardization was a common best practice and also appeared multiple times on the worst practices list. Specifically, organizations that are using social media in their selection process effectively will have articulated a policy for doing so that is enforced. Organizations that are using social media poorly will allow hiring managers to peruse social media at will and to incorporate the information they find there in unclear ways. Relatedly, another set of best/worst practices that appeared (although less frequently) was documentation. In addition to having an articulated policy, every element of that policy and adherence to it should be carefully documented, to create a paper trail that evidences the organization's decision-making process in relation to social media, because this provides a degree of support later, in the event of litigation. Poorly performing organizations will not only allow managers to do whatever they want, but will also keep no records of these actions.

The third common best practice was reliance upon traditional selection standards. Experts recommended following a traditional validation process, conducting a thorough job analyses, ensuring job relatedness of social media data collected, and other standard best practices of selection described in the SIOP (2003) Principles. One expert also noted that even if social media data are not broadly useful to the prediction of job performance, there may be special cases where social media data may be highly job-relevant. For example, for the job of social media manager, social media presence and social media content posted might be considered a work sample test, which has a significant research literature demonstrating its relationship with job performance (Roth, Bobko, & McFarland, 2005). Those considering social media should be careful to neither embrace nor reject social media data completely; the situations where social media data are useful to selection itself are likely to be quite nuanced.

Three practices also appeared multiple times in response to the worst practices question. As mentioned before, standardization was the first of these. The second was a lack of attention paid to legality. Although social media may not be predictive of job performance, an organization can use any selection measure they would like as long as they are not unfair across membership in legally protected classes. In short, no legal system requires employees to only be hired on job-related characteristics, but many legal systems require that the process used does not result in differential hiring within particular classes, such as race, sex, religion, color, national origin, disability, age, and pregnancy. The worst practice that emerged here occurs when organizations not only use social media data without evidence, but also fail to even evaluate the legality of the resulting hiring decisions. We can imagine, for example, a hiring manager who in a casual perusal of a social media profile notices that a job candidate is pregnant and makes a hiring decision illegally based upon that information.

The third worst practice was both a practical and ethical one. Experts condemned the use of social media to make decisions based upon information that is not job-relevant. Practically speaking, this suggests that in the absence of reliability and validity evidence, social media should not be used. Ethically speaking, this suggests that even if reliability and validity evidence is available, there are situations where social media data should still be off-limits. For example, although consumption of alcohol in leisure time might be correlated with various outcomes potentially of interest (Eftekhar, Fullwood, & Morris, 2014; Karl, Peluchette, & Schlaegel, 2010), such behavior is not job-related, on the face of it.

Other worst practices mentioned included adopting new social media as selection procedures simply because they are trendy, making attributions based upon social media postings, failing to document, allowing people making hiring decisions access to information about protected class membership via social media screening, and inconsistency across individuals in terms of both decision-making and access. For example, some job applicants may be less likely to have particular social media profiles than others, and deciding based upon this information may be unfair.

16.3 Crucial Areas for Further Study in Social Media in Selection and Recruitment

This book throughout its chapters has strived to significantly move forward our understanding and analysis of the use of social media in selection and recruitment. Despite this, there are still many areas that required additional examination. Given the results above, we present in this section some of the highest priority areas for additional empirical and theoretical examination. Some needed work represents incremental steps building forward from current research, whereas other questions will require significant foundational work and smaller steps.

Both short-term and long-term needs are important to consider. While we may want current practice to be well-informed, we must also consider how practice and development will be shaped and influenced by current research and practice. As discussed by Black et al. (2016), the details of social media use in selection change frequently as both the technologies and the way individuals use these technologies change. Understanding only the current environment of social media in selection and recruitment is a problem for long-term success, so we promote an approach incorporating both short- and long-term research goals.

To that end, we have developed and described below the four major questions most central to advancing research in this domain: (1) what useful information can be extracted from social media data, (2) how should this information be integrated into selection processes, (3) how can such data be used fairly and ethically, and (4) what about our answers to these questions change outside the context of the United States, where most research has been conducted to this point?

16.3.1 Question 1: What Useful Information Can Be Extracted from Social Media Data?

A major thrust of the existing work on social media use in selection and recruitment is related to determining its potential value for organizations. Can useful information be extracted from social media, and what does that information look like? This is the most common question addressed in many of the previous chapters and a major part of the discussion of the author survey. We anticipate that a significant portion of the future work undertaken exploring social media use in selection will likely be addressing this question, with our chapter authors being part of that charge.

Despite the great interest in and inherent value of the predictive value of social media data, empirical examination of the issue has been sparse to this point. Kluemper et al. (2012) found that the five-factor model personality ratings when assessed by rating social media profiles correlated with job performance, hirability ratings and academic performance, although with a small sample for job performance. In contrast, Van Iddekinge et al. (2013) found that recruiter ratings did not predict job performance or turnover intentions, with ratings also favoring whites and women, suggesting the potential for adverse impact. While both of these studies are informative, two studies are insufficient to draw any broad conclusions. Future studies need to both replicate these results as well as consider the various contextual factors varying between them, including population differences and procedural differences related to decision-making. Job performance is an important outcome for selection criteria and thus needs to be the focal outcome examined, but operationalizations of job performance vary widely and should be considered carefully. Studies across industries and job levels will also help to determine potential moderators and boundary conditions.

Kluemper et al. (2012) and Van Iddekinge et al. (2013) both asked raters to make evaluations of people based upon social media profiles, but asked them to do so for different variables. The raters in Kluemper et al.'s (2012) study were asked to look at social media content specifically as to how it related to personality characteristics, while the Van Iddekinge et al. (2013) recruiters were asked to make judgments on general suitability and specific KSAOs such as adaptability, creativity, and intelligence. The effectiveness of reviews targeted this way are likely to vary by both target factor and rater experience/training, and future research should consider this interaction.

Job-related tasks seem likely to impact the link between social media data use and job performance. For example, applicants to a job that involves online marketing might have social media data that is predictive of overall success. Jobs with vigilance-related tasks, such as security guard or quality controller, may have underlying KSAOs related to both vigilance and attention paid to information sharing that may be predicted by the quantity of social media content available. Researchers must consider both the KSAOs that social media behavior indicates and the behaviors themselves as potential predictors. Because social media behavior is the outcome of a person-by-situation interaction, there are two potential origins of useful information. First, information about KSAOs is represented by behaviors and can be measured if raters are able to extract information about those KSAOs while rating. Second, similarity between the social media context and the work context could result in superior prediction when predicting behavior from behavior. Specifically, greater similarity between the social media and work situations will result in a greater probability that social media "performance" will predict work performance. Future research must be careful to disentangle these and other approaches.

For example, a features approach would consider directly how and why applicant use different site features such as status updates, private messaging, groups, liking, privacy settings, and other features. Since features and labels for such actions vary from site to site, an affordances approach like that offered by Collmus, Armstrong, and Landers (2016) provides a strong theoretical basis to consider particular site tools and what behaviors they might facilitate. Such affordances or combinations of affordances should be examined in relation to selection outcomes such as job performance or particular task behaviors.

Site features could also have different relationships between selection and employment outcomes due to different motivations for their use. Smock, Ellison, Lampe, and Wohn (2011) found in a student sample that Facebook features that shared similar capabilities did not necessarily share similar motivations behind their use. For example, status updates were predicted by the motivation of expressive information shared, whereas writing on a Friend's wall was related to the motivations of passing time, professional advancement, and social interactions. In this way, the motives behind particular Facebook actions could be tied to specific work-related behaviors. Counts or percentage of total social media content creation done with particular features might give organizations information on underlying motivations that would play out in the workplace. Feature use associated with a motivation of professional advancement could relate to persistence or career focus.

Social media behaviors tied to particular contexts might also prove useful in the selection process, even contained within a larger set of content. One promising context is work-related social media content, even when posted among personal material. An applicant discussion about a previous position or social media interactions with other co-workers in a previous position may offer rich predictive data on how that person may behave in the organization that is considering his or her selection. This work-related or work-relevant social media content focus is one that has been the primary focus of research and analysis looking at organizations terminating current workers for social media content (O'Connor & Schmidt, 2015; O'Connor, Schmidt, & Drouin, in press; Schmidt & O'Connor, 2015). Organizations may want to more directly examine work-related posts as they are most directly applicable to a future work-setting.

Research by Van Zoonen, Verhoeven, and Vliegenthart (2016) looked to examine how often employees make social media posts related to work and create a typology of such behaviors for the site Twitter. In their sample, they found 36.5 % of participants' tweets were work-related in some way and that 86 % of participants had at least one work-related tweet, illustrating the extensiveness of this potential data source. The authors divided these work-related Twitter behaviors into six categories of work-related topics. Tweets that fit more than one category were counted in both, so overall percentages do add up to more than 100 %. The first and largest category (41.0 % of all work-related tweets) was profession-related, those talking about the field the employee works in but not specific to the person's job or organization. So, for example, a public school teacher tweeting about state laws threatening traditional tenure rules would fall into this category. The second category (24.7 %) was organization-related communication, tweets that focused on the organization the employee worked for and its actions. A tweet about how the organization won an award would fall into this category. The third category (8.5 %) was employee-public communication where communication was made to people outside the organization. An example of this would be a worker responding to a customer who had a problem with the company website or explaining how to find a particular piece of organization-related information. The fourth category (9.4 %) was persuasive communication, where the employee tried to convince the reader to perform a particular action. This includes instructing people to sign up for a contest or attend an event at the organization. The fifth category (24.6 %) was work behaviors, in which the employee was tweeting about what tasks they were doing in the job, often as they were taking place. For example, employees might announce their arrival at a meeting or that a job-related task has been completed (e.g., "finally done emptying all the recycle bins!"). The sixth category (12.6 %) was commentary, where employees commented on work-related issues and matters. This would include a worker complaining about his scheduled hours for the week. The seventh and final category (22.3 %) was in-group communication, which occurred when the person directly mentioned someone at the same organization or in the same field. These communications always included @ mentions or retweets, so there was interaction between the person and colleagues through Twitter. An example might be a worker telling about an activity he did on the shift with a couple co-workers who are also on Twitter (Van Zoonen et al., 2016).

These seven categories represent different ways employees discussed work and career-related manners on social media. Some of these categories may be more predictive of job performance than other, and the sentiment (i.e., positive, neutral, or negative) may also play a role. For just one potential application, individuals with more in-group communication on social media content might work better with others on a computer-mediated team, and that relationship may be moderated by sentiment. Such information could even be collected from employees of other organizations, before an invitation to apply has been extended. Social media data in this way could help to give greater knowledge of how that applicant would behave on the job.

Although job performance is the most evident outcome of value, going beyond it is also valuable, as advocated by Roth, Bobko, Van Iddekinge, and Thatcher (2016). Although job performance is crucial, organizations also may want to predict if applicants will be committed to the organization, stay on the job, engage in organizational citizenship behaviors, work well with others, behave ethically, or any of a host of other work-related constructs. Organizations might determine social media selection predicts some of these outcomes well but others not at all. A more fine grained examination of particular social media feature use or types of social media behaviors as discussed above may help to determine which aspects of social media impact which constructs. Depending on what an organization wants from an applicant, some features and behavior might be targeted while others ignored. This more in-depth approach would allow for quite targeted social media selection efforts not seen in current research.

Importantly, the predictive value of data from social media may vary significantly by industry and role, regardless of criterion. If so, social media-based screening would be beneficial for some jobs in an organization while a waste of resources in others. Managerial versus non-managerial roles is one important distinction that could be tested empirically. The need for managers to interact with subordinates and peers positively might be more valuable than for other employees, and thus looking at social media behaviors such as those in the Van Zoonen et al. (2016) article might predict relationship quality and managerial performance in particular.

Increased social media scrutiny might also be warranted for executives, for whom their online behaviors and past actions reflect on the organization. A major example of this was Brendan Eich's 9 days work as CEO of Mozilla in 2014 when a 2008 donation to a group supporting California's Proposition 8 ban on gay marriage received significant online attention and backlash leading to his resignation (Shankland, 2014). Organizations may want to conduct rigorous checks of social media profiles held by potential executives to prevent potential scandal and embarrassment.

Some organizations may also need to use social media data to identify candidate characteristics that would lead them to become problematic hires, which has legal consequences in some jurisdictions. As discussed by Schmidt and O'Connor (2016), employers may be liable if an employee commits a certain wrongful act while engaging in their employment. Employers may also be held to have made negligent hiring, retention, or supervision of an employee. If a court rules that the organization should have foreseen the illegal act yet nothing was done by the organization to stop it, organizational liability can result. This was seen in Howard v. Hertz (2014) in which a court ruled that based upon a Hertz employee's previous history of releasing private customer information on Facebook, Hertz was negligent for not taking appropriate action to prevent it from happening again. While this has not yet been applied to organizations that have hired a worker despite negative social media posts or evidence, the potential does exist. Jobs that involve a special care and protection duty such as hospitals and home healthcare may be at higher risk and therefore consider social media screening to be more of a necessity than choice.

One final important area related to determining what information social media might provide is in the distinction between external and internal selection of applicants. The existing literature has focused on individuals joining new organization as applicants, whereas organizations also often consider internal candidates for promotion. Given the much richer information potentially available from internal/enterprise social media than external social media (Landers & Goldberg, 2014), gathering information relevant to promotion from internal sources may be more fruitful than information relevant to hiring from outside sources. Organizations are also likely to have existing performance data for such candidates that could make such algorithms even more powerful.

16.3.2 Question 2: How Should Information from Social Media Be Used in Selection?

The second important question with regard to how social media selection processes will take place in the future concerns how data extracted from social media should be used. Although current social media selection processes are informal and commonly conducted directly by people making hiring decisions, new technology enables types of prediction not currently well-understood. Davison, Bing, Kluemper, and Roth (2016) briefly discuss the potential of innovative computer applications to assess factors such as personality based on social media data. Black et al. (2016) consider how technology might be used in the social media selection process as well as in auditing and modification of existing social media selection processes. Such approaches, either in combination or as a replacement for human judgment, may ultimately be demonstrated preferable. It is only through interdisciplinary research, as noted in our survey, that such gains can be demonstrated.

Looking to existing research outside of the organizational sciences, the most relevant computer applications making assessments on social media data are data science approaches investigating the prediction of user personality. Park et al. (2015) created an open-vocabulary analysis program for social media data for Big 5 personality factors. Using a sample of over 60,000 Facebook users, including site content and traditional self-report ratings for Big 5 personality factors, a model was developed and used to predict 4824 other Facebook users' Big 5 personality traits based on the users' social media data. Their results suggest that the language-based assessment application assessments did constitute valid personality measurement and added incremental validity over informant reports on the user's personality.

Youyou et al. (2015) compared the personality judgments made of an individual by his or her Facebook friends and those made by a computer application looking at his or her Facebook likes. These judgments were then compared to the user's self-report personality characteristics. Youyou et al. (2015) found that the algorithm developed was more accurate in judgment of personality than the user's Facebook friends when compared to the user's self-report values.

These two studies offer support for the potential of data science algorithms as better prediction of applicant personality than a staff member's personal and idiosyncratic assessment. The two studies are also experimental applications, whereas an organization would be able to refine and improve their algorithms over time, improving accuracy and increasing the type of data incorporated. In such a system, all analyses of social media data could also be automated, only providing the results of those analyses to those making the selection decision. This could help minimize concerns regarding the discovery of information that legally should not influence the hiring process.

Computer applications could also help organizations with the collection of social media data through data mining. When an applicant first applies, a computer application could automatically search social media and other online information potentially related to the candidate. This collected information could then be presented to staff members with some amount of information automatically filtered based on legal requirements, accuracy judgments, and/or perceived relevancy. Those making hiring decisions could receive links to online content, actual text pulled from social media posts, and/or overall ratings of candidates judged on a number of factors important to the organization.

One fruitful area to look to for ideas of how such system might function is modern educational plagiarism applications. These applications take a student assignment and compare it against other student's papers and online sources to compare if elements of the paper have been plagiarized (Straumsheim, 2015). One such system, SafeAssign, gives an overall score for the paper estimating what percentage of the paper is plagiarized. The instructor makes a judgment based upon that score, but could also examine the source of that score in more detail. In the software itself, SafeAssign underlines each part of the paper that is seen as possible plagiarism and provides a reference to where the assignment is believed to have been sourced, whether a website, journal article, or another student's paper. The instructor can then compare the student's paper part with the alleged sources to minimize false positives, with the application also giving a score on how likely plagiarism is in the current case. Another valuable feature of SafeAssign is that comparisons are not just made to online sources, but can be made to other student papers in the class, other student papers submitted to SafeAssign at the same university, and a global database of papers across institutions ("SafeAssign", June 2015). Thus, the student's work can be compared to a large number of peers and reveal sources plagiarized that may not come up with more general web searches.

While there is controversy surrounding how well such plagiarism applications actually correctly identify plagiarism (see Straumsheim, 2015), the concept has potential for application in automated social media selection systems. Instead of searching for plagiarized material online, selection-focused web scraping software might search for particular social media content that the organization deems relevant, such as illegal behavior, comments regarding employers with negative sentiment, the sharing of confidential information, and prejudicial statements made online. This could be done automatically upon receipt of a job application. The computer application could then organize and analyze the data, calculating scores based upon material found in various categories and then presenting details about the origins of that score to the person ultimately making the decision. Candidates who have scores in particular ranges might be labeled as high risk. Such standardization would allow for more consistent application of social media data, a critical consideration according to both our survey and several chapters.

That such data would build up over time would have potential benefits for employers. As discussed by Park et al. (2015), it was the large data set of Facebook users with self-report personality scores that allowed them to create an application that predicts personality well from just Facebook content. As the organization increases its database of applicant data, those data can be used to refine the algorithms used for prediction. For applicants that get hired, their initial social media-based scores could be compared to their actual work performance and related outcomes. How factors are weighed and used could change overtime as more data is gained to inform the process.

Organizations will also want to consider technology use in assessing and auditing social media use in selection processes. As noted by Black et al. (2016), social media selection processes need to be audited for continued effectiveness over time, and this auditing will likely need to be conducted more frequently than for traditionally validated selection systems. Automated systems could track in real time how well categories of social media content are predicting relevant organizational outcomes. Such applications could create data for HR professionals to consider as revisions or the system itself could make adjustments automatically (i.e., the data science concept of "incremental algorithms"). The quality of systems and the desires of organizational members can help determine the role such applications would play in social media selection system updating and revision.

16.3.3 Question 3: How Can Social Media Data Be Used Fairly and Ethically?

An important question that has driven a growing body of work regards applicant perceptions of organizational use of social media for selection (Davison, Maraist, & Bing, 2011). More broadly, this concerns the question of how organizations can use social media data fairly and ethically. Applicant reactions are often driven by perceptions of fairness (Hausknecht, Day, & Thomas 2004). Thus, researchers must better understand which organizational actions are perceived as fair. Because Stoughton (2016) covers privacy in great detail, we will focus on other concerns in this chapter; however, it is worth noting that privacy is at the forefront of considerations of fairness in the social media context.

Fairness of social media data use in selection is more likely when formal and transparent procedures are used, which has been previously argued by Black, Stone, and Johnson (2015) and by the Black et al. (2016). One way to do this is by creating formal procedures that evaluators and collectors of applicant social media data must follow. Clearly written policies and communication of those policies to employees and potentially applicants are a necessity. To date, discussion of social media-related policies has focused on policies of work-related social media use by current employees (O'Connor et al., 2016), so this represents a new area in need of research and applied work.

With formal procedures for how social media data should be examined, the question arises that, if applicants should be informed about the existence of such policies, how much information should be shared. Generally, applicants are neither told that their social media data will be examined nor when social media data has led to them being screened out of the selection process. Black et al. (2015) argued that applicants should know their social media data is being examined. This could be considered from both the practical level of applicant reactions as well as from an ethical level of what is morally appropriate for an organization to do.

If an organization informs applicants that social media data will be examined in the selection process, the next step is to decide how much information is given. Some organizations may only go so far as to inform applicants that social media data may be accessed during the process. Other organizations might offer information on what types of social media data will be sought, such as for assessing personality, discovering illegal actions, checking for racist statements, finding relevant colleague connections, or determining person–organization fit. Organizations could even provide information on the social media sites they look at in the process. Such elaboration may make applicants feel that social media data is being used in a fair way and for reasonable purposes, although it would increase the opportunity for faking.

Organizations may also consider how open they are related to the results of such searches. If an applicant has negative social media content arise during such a search does the employer inform the applicant? Does the employer inform someone who was screened out due to social media content? An organization could simply tell applicants they have been screened out or provide more direct feedback and guidance on why. Applicants may have greater acceptance when screened out if they are aware of the reason. In practice, many organizations assume withholding such information is the preferred approach. This, however, is an empirical question that needs to be tested.

Entwined with open social media data use policies are questions of accuracy and interpretation of information that appears contradictory (see Carr, 2016, for an example). Black et al. (2016) discuss this with regard to evaluations of the credibility of social media content. However, this represents a fairness question as well, as some social media might besmirch an individual's reputation while factually inaccurate. For example, a picture that could be interpreted as an individual engaging in drunken behavior may in fact be a picture of someone with a serious illness whose medication has led to such a presentation. Even if the image is presented with text providing context, there is no guarantee that a viewer will read, interpret, or believe such text.

This raises further fairness questions related to whether an applicant should be able to defend or explain social media content discovered. In an open process, an organization might directly ask an applicant about potentially disqualifying social media content found online. The applicant could then correct an error if one was made or give explanation, and this could be done before or after the screen was conducted. In a closed process where the applicant does not even know social media screening is happening, the misattributed picture or content might result in their exclusion without any chance for appeal. In considering fairness, organizations may want to consider instituting appeals processes for applicants.

Practical responses of applicants must be considered as well. If applicants are told that their social media content will be examined, applicants may close their social media accounts or engage in impression management. These are questions organizations will want to consider as they decide how open they want their processes to be and how "cleaned up" profiles help or hurt the degree social media content predicts important organizational outcomes from applicants. If the applicants with information most likely to flag them negatively are also the applicants most likely to change their profiles, this may have validity implications as well.

One potential result of knowledge of social media use in selection processes could be an arms race. Chiang and Suen (2015) found that social media content impacted recruiters' perceived fit of that candidate with the organization, and services have already appeared that modify social media profiles to increase hirability. Thus, on one side, organizations will try to secure accurate information about applicants. On the other, applicants will try to make good impressions, potentially regardless of accuracy. This may result in warring technologies, each attempting to outwit the other in each iteration. Roulin and Levashina (2016) delve into many of such issues created by applicant impression management.

Some organizations are already concerned about applicant faking, which makes the question of fairness more complicated. Such concern led to organizations asking applicants for passwords to their social media accounts, a practice described by Schmidt and O'Connor (2016) and subsequently banned in approximately 20 states in the United States (Drouin, O'Connor, Schmidt, & Miller, 2015; Pate, 2012). If organizations think that impression management will lead to fake profiles, organizations will be less likely to be transparent about their social media screening procedures. We are also likely to see organizations engage in new strategies and methods over time in order to combat this. Importantly, research is not yet clear on the degree or incidence rate of social media impression management tactics in the selection process, so organizations in such practices may be chasing shadows. This highlights the importance of further research in this area.

16.3.4 Question 4: What Changes Outside the Context of the United States?

A final and severely understudied question in this domain regards the generalizability of social media-based selection research conducted in the United States to other nations. We invited two contributions in this area. Shields and Levashina (2016) considered social media in BRIC (Brazil, Russia, India, and China) countries, whereas Schmidt and O'Connor (2016) provided examples of how non-US laws could impact social media selection processes. More needs to be done, however, with a significant need for empirical work. The three questions discussed above all may play out differently depending upon culture and legal system. In the present economy, dominant companies are multinationals with needs to balance workforces and customers all over the globe. As such, we need to couch our understanding of selection procedures within this global context, and the added dimension of social media which themselves vary in popularity by location makes this especially important in this context.

As noted by Shields and Levashina (2016), social media site popularity varies significantly by nation. In some cases, particular sites may not be allowed by national policy, such as the forbiddance of Facebook and Twitter in China (The Economist, 2013). This has significant effects on how organizations engage in social media data collections and examination. For example, Facebook data about a candidate from the United States may not provide the same information about that job candidate as data about a Chinese national job candidate on RenRen provides about that job candidate. The censorship environment in China in addition to cultural differences in long-term orientation (Hofstede, Hofstede, & Minkov, 1997) might result in substantial range restriction on numerous traits of interest.

Cross-cultural and cross-platform comparisons need to be made on social media data. A social media data analysis system that works well for Facebook data may not work as well for sites with different structures. Organizations may combat such issues by focusing their processes on the affordances of social media (Collmus et al., 2016) rather than specific features or by focusing upon particular types of work-related behaviors such as those of Van Zoonen et al. (2016), but the international context will work to complicate matters. Language structures, differences in language formality, and etiquette expectation differences all can make comparisons of social media data across nations difficult.

One area in particular need of additional research focuses upon differences in applicant reactions by culture and country. While there is existing evidence for some uniformity in selection tool reactions across countries (e.g. Ryan et al., 2009), different values and expectations (e.g., privacy) will play a role in how social media selection processes are seen. Organizations may need to balance national preferences with organizational desire for uniform systems of assessment. A social media process that is seen as fair in one country might be seen as unfair in another. Research comparing applicant reactions to social media data use in selection processes across different country contexts would be valuable for beginning to understand what differences exist.

International differences in candidate behaviors are also a high research priority. Cultures defined by restraint may be more likely to engage in impression management techniques in comparison to cultures that tend toward indulgence (Hofstede et al., 1997). Content seen as a "red flags" in a restrained culture may be innocuous in an indulgent one, influencing which candidates are screened out for objectively identical infractions. Behaviors engaged in by candidates may also be impacted by technology and infrastructure in a country. Job candidates from areas with limited Internet access are less likely to have robust online social media profiles and general online presence. Social media data collection policies completely standardized across nations may be detrimental to validity given such differences, depending upon the information sought.

Finally, differences in laws across countries will also have an impact on how social media selection processes are engaging in successfully and legally. Schmidt and O'Connor (2016) offer some illustrations of the impact of national laws, such as the European Union's Right to Be Forgotten, but more systematic legal examination is needed.

16.4 Conclusion

In this chapter, we used the results of our author survey to develop several stances on the current state of the literature. Specifically, experts are in general agreement that establishing a shared, interdisciplinary science is a high priority in order to determine the overall value and potential of social media in selection. Such tactics are necessary to remain relevant to modern organizational practices given the quickly changing nature of social media. It is additionally recognized that organizations are currently using social media in ways that are nonoptimal, if not harmful, to organizational goals, that there is pressure to continue doing so, and that practitioners face many of the same pressures that academics face. The difference is that practitioners are more likely to adopt these technologies despite the lack of evidence, while academics are likely to call for more research. All experts surveyed, whether practitioners or academics, expressed reservations about the use of social media in selection. Here, however, there was some disagreement; some experts condemned the use of social media outright, whereas others suggested great potential somewhere in the future. It is within the gap between those perspectives that future research in this domain will have the greatest impact.

From the chapters in this text, we furthermore developed four key questions of greatest importance for future research. First, we must determine what useful information can be obtained from social media data. This may be in the form of personal characteristics, like personality and cognitive ability, or it may be in the form of behaviors, such as social media endorsements and content counts. Second, we must explore the technical details of incorporating this information into selection systems. Specifically, we may take a more traditional organizational sciences approach, collecting specific theory-driven measures from existing social media, or we may take a more modern data science approach, extracting whatever information might be contained within social media data that is useful in parsimonious prediction of outcomes of interest. Third, even if we can figure out what to measure and how to implement it, we must consider how applicants will react to it, and if our implementations are ethical. Although great troves of data may be available, there may be lines that organizations simply should not cross. Some data, perhaps, should just be off-limits. Fourth and finally, we must consider how answers to the first three questions change as a result of location. Both culture and legal context influence how social media data might be used by organizations, and researchers should pay closer attention to such differences.

Overall, we conclude from this that the future is quite bright for research on social media in selection. Although this new predictor class is unproven and untested, there is sufficient enthusiasm from both academics and practitioners to suggest that future value may be obtained. Just as it took decades to develop rock solid recommendations for other selection methods, especially considering many of those debates are on-going even now, we should not expect that the challenges of social media-based selection should already be solved. If there is value to be found, it will take time to find it, and we hope that the questions posed here and the issues discussed will be a strong first step.

References

Antelman, K. (2004). Do open-access articles have a greater research impact? *College & Research Libraries, 65*, 372–382.

Black, S. L., Stone, D. L., & Johnson, A. F. (2015). Use of social networking websites on applicants' privacy. *Employee Responsibilities and Rights Journal, 27*(2), 115–159.

Black, S. L., Washington, M. L., & Schmidt, G. B. (2016). How to stay current in social media to be competitive in recruitment and selection. In R. N. Landers & G. B. Schmidt (Eds.), *Social media in employee selection and recruitment*. Cham, Switzerland: Springer.

Carr, C. T. (2016). An uncertainty reduction approach to applicant information-seeking in social media: Effects on attributions and hiring. In R. N. Landers & G. B. Schmidt (Eds.), *Social media in employee selection and recruitment*. Cham, Switzerland: Springer.

Chiang, J. K. H., & Suen, H. Y. (2015). Self-presentation and hiring recommendations in online communities: Lessons from LinkedIn. *Computers in Human Behavior, 48*, 516–524.

Collmus, A. B., Armstrong, M. B., & Landers, R. N. (2016). Game-thinking within social media to recruit and select job candidates. In R. N. Landers & G. B. Schmidt (Eds.), *Social media in employee selection and recruitment*. Cham, Switzerland: Springer.

Davison, H. K., Bing, M. N., Kluemper, D. H., & Roth, P. L. (2016). Social media as a personnel selection and hiring resources: Reservations and recommendations. In R. N. Landers & G. B. Schmidt (Eds.), *Social media in employee selection and recruitment*. Cham, Switzerland: Springer.

Davison, H. K., Maraist, C., & Bing, M. N. (2011). Friend or foe? The promise and pitfalls of using social networking sites for HR decisions. *Journal of Business & Psychology, 26*, 153–159.

Doherty, R. (2010). Getting social with recruitment. *Strategic HR Review, 9*(6), 11–15.

Drouin, M., O'Connor, K. W., Schmidt, G. B., & Miller, D. A. (2015). Facebook fired: Legal perspectives and young adults' opinions on the use of social media in employment decisions. *Computers in Human Behavior, 46*, 123–128.

Dunleavy, E., Morris, S., & Howard, E. (2015). Measuring adverse impact in employee selection decisions. In C. Hanvey & K. Sady (Eds.), *Practitioner's guide to legal issues in organizations* (pp. 1–26). Cham, Switzerland: Springer.

Dunnette, M. D. (1966). Fads, fashions, and folderol in psychology. *American Psychologist, 21*, 343–352.

Eftekhar, A., Fullwood, C., & Morris, N. (2014). Capturing personality from Facebook photos and photo-related activities: How much exposure do you need? *Computers in Human Behavior, 37*, 162–170.

Ernst, M. (2006). *Choosing a venue: Conference or journal?* Retrieved from https://homes.cs.washington.edu/~mernst/advice/conferences-vs-journals.html.

Grasz, J. (2014). Number of employers passing on applicants due to social media posts continues to rise, according to new CareerBuilder survey. Retrieved from http://www.careerbuilder.com/share/aboutus/pressreleasesdetail.aspx?sd=6%2F26%2F2014&id=pr829&ed=12%2F31%2F2014.

Hausknecht, J. P., Day, D. V., & Thomas, S. C. (2004). Applicant reactions to selection procedures: An updated model and meta-analysis. *Personnel Psychology, 57*, 639–683.

Henderson, A., & Bowley, R. (2010). Authentic dialog? The role of "friendship" in a social media recruitment campaign. *Journal of Communication Management, 14*, 237–257.

Hofstede, G., Hofstede, G. J., & Minkov, M. (1997). *Cultures and organizations*. New York: McGraw Hill.

Karl, K., Peluchette, J., & Schlaegel, C. (2010). Who's posting Facebook *faux pas*? A cross-cultural examination of personality differences. *International Journal of Selection and Assessment, 18*, 174–186.

Kelly, E., & Dobbin, F. (1998). How affirmative action became diversity management: Employer response to antidiscrimination law, 1961 to 1996. *American Behavioral Scientist, 41*, 960–984.

Kluemper, D. H., Rosen, P. A., & Mossholder, K. W. (2012). Social networking websites, personality ratings, and the organizational context: More than meets the eye? *Journal of Applied Social Psychology, 42*, 1143–1172.

Landers, R. N., & Goldberg, A. S. (2014). Online social media in the workplace: A conversation with employees. In M. D. Coovert & L. F. Thompson (Eds.), *Psychology of workplace technology* (pp. 284–306). New York: Routledge Academic.

Landers, R. N., & Schmidt, G. B. (2016). Social media in employee selection and recruitment: An overview. In R. N. Landers & G. B. Schmidt (Eds.), *Social media in employee selection and recruitment*. Cham, Switzerland: Springer.

Morse, W. C., Nielsen-Pincus, M., Force, J., & Wulfhorst, J. (2007). Bridges and barriers to developing and conducting interdisciplinary graduate-student team research. *Ecology and Society, 12*. Retrieved from http://www.ecologyandsociety.org/vol12/iss2/art8/.

O'Connor, K. W., & Schmidt, G. B. (2015). "Facebook fired": Legal standards for social media-based terminations of K-12 public school teachers. *Journal of Workplace Rights (Sage Open), 5*(1), 1–11. doi:10.1177/2158244015575636.

O'Connor, K. W., Schmidt, G. B., & Drouin, M. (2016). Helping workers understand and follow social media policies. *Business Horizons, 59*, 205–211.

Oravec, J. A. (2003). Blending by blogging: Weblogs in blended learning initiatives. *Journal of Educational Media, 28*, 225–233.

Park, G., Schwartz, H. A., Eichstaedt, J. C., Kern, M. L., Kosinski, M., Stillwell, D. J., et al. (2015). Automatic personality assessment through social media language. *Journal of Personality and Social Psychology, 108*, 934–952.

Pate, R. (2012). Invisible discrimination: Employers & social media sites. WCOB working papers. Paper 12. Retrieved June 11, 2015, from http://digitalcommons.sacredheart.edu/wcob_wp/12.

Patterson, D., Snyder, L., & Ullman, J. (1999). Evaluating computer scientists and engineers for promotion and tenure. *Computing Research News*. Retrieved from http://archive2.cra.org/uploads/documents/resources/bpmemos/tenure_review.pdf.

Roth, P. L., Bobko, P., Van Iddekinge, C. H., & Thatcher, J. B. (2016). Social media in employee-selection-related decisions: A research agenda for uncharted territory. *Journal of Management, 42*, 269–298.

Roth, P. L., Bobko, P., & McFarland, L. A. (2005). A meta-analysis of work sample test validity: Updating and integrating some classic literature. *Personnel Psychology, 58*, 1009–1037.

Roulin, N., & Levashina, J. (2016). Impression management and social media profiles. In R. N. Landers & G. B. Schmidt (Eds.), *Social media in employee selection and recruitment*. Cham, Switzerland: Springer.

Ryan, A. M., Boyce, A. S., Ghumman, S., Jundt, D., Schmidt, G. B., & Gibby, R. (2009). Going global: Cultural values and perceptions of selection procedures. *Applied Psychology: An International Review, 58*(4), 520–566.

"SafeAssign". (2015, June 19). Retrieved from http://www.niu.edu/blackboard/assess/safeassign.shtml.

Salgado, J. F., & Moscoso, S. (2002). Comprehensive meta-analysis of the construct validity of the employment interview. *European Journal of Work and Organizational Psychology, 11*(3), 299–324.

Schmidt, G. B., & O'Connor, K. W. (2015). Fired for Facebook: Using NLRB guidance to craft appropriate social media policies. *Business Horizons, 58*, 571–579.

Schmidt, G. B., & O'Connor, K. W. (2016). Legal concerns when considering social media data in selection. In R. N. Landers & G. B. Schmidt (Eds.), *Social media in employee selection and recruitment*. Cham, Switzerland: Springer.

Shankland, S. (2014). Mozilla under fire: Inside the 9-day reign of fallen CEO Brendan Eich. *CNET*. Retrieved December 12, 2015, from http://www.cnet.com/news/mozilla-under-fire-inside-the-9-day-reign-of-fallen-ceo-brendan-eich/.

Shields, B., & Levashina, J. (2016). Comparing the social media in the United State and BRIC nations, and the challenges faced in international selection. In R. N. Landers & G. B. Schmidt (Eds.), *Social media in employee selection and recruitment*. Cham, Switzerland: Springer.

Smock, A. D., Ellison, N. B., Lampe, C., & Wohn, D. Y. (2011). Facebook as a toolkit: A uses and gratification approach to unbundling feature use. *Computers in Human Behavior, 27*, 2322–2329.

Society for Industrial and Organizational Psychology [SIOP]. (2003). *Principles for the validation and use of personnel selection procedures* (4th ed.). Bowling Green, OH: Society for Industrial and Organizational Psychology.

Stoughton, J. W. (2016). Applicant reactions to social media in selection: Early returns and future directions. In R. N. Landers & G. B. Schmidt (Eds.), *Social media in employee selection and recruitment*. Cham, Switzerland: Springer.

Straumsheim, C. (2015). What is detected? Inside Higher Ed. Retrieved from https://www.insidehighered.com/news/2015/07/14/turnitinfaces-new-questions-about-efficacy-plagiarism-detection-software.

The Economist. (2013, April 6). The art of concealment. *The Economist*. Retrieved June 8, 2015, from http://www.economist.com/news/special-report/21574631-chinese-screening-online-material-abroad-becoming-ever-more-sophisticated.

Van Iddekinge, C. H., Lanivich, S. E., Roth, P. L., & Junco, E. (2013). Social media for selection? Validity and adverse impact potential of a Facebook-based assessment. *Journal of Management*. doi:10.1177/0149206313515524.

Van Zoonen, W., Verhoeven, J. W. M., & Vliegenthart, R. (2016). How employees use Twitter to talk about work: A typology of work-related tweets. *Computers in Human Behavior, 55*, 329–339.

Youyou, W., Kosinski, M., & Stillwell, D. (2015). Computer-based personality judgments are more accurate than those made by humans. *Proceedings of the National Academies of Science, 112*, 1036–1040.

Index

R.N. Landers, G.B. Schmidt (eds.), *Social Media in Employee Selection and Recruitment*, DOI 10.1007/978-3-319-29989-1

S

T